P9-EBY-330

# STRUCTURE - CONDUCT - PERFORMANCE

**What does the industry look like - What choices can be made - How do choices affect profit and growth**

Second Custom Edition

# MICROECONOMICS

## A BASIC PERSPECTIVE

Preface by Roger Mack

Taken from:

*Microeconomics*, Second Edition
by R. Glenn Hubbard and Anthony Patrick O'Brien

*Microeconomics: Principles, Applications, and Tools*, Fifth Edition
by Arthur O'Sullivan, Steven M. Sheffrin, and Stephen J. Perez

**Custom Publishing**

New York   Boston   San Francisco
London   Toronto   Sydney   Tokyo   Singapore   Madrid
Mexico City   Munich   Paris   Cape Town   Hong Kong   Montreal

Cover Art: Photodisc by Getty Images.

Taken from:

*Microeconomics*, Second Edition
by R. Glenn Hubbard and Anthony Patrick O'Brien
Copyright © 2008, 2006 by Pearson Education, Inc.Published by Prentice Hall
Upper Saddle River, New Jersey 07458

*Microeconomics: Principles, Applications, and Tools*, Fifth Edition
by Arthur O'Sullivan, Steven M. Sheffrin, and Stephen J. Perez
Copyright © 2008, 2006, 2003, 2001 by Pearson Education, Inc.
Published by Prentice Hall

Copyright © 2008, 1999 by Pearson Custom Publishing
All rights reserved.

Permission in writing must be obtained from the publisher before any part of this work may be
reproduced or transmitted in any form or by any means, electronic or mechanical, including
photocopying and recording, or by any information storage or retrieval system.

All trademarks, service marks, registered trademarks, and registered service marks are the property of
their respective owners and are used herein for identification purposes only.

Printed in the United States of America

ISBN 0-536-24745-5

2008400055

NM

Please visit our web site at *www.pearsoncustom.com*

PEARSON CUSTOM PUBLISHING
501 Boylston Street, Suite 900, Boston, MA 02116
A Pearson Education Company

# Brief Contents

Chapter 1 and Appendix A, pages 152-165, 188-200, and 318-338 taken from: *Microeconomics: Principles, Applications, and Tools*, Fifth Edition by Arthur O'Sullivan, Steven M. Sheffrin and Stephen J. Perez.

Appendix B and Chapters 2–13 taken from: *Microeconomics*, Second Edition by R. Glenn Hubbard and Anthony Patrick O'Brien.

# Contents

# Brief Contents

Chapter 1 and Appendix A, pages 152-165, 188-200, and 318-338 taken from: *Microeconomics: Principles, Applications, and Tools,* Fifth Edition by Arthur O'Sullivan, Steven M. Sheffrin and Stephen J. Perez.

Appendix B and Chapters 2–13 taken from: *Microeconomics,* Second Edition by R. Glenn Hubbard and Anthony Patrick O'Brien.

# Contents

# Brief Contents

Chapter 1 and Appendix A, pages 152-165, 188-200, and 318-338 taken from: *Microeconomics: Principles, Applications, and Tools,* Fifth Edition by Arthur O'Sullivan, Steven M. Sheffrin and Stephen J. Perez.

Appendix B and Chapters 2–13 taken from: *Microeconomics,* Second Edition by R. Glenn Hubbard and Anthony Patrick O'Brien.

# Contents

# Preface

"Annual income, twenty pounds; annual expenditure, nineteen pounds, happiness. Annual income, twenty pounds; annual expenditure, twenty-one pounds; result, misery"

–Charles Dickens

 ## MICROECONOMICS–A BASIC PERSPECTIVE

There is no doubt about it. For many of you, economics is among the most feared and most challenging courses that you will enroll in during your college experience. Despite this, economics is also a subject matter that will stay with you, be actively used and may well have the most impact throughout your life. Economics involves a way of thinking about choices and outcomes. In a very real sense, both the teaching and the learning of economics is "work in progress." Your choices and the choices of others around you, the resulting outcomes, and the opportunities, both chosen and given up, greatly determine much of the quality of your life.

Teaching *Microeconomic Principles* is indeed challenging. Classes are usually composed of students who have varying educational preparation, differences in abilities, desire and interest in understanding the subject matter. Many merely wish to pass the class. This text has been edited and designed to avoid as much intimidation as possible. A concern in teaching this class is the recognition that some students enter with varying degrees of *subject fear*. Nevertheless, economic literacy -that is, knowledge about the way economic decisions are made–matters and affects each of us daily. For this reason alone, it is important to have some understanding of economics.

The very basis of microeconomics is the decision-making process involving choices between alternative actions, involving both potential costs and potential rewards. These choices are assumed to be goal directed. That is, choices are made to achieve some outcome or reach some goal. The goal could be material, psychological or benevolent, but whatever it may be, we assume it involves "subjective well-being." The assumptions of economic thinking are based on the idea that people are rational and self interested, and that their tastes and preferences are consistent.

With any decision we make, we go through a series of thoughts. After we reach a decision, it seems rational to us, or we would not do it. Even though people sometimes show altruism, and complete selflessness, we all also show selfishness, and do things solely because of the impact their actions have on themselves. And while our tastes and preferences are constantly changing and adapting, they are consistent in the sense that we like things to stay the way they are, and we all have prejudices that favor some choices over others.

There exists nothing in the principle ideas of economics that specifies that people should not care about fairness, or that decisions are only made about the present, for the present. Unsophisticated critics often identify economic neoclassicism with models in which all agents are perfectly informed or fully instrumentally rational. Indeed, the last thirty years of neoclassical economics have been marked by an explosion of models in which economic actors are imperfectly informed, sometimes other-regarding, frequently irrational (or boundedly rational, jargon would have it) etc. In short, *homo economicus* has evolved to resemble us more. Many aspects of current theory simply acknowledge human limits on one's ability to reason analytically; to actually behave in one's self interest or have enough willpower to act rationally. Herbert Simon has coined the term 'procedurally rational' to indicate that we believe we act rationally when making extremely complex decisions.

Clearly, most economists would agree that the allocation of resources is an important aspect of economic thinking and of real economic systems and decision-making. Certainly a decision about the allocation of resources is important from the point of view

of this book. A school of thought in economics in the twentieth century, enormously influential especially in the United States, and often referred to as the *Chicago School*, believes that the allocation of resources is more than just one of the considerations.

This school of thought is called "neoclassical economics," and the "neo" means that it differs in important ways from the "classical economists" of the previous century. In this school of thought, economics is defined as "the study that considers human behavior as a relation between scarce means and alternative ends."

Neoclassical economists regard the study of the allocation of resources as essentially a scientific, not a normative, study. Revealed preferences are discovered by observing behavior and assuming rationality in decision-making. Neoclassical economists believe that free markets usually bring about an efficient allocation of resources.

Conversely, efficient allocation is the important thing about free markets. In those more or less rare cases when markets "fail" to bring about an efficient allocation of resources, it is appropriate for the government to intervene to correct the situation, if it can. Neoclassical economists have led the way in clearing up some key concepts almost all economists would rely on to explain and predict behavior. Microeconomics is most surely a behavioral study of decision-making.

Depending on the definition we prefer, we may say that economists are interested in the allocation of resources, in the nature and causes of wealth of nations or firms or individuals, or perhaps the efficient use of inputs to produce well being or to add value in the production of goods and services as outputs. We tend to share the positivist view that the ultimate test of a theory is the accuracy of its predictions. But, we also believe that predictions of good feelings and subjective well-being could also be considered an important goal of the decisions we all make.

All of those things depend on the actions and decisions of human beings. So, economists have to make some assumptions about human beings, about how human beings act and how human beings make decisions. We might turn to psychology for our assumptions — but in practice, most economists have not done that. Rather, most economists have begun from an assumption few modern psychologists would endorse. The assumption is that human beings are highly rational and self-interested.

Neoclassical economists usually assume, in other words, that human beings make the choices that give them the best possible advantage, given the circumstances they face. Circumstances include the prices of resources, goods and services, limited income, limited technology for transforming resources into goods and services, and taxes, regulations, and similar objective limitations on the choices they may make.

This is to say, economists assume that economic systems work as if they consisted of rational, self-interested persons. People are all types—sneaky and altruistic, smart and dumb—but if the average is a person who is rational and self-interested, then the system will act as if people in general were rational and self-interested.

Most of the current thinking in microeconomics represents a return to the basis of neoclassical economics after a century long detour. When economics first became identified as a distinct field of study, psychology did not exist as a discipline. However, Adam Smith, in his *other* famous book, *The Theory of Moral Sentiments*, has great insights about benevolence, loss aversion, willpower, and fairness that have proven to be the focus of modern behavioral economics.

Economics tends to study an economic system consisting of rational, self-interested persons; these are not particularly common-sense assumptions. We all know of examples of non-self-interested behavior - of people who give to the church and to good causes and who sacrifice themselves in other ways. There are two very different issues here. The first issue is that people are sometimes altruistic. It is hard to avoid the conclusion that people do sometimes act on ethical values, and it is hard to see how the selfishness of the (probable) majority can cancel out this self-sacrifice.

People often do act on non-self-interested values, but when they do, they act on their own values, not those of the government, some philosopher, or the observing social scientist. We might call this assumption "rational individualism" or "methodological individualism," the idea that socio-economic explanation must be sought at the level of the individual agent rather than rational self interest. This is complicated, but we shall avoid the complications here by adopting the analysis based on self-interest. A broader neoclassical economics assumes that people choose in the way that best advances their own values, altruistic or self-interested as those values may be. The suspicion that people are often irrational might be easier to deal with, since it is at least possible that deviations from rationality could be random and could cancel out.

In fact, there is a good deal of evidence that real choices can deviate from rationality in predictable ways. To the extent that they do, we can understand their choices in two stages: first, understand what the rational choices would be, and, second, adjust for any predictable irrationality. This leads us to the distinction of positive and normative economics. Critics of neoclassical economics sometimes claim that economics is a model for self-interest; that economics holds that "greed is good." This is a misunderstanding. The assumption of rational self-interest is positive economics, an attempt to describe what is, not what ought to be. The assumptions of rationality and self-interest may not really be questions of fact. I believe they make more sense if we think of them as guidelines for critical reasoning in economics. Take the assumption of rationality, for example. The assumption of self-interest works somewhat this way. When we assume self-interested motives we are reasoning as follows:

*"Self-interested motives are common among human beings.*
*Roger Mack is a human being.*
*Therefore, it is probable that Roger Mack's motives in this particular case are self-interested."*

Experience teaches us that self-interested motives are indeed pretty common. It's a good guideline for critical reasoning in economics, but we have to be aware that there are exceptions. I believe almost all modern economists would accept these assumptions as guidelines for sound critical reasoning in economics.

At the center is the idea that behavior is determined by the struggle between two processes which Adam Smith termed the "passions" and the "impartial spectator." The passions, in Smith's framework, included drives such as hunger and sex, emotions such as fear and anger, and motivational feeling states such as pain. Smith viewed behavior as under the control of passions, but believed that people have the ability to override sheer passion-driven behavior by evaluating it as if they were an "outsider'-the impartial spectator. The role of this "impartial spectator" was often that of "self-denial", of self-control; the role was that of long-term evaluator and planner in conflict with the shortsighted doer and actor.

Behavior is preference-driven or, more precisely, it is to be understood as a means for maximizing preference-satisfaction. Preference is given, current, fully determining, and strictly separate from both belief and from the means employed. Everything we do and say is instrumental to preference-satisfaction. Of course, the real world of economics is very complex. The allocation of resources in a market economy is the result of the interaction of thousands of decisions made by each of hundreds of millions of individual people. A rational choice occurs when a person uses the available resources to most effectively satisfy the wants of the person making the choice. A rational choice leads to rational behavior comparing costs and benefits presently and over time.

Economics deals with this complexity in part by thinking in terms of models. In a modern economic system, individuals, companies, markets and even nations are interdependent. A model is a description of these interdependencies in terms of graphs, mathematics, pictures, a computer language, or some similar descriptive language, together with a theory of the dynamics of the subsystem. Dynamics is the evolution of the subsystem as time passes.

New manifestations of what we term neoclassicism still subscribe to methodological individualism. While it is true that mainstream economists have, during the last few decades, acknowledged that the decision making agent is a creature of their social context, and thus that social structure and individual agency are messily intertwined, their models retain the distinction of placing the burden of explanation on the individual.

During the tumultuous 20th Century, neoclassicists invested greatly in taking all notions of psychology out of the rational agent's decision-making process. All hints of a philosophical discussion regarding the rationality of homo economicus were thus removed. People could, and should, be modeled as if they possessed consistent preferences that guide their behavior automatically.

During the past twenty-five years or so, homo economicus has developed a capacity to adapt his preferences in response to past outcomes. A more recent development has taken neoclassicism, and homo economicus, onto higher levels of sophistication. The advent of psychological *game theory* has brought on a reconsideration of the standard assumption that agents' current preferences are separate from the structure of the interaction in which they are involved.

Suddenly, what decision any individual wants to make is impacted by what he thinks others expect him to want. And when these second order beliefs about the expectations of others came to depend on the social structure in which the decision is made, the agent's very preferences could not be linked only with outcomes: they depended on the structure and history of the interaction as well.

Predictability for economics required something more: it required that decision makers' behavior is coordinated in a manner that aggregate decision making becomes sufficiently regular to give rise to solid predictions for the behavior of "the market." Thus, neoclassical theoretical exercises begin by postulating the agents' utility functions, specifying their constraints, and stating their 'information' or 'belief'. Then they pose the standard question: "What behavior should we expect in equilibrium?"

When A.A. Cournot constructed the first model of competition in 1838, he immediately noticed a gap in his explanation regarding the emergence of market equilibrium. Rather cunningly, instead of discussing this difficulty, he studied what happens when we begin from that equilibrium. Would the system have a tendency to move away from it or was the equilibrium stable? The proof of its stability secured his place in microeconomic theory. Moreover, it established this interesting practice:

First, one discovers an equilibrium. Second, one assumes (axiomatically) that agents (or their behavior) will find themselves at that equilibrium. Lastly, one demonstrates that, once at that equilibrium, any small perturbations are incapable of creating centrifugal forces able to dislodge self-interested behavior from the discovered equilibrium. This three-step theoretical move is tantamount to what has been described as methodological equilibrium.

It is uncontroversial to state that every aggregate phenomenon formulated by neoclassical thinkers is explained increasingly and exclusively as some imposed equilibrium emerging from the interaction of instrumentally rational individuals who are either optimizing consciously (as in rational choice or game theory) or are drawn to such behavior through a process of 'natural selection' (as in, for instance, evolutionary game theory). The bottom line, then, is clear: despite all denials, there is such a thing as a body of social economic theory that subscribes to the assumptions above and which we can legitimately, for want of a better term, label neoclassical.

Microeconomics is often referred to as the "theory of the firm", but there exists as many theories as there are firms. To simplify this, I have constructed the ideas of microeconomics around three primary concepts: *structure-conduct-performance*. It is the perspective of this work that firms exist within certain industry structures; each structure has differences of demand elasticity, product differentiation, resource availability and access. As a basic starting position, it is assumed that firms wish to be successful. Although success can be expressed in various ways, in microeconomics we often measure success of a firm as the level of monetary return on cost investment. Under most conditions and after carefully defining the concepts, the goal of firms is often the achievement of economic profit. This will be a basic concept for comparing and contrasting various industry structures in terms of what options are available to the decision makers managing the firms, and how their decisions determine the performance of the firm in terms of profit.

Microeconomics is in many ways a decision science about human behavior. It is a business, psychology, philosophy, sociology and political science course all rolled into one. Primarily we will be studying how individuals, households, industries and firms interact in making decisions about what to do, why do it, where to go, where to work, what to buy, what to sell and what to pay. We will discuss various market types; we will analyze differences between markets and between firms and industries.

We will analyze how the very structure of markets impacts the products we choose, the prices we pay, the income we receive and the quality of life we enjoy. We will discuss happiness and wellbeing. This is a course unlike almost any other course you have taken. This course will force you to analyze your surroundings and understand how the decisions you make and those options available to you affect your life on a daily basis.

By the conclusion of this course, you ought to be able to clearly and intelligently discuss economics from any of the following perspectives; international trade, internet shopping, local businesses, bars, restaurants, gas pricing, music downloading and well as implications of mergers and monopolies to why athletes and CEOs are so highly compensated. You will better understand the local, regional, national and global job market. You will better understand the trade-offs involved in decisions you make. You may shop smarter, work smarter, date smarter and generally better understand your own life and decisions you make.

In economics (and more generally social science), the nature of the role of the individual in the community or state has consistently been examined. Every society must address the question, either implicitly or explicitly, "How can the autonomy (or freedom or liberty) of an individual be maintained and at the same time provide for the commonwealth (social welfare)?" Whether the individual or the community is regarded as more important, the problem is one of balance. In some societies, the individual is regarded as more important than the community. In other societies, the community has priority over the individual. From a practical perspective, the problem is to balance the rights and freedom of the individual with the functions of the community. Different societies have attempted different approaches at different times.

Cooperation and conscription are opposite ends of a spectrum or range of behavioral patterns. Cooperation implies voluntary agreements and a coordinated approach to the solution of a problem. Conscription implies a non-voluntary or forced behavioral choice in the allocation process. An economic input (labor, capital, land) or an economic good or service can be conscripted. Conscription implies the ability of one person or group to force another to make choices they would not prefer. Conscription implies that some form of coercion has taken place. At another level voluntary and coerced behavior are at opposite ends of a spectrum of motivations.

Cooperation may be encouraged by strongly held common values or necessity. Each member of the society understands that their chance for survival is reduced if she or he is not a member of the community. If a government uses sanctions to force behavior or choice this is clearly coercion and conscription. Students in school may feel coerced by their peers, the class star or the rules of the system. Social pressure, other workers, the management of the firm, corporate rules or government regulations may coerce a worker.

Market oriented societies focus on competition to constrain individual behavior. In industrial societies, competition is regarded as the optimal way to coordinate economic behavior. A market exchange is a contract between sellers and buyers where each seeks to optimize their self-interest. The seller competes to get the highest possible price (or best deal), while the buyer competes to buy at the lowest possible price. The competition between the buyer and seller is influenced by the tastes (or preferences), information that each has, the alternatives that each has, their relative incomes and the rules of the game (customs, mores, laws, regulations, institutions, ideologies, values, principles, etc). Generally, societies use a mix of cooperation, conscription and competition. The difference among different economic systems is the degree to which one (or more) of these processes is emphasized.

In each case, the mix of cooperation, conscription and competition has been different and has resulted in fundamentally different societies with different solutions to the economic problems or allocation distribution and exchange. All societies develop social institutions (behavioral patterns) to coordinate the activities of production, distribution

and consumption. There is a wide range of forms these institutions may take depending on the physical environment, state of technical knowledge, social values and other factors. These institutions and behavioral patterns may rely on some combination of competition and cooperation. Market systems tend to focus on competition while other systems may have a larger role for cooperation or conscription.

This course is structured rather unusually. The most common discussion I have had with students is that they could follow and understood the concepts clearly from my class activities and lectures, but when they had to apply it to a new or different situation outside or on an exam, they were confused. This course is therefore structured as an "inverted classroom." You will learn the basic ideas and theories largely from the readings, assignments and web-based work outside the classroom. We will spend the majority of work inside the classroom doing hands-on explanations, problem sets (alone and in random groups), experiments and behavioral analysis, so that you can practice using microeconomic analysis for understanding and decision making.

This text is divided into five major sets of questions around a theme;

1   Economics and microeconomics and what are they all about? What is the focus of microeconomics? What is the theory of the firm? What kinds of firms are there and how do they differ? What is more important, revenue or costs?

2   What are those supply and demand curves all about? Where do they come from? What is the difference between quantity demanded, quantity supplied and demand and supply schedules? What are demand and supply curves? What is equilibrium? Why are these ideas important and what has elasticity have to do with slope and all the above?

3   What is a production function? What are the differences between fixed costs, variable costs and total costs? What are marginal costs and why are they important? Are total costs, average costs or marginal costs more important for decision making and why? What are the differences between long-run, short-run and market decisions? How does all this lead to a production decision for a firm? How hard can this be, firms only decide how many to produce and what price to charge?

4   What are the major types of industries? What are the differences between them? How do these differences impact the decisions managers can make? What is the difference between a competitor and a rival? Don't I always charge the highest price I can and pay the lowest costs I can?

5   How do the inputs to production get priced? What kind of things will affect the salary I receive? What decisions should I make when hiring labor or buying inputs?

The intent of this text is to help the introductory student unravel the logical way of thinking and theoretical framework found within the study of economics. This text will present economics as a reflection of the ever-changing world we live in, and views the ideas of economists as a pattern of thought to better understand certain aspects of that changing world. This course will attempt to excite your curiosity about an economic perspective to decision-making and then provide the tools needed to both develop and better understand such a perspective.

The economy is really just a metaphor for the enormously complex mix of daily personal and commercial transactions among more than 310 million Americans, the over 85 thousand households and more than six and one half billion world citizens. The deceptively precise numbers, reported daily, that purport to measure "savings" or "growth" or "income" are merely crude approximations compounded from the heap of samples, surveys, estimates, seasonal adjustments and sheer guesses. It takes months, even years, for economists to actually sort through the numbers and figure out what actually happened at any given time. The exact numbers are not the issue; the trends, the direction and the scope of the overall economic information are the basis of thought and discussions.

The main argument for the market system is the dual role played by prices. On the one hand, prices serve to ration demand: anyone unwilling to pay the market price does not get the good. On the other hand, prices serves to elicit production: any firm that can produce a good or service, for less than its market price has a powerful financial incentive to do so. What is produced goes to those who value it most. Those who produce and sell it are the most efficient companies that can produce it at the lowest price. What will be produced will be determined by whatever the ultimate user is willing and able to value at market price.

Economics is about the decisions we all face in meeting our needs and wants—material, sociopolitical, and psychological. All of these wants are in constant flux and change for most of us at a very rapid pace. Economics studies the activities arising from scarcity, both in what we want and what we have, in the dreams and hopes we form and in the means of achieving them within a socioeconomic order that itself is changing. We, both individually and collectively, as families, households or entire nations, cannot have all we desire and must choose between alternatives: alternative use of time, of effort, of monetary income, of wealth, revenue and/or expenses. We are always choosing between work and leisure and saving and spending.

One of the major ways microeconomics views society is to observe how individuals use knowledge and information, which, as Hayek and others have pointed out, is scattered in tiny fragments among millions and millions of people. When you have pricing systems, then all those people coordinate their efforts. Nobody can keep track of over 30 million different prices, or even the 2800 different prices in an average supermarket. If you have 100 million people and each one keeps track of a handful of prices that are relevant to their decisions, then it's manageable and it works.

One of the other things that become clear through knowledge of microeconomics is that knowledge with insight is important. Knowing what knowledge can mean, and how to apply it are skills which vary enormously. In a market economy, whoever shows that insight—when correct—it really doesn't matter that the other side might be better organized or even better financed. Think of someone like Henry Ford, who was so poor that he walked eight miles to Detroit to look for a job. But, when he conceived of mass-producing cars and designed a way to do it, it didn't matter that he was nobody well known. What mattered was that he could produce cars cheaper than anyone else could. The economy seems often to work fine without each part having perfect information about its working.

Almost two and a half centuries ago the Scottish moral philosopher Adam Smith used a particular metaphor to describe the competitive market system, a metaphor that still resonates today. He viewed the competitive economy as a system in which:

> "...every individual...endeavours as much as he can...to direct...industry so that its produce may be of the greatest value... neither intend(ing) to promote the public interest, nor know(ing) how much he is promoting it... He intends only his own gain, and he is in this, as in many other cases, led by an invisible hand to promote an end that was no part of his intention... By pursuing his own interest he frequently promotes that of society more effectually than when he really intends to promote it..."

ADAM SMITH, 1776

Price rations demand and elicits production. Production occurs when decisions are made to alter inputs in a process to make the resulting output more valuable, have more utility to demanders in the marketplace. Economic reasoning is applied to business and households and to public policy daily. This is the central concept of this course. Issues and ideas will be discussed in terms of relevance to these decision considerations and discussion will be encouraged on any "hot current topic or concern" as economics will always be a mixture of both art and science.

Roger W. Mack, Ph.D.
@Mackonomics.com, Mack Island
Summer, 2008

# Chapter 1
# Introduction: What is Economics?

# 1

# Introduction: What Is Economics?

Economics is the science of choice, exploring the choices made by individuals and organizations. Over the last few centuries, these choices have led to substantial gains in the standard of living around the globe. The typical American household today has roughly seven times the income and purchasing power of a household 100 years ago. Our prosperity is the result of choices made by all sorts of people, including inventors, workers, entrepreneurs, and the people who saved money and loaned it to others to invest in machines and other tools of production. One reason we have prospered is greater efficiency: We have discovered better ways to use our resources—raw materials, time, and energy—to produce the goods and services we value.

As an illustration of changes in the standard of living and our growing prosperity, let's compare the way people listened to music in 1891 with how we listen today. You can buy an iPod nano for $199 and fill it with 1,000 songs at $0.99 each. If you earn a wage of $15 per hour, it would take you about 80 hours of work to earn enough money to purchase and then fill an iPod. Back in 1891, the latest technological marvel was Thomas Edison's cylinder phonograph, which played music recorded on 4-inch cylinders. Imagine that you lived back then and wanted to get just as much music as you could fit on an iPod. Given the wages and prices in 1891, it would take you roughly 800 hours of work to earn enough money to buy the phonograph and all the cylinders. And if you wanted to keep your music with you, you would need 14 backpacks to carry all the cylinders.

Although prosperity and efficiency are widespread, they are not universal. In some parts of the world, many people live in poverty. For example, in sub-Saharan Africa 290 million people—almost half the population—live on less than $1 per day. And in all nations of the world, inefficiencies still exist, with valuable resources being wasted. For example, each year the typical urban commuter in the United States wastes more than 47 hours and $84 worth of gasoline trapped in rush hour traffic.

- **scarcity**
  The resources we use to produce goods and services are limited.

- **economics**
  The study of choices when there is scarcity.

- **factors of production**
  The resources used to produce goods and services; also known as *production inputs*.

- **natural resources**
  Resources provided by nature and used to produce goods and services.

- **labor**
  The physical and mental effort people use to produce goods and services.

- **physical capital**
  The stock of equipment, machines, structures, and infrastructure that is used to produce goods and services.

- **human capital**
  The knowledge and skills acquired by a worker through education and experience.

- **entrepreneurship**
  The effort used to coordinate the factors of production—natural resources, labor, physical capital, and human capital—to produce and sell products.

Economics provides a framework to diagnose all sorts of problems faced by society and then helps create and evaluate various proposals to solve them. Economics can help us develop strategies to replace poverty with prosperity, and to replace waste with efficiency. In this chapter, we explain what economics is and how we all can use economic analysis to think about practical problems and solutions.

# 1.1 | WHAT IS ECONOMICS?

Economists use the word **scarcity** to convey the idea that resources—the things we use to produce goods and services—are limited, while human wants are unlimited. Therefore, we cannot produce everything that everyone wants. In the words of the Rolling Stones, "You can't always get what you want." **Economics** studies the choices we make when there is scarcity; it is all about trade-offs. Here are some examples of scarcity and the trade-offs associated with making choices:

- You have a limited amount of time. If you take a part-time job, each hour on the job means one less hour for study or play.
- A city has a limited amount of land. If the city uses an acre of land for a park, it has one less acre for housing, retailers, or industry.
- You have limited income this year. If you spend $17 on a music CD, that's $17 less you have to spend on other products or to save.

People produce goods (music CDs, houses, and parks) and services (the advice of physicians and lawyers) by using one or more of the following five **factors of production**, or *production inputs*, or simply *resources*:

- **Natural resources** are provided by nature. Some examples are fertile land, mineral deposits, oil and gas deposits, and water. Some economists refer to all types of natural resources as *land*.
- **Labor** is the physical and mental effort people use to produce goods and services.
- **Physical capital** is the stock of equipment, machines, structures, and infrastructure that is used to produce goods and services. Some examples are forklifts, machines, computers, factories, airports, roads, and fiber-optic cables.
- **Human capital** is the knowledge and skills acquired by a worker through education and experience. Every job requires some human capital: To be a surgeon, you must learn anatomy and acquire surgical skills. To be an accountant, you must learn the rules of accounting and acquire computer skills. To be a musician, you must learn to play an instrument.
- **Entrepreneurship** is the effort used to coordinate the factors of production—natural resources, labor, physical capital, and human capital—to produce and sell products. An entrepreneur comes up with an idea for a product, decides how to produce it, and raises the funds to bring it to the market. Some examples of entrepreneurs are Bill Gates of Microsoft, Steve Jobs of Apple Computer, Inc., Howard Schultz of Starbucks, and McDonald's founder Ray Kroc.

Given our limited resources, we make our choices in a variety of ways. Sometimes we make our decisions as individuals, and other times we participate in collective decision making, allowing the government and other organizations to choose for us. Many of our choices happen within *markets*, institutions or arrangements that enable us to buy and sell things. For example, most of us participate in the labor market, exchanging our time for money, and we all participate in consumer markets, exchanging money for food and clothing. But we make other choices outside markets—from our personal decisions about everyday life to our political choices about matters that concern society as a whole. What unites all these decisions is the notion of scarcity: We can't have it all; there are trade-offs.

Economists are always reminding us that there is scarcity—that there are trade-offs in everything we do. Suppose that in a conversation with your economics instructor you share your enthusiasm about an upcoming launch of the space shuttle. The economist may tell you that the resources used for the shuttle could have been used instead for an unmanned mission to Mars.

By introducing the notion of scarcity into your conversation, your instructor is simply reminding you that there are trade-offs, that one thing (a shuttle mission) is sacrificed for another (a Mars mission). Talking about alternatives is the first step in a process that can help us make better choices about how to use our resources. For example, we could compare the scientific benefits of a shuttle mission to the benefits of a Mars mission and choose the mission with the greater benefit.

## Positive Versus Normative Analysis

Economics doesn't tell us what to choose—shuttle mission or Mars mission—but simply helps us to understand the trade-offs. President Harry S. Truman once remarked,

> All my economists say, "On the one hand, . . .; On the other hand, . . ." Give me a one-handed economist!

An economist might say, "On the one hand, we could use a shuttle mission to do more experiments in the gravity-free environment of Earth's orbit; on the other hand, we could use a Mars mission to explore the possibility of life on other planets." In using both hands, the economist is not being evasive, but simply doing economics, discussing the alternative uses of our resources. The ultimate decision about how to use our resources—shuttle mission or Mars exploration—is the responsibility of citizens or their elected officials.

Most modern economics is based on **positive analysis**, which predicts the consequences of alternative actions by answering the question "What *is*?" or "What *will be*?" A second type of economic reasoning is normative in nature. **Normative analysis** answers the question "What *ought to be*?"

In Table 1.1, we compare positive questions to normative questions. Normative questions lie at the heart of policy debates. Economists contribute to policy debates by conducting positive analyses of the consequences of alternative actions. For example, an economist could predict the effects of an increase in the minimum wage on the number of people employed nationwide, the income of families with minimum-wage workers, and consumer prices. Armed with the conclusions of the

- **positive analysis**
  Answers the question "What is?" or "What will be?"

- **normative analysis**
  Answers the question "What ought to be?"

## Table 1.1 | COMPARING POSITIVE AND NORMATIVE QUESTIONS

| Positive Questions | Normative Questions |
| --- | --- |
| • If the government increases the minimum wage, how many workers will lose their jobs? | • Should the government increase the minimum wage? |
| • If two office-supply firms merge, will the price of office supplies increase? | • Should the government block the merger of two office-supply firms? |
| • How does a college education affect a person's productivity and earnings? | • Should the government subsidize a college education? |
| • How do consumers respond to a cut in income taxes? | • Should the government cut taxes to stimulate the economy? |
| • If a nation restricts shoe imports, who benefits and who bears the cost? | • Should the government restrict imports? |

economist's positive analysis, citizens and policy makers could then make a normative decision about whether to increase the minimum wage. Similarly, an economist could study the projects that could be funded with $1 billion in foreign aid, predicting the effects of each project on the income per person in an African country. Armed with this positive analysis, policy makers could then decide which projects to support.

Economists don't always reach the same conclusions in their positive analyses. The disagreements often concern the magnitude of a particular effect. For example, most economists agree that an increase in the minimum wage will cause unemployment, but there is disagreement about how many people would lose their jobs. Similarly, economists agree that spending money to improve the education system in Africa will increase productivity and income, but there is disagreement about the size of the increase in income.

### The Three Key Economic Questions: What, How, and Who?

Economic decisions are made at every level in society. Individuals decide what products to buy, what occupations to pursue, and how much money to save. Firms decide what goods and services to produce and how to produce them. Governments decide what projects and programs to complete and how to pay for them. The choices made by individuals, firms, and governments answer three questions:

1 *What products do we produce?* Trade-offs exist: If a hospital uses its resources to perform more heart transplants, it has fewer resources to care for premature infants.

2 *How do we produce the products?* Alternative means of production are available: Power companies can produce electricity with coal, natural gas, or wind power. Professors can teach in large lecture halls or small classrooms.

3 *Who consumes the products?* We must decide how the products of society are distributed. If some people earn more money than others, should they consume more goods? How much money should the government take from the rich and give to the poor?

As we'll see later in the book, most of these decisions are made in markets, with prices playing a key role in determining what products we produce, how we produce them, and who gets the products. In Chapter 3, we'll examine the role of markets in modern economies and the role of government in market-based economies.

### Economic Models

Economists use *economic models* to explore the choices people make and the consequences of those choices. An economic model is a simplified representation of an economic environment, with all but the essential features of the environment eliminated. An **economic models** is an abstraction from reality that enables us to focus our attention on what really matters. As we'll see throughout the book, most economic models use graphs to represent the economic environment.

* **economic model**
A simplified representation of an economic environment, often employing a graph.

To see the rationale for economic modeling, consider an architectural model. An architect builds a scale model of a new building and uses the model to show how the building will fit on a plot of land and blend with nearby buildings. The model shows the exterior features of the building, but not the interior features. We can ignore the interior features because they are unimportant for the task at hand—seeing how the building will fit into the local environment.

Economists build models to explore decision making by individuals, firms, and other organizations. For example, we can use a model of a profit-maximizing firm to predict how a firm will respond to increased competition. If a new car-stereo

store opens up in your town, will the old firms be passive and simply accept smaller market shares, or will they aggressively cut their prices to try to drive the new rival out of business? The model of the firm includes the monetary benefits and costs of doing business, and assumes that firms want to make as much money as possible. Although there may be other motives in the business world—to have fun or help the world—the economic model ignores these other motives. The model focuses our attention on the profit motive and how it affects a firm's response to increased competition.

## 1.2 | ECONOMIC ANALYSIS AND MODERN PROBLEMS

Economic analysis provides important insights into real-world problems. To explain how we can use economic analysis in problem solving, we provide three examples. You'll see these examples again in more detail later in the book.

### Economic View of Traffic Congestion

Consider first the problem of traffic congestion. According to the Texas Transportation Institute, the typical U.S. commuter wastes about 47 hours per year because of traffic congestion.[1] In some cities, the time wasted by the typical commuter is much greater: 93 hours in Los Angeles, 72 hours in San Francisco, and 63 hours in Houston. In addition to time lost, we also waste 2.3 billion gallons of gasoline and diesel fuel each year.

To an economist, the diagnosis of the congestion problem is straightforward. When you drive onto a busy highway during rush hour, your car takes up space and decreases the distance between the vehicles on the highway. The normal reaction to a shorter distance between moving cars is to slow down. So when you enter the highway, you force other commuters to spend more time on the highway. If each of your 900 fellow commuters spends just 2 extra seconds on the highway, you will increase the total travel time by 30 minutes. In deciding whether to use the highway, you will presumably ignore these costs that you impose on others. Similarly, your fellow commuters ignore the cost they impose on you and others when they enter the highway. Because no single commuter pays the full cost, too many people use the highway, and everyone wastes time.

One possible solution to the congestion problem is to force people to pay for using the road, just as they pay for gasoline and tires. The government could impose a congestion tax of $8 per trip on rush-hour commuters and use a debit card system to collect the tax: Every time a car passes a checkpoint, a transponder would charge the commuter's card. Traffic volume during rush hours would then decrease as travelers (a) shift their travel to off-peak times, (b) switch to ride sharing and mass transit, and (c) shift their travel to less congested routes. The job for the economist is to compute the appropriate congestion tax and predict the consequences of imposing the tax.

### Economic View of Poverty in Africa

Consider next the issue of poverty in Africa. In the final two decades of the twentieth century, the world economy grew rapidly, and the average per capita income (income per person) increased by about 35 percent. By contrast, the economies of poverty-stricken sub-Saharan Africa shrank, and per capita income decreased by about 6 percent. Africa is the world's second-largest continent in both area and population and accounts for more than 12 percent of the world's human population. Figure 1.1 shows a map of Africa. The countries of sub-Saharan Africa are highlighted in yellow.

► **FIGURE 1.1**
**Map of Africa**
Africa is the world's second-largest continent in both area and population, and accounts for more than 12 percent of the world's human population. The countries of sub-Saharan Africa are highlighted in orange
*SOURCE: web.worldbank.org/WBSITE/ EXTERNAL/COUNTRIES/AFRICA*

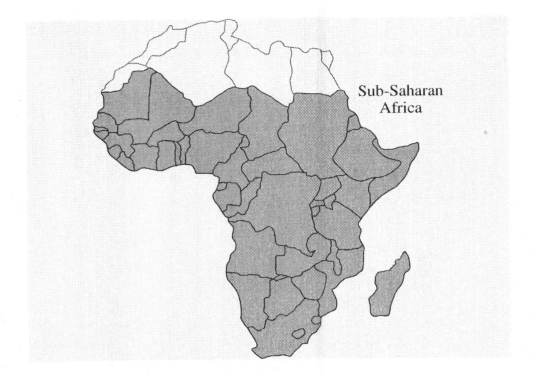

Sub-Saharan Africa

Economists have found that as a nation's economy grows, its poorest households share in the general prosperity.[2] Therefore, one way to reduce poverty in sub-Saharan Africa would be to increase economic growth. Economic growth occurs when a country expands its production facilities (machinery and factories), improves its public infrastructure (highways and water systems), widens educational opportunities, and adopts new technology.

The recent experience of sub-Saharan Africa is somewhat puzzling because in the last few decades the region has expanded educational opportunities and received large amounts of foreign aid. Some recent work by economists on the sources of growth suggests that institutions such as the legal system and the regulatory environment play key roles in economic growth.[3] In sub-Saharan Africa, a simple legal dispute about a small debt takes about 30 months to resolve, compared to five months in the United States. In Mozambique, it takes 174 days to complete the procedures required to set up a business, compared to just two days in Canada. In many cases, institutions impede rather than encourage the sort of investment and risk taking—entrepreneurship—that causes economic growth and reduces poverty. As a consequence, economists and policy makers are exploring ways to reform the region's institutions. They are also challenged with choosing among development projects that will generate the biggest economic boost per dollar spent—the biggest bang per buck.

## Economic View of Japan's Economic Problems

Consider next the economic problems experienced by Japan in the last decade. Following World War II, Japan grew rapidly, with per capita income increasing by about 4 percent per year between 1950 and 1992. But in 1992, the economy came to a screeching halt. For the next 10 years, per capita income either decreased or increased slightly. In 1995, the prices of all sorts of goods—including consumer goods and housing—actually started to decrease, and the downward slide continued for years. In an economy with declining prices, consumers expect lower prices tomorrow, so they are reluctant to buy goods and services today. Business managers are reluctant to borrow money to invest in production facilities, because if the prices of their products drop they might not have enough money to repay the loans.

The challenge for economists was to develop a set of policies to get the Japanese economy moving again. Economists responded by designing policies to stimulate spending by consumers and businesses and to make needed changes to the Japanese financial system. Although it was a slow process, economic and political reforms have put the Japanese economy on a sound footing that will support future economic growth.

# 1.3 | THE ECONOMIC WAY OF THINKING

How do economists think about problems and decision making? The economic way of thinking is best summarized by British economist John Maynard Keynes (1883–1946)[4]:

> The theory of economics does not furnish a body of settled conclusions immediately applicable to policy. It is a method rather than a doctrine, an apparatus of the mind, a technique of thinking which helps its possessor draw correct conclusions.

Let's look at the four elements of the economic way of thinking.

## 1. Use Assumptions to Simplify

Economists use assumptions to make things simpler and focus attention on what really matters. If you use a road map to plan a car trip from Seattle to San Francisco, you make two unrealistic assumptions to simplify your planning:

- The earth is flat: The flat road map doesn't show the curvature of the earth.
- The roads are flat: The standard road map doesn't show hills and valleys.

Instead of a map, you could use a globe that shows all the topographical features between Seattle and San Francisco, but you don't need those details to plan your trip. A map, with its unrealistic assumptions, will suffice, because the curvature of the earth and the topography of the highways are irrelevant to your trip. Although your analysis of the road trip is based on two unrealistic assumptions, that does not mean your analysis is invalid. Similarly, if economic analysis is based on unrealistic assumptions, that doesn't mean the analysis is faulty.

What if you decide to travel by bike instead of by automobile? Now the assumption of flat roads really matters, unless of course you are eager to pedal up and down mountains. If you use a standard map, and thus assume there are no mountains between the two cities, you may inadvertently pick a mountainous route instead of a flat one. In this case, the simplifying assumption makes a difference. The lesson is that we must think carefully about whether a simplifying assumption is truly harmless.

## 2. Isolate Variables—*Ceteris Paribus*

Economic analysis often involves *variables* and how they affect one another. A **variable** is a measure of something that can take on different values. Economists are interested in exploring relationships between two variables—for example, the relationship between the price of apples and the quantity of apples consumers purchase. Of course, the quantity of apples purchased depends on many other variables, including the consumer's income. To explore the relationship between the quantity and price of apples, we must assume that the consumer's income—and anything else that influences apple purchases—doesn't change.

* **variable**
A measure of something that can take on different values.

• **ceteris paribus**
The Latin expression meaning other
variables being held fixed.

Alfred Marshall (1842–1924) was a British economist who refined the economic model of supply and demand and provided a label for this process.[5] He picked one variable that affected apple purchases (price) and threw the other variable (income) into what he called the "pound" (in Marshall's time, the "pound" was an enclosure for holding stray cattle; nowadays, a pound is for stray dogs). That variable waited in the pound while Marshall examined the influence of the first variable. Marshall labeled the pound **ceteris paribus**, the Latin expression meaning that other variables are held fixed:

> . . . the existence of other tendencies is not denied, but their disturbing effect is neglected for a time. The more the issue is narrowed, the more exactly can it be handled.

This book contains many statements about the relationship between two variables. For example, the quantity of computers produced by Dell depends on the price of computers, the wage of computer workers, and the cost of microchips. When we say, "An increase in the price of computers increases the quantity of computers produced," we are assuming that the other two variables—the wage and the cost of microchips—do not change. That is, we apply the *ceteris paribus* assumption.

### 3. Think at the Margin

• **marginal change**
A small, one-unit change in value.

Economists often consider how a small change in one variable affects another variable and what impact that has on people's decision making. In other words, if circumstances change only slightly, how will people respond? A small, one-unit change in value is called a **marginal change**. The key feature of marginal change is that the first variable changes by only one unit. For example, you might ask, "If I study just one more hour, by how much will my exam score increase?" Economists call this process "thinking at the margin." Thinking at the margin is like thinking on the edge. You will encounter marginal thinking throughout this book. Here are some other marginal questions:

- If I study one more hour for an exam, by how much will my grade increase?
- If I stay in school and earn another degree, by how much will my lifetime earnings increase?
- If a car dealer hires one more sales associate, how many more cars will the dealer sell?

As we'll see in the next chapter, economists use the answer to a marginal question as a first step in deciding whether to do more or less of something.

### 4. Rational People Respond to Incentives

A key assumption of most economic analysis is that people act rationally, meaning that they act in their own self-interest. Scottish philosopher Adam Smith (1723–1790), who is also considered the founder of economics, wrote that he discovered within humankind:[6]

> a desire of bettering our condition, a desire which, though generally calm and dispassionate, comes with us from the womb, and never leaves us until we go to the grave.

Smith didn't say that people are motivated exclusively by self-interest, but rather that self-interest is more powerful than kindness or altruism. In this book, we will assume that people act in their own self-interest. Rational people respond to incentives. When the payoff, or benefit, from doing something changes, people change their behavior to get the benefit.

# Appendix A

# APPENDIX A
## USING GRAPHS AND PERCENTAGES

Economists use several types of graphs to present data, represent relationships between variables, and explain concepts. In this appendix, we review the mechanics of graphing variables. We'll also review the basics of computing percentage changes and using percentages to compute changes in variables.

## USING GRAPHS

A quick flip through the book will reveal the importance of graphs in economics. Every chapter has at least several graphs, and many chapters have more. Although it is possible to do economics without graphs, it's a lot easier with them in your toolbox.

### Graphing Single Variables

As we saw earlier in Chapter 1, a *variable* is a measure of something that can take on different values. Figure 1A.1 shows two types of graphs, each presenting data on a single variable. Panel A uses a pie graph to show the breakdown of U.S. music sales by type of music. The larger the sales of a type of music, the larger the pie slice. For example, the most popular type is Rock music, comprising 24 percent of the market. The next largest type is Rap/Hip-hop, followed by R&B/Urban, Country, and so on. Panel B of Figure 1A.1 uses a bar graph to show the revenue from foreign sales (exports) of selected U.S. industries. The larger the revenue, the taller the bar. For example, the bar for computer software, with export sales of about $60 billion, is over three times taller than the bar for motion pictures, TV, and video, with export sales of $17 billion.

A third type of single-variable graph shows how the value of a variable changes over time. Panel A of Figure 1A.2 shows a time-series graph, with the total dollar

► **FIGURE 1A.1**
**Graphs of Single Variables**

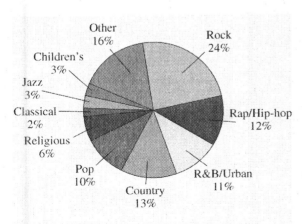

**(A) Pie Graph for Types of Recorded Music Sold in the United States**

SOURCE: Author's calculations based in Recording Industry Association of America, "2004 Consumer Profile."

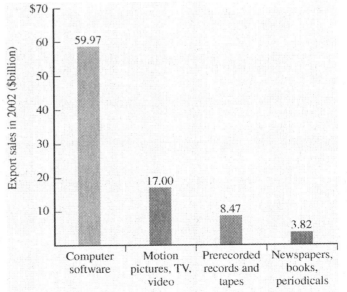

**(B) Bar Graph for U.S. Export Sales of Copyrighted Products**

SOURCE: Author's calculations based on International Intellectual Property Alliance, "Copyright Industries in the U.S. Economy, 2004 Report."

► FIGURE 1A.2
**Time-Series Graph**
SOURCE: Author's calculations based in
Recording Industry Association of
America, "2004 Consumer Profile."

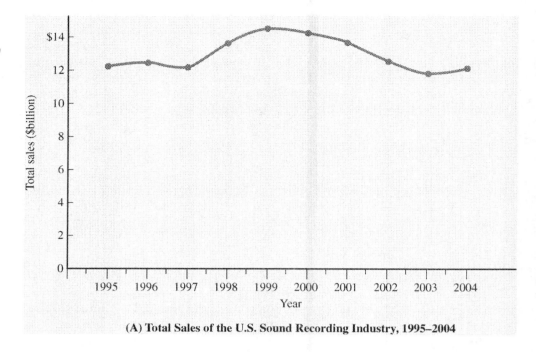

**(A) Total Sales of the U.S. Sound Recording Industry, 1995–2004**

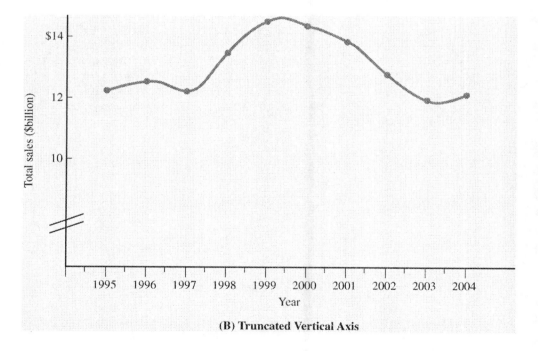

**(B) Truncated Vertical Axis**

value of the U.S. sound-recording industry from 1995 through 2004. Time is measured on the horizontal axis, and sales are measured on the vertical axis. The height of the line in a particular year shows the value in that year. For example, in 1995 the value was $12.32 billion. After reaching a peak of $14.59 billion in 1999, the value dropped over the next several years.

Panel B of Figure 1A.2 shows a truncated version of the graph in Panel A. The double hash marks in the lower part of the vertical axis indicate that the axis doesn't start from zero. The truncation of the vertical axis exaggerates the fluctuations in the value of production.

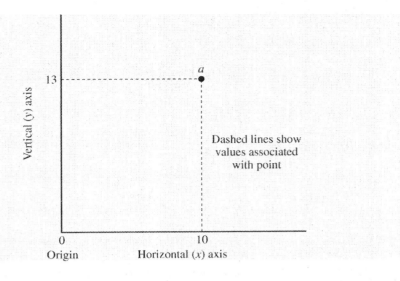

One variable is measured along the horizontal or x axis, while the other variable is measured along the vertical or y axis. The origin is defined as the intersection of the two axes, where the values of both variables are zero. The dashed lines show the values of the two variables at a particular point.

## Graphing Two Variables

We can also use a graph to show the relationship between two variables. Figure 1A.3 shows the basic elements of a two-variable graph. One variable is measured along the horizontal, or x, axis, while the other variable is measured along the vertical, or y, axis. The *origin* is defined as the intersection of the two axes, where the values of both variables are zero. Dashed lines show the values of the two variables at a particular point. For example, for point a, the value of the horizontal, or x, variable is 10, and the value of the vertical, or y, variable is 13.

To see how to draw a two-variable graph, suppose that you have a part-time job and you are interested in the relationship between the number of hours you work and your weekly income. The relevant variables are the hours of work per week and your weekly income. In Figure 1A.4, the table shows the relationship between the hours

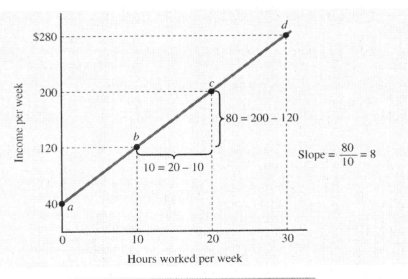

◄ **FIGURE 1A.4**
**Relationship Between Hours Worked and Income**

There is a positive relationship between work hours and income, so the income curve is positively sloped. The slope of the curve is $8: Each additional hour of work increases income by $8.

| Hours Worked per Week | Income per Week | Point on the Graph |
|---|---|---|
| 0 | $ 40 | a |
| 10 | 120 | b |
| 20 | 200 | c |
| 30 | 280 | d |

worked and income. Let's assume that your weekly allowance from your parents is $40 and your part-time job pays $8 per hour. If you work 10 hours per week, for example, your weekly income is $120 ($40 from your parents and $80 from your job). The more you work, the higher your weekly income: If you work 20 hours, your weekly income is $200; if you work 30 hours, it is $280.

Although a table with numbers is helpful in showing the relationship between work hours and income, a graph makes it easier to see the relationship. We can use data in a table to draw a graph. To do so, we perform five simple steps:

1. Draw a horizontal line to represent the first variable. In Figure 1A.4, we measure hours worked along the horizontal axis. As we move to the right along the horizontal axis, the number of hours worked increases, from zero to 30 hours.

2. Draw a vertical line intersecting the first line to represent the second variable. In Figure 1A.4, we measure income along the vertical axis. As we move up along the vertical axis, income increases from zero to $280.

3. Start with the first row of numbers in the table, which shows that with zero hours worked, income is $40. The value of the variable on the horizontal axis is zero, and the value of the variable on the vertical axis is $40, so we plot point *a* on the graph. This is the *vertical intercept*—the point where the curve cuts or intersects the vertical axis.

4. Pick a combination with a positive number for hours worked. For example, in the second row of numbers, if you work 10 hours, your income is $120.

   4.1 Find the point on the horizontal axis with that number of hours worked—10 hours—and draw a dashed line vertically straight up from that point.

   4.2 Find the point on the vertical axis with the income corresponding to those hours worked—$120—and draw a dashed line horizontally straight to the right from that point.

   4.3 The intersection of the dashed lines shows the combination of hours worked and income. Point *b* shows the combination of 10 hours worked and $120 in income.

5. Repeat step 4 for different combinations of work time and income shown in the table. Once we have a series of points on the graph (*a*, *b*, *c*, and *d*), we can connect them to draw a curve that shows the relationship between hours worked and income.

There is a **positive relationship** between two variables if they move in the same direction. As you increase your work time, your income increases, so there is a positive relationship between the two variables. In Figure 1A.4, as the number of hours worked increases, you move upward along the curve to higher income levels. Some people refer to a positive relationship as a *direct relationship*.

There is a **negative relationship** between two variables if they move in opposite directions. For example, there is a negative relationship between the amount of time you work and the time you have available for other activities such as recreation, study, and sleep. Some people refer to a negative relationship as an *inverse relationship*.

### Computing the Slope

How sensitive is one variable to changes in the other variable? We can use the slope of the curve to measure this sensitivity. To compute the **slope of a curve**, we pick two points and divide the vertical difference between the two points (the *rise*) by the horizontal difference (the *run*):

$$\text{Slope} = \frac{\text{Vertical difference between two points}}{\text{Horizontal difference between two points}} = \frac{\text{rise}}{\text{run}}$$

* **positive relationship**
A relationship in which two variables move in the same direction.

* **negative relationship**
A relationship in which two variables move in opposite directions.

* **slope of a curve**
The vertical difference between two points (the *rise*) divided by the horizontal difference (the *run*).

To compute the slope of a curve, we take four steps:

1  Pick two points on the curve, for example, points *b* and *c* in Figure 1A.4.
2  Compute the vertical difference between the two points (the rise). For points *b* and *c*, the vertical difference between the points is $80 ($200 − $120).
3  Compute the horizontal distance between the same two points (the run). For points *b* and *c*, the horizontal distance between the points is 10 hours (20 hours − 10 hours).
4  Divide the vertical distance by the horizontal distance to get the slope. The slope between points *b* and *c* is $8 per hour:

$$\text{Slope} = \frac{\text{Vertical difference}}{\text{Horizontal difference}} = \frac{\$200 - 120}{20 - 10} = \frac{\$80}{10} = \$8$$

In this case, a 10-hour increase in time worked increases income by $80, so the increase in income per hour of work is $8, which makes sense because this is the hourly wage. Because the curve is a straight line, the slope is the same at all points along the curve. You can check this yourself by computing the slope between points *c* and *d*.

We can use some shorthand to refer to the slope of a curve. The mathematical symbol Δ (delta) represents the change in a variable. So the slope of the curve in Figure 1A.4 could be written as

$$\text{Slope} = \frac{\Delta \text{Income}}{\Delta \text{Work hours}}$$

In general, if the variable on the vertical axis is *y* and the variable on the horizontal axis is *x*, we can express the slope as

$$\text{Slope} = \frac{\Delta y}{\Delta x}$$

## Moving Along the Curve Versus Shifting the Curve

Up to this point, we've explored the effect of changes in variables that cause movement along a given curve. In Figure 1A.4, we see the relationship between hours of work (on the horizontal axis) and income (on the vertical axis). Because the total income also depends on the allowance and the wage, we can make two observations about the curve in Figure 1A.4:

1  To draw this curve, we must specify the weekly allowance ($40) and the hourly wage ($8).
2  The curve shows that an increase in time worked increases the student's income, *ceteris paribus*. In this case, we are assuming that the allowance and the wage are both fixed.

A change in the weekly allowance will shift the curve showing the relationship between work time and income. In Figure 1A.5, when the allowance increases from $40 to $90, the curve shifts upward by $50: For a given number of work hours, income increases by $50. For example, the income associated with 10 hours of work is $170 (point *f*), compared to $120 with the original allowance (point *b*). The upward shift also means that to reach a given amount of income, fewer work hours are required. In other words, the curve shifts upward and to the left.

We can distinguish between movement along a curve and a shift of the entire curve. In Figure 1A.5, an increase in the hours worked causes movement along a single income curve. For example, if the allowance is $40, we are operating on the lower of the two curves, and if the hours worked increases from 10 to 20, we move from point *b* to point *c*. In contrast, if something other than the hours worked changes, we shift the entire curve, as we've seen with an increase in the allowance.

To draw a curve showing the relationship between hours worked and income, we fix the weekly allowance ($40) and the wage ($8 per hour). A change in the hours worked causes movement along the curve, for example, from point *b* to point *c*. A change in any other variable shifts the entire curve. For example, a $50 increase in the allowance (to $90) shifts the entire curve upward by $50.

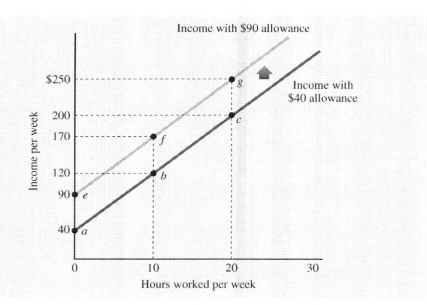

This book uses dozens of two-dimensional curves, each of which shows the relationship between *only two* variables. A common error is to forget that a single curve tells only part of the story. In Figure 1A.5, we needed two curves to explore the effects of changes in three variables. Here are some simple rules to keep in mind when you use two-dimensional graphs:

- A change in one of the variables shown on the graph causes movement along the curve. In Figure 1A.5, an increase in work time causes movement along the curve from point *a* to point *b*, to point *c*, and so on.

- A change in one of the variables that is not shown on the graph—one of the variables held fixed in drawing the curve—shifts the entire curve. In Figure 1A.5, an increase in the allowance shifts the entire curve upward.

## Graphing Negative Relationships

We can use a graph to show a negative relationship between two variables. Consider a consumer who has an annual budget of $360 to spend on CDs at a price of $12 per CD and downloaded music at a price of $1 per song. The table in Figure 1A.6 shows the relationship between the number of CDs and downloaded songs. A consumer who doesn't buy any CDs has $360 to spend on downloaded songs and can get 360 of them at a price of $1 each. A consumer who buys 10 CDs at $12 each has $240 left to spend on downloaded songs (point *b*). Moving down through the table, as the number of CDs increases, the number of downloaded songs decreases.

The graph in Figure 1A.6 shows the negative relationship between the number of CDs and the number of downloaded songs. The vertical intercept (point *a*) shows that a consumer who doesn't buy any CDs can afford 360 downloaded songs. There is a negative relationship between the number of CDs and downloaded songs, so the curve is negatively sloped. We can use points *b* and *c* to compute the slope of the curve:

$$\text{Slope} = \frac{\text{Vertical difference}}{\text{Horizontal difference}} = \frac{240 - 120}{10 - 20} = \frac{120}{-10} = -12$$

The slope is 12 downloaded songs per CD: For each additional CD, the consumer sacrifices 12 downloaded songs.

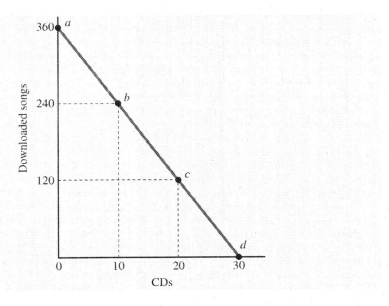

| Number of CDs Purchased | Number of Songs Downloaded | Point on the Graph |
|---|---|---|
| 0 | 360 | a |
| 10 | 240 | b |
| 20 | 120 | c |
| 30 | 0 | d |

▲ **FIGURE 1A.6**
**Negative Relationship Between CD Purchases and Downloaded Songs**
There is a negative relationship between the number of CDs and downloaded songs that a consumer can afford with a budget of $360. The slope of the curve is $12: Each additional CD (at a price of $12 each) decreases the number of downloadable songs (at $1 each) by 12 songs.

## Graphing Nonlinear Relationships

We can also use a graph to show a nonlinear relationship between two variables. Panel A of Figure 1A.7 shows the relationship between hours spent studying for an exam and the grade on the exam. As study time increases, the grade increases, but at a decreasing rate. In other words, each additional hour increases the exam grade by a smaller and smaller amount. For example, the second hour of study increases the grade by 4 points—from 6 to 10 points—but the ninth hour of study increases the grade by only 1 point—from 24 points to 25 points. This is a nonlinear relationship: The slope of the curve changes as we move along the curve. In Figure 1A.7, the slope decreases as we move to the right along the curve: The slope is 4 points per hour between points *a* and *b* but only 1 point per hour between points *c* and *d*.

Another possibility for a nonlinear curve is that the slope increases as we move to the right along the curve. Panel B of Figure 1A.7 shows the relationship between the amount of grain produced on the horizontal axis and the total cost of production on the vertical axis. The slope of the curve increases as the amount of grain increases, meaning that production cost increases at an increasing rate. On the lower part of the curve, increasing output from 1 ton to 2 tons increases production cost by $5, from $10 to $15. On the upper part of the curve, increasing output from 10 to 11 tons increases production cost by $25, from $100 to $125.

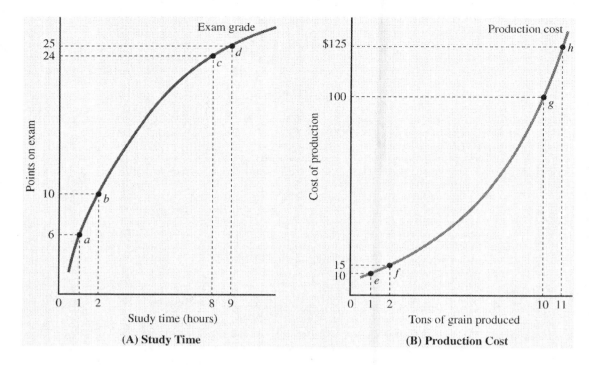

▲ **FIGURE 1A.7**
**Nonlinear Relationships**

**(A) Study time** There is a positive and nonlinear relationship between study time and the grade on an exam. As study time increases, the exam grade increases at a decreasing rate. For example, the second hour of study increased the grade by 4 points (from 6 points to 10 points), but the ninth hour of study increases the grade by only 1 point (from 24 points to 25 points).

**(B) Production cost** There is a positive and nonlinear relationship between the quantity of grain produced and total production cost. As the quantity increases, the total cost increases at an increasing rate. For example, to increase production from 1 ton to 2 tons, production cost increases by $5 (from $10 to $15) but to increase the production from 10 to 11 tons, total cost increases by $25 (from $100 to $125).

# COMPUTING PERCENTAGE CHANGES AND USING EQUATIONS

Economists often express changes in variables in terms of percentage changes. This part of the appendix provides a brief review of the mechanics of computing percentage changes. It also reviews some simple rules for solving equations to find missing values.

## Computing Percentage Changes

In many cases, the equations that economists use involve percentage changes. In this book, we use a simple approach to computing percentage changes: We divide the change in the variable by the initial value of the variable and then multiply by 100:

$$\text{Percentage change} = \frac{\text{New value} - \text{initial value}}{\text{Initial value}} \times 100$$

For example, if the price of a book increases from \$20 to \$22, the percentage change is 10 percent:

$$\text{Percentage change} = \frac{22 - 20}{20} \times 100 = \frac{2}{20} \times 100 = 10\%$$

Going in the other direction, suppose the price decreases from \$20 to \$19. In this case, the percentage change is −5 percent:

$$\text{Percentage change} = \frac{19 - 20}{20} \times 100 = -\frac{1}{20} \times 100 = -5\%$$

The alternative to this simple approach is to base the percentage change on the average value, or the midpoint, of the variable:

$$\text{Percentage change} = \frac{\text{New value} - \text{initial value}}{\text{Average value}} \times 100$$

For example, if the price of a book increases from \$20 to \$22, the computed percentage change under the midpoint approach would be 9.52 percent:

$$\text{Percentage change} = \frac{22 - 20}{(20 + 22) \div 2} \times 100 = \frac{2}{42 \div 2} \times 100 = \frac{2}{21} \times 100 = 9.52\%$$

If the change in the variable is relatively small, the extra precision associated with the midpoint approach is usually not worth the extra effort. The simple approach allows us to spend less time doing tedious arithmetic and more time doing economic analysis. In this book, we use the simple approach to compute percentage changes: If the price increases from \$20 to \$22, the price has increased by 10 percent.

If we know a percentage change, we can translate it into an absolute change. For example, if a price has increased by 10 percent and the initial price is \$20, then we add 10 percent of the initial price (\$2 is 10 percent of \$20) to the initial price (\$20), for a new price of \$22. If the price decreases by 5 percent, we subtract 5 percent of the initial price (\$1 is 5 percent of \$20) from the initial price (\$20), for a new price of \$19.

## Using Equations to Compute Missing Values

It will often be useful to compute the value of the numerator or the denominator of an equation. To do so, we use simple algebra to rearrange the equation to put the missing variable on the left side of the equation. For example, consider the relationship between time worked and income. The equation for the slope is

$$\text{Slope} = \frac{\Delta \text{ Income}}{\Delta \text{ Work hours}}$$

Suppose you want to compute how much income you'll earn by working more hours. We can rearrange the slope equation by multiplying both sides of the equation by the change in work hours:

$$\text{Work hours} \times \text{Slope} = \Delta \text{ Income}$$

By swapping sides of the equation, we get:

$$\Delta \text{ Income} = \Delta \text{ Work hours} \times \text{Slope}$$

For example, if you work seven extra hours and the slope is $8, your income will increase by $56:

$$\Delta \text{ Income} = \Delta \text{Work hours} \times \text{Slope} = 7 \times \$8 = \$56$$

We can use the same process to compute the difference in work time required to achieve a target change in income. In this case, we multiply both sides of the slope equation by the change in work time and then divide both sides by the slope. The result is

$$\Delta \text{Work hours} = \frac{\Delta \text{ Income}}{\text{Slope}}$$

For example, to increase your income by $56, you need to work seven hours:

$$\Delta \text{Work hours} = \frac{\Delta \text{ Income}}{\text{Slope}} = \frac{\$56}{\$8} = 7$$

## KEY TERMS

negative relationship          positive relationship          slope of a curve

## EXERCISES  Get Ahead of the Curve

Visit www.myeconlab.com to complete these exercises online and get instant feedback.

**A1.** Suppose you belong to a tennis club that has a monthly fee of $100 and a charge of $5 per hour to play tennis.

    **a.** Using Figure 1A.4 on page 19 as a model, prepare a table and draw a curve to show the relationship between the hours of tennis (on the horizontal axis) and the monthly club bill (on the vertical axis). For the table and graph, use 5, 10, 15, and 20 hours of tennis.

    **b.** The slope of the curve is _____ per _____.

    **c.** Suppose you start with 10 hours of tennis and then decide to increase your tennis time by 3 hours. On your curve, show the initial point and the new point. By how much will your monthly bill increase?

    **d.** Suppose you start with 10 hours and then decide to spend an additional $30 on tennis. On your curve, show the initial point and the new point. How many additional hours can you get?

**A2.** The following graph shows the relationship between the number of Frisbees produced and the cost of production. The vertical intercept is $\_\_\_\_\_, and the slope of the curve is $\_\_\_\_\_ per Frisbee. Point *b* shows that the cost of producing \_\_\_\_\_ Frisbees is $\_\_\_\_\_. The cost of producing 15 frisbees is $\_\_\_\_\_.

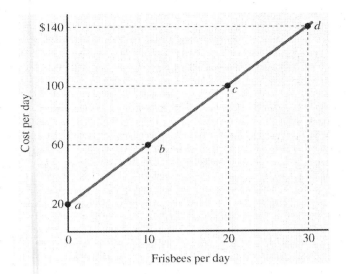

Cost per day / Frisbees per day

$140 ─ d
100 ─ c
60 ─ b
20 ─ a
0   10   20   30

**A3.** Suppose you have $120 to spend on CDs and movies. The price of a CD is $12, and the price of a movie is $6.

    **a.** Using Figure 1A.6 on page 19 as a model, prepare a table and draw a curve to show the relationship between the number of CDs (on the horizontal axis) and movies (on the vertical axis) you can afford to buy.

    **b.** The slope of the curve is _____ per _____.

**A4.** You manage Gofer Delivery Service. You rent a truck for $50 per day, and each delivery takes an hour of labor time. The hourly wage is $8.

    **a.** Draw a curve showing the relationship between the number of deliveries (on the horizontal axis) and your total cost (on the vertical axis). Draw the curve for between zero and 20 deliveries.

    **b.** The slope of the cost curve is _____ per _____.

    **c.** To draw the curve, what variables are held fixed?

    **d.** A change in _____ would cause a movement upward along the curve.

    **e.** Changes in _____ would cause the entire curve to shift upward.

**A5.** A change in a variable measured on an axis of a graph causes movement _____ a curve, while a change in a relevant variable that is not measured on an axis _____ the curve.

**A6.** Compute the percentage changes for the following :

| Initial Value | New Value | Percentage Change |
|---|---|---|
| 10 | 11 | _____ |
| 100 | 98 | _____ |
| 50 | 53 | _____ |

**A7.** Compute the new values for the following changes.

| Initial Value | Percentage Change | New Value |
|---|---|---|
| 100 | 12% | _____ |
| 50 | 8 | _____ |
| 20 | 15 | _____ |

# Appendix B

# Appendix B

## Using Graphs and Formulas

Review the use of **graphs** and **formulas**.

Graphs are used to illustrate key economics ideas. Graphs appear not just in economics textbooks but also on Web sites and in newspaper and magazine articles that discuss events in business and economics. Why the heavy use of graphs? Because they serve two useful purposes: (1) They simplify economic ideas, and (2) they make the ideas more concrete so they can be applied to real-world problems. Economic and business issues can be complicated, but a graph can help cut through complications and highlight the key relationships needed to understand the issue. In that sense, a graph can be like a street map.

For example, suppose you take a bus to New York City to see the Empire State Building. After arriving at the Port Authority Bus Terminal, you will probably use a map similar to the one shown below to find your way to the Empire State Building.

Maps are very familiar to just about everyone, so we don't usually think of them as being simplified versions of reality, but they are. This map does not show much more than the streets in this part of New York City and some of the most important buildings. The names, addresses, and telephone numbers of the people who live and work in the

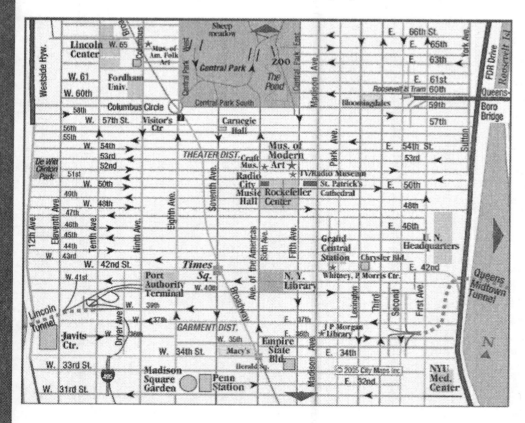

## A Preview of Important Economic Terms

# Summary

Becoming familiar with important terms is a necessary step in learning economics. These important economic terms include

*capital, entrepreneur, factors of production, firm, goods, house-hold, human capital, innovation, profit, revenue,* and *technology.*

area aren't given. Almost none of the stores and buildings those people work and live in are shown either. The map doesn't tell which streets allow curbside parking and which don't. In fact, the map tells almost nothing about the messy reality of life in this section of New York City, except how the streets are laid out, which is the essential information you need to get from the Port Authority to the Empire State Building.

Think about someone who says, "I know how to get around in the city, but I just can't figure out how to read a map." It certainly is possible to find your destination in a city without a map, but it's a lot easier with one. The same is true of using graphs in economics. It is possible to arrive at a solution to a real-world problem in economics and business without using graphs, but it is usually a lot easier if you do use them.

Often, the difficulty students have with graphs and formulas is a lack of familiarity. With practice, all the graphs and formulas in this text will become familiar to you. Once you are familiar with them, you will be able to use them to analyze problems that would otherwise seem very difficult. What follows is a brief review of how graphs and formulas are used.

# Graphs of One Variable

Figure 1A-1 displays values for *market shares* in the U.S. automobile market, using two common types of graphs. Market shares show the percentage of industry sales accounted for by different firms. In this case, the information is for groups of firms: the

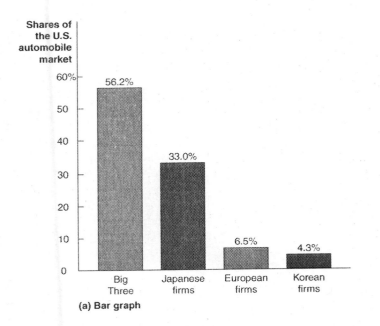

**(a) Bar graph**

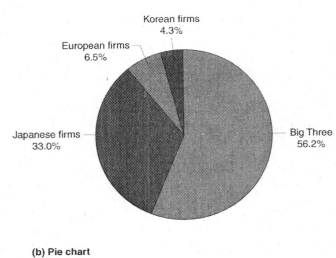

**(b) Pie chart**

Figure 1A-1 | Bar Graphs and Pie Charts

Values for an economic variable are often displayed as a bar graph or as a pie chart. In this case, panel (a) shows market share data for the U.S. automobile industry as a bar graph, where the market share of each group of firms is represented by the height of

its bar. Panel (b) displays the same information as a pie chart, with the market share of each group of firms represented by the size of its slice of the pie.

Source: "Auto Sales," *Wall Street Journal*, March 1, 2007.

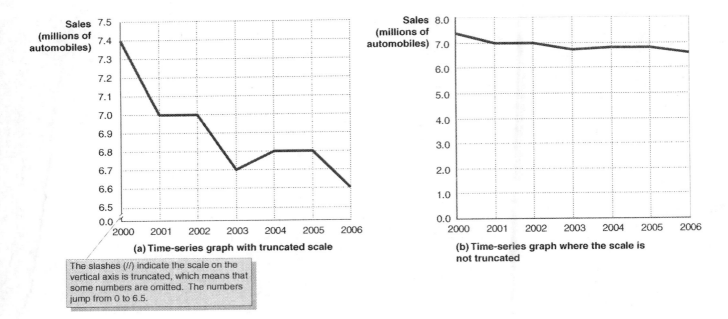

(a) Time-series graph with truncated scale

The slashes (//) indicate the scale on the vertical axis is truncated, which means that some numbers are omitted. The numbers jump from 0 to 6.5.

(b) Time-series graph where the scale is not truncated

## Figure 1A-2 | Time-Series Graphs

Both panels present time-series graphs of Ford Motor Company's worldwide sales during each year from 2000–2006. Panel (a) has a truncated scale on the vertical axis, and panel (b) does not. As a result, the fluctuations in Ford's sales appear smaller in panel (b) than in panel (a).
Source: Ford Motor Company, *Annual Report*, various years.

"Big Three"—Ford, General Motors, and DaimlerChrysler—as well as Japanese firms, European firms, and Korean firms. Panel (a) displays the information on market shares as a *bar graph*, where the market share of each group of firms is represented by the height of its bar. Panel (b) displays the same information as a *pie chart*, with the market share of each group of firms represented by the size of its slice of the pie.

Information on economic variables is also often displayed in *time-series graphs*. Time-series graphs are displayed on a coordinate grid. In a coordinate grid, we can measure the value of one variable along the vertical axis (or *y*-axis), and the value of another variable along the horizontal axis (or *x*-axis). The point where the vertical axis intersects the horizontal axis is called the *origin*. At the origin, the value of both variables is zero. The points on a coordinate grid represent values of the two variables. In Figure 1A-2, we measure the number of automobiles and trucks sold worldwide by the Ford Motor Company on the vertical axis, and we measure time on the horizontal axis. In time-series graphs, the height of the line at each date shows the value of the variable measured on the vertical axis. Both panels of Figure 1A-2 show Ford's worldwide sales during each year from 2000 to 2006. The difference between panel (a) and panel (b) illustrates the importance of the scale used in a time-series graph. In panel (a), the scale on the vertical axis is truncated, which means that it does not start with zero. The slashes (//) near the bottom of the axis indicate that the scale is truncated. In panel (b), the scale is not truncated. In panel (b), the decline in Ford's sales since 2000 appears smaller than in panel (a). (Technically, the horizontal axis is also truncated because we start with the year 2000, not the year 0.)

## Graphs of Two Variables

We often use graphs to show the relationship between two variables. For example, suppose you are interested in the relationship between the price of a pepperoni pizza and the quantity of pizzas sold per week in the small town of Bryan, Texas. A graph showing the relationship between the price of a good and the quantity of the good demanded at each price is called a *demand curve*. (As we will discuss later, in drawing a demand curve

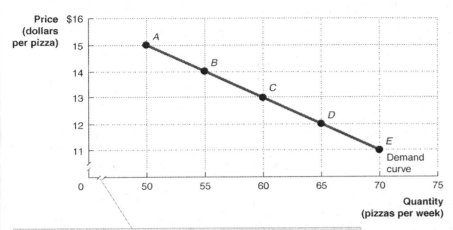

| Price<br>(dollars per pizza) | Quantity<br>(pizzas per week) | Points |
|:---:|:---:|:---:|
| $15 | 50 | A |
| 14 | 55 | B |
| 13 | 60 | C |
| 12 | 65 | D |
| 11 | 70 | E |

## Figure 1A-3

**Plotting Price and Quantity Points in a Graph**

The figure shows a two-dimensional grid on which we measure the price of pizza along the vertical axis (or *y*-axis) and the quantity of pizza sold per week along the horizontal axis (or *x*-axis). Each point on the grid represents one of the price and quantity combinations listed in the table. By connecting the points with a line, we can better illustrate the relationship between the two variables.

As you learned in Figure 1A-2, the slashes (//) indicate the scales on the axes are truncated, which means that numbers are omitted: On the horizontal axis numbers jump from 0 to 50, and on the vertical axis numbers jump from 0 to 11.

for a good, we have to hold constant any variables other than price that might affect the willingness of consumers to buy the good.) Figure 1A-3 shows the data you have collected on price and quantity. The figure shows a two-dimensional grid on which we measure the price of pizza along the *y*-axis and the quantity of pizza sold per week along the *x*-axis. Each point on the grid represents one of the price and quantity combinations listed in the table. We can connect the points to form the demand curve for pizza in Bryan, Texas. Notice that the scales on both axes in the graph are truncated. In this case, truncating the axes allows the graph to illustrate more clearly the relationship between price and quantity by excluding low prices and quantities.

## Slopes of Lines

Once you have plotted the data in Figure 1A-3, you may be interested in how much the quantity of pizza sold increases as the price decreases. The *slope* of a line tells us how much the variable we are measuring on the *y*-axis changes as the variable we are measuring on the *x*-axis changes. We can use the Greek letter delta ($\Delta$) to stand for the change in a variable. The slope is sometimes referred to as the rise over the run. So, we have several ways of expressing slope:

$$\text{Slope} = \frac{\text{Change in value on the vertical axis}}{\text{Change in value on the horizontal axis}} = \frac{\Delta y}{\Delta x} = \frac{\text{Rise}}{\text{Run}}.$$

Figure 1A-4 reproduces the graph from Figure 1A-3. Because the slope of a straight line is the same at any point, we can use any two points in the figure to calculate the slope of the line. For example, when the price of pizza decreases from $14 to $12, the quantity of pizza sold increases from 55 per week to 65 per week. Therefore, the slope is:

$$\text{Slope} = \frac{\Delta \text{Price of pizza}}{\Delta \text{Quantity of pizza}} = \frac{(\$12 - \$14)}{(65 - 55)} = \frac{-2}{10} = -0.2.$$

## Figure 1A-4

We can calculate the slope of a line as the change in the value of the variable on the y-axis divided by the change in the value of the variable on the x-axis. Because the slope of a straight line is constant, we can use any two points in the figure to calculate the slope of the line. For example, when the price of pizza decreases from $14 to $12, the quantity of pizza demanded increases from 55 per week to 65 per week. So, the slope of this line equals −2 divided by 10, or −0.2.

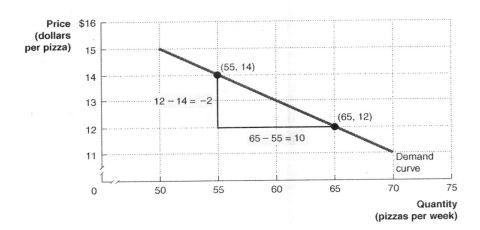

The slope of this line gives us some insight into how responsive consumers in Bryan, Texas, are to changes in the price of pizza. The larger the value of the slope (ignoring the negative sign), the steeper the line will be, which indicates that not many additional pizzas are sold when the price falls. The smaller the value of the slope, the flatter the line will be, which indicates a greater increase in pizzas sold when the price falls.

## Taking into Account More Than Two Variables on a Graph

The demand curve graph in Figure 1A-4 shows the relationship between the price of pizza and the quantity of pizza sold, but we know that the quantity of any good sold depends on more than just the price of the good. For example, the quantity of pizza sold in a given week in Bryan, Texas, can be affected by such other variables as the price of hamburgers, whether an advertising campaign by local pizza parlors has begun that week, and so on. Allowing the values of any other variables to change will cause the position of the demand curve in the graph to change.

Suppose, for example, that the demand curve in Figure 1A-4 was drawn holding the price of hamburgers constant at $1.50. If the price of hamburgers rises to $2.00, then some consumers will switch from buying hamburgers to buying pizza, and more pizzas will be sold at every price. The result on the graph will be to shift the line representing the demand curve to the right. Similarly, if the price of hamburgers falls from $1.50 to $1.00, some consumers will switch from buying pizza to buying hamburgers, and fewer pizzas will be sold at every price. The result on the graph will be to shift the line representing the demand curve to the left.

The table in Figure 1A-5 shows the effect of a change in the price of hamburgers on the quantity of pizza demanded. For example, suppose at first we are on the line labeled *Demand curve*$_1$. If the price of pizza is $14 (point *A*), an increase in the price of hamburgers from $1.50 to $2.00 increases the quantity of pizzas demanded from 55 to 60 per week (point *B*) and shifts us to *Demand curve*$_2$. Or, if we start on *Demand curve*$_1$ and the price of pizza is $12 (point *C*), a decrease in the price of hamburgers from $1.50 to $1.00 decreases the quantity of pizzas demanded from 65 to 60 per week (point *D*) and shifts us to *Demand curve*$_3$. By shifting the demand curve, we have taken into account the effect of changes in the value of a third variable—the price of hamburgers. We will use this technique of shifting curves to allow for the effects of additional variables many times in this book.

## Positive and Negative Relationships

We can use graphs to show the relationships between any two variables. Sometimes the relationship between the variables is *negative*, meaning that as one variable increases in value, the other variable decreases in value. This was the case with the

| Quantity (pizzas per week) | | | |
|---|---|---|---|
| Price (dollars per pizza) | When the Price of Hamburgers = $1.00 | When the Price of Hamburgers = $1.50 | When the Price of Hamburgers = $2.00 |
| $15 | 45 | 50 | 55 |
| 14 | 50 | 55 | 60 |
| 13 | 55 | 60 | 65 |
| 12 | 60 | 65 | 70 |
| 11 | 65 | 70 | 75 |

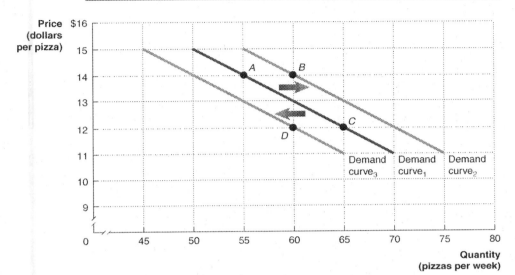

## Figure 1A-5

### Showing Three Variables on a Graph

The demand curve for pizza shows the relationship between the price of pizzas and the quantity of pizzas demanded, *holding constant other factors that might affect the willingness of consumers to buy pizza*. If the price of pizza is $14 (point *A*), an increase in the price of hamburgers from $1.50 to $2.00 increases the quantity of pizzas demanded from 55 to 60 per week (point *B*) and shifts us to Demand curve₂. Or, if we start on *Demand curve₁* and the price of pizza is $12 (point *C*), a decrease in the price of hamburgers from $1.50 to $1.00 decreases the quantity of pizza demanded from 65 to 60 per week (point *D*) and shifts us to *Demand curve₃*.

price of pizza and the quantity of pizzas demanded. The relationship between two variables can also be *positive*, meaning that the values of both variables increase or decrease together. For example, when the level of total income—or *disposable personal income*—received by households in the United States increases, the level of total *consumption spending*, which is spending by households on goods and services, also increases. The table in Figure 1A-6 shows the values for income and consumption spending for the years 2003–2006 (the values are in billions of dollars). The graph

| Year | Disposable Personal Income (billions of dollars) | Consumption Spending (billions of dollars) |
|---|---|---|
| 2003 | $8,163 | $7,704 |
| 2004 | 8,682 | 8,212 |
| 2005 | 9,036 | 8,742 |
| 2006 | 9,523 | 9,269 |

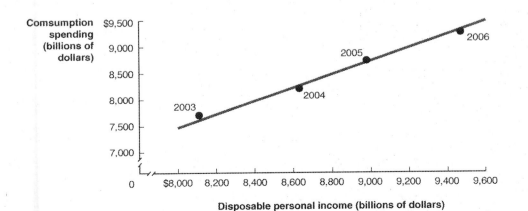

## Figure 1A-6

### Graphing the Positive Relationship between Income and Consumption

In a positive relationship between two economic variables, as one variable increases, the other variable also increases. This figure shows the positive relationship between disposable personal income and consumption spending. As disposable personal income in the United States has increased, so has consumption spending. Source: U.S. Department of Commerce, Bureau of Economic Analysis.

plots the data from the table, with national income measured along the horizontal axis and consumption spending measured along the vertical axis. Notice that the four points do not all fall exactly on the line. This is often the case with real-world data. To examine the relationship between two variables, economists often use the straight line that best fits the data.

## Determining Cause and Effect

When we graph the relationship between two variables, we often want to draw conclusions about whether changes in one variable are causing changes in the other variable. Doing so, however, can lead to incorrect conclusions. For example, suppose you graph the number of homes in a neighborhood that have a fire burning in the fireplace and the number of leaves on trees in the neighborhood. You would get a relationship like that shown in panel (a) of Figure 1A-7: The more fires burning in the neighborhood, the fewer leaves the trees have. Can we draw the conclusion from this graph that using a fireplace causes trees to lose their leaves? We know, of course, that such a conclusion would be incorrect. In spring and summer, there are relatively few fireplaces being used, and the trees are full of leaves. In the fall, as trees begin to lose their leaves, fireplaces are used more frequently. And in winter, many fireplaces are being used and many trees have lost all their leaves. The reason that the graph in Figure 1A-7 is misleading about cause and effect is that there is obviously an *omitted variable* in the analysis—the season of the year. An omitted variable is one that affects other variables, and its omission can lead to false conclusions about cause and effect.

Although in our example the omitted variable is obvious, there are many debates about cause and effect where the existence of an omitted variable has not been clear. For instance, it has been known for many years that people who smoke cigarettes suffer from higher rates of lung cancer than do nonsmokers. For some time, tobacco companies and some scientists argued that there was an omitted variable—perhaps psychological temperament—that made some people more likely to smoke and more likely to develop lung cancer. If this omitted variable existed, then the finding that smokers were

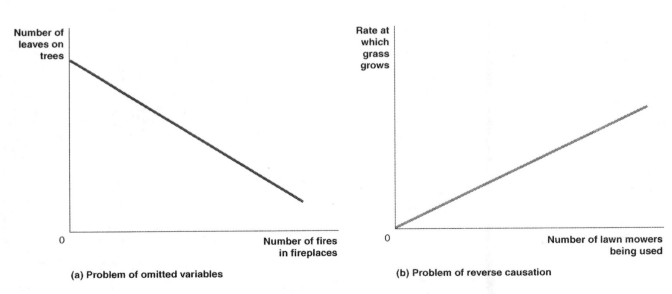

**(a) Problem of omitted variables**      **(b) Problem of reverse causation**

## Figure 1A-7 | Determining Cause and Effect

Using graphs to draw conclusions about cause and effect can be hazardous. In panel (a), we see that there are fewer leaves on the trees in a neighborhood when many homes have fires burning in their fireplaces. We cannot draw the conclusion that the fires cause the leaves to fall because we have an *omitted variable*—the season of the year. In panel (b), we see that more lawn mowers are used in a neighborhood during times when the grass grows rapidly and fewer lawn mowers are used when the grass grows slowly. Concluding that using lawn mowers *causes* the grass to grow faster would be making the error of *reverse causality*.

more likely to develop lung cancer would not have been evidence that smoking *caused* lung cancer. In this case, however, nearly all scientists eventually concluded that the omitted variable did not exist and that, in fact, smoking does cause lung cancer.

A related problem in determining cause and effect is known as *reverse causality*. The error of reverse causality occurs when we conclude that changes in variable *X* cause changes in variable *Y* when, in fact, it is actually changes in variable *Y* that cause changes in variable *X*. For example, panel (b) of Figure 1A-7 plots the number of lawn mowers being used in a neighborhood against the rate at which grass on lawns in the neighborhood is growing. We could conclude from this graph that using lawn mowers *causes* the grass to grow faster. We know, however, that in reality, the causality is in the other direction: Rapidly growing grass during the spring and summer causes the increased use of lawn mowers. Slowly growing grass in the fall or winter or during periods of low rainfall causes decreased use of lawn mowers.

Once again, in our example, the potential error of reverse causality is obvious. In many economic debates, however, cause and effect can be more difficult to determine. For example, changes in the money supply, or the total amount of money in the economy, tend to occur at the same time as changes in the total amount of income people in the economy earn. A famous debate in economics was about whether the changes in the money supply caused the changes in total income or whether the changes in total income caused the changes in the money supply. Each side in the debate accused the other side of committing the error of reverse causality.

## Are Graphs of Economic Relationships Always Straight Lines?

The graphs of relationships between two economic variables that we have drawn so far have been straight lines. The relationship between two variables is *linear* when it can be represented by a straight line. Few economic relationships are actually linear. For example, if we carefully plot data on the price of a product and the quantity demanded at each price, holding constant other variables that affect the quantity demanded, we will usually find a curved—or *nonlinear*—relationship rather than a linear relationship. In practice, however, it is often useful to approximate a nonlinear relationship with a linear relationship. If the relationship is reasonably close to being linear, the analysis is not significantly affected. In addition, it is easier to calculate the slope of a straight line, and it also is easier to calculate the area under a straight line. So, in this textbook, we often assume that the relationship between two economic variables is linear even when we know that this assumption is not precisely correct.

## Slopes of Nonlinear Curves

In some situations, we need to take into account the nonlinear nature of an economic relationship. For example, panel (a) of Figure 1A-8 shows the hypothetical relationship between Apple's total cost of producing iPods and the quantity of iPods produced. The relationship is curved, rather than linear. In this case, the cost of production is increasing at an increasing rate, which often happens in manufacturing. Put a different way, as we move up the curve, its slope becomes larger. (Remember that with a straight line, the slope is always constant.) To see this effect, first remember that we calculate the slope of a curve by dividing the change in the variable on the *y*-axis by the change in the variable on the *x*-axis. As we move from point *A* to point *B*, the quantity produced increases by 1 million iPods, while the total cost of production increases by $50 million. Farther up the curve, as we move from point *C* to point *D*, the change in quantity is the same—1 million iPods—but the change in the total cost of production is now much larger: $250 million. Because the change in the *y* variable has increased, while the change in the *x* variable has remained the same, we know that the slope has increased.

To measure the slope of a nonlinear curve at a particular point, we must measure the slope of the *tangent line* to the curve at that point. A tangent line will only touch the curve at that point. We can measure the slope of the tangent line just as we would

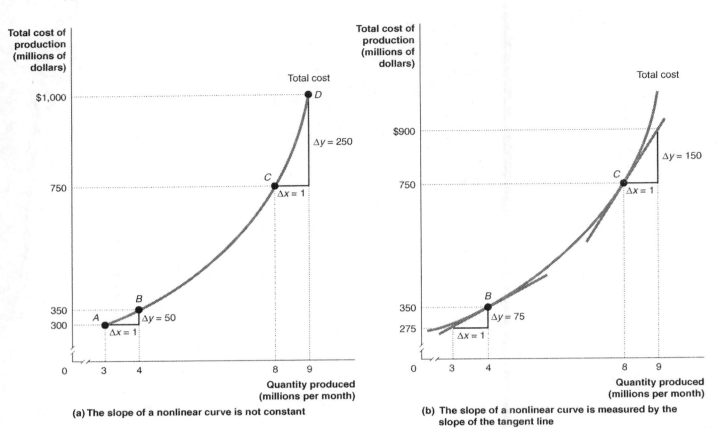

**Figure 1A-8** | The Slope of a Nonlinear Curve

The relationship between the quantity of iPods produced and the total cost of production is curved, rather than liner. In panel (a), in moving from point A to point B, the quantity produced increases by 1 million iPods, while the total cost of production increases by $50 million. Farther up the cure, as we move from point C to point D, the change in quantity is the same—1 million iPods—but the change in the total cost of production is now much larger: $250 million.

Because the change in the y variable has increased, while the change in the x variable has remained the same, we know that the slope has increased. In panel (b), we measure the slope of the curve at a particular point by the slope of the tangent line. The slope of the tangent line at point B is 75, and the slope of the tangent line at point C is 150.

the slope of any straight line. In panel (b), the tangent line at point B has a slope equal to:

$$\frac{\Delta \text{Cost}}{\Delta \text{Quantity}} = \frac{75}{1} = 75.$$

The tangent line at point C has a slope equal to:

$$\frac{\Delta \text{Cost}}{\Delta \text{Quantity}} = \frac{150}{1} = 150.$$

Once again, we see that the slope of the curve is larger at point C than at point B.

## Formulas

We have just seen that graphs are an important economic tool. In this section, we will review several useful formulas and show how to use them to summarize data and to calculate important relationships.

## Formula for a Percentage Change

One important formula is the percentage change. The *percentage change* is the change in some economic variable, usually from one period to the next, expressed as a percentage. An important macroeconomic measure is the real gross domestic product (GDP). *GDP* is the value of all the final goods and services produced in a country during a year. "Real" GDP is corrected for the effects of inflation. When economists say that the U.S. economy grew 3.3 percent during 2006, they mean that real GDP was 3.3 percent higher in 2006 than it was in 2005. The formula for making this calculation is:

$$\left( \frac{GDP_{2006} - GDP_{2005}}{GDP_{2005}} \right) \times 100$$

or, more generally, for any two periods:

$$\text{Percentage change} = \frac{\text{Value in the second period} - \text{Value in the first period}}{\text{Value in the first period}} \times 100.$$

In this case, real GDP was $11,049 billion in 2005 and $11,415 billion in 2006. So, the growth rate of the U.S. economy during 2006 was:

$$\left( \frac{\$11,415 - \$11,049}{\$11,049} \right) \times 100 = 3.3\%.$$

Notice that it didn't matter that in using the formula, we ignored the fact that GDP is measured in billions of dollars. In fact, when calculating percentage changes, *the units don't matter*. The percentage increase from $11,049 billion to $11,415 billion is exactly the same as the percentage increase from $11,049 to $11,415.

## Formulas for the Areas of a Rectangle and a Triangle

Areas that form rectangles and triangles on graphs can have important economic meaning. For example, Figure 1A-9 shows the demand curve for Pepsi. Suppose that the price is currently $2.00 and that 125,000 bottles of Pepsi are sold at that price. A firm's *total revenue* is equal to the amount it receives from selling its product, or the quantity sold multiplied by the price. In this case, total revenue will equal 125,000 bottles times $2.00 per bottle, or $250,000.

The formula for the area of a rectangle is:

$$\text{Area of a rectangle} = \text{Base} \times \text{Height}$$

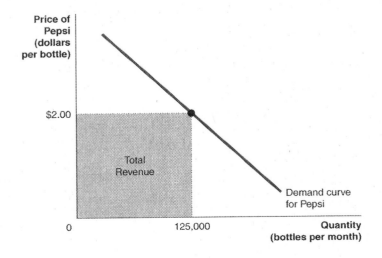

### Figure 1A-9

**Showing a Firm's Total Revenue on a Graph**

The area of a rectangle is equal to its base multiplied by its height. Total revenue is equal to quantity multiplied by price. Here, total revenue is equal to the quantity of 125,000 bottles times the price of $2.00 per bottle, or $250,000. The area of the green-shaded rectangle shows the firm's total revenue.

## Figure 1A-10

**The Area of a Triangle**

The area of a triangle is equal to $\frac{1}{2}$ multiplied by its base multiplied by its height. The area of the blue-shaded triangle has a base equal to 150,000 − 125,000, or 25,000, and a height equal to $2.00 − $1.50, or $0.50. Therefore, its area equals $\frac{1}{2}$ × 25,000 × $0.50, or $6,250.

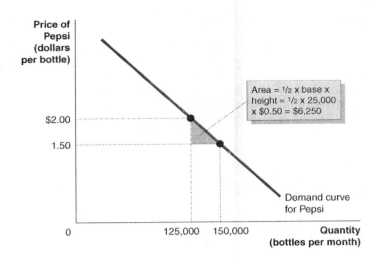

Area = ½ x base x height = ½ x 25,000 x $0.50 = $6,250

In Figure 1A-9, the green-shaded rectangle also represents the firm's total revenue because its area is given by the base of 125,000 bottles multiplied by the price of $2.00 per bottle.

We will see in later chapters that areas that are triangles can also have economic significance. The formula for the area of a triangle is:

$$\text{Area of a triangle} = \frac{1}{2} \times \text{Base} \times \text{Height}.$$

The blue-shaded area in Figure 1A-10 is a triangle. The base equals 150,000 − 125,000, or 25,000. Its height equals $2.00 − $1.50, or $0.50. Therefore, its area equals $\frac{1}{2}$ × 25,000 × $0.50, or $6,250. Notice that the blue area is a triangle only if the demand curve is a straight line, or linear. Not all demand curves are linear. However, the formula for the area of a triangle will usually still give a good approximation, even if the demand curve is not linear.

## Summary of Using Formulas

You will encounter several other formulas in this book. Whenever you must use a formula, you should follow these steps:

1 Make sure you understand the economic concept that the formula represents.

2 Make sure you are using the correct formula for the problem you are solving.

3 Make sure that the number you calculate using the formula is economically reasonable. For example, if you are using a formula to calculate a firm's revenue and your answer is a negative number, you know you made a mistake somewhere.

**LEARNING OBJECTIVE**  Review the use of graphs and formulas, **pages 24-34.**

myeconlab  Visit www.myeconlab.com to complete these exercises
*Get Ahead of the Curve* online and get instant feedback.

## Problems and Applications

1A.1 The following table gives the relationship between the price of custard pies and the number of pies Jacob buys per week.

| PRICE | QUANTITY OF PIES | WEEK |
|-------|------------------|-----------|
| $3.00 | 6 | July 2 |
| 2.00 | 7 | July 9 |
| 5.00 | 4 | July 16 |
| 6.00 | 3 | July 23 |
| 1.00 | 8 | July 30 |
| 4.00 | 5 | August 6 |

a. Is the relationship between the price of pies and the number of pies Jacob buys a positive relationship or a negative relationship?

b. Plot the data from the table on a graph similar to Figure 1A-3. Draw a straight line that best fits the points.

c. Calculate the slope of the line.

**1A.2** The following table gives information on the quantity of glasses of lemonade demanded on sunny and overcast days. Plot the data from the table on a graph similar to Figure 1A-5. Draw two straight lines representing the two demand curves—one for sunny days and one for overcast days.

| PRICE (DOLLARS PER GLASS) | QUANTITY (GLASSES OF LEMONADE PER DAY) | WEATHER |
|---|---|---|
| $0.80 | 30 | Sunny |
| 0.80 | 10 | Overcast |
| 0.70 | 40 | Sunny |
| 0.70 | 20 | Overcast |
| 0.60 | 50 | Sunny |
| 0.60 | 30 | Overcast |
| 0.50 | 60 | Sunny |
| 0.50 | 40 | Overcast |

**1A.3** Using the information in Figure 1A-2, calculate the percentage change in auto sales from one year to the next. Between which years did sales fall at the fastest rate?

**1A.4** Real GDP in 1981 was $5,292 billion. Real GDP in 1982 was $5,189 billion. What was the percentage change in real GDP from 1981 to 1982? What do economists call the percentage change in real GDP from one year to the next?

**1A.5** Assume that the demand curve for Pepsi passes through the following two points:

| PRICE PER BOTTLE OF PEPSI | NUMBER OF BOTTLES OF PEPSI SOLD |
|---|---|
| $2.50 | 100,000 |
| 1.25 | 200,000 |

a. Draw a graph with a linear demand curve that passes through these two points.

b. Show on the graph the areas representing total revenue at each price. Give the value for total revenue at each price.

**1A.6** What is the area of the blue triangle shown in the following figure?

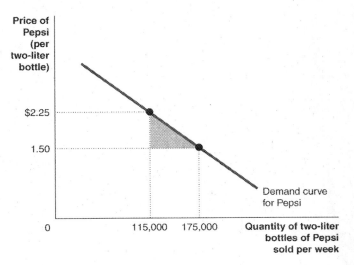

**1A.7** Calculate the slope of the total cost curve at point *A* and at point *B* in the following figure.

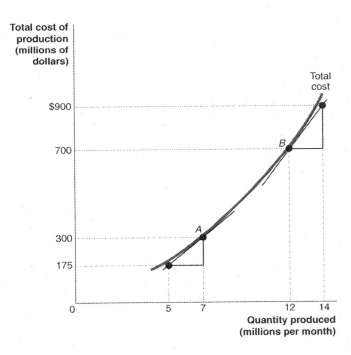

**>> End Appendix Learning Objective**

# Chapter 2
# Introduction to Markets

**Scarcity** The situation in which unlimited wants exceed the limited resources available to fulfill those wants.

I n a market system, managers at most firms must make decisions like those made by BMW's managers. The decisions managers face reflect a key fact of economic life: *Scarcity requires trade-offs.* **Scarcity** exists because we have unlimited wants but only limited resources available to fulfill those wants. Goods and services are scarce. So, too, are the economic resources, or *factors of production*—workers, capital, natural resources, and entrepreneurial ability—used to make goods and services. Your time is scarce, which means you face trade-offs: If you spend an hour studying for an economics exam, you have one less hour to spend studying for a psychology exam or going to the movies. If your university decides to use some of its scarce budget funds to buy new computers for the computer labs, those funds will not be available to buy new books for the library or to resurface the student parking lot. If BMW decides to devote some of the scarce workers and machinery in its Spartanburg assembly plant to producing more Z4 roadsters, those resources will not be available to produce more X5 SUVs.

Many of the decisions of households and firms are made in markets. One key activity that takes place in markets is trade. Trade involves the decisions of millions of households and firms spread around the world. By engaging in trade, people can raise their standard of living. In this chapter, we provide an overview of how the market system coordinates the independent decisions of these millions of households and firms. We begin our analysis of the economic consequences of scarcity and the working of the market system by introducing an important economic model: the *production possibilities frontier.*

---

**2.1 LEARNING OBJECTIVE**

2.1 | Use a production possibilities frontier to analyze opportunity costs and trade-offs.

# Production Possibilities Frontiers and Opportunity Costs

As we saw in the opening to this chapter, BMW operates an automobile factory in Spartanburg, South Carolina, where it assembles Z4 roadsters and X5 SUVs. Because the firm's resources—workers, machinery, materials, and entrepreneurial skills—are limited, BMW faces a trade-off: Resources devoted to producing Z4s are not available for producing X5s and vice versa. Chapter 1 explained that economic models can be useful in analyzing many questions. We can use a simple model called the *production possibilities frontier* to analyze the trade-offs BMW faces in its Spartanburg plant. A **production possibilities frontier** (*PPF*) is a curve showing the maximum attainable combinations of two products that may be produced with available resources and current technology. In BMW's case, the two products are Z4 roadsters and X5 SUVs, and the resources are BMW's workers, materials, robots, and other machinery.

**Production possibilities frontier** (*PPF*) A curve showing the maximum attainable combinations of two products that may be produced with available resources and current technology.

## Graphing the Production Possibilities Frontier

Figure 2-1 uses a production possibilities frontier to illustrate the trade-offs that BMW faces. The numbers from the table are plotted in the graph. The line in the graph is BMW's production possibilities frontier. If BMW uses all its resources to produce roadsters, it can produce 800 per day—point *A* at one end of the production possibilities frontier. If BMW uses all its resources to produce SUVs, it can produce 800 per day—point *E* at the other end of the production possibilities frontier. If BMW devotes resources to producing both vehicles, it could be at a point like *B*, where it produces 600 roadsters and 200 SUVs.

All the combinations either on the frontier—like *A*, *B*, *C*, *D*, and *E*—or inside the frontier—like point *F*—are *attainable* with the resources available. Combinations on

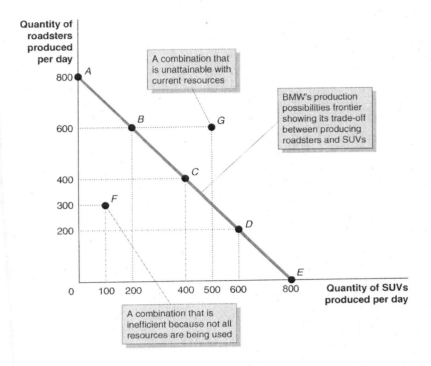

| BMW's Production Choices at Its Spartanburg Plant | | |
|---|---|---|
| Choice | Quantity of Roadsters Produced | Quantity of SUVs Produced |
| A | 800 | 0 |
| B | 600 | 200 |
| C | 400 | 400 |
| D | 200 | 600 |
| E | 0 | 800 |

A combination that is unattainable with current resources

BMW's production possibilities frontier showing its trade-off between producing roadsters and SUVs

A combination that is inefficient because not all resources are being used

## Figure 2-1

### BMW's Production Possibilities Frontier

BMW faces a trade-off: To build one more roadster, it must build one less SUV. The production possibilities frontier illustrates the trade-off BMW faces. Combinations on the production possibilities frontier—like points A, B, C, D, and E—are *technically efficient* because the maximum output is being obtained from the available resources. Combinations inside the frontier—like point F—are *inefficient* because some resources are not being used. Combinations outside the frontier—like point G—are *unattainable* with current resources.

the frontier are *efficient* because all available resources are being fully utilized, and the fewest possible resources are being used to produce a given amount of output. Combinations inside the frontier—like point F—are *inefficient* because maximum output is not being obtained from the available resources—perhaps because the assembly line is not operating at capacity. BMW might like to be beyond the frontier—at a point like G, where it would be producing 600 roadsters and 500 SUVs—but points beyond the production possibilities frontier are *unattainable*, given the firm's current resources. To produce the combination at G, BMW would need more machines or more workers.

Notice that if BMW is producing efficiently and is on the production possibilities frontier, the only way to produce more of one vehicle is to produce less of the other vehicle. Recall from Chapter 1 that the **opportunity cost** of any activity is the highest valued alternative that must be given up to engage in that activity. For BMW, the opportunity cost of producing one more SUV is the number of roadsters the company will not be able to produce because it has shifted those resources to producing SUVs. For example, in moving from point B to point C, the opportunity cost of producing 200 more SUVs per day is the 200 fewer roadsters that can be produced.

What point on the production possibilities frontier is best? We can't tell without further information. If consumer demand for SUVs is greater than demand for roadsters, the company is likely to choose a point closer to E. If demand for roadsters is greater than demand for SUVs, the company is likely to choose a point closer to A.

**Opportunity cost** The highest-valued alternative that must be given up to engage in an activity.

# Solved Problem | 2-1

## Drawing a Production Possibilities Frontier for Rosie's Boston Bakery

Rosie's Boston Bakery specializes in cakes and pies. Rosie has 5 hours per day to devote to baking. In 1 hour, Rosie can prepare 2 pies or 1 cake.

a. Use the information given to complete the following table:

| | HOURS SPENT MAKING | | QUANTITY MADE | |
|---|---|---|---|---|
| CHOICE | CAKES | PIES | CAKES | PIES |
| A | 5 | 0 | | |
| B | 4 | 1 | | |
| C | 3 | 2 | | |
| D | 2 | 3 | | |
| E | 1 | 4 | | |
| F | 0 | 5 | | |

b. Use the data in the table to draw a production possibilities frontier graph illustrating Rosie's trade-offs between making cakes and making pies. Label the vertical axis "Quantity of cakes made." Label the horizontal axis "Quantity of pies made." Make sure to label the values where Rosie's production possibilities frontier intersects the vertical and horizontal axes.

c. Label the points representing choice $D$ and choice $E$. If Rosie is at choice $D$, what is her opportunity cost of making more pies?

## SOLVING THE PROBLEM:

**Step 1:** **Review the chapter material.** This problem is about using production possibilities frontiers to analyze trade-offs, so you may want to review the section "Graphing the Production Possibilities Frontier," which begins on page 38.

**Step 2:** **Answer question (a) by filling in the table.** If Rosie can produce 1 cake in 1 hour, then with choice $A$, she will make 5 cakes and 0 pies. Because she can produce 2 pies in 1 hour, with choice $B$, she will make 4 cakes and 2 pies. Using similar reasoning, you can fill in the remaining cells in the table as follows:

| | HOURS SPENT MAKING | | QUANTITY MADE | |
|---|---|---|---|---|
| CHOICE | CAKES | PIES | CAKES | PIES |
| A | 5 | 0 | 5 | 0 |
| B | 4 | 1 | 4 | 2 |
| C | 3 | 2 | 3 | 4 |
| D | 2 | 3 | 2 | 6 |
| E | 1 | 4 | 1 | 8 |
| F | 0 | 5 | 0 | 10 |

**Step 3:** **Answer question (b) by drawing the production possibilities frontier graph.** Using the data in the table in Step 2, you should draw a graph that looks like this:

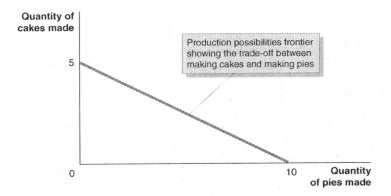

If Rosie devotes all 5 hours to making cakes, she will make 5 cakes. Therefore, her production possibilities frontier will intersect the vertical axis at 5 cakes made. If Rosie devotes all 5 hours to making pies, she will make 10 pies. Therefore, her production possibilities frontier will intersect the horizontal axis at 10 pies made.

Step 4: **Answer question (c) by showing choices *D* and *E* on your graph.** The points for choices *D* and *E* can be plotted using the information from the table:

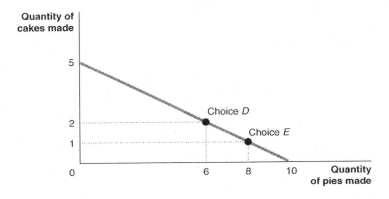

Moving from choice *D* to choice *E* increases Rosie's production of pies by 2 but lowers her production of cakes by 1. Therefore, her opportunity cost of making 2 more pies is making 1 less cake.

>> **End Solved Problem 2-1**

## Making the Connection | Trade-offs: Hurricane Katrina, Tsunami Relief, and Charitable Giving

When Hurricane Katrina hit the Gulf Coast region in August 2005, it resulted in massive flooding that destroyed large sections of New Orleans and other towns in Louisiana, Mississippi, Alabama, and Texas. More than 1,800 people lost their lives. In response, there was a massive outpouring of charitable donations to aid the victims. More than two-thirds of Americans donated money to hurricane relief. Although these funds helped to reduce the suffering of many hurricane victims, donations to some other causes actually declined. For instance, the head of the United Way in Alleghany County, Pennsylvania, indicated that it had suffered a decline in donations during 2005: "We're seeing declines this year, not all entirely due to the economy but also due to the effect of so much fund raising in August and September for hurricanes Katrina and Rita." The director of the Women's Center and Shelter of Great Pittsburgh

*More funds for Katrina relief meant less funds for other charities.*

had a similar experience: "What they've told us is there are so many important causes that they are aware of that they want to support. The choices are greater than what they've been faced with before."

Unfortunately, the trade-off of an increase in charitable giving to one cause resulting in a decrease in charitable giving to other causes is common following a disaster. In December 2004, an earthquake caused a tidal wave—or tsunami—to flood coastal areas of Indonesia, Thailand, Sri Lanka, and other countries bordering the Indian Ocean. More than 280,000 people died, and billions of dollars worth of property was destroyed. Governments and individuals around the world moved quickly to donate to relief efforts. The U.S. government donated $950 million, and individual U.S. citizens donated an additional $500 million. Both governments and individuals face limited budgets, however, and funds used for one purpose are unavailable to be used for another purpose. Although governments and individuals did increase their total charitable giving following the tsunami disaster, much of the funds spent on tsunami relief appear to have been diverted from other uses. A difficult trade-off resulted: Giving funds to victims of the tsunami meant fewer funds were available to aid other good causes.

For example, some of the funds provided by the U.S. government for reconstruction in the tsunami-devastated areas came from existing aid programs. As a result, spending on other aid projects in the region declined. Similarly, nonprofit organizations in New York City reported sharp declines in donations to the homeless and the poor, as donors gave funds for tsunami relief instead. According to a report in the newspaper *Crain's New York Business*, "Some groups such as Bailey House, which helps homeless people who have AIDS, have even started receiving letters from longtime donors warning that this year's gifts are being redirected to the tsunami relief effort." As one commentator observed, "The milk of human kindness is probably flowing at the usual rate in the United States. It's just getting channeled in different directions."

Source: Steve Levin, "Disaster Aid Is Extra Giving," *Pittsburgh Post Gazette*, April 22, 2006; Jacqueline L. Salmon, "Katrina Compassion Drives Disaster Donations to a Record," *Washington Post*, June 19, 2006, p. A05; and Daniel Gross, "Zero-Sum Charity," *Slate*, January 20, 2005.

## Increasing Marginal Opportunity Costs

We can use the production possibilities frontier to explore issues related to the economy as a whole. For example, suppose we divide all the goods and services produced in the economy into just two types: military goods and civilian goods. In Figure 2-2, we let tanks represent military goods and automobiles represent civilian goods. If all the coun-

### Figure 2-2

**Increasing Marginal Opportunity Cost**

As the economy moves down the production possibilities frontier, it experiences *increasing marginal opportunity costs* because increasing automobile production by a given quantity requires larger and larger decreases in tank production. For example, to increase automobile production from 0 to 200—moving from point *A* to point *B*—the economy has to give up only 50 tanks. But to increase automobile production by another 200 vehicles—moving from point *B* to point *C*—the economy has to give up 150 tanks.

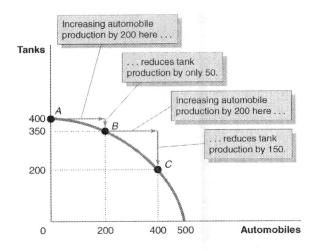

try's resources are devoted to producing military goods, 400 tanks can be produced in one year. If all resources are devoted to producing civilian goods, 500 automobiles can be produced in one year. Devoting resources to producing both goods results in the economy being at other points along the production possibilities frontier.

Notice that this production possibilities frontier is bowed outward rather than being a straight line. Because the curve is bowed out, the opportunity cost of automobiles in terms of tanks depends on where the economy currently is on the production possibilities frontier. For example, to increase automobile production from 0 to 200—moving from point *A* to point *B*—the economy has to give up only 50 tanks. But to increase automobile production by another 200 vehicles—moving from point *B* to point *C*—the economy has to give up 150 tanks.

As the economy moves down the production possibilities frontier, it experiences *increasing marginal opportunity costs* because increasing automobile production by a given quantity requires larger and larger decreases in tank production. Increasing marginal opportunity costs occurs because some workers, machines, and other resources are better suited to one use than to another. At point *A*, some resources that are well suited to producing automobiles are forced to produce tanks. Shifting these resources into producing automobiles by moving from point *A* to point *B* allows a substantial increase in automobile production, without much loss of tank production. But as the economy moves down the production possibilities frontier, more and more resources that are better suited to tank production are switched into automobile production. As a result, the increases in automobile production become increasingly smaller, while the decreases in tank production become increasingly larger. We would expect in most situations that production possibilities frontiers will be bowed outward rather than linear, as in the BMW example discussed earlier.

The idea of increasing marginal opportunity costs illustrates an important economic concept: *The more resources already devoted to any activity, the smaller the payoff to devoting additional resources to that activity.* For example, the more hours you have already spent studying economics, the smaller the increase in your test grade from each additional hour you spend—and the greater the opportunity cost of using the hour in that way. The more funds a firm has devoted to research and development during a given year, the smaller the amount of useful knowledge it receives from each additional dollar—and the greater the opportunity cost of using the funds in that way. The more funds the federal government spends cleaning up the environment during a given year, the smaller the reduction in pollution from each additional dollar—and, once again, the greater the opportunity cost of using the funds in that way.

## Economic Growth

At any given time, the total resources available to any economy are fixed. Therefore, if the United States produces more automobiles, it must produce less of something else—tanks in our example. Over time, though, the resources available to an economy may increase. For example, both the labor force and the capital stock—the amount of physical capital available in the country—may increase. The increase in the available labor force and the capital stock shifts the production possibilities frontier outward for the U.S. economy and makes it possible to produce both more automobiles and more tanks. Panel (a) of Figure 2-3 shows that the economy can move from point *A* to point *B*, producing more tanks and more automobiles.

Similarly, technological advance makes it possible to produce more goods with the same amount of workers and machinery, which also shifts the production possibilities frontier outward. Technological advance need not affect all sectors equally. Panel (b) of Figure 2-3 shows the results of technological advance in the automobile industry that increases the quantity of automobile workers can produce per year while leaving unchanged the quantity of tanks that can be produced.

Shifts in the production possibilities frontier represent **economic growth** because they allow the economy to increase the production of goods and services, which ultimately raises the standard of living. In the United States and other high-income countries, the

**Economic growth** The ability of the economy to produce increasing quantities of goods and services.

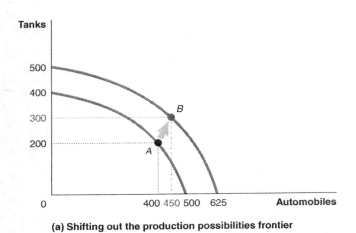

(a) Shifting out the production possibilities frontier

(b) Technological change in the automobile undustry

## Figure 2-3 | Economic Growth

Panel (a) shows that as more economic resources become available and technological change occurs, the economy can move from point *A* to point *B*, producing more tanks and more automobiles. Panel (b) shows the results of technological advance in the automobile industry that increases the quantity of vehicles workers can produce per year while leaving the maximum quantity of tanks that can be produced unchanged. Shifts in the production possibilities frontier represent *economic growth*.

market system has aided the process of economic growth, which over the past 200 years has greatly increased the well-being of the average person.

2.2 | Understand comparative advantage and explain how it is the basis for trade.

# Comparative Advantage and Trade

We can use the ideas of production possibilities frontiers and opportunity costs to understand the basic economic activity of *trade*. Markets are fundamentally about **trade**, which is the act of buying and selling. Sometimes we trade directly, as when children trade one baseball card for another baseball card. But often we trade indirectly: We sell our labor services as, say, an accountant, a salesperson, or a nurse for money, and then we use the money to buy goods and services. Although in these cases, trade takes place indirectly, ultimately the accountant, salesperson, or nurse is trading his or her services for food, clothing, and other goods and services. One of the great benefits to trade is that it makes it possible for people to become better off by increasing both their production and their consumption.

**Trade** The act of buying or selling.

## Specialization and Gains from Trade

Consider the following situation: You and your neighbor both have fruit trees on your property. Initially, suppose you have only apple trees and your neighbor has only cherry trees. In this situation, if you both like apples and cherries, there is an obvious opportunity for both of you to gain from trade: You trade some of your apples for some of your neighbor's cherries, making you both better off. But what if there are apple and cherry trees growing on both of your properties? In that case, there can still be gains from trade. For example, your neighbor might be very good at picking apples, and you might be very good at picking cherries. It would make sense for your neighbor to concentrate on picking apples and for you to concentrate on picking cherries. You can then trade some of the cherries you pick for some of the apples your neighbor picks. But what if your neighbor is actually better at picking both apples and cherries than you are?

We can use production possibilities frontiers (*PPFs*) to show how your neighbor can benefit from trading with you even though she is better than you are at picking both apples and cherries. (For simplicity, and because it will not have any effect on the conclusions we draw, we will assume that the *PPFs* in this example are straight lines.) The table in Figure 2-4 shows how many apples and how many cherries you and your neighbor can pick in one week. The graph in the figure uses the data from the table to construct *PPFs*. Panel (a) shows your *PPF*. If you devote all your time to picking apples, you can pick 20 pounds of apples per week. If you devote all your time to picking cherries, you can pick 20 pounds per week. Panel (b) shows that if your neighbor devotes all her time to picking apples, she can pick 30 pounds. If she devotes all her time to picking cherries, she can pick 60 pounds.

The production possibilities frontiers in Figure 2-4 show how many apples and cherries you and your neighbor can consume, *without trade*. Suppose that when you don't trade with your neighbor, you pick and consume 8 pounds of apples and 12 pounds of cherries per week. This combination of apples and cherries is represented by point *A* in panel (a) of Figure 2-5, on page 46. When your neighbor doesn't trade with you, she picks and consumes 9 pounds of apples and 42 pounds of cherries per week. This combination of apples and cherries is represented by point *B* in panel (b) of Figure 2-5.

After years of picking and consuming your own apples and cherries, suppose your neighbor comes to you one day with the following proposal: She offers to trade you 15 pounds of her cherries for 10 pounds of your apples next week. Should you accept this offer? You should accept because you will end up with more apples and more cherries to consume. To take advantage of her proposal, you should specialize in picking only apples rather than splitting your time between picking apples and picking cherries. We know this will allow you to pick 20 pounds of apples. You can trade 10 pounds of apples to your neighbor for 15 pounds of her cherries. The result is that you will be able to consume 10 pounds of apples and 15 pounds of cherries (point *A'* in panel (a) of Figure 2-5). You are clearly better off as a result of trading with your neighbor: You now can consume 2 more pounds of apples and 3 more pounds of cherries than you were consuming without trading. You have moved beyond your *PPF*!

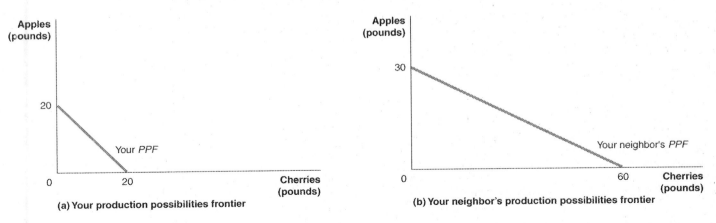

|  | **You** | | **Your Neighbor** | |
|---|---|---|---|---|
|  | Apples | Cherries | Apples | Cherries |
| Devote all time to picking apples | 20 pounds | 0 pounds | 30 pounds | 0 pounds |
| Devote all time to picking cherries | 0 pounds | 20 pounds | 0 pounds | 60 pounds |

**(a) Your production possibilities frontier**

**(b) Your neighbor's production possibilities frontier**

Figure 2-4 | Production Possibilities for You and Your Neighbor, without Trade

The table in this figure shows how many pounds of apples and how many pounds of cherries you and your neighbor can each pick in one week. The graphs in the figure use the data from the table to construct production possibilities frontiers (*PPFs*) for you and your neighbor. Panel (a) shows your *PPF*. If you devote all your time to pick-ing apples and none of your time to picking cherries, you can pick 20 pounds. If you devote all your time to picking cherries, you can pick 20 pounds. Panel (b) shows that if your neighbor devotes all her time to picking apples, she can pick 30 pounds. If she devotes all her time to picking cherries, she can pick 60 pounds.

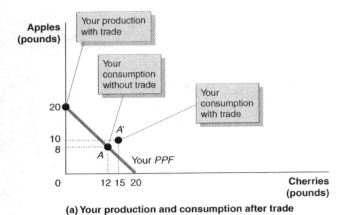

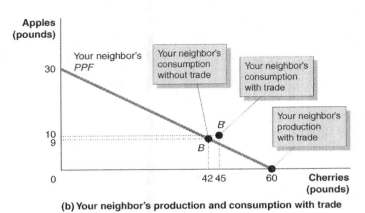

## Figure 2-5 | Gains from Trade

When you don't trade with your neighbor, you pick and consume 8 pounds of apples and 12 pounds of cherries per week—point *A* in panel (a). When your neighbor doesn't trade with you, she picks and consumes 9 pounds of apples and 42 pounds of cherries per week—point *B* in panel (b). If you specialize in picking apples, you can pick 20 pounds. If your neighbor specializes in picking cherries, she can pick 60 pounds. If

you trade 10 pounds of your apples for 15 pounds of your neighbor's cherries, you will be able to consume 10 pounds of apples and 15 pounds of cherries—point *A'* in panel (a). Your neighbor can now consume 10 pounds of apples and 45 pounds of cherries—point *B'* in panel (b). You and your neighbor are both better off as a result of trade.

Your neighbor has also benefited from the trade. By specializing in picking only cherries, she can pick 60 pounds. She trades 15 pounds of cherries to you for 10 pounds of apples. The result is that she can consume 10 pounds of apples and 45 pounds of cherries (point *B'* in panel (b) of Figure 2-5). This is 1 more pound of apples and 3 more pounds of cherries than she was consuming before trading with you. She also has moved beyond her *PPF*. Table 2-1 summarizes the changes in production and consumption that result from your trade with your neighbor. (In this example, we chose one specific rate of trading cherries for apples—15 pounds of cherries for 10 pounds of apples. There are, however, many other rates of trading cherries for apples that would also make you and your neighbor better off.)

## Absolute Advantage versus Comparative Advantage

**Absolute advantage** The ability of an individual, a firm, or a country to produce more of a good or service than competitors, using the same amount of resources.

Perhaps the most remarkable aspect of the preceding example is that your neighbor benefits from trading with you even though she is better than you at picking both apples and cherries. **Absolute advantage** is the ability of an individual, a firm, or a country to

## TABLE 2-1

### A Summary of the Gains from Trade

|  | YOU | | YOUR NEIGHBOR | |
|---|---|---|---|---|
|  | APPLES (IN POUNDS) | CHERRIES (IN POUNDS) | APPLES (IN POUNDS) | CHERRIES (IN POUNDS) |
| Production *and* consumption *without* trade | 8 | 12 | 9 | 42 |
| Production *with* trade | 20 | 0 | 0 | 60 |
| Consumption *with* trade | 10 | 15 | 10 | 45 |
| Gains from trade (increased consumption) | 2 | 3 | 1 | 3 |

produce more of a good or service than competitors, using the same amount of resources. Your neighbor has an absolute advantage over you in producing both apples and cherries because she can pick more of each fruit than you can in the same amount of time. Although it seems that your neighbor should pick her own apples *and* her own cherries, we have just seen that she is better off specializing in cherry picking and leaving the apple picking to you.

We can consider further why both you and your neighbor benefit from specializing in picking only one fruit. First, think about the opportunity cost to each of you of picking the two fruits. We saw from the *PPF* in Figure 2-4 that if you devoted all your time to picking apples, you would be able to pick 20 pounds of apples per week. As you move down your *PPF* and shift time away from picking apples to picking cherries, you have to give up 1 pound of apples for each pound of cherries you pick (the slope of your *PPF* is −1). (For a review of calculating slopes, see the appendix to Chapter 1.) Therefore, your opportunity cost of picking 1 pound of cherries is 1 pound of apples. By the same reasoning, your opportunity cost of picking 1 pound of apples is 1 pound of cherries. Your neighbor's *PPF* has a different slope, so she faces a different trade-off: As she shifts time from picking apples to picking cherries, she has to give up 0.5 pound of apples for every 1 pound of cherries she picks (the slope of your neighbor's *PPF* is −0.5). As she shifts time from picking cherries to picking apples, she gives up 2 pounds of cherries for every 1 pound of apples she picks. Therefore, her opportunity cost of picking 1 pound of apples is 2 pounds of cherries, and her opportunity cost of picking 1 pound of cherries is 0.5 pound of apples.

Table 2-2 summarizes the opportunity costs for you and your neighbor of picking apples and cherries. Note that even though your neighbor can pick more apples in a week than you can, the *opportunity cost* of picking apples is higher for her than for you because when she picks apples, she gives up more cherries than you do. So, even though she has an absolute advantage over you in picking apples, it is more costly for her to pick apples than it is for you. The table also shows that her opportunity cost of picking cherries is lower than your opportunity cost of picking cherries. **Comparative advantage** is the ability of an individual, a firm, or a country to produce a good or service at a lower opportunity cost than competitors. In apple picking, your neighbor has an *absolute advantage* over you, but you have a *comparative advantage* over her. Your neighbor has both an absolute and a comparative advantage over you in picking cherries. As we have seen, you are better off specializing in picking apples, and your neighbor is better off specializing in picking cherries.

## Comparative Advantage and the Gains from Trade

We have just derived an important economic principle: *The basis for trade is comparative advantage, not absolute advantage.* The fastest apple pickers do not necessarily do much apple picking. If the fastest apple pickers have a comparative advantage in some other activity——picking cherries, playing major league baseball, or being industrial engineers—— they are better off specializing in that other activity. Individuals, firms, and countries are better off if they specialize in producing goods and services for which they have a comparative advantage and obtain the other goods and services they need by trading. We will return to the important concept of comparative advantage in Chapter 8, which is devoted to the subject of international trade.

**Comparative advantage** The ability of an individual, a firm, or a country to produce a good or service at a lower opportunity cost than competitors.

| | OPPORTUNITY COST OF PICKING 1 POUND OF APPLES | OPPORTUNITY COST OF PICKING 1 POUND OF CHERRIES |
|---|---|---|
| **YOU** | 1 pound of cherries | 1 pound of apples |
| **YOUR NEIGHBOR** | 2 pounds of cherries | 0.5 pound of apples |

**TABLE 2-2**

**Opportunity Costs of Picking Apples and Cherries**

2.3 | Explain the basic idea of how a market system works.

# The Market System

We have seen that households, firms, and the government face trade-offs and incur opportunity costs because of the scarcity of resources. We have also seen that trade allows people to specialize according to their comparative advantage. By engaging in trade, people can raise their standard of living. Of course, trade in the modern world is much more complex than the examples we have considered so far. Trade today involves the decisions of millions of people spread around the world. But how does an economy make trade possible, and how are the decisions of these millions of people coordinated? In the United States and most other countries, trade is carried out in markets. Markets also determine the answers to the three fundamental questions discussed in Chapter 1: *What* goods and services will be produced? *How* will the goods and services be produced? and *Who* will receive the goods and services?

> **Market** A group of buyers and sellers of a good or service and the institution or arrangement by which they come together to trade.

Recall that the definition of **market** is a group of buyers and sellers of a good or service and the institution or arrangement by which they come together to trade. Markets take many forms: They can be physical places, like a local pizza parlor or the New York Stock Exchange, or virtual places, like eBay. In a market, the buyers are demanders of goods or services, and the sellers are suppliers of goods or services. Households and firms interact in two types of markets: *product markets* and *factor markets*. **Product markets** are markets for goods—such as computers—and services—such as medical treatment. In product markets, households are demanders, and firms are suppliers. **Factor markets** are markets for the *factors of production*. **Factors of production** are the inputs used to make goods and services. Factors of production are divided into four broad categories:

> **Product markets** Markets for goods—such as computers—and services—such as medical treatment.

> **Factor markets** Markets for the factors of production, such as labor, capital, natural resources, and entrepreneurial ability.

> **Factors of production** The inputs used to make goods and services.

- *Labor* includes all types of work, from the part-time labor of teenagers working at McDonald's to the work of top managers in large corporations.

- *Capital* refers to physical capital, such as computers and machine tools, that is used to produce other goods.

- *Natural resources* include land, water, oil, iron ore, and other raw materials (or "gifts of nature") that are used in producing goods.

- An *entrepreneur* is someone who operates a business. *Entrepreneurial ability* is the ability to bring together the other factors of production to successfully produce and sell goods and services.

## The Circular Flow of Income

Two key groups participate in markets:

- A *household* consists of all the individuals in a home. Households are suppliers of factors of production—particularly labor—used by firms to make goods and services. Households use the income they receive from selling the factors of production to purchase the goods and services supplied by firms. We are used to thinking of households as suppliers of labor because most people earn most of their income by going to work, which means they are selling their labor services to firms in the labor market. But households own the other factors of production, as well, either directly or indirectly, by owning the firms that have these resources. All firms are owned by households. Small firms, like a neighborhood restaurant, might be owned by one person. Large firms, like Microsoft or BMW, are owned by millions of households who own shares of stock in them. (We discuss the stock market in Chapter 7.) When firms pay profits to the people who own them, the firms are paying for using the capital and natural resources that are supplied to them by those owners. So, we can generalize by saying that in factor markets, households are suppliers, and firms are demanders.

- *Firms* are suppliers of goods and services. Firms use the funds they receive from selling goods and services to buy the factors of production needed to make the goods and services.

We can use a simple economic model called the **circular-flow diagram** to see how participants in markets are linked. Figure 2-6 shows that in factor markets, households supply labor and other factors of production in exchange for wages and other payments from firms. In product markets, households use the payments they earn in factor markets to purchase the goods and services supplied by firms. Firms produce these goods and services using the factors of production supplied by households. In the figure, the blue arrows show the flow of factors of production from households through factor markets to firms. The red arrows show the flow of goods and services from firms through product markets to households. The green arrows show the flow of funds from firms through factor markets to households and the flow of spending from households through product markets to firms.

Like all economic models, the circular-flow diagram is a simplified version of reality. For example, Figure 2-6 leaves out the important role of government in buying goods from firms and in making payments, such as Social Security or unemployment insurance payments, to households. The figure also leaves out the roles played by banks, the stock and bond markets, and other parts of the *financial system* in aiding the flow of funds from lenders to borrowers. Finally, the figure does not show that some goods and services purchased by domestic households are produced in foreign countries and some goods and services produced by domestic firms are sold to foreign households. The government, the financial system, and the international sector are explored further in later chapters. Despite these simplifications, the circular-flow diagram in Figure 2-6 is useful for seeing how product markets, factor markets, and their participants are linked

**Circular-flow diagram** A model that illustrates how participants in markets are linked.

## Figure 2-6

**The Circular-Flow Diagram**

Households and firms are linked together in a circular flow of production, income, and spending. The blue arrows show the flow of the factors of production. In factor markets, households supply labor, entrepreneurial ability, and other factors of production to firms. Firms use these factors of production to make goods and services that they supply to households in product markets. The red arrows show the flow of goods and services from firms to households. The green arrows show the flow of funds. In factor markets, households receive wages and other payments from firms in exchange for supplying the factors of production. Households use these wages and other payments to purchase goods and services from firms in product markets. Firms sell goods and services to households in product markets, and they use the funds to purchase the factors of production from households in factor markets.

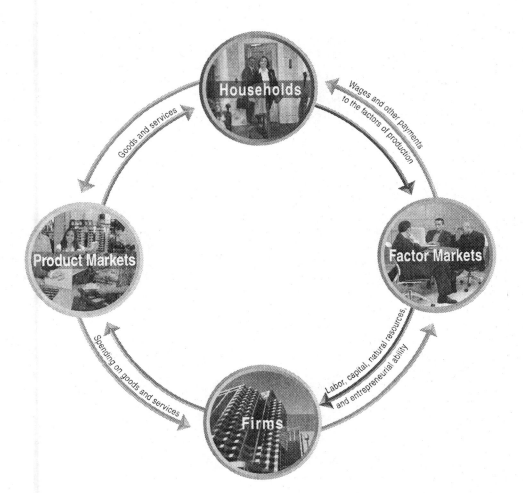

together. One of the great mysteries of the market system is that it manages to successfully coordinate the independent activities of so many households and firms.

## The Gains from Free Markets

**Free market** A market with few government restrictions on how a good or service can be produced or sold or on how a factor of production can be employed.

A **free market** exists when the government places few restrictions on how a good or a service can be produced or sold or on how a factor of production can be employed. Governments in all modern economies intervene more than is consistent with a fully free market. In that sense, we can think of the free market as being a benchmark against which we can judge actual economies. There are relatively few government restrictions on economic activity in the United States, Canada, the countries of Western Europe, Hong Kong, Singapore, and Estonia. So these countries come close to the free market benchmark. In countries such as Cuba and North Korea, the free market system has been rejected in favor of centrally planned economies with extensive government control over product and factor markets. Countries that come closest to the free-market benchmark have been more successful than countries with centrally planned economies in providing their people with rising living standards.

The Scottish philosopher Adam Smith is considered the father of modern economics because his book *An Inquiry into the Nature and Causes of the Wealth of Nations*, published in 1776, was an early and very influential argument for the free market system. Smith was writing at a time when extensive government restrictions on markets were still very common. In many parts of Europe, the *guild system* still prevailed. Under this system, governments would give guilds, or organizations of producers, the authority to control the production of a good. For example, the shoemakers' guild controlled who was allowed to produce shoes, how many shoes they could produce, and what price they could charge. In France, the cloth makers' guild even dictated the number of threads in the weave of the cloth.

Smith argued that such restrictions reduced the income, or wealth, of a country and its people by restricting the quantity of goods produced. Some people at the time supported the restrictions of the guild system because it was in their financial interest to do so. If you were a member of a guild, the restrictions served to reduce the competition you faced. But other people sincerely believed that the alternative to the guild system was economic chaos. Smith argued that these people were wrong and that a country could enjoy a smoothly functioning economic system if firms were freed from guild restrictions.

## The Market Mechanism

In Smith's day, defenders of the guild system worried that if, for instance, the shoemakers' guild did not control shoe production, either too many or too few shoes would be produced. Smith argued that prices would do a better job of coordinating the activities of buyers and sellers than the guilds could. A key to understanding Smith's argument is the assumption that *individuals usually act in a rational, self-interested way*. In particular, individuals take those actions most likely to make themselves better off financially. This assumption of rational, self-interested behavior underlies nearly all economic analysis. In fact, economics can be distinguished from other fields that study human behavior—such as sociology and psychology—by its emphasis on the assumption of self-interested behavior. Adam Smith understood—as economists today understand—that people's motives can be complex. But in analyzing people in the act of buying and selling, the motivation of financial reward usually provides the best explanation for the actions people take.

For example, suppose that a significant number of consumers switch from buying regular gasoline-powered cars to buying gasoline/electric-powered hybrid cars, such as the Toyota Prius, as in fact happened in the United States during the 2000s. Firms will find that they can charge relatively higher prices for hybrid cars than they can for regular cars. The self-interest of these firms will lead them to respond to consumers' wishes by producing more hybrids and fewer regular cars. Or suppose that consumers decide that they want to eat less bread, pasta, and other foods high in carbohydrates, as many did following the increase in popularity of the Atkins and South Beach diets. Then the prices firms can charge for bread and pasta will fall. The self-interest of firms will lead them to produce less bread and pasta, which in fact is what happened.

In the case where consumers want more of a product, and in the case where they want less of a product, the market system responds without a guild or the government giving orders about how much to produce or what price to charge. In a famous phrase, Smith said that firms would be led by the "invisible hand" of the market to provide consumers with what they wanted. Firms would respond to changes in prices by making decisions that ended up satisfying the wants of consumers.

### Making the Connection | A Story of the Market System in Action: How Do You Make an iPod?

*The market coordinates the activities of the many people spread around the world who contribute to the making of an iPod.*

The iPod is a product of Apple, which has its headquarters in Cupertino, California. It seems reasonable to assume that iPods are also manufactured in California. In fact, Apple produces none of the components of the iPod, nor does it assemble the components into a finished product. Far from being produced entirely by one company in one place, the iPod requires the coordinated activities of thousands of workers and dozens of firms, spread around the world.

Several Asian firms, including Asustek, Inventec Appliances, and Foxconn, assemble the iPod, which is then shipped to Apple for sale in the United States. But the firms doing final assembly don't make any of the components. For example, the iPod's hard drive is manufactured by the Japanese firm, Toshiba, although Toshiba actually assembles the hard drive in factories in China and the Philippines. Apple purchases the controller chip that manages the iPod's functions from PortalPlayer, which is based in Santa Clara, California. But PortalPlayer actually has the chip manufactured for it by Taiwan Semiconductor Manufacturing Corporation, and the chip's processor core was designed by ARM, a British company. Taiwan Semiconductor Manufacturing Corporation's factories are for the most part not in Taiwan, but in mainland China and Eastern Europe.

All told, the iPod contains 451 parts, designed and manufactured by firms around the world. Many of these firms are not even aware of which other firms are also producing components for the iPod. Few of the managers of these firms have met managers of the other firms or shared knowledge of how their particular components are produced. In fact, no one person from Steve Jobs, the head of Apple, on down possesses the knowledge of how to produce all of the components that are assembled into an iPod. Instead, the invisible hand of the market has led these firms to contribute their knowledge to the process that ultimately results in an iPod available for sale in a store in the United States. Apple has so efficiently organized the process of producing the iPod that you can order a custom iPod with a personal engraving and have it delivered from an assembly plant in China to your doorstep in the United States in as little as three days.

Hal Varian, an economist at the University of California, Berkeley, has summarized the iPod story: "Those clever folks at Apple figured out how to combine 451 mostly generic parts into a valuable product. They may not make the iPod, but they created it."

Sources: Hal Varian, "An iPod Has Global Value. Ask the (Many) Countries That Make It," *New York Times*, June 28, 2007; and Greg Linden, Kenneth L. Kraemer, Jaon Dedrick, "Who Captures Value in a Global Innovation System? The Case of Apple's iPod," Personal Computing Industry Center, June 2007.

## The Role of the Entrepreneur

*Entrepreneurs* are central to the working of the market system. An **entrepreneur** is someone who operates a business. Entrepreneurs must first determine what goods and services they believe consumers want, and then they must decide how to produce those goods and services most profitably. Entrepreneurs bring together the factors of production—labor, capital, and natural resources—to produce goods and services. They put their own funds

**Entrepreneur** Someone who operates a business, bringing together the factors of production—labor, capital, and natural resources—to produce goods and services.

at risk when they start businesses. If they are wrong about what consumers want or about the best way to produce goods and services, they can lose those funds. In fact, it is not unusual for entrepreneurs who eventually achieve great success to fail at first. For instance, early in their careers, both Henry Ford and Sakichi Toyoda, who eventually founded the Toyota Motor Corporation, started companies that quickly failed.

## The Legal Basis of a Successful Market System

In a free market, government does not restrict how firms produce and sell goods and services or how they employ factors of production, but the absence of government intervention is not enough for a market system to work well. Government has to provide secure rights to private property for a market system to work at all. In addition, government can aid the working of the market by enforcing contracts between private individuals through an independent court system. Many economists would also say the government has a role in facilitating the development of an efficient financial system as well as systems of education, transportation, and communication. The protection of private property and the existence of an independent court system to impartially enforce the law provide a *legal environment* that will allow a market system to succeed.

***Protection of Private Property*** For a market system to work well, individuals must be willing to take risks. Someone with $250,000 can be cautious and keep it safely in a bank—or even in cash, if the person doesn't trust the banking system. But the market system won't work unless a significant number of people are willing to risk their funds by investing them in businesses. Investing in businesses is risky in any country. Many businesses fail every year in the United States and other high-income countries. But in the high-income countries, someone who starts a new business or invests in an existing business doesn't have to worry that the government, the military, or criminal gangs might decide to seize the business or demand payments for not destroying the business. Unfortunately, in many poor countries, owners of businesses are not well protected from having their businesses seized by the government or from having their profits taken by criminals. Where these problems exist, opening a business can be extremely risky. Cash can be concealed easily, but a business is difficult to conceal and difficult to move.

**Property rights** The rights individuals or firms have to the exclusive use of their property, including the right to buy or sell it.

**Property rights** are the rights individuals or firms have to the exclusive use of their property, including the right to buy or sell it. Property can be tangible, physical property, such as a store or factory. Property can also be intangible, such as the right to an idea.

Two amendments to the U.S. Constitution guarantee property rights: The 5th Amendment states that the federal government shall not deprive any person "of life, liberty, or property, without due process of law." The 14th Amendment extends this guarantee to the actions of state governments: "No state . . . shall deprive any person of life, liberty, or property, without due process of law." Similar guarantees exist in every high-income country. Unfortunately, in many developing countries, such guarantees do not exist or are poorly enforced.

In any modern economy, *intellectual property rights* are very important. Intellectual property includes books, films, software, and ideas for new products or new ways of producing products. To protect intellectual property, the federal government grants a *patent* that gives an inventor—which is often a firm—the exclusive right to produce and sell a new product for a period of 20 years from the date the product was invented. For instance, because Microsoft has a patent on the Windows operating system, other firms cannot sell their own versions of Windows. The government grants patents to encourage firms to spend money on the research and development necessary to create new products. If other companies could freely copy Windows, Microsoft would not have spent the funds necessary to develop it. Just as a new product or a new method of making a product receives patent protection, books, films, and software receive *copyright* protection. Under U.S. law, the creator of a book, film, or piece of music has the exclusive right to use the creation during the creator's lifetime. The creator's heirs retain this exclusive right for 50 years after the death of the creator.

## Making the Connection

## Property Rights in Cyberspace: YouTube and MySpace

The development of the Internet has led to new problems in protecting intellectual property rights. People can copy and e-mail songs, newspaper and magazine articles, and even entire motion pictures and television programs or post them on Web sites. Controlling unauthorized copying is more difficult today than it was when "copying" meant making a physical copy of a book, CD, or DVD. The popularity of YouTube and MySpace highlights the problem of unauthorized copying of videos and music. YouTube, founded in 2005, quickly became an enormous success because it provided an easy way to upload videos, which could then be viewed by anyone with an Internet connection. By 2007, thousands of new videos were being uploaded each day, and the site was receiving more than 20 million visitors per month. YouTube earned substantial profits from selling online advertising. Unfortunately, many of the videos on the site contained copyrighted material.

At first, YouTube's policy was to remove any video containing unauthorized material if the holder of the copyright complained. Then YouTube began to negotiate with the copyright holders to pay a fee in return for allowing the copyrighted material to remain on the site. For music videos, YouTube was usually able to obtain the needed permission directly from the

*Some recording artists worry that the copyrights for their songs are not being protected on the Internet.*

recording company. Things were more complicated when videos on YouTube used copyrighted songs as background music. In those cases, YouTube needed to obtain permissions from the songwriters as well as the record company, which could be a time-consuming process. Obtaining permission to use videos that contained material from television shows or movies was even more complicated because sometimes dozens of people—including the actors, directors, and composers of music—held rights to the television show or movie. YouTube's vice president for business development was quoted as saying, "It's almost like technology has pushed far beyond the business practices and the law, and now everything needs to kind of catch up." In November 2006, YouTube agreed to be purchased by Google for $1.65 billion, which made the young entrepreneurs who started the company very wealthy. The willingness of YouTube's owners to sell their company to Google was motivated at least partly by the expectation that Google had the resources to help them resolve their copyright problems.

MySpace had similar problems because many Web pages on the site contained copyrighted music or videos. Universal Music sued MySpace after music from rapper Jay-Z's latest album started appearing on the site even before the album was released. In its lawsuit, Universal claimed that the illegal use of its copyrighted music had "created hundreds of millions of dollars of value for the owners of MySpace."

Music, television, and movie companies believe that the failure to give the full protection of property rights to the online use of their material reduces their ability to sell CDs and DVDs.

Sources: Kevin J. Delaney, Ethan Smith, and Brooks Barnes, "YouTube Finds Signing Rights Deals Complex, Frustrating," *Wall Street Journal*, November 3, 2006, p. B1; and Ethan Smith and Julia Angwin, "Universal Music Sues MySpace Claiming Copyright Infringement," *Wall Street Journal*, November 18, 2006, p. A3.

***Enforcement of Contracts and Property Rights*** Much business activity involves someone agreeing to carry out some action in the future. For example, you may borrow $20,000 to buy a car and promise the bank—by signing a loan contract—that you will pay back the money over the next five years. Or Microsoft may sign a licensing agreement with a small technology company, agreeing to use that company's technology for a period of several years in return for a fee. Usually these agreements take the form of legal contracts. For a market system to work, businesses and individuals have to rely on these contracts being carried out. If one party to a legal contract does not fulfill its obligations—perhaps the small company had promised Microsoft exclusive use of its technology but then began licensing it to other companies—the other party could go to court to have the agreement enforced. Similarly, if property owners in the United States believe that the federal or state government has violated their rights under the 5th or 14th Amendments, they can go to court to have their rights enforced.

But going to court to enforce a contract or private property rights will be successful only if the court system is independent and judges are able to make impartial decisions on the basis of the law. In the United States and other high-income countries, the court systems have enough independence from other parts of the government and enough protection from intimidation by outside forces—such as criminal gangs—that they are able to make their decisions based on the law. In many developing countries, the court systems lack this independence and will not provide a remedy if the government violates private property rights or if a person with powerful political connections decides to violate a business contract.

If property rights are not well enforced, fewer goods and services will be produced. This reduces economic efficiency, leaving the economy inside its production possibilities frontier.

# Conclusion

We have seen that by trading in markets, people are able to specialize and pursue their comparative advantage. Trading on the basis of comparative advantage makes all participants in trade better off. The key role of markets is to facilitate trade. In fact, the market system is a very effective means of coordinating the decisions of millions of consumers, workers, and firms. At the center of the market system is the consumer. To be successful, firms must respond to the desires of consumers. These desires are communicated to firms through prices. To explore how markets work, we must study the behavior of consumers and firms. We continue this exploration of markets in Chapter 3, when we develop the model of demand and supply.

# Chapter 3
# Demand Side

I n Chapter 1, we explored how economists use models to predict human behavior Chapter 2, we used the model of production possibilities frontiers to analyze scarcity and trade-offs. In this chapter and the next, we explore the model of demand and supply, which is the most powerful tool in economics, and use it to explain how prices are determined.

Recall from Chapter 1 that economic models rely on assumptions and that these assumptions are simplifications of reality. In some cases, the assumptions of the model may not seem to describe exactly the economic situation being analyzed. For example, the model of demand and supply assumes that we are analyzing a *perfectly competitive market*. In a **perfectly competitive market**, there are many buyers and sellers, all the products sold are identical, and there are no barriers to new firms entering the market. These assumptions are very restrictive and apply exactly to only a few markets, such as the markets for wheat and other agricultural products. Experience has shown, however, that the model of demand and supply can be very useful in analyzing markets where competition among sellers is intense, even if there are relatively few sellers and the products being sold are not identical. In fact, in recent studies the model of demand and supply has been successful in analyzing markets with as few as four buyers and four sellers. In the end, the usefulness of a model depends on how well it can predict outcomes in a market. As we will see in this chapter, the model of demand and supply is often very useful in predicting changes in quantities and prices in many markets.

We begin considering the model of demand and supply by discussing consumers and the demand side of the market, then we turn to firms and the supply side. As you will see, we will apply this model throughout this book to understand business, the economy, and economic policy.

**Perfectly competitive market**
A market that meets the conditions of (1) many buyers and sellers, (2) all firms selling identical products, and (3) no barriers to new firms entering the market.

---

3.1 | Discuss the variables that influence demand.

# The Demand Side of the Market

Chapter 2 explained that in a market system, consumers ultimately determine which goods and services will be produced. The most successful businesses are the ones that respond best to consumer demand. But what determines consumer demand for a product? Certainly, many factors influence the willingness of consumers to buy a particular product. For example, consumers who are considering buying a digital music player, such as Apple's iPod or Microsoft's Zune, will make their decisions based on, among other factors, the income they have available to spend and the effectiveness of the advertising campaigns of the companies that sell digital music players. The main factor in consumer decisions, though, will be the price of the digital music player. So, it makes sense to begin with price when analyzing the decisions of consumers to buy a product. It is important to note that when we discuss demand, we are considering not what a consumer *wants* to buy but what the consumer is both willing and *able* to buy.

## Demand Schedules and Demand Curves

Tables that show the relationship between the price of a product and the quantity of the product demanded are called **demand schedules**. The table in Figure 3-1 shows the number of players consumers would be willing to buy over the course of a month at five different prices. The amount of a good or a service that a consumer is willing and able to purchase at a given price is referred to as the **quantity demanded**. The graph in Figure 3-1 plots the numbers from the table as a **demand curve**, a curve that shows the relationship between the price of a product and the quantity of the product demanded. (Note that for convenience, we made the demand curve in Figure 3-1 a straight line, or linear. There is no reason that all demand curves need to be straight lines.) The demand curve in Figure 3-1 shows the **market demand**, or the demand by all the consumers of a

**Demand schedule** A table showing the relationship between the price of a product and the quantity of the product demanded.

**Quantity demanded** The amount of a good or service that a consumer is willing and able to purchase at a given price.

**Demand curve** A curve that shows the relationship between the price of a product and the quantity of the product demanded.

**Market demand** The demand by all the consumers of a given good or service.

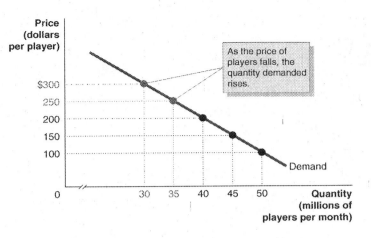

| Demand Schedule | |
|---|---|
| Price (dollars per player) | Quantity (millions of players per month) |
| $300 | 30 |
| 250 | 35 |
| 200 | 40 |
| 150 | 45 |
| 100 | 50 |

As the price of players falls, the quantity demanded rises.

**Figure 3-1**

**A Demand Schedule and Demand Curve**

As the price changes, consumers change the quantity of digital music players they are willing to buy. We can show this as a *demand schedule* in a table or as a *demand curve* on a graph. The table and graph both show that as the price of players falls, the quantity demanded rises. When the price of a player is $300, consumers buy 30 million. When the price drops to $250, consumers buy 35 million. Therefore, the demand curve for digital music players is downward sloping.

given good or service. The market for a product, such as restaurant meals, that is purchased locally would include all the consumers in a city or a relatively small area. The market for a product that is sold internationally, such as digital music players, would include all the consumers in the world.

The demand curve in Figure 3-1 slopes downward because consumers will buy more players as the price falls. When the price of players is $300, consumers buy 30 million players per month. If the price of players falls to $250, consumers buy 35 million players. Buyers demand a larger quantity of a product as the price falls because the product becomes less expensive relative to other products and because they can afford to buy more at a lower price.

## The Law of Demand

The inverse relationship between the price of a product and the quantity of the product demanded is known as the **law of demand**: Holding everything else constant, when the price of a product falls, the quantity demanded of the product will increase, and when the price of a product rises, the quantity demanded of the product will decrease. The law of demand holds for any market demand curve. Economists have never found an exception to it. In fact, Nobel Prize–winning economist George Stigler once remarked that the surest way for an economist to become famous would be to discover a market demand curve that sloped upward rather than downward.

## What Explains the Law of Demand?

It makes sense that consumers will buy more of a good when the price falls and less of a good when the price rises, but let's look more closely at why this is true. When the price of digital music players falls, consumers buy a larger quantity because of the *substitution effect* and the *income effect*.

***Substitution Effect*** The **substitution effect** refers to the change in the quantity demanded of a good that results from a change in price, making the good more or less expensive *relative* to other goods that are *substitutes*. When the price of digital music players falls, consumers will substitute buying music players for buying other goods, such as radios or compact stereos.

***The Income Effect*** The **income effect** of a price change refers to the change in the quantity demanded of a good that results from the effect of a change in the good's price on consumers' purchasing power. Purchasing power is the quantity of goods a consumer can buy with a fixed amount of income. When the price of a good falls, the increased purchasing power of consumers' incomes will usually lead them to purchase a larger quantity of the good. When the price of a good rises, the decreased purchasing power of consumers' incomes will usually lead them to purchase a smaller quantity of the good.

Note that although we can analyze them separately, the substitution effect and the income effect happen simultaneously whenever a price changes. Thus, a fall in the price

**Law of demand** The rule that, holding everything else constant, when the price of a product falls, the quantity demanded of the product will increase, and when the price of a product rises, the quantity demanded of the product will decrease.

**Substitution effect** The change in the quantity demanded of a good that results from a change in price, making the good more or less expensive relative to other goods that are substitutes.

**Income effect** The change in the quantity demanded of a good that results from the effect of a change in the good's price on consumers' purchasing power.

of digital music players leads consumers to buy more players, both because the players are now cheaper relative to substitute products and because the purchasing power of the consumers' incomes has increased.

## Holding Everything Else Constant: The *Ceteris Paribus* Condition

Notice that the definition of the law of demand contains the phrase *holding everything else constant*. In constructing the market demand curve for digital music players, we focused only on the effect that changes in the price of players would have on the quantity of players consumers would be willing and able to buy. We were holding constant other variables that might affect the willingness of consumers to buy players. Economists refer to the necessity of holding all variables other than price constant in constructing a demand curve as the **ceteris paribus** condition; *ceteris paribus* is Latin for "all else equal."

What would happen if we allowed a change in a variable—other than price—that might affect the willingness of consumers to buy music players? Consumers would then change the quantity they demand at each price. We can illustrate this effect by shifting the market demand curve. A shift of a demand curve is *an increase or a decrease in demand*. A movement along a demand curve is *an increase or a decrease in the quantity demanded*. As Figure 3-2 shows, we shift the demand curve to the right if consumers decide to buy more of the good at each price, and we shift the demand curve to the left if consumers decide to buy less at each price.

## Variables That Shift Market Demand

Many variables other than price can influence market demand. These five are the most important:

*   Income

*   Prices of related goods

*   Tastes

*   Population and demographics

*   Expected future prices

We next discuss how changes in each of these variables affect the market demand curve for digital music players.

**Ceteris paribus ("all else equal")** The requirement that when analyzing the relationship between two variables—such as price and quantity demanded—other variables must be held constant.

## Figure 3-2

**Shifting the Demand Curve**

When consumers increase the quantity of a product they wish to buy at a given price, the market demand curve shifts to the right, from $D_1$ to $D_2$. When consumers decrease the quantity of a product they wish to buy at any given price, the demand curve shifts to the left, from $D_1$ to $D_3$.

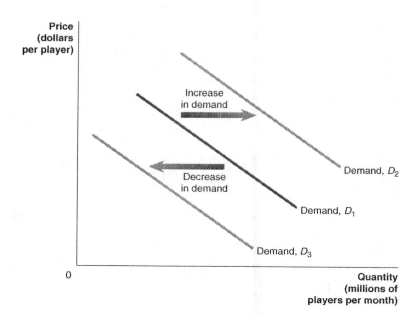

*Income* The income that consumers have available to spend affects their willingness and ability to buy a good. Suppose that the market demand curve in Figure 3-1 represents the willingness of consumers to buy digital music players when average household income is $43,000. If household income rises to $45,000, the demand for players will increase, which we show by shifting the demand curve to the right. A good is a **normal good** when demand increases following a rise in income and decreases following a fall in income. Most goods are normal goods, but the demand for some goods falls when income rises and rises when income falls. For instance, as your income rises, you might buy less canned tuna fish or fewer hot dogs and buy more shrimp or prime rib. A good is an **inferior good** when demand decreases following a rise in income and increases following a fall in income. So, for you hot dogs and tuna fish would be examples of inferior goods—not because they are of low quality but because you buy less of them as your income increases.

**Normal good** A good for which the demand increases as income rises and decreases as income falls.

**Inferior good** A good for which the demand increases as income falls and decreases as income rises.

*Prices of Related Goods* The prices of other goods can also affect consumers' demand for a product. Suppose that the market demand curve in Figure 3-1 represents the willingness and ability of consumers to buy digital music players during a year when the average price of compact stereos, such as the Bose Wave music system, is $500. If the average price of these stereo systems falls to $400, how will the market demand for digital music players change? Fewer players will be demanded at every price. We show this by shifting the demand curve for players to the left.

Goods and services that can be used for the same purpose—such as digital music players and compact stereos—are **substitutes**. When two goods are substitutes, the more you buy of one, the less you will buy of the other. A decrease in the price of a substitute causes the demand curve for a good to shift to the left. An increase in the price of a substitute causes the demand curve for a good to shift to the right.

**Substitutes** Goods and services that can be used for the same purpose.

Many consumers play songs downloaded from a Web site, such as iTunes or Zune Marketplace, on their digital music players. Suppose the market demand curve in Figure 3-1 represents the willingness of consumers to buy players at a time when the average price to download a song is $0.99. If the price to download a song falls to $0.49, consumers will buy more song downloads *and* more digital music players: The demand curve for music players will shift to the right.

Products that are used together—such as digital music players and song downloads—are **complements**. When two goods are complements, the more consumers buy of one, the more they will buy of the other. A decrease in the price of a complement causes the demand curve for a good to shift to the right. An increase in the price of a complement causes the demand curve for a good to shift to the left.

**Complements** Goods and services that are used together.

## Making *the* Connection | Why Supermarkets Need to Understand Substitutes and Complements

Supermarkets sell what sometimes seems like a bewildering variety of goods. The first row of the following table shows the varieties of eight products stocked by five Chicago supermarkets.

| | COFFEE | FROZEN PIZZA | HOT DOGS | ICE CREAM | POTATO CHIPS | REGULAR CEREAL | SPAGHETTI SAUCE | YOGURT |
|---|---|---|---|---|---|---|---|---|
| Varieties in five Chicago supermarkets | 391 | 337 | 128 | 421 | 285 | 242 | 194 | 288 |
| Varieties introduced in a 2-year period | 113 | 109 | 47 | 129 | 93 | 114 | 70 | 107 |
| Varieties removed in a 2-year period | 135 | 86 | 32 | 118 | 77 | 75 | 36 | 51 |

Source: Juin-Kuan Chong, Teck-Hua Ho, and Christopher S. Tang, "A Modeling Framework for Category Assortment Planning," *Manufacturing & Service Operations Management*, 2001, Vol. 3, No. 3, pp. 191–210.

Supermarkets are also constantly adding new varieties of goods to their shelves and removing old varieties. The second row of the table shows that these five Chicago supermarkets added 113 new varieties of coffee over a two-year period, while the third row shows that they eliminated 135 existing varieties. How do supermarkets decide which varieties to add and which to remove?

Christopher Tang is a professor at the Anderson Graduate School of Management at the University of California, Los Angeles (UCLA). In an interview with the *Baltimore Sun*, Tang argues that supermarkets should not necessarily remove the slowest-selling goods from their shelves but should consider the relationships among the goods. In particular, they should consider whether the goods being removed are substitutes or complements with the remaining goods. A lobster bisque soup, for example, could be a relatively slow seller but might be a complement to other soups because it can be used with them to make a sauce. In that case, removing the lobster bisque would hurt sales of some of the remaining soups. Tang suggests the supermarket would be better off removing a slow-selling soup that is a substitute for another soup. For example, the supermarket might want to remove one of two brands of cream of chicken soup.

Source: Lobster bisque example from Lorraine Mirabella, "Shelf Science in Supermarkets," *Baltimore Sun*, March 17, 2002, p. 16.

---

***Tastes*** Consumers can be influenced by an advertising campaign for a product. If Apple, Microsoft, Toshiba, and other makers of digital music players begin to heavily advertise on television and online, consumers are more likely to buy players at every price, and the demand curve will shift to the right. An economist would say that the advertising campaign has affected consumers' *taste* for digital music players. Taste is a catchall category that refers to the many subjective elements that can enter into a consumer's decision to buy a product. A consumer's taste for a product can change for many reasons. Sometimes trends play a substantial role. For example, the popularity of low-carbohydrate diets caused a decline in demand for some goods, such as bread and donuts, and an increase in demand for beef. In general, when consumers' taste for a product increases, the demand curve will shift to the right, and when consumers' taste for a product decreases, the demand curve for the product will shift to the left.

***Population and Demographics*** Population and demographic factors can affect the demand for a product. As the population of the United States increases, so will the number of consumers, and the demand for most products will increase. The **demographics** of a population refers to its characteristics, with respect to age, race, and gender. As the demographics of a country or region change, the demand for particular goods will increase or decrease because different categories of people tend to have different preferences for those goods. For instance, in 2006, a record 17 percent of the U.S. population was 60 years of age or older increasing the demand for health care and other products heavily used by older people.

**Demographics** The characteristics of a population with respect to age, race, and gender.

## Making the Connection | Companies Respond to a Growing Hispanic Population

The spending power of Hispanic Americans is rapidly increasing. So, it is no surprise that firms have begun to respond: When Apple announced in early 2007 that it would sell a 90-minute video of highlights of the 2007 Super Bowl on its iTunes store, the download was made available in Spanish as well as in English. In late 2006, "Coffee Break Spanish," a weekly Spanish language podcast, was one of the most frequently downloaded podcasts on iTunes. Today, more than one third of all DVDs are sold to consumers whose first language is Spanish, and Blockbuster has responded by increasing its offerings of Spanish-language films. Kmart sells a clothing line named after Thalia, a Mexican singer. The Ford Motor Company hired Mexican actress Salma Hayek to appear in commercials. A used car dealer in Pennsylvania displayed a sign stating "Salga Manejando Hoy Mismo" (or "Drive Out Today" in English).

*Blockbuster responds to a growing Hispanic population by featuring DVDs dubbed in Spanish.*

The increase in spending by Hispanic households was due partly to increased population growth and partly to rising incomes. By 2020, the Hispanic share of the U.S. consumer market is expected to grow to more than 13 percent—almost twice what it was in 2000. The Selig Center for Economic Growth at the University of Georgia has forecast that spending by Hispanic households will increase about 70 percent more between 2006 and 2011 than spending by non-Hispanic households.

As the demand for goods purchased by Hispanic households increases, a larger quantity can be sold at every price. Firms have responded by devoting more resources to serving this demographic group.

Sources: "Apple Completes Pass for Super Bowl Highlights," *St. Petersburg* (Florida) *Times*, February 1, 2007; Catherine E. Shoichet and John Martin, "Downloading," *Houston Chronicle*, January 7, 2007; Jeffrey M. Humphreys, "The Multicultural Economy 2006," *Georgia Business and Economic Conditions*, Third Quarter 2006, Vol. 66, No. 3; and Eduardo Porter, "Buying Power of Hispanics Is Set to Soar," *Wall Street Journal*, April 18, 2003, p. B1.

*Expected Future Prices* Consumers choose not only which products to buy but also when to buy them. If enough consumers become convinced that digital music players will be selling for lower prices three months from now, the demand for players will decrease now, as some consumers postpone their purchases to wait for the expected price decrease. Alternatively, if enough consumers become convinced that the price of players will be higher three months from now, the demand for players will increase now, as some consumers try to beat the expected price increase.

Table 3-1 on page 74 summarizes the most important variables that cause market demand curves to shift. You should note that the table shows the shift in the demand curve that results from an *increase* in each of the variables. A *decrease* in these variables would cause the demand curve to shift in the opposite direction.

## A Change in Demand versus a Change in Quantity Demanded

It is important to understand the difference between a *change in demand* and a *change in quantity demanded*. A change in demand refers to a shift of the demand curve. A shift occurs if there is a change in one of the variables, *other than the price of the product*, that affects the willingness of consumers to buy the product. A change in quantity demanded refers to a movement along the demand curve as a result of a change in the product's price. Figure 3-3 illustrates this important distinction. If the price of digital music players falls from $300 to $250, the result will be a movement along the demand curve from

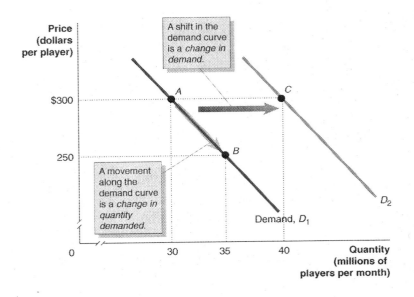

### Figure 3-3

**A Change in Demand versus a Change in the Quantity Demanded**

If the price of digital music players falls from $300 to $250, the result will be a movement along the demand curve from point *A* to point *B*—an increase in quantity demanded from 30 million to 35 million. If consumers' income increases, or if another factor changes that makes consumers want more of the product at every price, the demand curve will shift to the right—an increase in demand. In this case, the increase in demand from $D_1$ to $D_2$ causes the quantity of players demanded at a price of $300 to increase from 30 million at point *A* to 40 million at point *C*.

## TABLE 3-1

**Variables That Shift Market Demand Curves**

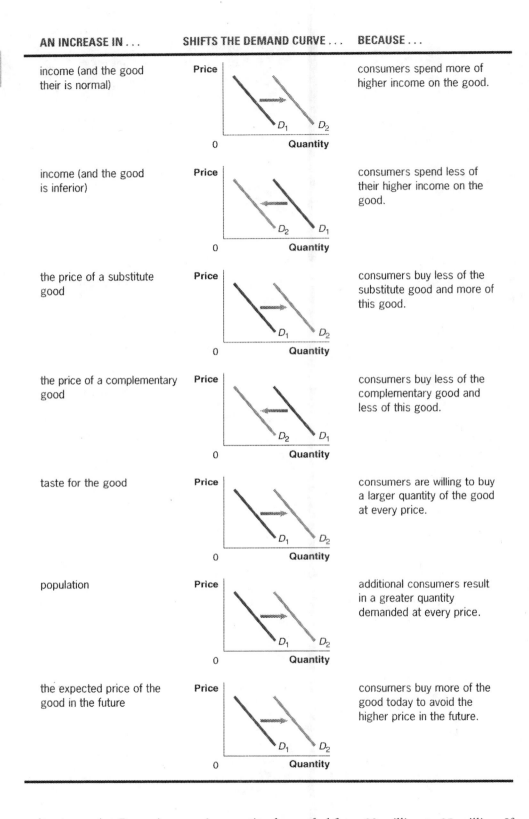

| AN INCREASE IN . . . | SHIFTS THE DEMAND CURVE . . . | BECAUSE . . . |
| --- | --- | --- |
| income (and the good their is normal) | | consumers spend more of higher income on the good. |
| income (and the good is inferior) | | consumers spend less of their higher income on the good. |
| the price of a substitute good | | consumers buy less of the substitute good and more of this good. |
| the price of a complementary good | | consumers buy less of the complementary good and less of this good. |
| taste for the good | | consumers are willing to buy a larger quantity of the good at every price. |
| population | | additional consumers result in a greater quantity demanded at every price. |
| the expected price of the good in the future | | consumers buy more of the good today to avoid the higher price in the future. |

point *A* to point *B*—an increase in quantity demanded from 30 million to 35 million. If consumers' incomes increase, or if another factor changes that makes consumers want more of the product at every price, the demand curve will shift to the right—an increase in demand. In this case, the increase in demand from $D_1$ to $D_2$ causes the quantity of digital music players demanded at a price of $300 to increase from 30 million at point *A* to 40 million at point *C*.

*Will Apple's iPhone match the success of its iPod?*

Making the Connection | **Apple Forecasts the Demand for iPhones and other Consumer Electronics**

One of the most important decisions that the managers of any large firm have to make is which new products to develop. A firm must devote people, time, and money to designing the product, negotiating with suppliers, formulating a marketing campaign, and many other tasks. But any firm has only limited resources and so faces a trade-off: Resources used to develop one product will not be available to develop another product. Ultimately, the products a firm chooses to develop will be those which it believes will be the most profitable. So, to decide which products to develop, firms need to forecast the demand for those products.

David Sobotta, who worked at Apple for 20 years, eventually becoming its national sales manager, has described the strategy Apple has used to decide which consumer electronics products will have the greatest demand. Sobotta describes discussions at Apple during 2002 about whether to develop a tablet personal computer. A tablet PC is a laptop with a special screen that allows the computer to be controlled with a stylus or pen and that has the capability of converting handwritten input into text. The previous year, Bill Gates, chairman of Microsoft, had predicted that "within five years . . . [tablet PCs] will be the most popular form of PC sold in America." Representatives of the federal government's National Institutes of Health also urged Apple to develop a tablet PC, arguing that it would be particularly useful to doctors, nurses, and hospitals. Apple's managers decided not to develop a tablet PC, however, because they believed the technology was too complex for the average computer user and did not believe that the demand from doctors and nurses would be very large. This forecast turned out to be correct. Despite Bill Gates's prediction, in 2006, tablets made up only 1 percent of the computer market, and they were forecast to increase to only 5 percent by 2009.

According to Sobotta, "Apple executives had a theory that the route to success will not be through selling thousands of relatively expensive things, but millions of very inexpensive things like iPods." In fact, although many business analysts were skeptical that the iPod would succeed, demand grew faster than even Apple's most optimistic forecasts. By the beginning of 2007, 100 million iPods had been sold. So, it was not very surprising when in early 2007, Apple Chief Executive Officer Steve Jobs announced that the company would be combining the iPod with a cell phone to create the iPhone. With more than 900 million cell phones sold each year, Apple expects the demand for the iPhone to be very large. As Sobotta noted, "And there's an 'Apple gap': mobile phone users often find their interfaces confusing. . . . Apple's unique ability to simplify while innovating looks like a good fit there."

Apple forecast that it would sell 10 million iPhones during the product's first year on the market, with much larger sales expected in future years. Time will tell whether Apple's forecast of a large demand for the iPhone will turn out to be correct.

Source: David Sobotta, "Technology: What Jobs Told Me on the iPhone," *The Guardian* (London), January 4, 2007, p. 1; and Connie Guglielmo, "Apple First-Quarter Profit Rises on IPod, Mac Sales," Bloomberg.com, January 17, 2007.

3.2 | Discuss the variables that influence supply.

# The Supply Side of the Market

Just as many variables influence the willingness and ability of consumers to buy a particular good or service, many variables also influence the willingness and ability of firms to sell a good or service. The most important of these variables is price. The amount of a good or service that a firm is willing and able to supply at a given price is the **quantity supplied**. Holding other variables constant, when the price of a good rises, producing

**Quantity supplied** The amount of a good or service that a firm is willing and able to supply at a given price.

the good is more profitable, and the quantity supplied will increase. When the price of a good falls, the good is less profitable, and the quantity supplied will decrease. In addition, as we saw in Chapter 2, devoting more and more resources to the production of a good results in increasing marginal costs. So, if, for example, Apple, Microsoft, and Toshiba increase production of digital music players during a given time period, they are likely to find that the cost of producing the additional players increases as they run existing factories for longer hours and pay higher prices for components and higher wages for workers. With higher marginal costs, firms will supply a larger quantity only if the price is higher.

## Supply Schedules and Supply Curves

**Supply schedule** A table that shows the relationship between the price of a product and the quantity of the product supplied.

**Supply curve** A curve that shows the relationship between the price of a product and the quantity of the product supplied.

A **supply schedule** is a table that shows the relationship between the price of a product and the quantity of the product supplied. The table in Figure 3-4 is a supply schedule showing the quantity of digital music players that firms would be willing to supply per month at different prices. The graph in Figure 3-4 plots the numbers from the supply schedule as a *supply curve*. A **supply curve** shows the relationship between the price of a product and the quantity of the product supplied. The supply schedule and supply curve both show that as the price of players rises, firms will increase the quantity they supply. At a price of $250 per player, firms will supply 45 million players per year. At the higher price of $300, they will supply 50 million. (Once again, we are assuming for convenience that the supply curve is a straight line, even though not all supply curves are actually straight lines.)

## The Law of Supply

**Law of supply** The rule that, holding everything else constant, increases in price cause increases in the quantity supplied, and decreases in price cause decreases in the quantity supplied.

The *market supply curve* in Figure 3-4 is upward sloping. We expect most supply curves to be upward sloping according to the **law of supply**, which states that, holding everything else constant, increases in price cause increases in the quantity supplied, and decreases in price cause decreases in the quantity supplied. Notice that the definition of the law of supply—like the definition of the law of demand—contains the phrase *holding everything else constant*. If only the price of the product changes, there is a movement along the supply curve, which is *an increase or a decrease in the quantity supplied*. As Figure 3-5 shows, if any other variable that affects the willingness of firms to supply a good changes, the supply curve will shift, which is *an increase or decrease in supply*. When firms increase the quantity of a product they wish to sell at a given price, the supply curve shifts to the right. The shift from $S_1$ to $S_3$ represents *an increase in supply*. When firms decrease the quantity of a product they wish to sell at a given price, the supply curve shifts to the left. The shift from $S_1$ to $S_2$ represents *a decrease in supply*.

## Figure 3-4

**Supply Schedule and Supply Curve**

As the price changes, Apple, Microsoft, Toshiba, and the other firms producing digital music players change the quantity they are willing to supply. We can show this as a *supply schedule* in a table or as a *supply curve* on a graph. The supply schedule and supply curve both show that as the price of players rises, firms will increase the quantity they supply. At a price of $250, firms will supply 45 million players. At a price of $300 per player, firms will supply 50 million players.

| Supply Schedule | |
| --- | --- |
| Price (dollars per player) | Quantity (millions of players per month) |
| $300 | 50 |
| 250 | 45 |
| 200 | 40 |
| 150 | 35 |
| 100 | 30 |

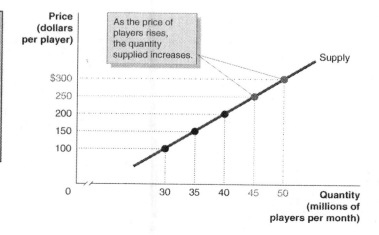

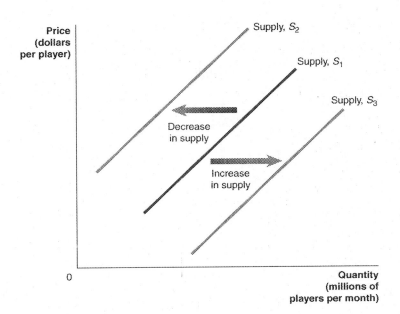

## Figure 3-5

### Shifting the Supply Curve

When firms increase the quantity of a product they wish to sell at a given price, the supply curve shifts to the right. The shift from $S_1$ to $S_3$ represents an *increase in supply*. When firms decrease the quantity of a product they wish to sell at a given price, the supply curve shifts to the left. The shift from $S_1$ to $S_2$ represents a *decrease in supply*.

## Variables That Shift Supply

The following are the most important variables that shift supply:

- Prices of inputs
- Technological change
- Prices of substitutes in production
- Number of firms in the market
- Expected future prices

We next discuss how each of these variables affects the supply of digital music players.

***Prices of Inputs*** The factor most likely to cause the supply curve for a product to shift is a change in the price of an *input*. An input is anything used in the production of a good or service. For instance, if the price of a component of digital music players, such as the microprocessor, rises, the cost of producing music players will increase, and players will be less profitable at every price. The supply of players will decline, and the market supply curve for players will shift to the left. Similarly, if the price of an input declines, the supply of players will increase, and the supply curve will shift to the right.

***Technological Change*** A second factor that causes a change in supply is *technological change*. **Technological change** is a positive or negative change in the ability of a firm to produce a given level of output with a given quantity of inputs. Positive technological change occurs whenever a firm is able to produce more output using the same amount of inputs. This shift will happen when the *productivity* of workers or machines increases. If a firm can produce more output with the same amount of inputs, its costs will be lower, and the good will be more profitable to produce at any given price. As a result, when positive technological change occurs, the firm will increase the quantity supplied at every price, and its supply curve will shift to the right. Normally, we expect technological change to have a positive impact on a firm's willingness to supply a product. Negative technological change is relatively rare, although it could result from a natural disaster or a war that reduces the ability of a firm to supply as much output with a given amount of inputs. Negative technological change will raise a firm's costs, and the good will be less profitable to produce. Therefore, negative technological change causes a firm's supply curve to shift to the left.

**Technological change** A positive or negative change in the ability of a firm to produce a given level of output with a given quantity of inputs.

***Prices of Substitutes in Production*** Firms often choose which good or service they will produce. Alternative products that a firm could produce are called *substitutes in production*. To this point, we have considered the market for all types of digital music players. But suppose we now consider separate markets for music players with screens capable of showing videos and for smaller players, without screens, that play only music. If the price of video music players increases, video music players will become more profitable, and Apple, Microsoft, and the other companies making music players will shift some of their productive capacity away from smaller players and toward video players. The companies will offer fewer smaller players for sale at every price, so the supply curve for smaller players will shift to the left.

***Number of Firms in the Market*** A change in the number of firms in the market will change supply. When new firms *enter* a market, the supply curve shifts to the right, and when existing firms leave, or *exit*, a market, the supply curve for digital music players shifts to the left. For instance, when Microsoft introduced the Zune, the market supply curve for digital music players shifted to the right.

***Expected Future Prices*** If a firm expects that the price of its product will be higher in the future than it is today, it has an incentive to decrease supply now and increase it in the future. For instance, if Apple believes that prices for digital music players are temporarily

**TABLE 3-2**

**Variables That Shift Market Supply Curves**

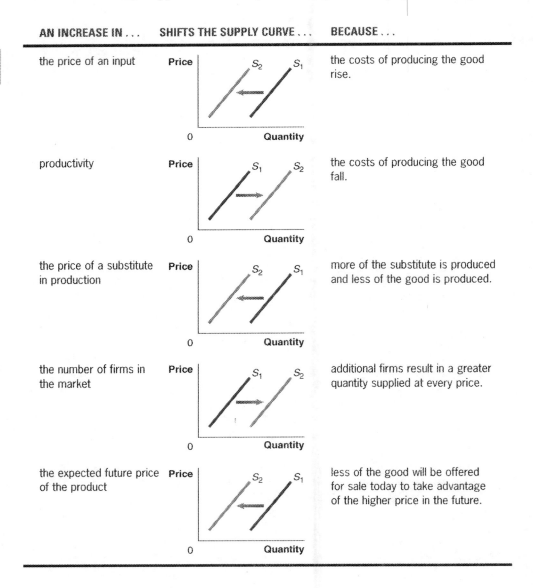

| AN INCREASE IN . . . | SHIFTS THE SUPPLY CURVE . . . | BECAUSE . . . |
| --- | --- | --- |
| the price of an input | | the costs of producing the good rise. |
| productivity | | the costs of producing the good fall. |
| the price of a substitute in production | | more of the substitute is produced and less of the good is produced. |
| the number of firms in the market | | additional firms result in a greater quantity supplied at every price. |
| the expected future price of the product | | less of the good will be offered for sale today to take advantage of the higher price in the future. |

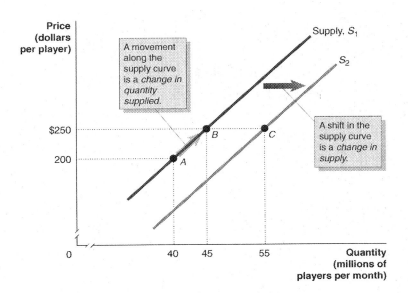

## Figure 3-6

**A Change in Supply versus a Change in the Quantity Supplied**

If the price of digital music players rises from $200 to $250, the result will be a movement up the supply curve from point A to point B—an increase in quantity supplied by Apple, Microsoft, and Toshiba and the other firms from 40 million to 45 million. If the price of an input decreases or another factor changes that makes sellers supply more of the product at every price, the supply curve will shift to the right—an increase in supply. In this case, the increase in supply from $S_1$ to $S_2$ causes the quantity of digital music players supplied at a price of $250 to increase from 45 million at point B to 55 million at point C.

low—perhaps because of a price war among firms making players—it may store some of its production today to sell tomorrow, when it expects prices will be higher.

Table 3-2 on page 78 summarizes the most important variables that cause market supply curves to shift. You should note that the table shows the shift in the supply curve that results from an *increase* in each of the variables. A *decrease* in these variables would cause the supply curve to shift in the opposite direction.

## A Change in Supply versus a Change in Quantity Supplied

We noted earlier the important difference between a change in demand and a change in quantity demanded. There is a similar difference between a *change in supply* and a *change in quantity supplied*. A change in supply refers to a shift of the supply curve. The supply curve will shift when there is a change in one of the variables, *other than the price of the product*, that affects the willingness of suppliers to sell the product. A change in quantity supplied refers to a movement along the supply curve as a result of a change in the product's price. Figure 3-6 illustrates this important distinction. If the price of music players rises from $200 to $250, the result will be a movement up the supply curve from point A to point B—an increase in quantity supplied from 40 million to 45 million. If the price of an input decreases or another factor makes sellers supply more of the product at every price change, the supply curve will shift to the right—an increase in supply. In this case, the increase in supply from $S_1$ to $S_2$ causes the quantity of digital music players supplied at a price of $250 to increase from 45 million at point B to 55 million at point C.

3.3 | Use a graph to illustrate market equilibrium.

**3.3 LEARNING** OBJECTIVE

# Market Equilibrium: Putting Demand and Supply Together

The purpose of markets is to bring buyers and sellers together. As we saw in Chapter 2, instead of being chaotic and disorderly, the interaction of buyers and sellers in markets ultimately results in firms being led to produce those goods and services consumers desire most. To understand how this process happens, we first need to see how markets work to reconcile the plans of buyers and sellers.

In Figure 3-7, we bring together the market demand curve for digital music players and the market supply curve. Notice that the demand curve crosses the supply curve at

## Figure 3-7

**Market Equilibrium**

Where the demand curve crosses the supply curve determines market equilibrium. In this case, the demand curve for digital music players crosses the supply curve at a price of $200 and a quantity of 40 million. Only at this point is the quantity of players consumers are willing to buy equal to the quantity of players Apple, Microsoft, Toshiba, and the other firms are willing to sell: The quantity demanded is equal to the quantity supplied.

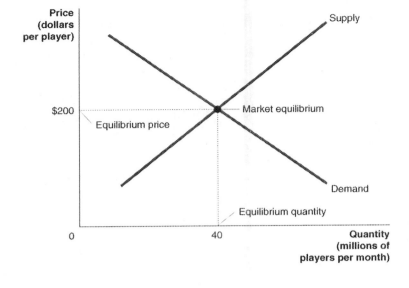

**Market equilibrium** A situation in which quantity demanded equals quantity supplied.

**Competitive market equilibrium** A market equilibrium with many buyers and many sellers.

**Surplus** A situation in which the quantity supplied is greater than the quantity demanded.

**Shortage** A situation in which the quantity demanded is greater than the quantity supplied.

only one point. This point represents a price of $200 and a quantity of 40 million players. Only at this point is the quantity of players consumers are willing to buy equal to the quantity of players firms are willing to sell. This is the point of **market equilibrium**. Only at market equilibrium will the quantity demanded equal the quantity supplied. In this case, the *equilibrium price* is $200, and the *equilibrium quantity* is 40 million. As we noted at the beginning of the chapter, markets that have many buyers and many sellers are competitive markets, and equilibrium in these markets is a **competitive market equilibrium**. In the market for digital music players, there are many buyers but fewer than 20 firms. Whether 20 firms is enough for our model of demand and supply to apply to this market is a matter of judgment. In this chapter, we are assuming that the market for digital music players has enough sellers to be competitive.

## How Markets Eliminate Surpluses and Shortages

A market that is not in equilibrium moves toward equilibrium. Once a market is in equilibrium, it remains in equilibrium. To see why, consider what happens if a market is not in equilibrium. For instance, suppose that the price in the market for digital music players was $250, rather than the equilibrium price of $200. As Figure 3-8 shows, at a price of $250, the quantity of players supplied would be 45 million, and the quantity of players demanded would be 35 million. When the quantity supplied is greater than the quantity demanded, there is a **surplus** in the market. In this case, the surplus is equal to 10 million players (45 million − 35 million = 10 million). When there is a surplus, firms have unsold goods piling up, which gives them an incentive to increase their sales by cutting the price. Cutting the price will simultaneously increase the quantity demanded and decrease the quantity supplied. This adjustment will reduce the surplus, but as long as the price is above $200, there will be a surplus, and downward pressure on the price will continue. Only when the price has fallen to $200 will the market be in equilibrium.

If, however, the price were $100, the quantity supplied would be 30 million, and the quantity demanded would be 50 million, as shown in Figure 3-8. When the quantity demanded is greater than the quantity supplied, there is a **shortage** in the market. In this case, the shortage is equal to 20 million digital music players (50 million − 30 million = 20 million). When a shortage occurs, some consumers will be unable to buy a digital music player at the current price. In this situation, firms will realize that they can raise the price without losing sales. A higher price will simultaneously increase the quantity supplied and decrease the quantity demanded. This adjustment will reduce the shortage, but as long as the price is below $200, there will be a shortage, and upward pressure on the price will continue. Only when the price has risen to $200 will the market be in equilibrium.

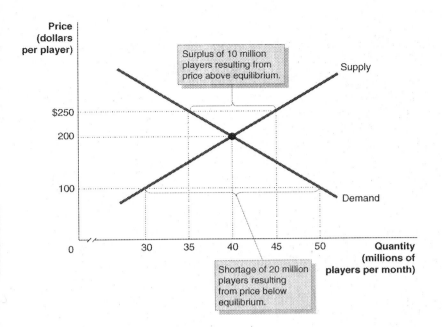

Figure 3-8

**The Effect of Surpluses and Shortages on the Market Price**

When the market price is above equilibrium, there will be a *surplus*. In the figure, a price of $250 for digital music players results in 45 million being supplied but only 35 million being demanded, or a surplus of 10 million. As Apple, Microsoft, Toshiba, and the other firms cut the price to dispose of the surplus, the price will fall to the equilibrium of $200. When the market price is below equilibrium, there will be a *shortage*. A price of $100 results in 50 million players being demanded but only 30 million being supplied, or a shortage of 20 million. As consumers who are unable to buy a player offer to pay higher prices, the price will rise to the equilibrium of $200.

At a competitive market equilibrium, all consumers willing to pay the market price will be able to buy as much of the product as they want, and all firms willing to accept the market price will be able to sell as much of the product as they want. As a result, there will be no reason for the price to change unless either the demand curve or the supply curve shifts.

## Demand and Supply Both Count

Always keep in mind that it is the interaction of demand and supply that determines the equilibrium price. Neither consumers nor firms can dictate what the equilibrium price will be. No firm can sell anything at any price unless it can find a willing buyer, and no consumer can buy anything at any price without finding a willing seller.

# Solved Problem | 3-3

## Demand and Supply Both Count: A Tale of Two Letters

Which letter is likely to be worth more: one written by Abraham Lincoln or one written by his assassin, John Wilkes Booth? Lincoln is one of the greatest presidents, and many people collect anything written by him. The demand for letters written by Lincoln surely would seem to be much greater than the demand for letters written by Booth. Yet when R. M. Smythe and Co. auctioned off on the same day a letter written by Lincoln and a letter written by Booth, the Booth letter sold for $31,050, and the Lincoln letter sold for only $21,850. Use a demand and supply graph to explain how the Booth letter has a higher market price than the Lincoln letter, even though the demand for letters written by Lincoln is greater than the demand for letters written by Booth.

## SOLVING THE PROBLEM:

**Step 1:** **Review the chapter material.** This problem is about prices being determined at market equilibrium, so you may want to review the section "Market Equilibrium: Putting Demand and Supply Together," which begins on page 79.

**Step 2:** **Draw demand curves that illustrate the greater demand for Lincoln's letters.** Begin by drawing two demand curves. Label one "Demand for Lincoln's letters" and the other "Demand for Booth's letters." Make sure that the Lincoln demand curve is much farther to the right than the Booth demand curve.

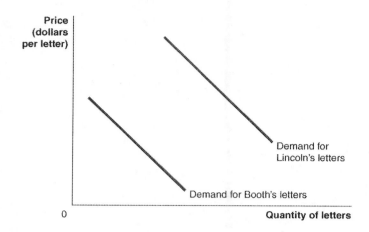

**Step 3:** **Draw supply curves that illustrate the equilibrium price of Booth's letters being higher than the equilibrium price of Lincoln's letters.** Based on the demand curves you have just drawn, think about how it might be possible for the market price of Lincoln's letters to be lower than the market price of Booth's letters. The only way this can be true is if the supply of Lincoln's letters is much greater than the supply of Booth's letters. Draw on your graph a supply curve for Lincoln's letters and a supply curve for Booth's letters that will result in an equilibrium price of Booth's letters of $31,050 and an equilibrium price of Lincoln's letters of $21,850. You have now solved the problem.

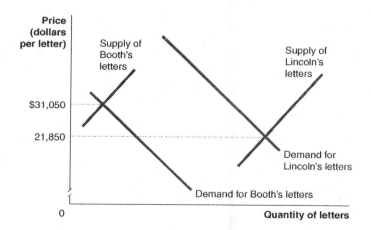

**EXTRA CREDIT:** The explanation for this puzzle is that both demand and supply count when determining market price. The demand for Lincoln's letters is much greater than the demand for Booth's letters, but the supply of Booth's letters is very small. Historians believe that only eight letters written by Booth exist today. (Note that the supply curves for letters written by Booth and by Lincoln slope up even though only a fixed number of each of these types of letters is available and, obviously, no more can be produced. The upward slope of the supply curves occurs because the higher the price, the larger the quantity of letters that will be offered for sale by people who currently own them.)

3.4 | Use demand and supply graphs to predict changes in prices and quantities.

# The Effect of Demand and Supply Shifts on Equilibrium

We have seen that the interaction of demand and supply in markets determines the quantity of a good that is produced and the price at which it sells. We have also seen that several variables cause demand curves to shift, and other variables cause supply curves to shift. As a result, demand and supply curves in most markets are constantly shifting, and the prices and quantities that represent equilibrium are constantly changing. In this section, we see how shifts in demand and supply curves affect equilibrium price and quantity.

## The Effect of Shifts in Supply on Equilibrium

When Microsoft decided to start selling the Zune music player, the market supply curve for music players shifted to the right. Figure 3-9 shows the supply curve shifting from $S_1$ to $S_2$. When the supply curve shifts to the right, there will be a surplus at the original equilibrium price, $P_1$. The surplus is eliminated as the equilibrium price falls to $P_2$, and the equilibrium quantity rises from $Q_1$ to $Q_2$. If existing firms exit the market, the supply curve will shift to the left, causing the equilibrium price to rise and the equilibrium quantity to fall.

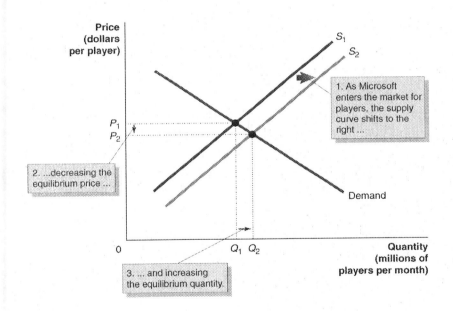

### Figure 3-9

**The Effect of an Increase in Supply on Equilibrium**

If a firm enters a market, as Microsoft entered the market for digital music players when it launched the Zune, the equilibrium price will fall, and the equilibrium quantity will rise.

1. As Microsoft enters the market for digital music players, a larger quantity of players will be supplied at every price, so the market supply curve shifts to the right, from $S_1$ to $S_2$, which causes a surplus of players at the original price, $P_1$.
2. The equilibrium price falls from $P_1$ to $P_2$.
3. The equilibrium quantity rises from $Q_1$ to $Q_2$.

## Making the Connection | The Falling Price of LCD Televisions

Research on flat-screen televisions using liquid crystal displays (LCDs) began in the 1960s. However, it was surprisingly difficult to use this research to produce a television priced low enough for many consumers to purchase. One researcher noted, "In the 1960s, we used to say 'In ten years, we're going to have the TV on the wall.' We said the same thing in the seventies and then in the eighties." A key technical problem in manufacturing LCD televisions was making glass sheets large enough, thin enough, and clean enough to be used as LCD screens. Finally, in 1999, Corning, Inc., developed a process to manufacture glass that was less than 1 millimeter thick and very clean because it was produced without being touched by machinery.

Corning's breakthrough led to what the *Wall Street Journal* described as a "race to build new, better factories." The firms producing the flat screens are all located in Taiwan, South Korea, and Japan. The leading firms are Korea's Samsung Electronics and LG Phillips LCD, Taiwan's AU Optronics, and Japan's Sharp Corporation. In 2004, AU Optronics opened a new factory with 2.4 million square feet of clean room in which the LCD screens are manufactured. This factory is nearly five times as large as the largest factory in which Intel makes computer chips. In all, 10 new factories manufacturing LCD screens came into operation between late 2004 and late 2005. The figure shows that this increase in supply drove the price of a typical large LCD television from $4,000 in the fall of 2004 to $1,600 at the end of 2006, increasing the quantity demanded worldwide from 8 million to 46 million.

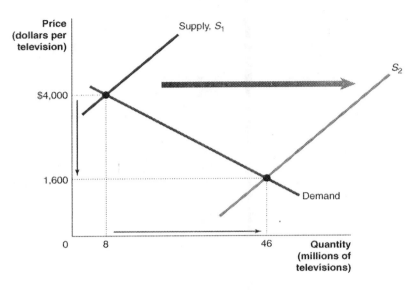

Sources: David Richards, "Sony and Panasonic Flat Screen Kings," Smarthouse.com, February 13, 2007; Evan Ramstad, "Big Display: Once a Footnote, Flat Screens Grow into Huge Industry," *Wall Street Journal*, August 30, 2004, p. A1; and Michael Schuman, "Flat Chance: Prices on Cool TVs Are Dropping as New Factories Come on Line," *Time*, October 18, 2004, pp. 64–66.

## The Effect of Shifts in Demand on Equilibrium

When population growth and income growth occur, the market demand for music players shifts to the right. Figure 3-10 shows the effect of a demand curve shifting to the right, from $D_1$ to $D_2$. This shift causes a shortage at the original equilibrium price, $P_1$. To eliminate the shortage, the equilibrium price rises to $P_2$, and the equilibrium quantity

### Figure 3-10

**The Effect of an Increase in Demand on Equilibrium**

Increases in income and population will cause the equilibrium price and quantity to rise:
1. As population and income grow, the quantity demanded increases at every price, and the market demand curve shifts to the right, from $D_1$ to $D_2$, which causes a shortage of digital music players at the original price, $P_1$.
2. The equilibrium price rises from $P_1$ to $P_2$.
3. The equilibrium quantity rises from $Q_1$ to $Q_2$.

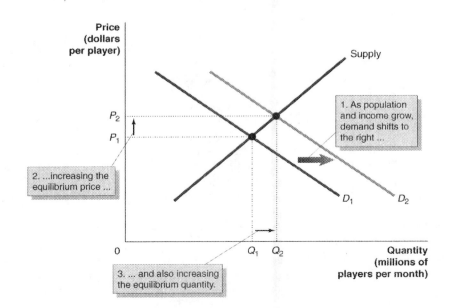

rises from $Q_1$ to $Q_2$. By contrast, if the price of a complementary good, such as downloads from music Web sites, were to rise, the demand for music players would decrease. This change would cause the demand curve for players to shift to the left, and the equilibrium price and quantity would both decrease.

## The Effect of Shifts in Demand and Supply over Time

Whenever only demand or only supply shifts, we can easily predict the effect on equilibrium price and quantity. But what happens if *both* curves shift? For instance, in many markets, the demand curve shifts to the right over time, as population and income grow. The supply curve also often shifts to the right as new firms enter the market and positive technological change occurs. Whether the equilibrium price in a market rises or falls over time depends on whether demand shifts to the right more than does supply. Panel (a) of Figure 3-11 shows that when demand shifts to the right more than supply, the equilibrium price rises. But, as panel (b) shows, when supply shifts to the right more than demand, the equilibrium price falls.

Table 3-3 on page 86 summarizes all possible combinations of shifts in demand and supply over time and the effects of the shifts on equilibrium price ($P$) and quantity ($Q$). For example, the entry in red in the table shows that if the demand curve shifts to the right and the supply curve also shifts to the right, then the equilibrium quantity will increase, while the equilibrium price may increase, decrease, or remain unchanged. To make sure you understand each entry in the table, draw demand and supply graphs to check whether you can reproduce the predicted changes in equilibrium price and quantity. If the entry in the table says the predicted change in equilibrium price or quantity can be either an increase or a decrease, draw two graphs similar to panels (a) and (b) of Figure 3-11, one showing the equilibrium price or quantity increasing and the other showing it decreasing. Note also that in the ambiguous cases where either price or quantity might increase or decrease, it is also possible that price or quantity might remain unchanged. Be sure you understand why this is true.

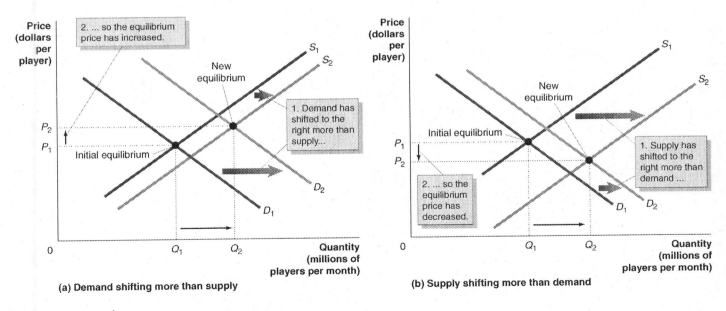

**(a) Demand shifting more than supply**

**(b) Supply shifting more than demand**

Figure 3-11 | Shifts in Demand and Supply over Time

Whether the price of a product rises or falls over time depends on whether demand shifts to the right more than supply.

In panel (a), demand shifts to the right more than supply, and the equilibrium price rises.

1. Demand shifts to the right more than supply.
2. Equilibrium price rises from $P_1$ to $P_2$.

In panel (b), supply shifts to the right more than demand, and the equilibrium price falls.

1. Supply shifts to the right more than demand.
2. Equilibrium price falls from $P_1$ to $P_2$.

TABLE 3-3

| How Shifts in Demand and Supply Affect Equilibrium Price (P) and Quantity (Q) | SUPPLY CURVE UNCHANGED | SUPPLY CURVE SHIFTS TO THE RIGHT | SUPPLY CURVE SHIFTS TO THE LEFT |
|---|---|---|---|
| **DEMAND CURVE UNCHANGED** | Q unchanged<br>P unchanged | Q increases<br>P decreases | Q decreases<br>P increases |
| **DEMAND CURVE SHIFTS TO THE RIGHT** | Q increases<br>P increases | Q increases<br>P increases or decreases | Q increases or decreases<br>P increases |
| **DEMAND CURVE SHIFTS TO THE LEFT** | Q decreases<br>P decreases | Q increases or decreases<br>P decreases | Q decreases<br>P decreases or decreases |

# Solved Problem | 3-4

## High Demand and Low Prices in the Lobster Market?

During the spring, when demand for lobster is relatively low, Maine lobstermen are able to sell their lobster catches for about $4.50 per pound. During the summer, when demand for lobster is much higher, Maine lobstermen are able to sell their lobster catches for only about $3.00 per pound. It may seem strange that the market price is higher when demand is low than when demand is high. Can you resolve this paradox with the help of a demand and supply graph?

### SOLVING THE PROBLEM:

Step 1: **Review the chapter material.** This problem is about how shifts in demand and supply curves affect the equilibrium price, so you may want to review the section "The Effect of Shifts in Demand and Supply over Time," which begins on page 85.

Step 2: **Draw the demand and supply graph.** Draw a demand and supply graph, showing the market equilibrium in the spring. Label the equilibrium price $4.50. Label both the demand and supply curves "spring."

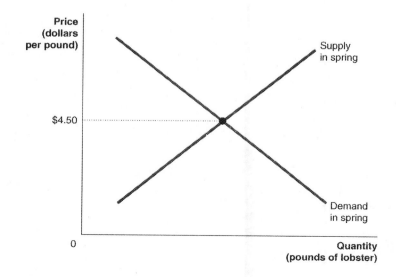

**Step 3:   Add to your graph a demand curve for summer.**

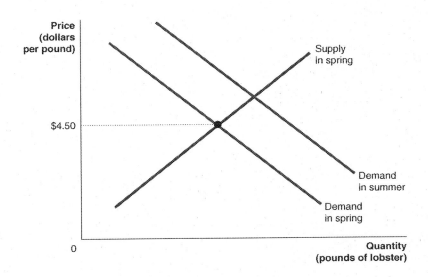

**Step 4:   Explain the graph.** After studying the graph, it is possible to see how the equilibrium price can fall from $4.50 to $3.00, despite the increase in demand: The supply curve must have shifted to the right by enough to cause the equilibrium price to fall to $3.00. Draw the new supply curve, label it "summer," and label the new equilibrium price $3.00. The demand for lobster does increase in summer compared with the spring. But the increase in the supply of lobster between spring and summer is even greater. So, the equilibrium price falls.

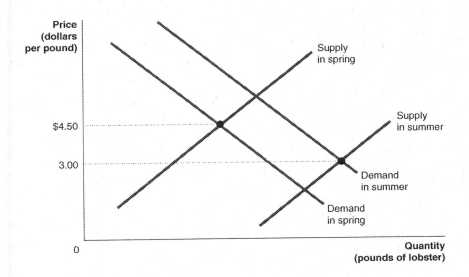

Source. Carey Goldberg, "Down East, the Lobster Hauls Are Up Big," *New York Times*, May 31, 2001.

**>> End Solved Problem 3-4**

## Shifts in a Curve versus Movements along a Curve

When analyzing markets using demand and supply curves, it is important to remember that *when a shift in a demand or supply curve causes a change in equilibrium price, the change in price does not cause a further shift in demand or supply.* For instance, suppose an increase in supply causes the price of a good to fall, while everything else that affects the willingness of consumers to buy the good is constant. The result will be an increase in the quantity demanded but not an increase in demand. For demand to increase, the whole curve must shift. The point is the same for supply: If the price of the good falls but everything else that affects the willingness of sellers to supply the good is constant, the quantity supplied decreases, but the supply does not. For supply to decrease, the whole curve must shift.

# Don't Let This Happen to **YOU!**

### Remember: A Change in a Good's Price Does *Not* Cause the Demand or Supply Curve to Shift

Suppose a student is asked to draw a demand and supply graph to illustrate how an increase in the price of oranges would affect the market for apples, other variables being constant. He draws the graph on the left below and explains it as follows: "Because apples and oranges are substitutes, an increase in the price of oranges will cause an initial shift to the right in the demand curve for apples, from $D_1$ to $D_2$. However, because this initial shift in the demand curve for apples results in a higher price for apples, $P_2$, consumers will find apples less desirable, and the demand curve will shift to the left, from $D_2$ to $D_3$, resulting in a final equilibrium price of $P_3$." Do you agree or disagree with the student's analysis?

You should disagree. The student has correctly understood that an increase in the price of oranges will cause the demand curve for apples to shift to the right. But the sec-

ond demand curve shift the student describes, from $D_2$ to $D_3$, will not take place. Changes in the price of a product do not result in shifts in the product's demand curve. Changes in the price of a product result only in movements along a demand curve.

The graph on the right below shows the correct analysis. The increase in the price of oranges causes the demand curve for apples to increase from $D_1$ to $D_2$. At the original price, $P_1$, the increase in demand initially results in a shortage of apples equal to $Q_3 - Q_1$. But, as we have seen, a shortage causes the price to increase until the shortage is eliminated. In this case, the price will rise to $P_2$, where the quantity demanded and the quantity supplied are both equal to $Q_2$. Notice that the increase in price causes a decrease in the *quantity demanded* from $Q_3$ to $Q_2$, but does *not* cause a decrease in demand.

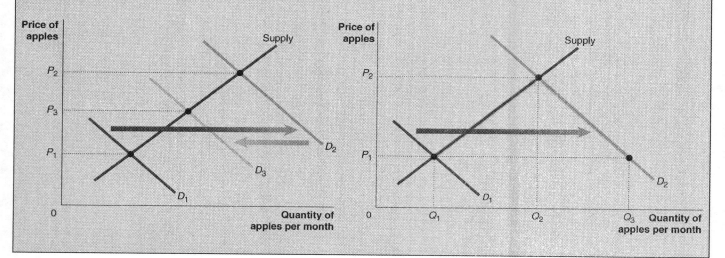

# Conclusion

The interaction of demand and supply determines market equilibrium. The model of demand and supply provides us with a powerful tool for predicting how changes in the actions of consumers and firms will cause changes in equilibrium prices and quantities. As we have seen in this chapter, the model can often be used to analyze markets that do not meet all the requirements for being perfectly competitive. As long as there is intense competition among sellers, the model of demand and supply can often successfully predict changes in prices and quantities. We will use the model in the next chapter to analyze economic efficiency and the results of government-imposed price floors and price ceilings. Before moving on, read *An Inside Look* on the next page to learn how Apple and AT&T benefit from collaborating on the iPhone.

## WALL STREET JOURNAL, FEBRUARY 17, 2007

## Apple Coup: How Steve Jobs Played Hardball in iPhone Birth

During a visit to Las Vegas last December for a rodeo event, Cingular Wireless chief executive Stan Sigman received a welcome guest: Steve Jobs. The Apple Inc. chief stopped by Mr. Sigman's Four Seasons hotel suite to show off the iPhone, a sleek cellphone designed to surf the Web and double as an iPod music player.

The phone had been in development by Apple and Cingular [now AT&T] for two years and was weeks away from being revealed to the world. And yet this was the first time Mr. Sigman got to see it. For three hours, Mr. Jobs played with the device, with its touch-screen that allows users to view contacts, dial numbers and flip through photos with the swipe of a finger. Mr. Sigman looked on in awe, according to a person familiar with the meeting . . .

Mr. Jobs is famous for making a splash with new products that upend industry models. Several years ago, he personally lobbied music industry executives and obtained licenses for songs that gave Apple the flexibility to build its successful iTunes store.

**(a)** Apple eyed the cellphone market as both an opportunity to expand its iPod business and, if ignored, a potential threat to the company, people familiar with its strategy say. Cellphones are gradually offering more sophisticated capabilities and features, including increased storage capacity and entertainment functions. That stands to make them more competitive with iPods over time. Already, music phones like Samsung Electronics Co.'s BlackJack, Sony Ericsson's Walkman models and LG Electronic Inc.'s Chocolate are edging onto Apple's turf . . .

In early 2005, Mr. Jobs called Mr. Sigman to pitch the initial concept of the iPhone. The two executives later met in New York, and agreed to pursue the idea. Mr. Sigman is a Texan who wears cowboy boots and business suits, while Mr. Jobs is a former hippie who sports black turtlenecks and jeans. Despite their vastly different styles, the two executives found common ground. Over the next year and a half, the two sides negotiated to reach an agreement that would make sense for both of them . . .

**(b)** While Mr. Jobs considered Cingular a logical choice as a partner to carry the device—its GSM technology is the prevailing standard in much of the world—Apple continued to shop its ideas to other carriers. Mr. Jobs reached out to Verizon Wireless chief executive Denny Strigl in the middle of 2005 and proposed a partnership with the carrier, a joint venture of Verizon Communications Inc. and Vodafone Group PLC. The companies held a few discussions over the next year, but the talks eventually soured.

There were a few sticking points. Verizon balked at the notion of cutting out its big retail partners, like Circuit City, who would not be allowed to sell the phone. And the company's chief marketing officer, John Stratton, was firm that Verizon wouldn't give up its ability to sell content like music and videos through its proprietary V Cast service, people familiar with the discussions say. . . .

In January, Mr. Jobs finally unveiled the phone at Macworld, the conference he has used to launch such key products as the iPod Mini. Since then, the two companies have continued to test the iPhone at an undisclosed facility, a person familiar with the matter said. The handful of Cingular people who have access to the sample phones at the company's headquarters were required to sign confidentiality agreements, a person familiar with the matter says. Meanwhile, competitors already are responding. Samsung and LG both have announced phones in recent weeks with designs that look similar to the iPhone. Apple has said it intends to sell 10 million of the devices by 2008, with price tags for two different versions set steeply at $499 and $599.

**(c)** Cingular, which has more than 60 million customers, hopes the iPhone will give it a lift when it hits stores in June, at a time when attracting new subscribers is getting more difficult for all operators.

*Source: Amol Sharma, Nick Wingfield, and Li Yuan, "Apple Coup: How Steve Jobs Played Hardball in iPhone Birth," Wall Street Journal, February 17, 2007, p. A1. Copyright © 2007 Dow Jones. Reprinted by permission of Dow Jones.*

## Key Points in the Article

The article discusses Apple's new iPhone, which combines features of the iPod and a cell phone. Apple has teamed up with Cingular, now AT&T, to provide cell phone service for the iPhone. The phone will also function as an iPod that plays music in Apple's proprietary format. The iPhone helps both companies. Apple gains because it now has a digital music player that doubles as a cell phone and competes with the other music phones on the market. AT&T gains a potentially large customer base for its cell phone services.

## Analyzing the News

**a** Apple has viewed the evolution of the cell phone as a threat to the iPod because over time, cell phone manufacturers have added features that are similar to those of the iPod. For example, manufacturers have increased the storage capacity of cell phones so that people can store their music, pictures, and videos. Cell phones can also function as cameras and video recorders. These cell phones are a threat to the iPod because they are substitute goods that offer many of the same features.

If people are forced to choose just one product, then they might choose a cell phone that can play music over an iPod that cannot function as a phone. The figure shows the result. The demand curve for iPods shifts to the left, which reduces the price and quantity sold of iPods. Because the iPod is a critical product for Apple, this would significantly harm the entire company. Introducing the iPhone is a strategy to protect a very lucrative market for Apple.

**b** Apple could have worked with a number of different cell phone service providers. Ultimately, Apple chose to partner with Cingular for a couple of reasons. First, Cingular uses technology that is the industry standard. Second, Cingular was willing to make concessions that other cell phone service providers were not willing to make. The chapter opener pointed out that one of the key factors in the iPod's success was that Apple both made the iPod and sold music through iTunes. This means that

the two products were developed by the same company and worked seamlessly together. One reason that Apple did not end up partnering with Verizon is that Verizon insisted on the right to continue to sell downloads of music and videos. This raised the possibility of compatibility problems with downloads available through iTunes.

**c** AT&T also benefits from the introduction of the iPhone. The iPhone will work only with AT&T's cellular phone service, so if you want to purchase an iPhone, you have to purchase AT&T's service. That means the iPhone and AT&T's services are complementary goods—and as sales of iPhones increase, the demand for AT&T's services should also increase.

## Thinking Critically

1. What effect will the introduction of the iPhone have on sales of the iPod? Are there any reasons why someone might want to own both an iPhone and an iPod? Would it be better to think of the iPhone and the iPod as substitutes or complements? Briefly explain.

2. Apple plans to sell two versions of the iPhone: one for $499 and one for $599, which are significantly higher than the price of the most expensive iPod and much higher than the prices of cell phones. Are most customers likely to see the iPhone as a closer substitute for other cell phones or for other digital music players? Is the high price of the iPhone relevant to your answer? Briefly explain.

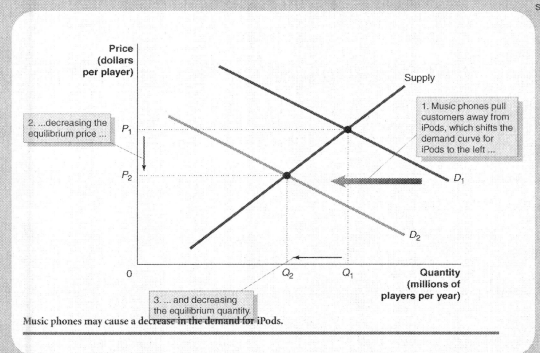

2. ...decreasing the equilibrium price ...

1. Music phones pull customers away from iPods, which shifts the demand curve for iPods to the left ...

3. ... and decreasing the equilibrium quantity.

*Music phones may cause a decrease in the demand for iPods.*

# Chapter 4
# Economic Efficiency

We saw in Chapter 3 that, in a competitive market, the price adjusts to ensure that the quantity demanded equals the quantity supplied. Stated another way, in equilibrium, every consumer willing to pay the market price is able to buy as much of the product as the consumer wants, and every firm willing to accept the market price can sell as much as it wants. Even so, consumers would naturally prefer to pay a lower price, and sellers would prefer to receive a higher price. Normally, consumers and firms have no choice but to accept the equilibrium price if they wish to participate in the market. Occasionally, however, consumers succeed in having the government impose a **price ceiling**, which is a legally determined maximum price that sellers may charge. Rent control is an example of a price ceiling. Firms also sometimes succeed in having the government impose a **price floor**, which is a legally determined minimum price that sellers may receive. In markets for farm products such as milk, the government has been setting price floors that are above the equilibrium market price since the 1930s.

Another way in which the government intervenes in markets is by imposing taxes. The government relies on the revenue raised from taxes to finance its operations. As we will see, though, imposing taxes alters the equilibrium in a market.

Unfortunately, whenever the government imposes a price ceiling, a price floor, or a tax, there are predictable negative economic consequences. It is important for government policymakers and voters to understand these negative consequences when evaluating the effects of these policies. Economists have developed the concepts of *consumer surplus, producer surplus,* and *economic surplus,* which we discuss in the next section. In the sections that follow, we use these concepts to analyze the economic effects of price ceilings, price floors, and taxes. (As we will see in later chapters, these concepts are also useful in many other contexts.)

**Price ceiling** A legally determined maximum price that sellers may charge.

**Price floor** A legally determined minimum price that sellers may receive.

---

**4.1 LEARNING OBJECTIVE**

4.1 | Distinguish between the concepts of consumer surplus and producer surplus.

# Consumer Surplus and Producer Surplus

Consumer surplus measures the dollar benefit consumers receive from buying goods or services in a particular market. Producer surplus measures the dollar benefit firms receive from selling goods or services in a particular market. Economic surplus in a market is the sum of consumer surplus plus producer surplus. As we will see, *when the government imposes a price ceiling or a price floor, the amount of economic surplus in a market is reduced*—in other words, price ceilings and price floors reduce the total benefit to consumers and firms from buying and selling in a market. To understand why this is true, we need to understand how consumer surplus and producer surplus are determined.

## Consumer Surplus

**Consumer surplus** measures the difference between the highest price a consumer is willing to pay and the price the consumer actually pays. For example, suppose you are in Wal-Mart and you see a DVD of *Spider-Man 3* on the rack. No price is indicated on the package, so you bring it over to the register to check the price. As you walk to the register, you think to yourself that $20 is the highest price you would be willing to pay. At the register, you find out that the price is actually $12, so you buy the DVD. Your consumer surplus in this example is $8: the difference between the $20 you were willing to pay and the $8 you actually paid.

We can use the demand curve to measure the total consumer surplus in a market. Demand curves show the willingness of consumers to purchase a product at different prices. Consumers are willing to purchase a product up to the point where the marginal benefit of consuming a product is equal to its price. The **marginal benefit** is the addi-

**Consumer surplus** The difference between the highest price a consumer is willing to pay and the price the consumer actually pays.

**Marginal benefit** The additional benefit to a consumer from consuming one more unit of a good or service.

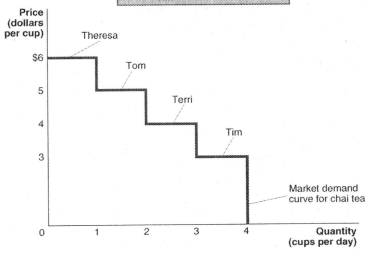

| Consumer | Highest Price Willing to Pay |
|---|---|
| Theresa | $6 |
| Tom | 5 |
| Terri | 4 |
| Tim | 3 |

## Figure 4-1

**Deriving the Demand Curve for Chai Tea**

With four consumers in the market for chai tea, the demand curve is determined by the highest price each consumer is willing to pay. For prices above $6, no tea is sold because $6 is the highest price any consumer is willing to pay. For prices of $3 and below, all four consumers are willing to buy a cup of tea.

tional benefit to a consumer from consuming one more unit of a good or service. As a simple example, suppose there are only four consumers in the market for chai tea: Theresa, Tom, Terri, and Tim. Because these four consumers have different tastes for tea and different incomes, the marginal benefit each of them receives from consuming a cup of tea will be different. Therefore, the highest price each is willing to pay for a cup of tea is also different. In Figure 4-1, the information from the table is used to construct a demand curve for chai tea. For prices above $6 per cup, no tea is sold because $6 is the highest price any of the consumers is willing to pay. At a price of $5, both Theresa and Tom are willing to buy, so two cups are sold. At prices of $3 and below, all four consumers are willing to buy, and four cups are sold.

Suppose the market price of tea is $3.50 per cup. As Figure 4-2 on page 102 shows, the demand curve allows us to calculate the total consumer surplus in this market. In panel (a), we can see that the highest price Theresa is willing to pay is $6, but because she pays only $3.50, her consumer surplus is $2.50 (shown by the area of rectangle *A*). Similarly, Tom's consumer surplus is $1.50 (rectangle *B*), and Terri's consumer surplus is $0.50 (rectangle *C*). Tim is unwilling to buy a cup of tea at a price of $3.50, so he doesn't participate in this market and receives no consumer surplus. In this simple example, the total consumer surplus is equal to $2.50 + $1.50 + $0.50 = $4.50 (or the sum of the areas of rectangles *A*, *B*, and *C*). Panel (b) shows that a lower price will increase consumer surplus. If the price of tea drops from $3.50 per cup to $3.00, Theresa, Tom, and Terri each receive $0.50 more in consumer surplus (shown by the shaded areas), so total consumer surplus in the market rises to $6.00. Tim now buys a cup of tea but doesn't receive any consumer surplus because the price is equal to the highest price he is willing to pay. In fact, Tim is indifferent between buying the cup or not—his well-being is the same either way.

The market demand curves shown in Figures 4-1 and 4-2 do not look like the smooth curves we saw in Chapter 3. This is because this example uses a small number of consumers, each consuming a single cup of tea. With many consumers, the market demand curve for chai tea will have the normal smooth shape shown in Figure 4-3. In this figure, the quantity demanded at a price of $2.00 is 15,000 cups per day. We can calculate total consumer surplus in Figure 4-3 the same way we did in Figures 4-1 and

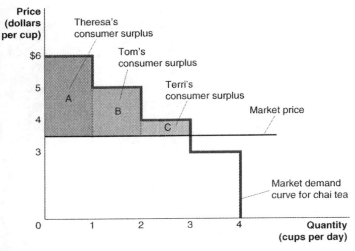

(a) Consumer surplus with a market price of $3.50

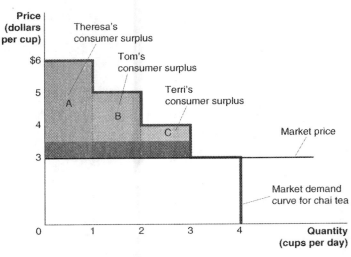

(b) Consumer surplus with a market price of $3.00

**Figure 4-2** | Measuring Consumer Surplus

Panel (a) shows the consumer surplus for Theresa, Tom, and Terri when the price of tea is $3.50 per cup. Theresa's consumer surplus is equal to the area of rectangle *A* and is the difference between the highest price she would pay—$6—and the market price of $3.50. Tom's consumer surplus is equal to the area of rectangle *B*, and Terri's con-

sumer surplus is equal to the area of rectangle *C*. Total consumer surplus in this market is equal to the sum of the areas of rectangles *A*, *B*, and *C*, or the total area below the demand curve and above the market price. In panel (b), consumer surplus increases by the shaded area as the market price declines from $3.50 to $3.00.

4-2: by adding up the consumer surplus received on each unit purchased. Once again, we can draw an important conclusion: *The total amount of consumer surplus in a market is equal to the area below the demand curve and above the market price.* Consumer surplus is shown as the blue area in Figure 4-3 and represents the benefit to consumers in excess of the price they paid to purchase the product—in this case, chai tea.

**Figure 4-3**

**Total Consumer Surplus in the Market for Chai Tea**

The demand curve tells us that most buyers of chai tea would have been willing to pay more than the market price of $2.00. For each buyer, consumer surplus is equal to the difference between the highest price he or she is willing to pay and the market price actually paid. Therefore, the total amount of consumer surplus in the market for chai tea is equal to the area below the demand curve and above the market price. Consumer surplus represents the benefit to consumers in excess of the price they paid to purchase the product.

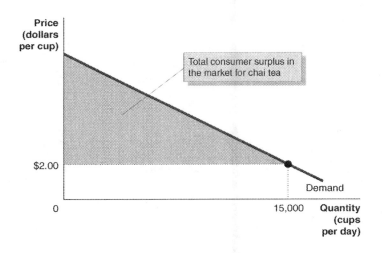

**Making** the **Connection** | **The Consumer Surplus from Satellite Television**

Consumer surplus allows us to measure the benefit consumers receive in excess of the price they paid to purchase a product. Recently, Austan Goolsbee and Amil Petrin, economists at the Graduate

School of Business at the University of Chicago, estimated the consumer surplus that households receive from subscribing to satellite television. To do this, they estimated the demand curve for satellite television and then computed the shaded area shown in the graph.

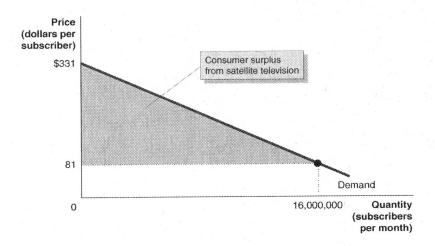

In 2001, the year for which the study was conducted, 16 million consumers paid an average price of $81 per month to subscribe to DIRECTV or DISH Network, the two main providers of satellite television. The demand curve shows that many consumers would have been willing to pay more than $81 rather than do without satellite television. Goolsbee and Petrin calculated that the consumer surplus for households subscribing to satellite television averaged $127 per month, which is the difference between the price they would have paid and the $81 they did pay. The shaded area on the graph represents the total consumer surplus in the market for satellite television. Goolsbee and Petrin estimate that the value of this area is $2 billion. This is one year's benefit to the consumers who subscribe to satellite television.

Source: Austan Goolsbee and Amil Petrin, "The Consumer Gains from Direct Broadcast Satellites and the Competition with Cable TV," *Econometrica*, Vol. 72, No. 2, March 2004, pp. 351–381.

## Producer Surplus

Just as demand curves show the willingness of consumers to buy a product at different prices, supply curves show the willingness of firms to supply a product at different prices. The willingness to supply a product depends on the cost of producing it. Firms will supply an additional unit of a product only if they receive a price equal to the additional cost of producing that unit. **Marginal cost** is the additional cost to a firm of producing one more unit of a good or service. Consider the marginal cost to the firm Heavenly Tea of producing one more cup: In this case, the marginal cost includes the ingredients to make the tea and the wages paid to the worker preparing the tea. Often, the marginal cost of producing a good increases as more of the good is produced during a given period of time. This is the key reason—as we saw in Chapter 3—that supply curves are upward sloping.

Panel (a) of Figure 4-4 shows Heavenly Tea's producer surplus. For simplicity, we show Heavenly producing only a small quantity of tea. The figure shows that Heavenly's marginal cost of producing the first cup of tea is $1.00. Its marginal cost of producing

**Marginal cost** The additional cost to a firm of producing one more unit of a good or service.

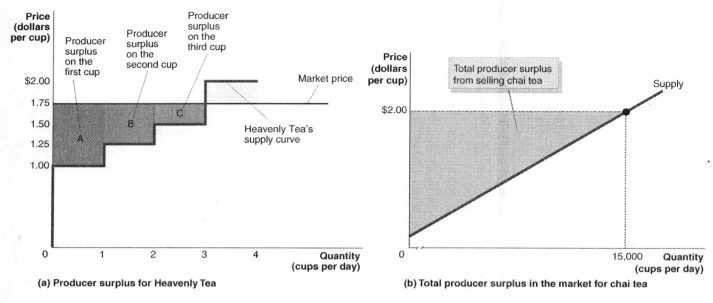

**Figure 4-4** | Calculating Producer Surplus

Panel (a) shows Heavenly Tea's producer surplus. Producer surplus is the difference between the lowest price a firm would be willing to accept and the price it actually receives. The lowest price Heavenly Tea is willing to accept to supply a cup of tea is equal to its marginal cost of producing that cup. When the market price of tea is $1.75, Heavenly receives producer surplus of $0.75 on the first cup (the area of rectan- gle *A*), $0.50 on the second cup (rectangle *B*), and $0.25 on the third cup (rectangle *C*). In panel (b), the total amount of producer surplus tea sellers receive from selling chai tea can be calculated by adding up for the entire market the producer surplus received on each cup sold. In the figure, total producer surplus is equal to the area above the supply curve and below the market price, shown in red.

**Producer surplus** The difference between the lowest price a firm would be willing to accept and the price it actually receives.

the second cup is $1.25, and so on. The marginal cost of each cup of tea is the lowest price Heavenly is willing to accept to supply that cup. The supply curve, then, is also a marginal cost curve. Suppose the market price of tea is $1.75 per cup. On the first cup of tea, the price is $0.75 higher than the lowest price Heavenly is willing to accept. **Producer surplus** is the difference between the lowest price a firm would be willing to accept and the price it actually receives. Therefore, Heavenly's producer surplus on the first cup is $0.75 (shown by the area of rectangle *A*). Its producer surplus on the second cup is $0.50 (rectangle *B*). Its producer surplus on the third cup is $0.25 (rectangle *C*). Heavenly will not be willing to supply the fourth cup because the marginal cost of producing it is less than the market price. Heavenly Tea's total producer surplus is equal to $0.75 + $0.50 + $0.25 = $1.50 (or the sum of rectangles *A, B,* and *C*). A higher price will increase producer surplus. For example, if the market price of chai tea rises from $1.75 to $2.00, Heavenly Tea's producer surplus will increase from $1.50 to $2.25. (Make sure you understand how the new level of producer surplus was calculated.)

The supply curve shown in panel (a) of Figure 4-4 does not look like the smooth curves we saw in Chapter 3 because this example uses a single firm producing only a small quantity of tea. With many firms, the market supply curve for chai tea will have the normal smooth shape shown in panel (b) of Figure 4-4. In panel (b), the quantity supplied at a price of $2.00 is 15,000 cups per day. We can calculate total producer sur- plus in panel (b) the same way we did in panel (a): by adding up the producer surplus received on each cup sold. Therefore, *the total amount of producer surplus in a market is equal to the area above the market supply curve and below the market price.* The total producer surplus tea sellers receive from selling chai tea is shown as the red area in panel (b) of Figure 4-4.

## What Consumer Surplus and Producer Surplus Measure

We have seen that consumer surplus measures the benefit to consumers from participating in a market, and producer surplus measures the benefit to producers from participating in a market. It is important, however, to be clear what we mean by this. In a sense, consumer surplus measures the *net* benefit to consumers from participating in a market rather than the *total* benefit. That is, if the price of a product were zero, the consumer surplus in a market would be all of the area under the demand curve. When the price is not zero, consumer surplus is the area below the demand curve and above the market price. So, consumer surplus in a market is equal to the total benefit received by consumers minus the total amount they must pay to buy the good.

Similarly, producer surplus measures the *net* benefit received by producers from participating in a market. If producers could supply a good at zero cost, the producer surplus in a market would be all of the area below the market price. When cost is not zero, producer surplus is the area below the market price and above the supply curve. So, producer surplus in a market is equal to the total amount firms receive from consumers minus the cost of producing the good.

---

4.2 | Understand the concept of economic efficiency.

# The Efficiency of Competitive Markets

In Chapter 3, we defined a *competitive market* as a market with many buyers and many sellers. An important advantage of the market system is that it results in efficient economic outcomes. But what do we mean by *economic efficiency?* The concepts we have developed so far in this chapter give us two ways to think about the economic efficiency of competitive markets. We can think in terms of marginal benefit and marginal cost. We can also think in terms of consumer surplus and producer surplus. As we will see, these two approaches lead to the same outcome, but using both can increase our understanding of economic efficiency.

## Marginal Benefit Equals Marginal Cost in Competitive Equilibrium

Figure 4-5 again shows the market for chai tea. Recall from our discussion that the demand curve shows the marginal benefit received by consumers, and the supply curve shows the marginal cost of production. To achieve economic efficiency in this market, the marginal

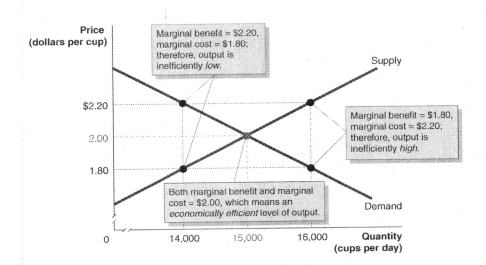

## Figure 4-5

**Marginal Benefit Equals Marginal Cost Only at Competitive Equilibrium**

In a competitive market, equilibrium occurs at a quantity of 15,000 cups and price of $2.00 per cup, where marginal benefit equals marginal cost. This is the economically efficient level of output because every cup has been produced where the marginal benefit to buyers is greater than or equal to the marginal cost to producers.

benefit from the last unit sold should equal the marginal cost of production. The figure shows that this equality occurs at competitive equilibrium where 15,000 cups per day are produced, and marginal benefit and marginal cost are both equal to $2.00. Why is this outcome economically efficient? Because every cup of chai tea has been produced where the marginal benefit to buyers is greater than or equal to the marginal cost to producers.

Another way to see why the level of output at competitive equilibrium is efficient is to consider what would be true if output were at a different level. For instance, suppose that output of chai tea were 14,000 cups per day. Figure 4-5 shows that at this level of output, the marginal benefit from the last cup sold is $2.20, whereas the marginal cost is only $1.80. This level of output is not efficient because 1,000 more cups could be produced for which the additional benefit to consumers would be greater than the additional cost of production. Consumers would willingly purchase those cups, and tea sellers would willingly supply them, making both consumers and sellers better off. Similarly, if the output of chai tea were 16,000 cups per day, the marginal cost of the 16,000th cup is $2.20, whereas the marginal benefit is only $1.80. Tea sellers would only be willing to supply this cup at a price of $2.20, which is $0.40 higher than consumers would be willing to pay. In fact, consumers would not be willing to pay the price tea sellers would need to receive for any cup beyond the 15,000th.

To summarize, we can say this: *Equilibrium in a competitive market results in the economically efficient level of output, where marginal benefit equals marginal cost.*

## Economic Surplus

**Economic surplus** The sum of consumer surplus and producer surplus.

**Economic surplus** in a market is the sum of consumer surplus and producer surplus. In a competitive market, with many buyers and sellers and no government restrictions, economic surplus is at a maximum when the market is in equilibrium. To see this, let's look one more time at the market for chai tea shown in Figure 4-6. The consumer surplus in this market is the blue area below the demand curve and above the line indicating the equilibrium price of $2.00. The producer surplus is the red area above the supply curve and below the price line.

## Deadweight Loss

To show that economic surplus is maximized at equilibrium, consider the situation in which the price of chai tea is *above* the equilibrium price, as shown in Figure 4-7. At a price of $2.20 per cup, the number of cups consumers are willing to buy per day drops from 15,000 to 14,000. At competitive equilibrium, consumer surplus is equal to the sum of areas A, B, and C. At a price of $2.20, fewer cups are sold at a higher price, so consumer surplus declines to just the area of A. At competitive equilibrium, producer surplus is equal to the sum of areas D and E. At the higher price of $2.20, producer surplus changes to be equal to the sum of areas B and D. The sum of consumer and producer surplus—economic surplus—has been reduced to the sum of areas A, B, and D. Notice that this is less than the original economic surplus by an amount equal to areas C and E.

## Figure 4-6

### Economic Surplus Equals the Sum of Consumer Surplus and Producer Surplus

The economic surplus in a market is the sum of the blue area representing consumer surplus and the red area representing producer surplus.

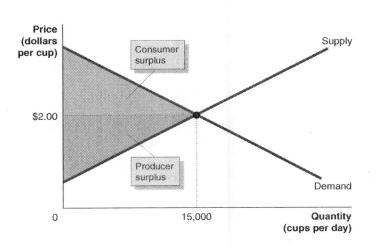

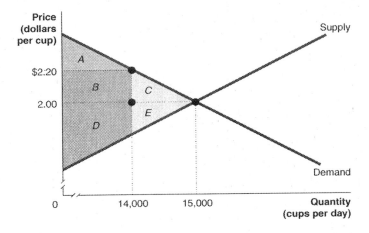

|  | At Competitive Equilibrium | At a Price of $2.20 |
|---|---|---|
| Consumer Surplus | A + B + C | A |
| Producer Surplus | D + E | B + D |
| Deadweight Loss | None | C + E |

## Figure 4-7

**When a Market Is Not in Equilibrium, There Is a Deadweight Loss**

Economic surplus is maximized when a market is in competitive equilibrium. When a market is not in equilibrium, there is a deadweight loss. When the price of chai tea is $2.20, instead of $2.00, consumer surplus declines from an amount equal to the sum of areas *A, B,* and *C* to just area *A.* Producer surplus increases from the sum of areas *D* and *E* to the sum of areas *B* and *D.* At competitive equilibrium, there is no deadweight loss. At a price of $2.20, there is a deadweight loss equal to the sum of areas *C* and *E.*

Economic surplus has declined because at a price of $2.20, all the cups between the 14,000th and the 15,000th, which would have been produced in competitive equilibrium, are not being produced. These "missing" cups are not providing any consumer or producer surplus, so economic surplus has declined. The reduction in economic surplus resulting from a market not being in competitive equilibrium is called the **deadweight loss.** In the figure, it is equal to the sum of areas *C* and *E*.

**Deadweight loss** The reduction in economic surplus resulting from a market not being in competitive equilibrium.

## Economic Surplus and Economic Efficiency

Consumer surplus measures the benefit to consumers from buying a particular product, such as chai tea. Producer surplus measures the benefit to firms from selling a particular product. Therefore, economic surplus—which is the sum of the benefit to firms plus the benefit to consumers—is the best measure we have of the benefit to society from the production of a particular good or service. This gives us a second way of characterizing the economic efficiency of a competitive market: *Equilibrium in a competitive market results in the greatest amount of economic surplus, or total net benefit to society, from the production of a good or service.* Anything that causes the market for a good or service not to be in competitive equilibrium reduces the total benefit to society from the production of that good or service.

Now we can give a more general definition of *economic efficiency* in terms of our two approaches: **Economic efficiency** is a market outcome in which the marginal benefit to consumers of the last unit produced is equal to its marginal cost of production and in which the sum of consumer surplus and producer surplus is at a maximum.

**Economic efficiency** A market outcome in which the marginal benefit to consumers of the last unit produced is equal to its marginal cost of production and in which the sum of consumer surplus and producer surplus is at a maximum.

**4.3 LEARNING** OBJECTIVE

4.3 | Explain the economic effect of government-imposed price ceilings and price floors.

## Government Intervention in the Market: Price Floors and Price Ceilings

Notice that we have *not* concluded that every *individual* is better off if a market is at competitive equilibrium. We have only concluded that economic surplus, or the *total* net benefit to society, is greatest at competitive equilibrium. Any individual producer would rather charge a higher price, and any individual consumer would rather pay a lower price, but usually producers can sell and consumers can buy only at the competitive equilibrium price.

Producers or consumers who are dissatisfied with the competitive equilibrium price can lobby the government to legally require that a different price be charged. The U.S. government only occasionally overrides the market outcome by setting prices. When the government does intervene, it can either attempt to aid sellers by requiring that a price be above equilibrium—a price floor—or aid buyers by requiring that a price be below equilibrium—a price ceiling. To affect the market outcome, a price floor must be set above the equilibrium price and a price ceiling must be set below the equilibrium price. Otherwise, the price ceiling or price floor will not be *binding* on buyers and sellers. The preceding section demonstrates that moving away from competitive equilibrium will reduce economic efficiency. We can use the concepts of consumer surplus, producer surplus, and deadweight loss to see more clearly the economic inefficiency of binding price floors and price ceilings.

## Price Floors: Government Policy in Agricultural Markets

The Great Depression of the 1930s was the greatest economic disaster in U.S. history, affecting every sector of the U.S. economy. Many farmers were unable to sell their products or could sell them only at very low prices. Farmers were able to convince the federal government to intervene to raise prices by setting price floors for many agricultural products. Government intervention in agriculture—often referred to as the "farm program"—has continued ever since. To see how a price floor in an agricultural market works, suppose that the equilibrium price in the wheat market is $3.00 per bushel but the government decides to set a price floor of $3.50 per bushel. As Figure 4-8 shows, the price of wheat rises from $3.00 to $3.50, and the quantity of wheat sold falls from 2.0 billion bushels per year to 1.8 billion. Initially, suppose that production of wheat also falls to 1.8 billion bushels.

Just as we saw in the earlier example of the market for chai tea (refer to Figure 4-7), the producer surplus received by wheat farmers increases by an amount equal to the area of the red rectangle *A* and falls by an amount equal to the area of the yellow triangle *C*. The area of the red rectangle *A* represents a transfer from consumer surplus to producer surplus. The total fall in consumer surplus is equal to the area of the red rectangle *A* plus the area of the yellow triangle *B*. Wheat farmers benefit from this program, but consumers lose. There is also a deadweight loss equal to the areas of the yellow triangles *B* and *C*, which represents the decline in economic efficiency due to the price floor. There

## Figure 4-8

**The Economic Effect of a Price Floor in the Wheat Market**

If wheat farmers convince the government to impose a price floor of $3.50 per bushel, the amount of wheat sold will fall from 2.0 billion bushels per year to 1.8 billion. If we assume that farmers produce 1.8 billion bushels, producer surplus then increases by the red rectangle *A*—which is transferred from consumer surplus—and falls by the yellow triangle *C*. Consumer surplus declines by the red rectangle *A* plus the yellow triangle *B*. There is a deadweight loss equal to the yellow triangles *B* and *C*, representing the decline in economic efficiency due to the price floor. In reality, a price floor of $3.50 per bushel will cause farmers to expand their production from 2.0 billion to 2.2 billion bushels, resulting in a surplus of wheat.

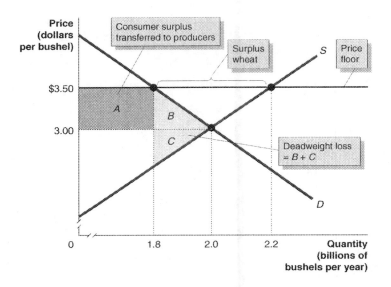

is a deadweight loss because the price floor has reduced the amount of economic surplus in the market for wheat. Or, looked at another way, the price floor has caused the marginal benefit of the last bushel of wheat to be greater than the marginal cost of producing it. We can conclude that a price floor reduces economic efficiency.

The actual federal government farm programs have been more complicated than just legally requiring farmers not to sell their output below a minimum price. We assumed initially that farmers reduce their production of wheat to the amount consumers are willing to buy. In fact, as Figure 4-8 shows, a price floor will cause the quantity of wheat that farmers want to supply to increase from 2.0 billion to 2.2 billion bushels. Because the higher price also reduces the amount of wheat consumers wish to buy, the result is a surplus of 0.4 billion bushels of wheat (the 2.2 billion bushels supplied minus the 1.8 billion demanded).

The federal government's farm programs have often resulted in large surpluses of wheat and other agricultural products. The government has usually either bought the surplus food or paid farmers to restrict supply by taking some land out of cultivation. Because both of these options are expensive, Congress passed the Freedom to Farm Act of 1996. The intent of the act was to phase out price floors and government purchases of surpluses and return to a free market in agriculture. To allow farmers time to adjust, the federal government began paying farmers *subsidies*, or cash payments based on the number of acres planted. Although the subsidies were originally scheduled to be phased out, Congress has continued to pay them.

## Making the Connection | Price Floors in Labor Markets: The Debate over Minimum Wage Policy

The minimum wage may be the most controversial "price floor." Supporters see the minimum wage as a way of raising the incomes of low-skilled workers. Opponents argue that it results in fewer jobs and imposes large costs on small businesses.

In summer 2008, the national minimum wage as set by Congress is $6.55 per hour for most occupations. (The minimum wage is scheduled to increase to $7.25 per hour in 2009.) It is illegal for an employer to pay less than this wage in those occupations. For most workers, the minimum wage is irrelevant because it is well below the wage employers are voluntarily willing to pay them. But for low-skilled workers——such as workers in fast-food restaurants——the minimum wage is above the wage they would otherwise receive. The following figure shows the effect of the minimum wage on employment in the market for low-skilled labor.

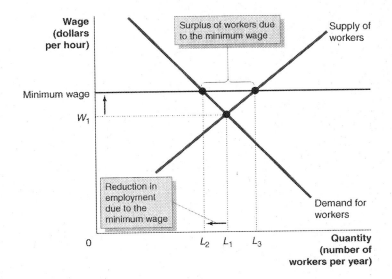

Without a minimum wage, the equilibrium wage would be $W_1$, and the number of workers hired would be $L_1$. With a minimum wage set above the equilibrium wage, the quantity of workers demanded by employers declines from $L_1$ to $L_2$, and the quantity of labor supplied increases to $L_3$, leading to a surplus of workers unable to find jobs equal to $L_3 - L_2$. The quantity of labor supplied increases because the higher wage attracts more people to work. For instance, some teenagers may decide that working after school is worthwhile at the minimum wage of $6.55 per hour but would not be worthwhile at a lower wage.

This analysis is very similar to our analysis of the wheat market in Figure 4-8. Just as a price floor in the wheat market leads to less wheat consumed, a price floor in the labor market should lead to fewer workers hired. Views differ sharply among economists, however, concerning how large a reduction in employment the minimum wage causes. For instance, David Card of the University of California, Berkeley, and Alan Krueger of Princeton University conducted a study of fast-food restaurants in New Jersey and Pennsylvania that indicates that the effect of minimum wage increases on employment is very small. Card and Krueger's study has been very controversial, however. Other economists have examined similar data and have come to the different conclusion that the minimum wage leads to a significant decrease in employment.

Whatever the extent of employment losses from the minimum wage, because it is a price floor, it will cause a deadweight loss, just as a price floor in the wheat market does. Therefore, many economists favor alternative policies for attaining the goal of raising the incomes of low-skilled workers. One policy many economists support is the *earned income tax credit*. The earned income tax credit reduces the amount of tax that low-income wage earners would otherwise pay to the federal government. Workers with very low incomes who do not owe any tax receive a payment from the government. Compared with the minimum wage, the earned income tax credit can increase the incomes of low-skilled workers without reducing employment. The earned income tax credit also places a lesser burden on the small businesses that employ many low-skilled workers, and it might cause a smaller loss of economic efficiency.

Sources: David Card and Alan B. Krueger, *Myth and Measurement: The New Economics of the Minimum Wage*, Princeton, NJ: Princeton University Press, 1995; David Neumark and William Wascher, "Minimum Wages and Employment: A Case Study of the Fast-Food Industry in New Jersey and Pennsylvania: Comment," *American Economic Review*, Vol. 90, No. 5, December 2000, pp. 1362–1396; and David Card and Alan B. Krueger, "Minimum Wages and Employment: A Case Study of the Fast-Food Industry in New Jersey and Pennsylvania: Reply," *American Economic Review*, Vol. 90, No. 5, December 2000, pp. 1397–1420.

## Price Ceilings: Government Rent Control Policy in Housing Markets

Support for governments setting price floors typically comes from sellers, and support for governments setting price ceilings typically comes from consumers. For example, when there is a sharp increase in gasoline prices, there are often proposals for the government to impose a price ceiling on the market for gasoline. As we saw in the opener to this chapter, New York is one of the cities that imposes rent controls, which put a ceiling on the maximum rent that landlords can charge for an apartment. Figure 4-9 shows the market for apartments in a city that has rent controls.

Without rent control, the equilibrium rent would be $1,500 per month, and 2,000,000 apartments would be rented. With a maximum legal rent of $1,000 per month, landlords reduce the quantity of apartments supplied to 1,900,000. The fall in the quantity of apartments supplied is the result of some apartments being converted to offices or sold off as condominiums, some small apartment buildings being converted to single-family homes, and, over time, some apartment buildings being abandoned. In New York City, rent control has resulted in whole city blocks being abandoned by

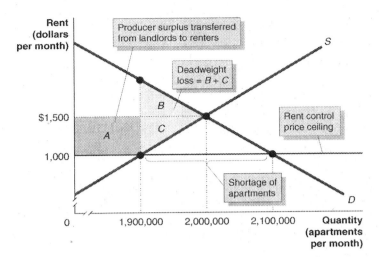

**Figure 4-9**

**The Economic Effect of a Rent Ceiling**

Without rent control, the equilibrium rent is $1,500 per month. At that price, 2,000,000 apartments would be rented. If the government imposes a rent ceiling of $1,000, the quantity of apartments supplied falls to 1,900,000, and the quantity of apartments demanded increases to 2,100,000, resulting in a shortage of 200,000 apartments. Producer surplus equal to the area of the blue rectangle A is transferred from landlords to renters, and there is a deadweight loss equal to the areas of yellow triangles B and C.

landlords who were unable to cover their costs with the rents they were allowed to charge. In London, when rent controls were applied to rooms and apartments located in a landlord's own home, the quantity of these apartments supplied dropped by 75 percent.

In Figure 4-9, with the rent ceiling of $1,000, the quantity of apartments demanded rises to 2,100,000. There is a shortage of 200,000 apartments. Consumer surplus increases by rectangle A and falls by triangle B. Rectangle A would have been part of producer surplus if rent control were not in place. With rent control, it is part of consumer surplus. Rent control causes the producer surplus received by landlords to fall by rectangle A plus triangle C. Triangles B and C represent the deadweight loss. There is a deadweight loss because rent control has reduced the amount of economic surplus in the market for apartments. Rent control has caused the marginal benefit of the last apartment rented to be greater than the marginal cost of supplying it. We can conclude that a price ceiling, such as rent control, reduces economic efficiency. The appendix to this chapter shows how we can make quantitative estimates of the deadweight loss, and it shows the changes in consumer surplus and producer surplus that result from rent control.

Renters as a group benefit from rent controls—total consumer surplus is larger—but landlords lose. Because of the deadweight loss, the total loss to landlords is greater than the gain to renters. Notice also that although renters as a group benefit, the number of renters is reduced, so some renters are made worse off by rent controls because they are unable to find an apartment at the legal rent.

# Don't Let This Happen to **YOU!**

## Don't Confuse "Scarcity" with a "Shortage"

At first glance, the following statement seems correct: "There is a shortage of every good that is scarce." In everyday conversation, we describe a good as "scarce" if we have trouble finding it. For instance, if you are looking for a present for a child, you might call the latest hot toy "scarce" if you are willing to buy it at its listed price but can't find it online or in any store. But recall from Chapter 2 that econ-

omists have a broad definition of *scarce*. In the economic sense, almost everything—except undesirable things like garbage—is scarce. A shortage of a good occurs only if the quantity demanded is greater than the quantity supplied at the current price. Therefore, the preceding statement—"There is a shortage of every good that is scarce"—is incorrect. In fact, there is no shortage of most scarce goods.

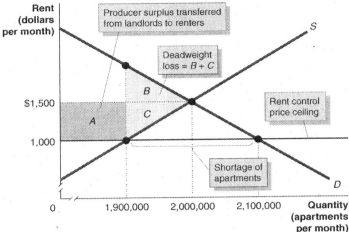

Figure 4-9

**The Economic Effect of a Rent Ceiling**

Without rent control, the equilibrium rent is $1,500 per month. At that price, 2,000,000 apartments would be rented. If the government imposes a rent ceiling of $1,000, the quantity of apartments supplied falls to 1,900,000, and the quantity of apartments demanded increases to 2,100,000, resulting in a shortage of 200,000 apartments. Producer surplus equal to the area of the blue rectangle *A* is transferred from landlords to renters, and there is a deadweight loss equal to the areas of yellow triangles *B* and *C*.

landlords who were unable to cover their costs with the rents they were allowed to charge. In London, when rent controls were applied to rooms and apartments located in a landlord's own home, the quantity of these apartments supplied dropped by 75 percent.

In Figure 4-9, with the rent ceiling of $1,000, the quantity of apartments demanded rises to 2,100,000. There is a shortage of 200,000 apartments. Consumer surplus increases by rectangle *A* and falls by triangle *B*. Rectangle *A* would have been part of producer surplus if rent control were not in place. With rent control, it is part of consumer surplus. Rent control causes the producer surplus received by landlords to fall by rectangle *A* plus triangle *C*. Triangles *B* and *C* represent the deadweight loss. There is a deadweight loss because rent control has reduced the amount of economic surplus in the market for apartments. Rent control has caused the marginal benefit of the last apartment rented to be greater than the marginal cost of supplying it. We can conclude that a price ceiling, such as rent control, reduces economic efficiency. The appendix to this chapter shows how we can make quantitative estimates of the deadweight loss, and it shows the changes in consumer surplus and producer surplus that result from rent control.

Renters as a group benefit from rent controls—total consumer surplus is larger—but landlords lose. Because of the deadweight loss, the total loss to landlords is greater than the gain to renters. Notice also that although renters as a group benefit, the number of renters is reduced, so some renters are made worse off by rent controls because they are unable to find an apartment at the legal rent.

# Don't Let This Happen to YOU!

## Don't Confuse "Scarcity" with a "Shortage"

At first glance, the following statement seems correct: "There is a shortage of every good that is scarce." In everyday conversation, we describe a good as "scarce" if we have trouble finding it. For instance, if you are looking for a present for a child, you might call the latest hot toy "scarce" if you are willing to buy it at its listed price but can't find it online or in any store. But recall from Chapter 2 that econ-

omists have a broad definition of *scarce*. In the economic sense, almost everything—except undesirable things like garbage—is scarce. A shortage of a good occurs only if the quantity demanded is greater than the quantity supplied at the current price. Therefore, the preceding statement—"There is a shortage of every good that is scarce"—is incorrect. In fact, there is no shortage of most scarce goods.

# Quantitative Demand and Supply Analysis

Graphs help us understand economic change *qualitatively*. For instance, a demand and supply graph can tell us that if household incomes rise, the demand curve for a normal good will shift to the right, and its price will rise. Often, though, economists, business managers, and policymakers want to know more than the qualitative direction of change; they want a *quantitative estimate* of the size of the change.

In Chapter 4, we carried out a qualitative analysis of rent controls. We saw that imposing rent controls involves a trade-off: Renters as a group gain, but landlords lose, and the market for apartments becomes less efficient, as shown by the deadweight loss. To better evaluate rent controls, we need to know more than just that these gains and losses exist; we need to know how large they are. A quantitative analysis of rent controls will tell us how large the gains and losses are.

Use **quantitative** demand and supply **analysis**.

## Demand and Supply Equations

The first step in a quantitative analysis is to supplement our use of demand and supply curves with demand and supply *equations*. We noted briefly in Chapter 3 that economists often statistically estimate equations for demand curves. Supply curves can also be statistically estimated. For example, suppose that economists have estimated that the demand for apartments in New York City is:

$$Q^D = 3,000,000 - 1,000P,$$

and the supply of apartments is:

$$Q^S = -450,000 + 1,300P.$$

We have used $Q^D$ for the quantity of apartments demanded per month, $Q^S$ for the quantity of apartments supplied per month, and $P$ for the apartment rent in dollars per month. In reality, both the quantity of apartments demanded and the quantity of apartments supplied will depend on more than just the rental price of apartments in New York City. For instance, the demand for apartments in New York City will also depend on the average incomes of families in the New York area and on the rents of apartments in surrounding cities. For simplicity, we will ignore these other factors.

With no government intervention, we know that at competitive market equilibrium, the quantity demanded must equal the quantity supplied, or:

$$Q^D = Q^S.$$

We can use this equation, which is called an *equilibrium condition*, to solve for the equilibrium monthly apartment rent by setting the demand equation equal to the supply equation:

$$3,000,000 - 1,000P = -450,000 + 1,300P$$

$$3,450,000 = 2,300P$$

$$P = \frac{3,450,000}{2,300} = \$1,500.$$

## Figure 4A-1

### Graphing Supply and Demand Equations

After statistically estimating supply and demand equations, we can use the equations to draw supply and demand curves. In this case, the equilibrium rent for apartments is $1,500 per month, and the equilibrium quantity of apartments rented is 1,500,000. The supply equation tells us that at a rent of $346, the quantity of apartments supplied will be zero. The demand equation tells us that at a rent of $3,000, the quantity of apartments demanded will be zero. The areas representing consumer surplus and producer surplus are also indicated on the graph.

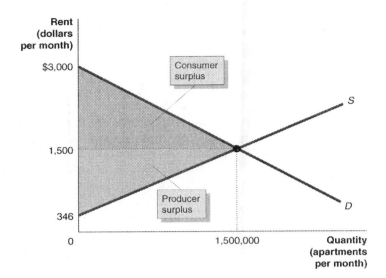

We can then substitute this price back into either the supply equation or the demand equation to find the equilibrium quantity of apartments rented:

$$Q^D = 3,000,000 - 1,000P = 3,000,000 - 1,000(1,500) = 1,500,000$$

$$Q^S = -450,000 + 1,300P = -450,000 + 1,300(1,500) = 1,500,000.$$

Figure 4A-1 illustrates the information from these equations in a graph. The figure shows the values for rent when the quantity supplied is zero and when the quantity demanded is zero. These values can be calculated from the demand equation and the supply equation by setting $Q^D$ and $Q^S$ equal to zero and solving for price:

$$Q^D = 0 = 3,000,000 - 1,000P$$

$$P = \frac{3,000,000}{1,000} = \$3,000$$

and:

$$Q^S = 0 = -450,000 + 1,300P$$

$$P = \frac{-450,000}{-1,300} = \$346.15.$$

## Calculating Consumer Surplus and Producer Surplus

Figure 4A-1 shows consumer surplus and producer surplus in this market. Recall that the sum of consumer surplus and producer surplus equals the net benefit that renters and landlords receive from participating in the market for apartments. We can use the values from the demand and supply equations to calculate the value of consumer surplus and producer surplus. Remember that consumer surplus is the area below the demand curve and above the line representing market price. Notice that this area forms a right triangle because the demand curve is a straight line—it is *linear*. As we noted in the appendix to Chapter 1, the area of a triangle is equal to ½ multiplied by the base of the triangle multiplied by the height of the triangle. In this case, the area is:

$$\frac{1}{2} \times (1,500,000) \times (3,000 - 1,500) = \$1,125,000,000.$$

So, this calculation tells us that the consumer surplus in the market for rental apartments in New York City would be about $1.125 billion.

We can calculate producer surplus in a similar way. Remember that producer surplus is the area above the supply curve and below the line representing market price. Because our supply curve is also a straight line, producer surplus on the figure is equal to the area of the right triangle:

$$\frac{1}{2} \times 1{,}500{,}000 \times (1{,}500 - 346) = \$865{,}500{,}000.$$

This calculation tells us that the producer surplus in the market for rental apartments in New York City is about $865 million.

We can use this same type of analysis to measure the impact of rent control on consumer surplus, producer surplus, and economic efficiency. For instance, suppose the city imposes a rent ceiling of $1,000 per month. Figure 4A-2 can help guide us as we measure the impact.

First, we can calculate the quantity of apartments that will actually be rented by substituting the rent ceiling of $1,000 into the supply equation:

$$Q^S = -450{,}000 + (1{,}300 \times 1{,}000) = 850{,}000.$$

We also need to know the price on the demand curve when the quantity of apartments is 850,000. We can do this by substituting 850,000 for quantity in the demand equation and solving for price:

$$850{,}000 = 3{,}000{,}000 - 1{,}000P$$

$$P = \frac{-2{,}150{,}000}{-1{,}000} = \$2{,}150.$$

Compared with its value in competitive equilibrium, consumer surplus has been reduced by a value equal to the area of the yellow triangle *B* but increased by a value equal to the area of the blue rectangle *A*. The area of the yellow triangle *B* is:

$$\frac{1}{2} \times (1{,}500{,}000 - 850{,}000) \times (2{,}150 - 1{,}500) = \$211{,}250{,}000,$$

and the area of the blue rectangle *A* is base multiplied by height, or:

$$(\$1{,}500 - \$1{,}000) \times (850{,}000) = \$425{,}000{,}000.$$

The value of consumer surplus in competitive equilibrium was $1,125,000,000. As a result of the rent ceiling, it will be increased to:

$$(\$1{,}125{,}000{,}000 + \$425{,}000{,}000) - \$211{,}250{,}000 = \$1{,}338{,}750{,}000.$$

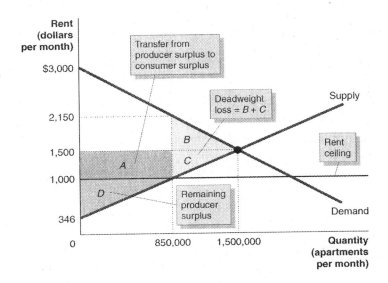

## Figure 4A-2

### Calculating the Economic Effect of Rent Controls

Once we have estimated equations for the demand and supply of rental housing, a diagram can guide our numeric estimates of the economic effects of rent control. Consumer surplus falls by an amount equal to the area of the yellow triangle *B* and increases by an amount equal to the area of the blue rectangle *A*. The difference between the values of these two areas is $213,750,000. Producer surplus falls by an amount equal to the area of the blue rectangle *A* plus the area of the yellow triangle *C*. The value of these two areas is $587,500,000. The remaining producer surplus is equal to the area of triangle *D*, or $278,000,000. Deadweight loss is equal to the area of triangle *B* plus the area of triangle *C*, or $373,750,000.

Compared with its value in competitive equilibrium, producer surplus has been reduced by a value equal to the area of the yellow triangle *C* plus a value equal to the area of the blue rectangle. The area of the yellow triangle *C* is:

$$\frac{1}{2} \times 1{,}500{,}000 - 850{,}000) \times (1{,}500 - 1{,}000) = \$162{,}500{,}000.$$

We have already calculated the area of the blue rectangle *A* as \$425,000,000. The value of producer surplus in competitive equilibrium was \$865,500,000. As a result of the rent ceiling, it will be reduced to:

$$\$865{,}500{,}000 - \$162{,}500{,}000 - \$425{,}000{,}000 = \$278{,}000{,}000.$$

The loss of economic efficiency, as measured by the deadweight loss, is equal to the value represented by the areas of the yellow triangles *B* and *C*, or:

$$\$211{,}250{,}000 + \$162{,}500{,}000 = \$373{,}750{,}000.$$

The following table summarizes the results of the analysis (the values are in millions of dollars).

| CONSUMER SURPLUS | | PRODUCER SURPLUS | | DEADWEIGHT LOSS | |
|---|---|---|---|---|---|
| COMPETITIVE EQUILIBRIUM | RENT CONTROL | COMPETITIVE EQUILIBRIUM | RENT CONTROL | COMPETITIVE EQUILIBRIUM | RENT CONTROL |
| $1,125 | $1,338.75 | $865.50 | $278 | $0 | $373.75 |

Qualitatively, we know that imposing rent controls will make consumers better off, make landlords worse off, and decrease economic efficiency. The advantage of the analysis we have just gone through is that it puts dollar values on the qualitative results. We can now see how much consumers have gained, how much landlords have lost, and how great the decline in economic efficiency has been. Sometimes the quantitative results can be surprising. Notice, for instance, that after the imposition of rent control, the deadweight loss is actually greater than the remaining producer surplus.

Economists often study issues where the qualitative results of actions are apparent, even to non-economists. You don't have to be an economist to understand who wins and loses from rent control or that if a company cuts the price of its product, its sales will increase. Business managers, policymakers, and the general public do, however, need economists to measure quantitatively the effects of different actions—including policies such as rent control—so that they can better assess the results of these actions.

---

**LEARNING** OBJECTIVE    Use Quantitative Demand and Supply Analysis, **pages 131–134.**

myeconlab Visit www.myeconlab.com to complete these exercises *Get Ahead of the Curve* online and get instant feedback.

## Review Questions

**4A.1** In a linear demand equation, what economic information is conveyed by the intercept on the price axis?

**4A.2** Suppose you were assigned the task of choosing a price that maximized economic surplus in a market. What price would you choose? Why?

**4A.3** Consumer surplus is used as a measure of a consumer's net benefit from purchasing a good or service. Explain why consumer surplus is a measure of net benefit.

**4A.4** Why would economists use the term *deadweight loss* to describe the impact on consumer and producer surplus from a price control?

## Problems and Applications

**4A.5** Suppose that you have been hired to analyze the impact on employment from the imposition of a minimum wage in the labor market. Further suppose that you estimate the supply and demand functions for labor, where *L* stands for the quantity of labor (measured in thousands of workers) and *W* stands for the wage rate (measured in dollars per hour):

Demand:  $L^D = 100 - 4W$
Supply:    $L^S = 6W$

First, calculate the free-market equilibrium wage and quantity of labor. Now suppose the proposed minimum wage is \$12. How large will the surplus of labor in this market be?

**4A.6** The following graphs illustrate the markets for two different types of labor. Suppose an identical minimum wage is imposed in both markets. In which market will the minimum wage have the largest impact on employment? Why?

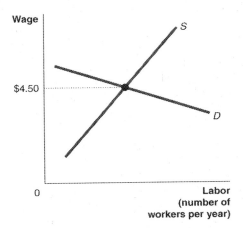

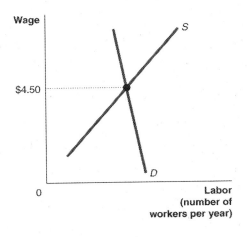

**4A.7** Suppose that you are the vice president of operations of a manufacturing firm that sells an industrial lubricant in a competitive market. Further suppose that your economist gives you the following supply and demand functions:

Demand: $Q^D = 45 - 2P$
Supply: $Q^S = -15 + P$

What is the consumer surplus in this market? What is the producer surplus?

**4A.8** The following graph shows a market in which a price floor of $3.00 per unit has been imposed. Calculate the values of each of the following.
  a. The deadweight loss
  b. The transfer of producer surplus to consumers or the transfer of consumer surplus to producers
  c. Producer surplus after the price floor is imposed
  d. Consumer surplus after the price floor is imposed

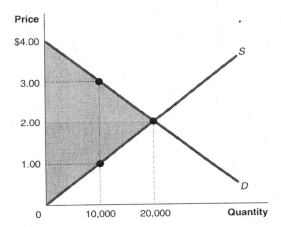

**4A.9** Construct a table like the one in this appendix on page 134, but assume that the rent ceiling is $1,200 rather than $1,000.

>> End Appendix Learning Objective

# Chapter 5
# Elasticity

Whether you are managing a publishing company, bookstore, or coffee shop, you need to know how an increase or decrease in the price of your products will affect the quantity consumers are willing to buy. We saw in Chapter 3 that cutting the price of a good increases the quantity demanded and that raising the price reduces the quantity demanded. But the critical question is this: *How much* will the quantity demanded change as a result of a price increase or decrease? Economists use the concept of **elasticity** to measure how one economic variable—such as the quantity demanded—responds to changes in another economic variable—such as the price. For example, the responsiveness of the quantity demanded of a good to changes in its price is called the *price elasticity of demand*. Knowing the price elasticity of demand allows you to compute the effect of a price change on the quantity demanded.

**Elasticity** A measure of how much one economic variable responds to changes in another economic variable.

We also saw in Chapter 3 that the quantity of a good that consumers demand depends not just on the price of the good but also on consumer income and on the prices of related goods. As a manager, you would also be interested in measuring the responsiveness of demand to these other factors. As we will see, we can use the concept of elasticity here as well. We also are interested in the responsiveness of the quantity supplied of a good to changes in its price, which is called the *price elasticity of supply*.

Elasticity is an important concept not just for business managers but for policymakers as well. If the government wants to discourage teenage smoking, it can raise the price of cigarettes by increasing the tax on them. If we know the price elasticity of demand for cigarettes, we can calculate how many fewer cigarettes will be demanded at a higher price. In this chapter, we will also see how policymakers use the concept of elasticity.

**6.1 LEARNING OBJECTIVE**

6.1 | Define the price elasticity of demand and understand how to measure it.

# The Price Elasticity of Demand and Its Measurement

We know from the law of demand that when the price of a product falls, the quantity demanded of the product increases. But the law of demand tells firms only that the demand curves for their products slope downward. More useful is a measure of the responsiveness of the quantity demanded to a change in price. This measure is called the **price elasticity of demand**.

**Price elasticity of demand** The responsiveness of the quantity demanded to a change in price, measured by dividing the percentage change in the quantity demanded of a product by the percentage change in the product's price.

## Measuring the Price Elasticity of Demand

We might measure the price elasticity of demand by using the slope of the demand curve because the slope of the demand curve tells us how much quantity changes as price changes. Using the slope of the demand curve to measure price elasticity has a drawback, however: The measurement of slope is sensitive to the units chosen for quantity and price. For example, suppose a $1 decrease in the price of *Harry Potter and the Deathly Hallows* leads to an increase in the quantity demanded from 10.1 million books to 10.2 million books. The change in quantity is 0.1 million books, and the change in price is −$1, so the slope is 0.1/−1 = −0.1. But if we measure price in cents, rather than dollars, the slope is 0.1/−100 = −0.001. If we measure price in dollars and books in thousands, instead of millions, the slope is 100/−1 = −100. Clearly, the value we compute for the slope can change dramatically, depending on the units we use for quantity and price.

To avoid this confusion over units, economists use *percentage changes* when measuring the price elasticity of demand. Percentage changes are not dependent on units. (For a review of calculating percentage changes, see the appendix to Chapter 1.) No matter what units we use to measure the quantity of wheat, 10 percent more wheat is 10 percent more wheat. Therefore, the price elasticity of demand is measured by dividing the percentage change in the quantity demanded by the percentage change in the price. Or:

$$\text{Price elasticity of demand} = \frac{\text{Percentage change in quantity demanded}}{\text{Percentage change in price}}.$$

It's important to remember that *the price elasticity of demand is not the same as the slope of the demand curve.*

If we calculate the price elasticity of demand for a price cut, the percentage change in price will be negative, and the percentage change in quantity demanded will be positive. Similarly, if we calculate the price elasticity of demand for a price increase, the percentage change in price will be positive, and the percentage change in quantity will be negative. Therefore, the price elasticity of demand is always negative. In comparing elasticities, though, we are usually interested in their relative size. So, we often drop the minus sign and compare their *absolute values*. In other words, although −3 is actually a smaller number than −2, a price elasticity of −3 is larger than a price elasticity of −2.

## Elastic Demand and Inelastic Demand

If the quantity demanded is responsive to changes in price, the percentage change in quantity demanded will be *greater* than the percentage change in price, and the price elasticity of demand will be greater than 1 in absolute value. In this case, demand is **elastic**. For example, if a 10 percent fall in the price of bagels results in a 20 percent increase in the quantity of bagels demanded, then:

$$\text{Price elasticity of demand} = \frac{20\%}{-10\%} = -2,$$

and we can conclude that the price of bagels is **elastic**.

When the quantity demanded is not very responsive to price, however, the percentage change in quantity demanded will be *less* than the percentage change in price, and the price elasticity of demand will be less than 1 in absolute value. In this case, demand is **inelastic**. For example, if a 10 percent fall in the price of wheat results in a 5 percent increase in the quantity of wheat demanded, then:

$$\text{Price elasticity of demand} = \frac{5\%}{-10\%} = -0.5,$$

and we can conclude that the demand for wheat is **inelastic**.

In the special case in which the percentage change in the quantity demanded is equal to the percentage change in price, the price elasticity of demand equals −1 (or 1 in absolute value). In this case, demand is **unit-elastic**.

**Elastic demand** Demand is elastic when the percentage change in quantity demanded is *greater* than the percentage change in price, so the price elasticity is *greater* than 1 in absolute value.

**Inelastic demand** Demand is inelastic when the percentage change in quantity demanded is *less* than the percentage change in price, so the price elasticity is *less* than 1 in absolute value.

**Unit-elastic demand** Demand is unit-elastic when the percentage change in quantity demanded is *equal to* the percentage change in price, so the price elasticity is equal to 1 in absolute value.

## An Example of Computing Price Elasticities

Suppose you own a small bookstore and you are trying to decide whether to cut the price you are charging for a new John Grisham mystery novel. You are currently at point $A$ in Figure 6-1: selling 16 copies of the novel per day at a price of $30 per copy. How many more copies you will sell by cutting the price to $20 depends on the price elasticity of demand for this novel. Let's consider two possibilities: If $D_1$ is the demand curve for this novel in your store, your sales will increase to 28 copies per day, point $B$. But if $D_2$ is your demand curve, your sales will increase only to 20 copies per day, point $C$. We might expect—correctly, as we will see—that between these points, demand curve $D_1$ is *elastic*, and demand curve $D_2$ is *inelastic*.

To confirm that $D_1$ is elastic between these points and that $D_2$ is inelastic, we need to calculate the price elasticity of demand for each curve. In calculating price elasticity between two points on a demand curve, though, we run into a problem because we get

## Figure 6-1

**Elastic and Inelastic Demand Curves**

Along $D_1$, cutting the price from $30 to $20 increases the number of copies sold from 16 per day to 28 per day, so demand is elastic between point $A$ and point $B$. Along $D_2$, cutting the price from $30 to $20 increases the number of copies sold from 16 per day to only 20 per day, so demand is inelastic between point $A$ and point $C$.

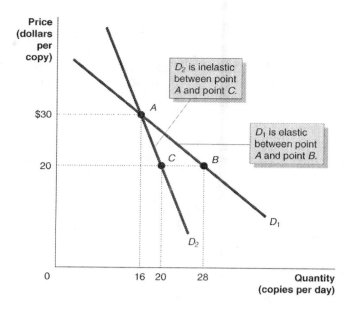

a different value for price increases than for price decreases. For example, suppose we calculate the price elasticity for $D_2$ as the price is cut from $30 to $20. This reduction is a 33 percent price cut that increases the quantity demanded from 16 books to 20 books, or by 25 percent. Therefore, the price elasticity of demand between points $A$ and $C$ is $25/-33 = -0.8$. Now let's calculate the price elasticity for $D_2$ as the price is *increased* from $20 to $30. This is a 50 percent price increase that decreases the quantity demanded from 20 books to 16 books, or by 20 percent. So, now our measure of the price elasticity of demand between points $A$ and $C$ is $-20/50 = -0.4$. It can be confusing to have different values for the price elasticity of demand between the same two points on the same demand curve.

## The Midpoint Formula

We can use the *midpoint formula* to ensure that we have only one value of the price elasticity of demand between the same two points on a demand curve. The midpoint formula uses the *average* of the initial and final quantities and the initial and final prices. If $Q_1$ and $P_1$ are the initial quantity and price and $Q_2$ and $P_2$ are the final quantity and price, the midpoint formula is:

$$\text{Price elasticity of demand} = \frac{(Q_2 - Q_1)}{\left(\dfrac{Q_1 + Q_2}{2}\right)} \div \frac{(P_2 - P_1)}{\left(\dfrac{P_1 + P_2}{2}\right)}.$$

The midpoint formula may seem challenging at first, but the numerator is just the change in quantity divided by the average of the initial and final quantities, and the denominator is just the change in price divided by the average of the initial and final prices.

Let's apply the formula to calculating the price elasticity of $D_2$ in Figure 6-1. Between point $A$ and point $C$ on $D_2$, the change in quantity is 4, and the average of the two quantities is 18. Therefore, there is a 22.2 percent change in quantity. The change in price is $-$10$, and the average of the two prices is $25. Therefore, there is a $-40$ percent change in price. So, the price elasticity of demand is $22.2/-40.0 = -0.6$. Notice these three results from calculating the price elasticity of demand using the midpoint formula: First, as we suspected from examining Figure 6-1, demand curve $D_2$ is inelastic between points $A$ and $C$. Second, our value for the price elasticity calculated using the midpoint formula is between the two values we calculated earlier. Third, the midpoint formula will give us the same value whether we are moving from the higher price to the lower price or from the lower price to the higher price.

more wheat. Therefore, the price elasticity of demand is measured by dividing the percentage change in the quantity demanded by the percentage change in the price. Or:

$$\text{Price elasticity of demand} = \frac{\text{Percentage change in quantity demanded}}{\text{Percentage change in price}}.$$

It's important to remember that *the price elasticity of demand is not the same as the slope of the demand curve.*

If we calculate the price elasticity of demand for a price cut, the percentage change in price will be negative, and the percentage change in quantity demanded will be positive. Similarly, if we calculate the price elasticity of demand for a price increase, the percentage change in price will be positive, and the percentage change in quantity will be negative. Therefore, the price elasticity of demand is always negative. In comparing elasticities, though, we are usually interested in their relative size. So, we often drop the minus sign and compare their *absolute values*. In other words, although −3 is actually a smaller number than −2, a price elasticity of −3 is larger than a price elasticity of −2.

## Elastic Demand and Inelastic Demand

If the quantity demanded is responsive to changes in price, the percentage change in quantity demanded will be *greater* than the percentage change in price, and the price elasticity of demand will be greater than 1 in absolute value. In this case, demand is **elastic**. For example, if a 10 percent fall in the price of bagels results in a 20 percent increase in the quantity of bagels demanded, then:

$$\text{Price elasticity of demand} = \frac{20\%}{-10\%} = -2,$$

and we can conclude that the price of bagels is **elastic**.

When the quantity demanded is not very responsive to price, however, the percentage change in quantity demanded will be *less* than the percentage change in price, and the price elasticity of demand will be less than 1 in absolute value. In this case, demand is **inelastic**. For example, if a 10 percent fall in the price of wheat results in a 5 percent increase in the quantity of wheat demanded, then:

$$\text{Price elasticity of demand} = \frac{5\%}{-10\%} = -0.5,$$

and we can conclude that the demand for wheat is **inelastic**.

In the special case in which the percentage change in the quantity demanded is equal to the percentage change in price, the price elasticity of demand equals −1 (or 1 in absolute value). In this case, demand is **unit-elastic**.

## An Example of Computing Price Elasticities

Suppose you own a small bookstore and you are trying to decide whether to cut the price you are charging for a new John Grisham mystery novel. You are currently at point *A* in Figure 6-1: selling 16 copies of the novel per day at a price of $30 per copy. How many more copies you will sell by cutting the price to $20 depends on the price elasticity of demand for this novel. Let's consider two possibilities: If $D_1$ is the demand curve for this novel in your store, your sales will increase to 28 copies per day, point *B*. But if $D_2$ is your demand curve, your sales will increase only to 20 copies per day, point *C*. We might expect—correctly, as we will see—that between these points, demand curve $D_1$ is *elastic*, and demand curve $D_2$ is *inelastic*.

To confirm that $D_1$ is elastic between these points and that $D_2$ is inelastic, we need to calculate the price elasticity of demand for each curve. In calculating price elasticity between two points on a demand curve, though, we run into a problem because we get

**Elastic demand** Demand is elastic when the percentage change in quantity demanded is *greater* than the percentage change in price, so the price elasticity is *greater* than 1 in absolute value.

**Inelastic demand** Demand is inelastic when the percentage change in quantity demanded is *less* than the percentage change in price, so the price elasticity is *less* than 1 in absolute value.

**Unit-elastic demand** Demand is unit-elastic when the percentage change in quantity demanded is *equal to* the percentage change in price, so the price elasticity is equal to 1 in absolute value.

## Figure 6-1

### Elastic and Inelastic Demand Curves

Along $D_1$, cutting the price from $30 to $20 increases the number of copies sold from 16 per day to 28 per day, so demand is elastic between point $A$ and point $B$. Along $D_2$, cutting the price from $30 to $20 increases the number of copies sold from 16 per day to only 20 per day, so demand is inelastic between point $A$ and point $C$.

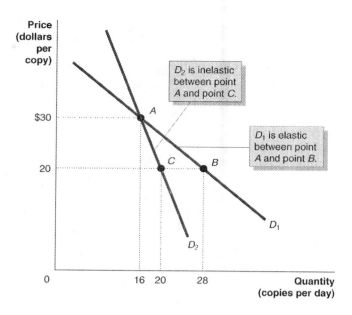

a different value for price increases than for price decreases. For example, suppose we calculate the price elasticity for $D_2$ as the price is cut from $30 to $20. This reduction is a 33 percent price cut that increases the quantity demanded from 16 books to 20 books, or by 25 percent. Therefore, the price elasticity of demand between points $A$ and $C$ is $25/-33 = -0.8$. Now let's calculate the price elasticity for $D_2$ as the price is *increased* from $20 to $30. This is a 50 percent price increase that decreases the quantity demanded from 20 books to 16 books, or by 20 percent. So, now our measure of the price elasticity of demand between points $A$ and $C$ is $-20/50 = -0.4$. It can be confusing to have different values for the price elasticity of demand between the same two points on the same demand curve.

## The Midpoint Formula

We can use the *midpoint formula* to ensure that we have only one value of the price elasticity of demand between the same two points on a demand curve. The midpoint formula uses the *average* of the initial and final quantities and the initial and final prices. If $Q_1$ and $P_1$ are the initial quantity and price and $Q_2$ and $P_2$ are the final quantity and price, the midpoint formula is:

$$\text{Price elasticity of demand} = \frac{(Q_2 - Q_1)}{\left(\dfrac{Q_1 + Q_2}{2}\right)} \div \frac{(P_2 - P_1)}{\left(\dfrac{P_1 + P_2}{2}\right)}.$$

The midpoint formula may seem challenging at first, but the numerator is just the change in quantity divided by the average of the initial and final quantities, and the denominator is just the change in price divided by the average of the initial and final prices.

Let's apply the formula to calculating the price elasticity of $D_2$ in Figure 6-1. Between point $A$ and point $C$ on $D_2$, the change in quantity is 4, and the average of the two quantities is 18. Therefore, there is a 22.2 percent change in quantity. The change in price is $-$10, and the average of the two prices is $25. Therefore, there is a $-40$ percent change in price. So, the price elasticity of demand is $22.2/-40.0 = -0.6$. Notice these three results from calculating the price elasticity of demand using the midpoint formula: First, as we suspected from examining Figure 6-1, demand curve $D_2$ is inelastic between points $A$ and $C$. Second, our value for the price elasticity calculated using the midpoint formula is between the two values we calculated earlier. Third, the midpoint formula will give us the same value whether we are moving from the higher price to the lower price or from the lower price to the higher price.

We can also use the midpoint formula to calculate the elasticity of demand between point *A* and point *B* on $D_1$. In this case, there is a 54.5 percent change in quantity and a –40 percent change in price. So, the elasticity of demand is 54.5/–40.0 = –1.4. Once again, as we suspected, demand curve $D_1$ is price elastic between points *A* and *B*.

# Solved Problem | 6-1

## Calculating the Price Elasticity of Demand

Scholastic Corporation's suggested retail price for *Harry Potter and the Deathly Hallows* is $35. Suppose you own a small bookstore, and you believe that if you keep the price of the book at $35, you will be able to sell 40 copies per day. You are considering cutting the price to $25. The graph below shows two possi-

ble increases in the quantity sold as a result of your price cut. Use the information in the graph to calculate the price elasticity between these two prices on each of the demand curves. Use the midpoint formula in your calculations. State whether each demand curve is elastic or inelastic between these two prices.

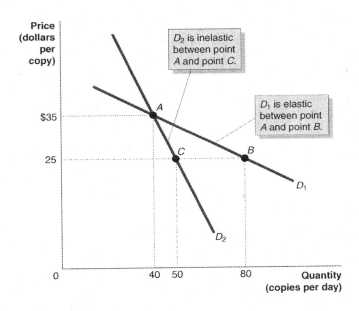

# SOLVING THE PROBLEM:

**Step 1:** **Review the chapter material.** This problem requires calculating the price elasticity of demand, so you may want to review the material in the section "The Midpoint Formula," which begins on page 176.

**Step 2:** **As the first step in using the midpoint formula, calculate the average quantity and the average price for demand curve $D_1$.**

$$\text{Average quantity} = \frac{40 + 80}{2} = 60$$

$$\text{Average price} = \frac{\$35 + \$25}{2} = \$30$$

**Step 3:** **Now calculate the percentage change in the quantity demanded and the percentage change in price for demand curve $D_1$.**

$$\text{Percentage change in quantity demanded} = \frac{80 - 40}{60} \times 100 = 66.7\%$$

$$\text{Percentage change in price} = \frac{\$25 - \$35}{\$30} \times 100 = -33.3\%$$

Step 4:   **Divide the percentage change in the quantity demanded by the percentage change in price to arrive at the price elasticity for demand curve $D_1$.**

$$\text{Price elasticity of demand} = \frac{66.7\%}{-33.3\%} = -2$$

Because the elasticity is greater than 1 in absolute value, $D_1$ is price *elastic* between these two prices.

Step 5:   **Calculate the price elasticity of demand curve $D_2$ between these two prices.**

$$\text{Percentage change in quantity demanded} = \frac{50 - 40}{45} \times 100 = 22.2\%$$

$$\text{Percentage change in price} = \frac{\$25 - \$35}{\$30} \times 100 = -33.3\%$$

$$\text{Price elasticity of demand} = \frac{22.2\%}{-33.3\%} = -0.7$$

Because the elasticity is less than 1 in absolute value, $D_2$ is price *inelastic* between these two prices.

>> **End Solved Problem 6-1**

## When Demand Curves Intersect, the Flatter Curve Is More Elastic

Remember that elasticity is not the same thing as slope. While slope is calculated using changes in quantity and price, elasticity is calculated using percentage changes. But it *is* true that if two demand curves intersect, the one with the smaller slope (in absolute value)—the flatter demand curve—is more elastic, and the one with the larger slope (in absolute value)—the steeper demand curve—is less elastic. In Figure 6-1, demand curve $D_1$ is more elastic than demand curve $D_2$.

## Polar Cases of Perfectly Elastic and Perfectly Inelastic Demand

**Perfectly inelastic demand** The case where the quantity demanded is completely unresponsive to price, and the price elasticity of demand equals zero.

Although they do not occur frequently, you should be aware of the extreme, or polar, cases of price elasticity. If a demand curve is a vertical line, it is **perfectly inelastic**. In this case, the quantity demanded is completely unresponsive to price, and the price elasticity of demand equals zero. However much price may increase or decrease, the quantity remains the same. For only a very few products will the quantity demanded be completely unresponsive to the price, making the demand curve a vertical line. The drug insulin is an example. Diabetics must take a certain amount of insulin each day. If the price of insulin declines, it will not affect the required dose and thus will not increase the quantity demanded. Similarly, a price increase will not affect the required dose or decrease the quantity demanded. (Of course, some diabetics will not be able to afford insulin at a higher price. If so, even in this case, the demand curve may not be completely vertical and, therefore, not perfectly inelastic.)

**Perfectly elastic demand** The case where the quantity demanded is infinitely responsive to price, and the price elasticity of demand equals infinity.

If a demand curve is a horizontal line, it is **perfectly elastic**. In this case, the quantity demanded would be infinitely responsive to price, and the price elasticity of demand equals infinity. If a demand curve is perfectly elastic, an increase in price causes the quantity demanded to fall to zero. Once again, perfectly elastic demand curves are rare, and it is important not to confuse *elastic* with *perfectly elastic*. Table 6-1 summarizes the different price elasticities of demand.

| IF DEMAND IS... | THEN THE ABSOLUTE VALUE OF PRICE ELASTICITY IS | |
|---|---|---|
| elastic | greater than 1 | 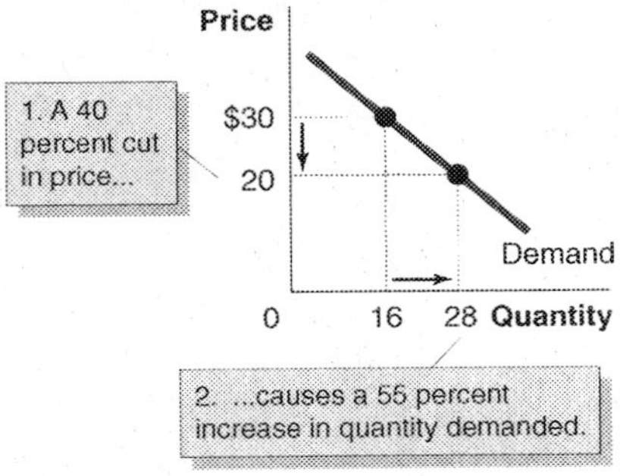 |

TABLE 6-1

**Summary of the Price Elasticities of Demand**

(Note that the percentage increases shown in the boxes in the graphs were calculated using the midpoint formula on page 176.)

**elastic** — greater than 1

1. A 40 percent cut in price...

Price
$30
20
Demand
0    16    28  Quantity

2. ...causes a 55 percent increase in quantity demanded.

**inelastic** — less than 1

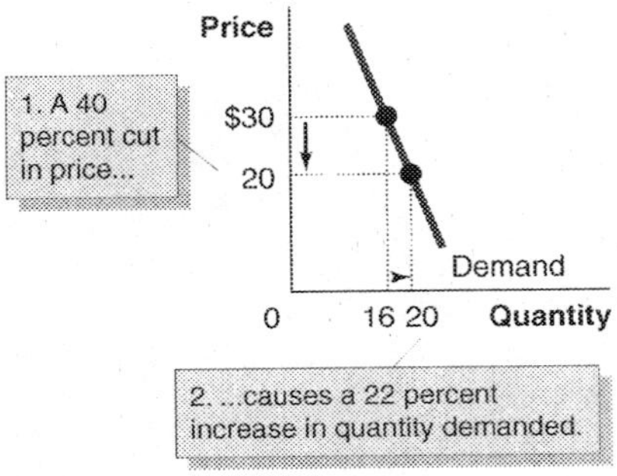

1. A 40 percent cut in price...

Price
$30
20
Demand
0    16 20  Quantity

2. ...causes a 22 percent increase in quantity demanded.

**unit-elastic** — equal to 1

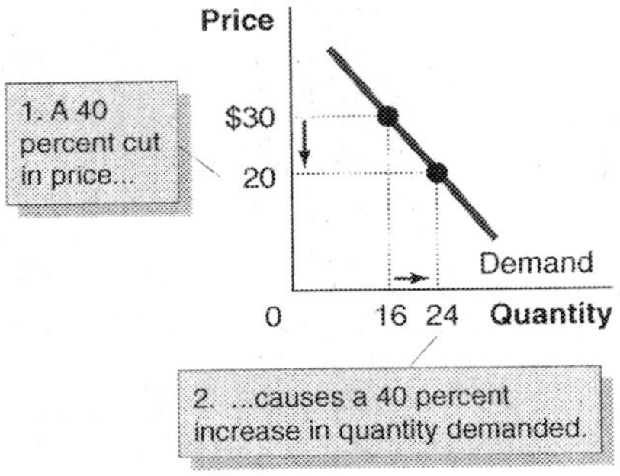

1. A 40 percent cut in price...

Price
$30
20
Demand
0    16 24  Quantity

2. ...causes a 40 percent increase in quantity demanded.

**perfectly elastic** — equal to infinity

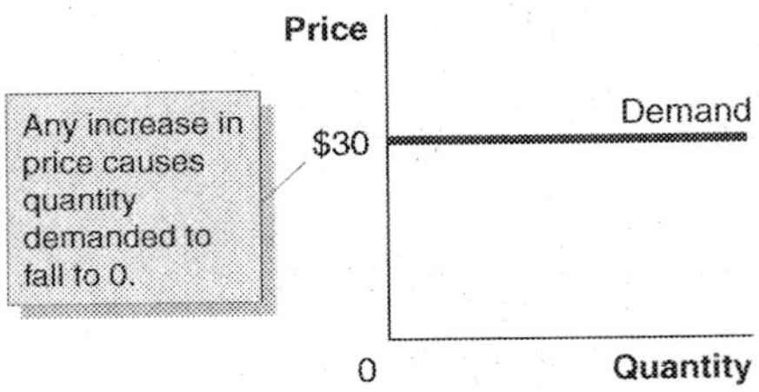

Any increase in price causes quantity demanded to fall to 0.

Price
Demand
$30
0    Quantity

**perfectly inelastic** — equal to 0

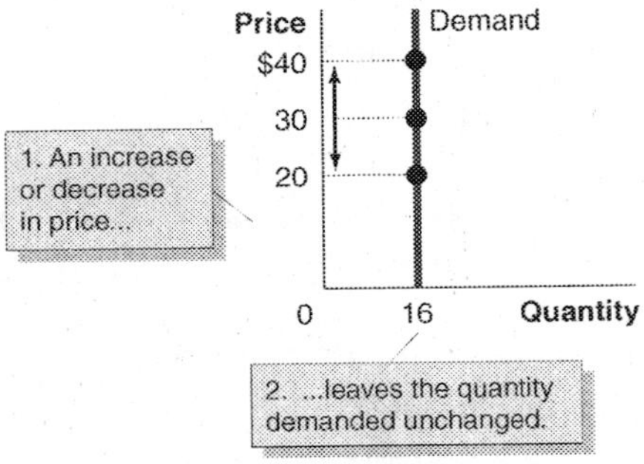

1. An increase or decrease in price...

Price    Demand
$40
30
20
0    16    Quantity

2. ...leaves the quantity demanded unchanged.

# Don't Let This Happen to **YOU!**

## Don't Confuse Inelastic with *Perfectly* Inelastic

You may be tempted to simplify the concept of elasticity by assuming that any demand curve described as being inelastic is *perfectly* inelastic. You should never assume this because perfectly inelastic demand curves are rare. For example, consider the following problem: "Use a demand and supply graph to show how a decrease in supply affects the equilibrium quantity of gasoline. Assume that the demand for gasoline is inelastic." The following graph would be an *incorrect* answer to this problem.

The demand for gasoline is inelastic, but it is not *perfectly* inelastic. When the price of gasoline rises, the quantity demanded falls. So, the graph that would be the correct answer to this problem would show a normal downward-sloping demand curve rather than a vertical demand curve.

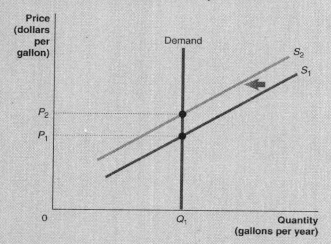

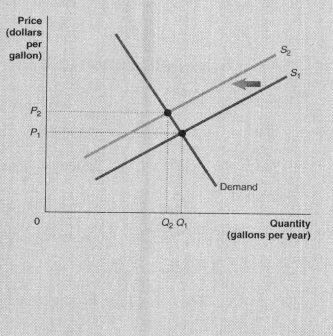

---

**6.2 LEARNING** OBJECTIVE

6.2 | Understand the determinants of the price elasticity of demand.

# The Determinants of the Price Elasticity of Demand

We have seen that the demand for some products may be elastic, while the demand for other products may be inelastic. In this section, we examine why price elasticities differ among products. The key determinants of the price elasticity of demand are as follows:

- Availability of close substitutes
- Passage of time
- Necessities versus luxuries
- Definition of the market
- Share of the good in the consumer's budget

## Availability of Close Substitutes

The availability of substitutes is the most important determinant of price elasticity of demand because how consumers react to a change in the price of a product depends on what alternatives they have. When the price of gasoline rises, consumers have few alternatives, so the quantity demanded falls only a little. But if Domino's raises the price of pizza, consumers have many alternatives, so the quantity demanded is likely to fall quite a lot. In fact, a key constraint on a firm's pricing policies is how many close substitutes exist for its product. In general, *if a product has more substitutes available, it will have more elastic demand. If a product has fewer substitutes available, it will have less elastic demand.*

## Passage of Time

It usually takes consumers some time to adjust their buying habits when prices change. If the price of chicken falls, for example, it takes a while before consumers decide to change from eating chicken for dinner once per week to eating it twice per week. If the price of gasoline increases, it also takes a while for consumers to decide to shift toward buying more fuel-efficient cars to reduce the quantity of gasoline they buy. *The more time that passes, the more elastic the demand for a product becomes.*

## Luxuries versus Necessities

Goods that are luxuries usually have more elastic demand curves than goods that are necessities. For example, the demand for milk is inelastic because milk is a necessity, and the quantity that people buy is not very dependent on its price. Tickets to a concert are a luxury, so the demand for concert tickets is much more elastic than the demand for milk. *The demand curve for a luxury is more elastic than the demand curve for a necessity.*

## Definition of the Market

In a narrowly defined market, consumers have more substitutes available. If the price of Kellogg's Raisin Bran rises, many consumers will start buying another brand of raisin bran. If the prices of all brands of raisin bran rise, the responsiveness of consumers will be lower. If the prices of all breakfast cereals rise, the responsiveness of consumers will be even lower. *The more narrowly we define a market, the more elastic demand will be.*

| Making the Connection | **The Price Elasticity of Demand for Breakfast Cereal** |
| --- | --- |

*What happens when the price of raisin bran increases?*

MIT economist Jerry Hausman has estimated the price elasticity of demand for breakfast cereal. He divided breakfast cereals into three categories: children's cereals, such as Trix and Froot Loops; adult cereals, such as Special K and Grape-Nuts; and family cereals, such as Corn Flakes and Raisin Bran. Some of the results of his estimates are given in the following table.

| CEREAL | PRICE ELASTICITY OF DEMAND |
| --- | --- |
| Post Raisin Bran | −2.5 |
| All family breakfast cereals | −1.8 |
| All types of breakfast cereals | −0.9 |

Source: Jerry A. Hausman, "The Price Elasticity of Demand for Breakfast Cereal," in Timothy F. Bresnahan and Robert J. Gordon, eds., *The Economics of New Goods*, Chicago: University of Chicago Press, 1997. Used with permission of The University of Chicago Press.

Just as we would expect, the price elasticity for a particular brand of raisin bran was larger in absolute value than the elasticity for all family cereals, and the elasticity for all family cereals was larger than the elasticity for all types of breakfast cereals. If Post increases the price of its Raisin Bran by 10 percent, sales will decline by 25 percent, as many consumers switch to another brand of raisin bran. If the prices of all family breakfast cereals rise by 10 percent, sales will decline by 18 percent, as consumers switch to child or adult cereals. In both of these cases, demand is elastic. But if the prices of all types of breakfast cereals rise by 10 percent, sales will decline by only 9 percent. Demand for all breakfast cereals is inelastic.

Source: Jerry A. Hausman, "Valuation of New Goods under Perfect and Imperfect Competition," in Timothy F. Bresnahan and Robert J. Gordon, eds., *The Economics of New Goods*, Chicago: University of Chicago Press, 1997.

## Share of a Good in a Consumer's Budget

Goods that take only a small fraction of a consumer's budget tend to have less elastic demand than goods that take a large fraction. For example, most people buy salt infrequently and in relatively small quantities. The share of the average consumer's budget that is spent on salt is very low. As a result, even a doubling of the price of salt is likely to result in only a small decline in the quantity of salt demanded. "Big-ticket items," such as houses, cars, and furniture, take up a larger share in the average consumer's budget. Increases in the prices of these goods are likely to result in significant declines in quantity demanded. In general, *the demand for a good will be more elastic the larger the share of the good in the average consumer's budget.*

## Is the Demand for Books Perfectly Inelastic?

At the beginning of the chapter we quoted Stephen Rubin, publisher of Doubleday, as saying, "I am just convinced that there is no difference between $22 and $23. . . . Price is not a factor if it is a book that you really want." Taken literally, Rubin seems to be arguing that the demand for books is perfectly inelastic because only when demand is perfectly inelastic is price "not a factor." It's unlikely that this is what he means because if demand were really perfectly inelastic, he could charge $200 or $2,000 instead of charging $23 and still sell the same number of books. It is more likely he is arguing that demand is inelastic, so that even though he will sell fewer books at a price of $23 than at a price of $22, the decline in sales will be small.

Notice also that the book he mentions is a "translation from a Czech writer." Specialized books of this type will have relatively few substitutes (although a consumer can buy a used copy or borrow a copy from the library). A cut in price is unlikely to attract many new customers, and an increase in price is unlikely to cause many existing customers to not buy. This lack of substitutes is the main factor that makes demand inelastic. The situation may be different for light fiction written by popular novelists, like John Grisham, Stephen King, or Dean Koontz. Many consumers see books written by these authors as close substitutes. Someone looking for a "good read" on an airplane trip or at the beach may switch from Stephen King to Dean Koontz if the price of the Stephen King book is significantly higher.

---

6.3 | Understand the relationship between the price elasticity of demand and total revenue.

# The Relationship between Price Elasticity of Demand and Total Revenue

**Total revenue** The total amount of funds received by a seller of a good or service, calculated by multiplying price per unit by the number of units sold.

A firm is interested in price elasticity because it allows the firm to calculate how changes in price will affect its **total revenue**, which is the total amount of funds it receives from selling a good or service. Total revenue is calculated by multiplying price per unit by the number of units sold. When demand is inelastic, price and total revenue move in the same direction: An increase in price raises total revenue, and a decrease in price reduces total revenue. When demand is elastic, price and total revenue move inversely: An increase in price reduces total revenue, and a decrease in price raises total revenue.

To understand the relationship between price elasticity and total revenue, consider Figure 6-2. Panel (a) shows a demand curve for a John Grisham novel (as in Figure 6-1 on page 176). This demand curve is inelastic between point *A* and point *B*. The total revenue received by a bookseller at point *A* equals the price of $30 multiplied by the 16 copies sold, or $480. This amount equals the areas of the rectangles *C* and *D* in the figure because together the rectangles have a height of $30 and a base of 16 copies. Because this demand curve is inelastic between point *A* and point *B* (it was demand curve $D_2$ in Figure 6-1), cutting the price to $20 (point *B*) reduces total revenue. The new total revenue is shown by the areas of rectangles *D* and *E*, and it is equal to $20 multiplied by 20 copies, or $400. Total revenue falls because the increase in the quantity demanded is not large enough to make up for the

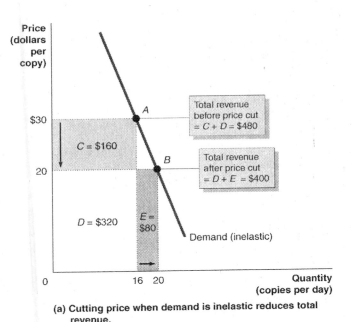

(a) Cutting price when demand is inelastic reduces total revenue.

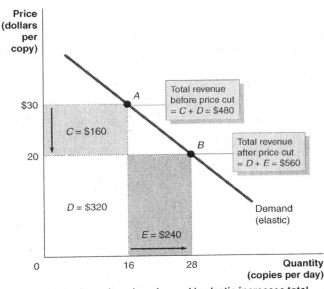

(b) Cutting price when demand is elastic increases total revenue.

**Figure 6-2 | The Relationship between Price Elasticity and Total Revenue**

When demand is inelastic, a cut in price will decrease total revenue. In panel (a), at point *A*, the price is $30, 16 copies are sold, and total revenue received by the bookseller equals $30 × 16 copies, or $480. At point *B*, cutting price to $20 increases the quantity demanded to 20 copies, but the fall in price more than offsets the increase in quantity. As a result, revenue falls to $20 × 20 copies, or $400. When demand is elastic,

a cut in price will increase total revenue. In panel (b), at point *A*, the area of rectangles *C* and *D* is still equal to $480. But at point *B*, the area of rectangles *D* and *E* is equal to $20 × 28 copies, or $560. In this case, the increase in the quantity demanded is large enough to offset the fall in price, so total revenue increases.

decrease in price. As a result, the $80 increase in revenue gained as a result of the price cut—dark-green rectangle *E*—is less than the $160 in revenue lost—light-green rectangle *C*.

Panel (b) of Figure 6-2 shows a demand curve that is elastic between point *A* and point *B* (it was demand curve $D_1$ in Figure 6-1). In this case, cutting the price increases total revenue. At point *A*, the areas of rectangles *C* and *D* are still equal to $480, but at point *B*, the areas of rectangles *D* and *E* are equal to $20 multiplied by 28 copies, or $560. Here, total revenue rises because the increase in the quantity demanded is large enough to offset the lower price. As a result, the $240 increase in revenue gained as a result of the price cut—dark-green rectangle *E*—is greater than the $160 in revenue lost—light-green rectangle *C*.

The third, less common, possibility is that demand is unit elastic. In that case, a change in price is exactly offset by a proportional change in quantity demanded, leaving revenue unaffected. Therefore, when demand is unit elastic, neither a decrease in price nor an increase in price affects revenue. Table 6-2 summarizes the relationship between price elasticity and revenue.

## Elasticity and Revenue with a Linear Demand Curve

Along most demand curves, elasticity is not constant at every point. For example, a straight-line, or linear, demand curve for DVDs is shown in panel (a) of Figure 6-3. The numbers from the table are plotted in the graphs. The demand curve shows that when the price falls by $1, consumers always respond by buying 2 more DVDs per month. When the price is high and the quantity demanded is low, demand is elastic. This is true because a $1 fall in price is a smaller percentage change when the price is high, and an increase of 2 DVDs is a larger percentage change when the quantity of DVDs is small. By similar reasoning, we can see why demand is inelastic when the price is low and the quantity demanded is high. Panel (a) in Figure 6-3 shows that when price is between $8 and $4 and quantity is between 0 and 6, demand is elastic. Panel (b) shows that over this same range, total revenue will increase as price falls. For example, in panel (a), as price falls from $7 to $6,

TABLE 6-2

**The Relationship between Price Elasticity and Revenue**

| IF DEMAND IS . . . | THEN . . . | BECAUSE . . . |
|---|---|---|
| elastic | an increase in price reduces revenue | the decrease in quantity demanded is proportionally *greater* than the increase in price. |
| elastic | a decrease in price increases revenue | the increase in quantity demanded is proportionally *greater* than the decrease in price. |
| inelastic | an increase in price increases revenue | the decrease in quantity demanded is proportionally *smaller* than the increase in price. |
| inelastic | a decrease in price reduces revenue | the increase in quantity demanded is proportionally *smaller* than the decrease in price. |
| unit elastic | an increase in price does not affect revenue | the decrease in quantity demanded is proportionally *the same as* the increase in price. |
| unit elastic | a decrease in price does not affect revenue | the increase in quantity demanded is proportionally *the same as* the decrease in price. |

quantity demand increases from 2 to 4, and in panel (b), total revenue increases from $14 to $24. Similarly, when price is between $4 and zero and quantity is between 8 and 16, demand is inelastic. Over this same range, total revenue will decrease as price falls. For example, as price falls from $3 to $2 and quantity increases from 10 to 12, total revenue decreases from $30 to $24.

# Solved Problem | 6-3

## Price and Revenue Don't Always Move in the Same Direction

Briefly explain whether you agree or disagree with the following statement: "The only way to increase the revenue from selling a product is to increase the product's price."

### SOLVING THE PROBLEM:

**Step 1:** **Review the chapter material.** This problem deals with the effect of a price change on a firm's revenue, so you may want to review the section "The Relationship between Price Elasticity and Total Revenue," which begins on page 182.

**Step 2:** **Analyze the statement.** We have seen that a price increase will increase revenue only if demand is inelastic. In Figure 6-3, for example, increasing the rental price of DVDs from $1 to $2 *increases* revenue from $14 to $24 because demand is inelastic along this portion of the demand curve. But increasing the price from $5 to $6 *decreases* revenue from $30 to $24 because demand is elastic along this portion of the demand curve. If the price is currently $5, increasing revenue would require a price *cut*, not a price increase. As this example shows, the statement is incorrect and you should disagree with it.

**>> End Solved Problem 6-3**

| Price | Quantity Demanded | Total Revenue |
|---|---|---|
| $8 | 0 | $0 |
| 7 | 2 | 14 |
| 6 | 4 | 24 |
| 5 | 6 | 30 |
| 4 | 8 | 32 |
| 3 | 10 | 30 |
| 2 | 12 | 24 |
| 1 | 14 | 14 |
| 0 | 16 | 0 |

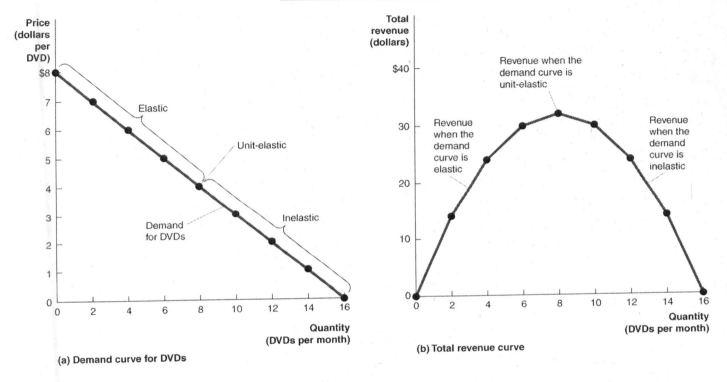

(a) Demand curve for DVDs

(b) Total revenue curve

**Figure 6-3** | Elasticity Is Not Constant Along a Linear Demand Curve

The data from the table are plotted in the graphs. Panel (a) shows that as we move down the demand curve for DVDs, the price elasticity of demand declines. In other words, at higher prices, demand is elastic, and at lower prices, demand is inelastic. Panel (b) shows that as the quantity of DVDs sold increases from zero, revenue will increase until it reaches a maximum of $32 when 8 DVDs are sold. As sales increase beyond 8 DVDs, revenue falls because demand is inelastic on this portion of the demand curve.

# Estimating Price Elasticity of Demand

To estimate the price elasticity of demand, economists need to know the demand curve for a product. To calculate the price elasticity of demand for new products, firms often rely on market experiments. With market experiments, firms try different prices and observe the change in quantity demanded that results.

**Making the Connection** | **Determining the Price Elasticity of Demand for DVDs by Market Experiment**

DVDs were a relatively new product in 2001. The movie studios producing them were unsure of the price elasticity of the demand curves they were facing, so they experimented with different prices to help determine the price elasticity.

Following are four films and the prices for DVDs and VHS tapes that the studios suggested stores such as Blockbuster Video charge for them:

| FILM | DVD PRICE | VHS PRICE |
| --- | --- | --- |
| *Rugrats in Paris* | $22.46 | $22.99 |
| *The Mummy Returns* | 26.98 | 22.98 |
| *Miss Congeniality* | 16.69 | 22.98 |
| *The Perfect Storm* | 24.98 | 22.99 |

*When DVDs were first introduced, the movie studios were uncertain about their price elasticity of demand.*

VHS tapes had been on the market for many years, and the studios had determined their pricing strategies, given their estimates of the price elasticity of demand. As a result, the prices of VHS tapes were usually very similar; for these four films, the prices were almost identical. The prices of DVDs were much less standardized because the studios were unsure of their price elasticities. Tom Adams, the head of Adams Market Research, a company that does research on the home video market, summed up the situation: "The studios have different views of the market, so they are setting different suggested retail prices, and the stores are discounting those prices to different degrees."

After several years of market experiments, the move studios had more accurate estimates of the price elasticity of DVDs, and the prices of most DVDs became similar. For instance, in 2007, nearly all newly released DVDs had a list price of about $29, which was often discounted to about $17 when they were sold online or in discount department stores, such as Wal-Mart. When HD-DVDs were introduced, the studios apparently felt confident that they understood their price elasticity, because in 2007 most had list prices of $39.95, discounted to $27.95 in many online stores.

Sources: Geraldine Fabrikant, "Sale of DVDs Are Challenging Movie Rental Business," *New York Times*, April 16, 2001; prices from Amazon.com.

---

**6.4 LEARNING** OBJECTIVE

6.4 | Define the cross-price elasticity of demand and the income elasticity of demand, and understand their determinants and how they are measured.

# Other Demand Elasticities

Elasticity is an important concept in economics because it allows us to quantify the responsiveness of one economic variable to changes in another economic variable. In addition to price elasticity, two other demand elasticities are important: *cross-price elasticity of demand* and *income elasticity of demand*.

## Cross-Price Elasticity of Demand

**Cross-price elasticity of demand**
The percentage change in quantity demanded of one good divided by the percentage change in the price of another good.

Suppose you work at Apple and you need to predict the effect of an increase in the price of Microsoft's Zune on the quantity of iPods demanded, holding other factors constant. You can do this by calculating the **cross-price elasticity of demand**, which is the percentage change in the quantity of iPods demanded divided by the percentage change in the price of Zunes—or, in general:

$$\text{Cross-price elasticity of demand} = \frac{\text{Percentage change in quantity demanded of one good}}{\text{Percentage change in price of another good}}.$$

| IF THE PRODUCTS ARE . . . | THEN THE CROSS-PRICE ELASTICITY OF DEMAND WILL BE . . . | EXAMPLE |
|---|---|---|
| substitutes | positive | Two brands of digital music players |
| complements | negative | Digital music players and song downloads from online music stores |
| unrelated | zero | Digital music players and peanut butter |

**TABLE 6-3**

**Summary of Cross-Price Elasticity of Demand**

The cross-price elasticity of demand is positive or negative, depending on whether the two products are substitutes or complements. Recall that substitutes are products that can be used for the same purpose, such as two brands of digital music players. Complements are products that are used together, such as digital music players and song downloads from online music sites. An increase in the price of a substitute will lead to an increase in quantity demanded, so the cross-price elasticity of demand will be positive. An increase in the price of a complement will lead to a decrease in the quantity demanded, so the cross-price elasticity of demand will be negative. Of course, if the two products are unrelated—such as digital music players and peanut butter—the cross-price elasticity of demand will be zero. Table 6-3 summarizes the key points concerning the cross-price elasticity of demand.

Cross-price elasticity of demand is important to firm managers because it allows them to measure whether products sold by other firms are close substitutes for their products. For example, Amazon.com and Barnesandnoble.com are the leading online booksellers. We might predict that if Amazon raises the price of a new John Grisham novel, many consumers will buy it from Barnesandnoble.com instead. But Jeff Bezos, Amazon's chief executive officer, has argued that because of Amazon's reputation for good customer service and because more customers are familiar with the site, ordering a book from Barnesandnoble.com is not a good substitute for ordering a book from Amazon. In effect, Bezos is arguing that the cross-price elasticity between Amazon's books and Barnesandnoble.com's books is low. Economists Judith Chevalier of Yale University and Austan Goolsbee of the University of Chicago used data on prices and quantities of books sold on these Web sites to estimate the cross-price elasticity. They found that the cross-price elasticity of demand between books at Amazon and books at Barnesandnoble.com was 3.5. This estimate means that if Amazon raises its prices by 10 percent, the quantity of books demanded on Barnesandnoble.com will increase by 35 percent. This result indicates that, contrary to Jeff Bezos's argument, consumers do consider books sold on the two Web sites to be close substitutes.

## Income Elasticity of Demand

The **income elasticity of demand** measures the responsiveness of quantity demanded to changes in income. It is calculated as follows:

$$\text{Income elasticity of demand} = \frac{\text{Percentage change in quantity demanded}}{\text{Percentage change in income}}.$$

**Income elasticity of demand**
A measure of the responsiveness of quantity demanded to changes in income, measured by the percentage change in quantity demanded divided by the percentage change in income.

As we saw in Chapter 3, if the quantity demanded of a good increases as income increases, then the good is a *normal good*. Normal goods are often further subdivided into *luxury goods* and *necessity goods*. A good is a luxury if the quantity demanded is very responsive to changes in income, so that a 10 percent increase in income results in more than a 10 percent increase in quantity demanded. Expensive jewelry and vacation homes are examples of luxuries. A good is a necessity if the quantity demanded is not very responsive to changes in income, so that a 10 percent increase in income results in less than a 10 percent increase in quantity demanded. Food and clothing are examples of

**TABLE 6-4**

**Summary of Income Elasticity of Demand**

| IF THE INCOME ELASTICITY OF DEMAND IS . . . | THEN THE GOOD IS . . . | EXAMPLE |
| --- | --- | --- |
| positive but less than 1 | normal and a necessity | Milk |
| positive and greater than 1 | normal and a luxury | Caviar |
| negative | inferior | High-fat meat |

necessities. A good is *inferior* if the quantity demanded falls when income increases. Ground beef with a high fat content is an example of an inferior good. We should note that normal goods, inferior goods, necessities, and luxuries are just labels economists use for goods with different income elasticities; they are not intended to be value judgments about the worth of these goods.

Because most goods are normal goods, during periods of economic expansion, when consumer income is rising, most firms can expect—holding other factors constant—that the quantity demanded of their products will increase. Sellers of luxuries can expect particularly large increases. During the late 1990s, rapid increases in income resulted in large increases in demand for luxuries, such as meals in expensive restaurants, luxury apartments, and high-performance automobiles. During recessions, falling consumer income can cause firms to experience increases in demand for inferior goods. For example, the demand for bus trips increases as consumers cut back on air travel, and supermarkets find the demand for hamburger increases relative to the demand for steak. Table 6-4 summarizes the key points about the income elasticity of demand.

**Making the Connection**

## Price Elasticity, Cross-Price Elasticity, and Income Elasticity in the Market for Alcoholic Beverages

Many public policy issues are related to the consumption of alcoholic beverages. These issues include underage drinking, drunk driving, and the possible beneficial effects of red wine in lowering the risk of heart disease. X. M. Gao, an economist who works at American Express, and two colleagues have estimated statistically the following elasticities. (*Spirits* refers to all beverages that contain alcohol, other than beer and wine.)

| | |
| --- | --- |
| Price elasticity of demand for beer | −0.23 |
| Cross-price elasticity of demand between beer and wine | 0.31 |
| Cross-price elasticity of demand between beer and spirits | 0.15 |
| Income elasticity of demand for beer | −0.09 |
| Income elasticity of demand for wine | 5.03 |
| Income elasticity of demand for spirits | 1.21 |

The demand for beer is inelastic. A 10 percent increase in the price of beer will result in a 2.3 percent decline in the quantity of beer demanded. Not surprisingly, both wine and spirits are substitutes for beer. A 10 percent increase in the price of wine will result in a 3.1 percent *increase* in the quantity of beer demanded. A 10 percent increase in income will result in a little less than a 1 percent *decline* in the quantity of beer demanded. So, beer is an inferior good. Both wine and spirits are categorized as luxuries because their income elasticities are greater than 1.

Source: X. M. Gao, Eric J. Wailes, and Gail L. Cramer, "A Microeconometric Model Analysis of U.S. Consumer Demand for Alcoholic Beverages," *Applied Economics*, January 1995.

# The Price Elasticity of Supply and Its Measurement

We can use the concept of elasticity to measure the responsiveness of firms to a change in price just as we used it to measure the responsiveness of consumers. We know from the law of supply that when the price of a product increases, the quantity supplied increases. To measure how much quantity supplied increases when price increases, we use the *price elasticity of supply.*

## Measuring the Price Elasticity of Supply

Just as with the price elasticity of demand, we calculate the **price elasticity of supply** using percentage changes:

$$\text{Price elasticity of demand} = \frac{\text{Percentage change in quantity demanded}}{\text{Percentage change in price}}.$$

**Price elasticity of supply**
The responsiveness of the quantity supplied to a change in price, measured by dividing the percentage change in the quantity supplied of a product by the percentage change in the product's price.

Notice that because supply curves are upward sloping, the price elasticity of supply will be a positive number. We categorize the price elasticity of supply the same way we categorized the price elasticity of demand: If the price elasticity of supply is less than 1, then supply is *inelastic.* For example, the price elasticity of supply of gasoline from U.S. oil refineries is about 0.20, and so it is inelastic. A 10 percent increase in the price of gasoline will result in only a 2 percent increase in the quantity supplied. If the price elasticity of supply is greater than 1, then supply is *elastic.* If the price elasticity of supply is equal to 1, then supply is *unit elastic.* As with other elasticity calculations, when we calculate the price elasticity of supply, we hold the values of other factors constant.

## Determinants of the Price Elasticity of Supply

Whether supply is elastic or inelastic depends on the ability and willingness of firms to alter the quantity they produce as price increases. Often, firms have difficulty increasing the quantity of the product they supply during any short period of time. For example, a pizza parlor cannot produce more pizzas on any one night than is possible using the ingredients on hand. Within a day or two it can buy more ingredients, and within a few months it can hire more cooks and install additional ovens. As a result, the supply curve for pizza and most other products will be inelastic if we measure it over a short period of time, but increasingly elastic the longer the period of time over which we measure it. Products that require resources that are themselves in fixed supply are an exception to this rule. For example, a French winery may rely on a particular variety of grape. If all the land on which that grape can be grown is already planted in vineyards, then the supply of that wine will be inelastic even over a long period.

Making the Connection | **Why Are Oil Prices So Unstable?**

Bringing oil to market is a long process. Oil companies hire geologists to locate fields for exploratory oil well drilling. If an exploratory well indicates that significant amounts of oil are present, the company begins full-scale development of the field. The process from exploration to pumping significant amounts of oil can take years. Because it takes so long to bring additional quantities of oil to market, the price elasticity of supply for oil is very low. Substitutes are limited for oil-based products—such as gasoline—so the price elasticity of demand for oil is also low.

As the following graph shows, the combination of inelastic supply and inelastic demand results in shifts in supply causing large changes in price. In the graph, a reduction in supply that shifts the market supply curve from $S_1$ to $S_2$ causes the equilibrium quantity of oil to fall only by 5 percent, from 80 million barrels per day to 76 million, but the equilibrium price rises by 22 percent, from $40 per barrel to $50 per barrel.

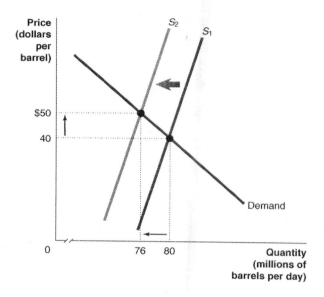

The world oil market is heavily influenced by the Organization of Petroleum Exporting Countries (OPEC). OPEC has 11 members, including Saudi Arabia, Kuwait, and other Arab countries, as well as Iran, Venezuela, Nigeria, and Indonesia. Together these countries own 75 percent of the world's proven oil reserves. Periodically, OPEC has attempted to force up the price of oil by reducing the quantity of oil its members supply. As we will discuss further in Chapter 13, since the 1970s, the attempts by OPEC to reduce the quantity of oil on world markets have been successful only sporadically: Periods during which OPEC members cooperate and reduce supply alternate with periods in which the members fail to cooperate and supply increases. As a result, the supply curve for oil shifts fairly frequently. Combined with the low price elasticities of oil supply and demand, these shifts in supply have caused the price of oil to fluctuate significantly over the past 30 years, from as low as $11 per barrel to more than $75 per barrel.

Over longer periods of time, higher oil prices also lead to greater increases in the quantity supplied; in other words, the price elasticity of supply for oil increases. This increase happens because higher prices increase the economic incentive to explore for oil and to recover oil from more costly sources, such as under the oceans, in the Arctic, or at greater depths in the earth. When supply is more elastic, a given shift in supply results in a smaller increase in price. This effect is illustrated in the following graph. Compared with the preceding graph, the same decrease in supply increases the equilibrium price to $45 per barrel rather than $50 per barrel (and also causes a smaller decrease in the equilibrium quantity).

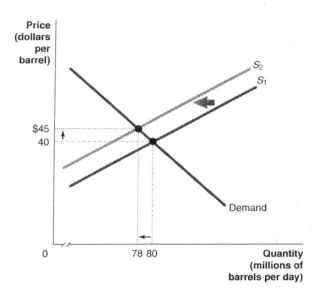

## Polar Cases of Perfectly Elastic and Perfectly Inelastic Supply

Although it occurs infrequently, it is possible for supply to fall into one of the polar cases of price elasticity. If a supply curve is a vertical line, it is *perfectly inelastic*. In this case, the quantity supplied is completely unresponsive to price, and the price elasticity of supply equals zero. However much price may increase or decrease, the quantity remains the same. Over a brief period of time, the supply of some goods and services may be perfectly inelastic. For example, a parking lot may have only a fixed number of parking spaces. If demand increases, the price to park in the lot may rise, but no more spaces will become available. Of course, if demand increases permanently, over a longer period of time, the owner of the lot may buy more land to add additional spaces.

If a supply curve is a horizontal line, it is *perfectly elastic*. In this case, the quantity supplied is infinitely responsive to price, and the price elasticity of supply equals infinity. If a supply curve is perfectly elastic, a very small increase in price causes a very large increase in quantity supplied. Just as with demand curves, it is important not to confuse a supply curve being elastic with its being perfectly elastic and not to confuse a supply curve being inelastic with its being perfectly inelastic. Table 6-5 summarizes the different price elasticities of supply.

## Using Price Elasticity of Supply to Predict Changes in Price

Figure 6-5 illustrates the important point that, when demand increases, the amount that price increases depends on the price elasticity of supply. The figure shows the demand and supply for parking spaces at a beach resort. In panel (a), on a typical summer weekend, equilibrium occurs at point *A*, where Demand (typical) intersects a supply curve that is inelastic. The increase in demand for parking spaces on the Fourth of July shifts the demand curve to the right, moving the equilibrium to point *B*. Because the supply curve is inelastic, the increase in demand results in a large increase in price—from $2.00 per hour to $4.00—but only a small increase in the quantity of spaces supplied—from 1,200 to 1,400.

In panel (b), supply is elastic, perhaps because the resort has vacant land that can be used for parking during periods of high demand. As a result, the shift in equilibrium from point A to point B results in a smaller increase in price and a larger increase in the quantity supplied. An increase in price from $2.00 per hour to $2.50 is sufficient to increase the quantity of parking supplied from 1,200 to 2,100. Knowing the price elasticity of supply makes it possible to predict more accurately how much price will change following an increase or a decrease in demand.

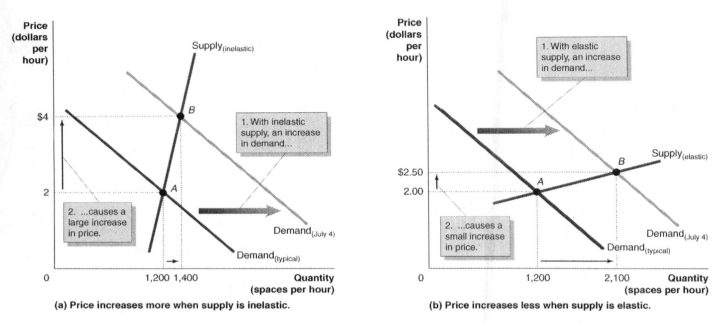

(a) Price increases more when supply is inelastic.

(b) Price increases less when supply is elastic.

**Figure 6-5** | Changes in Price Depend on the Price Elasticity of Supply

In panel (a), Demand (typical) represents the typical demand for parking spaces on a summer weekend at a beach resort. Demand (July 4) represents demand on the Fourth of July. Because supply is inelastic, the shift in equilibrium from point A to point B results in a large increase in price—from $2.00 per hour to $4.00—but only a small increase in the quantity of spaces supplied—from 1,200 to 1,400. In panel (b),

supply is elastic. As a result, the shift in equilibrium from point A to point B results in a smaller increase in price and a larger increase in the quantity supplied. An increase in price from $2.00 per hour to $2.50 is sufficient to increase the quantity of parking supplied from 1,200 to 2,100.

| IF SUPPLY IS... | THEN THE VALUE OF PRICE ELASTICITY IS |
| --- | --- |

Table 6-5

**Summary of the Price Elasticities of Supply**

(Note that the percentage increases shown in the boxes in the graphs were calculated using the midpoint formula on page 176.)

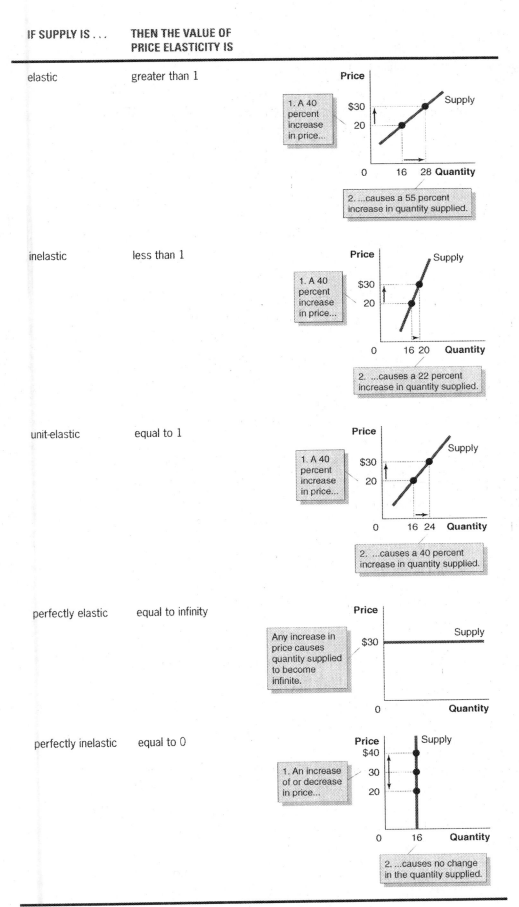

elastic — greater than 1

1. A 40 percent increase in price...

2. ...causes a 55 percent increase in quantity supplied.

inelastic — less than 1

1. A 40 percent increase in price...

2. ...causes a 22 percent increase in quantity supplied.

unit-elastic — equal to 1

1. A 40 percent increase in price...

2. ...causes a 40 percent increase in quantity supplied.

perfectly elastic — equal to infinity

Any increase in price causes quantity supplied to become infinite.

perfectly inelastic — equal to 0

1. An increase of or decrease in price...

2. ...causes no change in the quantity supplied.

## Conclusion

In this chapter, we have explored the important concept of elasticity. Table 6-6 summarizes the various elasticities we discussed in this chapter. Computing elasticities is important in economics because it allows us to measure how one variable changes in response to changes in another variable. For example, by calculating the price elasticity of demand for its product, a firm can make a quantitative estimate of the effect of a price change on the revenue it receives. Similarly, by calculating the price elasticity of demand for cigarettes, the government can better estimate the effect of an increase in cigarette taxes on smoking.

## PRICE ELASTICITY OF DEMAND

TABLE 6-6

**Summary of Elasticities**

$$\text{Formula: } \frac{\text{Percentage change in quantity demanded}}{\text{Percentage change in price}}$$

$$\text{Midpoint Formula: } \frac{(Q_2 - Q_1)}{\left(\dfrac{Q_1 + Q_2}{2}\right)} \div \frac{(P_2 - P_1)}{\left(\dfrac{P_1 + P_2}{2}\right)}$$

| | ABSOLUTE VALUE OF PRICE ELASTICITY | EFFECT ON TOTAL REVENUE OF AN INCREASE IN PRICE |
|---|---|---|
| Elastic | Greater than 1 | Total revenue falls |
| Inelastic | Less than 1 | Total revenue rises |
| Unit elastic | Equal to 1 | Total revenue unchanged |

## CROSS-PRICE ELASTICITY OF DEMAND

$$\text{Formula: } \frac{\text{Percentage change in quantity demanded of one good}}{\text{Percentage change in price of another good}}$$

| TYPES OF PRODUCTS | VALUE OF CROSS-PRICE ELASTICITY |
|---|---|
| Substitutes | Positive |
| Complements | Negative |
| Unrelated | Zero |

## INCOME ELASTICITY OF DEMAND

$$\text{Formula: } \frac{\text{Percentage change in quantity demanded}}{\text{Percentage change in income}}$$

| TYPES OF PRODUCTS | VALUE OF INCOME ELASTICITY |
|---|---|
| Normal and a necessity | Positive but less than 1 |
| Normal and a luxury | Positive and greater than 1 |
| Inferior | Negative |

## PRICE ELASTICITY OF SUPPLY

$$\text{Formula: } \frac{\text{Percentage change in quantity supplied}}{\text{Percentage change in price}}$$

| | VALUE OF PRICE ELASTICITY |
|---|---|
| Elastic | Greater than 1 |
| Inelastic | Less than 1 |
| Unit elastic | Equal to 1 |

# Chapter 6
# Behavioral Economics

We begin this chapter by exploring how consumers make decisions. In Chapter 1, we saw that economists usually assume that people act in a rational, self-interested way. In explaining consumer behavior, this means economists believe consumers make choices that will leave them as satisfied as possible, given their *tastes*, their *incomes*, and the *prices* of the goods and services available to them. We will see how the downward-sloping demand curves we encountered in Chapters 3 through 5 result from the economic model of consumer behavior. We will also see that in certain situations, knowing the best decision to make can be difficult. In these cases, economic reasoning provides a powerful tool for consumers to improve their decision making. Finally, we will see that *experimental economics* has shown that factors such as social pressure and notions of fairness can affect consumer behavior. We will look at how businesses take these factors into account when setting prices. In the appendix to this chapter, we extend the analysis by using indifference curves and budget lines to understand consumer behavior.

9.1 | Define utility and explain how consumers choose goods and services to maximize their utility.

# Utility and Consumer Decision Making

We saw in Chapter 3 that the model of demand and supply is a powerful tool for analyzing how prices and quantities are determined. We also saw that, according to the *law of demand*, whenever the price of a good falls, the quantity demanded increases. In this section, we will show how the economic model of consumer behavior leads to the law of demand.

## The Economic Model of Consumer Behavior in a Nutshell

Imagine walking through a shopping mall, trying to decide how to spend your clothing budget. If you had an unlimited budget, your decision would be easy: Just buy as much of everything as you want. Given that you have a limited budget, what do you do? Economists assume that consumers act so as to make themselves as well off as possible. Therefore, you should choose the one combination of clothes that makes you as well off as possible from among those combinations that you can afford. Stated more generally, the economic model of consumer behavior predicts that consumers will choose to buy the combination of goods and services that makes them as well off as possible from among all the combinations that their budgets allow them to buy.

This prediction may seem obvious and not particularly useful. But as we explore the implication of this prediction, we will see that it leads to conclusions that are both useful and not obvious.

## Utility

Ultimately, how well off you are from consuming a particular combination of goods and services depends on your tastes, or preferences. There is an old saying—"There's no accounting for tastes"—and economists don't try to. If you buy Cherry Coke instead of Pepsi, even though Pepsi has a lower price, you must receive more enjoyment or satisfaction from drinking Cherry Coke. Economists refer to the enjoyment or satisfaction people receive from consuming goods and services as **utility**. So we can say that the goal of a consumer is to spend available income so as to maximize utility. But utility is a difficult concept to measure because there is no way of knowing exactly how much enjoyment or satisfaction someone receives from consuming a product. Similarly, it is not possible to compare utility across consumers. There is no way of knowing for sure whether Jill receives more or less satisfaction than Jack from drinking a bottle of Cherry Coke.

**Utility** The enjoyment or satisfaction people receive from consuming goods and services.

Two hundred years ago, economists hoped to measure utility in units called "utils." The util would be an objective measure in the same way that temperature is: If it is 70 degrees in New York and 70 degrees in Los Angeles, it is just as warm in both cities. These economists wanted to say that if Jack's utility from eating a hamburger is 10 utils and Jill's utility is 5 utils, then Jack receives exactly twice the satisfaction from eating a hamburger that Jill does. In fact, it is *not* possible to measure utility across people. It turns out that none of the important conclusions of the economic model of consumer behavior depend on utility being directly measurable (a point we demonstrate in the appendix to this chapter). Nevertheless, the economic model of consumer behavior is easier to understand if we assume that utility is something directly measurable, like temperature.

## The Principle of Diminishing Marginal Utility

To make the model of consumer behavior more concrete, let's see how a consumer makes decisions in a case involving just two products: pepperoni pizza and Coke. To begin, consider how the utility you receive from consuming a good changes with the amount of the good you consume. For example, suppose that you have just arrived at a Super Bowl party where the hosts are serving pepperoni pizza, and you are very hungry. In this situation, you are likely to receive quite a lot of enjoyment, or utility, from consuming the first slice of pizza. Suppose this satisfaction is measurable and is equal to 20 units of utility, or *utils*. After eating the first slice, you decide to have a second slice. Because you are no longer as hungry, the satisfaction you receive from eating the second slice of pizza is less than the satisfaction you received from eating the first slice. Consuming the second slice increases your utility by only an *additional* 16 utils, which raises your *total* utility from eating the two slices to 36 utils. If you continue eating slices, each additional slice gives you less and less additional satisfaction.

The table in Figure 9-1 shows the relationship between the number of slices of pizza you consume while watching the Super Bowl and the amount of utility you receive. The second column in the table shows the total utility you receive from eating a particular number of slices. The third column shows the additional utility, or **marginal utility** (*MU*), you receive from consuming one additional slice. (Remember that in economics, "marginal" means additional.) For example, as you increase your consumption from 2 slices to 3 slices, your total utility increases from 36 to 46, so your marginal utility from consuming the third slice is 10 utils. As the table shows, by the time you eat the fifth slice of pizza that evening, your marginal utility is very low: only 2 utils. If you were to eat a sixth slice, you would become slightly nauseated, and your marginal utility would actually be a *negative* 3 utils.

Figure 9-1 also plots the numbers from the table as graphs. Panel (a) shows how your total utility rises as you eat the first five slices of pizza and then falls as you eat the sixth slice. Panel (b) shows how your marginal utility declines with each additional slice you eat and finally becomes negative when you eat the sixth slice. The height of the marginal utility line at any quantity of pizza in panel (b) represents the change in utility as a result of consuming that additional slice. For example, the change in utility as a result of consuming 4 slices instead of 3 is 6 utils, so the height of the marginal utility line in panel (b) is 6 utils.

The relationship illustrated in Figure 9-1 between consuming additional units of a product during a period of time and the marginal utility received from consuming each additional unit is referred to as the **law of diminishing marginal utility**. For nearly every good or service, the more you consume during a period of time, the less you increase your total satisfaction from each additional unit you consume.

**Marginal utility (*MU*)** The change in total utility a person receives from consuming one additional unit of a good or service.

**Law of diminishing marginal utility** The principle that consumers experience diminishing additional satisfaction as they consume more of a good or service during a given period of time.

## The Rule of Equal Marginal Utility per Dollar Spent

The key challenge for consumers is to decide how to allocate their limited incomes among all the products they wish to buy. Every consumer has to make trade-offs: If you have $100 to spend on entertainment for the month, then the more DVDs you buy, the

# Figure 9-1

**Total and Marginal Utility from Eating Pizza on Super Bowl Sunday**

The table shows that for the first 5 slices of pizza, the more you eat, the more your total satisfaction or utility increases. If you eat a sixth slice, you start to feel ill from eating too much pizza, and your total utility falls. Each additional slice increases your utility by less than the previous slice, so your marginal utility from each slice is less than the one before. Panel (a) shows your total utility rising as you eat the first 5 slices and falling with the sixth slice. Panel (b) shows your marginal utility falling with each additional slice you eat and becoming negative with the sixth slice. The height of the marginal utility line at any quantity of pizza in panel (b) represents the change in utility as a result of consuming that additional slice. For example, the change in utility as a result of consuming 4 slices instead of 3 is 6 utils, so the height of the marginal utility line in panel (b) for the fourth slice is 6 utils.

| Number of Slices | Total Utility from Eating Pizza | Marginal Utility from the Last Slice Eaten |
|---|---|---|
| 0 | 0 | -- |
| 1 | 20 | 20 |
| 2 | 36 | 16 |
| 3 | 46 | 10 |
| 4 | 52 | 6 |
| 5 | 54 | 2 |
| 6 | 51 | -3 |

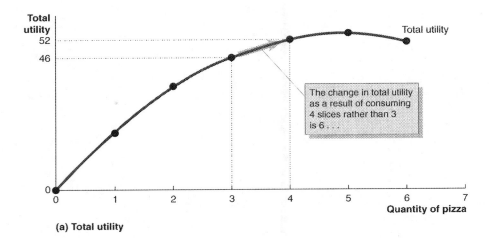

The change in total utility as a result of consuming 4 slices rather than 3 is 6 . . .

**(a) Total utility**

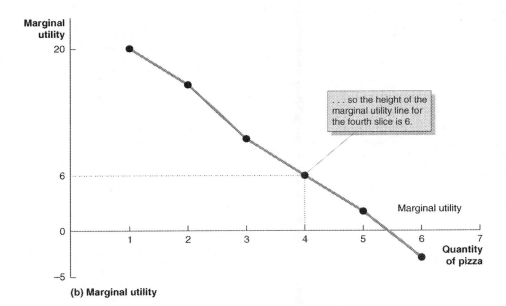

. . . so the height of the marginal utility line for the fourth slice is 6.

**(b) Marginal utility**

fewer movies you can see in the theater. Economists refer to the limited amount of income you have available to spend on goods and services as your **budget constraint.** The principle of diminishing marginal utility helps us understand how consumers can best spend their limited incomes on the products available to them.

Suppose you attend a Super Bowl party at a restaurant, and you have $10 to spend on refreshments. Pizza is selling for $2 per slice, and Coke is selling for $1 per cup. Table 9-1 shows the relationship between the amount of pizza you eat, the amount of Coke you drink, and the amount of satisfaction, or utility, you receive. The values for pizza are repeated from the table in Figure 9-1. The values for Coke also follow the principle of diminishing marginal utility.

How many slices of pizza and how many cups of Coke do you buy if you want to maximize your utility? If you did not have a budget constraint, you would buy 5 slices of pizza and 5 cups of Coke because that would give you total utility of 107 (54 + 53), which is the maximum utility you can achieve. Eating another slice of pizza or drinking another cup of Coke during the evening would lower your utility. Unfortunately, you do have a budget constraint: You have only $10 to spend. To buy 5 slices of pizza (at $2 per slice) and 5 cups of Coke (at $1 per cup), you would need $15.

To select the best way to spend your $10, remember this key economic principle: *Optimal decisions are made at the margin.* That is, most of the time, economic decision makers—consumers, firms, and the government—are faced with decisions about whether to do a little more of one thing or a little more of an alternative. In this case, you are choosing to consume a little more pizza or a little more Coke. BMW chooses to manufacture more roadsters or more SUVs in its South Carolina factory. Congress and the president choose to spend more for research on heart disease or more for research on breast cancer. Every economic decision maker faces a budget constraint, and every economic decision maker faces trade-offs.

The key to making the best consumption decision is to maximize utility by following the *rule of equal marginal utility per dollar spent.* As you decide how to spend your income, you should buy pizza and Coke up to the point where the last slice of pizza purchased and the last cup of Coke purchased give you equal increases in utility *per dollar.* By doing this, you will have maximized your total utility.

It is important to remember that to follow this rule, you must equalize your marginal utility per dollar spent, *not* your marginal utility from each good. Buying season tickets for your favorite NFL team or for the opera or buying a BMW may give you a lot more satisfaction than drinking a cup of Coke, but the NFL tickets may well give you less

**Budget constraint** The limited amount of income available to consumers to spend on goods and services.

TABLE 9-1 | **Total Utility and Marginal Utility from Eating Pizza and Drinking Coke**

| NUMBER OF SLICES OF PIZZA | TOTAL UTILITY FROM EATING PIZZA | MARGINAL UTILITY FROM THE LAST SLICE | NUMBER OF CUPS OF COKE | TOTAL UTILITY FROM DRINKING COKE | MARGINAL UTILITY FROM THE LAST CUP |
|---|---|---|---|---|---|
| 0 | 0 | — | 0 | 0 | — |
| 1 | 20 | 20 | 1 | 20 | 20 |
| 2 | 36 | 16 | 2 | 35 | 15 |
| 3 | 46 | 10 | 3 | 45 | 10 |
| 4 | 52 | 6 | 4 | 50 | 5 |
| 5 | 54 | 2 | 5 | 53 | 3 |
| 6 | 51 | −3 | 6 | 52 | −1 |

TABLE 9-2 | **Converting Marginal Utility to Marginal Utility per Dollar**

| (1)<br>SLICES<br>OF PIZZA | (2)<br>MARGINAL UTILITY<br>($MU_{PIZZA}$) | (3)<br>MARGINAL UTILITY<br>PER DOLLAR<br>$\left(\dfrac{MU_{pizza}}{P_{pizza}}\right)$ | (4)<br>CUPS<br>OF COKE | (5)<br>MARGINAL UTILITY<br>($MU_{COKE}$) | (6)<br>MARGINAL UTILITY<br>PER DOLLAR<br>$\left(\dfrac{MU_{Coke}}{P_{Coke}}\right)$ |
|---|---|---|---|---|---|
| 1 | 20 | 10 | 1 | 20 | 20 |
| 2 | 16 | 8 | 2 | 15 | 15 |
| 3 | 10 | 5 | 3 | 10 | 10 |
| 4 | 6 | 3 | 4 | 5 | 5 |
| 5 | 2 | 1 | 5 | 3 | 3 |
| 6 | –3 | –1.5 | 6 | –1 | –1 |

satisfaction *per dollar* spent. To decide how many slices of pizza and how many cups of Coke to buy, you must convert the values for marginal utility in Table 9-1 into marginal utility per dollar. You can do this by dividing marginal utility by the price of each good, as shown in Table 9-2.

In column (3), we calculate marginal utility per dollar spent on pizza. Because the price of pizza is $2 per slice, the marginal utility per dollar from eating one slice of pizza equals 20 divided by $2, or 10 utils per dollar. Similarly, we show in column (6) that because the price of Coke is $1 per cup, the marginal utility per dollar from drinking 1 cup of Coke equals 20 divided by $1, or 20 utils per dollar. To maximize the total utility you receive, you must make sure that the utility per dollar of pizza for the last slice of pizza is equal to the utility per dollar of Coke for the last cup of Coke. Table 9-2 shows that there are three combinations of slices of pizza and cups of Coke where marginal utility per dollar is equalized. Table 9-3 lists the combinations, the total amount of money needed to buy each combination, and the total utility received from consuming each combination.

If you buy 4 slices of pizza, the last slice gives you 3 utils per dollar. If you buy 5 cups of Coke, the last cup also gives you 3 utils per dollar, so you have equalized your marginal utility per dollar. Unfortunately, as the third column in the table shows, to buy 4 slices and 5 cups, you would need $13, and you have only $10. You could also equalize your marginal utility per dollar by buying 1 slice and 3 cups, but that would cost just $5, leaving you with $5 to spend. Only when you buy 3 slices and 4 cups have you equalized your marginal utility per dollar and spent neither more nor less than the $10 available.

TABLE 9-3 | **Equalizing Marginal Utility per Dollar Spent**

| COMBINATIONS OF PIZZA AND COKE<br>WITH EQUAL MARGINAL UTILITIES<br>PER DOLLAR | MARGINAL UTILITY PER DOLLAR<br>(MARGINAL UTILITY/PRICE) | TOTAL SPENDING | TOTAL UTILITY |
|---|---|---|---|
| 1 slice of pizza and 3 cups of Coke | 10 | $2 + $3 = $5 | 20 + 45 = 65 |
| 3 slices of pizza and 4 cups of Coke | 5 | $6 + $4 = $10 | 46 + 50 = 96 |
| 4 slices of pizza and 5 cups of Coke | 3 | $8 + $5 = $13 | 52 + 53 = 105 |

We can summarize the two conditions for maximizing utility:

1 $\dfrac{MU_{Pizza}}{P_{Pizza}} = \dfrac{MU_{Coke}}{P_{Coke}}$

2 Spending on pizza + Spending on Coke = Amount available to be spent

The first condition shows that the marginal utility per dollar spent must be the same for both goods. The second condition is the budget constraint, which states that total spending on both goods must equal the amount available to be spent. Of course, these conditions for maximizing utility apply not just to pizza and Coke but to any two pairs of goods.

# Solved Problem | 9-1

## Finding the Optimal Level of Consumption

The following table shows Lee's utility from consuming ice cream cones and cans of Lime Fizz soda.

| NUMBER OF ICE CREAM CONES | TOTAL UTILITY FROM ICE CREAM CONES | MARGINAL UTILITY FROM LAST CONE | NUMBER OF CANS OF LIME FIZZ | TOTAL UTILITY FROM CANS OF LIME FIZZ | MARGINAL UTILITY FROM LAST CAN |
|---|---|---|---|---|---|
| 0 | 0 | ---- | 0 | 0 | ---- |
| 1 | 30 | 30 | 1 | 40 | 40 |
| 2 | 55 | 25 | 2 | 75 | 35 |
| 3 | 75 | 20 | 3 | 101 | 26 |
| 4 | 90 | 15 | 4 | 119 | 18 |
| 5 | 100 | 10 | 5 | 134 | 15 |
| 6 | 105 | 5 | 6 | 141 | 7 |

a. Ed inspects this table and concludes, "Lee's optimal choice would be to consume 4 ice cream cones and 5 cans of Lime Fizz because with that combination, his marginal utility from ice cream cones is equal to his marginal utility from Lime Fizz." Do you agree with Ed's reasoning? Briefly explain.

b. Suppose that Lee has an unlimited budget to spend on ice cream cones and cans of Lime Fizz. Under these circumstances, how many ice cream cones and how many cans of Lime Fizz will he consume?

c. Suppose that Lee has $7 per week to spend on ice cream cones and Lime Fizz. The price of an ice cream cone is $2, and the price of a can of Lime Fizz is $1. If Lee wants to maximize his utility, how many ice cream cones and how many cans of Lime Fizz should he buy?

## SOLVING THE PROBLEM:

**Step 1: Review the chapter material.** This problem involves finding the optimal consumption of two goods, so you may want to review the section "The Rule of Equal Marginal Utility per Dollar Spent," which begins on page 287.

**Step 2: Answer question (a) by analyzing Ed's reasoning.** Ed's reasoning is incorrect. To maximize utility, Lee needs to equalize marginal utility per dollar for the two goods.

**Step 3:** **Answer question (b) by determining how Lee would maximize utility with an unlimited budget.** With an unlimited budget, consumers maximize utility by continuing to buy each good as long as their utility is increasing. In this case, Lee will maximize utility by buying 6 ice cream cones and 6 cans of Lime Fizz.

**Step 4:** **Answer question (c) by determining Lee's optimal combination of ice cream cones and cans of Lime Fizz.** Lee will maximize his utility if he spends his $7 per week so that the marginal utility of ice cream cones divided by the price of ice cream cones is equal to the marginal utility of Lime Fizz divided by the price of Lime Fizz. We can use the following table to solve this part of the problem:

| QUANTITY | ICE CREAM CONES | | CANS OF LIME FIZZ | |
|---|---|---|---|---|
| | MU | $\frac{MU}{P}$ | MU | $\frac{MU}{P}$ |
| 1 | 30 | 15 | 40 | 40 |
| 2 | 25 | 12.5 | 35 | 35 |
| 3 | 20 | 10 | 26 | 26 |
| 4 | 15 | 7.5 | 18 | 18 |
| 5 | 10 | 5 | 15 | 15 |
| 6 | 5 | 2.5 | 7 | 7 |

Lee will maximize his utility by buying 1 ice cream cone and 5 cans of Lime Fizz. At this combination, the marginal utility of each good divided by its price equals 15. He has also spent all of his $7.

>> **End Solved Problem 9-1**

## What if the Rule of Equal Marginal Utility per Dollar Does Not Hold?

The idea of getting the maximum utility by equalizing the ratio of marginal utility to price for the goods you are buying can be difficult to grasp, so it is worth thinking about in another way. Suppose that instead of buying 3 slices of pizza and 4 cups of Coke, you buy 4 slices and 2 cups. Four slices and 2 cups cost $10, so you would meet your budget constraint by spending all the money available to you, but would you have gotten the maximum amount of utility? No, you wouldn't have. From the information in Table 9-1, we can list the additional utility per dollar you are getting from the last slice and the last cup and the total utility from consuming 4 slices and 2 cups:

Marginal utility per dollar for the fourth slice of pizza = 3 utils per dollar

Marginal utility per dollar for the second cup of Coke = 15 utils per dollar

Total utility from 4 slices of pizza and 2 cups of Coke = 87 utils

Obviously, the marginal utilities per dollar are not equal. The last cup of Coke gave you considerably more satisfaction per dollar than did the last slice of pizza. You could raise your total utility by buying less pizza and more Coke. Buying 1 less slice of pizza frees up $2 that will allow you to buy 2 more cups of Coke. Eating 1 less slice of pizza reduces your utility by 6 utils, but drinking 2 additional cups of Coke raises your utility by 15 utils (make sure you see this), for a net increase of 9. You end up equalizing your marginal utility per dollar (5 utils per dollar for both the last slice and the last cup) and raising your total utility from 87 utils to 96 utils.

# Don't Let This Happen to **YOU!**

## Equalize Marginal Utilities *per Dollar*

Consider the information in the following table, which gives Harry's utility from buying CDs and DVDs.

**HARRY'S UTILITY FROM BUYING CDS AND DVDS**

| QUANTITY OF CDs | TOTAL UTILITY FROM CDs | MARGINAL UTILITY FROM LAST CD | QUANTITY OF DVDs | TOTAL UTILITY FROM DVDs | MARGINAL UTILITY FROM LAST DVD |
|---|---|---|---|---|---|
| 0 | 0 | — | 0 | 0 | — |
| 1 | 50 | 50 | 1 | 60 | 60 |
| 2 | 85 | 35 | 2 | 105 | 45 |
| 3 | 110 | 25 | 3 | 145 | 40 |
| 4 | 130 | 20 | 4 | 175 | 30 |
| 5 | 140 | 10 | 5 | 195 | 20 |
| 6 | 145 | 5 | 6 | 210 | 15 |

Can you determine from this information the optimal combination of CDs and DVDs for Harry? It is very tempting to say that Harry should buy 4 CDs and 5 DVDs because his marginal utility from CDs is equal to his marginal utility from DVDs with that combination. In fact, we can't be sure this is the best combination because we are lacking some critical information: Harry's budget constraint—how much he has available to spend on CDs and DVDs—and the prices of CDs and DVDs.

Let's say that Harry has $100 to spend this month, the price of CDs is $10, and the price of DVDs is $20. Using the information from the first table, we can now calculate Harry's marginal utility per dollar for both goods, as shown in the following table.

**HARRY'S MARGINAL UTILITY AND MARGINAL UTILITY PER DOLLAR FROM BUYING CDS AND DVDS**

| QUANTITY OF CDs | MARGINAL UTILITY FROM LAST CD ($MU_{CD}$) | MARGINAL UTILITY PER DOLLAR ($\frac{MU_{CD}}{P_{CD}}$) | QUANTITY OF DVDs | MARGINAL UTILITY FROM LAST DVD ($MU_{DVD}$) | MARGINAL UTILITY PER DOLLAR ($\frac{MU_{DVD}}{P_{DVD}}$) |
|---|---|---|---|---|---|
| 1 | 50 | 5 | 1 | 60 | 3 |
| 2 | 35 | 3.5 | 2 | 45 | 2.25 |
| 3 | 25 | 2.5 | 3 | 40 | 2 |
| 4 | 20 | 2 | 4 | 30 | 1.5 |
| 5 | 10 | 1 | 5 | 20 | 1 |
| 6 | 5 | 0.5 | 6 | 15 | 0.75 |

Harry's marginal utility per dollar is the same for two combinations of CDs and DVDs, as shown in the following table.

| COMBINATIONS OF CDs AND DVDs WITH EQUAL MARGINAL UTILITIES PER DOLLAR | MARGINAL UTILITY PER DOLLAR (MARGINAL UTILITY/PRICE) | TOTAL SPENDING | TOTAL UTILITY |
|---|---|---|---|
| 5 CDs and 5 DVDs | 1 | $50 + $100 = $150 | 140 + 195 = 335 |
| 4 CDs and 3 DVDs | 2 | $40 + $60 = $100 | 130 + 145 = 275 |

Unfortunately, 5 CDs and 5 DVDs would cost Harry $150, and he has only $100. The best Harry can do is to buy 4 CDs and 3 DVDs. This combination provides him with the maximum amount of utility attainable, given his budget constraint.

The key point, which we also saw in Solved Problem 9-1, is that consumers maximize their utility when they equalize marginal utility *per dollar* for every good they buy, not when they equalize marginal utility.

# The Income Effect and Substitution Effect of a Price Change

We can use the rule of equal marginal utility per dollar to analyze how consumers adjust their buying decisions when a price changes. Suppose you are back at the restaurant for the Super Bowl party, but this time the price of pizza is $1.50 per slice, rather than $2. You still have $10 to spend on pizza and Coke.

When the price of pizza was $2 per slice and the price of Coke was $1 per cup, your optimal choice was to consume 3 slices of pizza and 4 cups of Coke. The fall in the price of pizza to $1.50 per slice has two effects on the quantity of pizza you consume: the *income effect* and the *substitution effect*. First, consider the income effect. When the price of a good falls, you have more purchasing power. In our example, 3 slices of pizza and 4 cups of Coke now cost a total of only $8.50 instead of $10.00. An increase in purchasing power is essentially the same thing as an increase in income. The change in the quantity of pizza you will demand because of this increase in purchasing power—holding all other factors constant— is the **income effect** of the price change. Recall from Chapter 3 that if a product is a *normal good*, a consumer increases the quantity demanded as the consumer's income rises, but if a product is an *inferior good*, a consumer decreases the quantity demanded as the consumer's income rises. So, if we assume that for you pizza is a normal good, the income effect of a fall in price causes you to consume more pizza. If pizza had been an inferior good for you, the income effect of a fall in the price would have caused you to consume less pizza.

The second effect of the price change is the substitution effect. When the price of pizza falls, pizza becomes cheaper *relative* to Coke, and the marginal utility per dollar for each slice of pizza you consume increases. If we hold constant the effect of the price change on your purchasing power and just focus on the effect of the price being lower relative to the price of the other good, we have isolated the **substitution effect** of the price change. The lower price of pizza relative to the price of Coke has lowered the *opportunity cost* to you of consuming pizza because now you have to give up less Coke to consume the same quantity of pizza. Therefore, the substitution effect from the fall in the price of pizza relative to the price of Coke will cause you to eat more pizza and drink less Coke. In this case, both the income effect and the substitution effect of the fall in price cause you to eat more pizza. If the price of pizza had risen, both the income effect and the substitution effect would have caused you to eat less pizza. Table 9-4 summarizes the effect of a price change on the quantity demanded.

We can use Table 9-5 to determine the effect of the fall in the price of pizza on your optimal consumption. Table 9-5 has the same information as Table 9-2, with one change: The marginal utility per dollar from eating pizza has been changed to reflect the new lower price of $1.50 per slice. Examining the table, we can see that the fall in the price of pizza will result in your eating 1 more slice of pizza, so your optimal consumption now becomes 4 slices of pizza and 4 cups of Coke. You will be spending all of your $10, and the last dollar you spend on pizza will provide you with about the same marginal utility per dollar as the last dollar you spend on Coke. You will not be receiving

**Income effect** The change in the quantity demanded of a good that results from the effect of a change in price on consumer purchasing power, holding all other factors constant.

**Substitution effect** The change in the quantity demanded of a good that results from a change in price making the good more or less expensive relative to other goods, holding constant the effect of the price change on consumer purchasing power.

## TABLE 9-4

**Income Effect and Substitution Effect of a Price Change**

| | | INCOME EFFECT | | SUBSTITUTION EFFECT |
|---|---|---|---|---|
| **PRICE DECREASE** | Increases the consumer's purchasing power, which . . . | . . . if a normal good, causes the quantity demanded to increase. | . . . if an inferior good, causes the quantity demanded to decrease. | Lowers the opportunity cost of consuming the good, which causes the quantity of the good demanded to increase. |
| **PRICE INCREASE** | Decreases the consumer's purchasing power, which . . . | . . . if a normal good, causes the quantity demanded to decrease. | . . . if an inferior good, causes the quantity demanded to increase. | Raises the opportunity cost of consuming the good, which causes the quantity of the good demanded to decrease. |

TABLE 9-5 | **Adjusting Optimal Consumption to a Lower Price of Pizza**

| NUMBER OF SLICES OF PIZZA | MARGINAL UTILITY FROM LAST SLICE ($MU_{PIZZA}$) | MARGINAL UTILITY PER DOLLAR $\left(\dfrac{MU_{Pizza}}{P_{Pizza}}\right)$ | NUMBER OF CUPS OF COKE | MARGINAL UTILITY FROM LAST CUP ($MU_{COKE}$) | MARGINAL UTILITY PER DOLLAR $\left(\dfrac{MU_{Coke}}{P_{Coke}}\right)$ |
|---|---|---|---|---|---|
| 1 | 20 | 13.33 | 1 | 20 | 20 |
| 2 | 16 | 10.67 | 2 | 15 | 15 |
| 3 | 10 | 6.67 | 3 | 10 | 10 |
| 4 | 6 | 4 | 4 | 5 | 5 |
| 5 | 2 | 1.33 | 5 | 3 | 3 |
| 6 | −3 | — | 6 | −1 | — |

exactly the same marginal utility per dollar spent on the two products. As Table 9-5 shows, the last slice of pizza gives you 4 utils per dollar, and the last cup of Coke gives you 5 utils per dollar. But this is as close as you can come to equalizing marginal utility per dollar for the two products, unless you can buy a fraction of a slice of pizza or a fraction of a cup of Coke.

9.2 | Use the concept of utility to explain the law of demand.

# Where Demand Curves Come From

We saw in Chapter 3 that, according to the *law of demand*, whenever the price of a product falls, the quantity demanded increases. Now that we have covered the concepts of total utility, marginal utility, and the budget constraint, we can look more closely at why the law of demand holds.

In our example of optimal consumption of pizza and Coke at the Super Bowl party, we found the following:

> Price of pizza = $2 per slice ⇒ Quantity of pizza demanded = 3 slices
>
> Price of pizza = $1.50 per slice ⇒ Quantity of pizza demanded = 4 slices

In panel (a) of Figure 9-2, we plot the two points showing the optimal number of pizza slices you choose to consume at each price. In panel (b) of Figure 9-2, we draw a line connecting the two points. This downward-sloping line represents your demand curve for pizza. We could find more points on the line by changing the price of pizza and using the information in Table 9-2 to find the new optimal number of slices of pizza you would demand at each price.

To this point in this chapter, we have been looking at an individual demand curve. As we saw in Chapter 3, however, economists are typically interested in market demand curves. We can construct the market demand curve from the individual demand curves for all the consumers in the market. To keep things simple, let's assume that there are only three consumers in the market for pizza: you, David, and Sharon. The table in Figure 9-3 shows the individual demand schedules for the three consumers. Because consumers differ in their incomes and their preferences for products, we would not expect every consumer to demand the same quantity of a given product at each price. The final column gives the market demand, which is simply the sum of the quantities demanded by each of the three consumers at each price. For example, at a price of $1.50 per slice, your quantity demanded is 4 slices, David's quantity demanded is 6 slices, and Sharon's quantity demanded is 5 slices. So, at a price of $1.50, a quantity of 15 slices is demanded in the market. The graphs in the figure show that we can obtain the market demand curve by adding horizontally the individual demand curves.

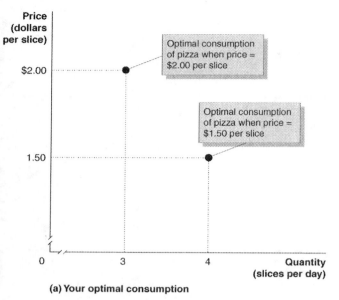

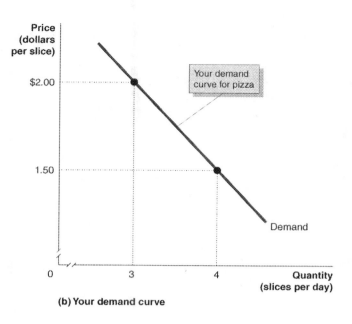

**(a) Your optimal consumption**

**(b) Your demand curve**

Figure 9-2 | Deriving the Demand Curve for Pizza

A consumer responds optimally to a fall in the price of a product by consuming more of that product. In panel (a), the price of pizza falls from $2 per slice to $1.50, and the optimal quantity of slices consumed rises from 3 to 4. When we graph this result in panel (b), we have the consumer's demand curve.

|  | Quantity (slices per day) | | | |
| Price (dollars per slice) | You | David | Sharon | Market |
| --- | --- | --- | --- | --- |
| $2.50 | 2 | 4 | 1 | 7 |
| 2.00 | 3 | 5 | 3 | 11 |
| 1.50 | 4 | 6 | 5 | 15 |
| 1.00 | 5 | 7 | 7 | 19 |
| 0.50 | 6 | 8 | 9 | 23 |

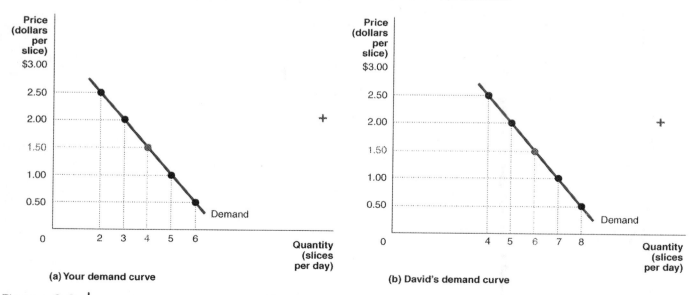

**(a) Your demand curve**

**(b) David's demand curve**

Figure 9-3 | Deriving the Market Demand Curve from Individual Demand Curves

The table shows that the total quantity demanded in a market is the sum of the quantities demanded by each buyer. We can find the market demand curve by adding horizontally the individual demand curves in parts (a), (b), and (c). For instance, at a price of $1.50, your quantity demanded is 4 slices, David's quantity demanded is 6 slices, and Sharon's quantity demanded is 5 slices. Therefore, part (d) shows a price of $1.50, and a quantity demanded of 15 is a point on the market demand curve.

Remember that according to the law of demand, market demand curves always slope downward. We now know that this is true because the income and substitution effects of a fall in price cause consumers to increase the quantity of the good they demand. There is a complicating factor, however. As we discussed earlier, only for normal goods will the income effect result in consumers increasing the quantity of the good they demand when the price falls. If the good is an inferior good, then the income effect leads consumers to *decrease* the quantity of the good they demand. The substitution effect, on the other hand, results in consumers increasing the quantity they demand of both normal and inferior goods when the price falls. So, when the price of an inferior good falls, the income and substitution effects work in opposite directions: The income effect causes consumers to decrease the quantity of the good they demand, whereas the substitution effect causes consumers to increase the quantity of the good they demand. Is it possible, then, that consumers might actually buy less of a good when the price falls? If this happened, the demand curve would be upward sloping.

For a demand curve to be upward sloping, the good would have to be an inferior good, and the income effect would have to be larger than the substitution effect. Goods that have both of these characteristics are called *Giffen goods.* Although we can conceive of there being Giffen goods, none has ever been discovered because for all actual goods, the substitution effect is larger than the income effect. Therefore, even for an inferior good, a fall in price leads to an increase in quantity demanded, and a rise in price leads to a decrease in the quantity demanded.

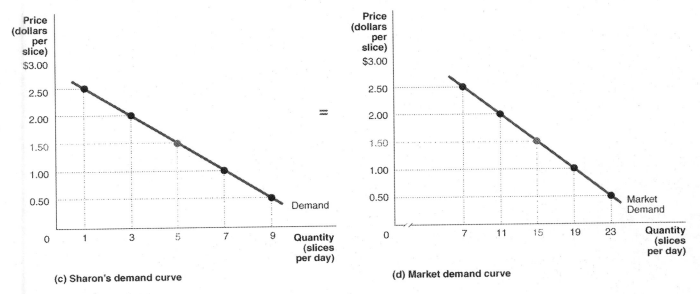

(c) Sharon's demand curve

(d) Market demand curve

Figure 9-3 | Continued

9.3 | Explain how social influences can affect consumption choices.

# Social Influences on Decision Making

Sociologists and anthropologists have argued that social factors such as culture, customs, and religion are very important in explaining the choices consumers make. Economists have traditionally seen such factors as being relatively unimportant, if they take them into consideration at all. Recently, however, some economists have begun to study how social factors influence consumer choice.

For example, people seem to receive more utility from consuming goods they believe are popular. As the economists Gary Becker and Kevin Murphy put it:

> The utility from drugs, crime, going bowling, owning a Rolex watch, voting Democratic, dressing informally at work, or keeping a neat lawn depends on whether friends and neighbors take drugs, commit crimes, go bowling, own Rolex watches, vote Democratic, dress informally, or keep their lawns neat.

This reasoning can help to explain why one restaurant is packed, while another restaurant that serves essentially the same food and has a similar décor has many fewer customers. Consumers decide which restaurant to go to partly on the basis of food and décor but also on the basis of the restaurant's popularity. People receive utility from being seen eating at a popular restaurant because they believe it makes them appear knowledgeable and fashionable. Whenever consumption takes place publicly, many consumers base their purchasing decisions on what other consumers are buying. Examples of public consumption include eating in restaurants, attending sporting events, wearing clothes or jewelry, and driving cars. In all these cases, the decision to buy a product depends partly on the characteristics of the product and partly on how many other people are buying the product.

## The Effects of Celebrity Endorsements

In many cases, it is not just the number of people who use a product that makes it desirable but the types of people who use it. If consumers believe that movie stars or professional athletes use a product, demand for the product will often increase. This may be partly because consumers believe public figures are particularly knowledgeable about products: "Tiger Woods knows more about cars than I do, so I'll buy the same car he drives." But many consumers also feel more fashionable and closer to famous people if they use the same products these people do. These considerations help to explain why companies are willing to pay millions of dollars to have celebrities endorse their products. As we saw at the beginning of this chapter, Coke has been using celebrities in its advertising for decades.

*In 2006, Tiger Woods earned $12 million from playing golf and $100 million from product endorsements.*

Making the Connection | **Why Do Firms Pay Tiger Woods to Endorse Their Products?**

Tiger Woods may be the best golfer who's ever lived. In his first five years as a professional, he won 27 tournaments on the Professional Golfers' Association (PGA) tour. When he won the Masters in 2001, he became the first golfer ever to win all four major professional golf championships in the same year. In late 2006 and early 2007, Tiger seemed hotter than ever when he won seven straight tournaments on the PGA tour. Even though Tiger Woods is a great golfer, should consumers care what products he uses? A number of major companies apparently believe consumers do care. The General Motors, Nike, Titleist, American Express, and Rolex companies collectively pay him more than $50 million per year to endorse their products.

There seems little doubt that consumers care what products Tiger uses, but *why* do they care? It might be that they believe Tiger has better information than they do about the products he endorses. The average weekend golfer might believe that if Tiger endorses Titleist golf clubs, maybe Titleist clubs are better than other golf clubs. But it seems more likely that people buy products associated with Tiger Woods or other celebrities because using these products makes them feel closer to the celebrity endorser or because it makes them appear to be fashionable.

---

## Network Externalities

Technology can play a role in explaining why consumers buy products that many other consumers are already buying. There is a **network externality** in the consumption of a product if the usefulness of the product increases with the number of consumers who use it. For example, if you owned the only cell phone in the world, it would not be very useful. The usefulness of cell phones increases with the number of people who own them. Similarly, your willingness to buy an iPod depends in part on the number of other people who own iPods. The more people who own iPods, the more music that will be available to download and the more useful an iPod is to you.

Some economists have suggested the possibility that network externalities may have a significant downside because they might result in consumers buying products that contain inferior technologies. This outcome could occur because network externalities can create significant *switching costs* to changing products: When a product becomes established, consumers may find it too costly to switch to a new product that contains a better technology. The selection of products may be *path dependent*. This means that because of switching costs, the technology that was first available may have advantages over better technologies that were developed later. In other words, the path along which the economy has developed in the past is important.

One example of path dependency and the use of an inferior technology is the QWERTY order of the letters along the top row of most computer keyboards. This order became widely used when manual typewriters were developed in the late nineteenth century. The metal keys on manual typewriters would stick together if a user typed too fast, and the QWERTY keyboard was designed to slow down typists and minimize the problem of the keys sticking together. With computers, the problem that QWERTY was developed to solve no longer exists, so keyboards could be changed easily to have letters in a more efficient layout. But because the overwhelming majority of people have learned to use keyboards with the QWERTY layout, there might be significant costs to them if they had to switch, even if a new layout ultimately made them faster typists.

Other products that supposedly embodied inferior technologies are VHS video recorders—supposedly inferior to Sony Betamax recorders—and the Windows computer operating system—supposedly inferior to the Macintosh operating system. Some economists have argued that because of path dependence and switching costs, network externalities can result in *market failures*. As we saw in Chapter 5, a market failure is a situation in which the market fails to produce the efficient level of output. If network externalities result in market failure, government intervention in these markets might improve economic efficiency. Many economists are skeptical, however, that network externalities really do lead to consumers being locked into products with inferior technologies. In particular, economists Stan Leibowitz of the University of Texas, Dallas, and Stephen Margolis of North Carolina State University have argued that in practice, the gains from using a superior technology are larger than the losses due to switching costs. After carefully studying the cases of the QWERTY keyboard, VHS video recorders, and the Windows computer operating system, they have concluded that there is no good evidence that the alternative technologies were actually superior. The implications of network externalities for economic efficiency remain controversial among economists.

**Network externality** This situation where the usefulness of a product increases with the number of consumers who use it.

## Does Fairness Matter?

If people were only interested in making themselves as well off as possible in a material sense, they would not be concerned with fairness. There is a great deal of evidence, however, that people like to be treated fairly and that they usually attempt to treat others fairly, even if doing so makes them worse off financially. Tipping servers in restaurants is an example. Diners in restaurants typically add 15 percent to their food bills as tips to their servers. Tips are not *required*, but most people see it as very unfair not to tip, unless the service has been exceptionally bad. You could argue that people leave tips not to be fair but because they are afraid that if they don't leave a tip, the next time they visit the restaurant, they will receive poor service. Studies have shown, however, that most people leave tips at restaurants even while on vacation or in other circumstances where they are unlikely to visit the restaurant again.

There are many other examples where people willingly part with money when they are not required to do so and when they receive nothing material in return. The most obvious example is making donations to charity. Apparently, donating money to charity or leaving tips in restaurants that they will never visit again gives people more utility than they would receive from keeping the money and spending it on themselves.

### *A Test of Fairness in the Economic Laboratory: The Ultimatum Game Experiment*

Economists have used experiments to increase their understanding of the role that fairness plays in consumer decision making. Experimental economics has been widely used during the past two decades, and a number of experimental economics laboratories exist in the United States and Europe. Economists Maurice Allais, Reinhard Selten, and Vernon Smith were awarded the Nobel Prize in Economics in part because of their contributions to experimental economics. Experiments make it possible to focus on a single aspect of consumer behavior. The *ultimatum game*, first popularized by Werner Güth of the Max Planck Institute of Economics, is an experiment that tests whether fairness is important in consumer decision making. Various economists have conducted the ultimatum game experiment under slightly different conditions, but with generally the same result. In this game, a group of volunteers—often college students—are divided into pairs. One member of each pair is the "allocator," and the other member of the pair is the "recipient."

Each pair is given an amount of money, say $20. The allocator decides how much of the $20 each member of the pair will get. There are no restrictions on how the allocator divides up the money. He or she could keep it all, give it all to the recipient, or anything in between. The recipient must then decide whether to accept the allocation or reject it. If the recipient decides to accept the allocation, each member of the pair gets to keep his or her share. If the recipient decides to reject the allocation, both members of the pair receive nothing.

If neither the allocator nor the recipient cared about fairness, optimal play in the ultimatum game is straightforward: The allocator should propose a division of the money in which the allocator receives $19.99 and the recipient receives $0.01. The allocator has maximized his or her gain. The recipient should accept the division because the alternative is to reject the division and receive nothing at all: Even a penny is better than nothing.

In fact, when the ultimatum game experiment is carried out, both allocators and recipients act as if fairness is important. Allocators usually offer recipients at least a 40 percent share of the money, and recipients almost always reject offers of less than a 10 percent share. Why do allocators offer recipients more than a negligible amount? It might be that allocators do not care about fairness but fear that recipients do care and will reject offers they consider unfair. This possibility was tested in an experiment known as the *dictator game* carried out by Daniel Kahneman (a psychologist who shared the Nobel Prize in Economics), Jack Knetsch, and Richard Thaler, using students at Cornell University. In this experiment, the allocators were given only two possible divisions of $20: either $18 for themselves and $2 for the recipient or an even division of $10 for themselves and $10 for the recipient. One important difference from the ultimatum game was that *the recipient was not allowed to reject the division.* Of the 161 allocators, 122 chose the even division of the $20. Because there was no possibility of the $18/$2 split being rejected, the allocators must have chosen the even split because they valued acting fairly.

Why would recipients in the ultimatum game ever reject any division of the money in which they receive even a very small amount, given that even a small amount of money is better than nothing? Apparently, most people value fairness enough that they will refuse to participate in transactions they consider unfair, even if they are worse off financially as a result.

**Business Implications of Fairness** If consumers value fairness, how does that affect firms? One consequence is that firms will sometimes not raise prices of goods and services, even when there is a large increase in demand, because they are afraid their customers will consider the price increases unfair and may buy elsewhere.

For example, the Broadway play *The Producers* was extremely popular during its first year in production. Even though ticket prices were an average of $75, on most nights, many more people wanted to buy tickets at that price than could be accommodated in the St. James Theater, where the play was running. Figure 9-4 illustrates this situation.

Notice that the supply curve in Figure 9-4 is a vertical line, which indicates that the capacity of the St. James Theater is fixed at 1,644 seats. At a price of $75 per ticket, there was a shortage of more than 400 tickets. Why didn't the theater raise ticket prices to $125, where the quantity supplied would equal the quantity demanded?

Let's look at two other examples in which it seems that businesses could increase their profits by raising prices. First, each year, many more people would like to buy tickets to see the Super Bowl than there are tickets for them to buy at the price the National Football League charges. Why doesn't the National Football League raise prices? Second, at popular restaurants, there are often long lines of people waiting to be served. Some of the people will wait hours to be served, and some won't be served at all before the restaurant closes. Why doesn't the restaurant raise prices high enough to eliminate the lines?

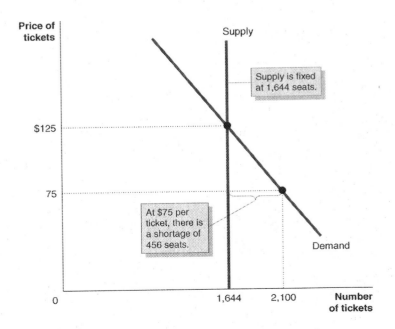

## Figure 9-4

**The Market for Tickets to *The Producers***

The St. James Theater could have raised prices for the Broadway musical *The Producers* to $125 per ticket and still sold all of the 1,644 tickets available. Instead, the theater kept the price of tickets at $75, even though the result was a shortage of more than 400 seats. Is it possible that this strategy maximized profits?

In each of these cases, it appears that a firm could increase its profits by raising prices. The seller would be selling the same quantity—of seats in a theater or a football stadium or meals in a restaurant—at a higher price, so profits should increase. Economists have provided two explanations why firms sometimes do not raise prices in these situations. Gary Becker, winner of the Nobel Prize in Economics, has suggested that the products involved—theatrical plays, football games, rock concerts, or restaurant meals—are all products that buyers consume together with other buyers. In those situations, the amount consumers wish to buy may be related to how much of the product other people are consuming. People like to consume, and be seen consuming, a popular product. In this case, a popular restaurant that increased its prices enough to eliminate lines might find that it had also eliminated its popularity.

Daniel Kahneman, Jack Knetsch, and Richard Thaler have offered another explanation for why firms don't always raise prices when doing so would seem to increase their profits. In surveys of consumers, these researchers found that most people considered it fair for firms to raise their prices following an increase in costs but unfair to raise prices following an increase in demand. For example, Kahneman, Knetsch, and Thaler conducted a survey in which people were asked their opinion of the following situation: "A hardware store has been selling snow shovels for $15. The morning after a large snowstorm, the store raises the price to $20." Eighty-two percent of those surveyed responded that they considered the hardware store's actions to be unfair. Kahneman, Knetsch, and Thaler have concluded that firms may sometimes not raise their prices even when the quantity demanded of their product is greater than the quantity supplied out of fear that in the long run, they will lose customers who believe the price increases were unfair.

These explanations share the same basic idea: Sometimes firms will give up some profits in the short run to keep their customers happy and increase their profits in the long run.

## Making the Connection | Professor Krueger Goes to the Super Bowl

Economist Alan Krueger of Princeton University has studied the question of why the National Football League does not charge a price for Super Bowl tickets that is high enough to make the quantity of tickets demanded equal to the quantity of tickets available. The prices may seem high—$400 for the best seats, $325 for the rest—but the quantity demanded still greatly exceeds the quantity supplied. Most Super Bowl tickets are allocated to the two teams playing in the game or to the league's corporate sponsors. To give ordinary fans a chance to attend the game, in 2001, the NFL set aside 500 pairs of tickets. They held a lottery for the opportunity to buy these tickets, and more than 36,000 people applied. Some fans were willing to pay as much as $5,000 to buy a ticket from ticket scalpers. (Scalpers buy tickets at their face value and then resell them at much higher prices, even though in Florida, where the 2001 Super Bowl was held, ticket scalping is illegal.)

Why didn't the NFL simply raise the price of tickets to clear the market? Krueger decided to survey football fans attending the game to see if their views could help explain this puzzle. Krueger's survey provides support for the Kahneman, Knetsch, and Thaler explanation of why companies do not always raise prices when the quantity demanded is greater than the quantity supplied. When asked whether it would "be fair for the NFL to raise the [price of tickets] to $1,500 if that is still less than the amount most people are willing to pay for tickets," 92 percent of the fans surveyed answered "no." Even 83 percent of the fans who had paid more than $1,500 for their tickets answered "no." Krueger concluded

*Should the NFL raise the price of Super Bowl tickets?*

that whatever the NFL might gain in the short run from raising ticket prices, it would more than lose in the long run by alienating football fans.

Source: Alan B. Krueger, "Supply and Demand: An Economist Goes to the Super Bowl," *Milken Institute Review*, Second Quarter 2001.

9.4 | Describe the behavioral economics approach to understanding decision making.

# Behavioral Economics: Do People Make Their Choices Rationally?

When economists say that consumers and firms are behaving "rationally," they mean that consumers and firms are taking actions that are appropriate to reach their goals, given the information available to them. In recent years, some economists have begun studying situations in which people do not appear to be making choices that are economically rational. This new area of economics is called **behavioral economics**. Why might consumers or businesses not act rationally? The most obvious reason would be that they do not realize that their actions are inconsistent with their goals. As we discussed in Chapter 1, one of the objectives of economics is to suggest ways to make better decisions. In this section, we discuss ways in which consumers can improve their decisions by avoiding some common pitfalls.

**Behavioral economics** The study of situations in which people make choices that do not appear to be economically rational.

Consumers commonly commit the following three mistakes when making decisions:

- They take into account monetary costs but ignore nonmonetary opportunity costs.

- They fail to ignore sunk costs.

- They are overly optimistic about their future behavior.

## Ignoring Nonmonetary Opportunity Costs

Remember from Chapter 2 that the **opportunity cost** of any activity is the highest-valued alternative that must be given up to engage in that activity. For example, if you own something you could sell, using it yourself involves an opportunity cost. It is often difficult for people to think of opportunity costs in these terms.

**Opportunity cost** The highest-valued alternative that must be given up to engage in an activity.

Consider the following example: Some of the fans at the 2001 Super Bowl participated in a lottery run by the National Football League that allowed the winners to purchase tickets at their face value, which was either $325 or $400, depending on where in the stadium the seats were located. Alan Krueger surveyed the lottery winners, asking them two questions:

*Question 1:* If you had not won the lottery, would you have been willing to pay $3,000 for your ticket?

*Question 2:* If after winning your ticket (and before arriving in Florida for the Super Bowl) someone had offered you $3,000 for your ticket, would you have sold it?

In answer to the first question, 94 percent said that if they had not won the lottery, they would not have paid $3,000 for a ticket. In answer to the second question, 92 percent said they would not have sold their ticket for $3,000. But these answers are contradictory! If someone offers you $3,000 for your ticket, then by using the ticket rather than selling it, you incur an opportunity cost of $3,000. There really is a $3,000 cost involved in using that ticket, even though you do not pay $3,000 in cash. The alternatives of either paying $3,000 or not receiving $3,000 amount to exactly the same thing.

**Endowment effect** The tendency of people to be unwilling to sell a good they already own even if they are offered a price that is greater than the price they would be willing to pay to buy the good if they didn't already own it.

If the ticket is really not worth $3,000 to you, you should sell it. If it is worth $3,000 to you, you should be willing to pay $3,000 in cash to buy it. Not being willing to sell a ticket you already own for $3,000, while at the same time not being willing to buy a ticket for $3,000 if you didn't already own one is inconsistent behavior. The inconsistency comes from a failure to take into account nonmonetary opportunity costs. Behavioral economists believe this inconsistency is caused by the **endowment effect**, which is the tendency of people to be unwilling to sell a good they already own even if they are offered a price that is greater than the price they would be willing to pay to buy the good if they didn't already own it.

The failure to take into account opportunity costs is a very common error in decision making. Suppose, for example, that a friend is in a hurry to have his room cleaned—it's the Friday before parents' weekend—and he offers you $50 to do it for him. You turn him down and spend the time cleaning your own room, even though you know somebody down the hall who would be willing to clean your room for $20. Leave aside complicating details—the guy who asked you to clean his room is a real slob, or you don't want the person who offered to clean your room for $20 to go through your stuff—and you should see the point we are making. The opportunity cost of cleaning your own room is $50—the amount your friend offered to pay you to clean his room. It is inconsistent to turn down an offer from someone else to clean your room for $20 when you are doing it for yourself at a cost of $50. The key point here is this: *Nonmonetary opportunity costs are just as real as monetary costs and should be taken into account when making decisions.*

## Business Implications of Consumers Ignoring Nonmonetary Opportunity Costs

Behavioral economist Richard Thaler has studied several examples of how businesses make use of consumers' failure to take into account opportunity costs. Whenever you buy something with a credit card, the credit card company charges the merchant a fee to process the bill. Credit card companies generally do not allow stores to charge higher prices to customers who use credit cards. A bill was introduced in Congress that would have made it illegal for credit card companies to enforce this rule. The credit card industry was afraid that if this law passed, credit card usage would drop because stores might begin charging a fee to credit card users. They attempted to have the law amended so that stores would be allowed to give a cash discount to people not using credit cards but would not be allowed to charge a fee to people using credit cards. There really is no difference in terms of opportunity cost between being charged a fee and not receiving a discount. The credit card industry was relying on the fact that *not* receiving a discount is a nonmonetary opportunity cost—and, therefore, likely to be ignored by consumers—but a fee is a monetary cost that people do take into account.

Film processing companies provide another example. Many of these companies have a policy of printing every picture on a roll of film, even if the picture is very fuzzy. Customers are allowed to ask for refunds on pictures they don't like. Once again, the companies are relying on the fact that passing up a refund once you have already paid for a picture is a nonmonetary opportunity cost rather than a direct monetary cost. In fact, customers rarely ask for refunds.

Making
the
Connection | ## Why Do Hilton Hotels and other Firms Hide Their Prices?

Economists recently began to use ideas from behavioral economics to understand a puzzling aspect of how some businesses price their products. David Laibson of Harvard University and Xavier Gabaix of New York University note that some products consist of a "base good" and "add-ons." For instance, to use a printer, you buy the printer itself—the base good—and replacement ink cartridges—the add-on. Typically, firms compete on the price of the base good but do their best to hide the prices of the add-ons. Because consumers sometimes spend more on the add-ons than on the base good, it may seem surprising that firms are able to successfully hide the prices of add-ons. For instance, over the life of a printer, consumers spend, on average, 10 times the price of the printer in buying ink cartridges. Yet one survey indicates that only 3 percent of consumers know the true cost of using a printer, including the cost of the ink cartridges. Similarly, many consumers are unaware of the add-on charges from using a checking account, such as ATM fees, returned check charges, and minimum balance fees. Many consumers making a hotel reservation are unaware of the hotel's charges for Internet access, for food from minibars, for breakfast at the hotel restaurant, or for local phone calls.

How are firms able to hide the prices of add-ons? Why doesn't competition lead some firms to offer lower-priced add-ons and advertise that their competitors' add-ons are higher priced? Laibson and Gabaix explain this puzzle by arguing that there are two types of consumers: sophisticated consumers, who pay attention to prices of add-ons, and myopic consumers, who ignore the prices of add-ons. It turns out that using advertising to convert myopic consumers into sophisticated consumers is not a profitable strategy. Consider the following example: Suppose that Hilton Hotels charges $80 per night for a room and the typical myopic consumer also spends $20 per night on local phone calls, food from the minibar, high-priced breakfasts, and other add-ons. Could a competing hotel, such as Marriott, attract Hilton's customers by advertising that Marriott's add-ons were more fairly priced than Hilton's? Laibson and Gabaix argue that this strategy would not work because its main effect would be to turn myopic consumers into sophisticated consumers. Once Hilton's customers become sophisticated, they will avoid the add-on fees, by, for instance, using their cell phones rather than the hotel phones to make calls or by eating breakfast in nearby restaurants rather than in the hotel. According to Laibson and Gabaix, Marriott's advertising campaign, "hurts Hilton—which sells fewer add-ons—but helps Hilton's customers, who are taught to substitute away from add-ons." But these sophisticated consumers are no more likely to switch from Hilton to Marriott than they were before Marriott incurred the cost of its advertising campaign. Exposing a competitor's hidden costs, say Laibson and Gabaix, "is good for the consumer and bad for both firms. Neither firm has an incentive to do it." As a result, many consumers remain unaware of the true prices of some of the products they purchase.

Sources: Christopher Shay, "The Hidden-Fee Economy," *New York Times*, December 10, 2006; and Xavier Gabaix and David Laibson, "Shrouded Attributes, Consumer Myopia, and Information Suppression in Competitive Markets," *Quarterly Journal of Economics*, Vol. 121, No. 2, May 2006, pp. 351–397.

*Some hotels hide what they charge for room service and Internet access.*

## Failing to Ignore Sunk Costs

A **sunk cost** is a cost that has already been paid and cannot be recovered. Once you have paid money and can't get it back, you should ignore that money in any later decisions you make. Consider the following two situations:

**Sunk cost** A cost that has already been paid and cannot be recovered.

*Situation 1:* You bought a ticket to a play for $75. The ticket is nonrefundable and must be used on Tuesday night, which is the only night the play will be performed. On Monday, a friend calls and invites you to a local comedy club to see a comedian you both like who is appearing only on Tuesday night. Your friend offers to pay the cost of going to the club.

*Situation 2:* It's Monday night, and you are about to buy a ticket for the Tuesday night performance of the same play as in situation 1. As you are leaving to buy the ticket, your friend calls and invites you to the comedy club.

Would your decision to go to the play or to the comedy club be different in situation 1 than in situation 2? Most people would say that in situation 1, they would go to the play, because otherwise they would lose the $75 they had paid for the ticket. In fact, though, the $75 is "lost" no matter what you do because the ticket is not refundable. The only real issue for you to decide is whether you would prefer to see the play or prefer to go with your friend to the comedy club. If you would prefer to go to the club, the fact that you have already paid $75 for the ticket to the play is irrelevant. Your decision should be the same in situation 1 and situation 2.

Psychologists Daniel Kahneman and Amos Tversky explored the tendency of consumers to not ignore sunk costs by asking two samples of people the following questions:

*Question 1:* One sample of people was asked the following question: "Imagine that you have decided to see a play and have paid the admission price of $10 per ticket. As you enter the theater, you discover that you have lost the ticket. The seat was not marked, and the ticket cannot be recovered. Would you pay $10 for another ticket?" Of those asked, 46 percent answered "yes," and 54 percent answered "no."

*Question 2:* A different sample of people was asked the following question: "Imagine that you have decided to see a play where admission is $10 per ticket. As you enter the theater, you discover that you have lost a $10 bill. Would you still pay $10 for a ticket to the play?" Of those asked, 88 percent answered "yes," and 12 percent answered "no."

The situations presented in the two questions are actually the same and should have received the same fraction of yes and no responses. Many people, though, have trouble seeing that in question 1, when deciding whether to see the play, they should ignore the $10 already paid for a ticket because it is a sunk cost.

## Being Unrealistic about Future Behavior

Studies have shown that a majority of adults in the United States are overweight. Why do many people choose to eat too much? One possibility is that they receive more utility from eating too much than they would from being thin. A more likely explanation, however, is that many people eat a lot today because they expect to eat less tomorrow. But they never do eat less, and so they end up overweight. (Of course, some people also suffer from medical problems that lead to weight gain.) Similarly, some people continue smoking today because they expect to be able to give it up sometime in the future. Unfortunately, for many people that time never comes, and they suffer the health consequences of prolonged smoking. In both these cases, people are overvaluing the utility from current choices—eating chocolate cake or smoking—and undervaluing the utility to be received in the future from being thin or not getting lung cancer.

Economists who have studied this question argue that many people have preferences that are not consistent over time. In the long run, you would like to be thin or give up smoking or achieve some other goal, but each day, you make decisions (such as to eat too much or to smoke) that are not consistent with this long-run goal. If you are unrealistic about your future behavior, you underestimate the costs of choices—like overeating or smoking—that you make today. A key way of avoiding this problem is to be realistic about your future behavior.

| Making the Connection | ## Why Don't Students Study More? |
|---|---|

Government statistics show that students who do well in college earn at least $10,000 more per year than students who fail to graduate or who graduate with low grades. So, over the course of a career of 40 years or more, students who do well in college will have earned upwards of $400,000 more than students who failed to graduate or who received low grades. Most colleges advise that students study at least two hours outside of class for every hour they spend in class. Surveys show that students often ignore this advice.

*If the payoff to studying is so high, why don't students study more?*

If the opportunity cost of not studying is so high, why do many students choose to study relatively little? Some students have work or family commitments that limit the amount of time they can study. But many other students study less than they would if they were more realistic about their future behavior. On any given night, a student has to choose between studying and other activities—like watching television, going to the movies, or going to a party—that may seem to provide higher utility in the short run. Many students choose one of these activities over studying because they expect to study tomorrow or the next day, but tomorrow they face the same choices and make similar decisions. As a result, they do not study enough to meet their long-run goal of graduating with high grades. If they were more realistic about their future behavior, they would not make the mistake of overvaluing the utility from activities like watching television or partying because they would realize that those activities can endanger their long-run goal of graduating with honors.

# Solved Problem | 9-4

## How Do You Get People to Save More of Their Income?

An article in the *New York Times* states the following:

> When it comes to saving for retirement, Americans . . . know they do not put away enough. . . . But ask them to save more in their [retirement] plans and they balk. A buck in the hand is irresistibly spent. Try a different approach. Ask them to commit now to increasing their savings in the future, make the increase coincide with the next raise, and they cheerfully sign up.

Why would people refuse to increase their savings now but agree to increase their savings in the future?

Source: Louis Uchitelle, "Why It Takes Psychology to Make People Save," *New York Times*, January 13, 2002.

## SOLVING THE PROBLEM:

Step 1: **Review the chapter material.** This problem is about how people are not always realistic about their future behavior, so you may want to review the section "Being Unrealistic about Future Behavior," which begins on page 306.

Step 2: **Use your understanding of consumer decision making to show that this plan may work.** We have seen that many people are unrealistic about their future behavior. They spend money today that they should be saving for retirement, partly because they expect to increase their saving in the future. A savings plan that gets people to commit today to saving in the future takes advantage of people's optimism about their future behavior. They agree to save more in the future because they expect to be doing that anyway. In fact, without being part of a plan that automatically saves their next raise, they probably would not have increased their savings.

>> **End Solved Problem 9-2**

Taking into account nonmonetary opportunity costs, ignoring sunk costs, and being more realistic about future behavior are three ways in which consumers are able to improve the decisions they make.

# Conclusion

In a market system, consumers are in the driver's seat. Goods are produced only if consumers want them to be. Therefore, how consumers make their decisions is an important area for economists to study, a fact that was highlighted when Daniel Kahneman—whose research was mentioned several times in this chapter—shared the Nobel Prize in Economics. Economists expect that consumers will spend their incomes so that the last dollar spent on each good provides them with equal additional amounts of satisfaction, or utility. In practice, there are significant social influences on consumer decision making, particularly when a good or service is consumed in public. Fairness also seems to be an important consideration for most consumers. Finally, many consumers could improve the decisions they make if they would take into account nonmonetary opportunity costs and ignore sunk costs.

## MORE BEHAVIORAL IDEAS

This chapter explores the role of information in markets and what happens when one side of the market has better information than the other. In the market for used cars, sellers know more about the quality of the product than buyers do. In the market for life insurance, buyers know more about the risks they face than sellers do. As we saw earlier in the book, the model of supply and demand is based on several assumptions, one of which is that buyers and sellers have enough information to make informed choices. In a world of fully informed buyers and sellers, markets operate smoothly, generating an equilibrium price and an equilibrium quantity for each good. In a world with imperfect information, some goods will be sold in very small numbers, or not sold at all. In addition, buyers and sellers will use resources to acquire information to help make better decisions. The 2001 Nobel Prize in economics was awarded to three economists—George Akerlof, Michael Spence, and Joseph Stiglitz—who studied the effects of imperfect information on all sorts of markets.

## 14.1 | THE LEMONS PROBLEM

The classic example of a market with imperfect information is the market for used cars.[1] Suppose there are two types of cars, low quality and high quality. A low-quality car, also known as a "lemon," breaks down frequently and has relatively high repair costs. A high-quality car, also known as a "plum," is reliable and has relatively low repair costs. Suppose buyers cannot distinguish between lemons and plums. Although a buyer can get some information about a particular car by looking at the car and taking it for a test drive, the information gleaned from this kind of inspection is not enough to determine the quality of the car. In contrast, a person selling a car after owning it for a while knows from experience whether the car is a lemon or a plum. We say that there is **asymmetric information** in a market if one side of the market—either buyers or sellers—has better information than the other side. Because buyers cannot distinguish between lemons and plums, there will be a single market for used automobiles: Both types of cars will be sold together in a **mixed market** for the same price.

### Uninformed Buyers and Knowledgeable Sellers

How much is a consumer willing to pay for a used car that could be either a lemon or a plum? To determine a consumer's willingness to pay in a mixed market with both lemons and plums, we must answer three questions:

1 How much is the consumer willing to pay for a plum?
2 How much is the consumer willing to pay for a lemon?
3 What is the chance that a used car purchased in the mixed market will be of low quality?

Suppose the typical buyer is willing to pay $4,000 for a plum and $2,000 for a lemon. The buyer is willing to pay less for a lemon because it is less reliable and has higher repair costs. For someone who is willing to put up with the hassle and repair expense, a lemon is a reasonable car. That's why the typical buyer is willing to pay $2,000, not zero, for a low-quality car that we tag with the label "lemon." Someone who pays $2,000 and gets a lemon is just as happy as someone who pays $4,000 and gets a plum.

Consumer expectations play a key role in determining the market outcome when there is imperfect information. Suppose that half the used cars *on the road* are lemons, and consumers know this. A reasonable expectation for consumers is that half the cars *on the used-car market* will be lemons, too. In other words, buyers initially expect a

### asymmetric information
A situation in which one side of the market—either buyers or sellers—has better information than the other.

### mixed market
A market in which goods of different qualities are sold for the same price.

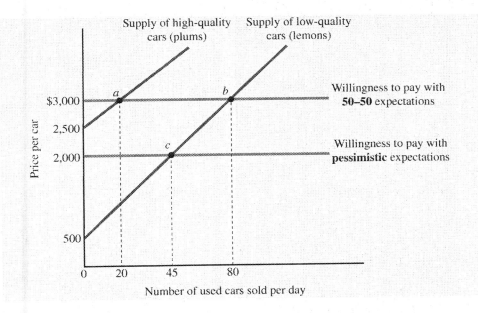

**All Used Cars on the Market Are Lemons**

If buyers assume that there is a 50–50 chance of getting a lemon or a plum, they are willing to pay $3,000 for a used car. At this price, 20 plums are supplied (point *a*) along with 80 lemons (point *b*). This is not an equilibrium because consumers' expectation of a 50–50 split are not realized. If consumers become pessimistic and assume that all cars on the market will be lemons, they are willing to pay $2,000 for a used car. At this price, only lemons will be supplied (point *c*). Consumer expectations are realized, so the equilibrium is shown by point *c*, with an equilibrium price of $2,000.

50–50 split between the two types of cars. A reasonable assumption is that a buyer in the mixed market is willing to pay the average value of the two types of cars, or $3,000. In other words, a buyer is willing to pay $3,000 for a 50–50 chance of getting either a plum or a lemon.

The current owner of a used car knows from everyday experience whether the car is a lemon or a plum. For each owner, the question is, given the single market price for all used cars, lemons and plums alike, should I sell my car? The answers to this question are shown by the two supply curves in Figure 14.1, one for lemons and one for plums:

- **Lemon supply.** As shown by the lower curve, the minimum supply price for lemons is $500: At any price less than $500, no lemons will be supplied. Lemons have a lower minimum price because they are worth less to their current owners. The number of lemons supplied increases with price. For example, 80 cars will be supplied at a price of $3,000 (point *b*).

- **Plum supply.** As shown by the upper curve, the minimum supply price for plums is $2,500: At any price less than $2,500, no plums will be supplied. Consistent with the law of supply, the higher the price of used cars, the larger the number of plums supplied. For example, 20 plums will be supplied at a price of $3,000 (point *a*).

## Equilibrium with All Low-Quality Goods

Table 14.1 shows two scenarios for our hypothetical used-car market, based on the supply curves shown in Figure 14.1. In the first column, we assume that buyers have 50–50 expectations about the quality of used cars. As we saw earlier, if buyers expect a 50–50 split between lemons and plums, the typical buyer will be willing to pay $3,000 for a used car. From the supply curves in Figure 14.1, we know that at this price 20 plums and 80 lemons will be supplied, so 80 percent of the used cars (80 of 100) will be lemons. In this case, consumers are too optimistic and underestimate the chance of getting a lemon.

The experiences of these 100 consumers show that the actual chance of getting a lemon is 80 percent, not 50 percent as initially assumed. Once future buyers realize this, they will of course become more pessimistic about the used-car market. Suppose they assume that all the used cars on the market will be lemons. Under this assumption, the typical buyer will be willing to pay only $2,000 (the value of a lemon) for a used car. As shown in Figure 14.1, this price is less than the $2,500 minimum price for

Table 14.1 | EQUILIBRIUM WITH ALL LOW-QUALITY GOODS

| | Buyers Initially Have 50–50 Expectations | Equilibrium: Pessimistic Expectations |
|---|---|---|
| **Demand Side of Market** | | |
| Amount buyer is willing to pay for a lemon | $2,000 | $2,000 |
| Amount buyer is willing to pay for a plum | $4,000 | $4,000 |
| Assumed chance of getting a lemon | 50% | 100% |
| Assumed chance of getting a plum | 50% | 0% |
| Amount buyer is willing to pay for a used car in mixed market | $3,000 | $2,000 |
| **Supply Side of Market** | | |
| Number of lemons supplied | 80 | 45 |
| Number of plums supplied | 20 | 0 |
| Total number of used cars supplied | 100 | 45 |
| Actual chance of getting a lemon | 80% | 100% |

supplying plums, so plums will disappear from the used-car market. At a price of $2,000, the quantity of plums supplied is zero, but the quantity of lemons supplied is 45 (point *c*). In other words, all the used cars will be lemons, so consumers' pessimism is justified. Because consumers' expectations are consistent with their actual experiences in the market, the equilibrium price of used cars is $2,000. The equilibrium in the used-car market is shown in the second column of Table 14.1.

In this equilibrium, no plums are bought or sold, so every buyer will get a lemon. People get exactly what they pay for: They are willing to pay $2,000 for a serviceable but low-quality car, and that's what each consumer gets. The domination of the used-car market by lemons is an example of the **adverse-selection problem**. The uninformed side of the market (buyers in this case) must choose from an undesirable or adverse selection of used cars. The asymmetric information in the market generates a downward spiral of price and quality:

- The presence of low-quality goods on the market pulls down the price that consumers are willing to pay.
- A decrease in price decreases the number of high-quality goods supplied, decreasing the average quality of goods on the market.
- The decrease in the average quality of goods on the market pulls down the price that consumers are willing to pay again.

In the extreme case, this downward spiral continues until all the cars on the market are lemons.

### A Thin Market: Equilibrium with Some High-Quality Goods

The disappearance of plums from our hypothetical used-car market is an extreme case. The plums disappeared from the market because informed plum owners decided to keep their cars rather than selling them at a relatively low price in the used-car market. This outcome would change if the minimum supply price of plums were lower, specifically if it is below $2,000. In this case, most but not all the used cars on the market will be lemons, and some lucky buyers will get plums. In this case, we say that asymmetric information generates a **thin market**: Some high-quality goods are sold, but fewer than would be sold in a market with perfect information.

Figure 14.2 shows the situation that leads to a thin market. The minimum supply price for plums is $1,833, and the quantity of plums supplied increases with the price of used cars. Suppose that consumers are initially pessimistic, assuming that

**• adverse-selection problem**
A situation in which the uninformed side of the market must choose from an undesirable or adverse selection of goods.

**• thin market**
A market in which some high-quality goods are sold but fewer than would be sold in a market with perfect information.

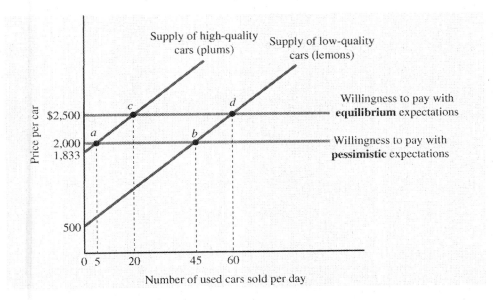

**The Market for High-Quality Cars (Plums) Is Thin**
If buyers are pessimistic and assume that only lemons will be sold, they are willing to pay $2,000 for a used car. At this price, 5 plums are supplied (point *a*), along with 45 lemons (point *b*). This is not an equilibrium because 10% of consumers get plums, contrary to their expectations. If consumers assume that there is a 25% change of getting a plum, they are willing to pay $2,500 for a used car. At this price, 20 plums are supplied (point *c*), along with 60 lemons (point *d*). This is an equilibrium because 25% of consumers get plums, consistent with their expectations. Consumer expectations are realized, so the equilibrium is shown by points *c* and *d*.

all cars for sale will be lemons. This means that consumers are willing to pay only $2,000 for a used car. Because the minimum supply price for plums ($1,833) is now less than the willingness to pay for a lemon, some plums will be supplied at a price of $2,000. In Figure 14.2, 5 plums and 45 lemons are supplied at this price, so 1 out of every 10 buyers will get a plum. In this case, pessimism is not an equilibrium, because some buyers will get plums when they expect lemons. This is also shown in the first column of Table 14.2.

In equilibrium, consumer expectations about the chances of getting the two types of cars are realized. Suppose that consumers expect 1 of every 4 cars to be a plum. Let's assume that each consumer is willing to pay $2,500 for a used car under these circumstances. Consumers are willing to pay a bit more than the value of a lemon because there is a small chance of getting a plum. In Figure 14.2, at this price 20 plums are supplied (point *c*) and 60 lemons are supplied (point *d*), so in fact 1 in 4 consumers actually gets a plum. This is an equilibrium because 25 percent of the cars sold are plums and 75 percent are lemons, consistent with consumers' expectations. This is also shown in the second column of Table 14.2.

Table 14.2 | A THIN MARKET FOR HIGH-QUALITY GOODS

| | Initial Pessimistic Expectations | Equilibrium: 75–25 Expectations |
|---|---|---|
| **Demand Side of Market** | | |
| Amount buyer is willing to pay for a lemon | $2,000 | $2,000 |
| Amount buyer is willing to pay for a plum | $4,000 | $4,000 |
| Assumed chance of getting a lemon | 100% | 75% |
| Assumed chance of getting a plum | 0% | 25% |
| Amount buyer is willing to pay for a used car in mixed market | $2,000 | $2,500 |
| **Supply Side of Market** | | |
| Number of lemons supplied | 45 | 60 |
| Number of plums supplied | 5 | 20 |
| Total number of used cars supplied | 50 | 80 |
| Actual chance of getting a lemon | 90% | 75% |

# 14.2 | RESPONDING TO THE LEMONS PROBLEM

In a market with asymmetric information, there are strong incentives for buyers and sellers to solve the lemons problem. In our example of a thin market, the price of a used car is $2,500, but consumers are willing to pay $4,000 for a plum. This $1,500 gap between the willingness to pay for a plum and the price in the mixed market provides an incentive for buyers to acquire information to help identify plums. It also provides an incentive for plum owners to prove that they are selling high-quality cars.

## Buyers Invest in Information

In our model of the thin market, 1 of 4 buyers pays $2,500 to get a plum worth $4,000. The more information a buyer has, the greater the chance of picking a plum from the cars in the mixed market. Suppose a buyer gets enough information to identify the plums in a market. The buyer could purchase a plum worth $4,000 at the prevailing price of $2,500, generating a gain of $1,500. A buyer can get information about individual cars by taking the car to a mechanic for a careful inspection. In addition, a buyer can get general information about the reliability of different models from magazines and the Internet. *Consumer Reports* publishes information on repair histories of different models and even computes a "Trouble" index, scoring each model on a scale of 1 to 5. By consulting these information sources, a buyer improves the chances of getting a high-quality car.

## Consumer Satisfaction Scores from ValueStar and eBay

The problem of asymmetric information in consumer goods such as cars also occurs for some types of consumer services. Most consumers can't easily determine the quality of service they will receive from an auto repair shop, a landscaper, or a plumber. How can a high-quality service provider distinguish itself from low-quality providers?

If you live in the San Francisco Bay area, you can get information about the performance of firms providing consumer services such as medical and dental care, gardening and landscaping, pet grooming, auto repair, and home improvement. ValueStar is a consumer guide and business directory that uses customer satisfaction surveys to determine how well a firm does relative to its competitors in providing quality service. To earn the right to display a Customer-Rated seal from ValueStar, a firm must prove that it has all the required licenses and insurance and must agree to pay for a survey of its past customers. ValueStar uses consumer surveys to compute a consumer-satisfaction score for each company. Any company receiving a score of at least 85 out of 100 has the right to display a Customer-Rated Gold seal for a one-year period.

Another example of consumer satisfaction scores is evident on eBay, the Internet auction site. On eBay, buyers must rely on sellers to honestly disclose the quality of the goods they are auctioning and to promptly ship them once a consumer pays. Buyers help other purchasers distinguish "good" from "bad" sellers on eBay by rating them online with "stars," indicating their satisfaction with their transactions.

## Guarantees and Lemons Laws

Used-car sellers also have an incentive to solve the lemons problem. If a plum owner persuades a buyer that her car is a plum and then sells the car for $4,000 rather than $2,500, the seller's gain is $1,500. Sellers can identify a car as a plum in a sea of lemons by offering one of the following guarantees:

- *Money-back guarantees.* The seller could promise to refund the $4,000 price if the car turned out to be a lemon. Because the car is in fact a plum—a fact known by the seller—the buyer will not ask for a refund, so both the buyer and the seller will be happy with the transaction.

- *Warranties and repair guarantees.* The seller could promise to cover any extraordinary repair costs for one year. Because the car is a plum, there won't be any extraordinary costs, so both the buyer and the seller will be happy with the transaction.

Many states have laws that require automakers to buy back cars that experience frequent problems in the first year of use. For example, under California's Song–Beverly Consumer Warranty Act, also known as the "Lemons Law," auto dealers are required to repurchase vehicles that have been brought back for repair at least four times for the same problem or have been in the mechanic's shop for at least 30 calendar days in the first year following purchase. A vehicle repurchased under the lemons law must be fixed before it is sold to another customer and must be identified as a lemon with a stamp on the title and a sticker on the car that says "lemons law buyback." One problem with enforcing these laws is that lemons can cross state lines without a paper trail. The interstate commerce in lemons has led to new laws in some states requiring the branding of lemons on vehicle titles to follow the car when it crosses state lines.

# 14.3 | EVIDENCE OF THE LEMONS EFFECT

The lemons model makes two predictions about markets with asymmetric information. First, the presence of low-quality goods in a market will at least reduce the number of high-quality goods in the market and may even eliminate them. Second, buyers and sellers will respond to the lemons problem by investing in information and other means of distinguishing between low-quality and high-quality goods. What's the evidence for the lemons model?

# APPLICATION

## THE RESALE VALUE OF A WEEK-OLD CAR

APPLYING THE CONCEPTS #1: Why does a new car lose about 20 percent of its value in the first week?

If you buy a new car for $20,000 today and then try to sell it a week later, you probably won't get more than $16,000 for it. Even if you drove it just a couple hundred miles, cleaned it up, and returned it to the dealer with that new-car smell, the car will lose about 20 percent of its value in the first week. You won't fare any better by putting an advertisement in the newspaper or trying to sell the car on eBay. Why does the typical new car lose so much of its value in the first week?

A potential buyer of a week-old car might believe that a person who returns a car after only one week could have discovered it was a lemon and may be trying to get rid of it. Alternatively, the seller could have simply changed his or her mind about the car. The problem is that buyers don't know why the car is being sold, and as long as there is a chance that the car is a lemon they won't be willing to pay the full "new" price for it. In general, buyers are willing to pay a lot less for a week-old car, and so the owners of high-quality, week-old cars are less likely to put them on the market. This downward spiral ultimately reduces the price of week-old cars by about 20 percent. *Related to Exercises 3.1 and 3.6.*

### Used Pickup Trucks

Studies of the market for used pickup trucks have provided mixed results concerning the lemons problem.[2] It appears that for trucks less than 10 years old, those sold on the market are just as reliable, on average, as those that remain with their current owners. These studies provide support for the second implication of the theory of lemons, that people acquire information and develop effective means to deal with the problem of asymmetric information. In contrast, there does seem to be a lemons problem for trucks at least 10 years old, which represent about one-third of transactions. Compared to old trucks that remain with their current owners, old trucks that are sold have significantly higher repair costs, with a difference in cost of about 45 percent. Old trucks that are sold have a much higher probability of requiring engine and transmission repairs.

# APPLICATION

## REGULATION OF THE CALIFORNIA KIWIFRUIT MARKET

APPLYING THE CONCEPTS #2: How can government solve the adverse-selection problem?

Kiwifruit is subject to imperfect information because buyers cannot determine its sweetness—its quality level—by simple inspection. The sweetness level at the time of consumption is determined by the fruit's "maturity"—its sugar content at the time of harvest. Kiwifruit continues to convert starch into sugar after it is picked, so a harvest-time sugar content of 6.5 percent leads to a sugar content of about 14 percent at the time of consumption. Fruit that is picked early has a low sugar content at harvest time and never tastes sweet. There is asymmetric information because producers know the maturity of the fruit, but fruit wholesalers and grocery stores, who buy fruit at the time of harvest, cannot determine whether a piece of fruit will ultimately be sweet or sour.

Before 1987, kiwifruit from California suffered from the "lemons" problem. Maturity levels of the fruit varied across producers. On average, the sugar content at the time of harvest was below the industry standard, established by kiwifruit from New Zealand. Given the large number of "lemons" among California kiwifruit, grocery stores were not willing to pay as much for California fruit. In other words, the presence of low-quality (immature) fruit in the mixed market pulled down the price of California fruit. Mature kiwifruit is more costly to produce than immature fruit, and the low price decreased the production of mature fruit. This is similar to low used-car prices decreasing the number of high-quality used cars on the market. In general, adverse selection led to low prices and a relatively large volume of low-quality kiwifruit from California.

In 1987, California producers implemented a federal marketing order to address the lemon–kiwi problem. The federal order specified a minimum maturity standard (6.5 percent sugar content at the time of harvest), and as the average quality of California fruit increased, so did the price. Within a few years, the gap between California and New Zealand prices had decreased significantly.
*Related to Exercises 3.3 and 3.7.*

SOURCE: Christopher Ferguson and Hoy Carman, "Kiwifruit and the 'Lemon' Problem: Do Minimum Quality Standards Work?" Working Paper, 1999. International Food and Agribusiness Management Association.

# APPLICATION

## BASEBALL PITCHERS ARE LIKE USED CARS

APPLYING THE CONCEPTS #3: Does the market for baseball pitchers suffer from the adverse-selection problem?

Professional baseball teams compete with each other for players. After six years of play in the major leagues, a player has the option of becoming a free agent and offering his services to the highest bidder. A player is likely to switch teams if the new team offers him a higher salary than his original team. One of the puzzling features of the free-agent market is that pitchers who switch teams are more prone to injuries than pitchers who don't. On average, pitchers who switch teams spend 28 days per season on the disabled list, compared to only 5 days for pitchers who do not switch teams. This doesn't mean that all the switching pitchers are lemons; many of them are injury-free and are valuable additions to their new teams. But on average, the switching pitchers spend five times longer recovering from injuries.

This puzzling feature of the free-agent market for baseball players is explained by asymmetric information and adverse selection. Because the coaches, physicians, and trainers from the player's original team have interacted with the player on a daily basis for several years, they know from experience whether he is likely to suffer from injuries that prevent him from playing. In contrast, the new team has much less information. Its physicians can examine the pitcher, and the team can check league records to see how long the pitcher has spent on the disabled list, but these measures do not eliminate the asymmetric information. The original team has several years of daily experience with the pitcher and has better information about the pitcher's physical health.

To illustrate the lemons problem for pitchers, consider the incentives for a team to outbid another team for a pitcher. Suppose the market price for pitchers is $1 million per year, and a pitcher who is currently with the Detroit Tigers is offered this salary by another team. If the Tigers think the pitcher is likely to spend a lot of time next season recovering from injuries, they won't try to outbid the other team for the pitcher: They will let the pitcher switch teams. But if the Tigers think the pitcher will be injury-free and productive, he will be worth more than $1 million to the Tigers, so they will outbid other teams and keep him. In general, an injury-prone pitcher is more likely to switch teams. As in the used-car market, there are many "lemons" on the used-pitcher market. The market for baseball players playing other positions does not suffer from the adverse selection, perhaps because the injuries that affect their performance are easier for other teams to detect.

Although you may think it's bizarre to compare baseball pitchers to used cars, people in baseball don't think so. They recognize the similarity between the two markets. Jackie Moore, who managed a free-agent camp where teams looking for players can see free agents in action, sounds like a used-car salesman: "We want to get players off the lot. We want to cut a deal. How many camps can you go into where you can look at a player and take him home with you?" *Related to Exercises 3.4 and 3.8.*

SOURCES: Kenneth Lehn, "Information Asymmetries in Baseball's Free Agent Market," *Economic Inquiry*, vol. 22, January 1984, pp. 37–44; Chris Sheridan, "Free Agents at End of Baseball's Earth," Associated Press, printed in *Corvallis Gazette-Times*, April 15, 1995, p. B1.

# 14.4 | UNINFORMED SELLERS AND KNOWLEDGEABLE BUYERS: INSURANCE

So far, we have explored the effects of asymmetric information when sellers are more knowledgeable than buyers. The same sort of problems occur when buyers are more knowledgeable than sellers. The best example of superior knowledge on the demand side of the market is insurance. A person who buys an insurance policy knows much more about his or her risks and needs for insurance than the insurance company knows. For example, when you buy an auto insurance policy, you know more than your insurance company about your driving habits and your chances of getting into an accident. We'll see that insurance markets suffer from the adverse-selection problem: Insurance companies must pick from an adverse or undesirable selection of customers.

## Health Insurance

To illustrate the information problems in the market for insurance, consider health insurance provided to individual consumers. Suppose there are two types of consumers: low-cost consumers with relatively low medical expenses of $2,000 per year and high-cost consumers with relatively high medical expenses $6,000 per year. The amount a consumer is willing to pay for an insurance policy covering all medical expenses increases with the anticipated medical expenses, so high-cost people are willing to pay more for health insurance.

The insurance company cannot distinguish between high-cost and low-cost people, but it still must pick a price for its coverage. To simplify matters, let's assume that there are no administrative costs, so the only cost for the insurance company is the medical bills it pays for its customers. Let's also assume that the insurance company sets the price equal to its average cost per customer, equal to the total medical bills paid by the insurance company divided by the number of customers. These assumptions simplify the math without affecting the basic results.

What is the insurance company's average cost per customer? To determine the average cost in a mixed market, we must answer three questions:

- What is the cost of providing medical care to a high-cost person?

- What is the cost of providing medical care to a low-cost person?

- What fraction of the customers are low-cost people?

Suppose that half the population is high cost and the other half is low cost. Let's assume that the insurance company is somewhat naive and initially assumes that the mix of insurance buyers will be the same as the population mix. In other words, the insurance company initially assumes that half its customers will be high cost and half will be low cost. In this case, the average cost per customer is $4,000, that is, the average of $2,000 for each low-cost customer and $6,000 for each high-cost customer.

There is asymmetric information in the insurance market because potential buyers know from everyday experience and family histories what type of customer they are, either low cost or high cost. For each person, the question is: Given the single market price for all insurance, for low-cost and high-cost people alike, should I buy insurance? The answers to this question are shown in two demand curves in Figure 14.3. The demand curve for the high-cost people is higher than the curve for the low-cost people, reflecting their larger benefits from having medical insurance.

## Equilibrium with All High-Cost Consumers

Table 14.3 shows two scenarios for our hypothetical insurance market, with numbers based on the demand curves shown in Figure 14.3. In the first column, we assume that firms initially assume a 50–50 mix of customers. As we saw earlier, if sellers expect a

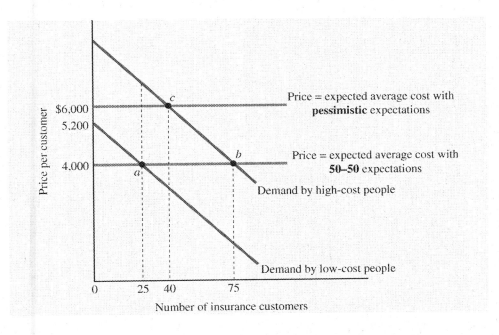

If insurance companies assume there will be a 50–50 split between high-cost and low-cost customers, the average cost of insurance and its price is $4,000. At this price, there are 25 low-cost customers (point *a*) and 75 high-cost customers (point *b*). This is not an equilibrium because 75 percent of insurance buyers are high-cost customers, contrary to the expectations of a 50–50 split. If insurance companies become pessimistic and assume that all buyers will be high-cost consumers, the average cost and price is $6,000. The insurance company's expectations are realized, so the equilibrium is shown by point *c*.

## Table 14.3 | EQUILIBRIUM WITH ALL HIGH-COST CUSTOMERS

|  | 50–50 Expectations | Equilibrium: Pessimistic Expectations |
|---|---|---|
| **Supply Side of Market** |  |  |
| Cost of serving a high-cost customer | $6,000 | $6,000 |
| Cost of serving a low-cost customer | $2,000 | $2,000 |
| Assumed fraction of high-cost customers | 50% | 100% |
| Assumed chance of low-cost customers | 50% | 0% |
| Expected average cost per customer (price) | $4,000 | $6,000 |
| **Demand Side of Market** |  |  |
| Number of high-cost customers | 75 | 40 |
| Number of low-cost customers | 25 | 0 |
| Total number of customers | 100 | 40 |
| Actual fraction of high-cost customers | 75% | 100% |
| Actual average cost per customer | $5,000 | $6,000 |

50–50 split between the two types, the average cost per customer is $4,000, and that's the price they charge for medical insurance. From the demand curves in Figure 14.3, we know that at this price 25 low-cost people will buy insurance (point *a*), along with 75 high-cost people (point *b*). In this case, insurance companies are too optimistic and underestimate the fraction of customers with large medical bills. The actual fraction of high-cost customers is 75 percent, and the actual average cost is $5,000 (equal to 0.25 times $2,000, plus 0.75 times $6,000). The company's average cost of $5,000 exceeds its price of $4,000, so the firm will lose money.

Suppose that after observing the outcome in the first column, insurance companies become very pessimistic. They assume that all their customers will be high-cost people. Under this assumption, the average cost per customer is $6,000, the average cost per high-cost customer, and that's the pessimistic price. As shown in Figure 14.3, this price exceeds the maximum that low-cost people are willing to pay for insurance ($5,200), so none of the low-cost consumers will buy insurance at this price. But a total of 40 high-cost consumers will buy insurance at this price (point *c*). In other words, all the customers will be high-cost people, so the company's pessimism is justi-fied. The price chosen by the insurance company equals the actual average cost of providing service, so the equilibrium is shown by point $c$, with an equilibrium price of $6,000. This equilibrium is shown in the second column of Table 14.3.

The domination of the insurance market by high-cost people is another example of the adverse-selection problem. The uninformed side of the market (sellers in this case) must choose from an undesirable or adverse selection of consumers. The asym-metric information in the market generates an upward spiral of price and average cost of service:

- The presence of high-cost consumers in the market pulls up the average cost of service, pulling up the price.
- An increase in price decreases the number of low-cost consumers who purchase insurance.
- The decrease in the number of low-cost consumers pulls up the average cost of insurance.
- In the extreme case, this upward spiral continues until all insurance customers are high-cost people.

Our example of health insurance indicates that only high-cost people buy insur-ance. A more realistic outcome is a thin market, with a relatively small number of low-cost people buying insurance. The adverse-selection problem could be less severe, but still will be present as long as insurance companies cannot distinguish perfectly between low-cost and high-cost people.

### Responding to Adverse Selection in Insurance: Group Insurance

Insurance companies use group insurance plans to diminish the adverse-selection prob-lem. By enrolling all the employees of an organization in one or two insurance plans, they ensure that all workers, not just high-cost people, join the pool of consumers.

In our example, group insurance would generate a 50–50 mix of low-cost and high-cost customers, and the break-even price would be $6,000. In contrast, when a firm sells insurance to individuals, the low-cost people have an incentive to go without insurance, leading to the adverse-selection problem and higher prices.

Most insurance companies use **experience rating** to set their prices for group insurance. They charge different prices to different firms, depending on the past medical bills of the firm's employees. A firm whose employees have low medical bills pays a low price for its employees' health insurance. Experience rating gives firms an incentive to decrease the health costs of their workers. As a result, they have an incen-tive to invest in safety and health programs for their workers. They also have an incen-tive to avoid hiring applicants with health problems. Under experience rating, a firm that hires a worker with above-average medical costs will ultimately pay a higher price for its group insurance.

### The Uninsured

One implication of asymmetric information in the insurance market is that many low-cost consumers who are not eligible for a group plan will not carry insurance. Given the adverse-selection problem, the price for an individual insurance plan is relatively high, and many consumers go without insurance. This is a contributing factor to the problem of the "uninsured." In 2004, about 46 million people (about 14 percent of the U.S. population) were not covered by health insurance. About 70 percent of working-age people have private insurance, and another 10 percent have some sort of govern-ment insurance, leaving 20 percent without health insurance. In general, the unin-sured are the people and their families who do not receive insurance through their employers, are unemployed or between jobs, or are poor but do not qualify for

* **experience rating**
A situation in which insurance companies charge different prices for medical insurance to different firms depending on the past medical bills of a firm's employees.

Medicaid. The uninsured obtain care for medical emergencies but typically do not receive routine—and less costly—preventive care.

The problem of uninsured people does not show any signs of improving. A proposal for universal coverage from the national government, which would have required each employer to provide health insurance for all its workers, was soundly defeated. Stanford health economist Victor Fuchs has suggested a plan under which everyone would receive a voucher—a coupon from the government they could use toward the purchase of their own health insurance.[3] The difficulty with any voucher plan is that new taxes would be necessary to finance it. Most European countries that provide universal coverage to their citizens finance it with a value-added tax—essentially a national sales tax. Clearly, introducing a new tax or raising existing tax rates to finance a voucher plan would be very controversial.

4

# APPLICATION

## GENETIC TESTING BENEFITS LOW-RISK PEOPLE

APPLYING THE CONCEPTS #4: Who benefits from better information about risks?

You probably know someone who is impulsive and excitable, a thrill seeker who keeps life interesting for those of us who are more relaxed and mellow. Scientists recently identified one of the genes responsible for novelty-seeking behavior and discovered that about 15 percent of the people in Israel, Europe, and the United States carry the gene. Scientists estimate that about half of novelty-seeking behavior among people is linked to their genes, which might make them more inclined to take up skydiving or bungee jumping and engage in other risky behavior.

If you managed a life insurance company, would you like to know whether each customer has the novelty-seeking gene? It would reduce the problem of asymmetric information and allow you to charge different prices for insurance, leading to lower prices for people who are less inclined to take risks. In other words, people who don't have the novelty-seeking gene benefit from genetic testing because they will pay lower prices for life insurance.

The same logic applies to genetic tests that reveal an individual's likelihood of developing heart disease. In principle, an insurance company that has genetic information for its customers could distinguish between high-cost and low-cost customers and charge different prices to the two types of consumers. This is good news for people with a favorable genetic makeup because they would pay lower prices. But it's bad news for people whose genetic makeup makes them more likely to develop heart disease, because they would pay a higher price.

The development of genetic tests has led to fears that insurance companies will use the results of the tests to engage in genetic discrimination—denying insurance or charging higher prices to people with unfavorable genes. Federal employees are protected by an executive order that forbids genetic discrimination. Most states have laws that prevent insurance companies from using genetic information in determining prices and eligibility for insurance coverage. *Related to Exercises 4.3 and 4.4.*

SOURCE: "Genetic Discrimination Feared," Associated Press Online, June 26, 2000 www.ap.org, accessed 01/29/2001; Malcolm Ritter, "A Thrill a Minute: Geneticists Find Personality Link," The *Oregonian*, January 2, 1996, p. A1; National Conference of State Legislatures, "Genetics and Health Insurance: State Anti-Discrimination Laws," June 2005, available online at www.ncsl.org/programs/health/genetics/ndishlth.htm, accessed 07/05/2006.

### Other Types of Insurance

The same logic of adverse selection applies to the markets for other types of insurance, including life insurance, home insurance for theft and property damage, and automobile insurance. Buyers know more than sellers about their risks, so there is adverse selection, with high-risk individuals more likely to buy insurance. Life insurance companies provide group coverage to get a broader base of consumers and also try to distinguish between high-risk and low-risk people with physical exams. But because the companies are unable to distinguish between high-risk and low-risk people with sufficient precision, the adverse-selection problem persists.

## 14.5 | INSURANCE AND MORAL HAZARD

Does insurance affect people's risk-taking behavior? The answer is, yes. Insurance causes people to take greater risks because they know part of the cost of an undesirable outcome will be borne by their insurance companies. Here are some examples of people taking greater risks because they have insurance:

- Will Irma buy a fire extinguisher for her kitchen? If she had to pay for any property damage caused by a fire, she would definitely buy a fire extinguisher. But because her homeowner's insurance covers property damage from fires, she doesn't buy a fire extinguisher.
- Will Harry drive his car carefully? If he had to pay for all repairs resulting from a collision out of his own pocket, he would drive very carefully. But because his auto insurance covers some of the repair costs, he drives fast and recklessly.
- Will Flo fly on a commercial airline or hitch a ride with her pilot friend in a four-seat airplane? Traveling in small airplanes is much riskier. If Flo dies in an airplane crash, her family will lose the income she would otherwise earn. If she didn't have life insurance to offset these income losses, she would be less likely to risk harming her family by flying on the small plane instead of the commercial airline. But because she knows her family will collect $1 million in life insurance, she is willing to take the risk.

• **moral hazard**
A situation in which one side of an economic relationship takes undesirable or costly actions that the other side of the relationship cannot observe.

The risky behavior triggered by insurance is an example of the moral-hazard problem. **Moral hazard** occurs when one side of an economic relationship takes undesirable or costly actions that the other side of the relationship cannot observe. For example, Irma's insurance company doesn't know whether she has a fire extinguisher. She doesn't buy an extinguisher because her insurance will cover the cost of a kitchen fire. If there is a fire, Irma's hidden action—going without an extinguisher—is costly for the insurance company. Similarly, Harry's insurance company doesn't know how fast and recklessly he drives, and insurance encourages him to drive recklessly. His hidden action of reckless driving increases the likelihood of a costly accident. Just as collision insurance encourages risky driving, life insurance encourages risky activities such as flying small airplanes, parachuting, and bungee jumping. Similarly, health insurance encourages risky behavior such as smoking, drinking, and unhealthy diets.

Insurance companies use various measures to decrease the moral-hazard problem. Many insurance policies have a deductible—a dollar amount that a policy holder must pay before getting compensation from the insurance company. For example, if your car insurance policy has a $500 deductible and the damage from a collision is $900, the insurance company will pay you only $400. To compute its payment, the insurance company deducts your $500 deductible from the $900 damage figure, and then pays you $400. Deductibles reduces the moral-hazard problem because they shift part of the cost of a collision to the policy holder. Like a deductible, an insurance copayment shifts part of the cost of risky behavior to policy holders and thus reduces the moral-hazard problem.

## Deposit Insurance for Savings & Loans

For another example of moral hazard, consider the insurance provided for bank deposits. When you deposit money in a Savings and Loan (S&L), the money doesn't just sit in a vault. The S&L will invest the money, loaning it out and expecting to make a profit when loans are repaid with interest. Unfortunately, some loans are not repaid, and the S&L could lose money and be unable to return your money. To protect people who put their money in S&Ls and other banks, the Federal Deposit Insurance Corporation (FDIC) insures the first $100,000 of your deposit, so if the S&L goes bankrupt, you'll still get your money back. The government enacted the federal deposit insurance law in 1933 in response to the bank failures of the Great Depression.

How does deposit insurance affect you and the people who manage the S&L? If you know you'll get your money back no matter what happens to the S&L, you may deposit your money there without evaluating the performance of the S&L and the riskiness of its loans to borrowers and investments in the stock market. The manager of an S&L will also be more likely to make risky investments knowing that if it doesn't pay off and the S&L goes bankrupt, the federal government will reimburse depositors. Recognizing this moral hazard problem, the federal government has historically limited S&Ls to relatively safe investments.

In the 1980s, the federal government loosened some of the investment restrictions on S&Ls, and S&L managers began investing in volatile securities, including high-risk commercial mortgages and junk bonds. When these risky investments failed, many of the S&Ls went into bankruptcy. The government then bailed out the failed S&Ls, at a total cost to taxpayers of about $200 billion.

# 5

# APPLICATION

## PEOPLE WITH INSURANCE TAKE MORE RISKS

APPLYING THE CONCEPTS #5: How does insurance change behavior?

At fictional Wheeler State University, 1 out of every 10 bicycles was stolen in 2004. When a group of young entrepreneurs discovered that no one on campus had bicycle theft insurance, they decided to go into the insurance business, offering one-year theft insurance for $15 per bike. They sold 100 policies in 2005 and expected 10 of their 100 customers (10 percent of them) to lose their bicycles to theft. The entrepreneurs figured that their total revenue would more than cover the cost of replacing 10 bicycles, leaving a tidy profit. By the end of 2005, a total of 20 insured bicycles had been stolen, and the students lost a bundle of money on their little enterprise. What happened?

The key to solving this puzzle is the fact that the 10-percent theft rate occurred in 2004 when *no one* had theft insurance. When the entrepreneurs offered theft insurance the next year, they expected the same theft rate. Because of moral hazard, however, the students who bought theft insurance were less careful in protecting their bikes, perhaps using less secure locks or leaving their bikes on campus overnight. As a result, the theft rate for insured bikes was 20 percent, not 10 percent. The entrepreneurs lost money because they did not anticipate that insurance would increase risk-taking.

# Chapter 7
# Production Function

In Chapter 9, we looked behind the demand curve to better understand consumer decision making. In this chapter, we look behind the supply curve to better understand firm decision making. Earlier chapters showed that supply curves are upward sloping because marginal cost increases as firms increase the quantity of a good that they supply. In this chapter, we look more closely at why this is true. In the appendix to this chapter, we extend the analysis by using isoquants and isocost lines to understand the relationship between production and costs. Once we have a good understanding of production and cost, we can proceed in the following chapters to understand how firms decide what level of output to produce and what price to charge.

10.1 | Define technology and give examples of technological change.

# Technology: An Economic Definition

**Technology** The processes a firm uses to turn inputs into outputs of goods and services.

The basic activity of a firm is to use *inputs*, such as workers, machines, and natural resources, to produce *outputs* of goods and services. A pizza parlor, for example, uses inputs such as pizza dough, pizza sauce, cooks, and ovens to produce pizza. A firm's **technology** is the processes it uses to turn inputs into outputs of goods and services. Notice that this economic definition of technology is broader than the everyday definition. When we use the word *technology* in everyday language, we usually refer only to the development of new products. In the economic sense, a firm's technology depends on many factors, such as the skill of its managers, the training of its workers, and the speed and efficiency of its machinery and equipment. The technology of pizza production, for example, includes not only the capacity of the pizza ovens and how quickly they bake the pizza but also how quickly the cooks can prepare the pizza for baking, how well the manager motivates the workers, and how well the manager has arranged the facilities to allow the cooks to quickly prepare the pizzas and get them in the ovens.

**Technological change** A change in the ability of a firm to produce a given level of output with a given quantity of inputs.

Whenever a firm experiences positive **technological change**, it is able to produce more output using the same inputs or the same output using fewer inputs. Positive technological change can come from many sources. The firm's managers may rearrange the factory floor or the layout of a retail store, thereby increasing production and sales. The firm's workers may go through a training program. The firm may install faster or more reliable machinery or equipment. It is also possible for a firm to experience negative technological change. If a firm hires less-skilled workers or if a hurricane damages its facilities, the quantity of output it can produce from a given quantity of inputs may decline.

*Better inventory controls have helped reduce firms' costs.*

## Making the Connection | Improving Inventory Control at Wal-Mart

Inventories are goods that have been produced but not yet sold. For a retailer such as Wal-Mart, inventories at any point in time include the goods on the store shelves as well as goods in warehouses. Inventories are an input into Wal-Mart's output of goods sold to consumers. Having money tied up in holding inventories is costly, so firms have an incentive to hold as few inventories as possible and to *turn over* their inventories as rapidly as possible by ensuring that goods do not remain on the shelves long. Holding too few inventories, however, results in *stockouts*—that is, sales being lost because the goods consumers want to buy are not on the shelf.

Improvements in inventory control meet the economic definition of positive technological change because they allow firms to produce the same output with fewer inputs. In recent years, many firms have adopted *just-in-time* inventory systems in which firms accept shipments from suppliers as close as possible to the time they will be needed. The just-in-time system was pioneered by Toyota, which used it to reduce the inventories of parts in its automobile assembly plants. Wal-Mart has been a pioneer in using similar inventory control systems in its stores.

Wal-Mart actively manages its *supply chain*, which stretches from the manufacturers of the goods it sells to its retail stores. Entrepreneur Sam Walton, the company founder, built a series of distribution centers spread across the country to supply goods to the retail stores. As goods are sold in the stores, this *point-of-sale* information is sent electronically to the firm's distribution centers to help managers determine what products will be shipped to each store. Depending on a store's location relative to a distribution center, managers can use Wal-Mart's trucks to ship goods overnight. This distribution system allows Wal-Mart to minimize its inventory holdings without running the risk of many stockouts. Because Wal-Mart sells 15 percent to 25 percent of all the toothpaste, disposable diapers, dog food, and many other products sold in the United States, it has been able to involve many manufacturers closely in its supply chain. For example, a company such as Procter & Gamble, which is one of the world's largest manufacturers of toothpaste, laundry detergent, toilet paper, and other products, receives Wal-Mart's point-of-sale and inventory information electronically. Procter & Gamble uses that information to help determine its production schedules and the quantities it should ship to Wal-Mart's distribution centers.

Technological change has been a key to Wal-Mart's becoming one of the largest firms in the world, with 1.9 million employees and revenue of more than $348 billion in 2006.

---

10.2 | Distinguish between the economic short run and the economic long run.

# The Short Run and the Long Run in Economics

When firms analyze the relationship between their level of production and their costs, they separate the time period involved into the short run and the long run. In the **short run**, at least one of the firm's inputs is fixed. In particular, in the short run, the firm's technology and the size of its physical plant—its factory, store, or office—are both fixed, while the number of workers the firm hires is variable. In the **long run**, the firm is able to vary all its inputs and can adopt new technology and increase or decrease the size of its physical plant. Of course, the actual length of calendar time in the short run will be different from firm to firm. A pizza parlor may be able to increase its physical plant by adding another pizza oven and some tables and chairs in just a few weeks. BMW, in contrast, may take more than a year to increase the capacity of one of its automobile assembly plants by installing new equipment.

**Short run** The period of time during which at least one of a firm's inputs is fixed.

**Long run** The period of time in which a firm can vary all its inputs, adopt new technology, and increase or decrease the size of its physical plant.

## The Difference between Fixed Costs and Variable Costs

**Total cost** is the cost of all the inputs a firm uses in production. We have just seen that in the short run, some inputs are fixed and others are variable. The costs of the fixed inputs are *fixed costs*, and the costs of the variable inputs are *variable costs*. We can also think of **variable costs** as the costs that change as output changes. Similarly, **fixed costs** are costs that remain constant as output changes. A typical firm's variable costs include its labor costs, raw material costs, and costs of electricity and other utilities. Typical fixed costs include lease payments for factory or retail space, payments for fire insurance, and payments for newspaper and television advertising. All of a firm's costs are either fixed or variable, so we can state the following:

**Total cost** The cost of all the inputs a firm uses in production.

**Variable costs** Costs that change as output changes.

**Fixed costs** Costs that remain constant as output changes.

Total Cost = Fixed Cost + Variable Cost

or, using symbols:

$$TC = FC + VC.$$

*Publishers consider the salaries of editors to be a fixed cost.*

## Making the Connection

### Fixed Costs in the Publishing Industry

An editor at Cambridge University Press gives the following estimates of the annual fixed cost for a medium-size academic book publisher.

| COST | AMOUNT |
|---|---|
| Salaries and benefits | $437,500 |
| Rent | 75,000 |
| Utilities | 20,000 |
| Supplies | 6,000 |
| Postage | 4,000 |
| Travel | 8,000 |
| Subscriptions, etc. | 4,000 |
| Miscellaneous | 5,000 |
| Total | $559,500 |

Academic book publishers hire editors, designers, and production and marketing managers who help prepare books for publication. Because these employees work on several books simultaneously, the number of people the company hires does not go up and down with the quantity of books the company publishes during any particular year. Publishing companies therefore consider the salaries and benefits of people in these job categories as fixed costs.

In contrast, for a company that *prints* books, the quantity of workers varies with the quantity of books printed. The wages and benefits of the workers operating the printing presses, for example, would be a variable cost.

The other costs listed in the preceding table are typical of fixed costs at many firms.

Source: Beth Luey, *Handbook for Academic Authors*, 4th ed., Cambridge, UK: Cambridge University Press, 2002, p. 244.

## Implicit Costs versus Explicit Costs

**Opportunity cost** The highest-valued alternative that must be given up to engage in an activity.

**Explicit cost** A cost that involves spending money.

**Implicit cost** A nonmonetary opportunity cost.

It is important to remember that economists always measure costs as *opportunity costs*. The **opportunity cost** of any activity is the highest-valued alternative that must be given up to engage in that activity. As we saw in Chapter 7, costs are either *explicit* or *implicit*. When a firm spends money, it incurs an **explicit cost**. When a firm experiences a non-monetary opportunity cost, it incurs an **implicit cost**.

For example, suppose that Jill Johnson owns a pizza restaurant. In operating her store, Jill has explicit costs, such as the wages she pays her workers and the payments she makes for rent and electricity. But some of Jill's most important costs are implicit. Before opening her own restaurant, Jill earned a salary of $30,000 per year managing a restaurant for someone else. To start her restaurant, Jill quit her job, withdrew $50,000 from her bank account—where it earned her interest of $3,000 per year—and used the funds to equip her restaurant with tables, chairs, a cash register, and other equipment. To open her own business, Jill had to give up the $30,000 salary and the $3,000 in interest. This $33,000 is an implicit cost because it does not represent payments that Jill has to make. All the same, giving up this $33,000 per year is a real cost to Jill. In addition, during the course of the year, the $50,000 worth of tables, chairs, and other physical capital in Jill's store will lose some of its value due partly to wear and tear and partly to better furniture, cash registers, and so forth becoming available. *Economic depreciation* is the difference between what Jill paid for her capital at the beginning of the year and what she could sell the capital for at the end of the year. If Jill could sell the capital for $40,000 at the end of the year, then the $10,000 in economic depreciation represents another implicit cost.

TABLE 10-1

Jill Johnson's Costs per Year

| | |
|---|---|
| Pizza dough, tomato sauce, and other ingredients | $20,000 |
| Wages | 48,000 |
| Interest payments on loan to buy pizza ovens | 10,000 |
| Electricity | 6,000 |
| Lease payment for store | 24,000 |
| Foregone salary | 30,000 |
| Foregone interest | 3,000 |
| Economic depreciation | 10,000 |
| Total | $151,000 |

(Note that the whole $50,000 she spent on the capital is not a cost because she still has the equipment at the end of the year, although it is now worth only $40,000.)

Table 10-1 lists Jill's costs. The entries in red are explicit costs, and the entries in blue are implicit costs. As we saw in Chapter 7, the rules of accounting generally require that only explicit costs be used for purposes of keeping the company's financial records and for paying taxes. Therefore, explicit costs are sometimes called *accounting costs*. *Economic costs* include both accounting costs and implicit costs.

## The Production Function

Let's look at the relationship between the level of production and costs in the short run for Jill Johnson's restaurant. To keep things simpler than in the more realistic situation in Table 10-1, let's assume that Jill uses only labor—workers—and one type of capital—pizza ovens—to produce a single good: pizzas. Many firms use more than two inputs and produce more than one good, but it is easier to understand the relationship between output and cost by focusing on the case of a firm using only two inputs and producing only one good. In the short run, Jill doesn't have time to build a larger restaurant, install additional pizza ovens, or redesign the layout of her restaurant. So, in the short run, she can increase or decrease the quantity of pizzas she produces only by increasing or decreasing the quantity of workers she employs.

The first three columns of Table 10-2 show the relationship between the quantity of workers and ovens Jill uses each week and the quantity of pizzas she can produce. The relationship between the inputs employed by a firm and the maximum output it can

TABLE 10-2 | **Short-Run Production and Cost at Jill Johnson's Restaurant**

| QUANTITY OF WORKERS | QUANTITY OF PIZZA OVENS | QUANTITY OF PIZZAS PER WEEK | COST OF PIZZA OVENS (FIXED COST) | COST OF WORKERS (VARIABLE COST) | TOTAL COST OF PIZZAS | COST PER PIZZA (AVERAGE TOTAL COST) |
|---|---|---|---|---|---|---|
| 0 | 2 | 0 | $800 | $0 | $800 | — |
| 1 | 2 | 200 | 800 | 650 | 1,450 | $7.25 |
| 2 | 2 | 450 | 800 | 1,300 | 2,100 | 4.67 |
| 3 | 2 | 550 | 800 | 1,950 | 2,750 | 5.00 |
| 4 | 2 | 600 | 800 | 2,600 | 3,400 | 5.67 |
| 5 | 2 | 625 | 800 | 3,250 | 4,050 | 6.48 |
| 6 | 2 | 640 | 800 | 3,900 | 4,700 | 7.34 |

**Production function** The relationship between the inputs employed by a firm and the maximum output it can produce with those inputs.

produce with those inputs is called the firm's **production function**. Because a firm's technology is the processes it uses to turn inputs into output, the production function represents the firm's technology. In this case, Table 10-2 shows Jill's *short-run* production function because we are assuming that the time period is too short for Jill to increase or decrease the quantity of ovens she is using.

## A First Look at the Relationship between Production and Cost

Table 10-2 gives us information on Jill's costs. We can determine the total cost of producing a given quantity of pizzas if we know how many workers and ovens are required to produce that quantity of pizzas and what Jill has to pay for those workers and pizzas. Suppose Jill has taken out a bank loan to buy two pizza ovens. The cost of the loan is $800 per week. Therefore, her fixed costs are $800 per week. If Jill pays $650 per week to each worker, her variable costs depend on how many workers she hires. In the short run, Jill can increase the quantity of pizzas she produces only by hiring more workers. The table shows that if she hires 1 worker, she produces 200 pizzas during the week; if she hires 2 workers, she produces 450 pizzas; and so on. For a particular week, Jill's total cost of producing pizzas is equal to the $800 she pays on the loan for the ovens plus the amount she pays to hire workers. If Jill decides to hire 4 workers and produce 600 pizzas, her total cost is $3,400: $800 to lease the ovens and $2,600 to hire the workers. Her cost per pizza is equal to her total cost of producing pizzas divided by the quantity of pizzas produced. If she produces 600 pizzas at a total cost of $3,400, her cost per pizza, or *average total cost*, is $3,400/600 = $5.67. A firm's **average total cost** is always equal to its total cost divided by the quantity of output produced.

**Average total cost** Total cost divided by the quantity of output produced.

Panel (a) of Figure 10-1 uses the numbers in the next-to-last column of Table 10-2 to graph Jill's total cost. Panel (b) uses the numbers in the last column to graph her average

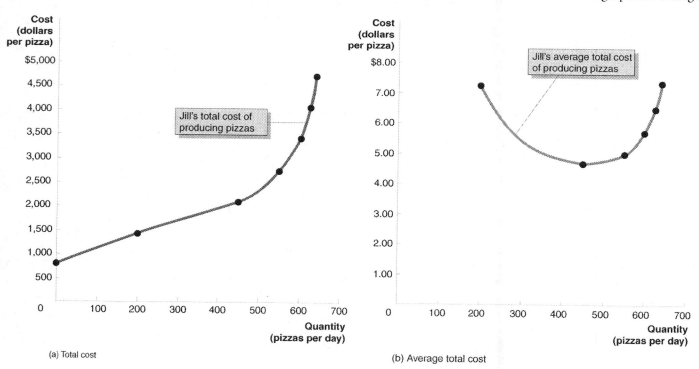

(a) Total cost

(b) Average total cost

Figure 10-1 | Graphing Total Cost and Average Total Cost at Jill Johnson's Restaurant

We can use the information from Table 10-2 to graph the relationship between the quantity of pizzas Jill produces and her total cost and average total cost. Panel (a) shows that total cost increases as the level of production increases. In panel (b), we see that the average total cost is roughly U-shaped: As production increases from low

levels, average cost falls before rising at higher levels of production. To understand why average cost has this shape, we must look more closely at the technology of producing pizzas, as shown by the production function.

total cost. Notice in panel (b) that Jill's average cost has roughly the same U shape as the average cost curve we saw Akio Morita calculate for Sony transistor radios at the beginning of this chapter. As production increases from low levels, average cost falls. Average cost then becomes fairly flat, before rising at higher levels of production. To understand why average cost has this U shape, we first need to look more closely at the technology of producing pizzas, as shown by the production function for Jill's restaurant. Then we need to look at how this technology determines the relationship between production and cost.

10.3 | Understand the relationship between the marginal product of labor and the average product of labor.

# The Marginal Product of Labor and the Average Product of Labor

To better understand the choices Jill faces, given the technology available to her, think first about what happens if she hires only one worker. That one worker will have to perform several different activities, including taking orders from customers, baking the pizzas, bringing the pizzas to the customers' tables, and ringing up sales on the cash register. If Jill hires two workers, some of these activities can be divided up: One worker could take the orders and ring up the sales, and one worker could bake the pizzas. With this division of tasks, Jill will find that hiring two workers actually allows her to produce more than twice as many pizzas as she could produce with just one worker.

The additional output a firm produces as a result of hiring one more worker is called the **marginal product of labor**. We can calculate the marginal product of labor by determining how much total output increases as each additional worker is hired. We do this for Jill's restaurant in Table 10-3.

**Marginal product of labor** The additional output a firm produces as a result of hiring one more worker.

When Jill hires only 1 worker, she produces 200 pizzas per week. When she hires 2 workers, she produces 450 pizzas per week. Hiring the second worker increases her production by 250 pizzas per week. So, the marginal product of labor for 1 worker is 200 pizzas. For 2 workers, the marginal product of labor rises to 250 pizzas. This increase in marginal product results from the *division of labor* and from *specialization*. By dividing the tasks to be performed—the division of labor—Jill reduces the time workers lose moving from one activity to the next. She also allows them to become more specialized at their tasks. For example, a worker who concentrates on baking pizzas will become skilled at doing so quickly and efficiently.

## The Law of Diminishing Returns

In the short run, the quantity of pizza ovens Jill leases is fixed, so as she hires more workers, the marginal product of labor eventually begins to decline. This happens because at some point, Jill uses up all the gains from the division of labor and from specialization

| QUANTITY OF WORKERS | QUANTITY OF PIZZA OVENS | QUANTITY OF PIZZAS | MARGINAL PRODUCT OF LABOR |
|---|---|---|---|
| 0 | 2 | 0 | — |
| 1 | 2 | 200 | 200 |
| 2 | 2 | 450 | 250 |
| 3 | 2 | 550 | 100 |
| 4 | 2 | 600 | 50 |
| 5 | 2 | 625 | 25 |
| 6 | 2 | 640 | 15 |

**TABLE 10-3**

The Marginal Product of Labor at Jill Johnson's Restaurant

**Law of diminishing returns** The principle that, at some point, adding more of a variable input, such as labor, to the same amount of a fixed input, such as capital, will cause the marginal product of the variable input to decline.

and starts to experience the effects of the **law of diminishing returns**. This law states that adding more of a variable input, such as labor, to the same amount of a fixed input, such as capital, will eventually cause the marginal product of the variable input to decline. For Jill, the marginal product of labor begins to decline when she hires the third worker. Hiring three workers raises the quantity of pizzas she produces from 450 per week to 550. But the increase in the quantity of pizzas—100—is less than the increase when she hired the second worker—250.

If Jill kept adding more and more workers to the same quantity of pizza ovens, eventually workers would begin to get in each other's way, and the marginal product of labor would actually become negative. When the marginal product is negative, the level of total output declines. No firm would actually hire so many workers as to experience a negative marginal product of labor and falling total output.

## Graphing Production

Panel (a) in Figure 10-2 shows the relationship between the quantity of workers Jill hires and her total output of pizzas, using the numbers from Table 10-3. Panel (b) shows the marginal product of labor. In panel (a), output increases as more workers are hired, but the increase in output does not occur at a constant rate. Because of specialization and the division of labor, output at first increases at an increasing rate, with each additional worker hired causing production to increase by a *greater* amount than did the hiring of the previous worker. But after the second worker has been hired, hiring more workers while keeping the quantity of ovens constant results in diminishing returns. When the point of diminishing returns is reached, production increases at a decreasing rate. Each additional worker hired after the second worker causes production to increase by a *smaller* amount than did the hiring of the previous worker. In panel (b), the marginal product of labor curve rises initially because of the effects of specialization and division of labor, and then it falls due to the effects of diminishing returns.

*The gains from division of labor and specialization are as important to firms today as they were in the eighteenth century, when Adam Smith first discussed them.*

Making the Connection | **Adam Smith's Famous Account of the Division of Labor in a Pin Factory**

In *The Wealth of Nations*, Adam Smith uses production in a pin factory as an example of the gains in output resulting from the division of labor. The following is an excerpt from his account of how pin making was divided into a series of tasks:

> One man draws out the wire, another straightens it, a third cuts it, a fourth points it, a fifth grinds it at the top for receiving the head; to make the head requires two or three distinct operations; to put it on is a [distinct operation], to whiten the pins is another; it is even a trade by itself to put them into the paper; and the important business of making a pin is, in this manner, divided into eighteen distinct operations.

Because the labor of pin making was divided up in this way, the average worker was able to produce about 4,800 pins per day. Smith speculated that a single worker using the pin-making machinery alone would make only about 20 pins per day. This lesson from more than 225 years ago, showing the tremendous gains from division of labor and specialization, remains relevant to most business situations today.

Source: Adam Smith, *An Inquiry into the Nature and Causes of the Wealth of Nations*, Vol. I, Oxford, UK: Oxford University Press edition, 1976, pp. 14–15.

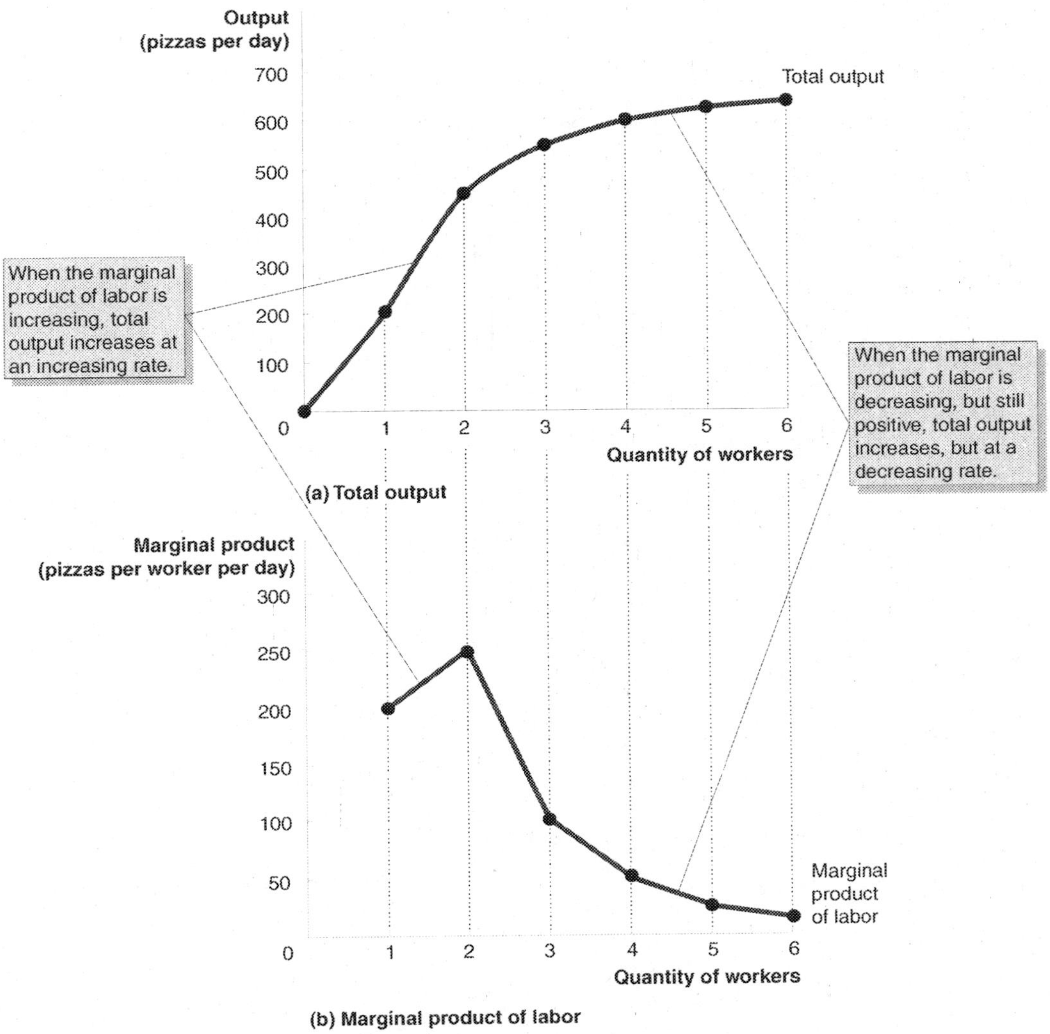

Figure 10-2 | Total Output and the Marginal Product of Labor

In panel (a), output increases as more workers are hired, but the increase in output does not occur at a constant rate. Because of specialization and the division of labor, output at first increases at an increasing rate, with each additional worker hired causing production to increase by a *greater* amount than did the hiring of the previous worker. After the third worker has been hired, hiring more workers while keeping the number of pizza ovens constant results in diminishing returns. When the point of diminishing returns is reached, production increases at a decreasing rate. Each additional worker hired after the third worker causes production to increase by a *smaller* amount than did the hiring of the previous worker. In panel (b), the *marginal product of labor* is the additional output produced as a result of hiring one more worker. The marginal product of labor rises initially because of the effects of specialization and division of labor, and then it falls due to the effects of diminishing returns.

## The Relationship between Marginal and Average Product

The marginal product of labor tells us how much total output changes as the quantity of workers hired changes. We can also calculate how many pizzas workers produce on average. The **average product of labor** is the total output produced by a firm divided by the quantity of workers. For example, using the numbers in Table 10-3, if Jill hires 4 workers to produce 600 pizzas, the average product of labor is 600/4 = 150.

We can state the relationship between the marginal and average products of labor this way: *The average product of labor is the average of the marginal products of labor.* For example, the numbers from Table 10-3 show that the marginal product of the first worker Jill hires is 200, the marginal product of the second worker is 250, and the

**Average product of labor** The total output produced by a firm divided by the quantity of workers.

marginal product of the third worker is 100. Therefore, the average product of labor for three workers is 183.3:

$$183.3 = (200 + 250 + 100) / 3$$

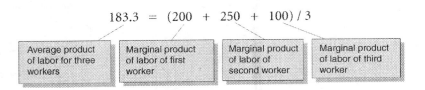

By taking the average of the marginal products of the first three workers, we have the average product of the three workers.

Whenever the marginal product of labor is greater than the average product of labor, the average product of labor must be increasing. This statement is true for the same reason that a person 6 feet, 2 inches tall entering a room where the average height is 5 feet, 9 inches raises the average height of people in the room. Whenever the marginal product of labor is less than the average product of labor, the average product of labor must be decreasing. The marginal product of labor equals the average product of labor for the quantity of workers where the average product of labor is at its maximum.

## An Example of Marginal and Average Values: College Grades

The relationship between the marginal product of labor and the average product of labor is the same as the relationship between the marginal and average values of any variable. To see this more clearly, think about the familiar relationship between a student's grade point average (GPA) in one semester and his overall, or cumulative, GPA. The table in Figure 10-3 shows Paul's college grades for each semester, beginning with fall 2005. The graph in Figure 10-3 plots the grades from the table. Just as each additional worker hired adds to a firm's total production, each additional semester adds to Paul's total grade points. We can calculate what each individual worker hired adds to total production (marginal product), and we can calculate the average production of the workers hired so far (average product).

Similarly, we can calculate the GPA Paul earns in a particular semester (his "marginal GPA"), and we can calculate his cumulative GPA for all the semesters he has completed so far (his "average GPA"). As the table shows, Paul gets off to a weak start in the fall semester of his freshman year, earning only a 1.50 GPA. In each subsequent semester through the fall of his junior year, his GPA for the semester increases from the previous semester——raising his cumulative GPA. As the graph shows, however, his cumulative GPA does not increase as rapidly as his semester-by-semester GPA because his cumulative GPA is held back by the low GPAs of his first few semesters. Notice that in Paul's junior year, even though his semester GPA declines from fall to spring, his cumulative GPA rises. Only in the fall of his senior year, when his semester GPA drops below his cumulative GPA, does his cumulative GPA decline.

**10.4 LEARNING** OBJECTIVE

10.4 | Explain and illustrate the relationship between marginal cost and average total cost.

# The Relationship between Short-Run Production and Short-Run Cost

We have seen that technology determines the values of the marginal product of labor and the average product of labor. In turn, the marginal and average products of labor affect the firm's costs. Keep in mind that the relationships we are discussing are *short-run* relationships: We are assuming that the time period is too short for the firm to change its technology or the size of its physical plant.

Figure 10-3

**Marginal and Average GPAs**

The relationship between marginal and average values for a variable can be illustrated using GPAs. We can calculate the GPA Paul earns in a particular semester (his "marginal GPA"), and we can calculate his cumulative GPA for all the semesters he has completed so far (his "average GPA"). Paul's GPA is only 1.50 in the fall semester of his freshman year. In each following semester through fall of his junior year, his GPA for the semester increases——raising his cumulative GPA. In Paul's junior year, even though his semester GPA declines from fall to spring, his cumulative GPA rises. Only in the fall of his senior year, when his semester GPA drops below his cumulative GPA, does his cumulative GPA decline.

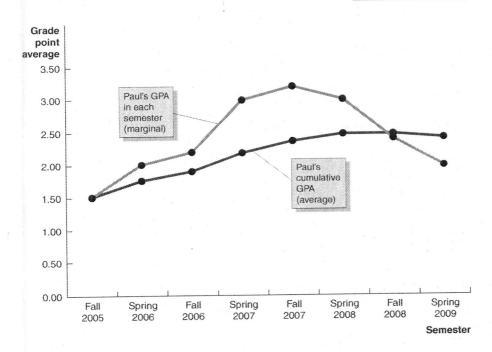

| | Semester GPA (Marginal) GPA | Cumulative GPA (Average) GPA |
|---|---|---|
| *Freshman Year* | | |
| Fall | 1.50 | 1.50 |
| Spring | 2.00 | 1.75 |
| *Sophomore Year* | | |
| Fall | 2.20 | 1.90 |
| Spring | 3.00 | 2.18 |
| *Junior Year* | | |
| Fall | 3.20 | 2.38 |
| Spring | 3.00 | 2.48 |
| *Senior Year* | | |
| Fall | 2.40 | 2.47 |
| Spring | 2.00 | 2.41 |

Average GPA continues to rise, although marginal GPA falls.

With the marginal GPA below the average, the average GPA falls.

Paul's GPA in each semester (marginal)

Paul's cumulative GPA (average)

At the beginning of this chapter, we saw how Akio Morita used an average total cost curve to determine the price of radios. The average total cost curve Morita used and the average total cost curve in Figure 10-1 for Jill Johnson's restaurant both have a U shape. As we will soon see, the U shape of the average total cost curve is determined by the shape of the curve that shows the relationship between *marginal cost* and the level of production.

## Marginal Cost

As we saw in Chapter 1, one of the key ideas in economics is that optimal decisions are made at the margin. Consumers, firms, and government officials usually make decisions about doing a little more or a little less. As Jill Johnson considers whether to hire additional workers to produce additional pizzas, she needs to consider how much she will add to her total cost by producing the additional pizzas. **Marginal cost** is the change in a firm's total cost from producing one more unit of a good or service. We can calculate marginal cost for a particular increase in output by dividing the change in cost by the

**Marginal cost** The change in a firm's total cost from producing one more unit of a good or service.

change in output. We can express this idea mathematically (remembering that the Greek letter delta, Δ, means "change in"):

$$MC = \frac{\Delta TC}{\Delta Q}.$$

In the table in Figure 10-4, we use this equation to calculate Jill's marginal cost of producing pizzas.

## Why Are the Marginal and Average Cost Curves U-Shaped?

Notice in the graph in Figure 10-4 that Jill's marginal cost of producing pizzas declines at first and then increases, giving the marginal cost curve a U shape. The table in Figure 10-4 also shows the marginal product of labor. This table helps us see the important relationship between the marginal product of labor and the marginal cost of production: The marginal product of labor is *rising* for the first two workers, but the marginal cost of the pizzas produced by these workers is *falling*. The marginal product of labor is *falling* for the last four workers, but the marginal cost of pizzas produced by these workers is *rising*. To summarize this point: *When the marginal product of labor is rising, the marginal cost of output is falling. When the marginal product of labor is falling, the marginal cost of production is rising.*

### Figure 10-4

Jill Johnson's Marginal Cost and Average Total Cost of Producing Pizzas

We can use the information in the table to calculate Jill's marginal cost and average total cost of producing pizzas. For the first two workers hired, the marginal product of labor is increasing. This increase causes the marginal cost of production to fall. For the last four workers hired, the marginal product of labor is falling. This causes the marginal cost of production to increase. Therefore, the marginal cost curve falls and then rises—that is, has a U shape—because the marginal product of labor rises and then falls. As long as marginal cost is below average total cost, average total cost will be falling. When marginal cost is above average total cost, average total cost will be rising. The relationship between marginal cost and average total cost explains why the average total cost curve also has a U shape.

| Quantity of Workers | Quantity of Ovens | Marginal Product of Labor | Total Cost of Pizzas | Marginal Cost of Pizzas | Average Total Cost of Pizzas |
|---|---|---|---|---|---|
| 0 | 0 | — | $800 | — | — |
| 1 | 200 | 200 | 1,450 | $3.25 | $7.25 |
| 2 | 450 | 250 | 2,100 | 2.60 | 4.67 |
| 3 | 550 | 100 | 2,750 | 6.50 | 5.00 |
| 4 | 600 | 50 | 3,400 | 13.00 | 5.67 |
| 5 | 625 | 25 | 4,050 | 26.00 | 6.48 |
| 6 | 640 | 15 | 4,700 | 43.33 | 7.34 |

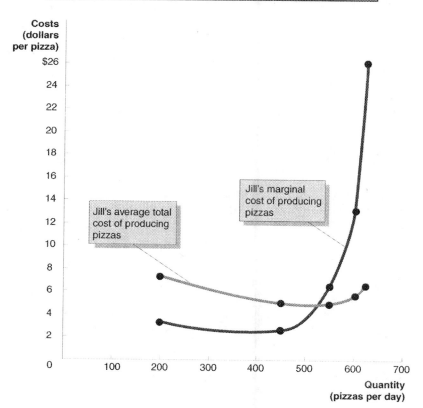

One way to understand why this point is true is first to notice that the only additional cost to Jill from producing more pizzas is the additional wages she pays to hire more workers. She pays each new worker the same $650 per week. So the marginal cost of the additional pizzas each worker makes depends on that worker's additional output, or marginal product. As long as the additional output from each new worker is rising, the marginal cost of that output is falling. When the additional output from each new worker is falling, the marginal cost of that output is rising. *We can conclude that the marginal cost of production falls and then rises—forming a U shape—because the marginal product of labor rises and then falls.*

The relationship between marginal cost and average total cost follows the usual relationship between marginal and average values. As long as marginal cost is below average total cost, average total cost falls. When marginal cost is above average total cost, average total cost rises. Marginal cost equals average total cost when average total cost is at its lowest point. Therefore, the average total cost curve has a U shape because the marginal cost curve has a U shape.

# Solved Problem | 10-4

## The Relationship between Marginal Cost and Average Cost

Is Jill Johnson right or wrong when she says the following? "I am currently producing 10,000 pizzas per month at a total cost of $500.00. If I produce 10,001 pizzas, my total cost will rise to $500.11. Therefore, my marginal cost of producing pizzas must be increasing." Draw a graph to illustrate your answer.

### SOLVING THE PROBLEM:

**Step 1:** **Review the chapter material.** This problem requires understanding the relationship between marginal and average cost, so you may want to review the section "Why Are the Marginal and Average Cost Curves U-Shaped?" which begins on page 344.

**Step 2:** **Calculate average total cost and marginal cost.** Average total cost is total cost divided by total output. In this case, average total cost is $500.11/10,001 = $0.05. Marginal cost is the change in total cost divided by the change in output. In this case, marginal cost is $0.11/1 = $0.11.

**Step 3:** **Use the relationship between marginal cost and average total cost to answer the question.** When marginal cost is greater than average total cost, marginal cost must be increasing. You have shown in step 2 that marginal cost is greater than average total cost. Therefore, Jill is right: Her marginal cost of producing pizzas must be increasing.

**Step 4:** **Draw the graph.**

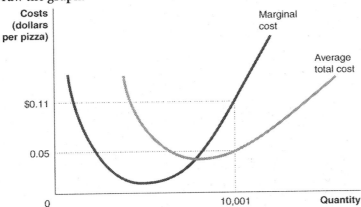

10.5 | Graph average total cost, average variable cost, average fixed cost, and marginal cost.

# Graphing Cost Curves

**Average fixed cost** Fixed cost divided by the quantity of output produced.

**Average variable cost** Variable cost divided by the quantity of output produced.

We have seen that we calculate average total cost by dividing total cost by the quantity of output produced. Similarly, we can calculate **average fixed cost** by dividing fixed cost by the quantity of output produced. And we can calculate **average variable cost** by dividing variable cost by the quantity of output produced. Or, mathematically, with $Q$ being the level of output, we have:

$$\text{Average total cost} = ATC = \frac{TC}{Q}$$

$$\text{Average fixed cost} = AFC = \frac{FC}{Q}$$

$$\text{Average variable cost} = AVC = \frac{VC}{Q}.$$

Finally, notice that average total cost is the sum of average fixed cost plus average variable cost:

$$ATC = AFC + AVC.$$

The only fixed cost Jill incurs in operating her restaurant is the $800 per week she pays on the bank loan for her pizza ovens. Her variable costs are the wages she pays her workers. The table and graph in Figure 10-5 show Jill's costs.

We will use graphs like the one in Figure 10-5 in the next several chapters to analyze how firms decide the level of output to produce and the price to charge. Before going further, be sure you understand the following three key facts about Figure 10-5:

1. The marginal cost (*MC*), average total cost (*ATC*), and average variable cost (*AVC*) curves are all U-shaped, and the marginal cost curve intersects the average variable cost and average total cost curves at their minimum points. When marginal cost is less than either average variable cost or average total cost, it causes them to decrease. When marginal cost is above average variable cost or average total cost, it causes them to increase. Therefore, when marginal cost equals average variable cost or average total cost, they must be at their minimum points.

2. As output increases, average fixed cost gets smaller and smaller. This happens because in calculating average fixed cost, we are dividing something that gets larger and larger—output—into something that remains constant—fixed cost. Firms often refer to this process of lowering average fixed cost by selling more output as "spreading the overhead." By "overhead" they mean fixed costs.

3. As output increases, the difference between average total cost and average variable cost decreases. This happens because the difference between average total cost and average variable cost is average fixed cost, which gets smaller as output increases.

10.6 | Understand how firms use the long-run average cost curve in their planning.

# Costs in the Long Run

The distinction between fixed cost and variable cost that we just discussed applies to the short run but *not* to the long run. For example, in the short run, Jill Johnson has fixed costs of $800 per week because she signed a loan agreement with a bank when she bought her pizza ovens. In the long run, the cost of purchasing more pizza ovens becomes variable because Jill can choose whether to expand her business by buying

| Quantity of Workers | Quantity of Ovens | Quantity of Pizzas | Cost of Ovens (Fixed Cost) | Cost of Workers (Variable Cost) | Total Cost of Pizzas | ATC | AFC | AVC | MC |
|---|---|---|---|---|---|---|---|---|---|
| 0 | 2 | 0 | $800 | $0 | $800 | – | – | – | – |
| 1 | 2 | 200 | 800 | 650 | 1,450 | $7.25 | $4.00 | $3.25 | $3.25 |
| 2 | 2 | 450 | 800 | 1,300 | 2,100 | 4.67 | 1.78 | 2.89 | 2.60 |
| 3 | 2 | 550 | 800 | 1,950 | 2,750 | 5.00 | 1.45 | 3.55 | 6.50 |
| 4 | 2 | 600 | 800 | 2,600 | 3,400 | 5.67 | 1.33 | 4.33 | 13.00 |
| 5 | 2 | 625 | 800 | 3,250 | 4,050 | 6.48 | 1.28 | 5.2 | 26.00 |
| 6 | 2 | 640 | 800 | 3,900 | 4,700 | 7.34 | 1.25 | 6.09 | 43.33 |

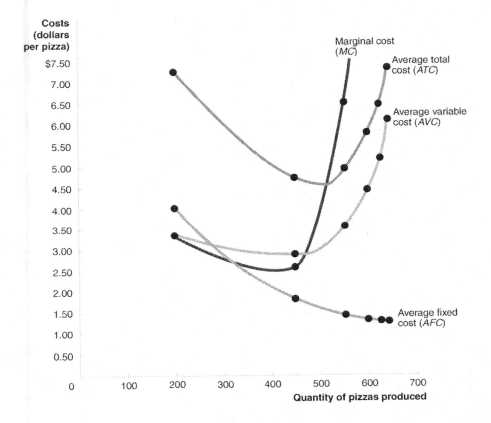

### Figure 10-5

**Costs at Jill Johnson's Restaurant**

Jill's costs of making pizzas are shown in the table and plotted in the graph. Notice three important facts about the graph: (1) The marginal cost (*MC*), average total cost (*ATC*), and average variable cost (*AVC*) curves are all U-shaped, and the marginal cost curve intersects both the average variable cost curve and average total cost curve at their minimum points. (2) As output increases, average fixed cost (*AFC*) gets smaller and smaller. (3) As output increases, the difference between average total cost and average variable cost decreases. Make sure you can explain why each of these three facts is true. You should spend time becoming familiar with this graph because it is one of the most important graphs in microeconomics.

more ovens. The same would be true of any other fixed costs a company like Jill's might have. Once a company has purchased a fire insurance policy, the cost of the policy is fixed. But when the policy expires, the company must decide whether to renew it, and the cost becomes variable. The important point here is this: *In the long run, all costs are variable. There are no fixed costs in the long run.* In other words, in the long run, total cost equals variable cost, and average total cost equals average variable cost.

Managers of successful firms simultaneously consider how they can most profitably run their current store, factory, or office and also whether in the long run they would be more profitable if they became larger or, possibly, smaller. Jill must consider how to run her current restaurant, which has only two pizza ovens, and she must also plan what to do when her current bank loan is paid off and the lease on her store ends. Should she buy more pizza ovens? Should she lease a larger restaurant?

## Economies of Scale

Short-run average cost curves represent the costs a firm faces when some input, such as the quantity of machines it uses, is fixed. The **long-run average cost curve** shows the lowest cost at which a firm is able to produce a given level of output in the long run, when no inputs are fixed. Many firms experience **economies of scale**, which means the

**Long-run average cost curve** A curve showing the lowest cost at which a firm is able to produce a given quantity of output in the long run, when no inputs are fixed.

**Economies of scale** The situation when a firm's long-run average costs fall as it increases output.

## Figure 10-6

The Relationship between
Short-Run Average Cost and
Long-Run Average Cost

If a small bookstore expects to sell only 1,000 books per month, then it will be able to sell that quantity of books at the lowest average cost of $22 per book if it builds the small store represented by the *ATC* curve on the left of the figure. A larger bookstore will be able to sell 20,000 books per month at a lower cost of $18 per book. A bookstore selling 20,000 books per month and a bookstore selling 40,000 books per month will experience constant returns to scale and have the same average cost. A bookstore selling 20,000 books per month will have reached minimum efficient scale. Very large bookstores will experience diseconomies of scale, and their average costs will rise as sales increase beyond 40,000 books per month.

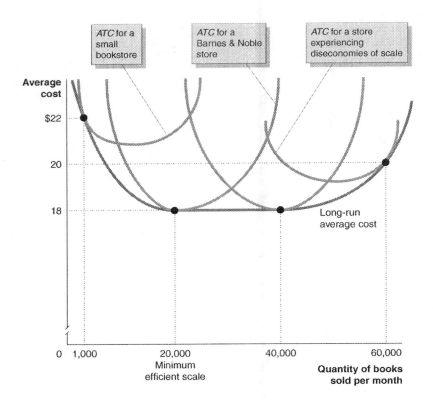

firm's long-run average costs fall as it increases the quantity of output it produces. We can see the effects of economies of scale in Figure 10-6, which shows the relationship between short-run and long-run average cost curves. Managers can use long-run average cost curves for planning because they show the effect on cost of expanding output by, for example, building a larger factory or store.

## Long-Run Average Total Cost Curves for Bookstores

Figure 10-6 shows long-run average cost in the retail bookstore industry. If a small bookstore expects to sell only 1,000 books per month, then it will be able to sell that quantity of books at the lowest average cost of $22 per book if it builds the small store represented by the *ATC* curve on the left of the figure. A much larger bookstore, such as one run by a national chain like Barnes & Noble, will be able to sell 20,000 books per month at a lower average cost of $18 per book. This decline in average cost from $22 to $18 represents the economies of scale that exist in bookselling. Why would the larger bookstore have lower average costs? One important reason is that the Barnes & Noble store is selling 20 times as many books per month as the small store but might need only six times as many workers. This saving in labor cost would reduce Barnes & Noble's average cost of selling books.

Firms may experience economies of scale for several reasons. First, as in the case of Barnes & Noble, the firm's technology may make it possible to increase production with a smaller proportional increase in at least one input. Second, both workers and managers can become more specialized, enabling them to become more productive, as output expands. Third, large firms, like Barnes & Noble, Wal-Mart, and General Motors, may be able to purchase inputs at lower costs than smaller competitors. In fact, as Wal-Mart expanded, its bargaining power with its suppliers increased, and its average costs fell. Finally, as a firm expands, it may be able to borrow money more inexpensively, thereby lowering its costs.

Economies of scale do not continue forever. The long-run average cost curve in most industries has a flat segment that often stretches over a substantial range of output. As Figure 10-6 shows, a bookstore selling 20,000 books per month and a bookstore selling 40,000 books per month have the same average cost. Over this range of output, firms in the industry experience **constant returns to scale**. As these firms increase their output, they have to increase their inputs, such as the size of the store and the quantity of

**Constant returns to scale** The situation when a firm's long-run average costs remain unchanged as it increases output.

workers, proportionally. The level of output at which all economies of scale are exhausted is known as **minimum efficient scale**. A bookstore selling 20,000 books per month has reached minimum efficient scale.

Very large bookstores experience increasing average costs as managers begin to have difficulty coordinating the operation of the store. Figure 10-6 shows that for sales above 40,000 books per month, firms in the industry experience **diseconomies of scale**. Toyota ran into diseconomies of scale in assembling automobiles. The firm found that as it expanded production at its Georgetown, Kentucky, plant and its plants in China, its managers had difficulty keeping costs from rising. The president of Toyota's Georgetown plant was quoted as saying, "Demand for . . . high volumes saps your energy. Over a period of time, it eroded our focus . . . [and] thinned out the expertise and knowledge we painstakingly built up over the years." One analysis of the problems Toyota faced in expanding production concluded: "It is the kind of paradox many highly successful companies face: Getting bigger doesn't always mean getting better."

**Minimum efficient scale** The level of output at which all economies of scale are exhausted.

**Diseconomies of scale** The situation when a firm's long-run average costs rise as the firm increases output.

# Solved Problem | 10-6

## Using Long-Run Average Cost Curves to Understand Business Strategy

In fall 2002, Motorola and Siemens were each manufacturing both mobile phone handsets and wireless infrastructure—the base stations needed to operate a wireless communications network. The firms discussed the following arrangement: Motorola would give Siemens its wireless infrastructure business in exchange for Siemens giving Motorola its mobile phone handsets business. The main factor motivating the trade was the hope of taking advantage of economies of scale in each business. Use long-run average total cost curves to explain why this trade might make sense for Motorola and Siemens.

## SOLVING THE PROBLEM:

Step 1:  **Review the chapter material.** This problem is about the long-run average cost curve, so you may want to review the material in the section "Costs in the Long Run," which begins on page 346.

Step 2:  **Draw long-run average cost graphs for Motorola and Siemens.** The question does not provide us with the details of the quantity of each product each firm is producing before the trade or the firms' average costs of production. If economies of scale were an important reason for the trade, we can assume that Motorola and Siemens were not yet at minimum efficient scale in the wireless infrastructure and phone handset businesses. Therefore, we can draw the following graphs:

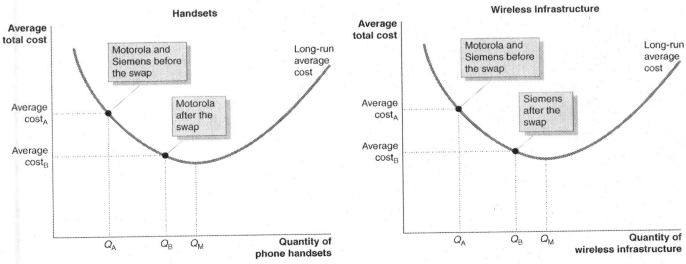

**Step 3:** **Explain the curves in the graphs.** Before the proposed trade, Motorola and Siemens are producing both products at less than the minimum efficient scale, which is $Q_M$ in both graphs. After the trade, Motorola's production of handsets will increase, moving it from $Q_A$ to $Q_B$ in the first graph. This increase in production will allow it to take advantage of economies of scale and reduce its average cost from Average Cost$_A$ to Average Cost$_B$. Similarly, production of wireless infrastructure by Siemens will increase from $Q_A$ to $Q_B$, lowering its average cost from Average Cost$_A$ to Average Cost$_B$. As drawn, the graphs show that both firms will still be short of minimum efficient scale after the trade, although their average costs will have fallen.

**EXTRA CREDIT:** These were new technologies at the time Motorola and Siemens discussed the trade. As a result, companies making these products were only beginning to understand how large minimum efficient scale was. To survive in the industry, the managements of both companies wanted to lower their costs by taking advantage of economies of scale. As one industry analyst put it: "Motorola and Siemens may be driven by the conviction that they have little choice. Most observers believe consolidation in both the [wireless] networking and handset areas is inevitable."

Source for quote: Ray Hegarty, *Rumored Motorola-Siemens Business Unit Swap? A Compelling M&A Story,* www.thefeature.com.

>> **End Solved Problem 10-6**

Over time, most firms in an industry will build factories or stores that are at least as large as the minimum efficient scale but not so large that diseconomies of scale occur. In the bookstore industry, stores will sell between 20,000 and 40,000 books per month. However, firms often do not know the exact shape of their long-run average cost curves. As a result, they may mistakenly build factories or stores that are either too large or too small.

Making | **The Colossal River Rouge:**
the |
Connection | **Diseconomies of Scale at**
| **Ford Motor Company**

When Henry Ford started the Ford Motor Company in 1903, automobile companies produced cars in small workshops, using highly skilled workers. Ford introduced two new ideas that allowed him to take advantage of economies of scale. First, Ford used identical—or, interchangeable—parts so that unskilled workers

could assemble the cars. Second, instead of having groups of workers moving from one stationary automobile to the next, he had the workers remain stationary while the automobiles moved along an assembly line. Ford built a large factory at Highland Park, outside Detroit, where he used these ideas to produce the famous Model T at an average cost well below what his competitors could match using older production methods in smaller factories.

Ford believed that he could produce automobiles at an even lower average cost by building a still larger plant along the River Rouge. Unfortunately, Ford's River Rouge plant was too large and suffered from diseconomies of scale. Ford's managers had great difficulty coordinating the production of automobiles in such a large plant. The following description of the River Rouge comes from a biography of Ford by Allan Nevins and Frank Ernest Hill:

A total of 93 separate structures stood on the [River Rouge] site. . . . Railroad trackage covered 93 miles, conveyors 27 [miles]. About 75,000 men worked in the great plant. A force of 5000 did

*Is it possible for a factory to be too big?*

nothing but keep it clean, wearing out 5000 mops and 3000 brooms a month, and using 86 tons of soap on the floors, walls, and 330 acres of windows. The Rouge was an industrial city, immense, concentrated, packed with power. . . . By its very massiveness and complexity, it denied men at the top contact with and understanding of those beneath, and gave those beneath a sense of being lost in inexorable immensity and power.

Beginning in 1927, Ford produced the Model A—its only car model at that time—at the River Rouge plant. Ford failed to achieve economies of scale and actually *lost money* on each of the four Model A body styles.

Ford could not raise the price of the Model A to make it profitable because at a higher price, the car could not compete with similar models produced by competitors such as General Motors and Chrysler. He eventually reduced the cost of making the Model A by constructing smaller factories spread out across the country. These smaller factories produced the Model A at a lower average cost than was possible at the River Rouge plant.

Source for quote: Allan Nevins and Frank Ernest Hill, *Ford: Expansion and Challenge, 1915–1933*, New York: Scribner, 1957, pp. 293, 295.

# Don't Let This Happen to **YOU!**

## DON'T CONFUSE DIMINISHING RETURNS WITH DISECONOMIES OF SCALE

The concepts of diminishing returns and diseconomies of scale may seem similar, but, in fact, they are unrelated. Diminishing returns applies only to the short run, when at least one of the firm's inputs, such as the quantity of machinery it uses, is fixed. The law of diminishing returns tells us that in the short run, hiring more workers will, at some point, result in less additional output. Diminishing returns explains why marginal cost curves eventually slope upward. Diseconomies of scale apply only in the long run, when the firm is free to vary all its inputs, can adopt new technology, and can vary the amount of machinery it uses and the size of its facility. Diseconomies of scale explain why long-run average cost curves eventually slope upward.

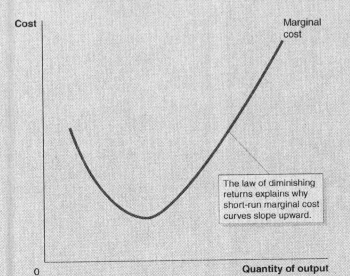

The law of diminishing returns explains why short-run marginal cost curves slope upward.

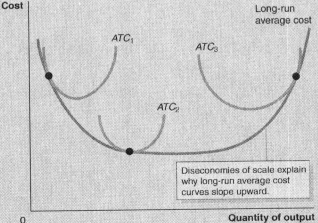

Diseconomies of scale explain why long-run average cost curves slope upward.

## Conclusion

In this chapter, we discussed the relationship between a firm's technology, production, and costs. In the discussion, we encountered a number of definitions of costs. Because we will use these definitions in later chapters, it is useful to bring them together in Table 10-4 for you to review.

We have seen the important relationship between a firm's level of production and its costs. Just as this information was vital to Akio Morita in deciding which price to charge for his transistor radios, so it remains vital today to all firms as they attempt to decide the optimal level of production and the optimal prices to charge for their products.

TABLE 10-4

**A Summary of Definitions of Cost**

| TERM | DEFINITION | SYMBOLS AND EQUATIONS |
|------|-----------|----------------------|
| Total cost | The cost of all the inputs used by a firm, or fixed cost plus variable cost | $TC$ |
| Fixed cost | Costs that remain constant when a firm's level of output changes | $FC$ |
| Variable cost | Costs that change when the firm's level of output changes | $VC$ |
| Marginal cost | Increase in total cost resulting from producing another unit of output | $MC = \dfrac{\Delta TC}{\Delta Q}$ |
| Average total cost | Total cost divided by the quantity of output produced | $ATC = \dfrac{TC}{Q}$ |
| Average fixed cost | Fixed cost divided by the quantity of output produced | $AFC = \dfrac{FC}{Q}$ |
| Average variable cost | Variable cost divided by the quantity of output produced | $AVC = \dfrac{VC}{Q}$ |
| Implicit cost | A nonmonetary opportunity cost | — |
| Explicit cost | A cost that involves spending money | — |

- **economic profit**
  Total revenue minus economic cost.

- **economic cost**
  The opportunity cost of the inputs used in the production process; equal to explicit cost plus implicit cost.

- **explicit cost**
  The actual monetary payment for inputs.

- **implicit cost**
  The opportunity cost of inputs that do not require a monetary payment.

This chapter explores the relationship between the quantity of output produced and the cost of production. As we'll see, a firm's production cost is determined by its production technology—the way the firm combines capital, labor, and materials to produce output. After we explain the link between technology and costs, we'll look at the actual cost curves of several products, including aluminum, hospital services, wind power, truck freight, and airplanes.

As we saw in Chapter 2, economists distinguish between the short run and the long run. The long run is a period long enough that a firm is perfectly flexible in its choice of all inputs, including its production facility. In contrast, when a firm cannot modify its facility, it is operating in the short run. In this chapter, we'll explore both short-run and long-run costs. In later chapters, we'll show how firms use short-run and long-run cost curves to make decisions about whether to enter a market and how much output to produce.

# 8.1 | ECONOMIC COST AND ECONOMIC PROFIT

This is the first of several chapters on the decisions firms make. A firm's objective is to maximize its **economic profit**, which equals its total revenue minus its economic cost:

$$\text{economic profit} = \text{total revenue} - \text{economic cost}$$

As we saw earlier in the book, a firm's total revenue is the money it gets from selling its product. If a firm charges the same price to every consumer, its total revenue equals the price per unit of output times the quantity sold.

This chapter explores the firm's cost of production. A firm's **economic cost** equals the cost of all the inputs used in the production process; it is measured as the opportunity cost of the inputs. Recall the first key principle of economics.

## PRINCIPLE OF OPPORTUNITY COST

The opportunity cost of something is what you sacrifice to get it.

To compute a firm's economic cost, we must determine what the firm sacrifices to use inputs in the production process. Economic cost is opportunity cost.

As shown in the first column of numbers in Table 8.1, a firm's economic cost can be divided into two types. A firm's **explicit cost** is its actual monetary payments for inputs. For example, if a firm spends a total of $10,000 per month on labor, capital, and materials, its explicit cost is $10,000. This is an opportunity cost because money spent on these inputs cannot be used to buy something else. A firm's **implicit cost** is the opportunity cost of the inputs that do not require a monetary payment. Here are two examples of inputs whose cost is implicit rather than explicit:

- *Opportunity cost of the entrepreneur's time.* If an entrepreneur could earn $5,000 per month in another job, the opportunity cost of the time spent running the firm is $5,000 per month.

**Table 8.1 | ECONOMIC COST VERSUS ACCOUNTING COST**

|  | Economic Cost | Accounting Cost |
|---|---|---|
| Explicit: monetary payments for labor, capital, materials | $10,000 | $10,000 |
| Implicit: opportunity cost of entrepreneur's time | 5,000 | — |
| Implicit: opportunity cost of funds | 2,000 | — |
| **Total** | 17,000 | 10,000 |

• *Opportunity cost of the entrepreneur's funds.* Many entrepreneurs use their own funds to set up and run their businesses. If an entrepreneur starts a business with $200,000 withdrawn from a savings account, the opportunity cost is the interest income the funds could have earned, for example, $2,000 per month.

Economic cost equals explicit cost plus implicit cost:

$$\text{economic cost} = \text{explicit cost} + \text{implicit cost}$$

In the first column of Table 8.1, the firm's economic cost is $17,000, equal to $10,000 in explicit cost plus $7,000 in implicit cost.

Accountants have a different approach to computing costs. Their narrower definition of cost includes only the explicit cost of inputs:

$$\text{accounting cost} = \text{explicit cost}$$

In other words, **accounting cost** includes the monetary payments for inputs, but ignores the opportunity cost of inputs that do not require an explicit monetary payment. In the second column of Table 8.1, the accounting cost is the $10,000 in monetary payments for labor, capital, and materials. **Accounting profit** equals total revenue minus accounting cost:

$$\text{accounting profit} = \text{total revenue} - \text{accounting cost}$$

A firm's accounting cost is always lower than its economic cost, so its accounting profit is always *higher* than its economic profit. For the rest of this book, when we refer to cost and profit, we mean *economic* cost and *economic* profit.

• **accounting cost**
The explicit costs of production.

• **accounting profit**
Total revenue minus accounting cost.

# 8.2 | A FIRM WITH A FIXED PRODUCTION FACILITY: SHORT-RUN COSTS

Consider first the case of a firm with a fixed production facility. Suppose that you have decided to start a small firm to produce plastic paddles for rafts. The production of paddles requires a workshop where workers use molds to form plastic material into paddles. Before we can discuss the cost of production, we need information about the nature of the production process.

## Production and Marginal Product

The table in Figure 8.1 shows how the quantity of paddles produced varies with the number of workers. A single worker in the workshop produces one paddle per day. Adding a second worker increases the quantity produced to five paddles per day. The **marginal product of labor** is the change in output from one additional unit of labor. In the table, the marginal product of the first worker is one paddle, compared to a marginal product of four paddles for the second worker.

Why does the marginal product increase as output increases? As we saw earlier in the book, when a firm increases its workforce, workers can specialize in production tasks. Productivity increases because of the benefits of continuity— each worker spends less time switching between production tasks. In addition, there are benefits from repetition—each worker becomes more proficient at an assigned task. A two-worker operation produces more than twice as many paddles as a one-person operation because the two workers can specialize, one being responsible for preparing the plastic for the mold and the other responsible for working the mold.

Starting with the third worker, the production process is subject to **diminishing returns**, one of the key principles of economics.

• **marginal product of labor**
The change in output from one additional unit of labor.

• **diminishing returns**
As one input increases while the other inputs are held fixed, output increases at a decreasing rate.

# PRINCIPLE OF DIMINISHING RETURNS

Suppose that output is produced with two or more inputs and we increase one input while holding the other inputs fixed. Beyond some point—called the *point of diminishing returns*—output will increase at a decreasing rate.

The third worker adds three paddles to total output, down from four paddles for the second worker. As the firm continues to hire more workers, the marginal product drops to two paddles for the fourth worker and one paddle for the fifth worker. As we saw earlier in the book, diminishing returns occurs because workers share a production facility. A larger workforce means that each worker gets a smaller share of the production facility. In the paddle example, the workers share a mold; as the number of workers increases, they will spend more time waiting to use the mold.

Figure 8.1 shows the firm's **total-product curve**, which represents the relationship between the quantity of labor (on the horizontal axis) and output (on the vertical axis), *ceteris paribus*. The total-product curve shows the effects of labor specialization as well as diminishing returns. For the first two workers, output increases at an increasing rate because labor specialization increases the marginal product of labor. Starting with the third worker, however, total output increases at a decreasing rate because of diminishing returns.

## Short-Run Total Cost

We've seen the production relationship between labor input and output, so we're ready to show the relationship between output and production cost. Suppose the opportunity cost of your time is $50 per day, and you can hire workers for your workshop at the market wage of $50 per day. You can purchase your workshop, including the building and the paddle mold, for $365,000. If the interest rate you could have earned on that money is 10 percent per year, the opportunity cost of tying up your $365,000 in the workshop is $36,500 per year, or $100 per day.

• **total-product curve**
A curve showing the relationship between the quantity of labor and the quantity of output produced, ceteris paribus.

▶ **FIGURE 8.1**
**Total-Product Curve**
The total-product curve shows the relationship between the quantity of labor and the quantity of output, given a fixed production facility. For the first 2 workers, output increases at an increasing rate because of labor specialization. Diminishing returns occurs for 3 or more workers, so output increases at a decreasing rate.

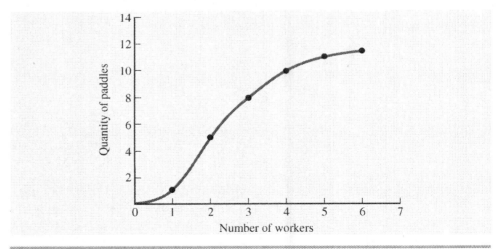

| Labor | Quantity of Output Produced | Marginal Product of Labor |
|---|---|---|
| 1 | 1 | 1 |
| 2 | 5 | 4 |
| 3 | 8 | 3 |
| 4 | 10 | 2 |
| 5 | 11 | 1 |
| 6 | 11.5 | 0.5 |

In the short-run analysis of costs, we divide production costs into two types, fixed cost and variable cost.

- **Fixed cost (FC)** is the cost that does not vary with the quantity produced. In our example, the fixed cost is the cost of the workshop, including the cost of the building and the mold. As shown in the third column of Table 8.2, the fixed cost is $100 per day, regardless of how much output is produced.

- **Variable cost (VC)** is the cost that varies with the quantity produced. For example, to produce more paddles, you must hire more workers. If the cost per worker is $50 per day, your daily variable cost is $50 times the number of workers, including you. As shown in the fourth column of Table 8.2, variable cost is $50 for one worker, $100 for two workers, and so on.

To compute the firm's total cost, we simply add the fixed and variable costs. The firm's **short-run total cost (TC)** equals the sum of fixed and variable costs:

$$TC = FC + VC$$

The fifth column in Table 8.2 shows the total cost for different quantities of output. For example, 1 worker produces 1 paddle at a total cost of $150, equal to the fixed cost of $100 plus a variable cost of $50. Hiring a second worker increases output to 5 paddles and increases total cost to $200, equal to $100 in fixed cost and $100 in variable cost. Moving down the fifth column, the total cost rises to $250 for 8 units of output, $300 for 10 units, and so on.

Figure 8.2 shows the short-run cost curves corresponding to columns 3, 4, and 5 of Table 8.2. The horizontal line on the graph shows the fixed cost of $100. The lower of the two positively sloped curves shows the variable cost (*VC*), and the higher of the two positively sloped curves is total cost (*TC*). Total cost is the sum of fixed cost and

**fixed cost (FC)**
Cost that does not vary with the quantity produced.

**variable cost (VC)**
Cost that varies with the quantity produced.

**short-run total cost (TC)**
The total cost of production when at least one input is fixed; equal to fixed cost plus variable cost.

**Table 8.2 | SHORT-RUN COSTS**

| 1 | 2 | 3 | 4 | 5 | 6 | 7 | 8 | 9 |
|---|---|---|---|---|---|---|---|---|
| Labor | Output | Fixed Cost (FC) | Variable Cost (VC) | Total Cost (TC) | Average Fixed Cost (AFC) | Average Variable Cost (AVC) | Average Total Cost (ATC) | Marginal Cost (MC) |
| 0 | 0 | $100 | $0 | $100 | — | — | — | — |
| 1 | 1 | 100 | $50 | 150 | $100.00 | $50.00 | $150.00 | $50.00 |
| 2 | 5 | 100 | 100 | 200 | 20.00 | 20.00 | 40.00 | 12.50 |
| 3 | 8 | 100 | 150 | 250 | 12.50 | 18.75 | 31.25 | 16.67 |
| 4 | 10 | 100 | 200 | 300 | 10.00 | 20.00 | 30.00 | 25.00 |
| 5 | 11 | 100 | 250 | 350 | 9.09 | 22.73 | 31.82 | 50.00 |
| 6 | 11.5 | 100 | 300 | 400 | 8.70 | 26.09 | 34.78 | 100.00 |

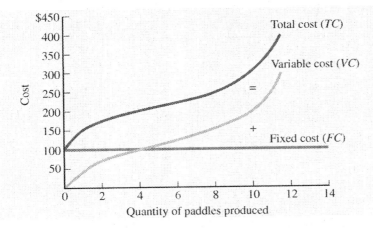

**◄ FIGURE 8.2**
**Short-Run Costs: Fixed Cost, Variable Cost, and Total Cost**
The short-run total-cost curve shows the relationship between the quantity of output and production costs, given a fixed production facility. Short-run total cost equals fixed cost (the cost that does not vary with the quantity produced) plus variable cost (the cost that varies with the quantity produced).

variable cost, so the vertical distance between the *TC* curve and the *VC* curve equals the firm's fixed cost. Notice that this distance is the same at any level of output.

## Short-Run Average Costs

• **average fixed cost (AFC)**
Fixed cost divided by the quantity produced.

There are three types of average cost. **Average fixed cost (AFC)** equals the fixed cost divided by the quantity produced:

$$AFC = \frac{FC}{Q}$$

To compute *AFC* for our paddle company, we simply divide the fixed cost ($100) by the quantity of paddles produced. In Table 8.2, we divide the number in column 3 by the number in column 2. This calculation gives us the values for *AFC*, which are shown in column 6. For example, the output in the second row is 1 paddle, so the average fixed cost is $100 = $100/1. In the third row, output is 5 paddles, so the average fixed cost is $5 = $100/5. As output increases, the $100 fixed cost is spread over more units, so *AFC* decreases.

• **average variable cost (AVC)**
Variable cost divided by the quantity produced.

A firm's **average variable cost (AVC)** incorporates the costs that vary with the quantity produced. Average variable cost equals the variable cost divided by the quantity produced:

$$AVC = \frac{VC}{Q}$$

To compute *AVC* for our paddle company, we simply divide the number in column 4 of Table 8.2 by the number in column 2. That calculation gives us the values for *AVC*, shown in column 7. For example, the output in the third row is 5 paddles and the variable cost is $100, so the average variable cost is $100/5 paddles, or $20. Notice that for small quantities of output, the *AVC* decreases as the quantity produced increases—from $50 for one paddle, $20 for 2 paddles, and so on. The *AVC* declines because of the benefits of labor specialization. Adding workers to a small workforce makes workers more productive on average, so the amount of labor required per unit of output drops, pushing down the average variable cost. In contrast, for large quantities of output, average variable cost increases as output increases because of diminishing returns. Adding workers to a large workforce makes workers less productive on average, pulling up the average variable cost. In Figure 8.3, the *AVC* curve is negatively sloped for small quantities, but positively sloped for large quantities.

▶ **FIGURE 8.3**
**Short-Run Average Costs**
The short-run average-total-cost curve (*ATC*) is U-shaped. As the quantity produced increases, fixed costs are spread over more and more units, pushing down the average total cost. In contrast, as the quantity increases, diminishing returns eventually pulls up the average total cost. The gap between *ATC* and *AVC* is the average fixed cost (*AFC*).

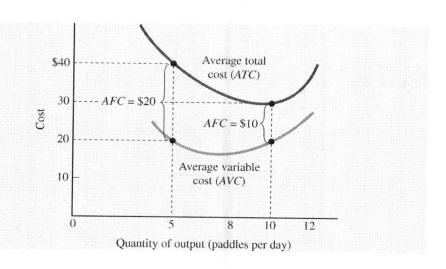

A firm's total cost is the sum of its fixed cost and variable cost, so the **short-run average total cost (ATC)**, or what we'll simply call "average cost," is the sum of the average fixed cost and the average variable cost:

$$ATC = \frac{TC}{Q} = \frac{FC}{Q} + \frac{VC}{Q} = AFC + AVC$$

* **short-run average total cost (ATC)** Short-run total cost divided by the quantity of output; equal to AFC plus AVC.

In Figure 8.3, we go from the *AVC* to *ATC* by adding the average fixed cost to *AVC*. For example, for five paddles *AFC* is $20 and *AVC* is $20, so *ATC* is equal to $40, the sum of $20 + $20. For 10 paddles, the average fixed cost is lower—only $10—while the average variable cost is $20, so *ATC* is $30, the sum of $10 + $20. In Figure 8.3, the gap between the *AVC* and *ATC* curves is the average fixed cost.

The *ATC* curve in Figure 8.2 is negatively sloped at quantities less than 10 paddles. The negative slope results from two forces that work together to push average cost down as output increases:

- *Spreading the fixed cost.* For small quantities of output, a one-unit increase in output reduces *AFC* by a large amount because the fixed cost is pretty "thick," being spread over just a few units of output. For example, going from 1 paddle to 5 paddles decreases *AFC* from $100 to $20 per paddle.
- *Labor specialization.* For small quantities of output, *AVC* decreases as output increases because labor specialization increases worker productivity.

These two forces both push *ATC* downward as output increases, so the curve is negatively sloped for small quantities of output.

What happens once the firm reaches the point at which the benefits of labor specialization are exhausted? As the firm continues to increase output beyond that point, the average variable cost increases because of diminishing returns. There is a tug-of-war between two forces: The spreading of fixed cost continues to push *ATC* down, while diminishing returns and rising average variable cost pull *ATC* up. The outcome of the tug-of-war varies with the quantity produced, giving the *ATC* curve its U shape:

- *Intermediate quantities of output, such as output between 3 and 10 paddles.* The tug-of-war is won by the spreading of fixed cost, because the fixed cost is still relatively "thick" and diminishing returns are not yet very strong. As a result, *ATC* decreases as output increases. For example, at 5 paddles *ATC* is $40, but at 10 paddles *ATC* drops to only $30.
- *Large quantities of output, such as 11 or more paddles.* The tug-of-war is won by diminishing returns and rising average variable cost. In this case, the reductions in *AFC* are relatively small because the fixed cost is already spread pretty thinly and diminishing returns are severe. As a result, *ATC* increases as output increases. For example, at 10 paddles *ATC* is $30, but at 11.5 paddles *ATC* jumps to $34.78.

## Short-Run Marginal Cost

The **short-run marginal cost (MC)** is the change in short-run total cost per unit change in output. In other words, it is the increase in total cost resulting from a one-unit increase in output. Mathematically, marginal cost is calculated by dividing the change in total cost (*TC*) by the change in output (*Q*):

* **short-run marginal cost (MC)** The change in short-run total cost resulting from a one-unit increase in output.

$$MC = \frac{\Delta TC}{\Delta Q} = \frac{\text{change in } TC}{\text{change in output}}$$

The marginal cost of the first paddle is the increase in cost when the firm produces the first paddle. To produce the first unit of output, the firm hires a single worker at $50. As shown in column 9 of Table 8.2, the marginal cost of the first paddle is $50. Moving down the ninth column, hiring the second worker for $50 increases

**Short-Run Marginal and Average Cost**

The marginal-cost curve (MC) is negatively sloped for small quantities of output, because of the benefits of labor specialization, and positively sloped for large quantities, because of diminishing returns. The MC curve intersects the average-cost curve (ATC) at the minimum point of the average curve. At this point ATC is neither falling nor rising.

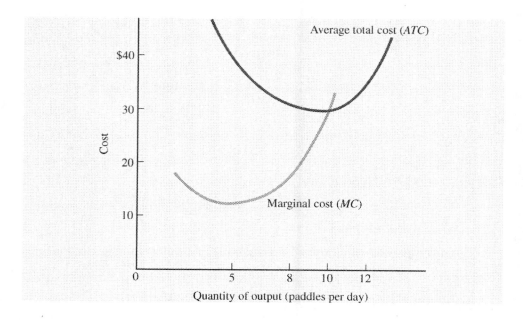

output to 5 paddles. A $50 increase in total cost increases output by 4 paddles, so the marginal cost is $12.50:

$$MC = \frac{\Delta TC}{\Delta Q} = \frac{\text{change in } TC}{\text{change in output}} = \frac{\$50}{4} = \$12.50$$

In this case, marginal cost decreases as output increases because of labor specialization and rising worker productivity. The first worker produces just one paddle, but adding a second worker increases output by four paddles. The $50 expense of adding the second worker translates into a $12.50 expense for each of the four extra paddles produced. We saw earlier that specialization leads to increasing marginal productivity. Now we know that specialization also leads to decreasing marginal cost. In Figure 8.4, the short-run marginal-cost curve is negatively sloped for the first five paddles.

The positively sloped portion of the marginal-cost curve is a result of diminishing returns. Hiring the third worker increases output from 5 to 8, so the $50 expense translates into a $16.67 expense for each of the 3 extra paddles produced. Diminishing returns has set in, so marginal cost increases as output increases. The marginal cost increases to $25 for between 8 and 10 paddles ($50/2 paddles), then increases to $50 for between 10 and 11 paddles ($50/1 paddle), and so on. In general, diminishing returns decreases labor productivity and causes rising marginal cost.

## The Relationship Between Marginal Cost and Average Cost

Figure 8.4 shows the relationship between short-run marginal cost and short-run average total cost. Whenever the marginal cost is less than the average cost (for fewer than 10 paddles), the average cost is falling. In contrast, whenever the marginal cost exceeds the average cost (for more than 10 paddles), the average cost is rising. Finally, when the marginal cost equals the average cost, the average cost is neither rising nor falling. Therefore, the marginal-cost curve intersects the short-run average total cost curve at its minimum point.

We can use some simple logic to explain the relationship between average and marginal cost. Suppose that you start the semester with 9 completed courses and a cumulative grade-point average of 3.0. In the first row of Table 8.3, you have 27 grade points (4 points for each A, 3 points for each B, and so on), so your GPA is 3.0, which is 27 points divided by 9 courses. You enroll in a single course this semester—a history course. Your new GPA will depend on your grade in the history course, the marginal grade. There are three possibilities:

**Table 8.3** | MARGINAL GRADE AND AVERAGE GRADE

|  | Marginal Grade | Number of Courses | Grade Points | Grade Point Average |
|---|---|---|---|---|
| Starting point | --- | 9 | 27 | 3.0 = 27/9 |
| Marginal grade < GPA | D | 10 | 28 = 27 + 1 | 2.8 = 28/10 |
| Marginal grade = GPA | B | 10 | 30 = 27 + 3 | 3.0 = 30/10 |
| Marginal grade > GPA | A | 10 | 31 = 27 + 4 | 3.1 = 31/10 |

- *Marginal grade less than the average grade.* In the second row of Table 8.3, if you get a D in history, your grade point total increases from 27 points to 28 points. Dividing the new total by 10 courses, your new GPA is 2.80. It's lower because your marginal grade of 1.0 is less than the old average grade of 3.0.

- *Marginal grade equal to the average grade.* In the second row of Table 8.3, if you get a B in history, your grade point total increases from 27 points to 30 points. Dividing the new total by 10 courses, your new GPA is 3.0. It hasn't changed because your marginal grade of 3.0 equals the old average grade of 3.0.

- *Marginal grade greater than the average grade.* In the second row of Table 8.3, if you get an A in history, your grade point total increases from 27 points to 31 points, so your new GPA is 3.10. It's higher because your marginal grade of 4.0 is greater than the old average grade of 3.0.

To summarize, whenever the marginal grade is less than the average grade, the average will fall; whenever the marginal grade exceeds the average grade, the average will rise; whenever the marginal grade equals the average grade, the average will not change.

# 8.3 | PRODUCTION AND COST IN THE LONG RUN

Up to this point, we've been exploring short-run cost curves, which show the cost of producing different quantities of output in a given production facility. We turn next to long-run cost curves, which show production costs in facilities of different sizes. The *long run* is defined as the period of time over which a firm is perfectly flexible in its choice of all inputs. In the long run, a firm can build a new production facility such as a factory, store, office, or restaurant. Another option in the long run is to modify an existing facility.

The key difference between the short run and the long run is that there are no diminishing returns in the long run. Recall that diminishing returns occur because workers share a fixed production facility, so the larger the number of workers in the facility, the smaller the share of the facility available for each worker. In the long run, a firm can expand its production facility as its workforce grows, so there are no diminishing returns.

## Expansion and Replication

Continuing the example of paddle production, suppose that you have decided to replace your existing workshop with a new one. You have been producing 10 paddles per day at a total cost of $300 per day, or an average cost of $30 per paddle. Suppose a company that sponsors rafting adventures orders new paddles, and you decide to produce twice as much output in your new facility. What should you do?

One possibility is simply to double the original operation. You could build two workshops that are identical to the original shop and hire two workforces, each identical to the original workforce. In the table in Figure 8.5, your firm moves from the third row of numbers (4 workers and $100 worth of capital produces 10 paddles per

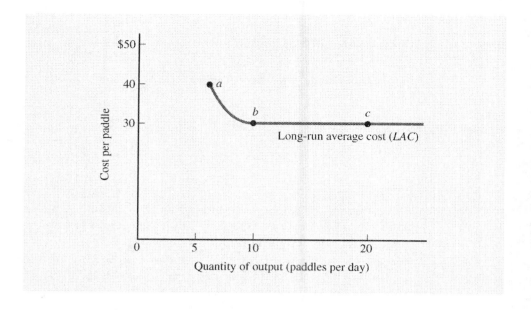

► **FIGURE 8.5**
**The Long-Run Average-Cost Curve and Scale Economies**
The long-run average-cost curve (*LAC*) is negatively sloped for up to 10 paddles per day, a result of indivisible inputs and the effects of labor specialization. If the firm replicates the operation that produces 10 paddles per day, the long-run average-cost curve will be horizontal beyond 10 paddles per day.

| | 1 | 2 | 3 | 4 | 5 |
|---|---|---|---|---|---|
| **Labor** | **Capital** | **Output** | **Labor Cost** | **Long-Run Total Cost (LTC)** | **Long-Run Average Cost (LAC)** |
| 1 | $100 | 1 | $50 | $150 | $150 |
| 2 | 100 | 5 | 100 | 200 | 40 |
| 4 | 100 | 10 | 200 | 300 | 30 |
| 8 | 200 | 20 | 400 | 600 | 30 |
| 12 | 300 | 30 | 600 | 900 | 30 |

• **long-run total cost (LTC)**
The total cost of production when a firm is perfectly flexible in choosing its inputs.

• **long-run average cost (LAC)**
The long-run cost divided by the quantity produced.

• **constant returns to scale**
A situation in which the long-run total cost increases proportionately with output, so average cost is constant.

day) to the fourth row, with twice as much labor, capital, and output. A firm's **long-run total cost (LTC)** is the total cost of production when the firm is perfectly flexible in choosing its inputs, including its production facility. As shown in column 5 of the table in Figure 8.5, if your firm doubles its output from 10 paddles to 20 paddles, the long-run total cost doubles too, from $300 to $600.

The firm's **long-run average cost (LAC)** equals the long-run cost divided by the quantity produced. As shown in column 6 of the table in Figure 8.5, doubling output from 10 to 20 paddles doesn't change the long-run average cost because doubling output by doubling both labor and capital increases costs proportionately. In the graph in Figure 8.5, point *b* shows the average cost with 10 paddles and point *c* shows the average cost with 20 paddles. As the quantity produced increases, the average cost doesn't change, so the average-cost curve is horizontal over this range of output. This is the case of **constant returns to scale**: As a firm scales up its operation, costs increase proportionately with output, so average cost is constant.

The same logic applies to larger output levels. Your firm could build a third workshop identical to the first two workshops, and its production costs will increase proportionately, from $600 to $900. In the table in Figure 8.5, the average cost for 30 paddles is $30, the same as for 10 and 20 paddles. In general, the replication process means the long-run total cost increases proportionately with the quantity produced, so the average cost is constant. In Figure 8.5, the long-run average-cost curve is horizontal for 10 or more paddles per day. In other words, there are constant returns to scale for output levels of 10 or more paddles.

We've seen that if a firm wants to double its output in the long run, replication is one option. By simply replicating an existing operation, a firm can double its output and its total costs, leaving average cost unchanged. Another possibility is to build a single larger workshop, one that can produce twice as much output at a lower cost than would be possible by simply replicating the original. If so, the long-run average cost of producing 20 or 30 paddles would be less than $30 per paddle.

A firm's **long-run marginal cost (LMC)** is the change in long-run cost resulting from producing one more unit of output. In the long run, the firm is perfectly flexible in choosing its inputs. Therefore, *LMC* is the increase in cost when the firm can change its production facility as well as its workforce.

* **long-run marginal cost (LMC)**
The change in long-run cost resulting from a one-unit increase in output.

## Reducing Output with Indivisible Inputs

What would happen if you decide to produce only 5 paddles per day instead of 10? Although it's tempting to think that your total costs would be cut in half, that's not necessarily the case. Remember that you use a single mold to produce 10 paddles per day. If you cut your output in half, you would still need the mold, so your capital costs won't be cut in half. In addition, if each mold requires a fixed amount of floor space, you would still need the same floor space. Therefore, cutting output in half wouldn't decrease the cost of your production facility at all. You would still have a cost of $100 per day for the mold and the workspace. Because cutting output in half doesn't cut capital costs in half, the average cost for producing 5 paddles will exceed the average cost for 10 paddles.

The mold is an example of an **indivisible input**, one that cannot be scaled down to produce a smaller quantity of output. When a production process requires the use of indivisible inputs, the average cost of production increases as output decreases, because the cost of the indivisible inputs is spread over a smaller quantity of output. Most production operations use some indivisible inputs, but the costs of these inputs vary. Here are some examples of firms and their indivisible inputs:

* **indivisible input**
An input that cannot be scaled down to produce a smaller quantity of output.

- A railroad company uses tracks to provide freight service between two cities. The company cannot scale down by laying a half set of tracks—a single rail.
- A shipping firm uses a large ship to carry TV sets from Japan to the United States. The company can't scale back by transporting TVs in rowboats.
- A steel producer uses a large blast furnace. The company can't scale back by producing steel in a toaster oven.
- A hospital uses imaging machines for x-rays, CAT scans, and MRIs. The hospital can't scale back by getting mini-MRI machines.
- A pizzeria uses a pizza oven. The company can't scale back by making pizza in a toaster oven.

The second row of the table in Figure 8.5 on page 194 shows labor and capital costs in the smaller operation. Suppose that to produce 5 paddles, you'll need 2 workers, including yourself. In this case, your labor cost will be $100. Adding the $100 cost of the indivisible input (the mold and shop space), the total cost of producing 5 paddles per day will be $200, or $40 per paddle. This cost exceeds the average cost of 10 paddles because in the smaller operation you still need the same amount of capital. In Figure 8.5 on page 194, point *a* shows that the average cost of 5 paddles per day exceeds the average cost for larger quantities.

## Scaling Down and Labor Specialization

A second possible reason for higher average long-run costs in a smaller operation is that labor will be less specialized in the small operation. As we saw earlier in the chapter, the labor specialization——each worker specializing in an individual production task—makes workers more productive because of continuity and repetition. Reversing this process, when we reduce the workforce each worker will become less specialized, performing a wider variety of production tasks. The loss of specialization will decrease labor productivity, leading to higher average cost.

To see the role of labor specialization, consider the first row of numbers in the table in Figure 8.6. To produce one paddle per day, the firm needs a full day of work by one worker. The single worker performs all production tasks and is less productive than the

- **economies of scale**
  A situation in which the long-run average cost of production decreases as output increases.

- **minimum efficient scale**
  The output at which scale economies are exhausted.

- **diseconomies of scale**
  A situation in which the long-run average cost of production increases as ouput increases.

specialized workers in larger operations. This is one reason for the relatively high average cost in a one-paddle operation ($150). The second reason is that the cost of the indivisible input is spread over fewer paddles.

## Economies of Scale

A firm experiences **economies of scale** if the long-run average cost of production decreases as output increases, meaning that the long-run average-cost curve is negatively sloped. In Figure 8.5 on page 194, the paddle producer experiences economies of scale between points *a* and *b*. At point *a*, the long-run average cost is $40, compared to $30 at point *b* and beyond. An increase in output from 5 to 10 paddles decreases the long-run average cost of production because the firm spreads the cost of an indivisible input over a larger quantity, decreasing average cost. In other words, there are some economies—cost savings—associated with scaling up the firm's operation.

One way to quantify the extent of scale economies in the production of a particular good is to determine the minimum efficient scale for producing the good. The **minimum efficient scale** is defined as the output at which scale economies are exhausted. In Figure 8.5, the long-run average-cost curve becomes horizontal at point *b*, so the minimum efficient scale is 10 paddles. If a firm starts out with a quantity of output below the minimum efficient scale, an increase in output will decrease the average cost. Once the minimum efficient scale has been reached, the average cost no longer decreases as output increases.

## Diseconomies of Scale

A positively sloped long-run average-cost curve indicates the presence of **diseconomies of scale**. In this case, average cost increases as output increases. Diseconomies of scale can occur for two reasons:

- *Coordination problems.* One of the problems of a large organization is that it requires several layers of management to coordinate the activities of the different parts of the organization. A large organization requires more meetings, reports, and administrative work, leading to higher unit cost. If an increase in the firm's output requires additional layers of management, the long-run average-cost curve may be positively sloped.

- *Increasing input costs.* When a firm increases its output, it will demand more of each of its inputs and *may* be forced to pay higher prices for some of these inputs.

For example, an expanding construction firm may be forced to pay higher wages to attract more workers. Alternatively, an expanding firm may be forced to hire workers who are less skilled than the original workers. An increase in wages or a decrease in productivity will increase the average cost of production, generating a positively sloped long-run average-cost curve.

Firms recognize the possibility of diseconomies of scale and adopt various strategies to avoid them. An example of a firm that adjusts its operations to avoid diseconomies of scale is 3M, a global technology company that produces products ranging from Post-it® notes to pharmaceuticals and telecommunications systems. The company makes a conscious effort to keep its production units as small as possible to keep them flexible. When a production unit gets too large, the company breaks it apart.

## Actual Long-Run Average-Cost Curves

Figure 8.6 shows the actual long-run average-cost curves for three products: aluminum production, truck freight, and hospital services.[1] In each case, the long-run average cost curve is negatively sloped for small quantities of output and relatively flat—almost horizontal—over a large range of output. In other words, these curves are

L-shaped. Other studies suggest that the long-run cost curves of a wide variety of goods and services have the same shape.

Why is the typical long-run average-cost curve L-shaped? The long-run average-cost curve is negatively sloped for small quantities of output because there are economies of scale resulting from indivisible inputs and labor specialization. As output increases, the average-cost curve eventually becomes horizontal and remains horizontal for a wide range of output. Over the horizontal portion of the cost curve, increases in inputs lead to proportionate increases in output, so the average cost doesn't change. In other words, the long-run average total cost (*LAC*) is constant and production is subject to constant returns to scale.

## Short-Run Versus Long-Run Average Cost

Why is the firm's short-run average-cost curve U-shaped, while the long-run average-cost curve is L-shaped? For large quantities of output, the short-run curve is positively sloped because of diminishing returns and the resulting decrease in labor productivity and increase in marginal cost. If a firm increases its output while at least one input is held fixed, diminishing returns eventually occur, pulling up the average cost of production.

The difference between the short run and long run is a firm's flexibility in choosing inputs. In the long run, a firm can increase all of its inputs, scaling up its operation by building a larger production facility. As a result, the firm will not suffer from diminishing returns. In most cases, the long-run average-cost curve will be negatively sloped or horizontal. In some cases, firms experience diseconomies of scale, so the long-run average-cost curve will be positively sloped for high output levels. Nonetheless, the long-run average cost will not be as steep as the short-run curve, which is relatively steep because of diminishing returns.

# 8.4 | APPLICATIONS OF PRODUCTION COST

In this chapter, we've explored the links between production technology and the cost of production. We've seen the firm's short-run cost curves, which show how production costs vary with the quantity produced when at least one input is fixed. We've also seen the long-run cost average-cost curve, which shows how the average cost of production varies when the firm is perfectly flexible in choosing its inputs. In this part of the chapter, we look at actual production costs for several products.

# APPLICATION

## THE PRODUCTION COST OF AN iPOD NANO

**APPLYING THE CONCEPTS #1:** What are the cost components for electronic products?

What's the cost of producing an iPod Nano, the ultra-thin digital music player with a storage capacity of 2 GB? As shown in Table 8.4, the cost per iPod is $98, which is divided between flash memory, other electronic components, other materials and parts, and assembly cost. The largest part of the cost is the $54 spent on flash memory.

Apple has sold millions of iPods, and its large sales volume gives the company an advantage in negotiating with its suppliers. For example, the flash memory that costs Apple $54 would cost smaller companies about $90. The large volume also provides a large reward for cost cutting. When the company switched the computer chip controlling the click wheel from a $1 chip from Synaptics to a $0.55 chip from Cypress Semiconductor, it saved only $0.45 per iPod, but with millions of units sold, that small savings per unit added up to a large increase in profit. **Related to Exercises 4.1 and 4.6.**

Table 8.4 | THE AVERAGE COST OF AN IPOD NANO

| Component | Cost per iPod |
| --- | --- |
| Flash memory | $54 |
| Other electronic components | 15 |
| Other materials and parts | 21 |
| Assembly | 8 |
| **TOTAL** | **98** |

SOURCE: Arik Hesseldahl, "Unpeeling Apple's Nano," *BusinessWeek Online*, September 22, 2005, available online at *www.businessweek.com/technology/*, accessed 06/27/2006.

# Chapter 8
# Competitive Market as an Ideal Type

Organic apple growing is an example of a *perfectly competitive* industry. Firms in perfectly competitive industries are unable to control the prices of the products they sell and are unable to earn an economic profit in the long run. There are two main reasons for this result: Firms in these industries sell identical products, and it is easy for new firms to enter these industries. Studying how perfectly competitive industries operate is the best way to understand how markets answer the fundamental economic questions discussed in Chapter 1:

- What goods and services will be produced?

- How will the goods and services be produced?

- Who will receive the goods and services produced?

In fact, though, most industries are not perfectly competitive. In most industries, firms do *not* produce identical products, and in some industries, it may be difficult for new firms to enter. There are thousands of industries in the United States. Although in some ways each industry is unique, industries share enough similarities that economists group them into four market structures. In particular, any industry has three key characteristics:

- The number of firms in the industry

- The similarity of the good or service produced by the firms in the industry

- The ease with which new firms can enter the industry

Economists use these characteristics to classify industries into the four market structures listed in Table 11-1.

Many industries, including restaurants, hardware stores, and other retailers, have a large number of firms selling products that are differentiated, rather than identical, and fall into the category of *monopolistic competition*. Some industries, such as computers and automobiles, have only a few firms and are *oligopolies*. Finally, a few industries, such as the delivery of first-class mail by the U.S. Postal Service, have only one firm and are *monopolies*. After discussing perfect competition in this chapter, we will devote a chapter to each of these other market structures.

TABLE 11-1  |  **The Four Market Structures**

| | MARKET STRUCTURE | | | |
|---|---|---|---|---|
| **CHARACTERISTIC** | **PERFECT COMPETITION** | **MONOPOLISTIC COMPETITION** | **OLIGOPOLY** | **MONOPOLY** |
| Number of firms | Many | Many | Few | One |
| Type of product | Identical | Differentiated | Identical or differentiated | Unique |
| Ease of entry | High | High | Low | Entry blocked |
| Examples of industries | • Wheat<br>• Apples | • Selling DVDs<br>• Restaurants | • Manufacturing computers<br>• Manufacturing automobiles | • First-class mail delivery<br>• Tap water |

11.1 | Define a perfectly competitive market and explain why a perfect competitor faces a horizontal demand curve.

# Perfectly Competitive Markets

Why are firms in a **perfectly competitive market** unable to control the prices of the goods they sell, and why are the owners of these firms unable to earn economic profits in the long run? We can begin our analysis by listing the three conditions that make a market perfectly competitive:

1　There must be many buyers and many firms, all of whom are small relative to the market.

2　The products sold by all firms in the market must be identical.

3　There must be no barriers to new firms entering the market.

All three of these conditions hold in the market for organic apples. No single consumer or producer of organic apples buys or sells more than a tiny fraction of the total apple crop. The apples sold by each apple grower are identical, and there are no barriers to a new firm entering the organic apple market by purchasing land and planting apple trees. As we will see, it is the existence of many firms, all selling the same good, that keeps any single organic apple farmer from affecting the price of organic apples.

Although the market for organic apples meets the conditions for perfect competition, the markets for most goods and services do not. In particular, the second and third conditions are very restrictive. In most markets that have many buyers and sellers, firms do not sell identical products. For example, not all restaurant meals are the same, nor is all women's clothing the same. In Chapter 12, we will explore the common situation of monopolistic competition where many firms are selling similar but not identical products. In Chapters 13 and 14, we will analyze industries that are oligopolies or monopolies, where it is difficult for new firms to enter. In this chapter, we concentrate on perfectly competitive markets so we can use as a benchmark the situation in which firms are facing the maximum possible competition.

**Perfectly competitive market**
A market that meets the conditions of (1) many buyers and sellers, (2) all firms selling identical products, and (3) no barriers to new firms entering the market.

## A Perfectly Competitive Firm Cannot Affect the Market Price

Prices in perfectly competitive markets are determined by the interaction of demand and supply. The actions of any single consumer or any single firm have no effect on the market price. Consumers and firms have to accept the market price if they want to buy and sell in a perfectly competitive market.

Because a firm in a perfectly competitive market is very small relative to the market and because it is selling exactly the same product as every other firm, it can sell as much as it wants without having to lower its price. But if a perfectly competitive firm tries to raise its price, it won't sell anything at all because consumers will switch to buying from the firm's competitors. Therefore, the firm will be a **price taker** and will have to charge the same price as every other firm in the market. Although we don't usually think of firms as being too small to affect the market price, consumers are often in the position of being price takers. For instance, suppose your local supermarket is selling bread for $1.50 per loaf. You can load up your shopping cart with 10 loaves of bread, and the supermarket will gladly sell them all to you for $1.50 per loaf. But if you go to the cashier and offer to buy the bread for $1.49 per loaf, he or she will not sell it to you. As a buyer, you are too small relative to the bread market to have any effect on the equilibrium price. Whether you leave the supermarket and buy no bread or you buy 10 loaves, you are unable to change the market price of bread by even 1 cent.

The situation you face as a bread buyer is the same one a wheat farmer faces as a wheat seller. More than 225,000 farmers grow wheat in the United States. The market price of wheat is determined not by any individual wheat farmer but by the interaction

**Price taker** A buyer or seller that is unable to affect the market price.

## Figure 11-1

**A Perfectly Competitive Firm Faces a Horizontal Demand Curve**

A firm in a perfectly competitive market is selling exactly the same product as many other firms. Therefore, it can sell as much as it wants at the current market price, but it cannot sell anything at all if it raises the price by even 1 cent. As a result, the demand curve for a perfectly competitive firm's output is a horizontal line. In the figure, whether the wheat farmer sells 3,000 bushels per year or 7,500 bushels has no effect on the market price of $4.

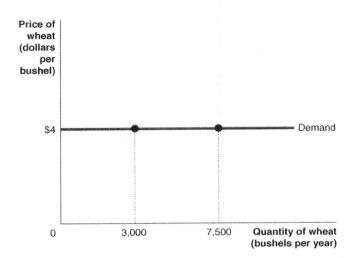

in the wheat market of all the buyers and all the sellers. If any one wheat farmer has the best crop the farmer has ever had, or if any one wheat farmer stops growing wheat altogether, the market price of wheat will not be affected *because the market supply curve for wheat will not shift by enough to change the equilibrium price by even 1 cent.*

## The Demand Curve for the Output of a Perfectly Competitive Firm

Suppose Bill Parker grows wheat on a 250-acre farm in Washington State. Farmer Parker is selling wheat in a perfectly competitive market, so he is a price taker. Because he can sell as much wheat as he chooses at the market price—but can't sell any wheat at all at a higher price—the demand curve for his wheat has an unusual shape: It is horizontal, as shown in Figure 11-1. With a horizontal demand curve, Farmer Parker must accept the market price, which in this case is $4. Whether Farmer Parker sells 3,000 bushels per year or 7,500 has no effect on the market price.

The demand curve for Farmer Parker's wheat is very different from the market demand curve for wheat. Panel (a) of Figure 11-2 shows the market for wheat. The

# Don't Let This Happen to **YOU!**

### Don't Confuse the Demand Curve for Farmer Parker's Wheat with the Market Demand Curve for Wheat

The demand curve for wheat has the normal downward-sloping shape. If the price of wheat goes up, the quantity of wheat demanded goes down, and if the price of wheat goes down, the quantity of wheat demanded goes up. But the demand curve for the output of a single wheat farmer is *not* downward sloping: It is a horizontal line. If an individual wheat farmer tries to increase the price he charges for his wheat, the quantity demanded falls to zero because buyers will purchase from one of the other 225,000 wheat farmers. But any one farmer can sell as much wheat as the farmer can produce without needing to cut the price. Both of these

things are true because each wheat farmer is very small relative to the overall market for wheat.

When we draw graphs of the wheat market, we usually show the market equilibrium quantity in millions or billions of bushels. When we draw graphs of the demand for wheat produced by one farmer, we usually show the quantity produced in smaller units, such as thousands of bushels. It is important to remember this difference in scale when interpreting these graphs.

Finally, it is not just wheat farmers who have horizontal demand curves for their products; any firm in a perfectly competitive market faces a horizontal demand curve.

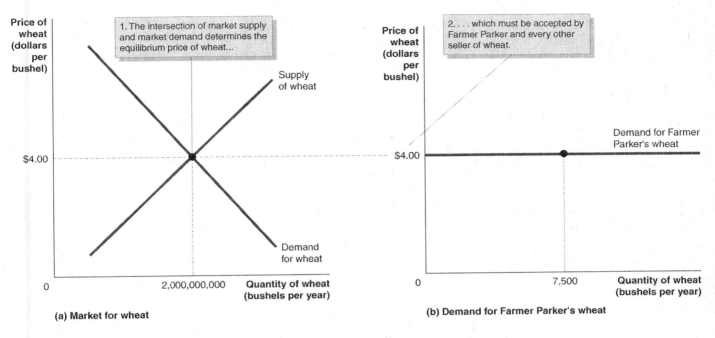

**Figure 11-2** | The Market Demand for Wheat versus the Demand for One Farmer's Wheat

In a perfectly competitive market, price is determined by the intersection of market demand and market supply. In panel (a), the demand and supply curves for wheat intersect at a price of $4 per bushel. An individual wheat farmer like Farmer Parker has no ability to affect the market price for wheat. Therefore, as panel (b) shows, the demand curve for Farmer Parker's wheat is a horizontal line. To understand this figure, it is important to notice that the scales on the horizontal axes in the two panels are very different. In panel (a), the equilibrium quantity of wheat is 2 *billion* bushels, and in panel (b), Farmer Parker is producing only 7,500 bushels of wheat.

demand curve in panel (a) is the *market demand curve for wheat* and has the normal downward slope we are familiar with from the market demand curves in Chapter 3. Panel (b) of Figure 11-2 shows the demand curve for Farmer Parker's wheat, which is a horizontal line. By viewing these graphs side by side, you can see that the price Farmer Parker receives for his wheat in panel (b) is determined by the interaction of all sellers and all buyers of wheat in the wheat market in panel (a). Keep in mind, however, that the scales on the horizontal axes in the two panels are very different. In panel (a), the equilibrium quantity of wheat is 2 *billion* bushels. In panel (b), Farmer Parker is producing only 7,500 bushels, or less than 0.0004 percent of market output. We need to use different scales in the two panels so we can display both of them on one page. Keep in mind the key point: Farmer Parker's output of wheat is very small relative to the total market output.

---

**11.2 LEARNING OBJECTIVE**

11.2 | Explain how a firm maximizes profits in a perfectly competitive market.

# How a Firm Maximizes Profit in a Perfectly Competitive Market

We have seen that Farmer Parker cannot control the price of his wheat. In this situation, how does he decide how much wheat to produce? We assume that Farmer Parker's objective is to maximize profits. This is a reasonable assumption for most firms, most of the time. Remember that **profit** is the difference between total revenue (*TR*) and total cost (*TC*):

**Profit** Total revenue minus total cost.

$$\text{Profit} = TR - TC.$$

To maximize his profit, Farmer Parker should produce the quantity of wheat where the difference between the total revenue he receives and his total cost is as large as possible.

**TABLE 11-2**

**Farmer Parker's Revenue from Wheat Farming**

| NUMBER OF BUSHELS (Q) | MARKET PRICE (PER BUSHEL) (P) | TOTAL REVENUE (TR) | AVERAGE REVENUE (AR) | MARGINAL REVENUE (MR) |
|---|---|---|---|---|
| 0 | $4 | $0 | — | — |
| 1 | 4 | 4 | $4 | $4 |
| 2 | 4 | 8 | 4 | 4 |
| 3 | 4 | 12 | 4 | 4 |
| 4 | 4 | 16 | 4 | 4 |
| 5 | 4 | 20 | 4 | 4 |
| 6 | 4 | 24 | 4 | 4 |
| 7 | 4 | 28 | 4 | 4 |
| 8 | 4 | 32 | 4 | 4 |
| 9 | 4 | 36 | 4 | 4 |
| 10 | 4 | 40 | 4 | 4 |

## Revenue for a Firm in a Perfectly Competitive Market

To understand how Farmer Parker maximizes profits, let's first consider his revenue. To keep the numbers simple, we will assume that he owns a very small farm and produces at most 10 bushels of wheat per year. Table 11-2 shows the revenue Farmer Parker will earn from selling various quantities of wheat if the market price for wheat is $4.

The third column in Table 11-2 shows that Farmer Parker's *total revenue* rises by $4 for every additional bushel he sells because he can sell as many bushels as he wants at the market price of $4 per bushel. The fourth and fifth columns in the table show Farmer Parker's *average revenue* and *marginal revenue* from selling wheat. His **average revenue** (*AR*) is his total revenue divided by the quantity of bushels he sells. For example, if he sells 5 bushels for a total of $20, his average revenue is $20/5 = $4. Notice that his average revenue is also equal to the market price of $4. In fact, for any level of output, a firm's average revenue is always equal to the market price. One way to see this is to note that total revenue equals price times quantity ($TR = P \times Q$), and average revenue equals total revenue divided by quantity ($AR = TR/Q$). So, $AR = TR/Q = (P \times Q)/Q = P$.

Farmer Parker's **marginal revenue** (*MR*) is the change in his total revenue from selling one more bushel:

$$\text{Marginal Revenue} = \frac{\text{Change in total revenue}}{\text{Change in quantity}}, \text{ or } MR = \frac{\Delta TR}{\Delta Q}.$$

**Average revenue (*AR*)** Total revenue divided by the quantity of the product sold.

**Marginal revenue (*MR*)** Change in total revenue from selling one more unit of a product.

Because for each additional bushel sold he always adds $4 to his total revenue, his marginal revenue is $4. Farmer Parker's marginal revenue is $4 per bushel because he is selling wheat in a perfectly competitive market and can sell as much as he wants at the market price. In fact, Farmer Parker's marginal revenue and average revenue are both equal to the market price. This is an important point: *For a firm in a perfectly competitive market, price is equal to both average revenue and marginal revenue.*

## Determining the Profit-Maximizing Level of Output

To determine how Farmer Parker can maximize profit, we have to consider his costs as well as his revenue. A wheat farmer has many costs, including seed, fertilizer, and the wages of farm workers. In Table 11-3, we bring together the revenue data from Table 11-1 with cost data for Farmer Parker's farm. Recall from Chapter 10 that a firm's *marginal cost* is the increase in total cost resulting from producing another unit of output.

| QUANTITY (BUSHELS) (Q) | TOTAL REVENUE (TR) | TOTAL COST (TC) | PROFIT (TR−TC) | MARGINAL REVENUE (MR) | MARGINAL COST (MC) |
|---|---|---|---|---|---|
| 0 | $0.00 | $1.00 | –$1.00 | — | — |
| 1 | 4.00 | 4.00 | 0.00 | $4.00 | $3.00 |
| 2 | 8.00 | 6.00 | 2.00 | 4.00 | 2.00 |
| 3 | 12.00 | 7.50 | 4.50 | 4.00 | 1.50 |
| 4 | 16.00 | 9.50 | 6.50 | 4.00 | 2.00 |
| 5 | 20.00 | 12.00 | 8.00 | 4.00 | 2.50 |
| 6 | 24.00 | 15.00 | 9.00 | 4.00 | 3.00 |
| 7 | 28.00 | 19.50 | 8.50 | 4.00 | 4.50 |
| 8 | 32.00 | 25.50 | 6.50 | 4.00 | 6.00 |
| 9 | 36.00 | 32.50 | 3.50 | 4.00 | 7.00 |
| 10 | 40.00 | 40.50 | –0.50 | 4.00 | 8.00 |

**TABLE 11-3**

**Farmer Parker's Profits from Wheat Farming**

We calculate profit in the fourth column by subtracting total cost in the third column from total revenue in the second column. The fourth column shows that as long as Farmer Parker produces between 2 and 9 bushels of wheat, he will earn a profit. His maximum profit is $9.00, which he will earn by producing 6 bushels of wheat. Because Farmer Parker wants to maximize his profits, we would expect him to produce 6 bushels of wheat. Producing more than 6 bushels reduces his profit. For example, if he produces 7 bushels of wheat, his profit will decline from $9.00 to $8.50. The values for marginal cost given in the last column of the table help us understand why Farmer Parker's profits will decline if he produces more than 6 bushels of wheat. After the sixth bushel of wheat, rising marginal cost causes Farmer Parker's profits to fall.

In fact, comparing the marginal cost and marginal revenue at each level of output is an alternative method of calculating Farmer Parker's profits. We illustrate the two methods of calculating profits in Figure 11-3 on the next page. We show the total revenue and total cost approach in panel (a) and the marginal revenue and marginal cost approach in panel (b). Total revenue is a straight line on the graph in panel (a) because total revenue increases at a constant rate of $4 for each additional bushel sold. Farmer Parker's profits are maximized when the vertical distance between the line representing total revenue and the total cost curve is as large as possible. Just as we saw in Table 11-3, this occurs at an output of 6 bushels.

The last two columns of Table 11-3 provide information on the marginal revenue (MR) Farmer Parker receives from selling another bushel of wheat and his marginal cost (MC) of producing another bushel of wheat. Panel (b) is a graph of Farmer Parker's marginal revenue and marginal cost. Because marginal revenue is always equal to $4, it is a horizontal line at the market price. We have already seen that the demand curve for a perfectly competitive firm is also a horizontal line at the market price. *Therefore, the marginal revenue curve for a perfectly competitive firm is the same as its demand curve.* Farmer Parker's marginal cost of producing wheat first falls and then rises, following the usual pattern we discussed in Chapter 10.

We know from panel (a) that profit is at a maximum at 6 bushels of wheat. In panel (b), profit is also at a maximum at 6 bushels of wheat. To understand why profit is maximized at the level of output where marginal revenue equals marginal cost, remember a key economic principle that we discussed in Chapter 1: *Optimal decisions are made at the margin.* Firms use this principle to decide the quantity of a good to produce. For example, in deciding how much wheat to produce, Farmer Parker needs

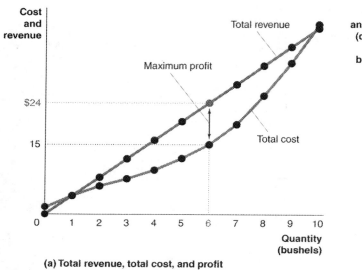

(a) Total revenue, total cost, and profit

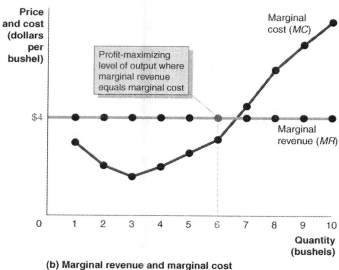

(b) Marginal revenue and marginal cost

## Figure 11-3 | The Profit-Maximizing Level of Output

In panel (a), Farmer Parker maximizes his profit where the vertical distance between total revenue and total cost is the largest. This happens at an output of 6 bushels. Panel (b) shows that Farmer Parker's marginal revenue ($MR$) is equal to a constant \$4 per bushel. Farmer Parker maximizes profits by producing wheat up to the point where the marginal revenue of the last bushel produced is equal to its marginal cost, or $MR = MC$.

In this case, at no level of output does marginal revenue exactly equal marginal cost. The closest Farmer Parker can come is to produce 6 bushels of wheat. He will not want to continue to produce once marginal cost is greater than marginal revenue because that would reduce his profits. Panels (a) and (b) show alternative ways of thinking about how Farmer Parker can determine the profit-maximizing quantity of wheat to produce.

to compare the marginal revenue he earns from selling another bushel of wheat to the marginal cost of producing that bushel. The difference between the marginal revenue and the marginal cost is the additional profit (or loss) from producing one more bushel. As long as marginal revenue is greater than marginal cost, Farmer Parker's profits are increasing, and he will want to expand production. For example, he will not stop producing at 5 bushels of wheat because producing and selling the sixth bushel adds \$4 to his revenue but only \$3 to his cost, so his profit increases by \$1. He wants to continue producing until the marginal revenue he receives from selling another bushel is equal to the marginal cost of producing it. At that level of output, he will make no *additional* profit by selling another bushel, so he will have maximized his profits.

By inspecting the table, we can see that at no level of output does marginal revenue exactly equal marginal cost. The closest Farmer Parker can come is to produce 6 bushels of wheat. He will not want to continue to produce once marginal cost is greater than marginal revenue because that would reduce his profits. For example, the seventh bushel of wheat adds \$4.50 to his cost but only \$4.00 to his revenue, so producing the seventh bushel *reduces* his profit by \$0.50.

From the information in Table 11-3 and Figure 11-3, we can draw the following conclusions:

1 The profit-maximizing level of output is where the difference between total revenue and total cost is the greatest.

2 The profit-maximizing level of output is also where marginal revenue equals marginal cost, or $MR = MC$.

Both these conclusions are true for any firm, whether or not it is in a perfectly competitive industry. We can draw one other conclusion about profit maximization that is true only of firms in perfectly competitive industries: For a firm in a perfectly competitive industry, price is equal to marginal revenue, or $P = MR$. So, we can restate the $MR = MC$ condition as $P = MC$.

11.3 | Use graphs to show a firm's profit or loss.

# Illustrating Profit or Loss on the Cost Curve Graph

We have seen that profit is the difference between total revenue and total cost. We can also express profit in terms of *average total cost* (*ATC*). This allows us to show profit on the cost curve graph we developed in Chapter 10.

To begin, we need to work through the several steps necessary to determine the relationship between profit and average total cost. Because profit is equal to total revenue minus total cost (*TC*) and total revenue is price times quantity, we can write the following:

$$\text{Profit} = (P \times Q) - TC.$$

If we divide both sides of this equation by $Q$, we have:

$$\frac{\text{Profit}}{Q} = \frac{(P \times Q)}{Q} - \frac{TC}{Q},$$

or:

$$\frac{\text{Profit}}{Q} = P - ATC,$$

because $TC/Q$ equals $ATC$. This equation tells us that profit per unit (or average profit) equals price minus average total cost. Finally, we obtain the expression for the relationship between total profit and average total cost by multiplying again by $Q$:

$$\text{Profit} = (P - ATC) \times Q.$$

This expression tells us that a firm's total profit is equal to the quantity produced multiplied by the difference between price and average total cost.

## Showing a Profit on the Graph

Figure 11-4 shows the relationship between a firm's average total cost and its marginal cost that we discussed in Chapter 10. In this figure, we also show the firm's marginal revenue curve (which is the same as its demand curve) and the area representing total profit. Using the relationship between profit and average total cost that we just determined, we can say that the area representing total profit has a height equal to $(P - ATC)$ and a base equal to $Q$. This area is shown by the green-shaded rectangle.

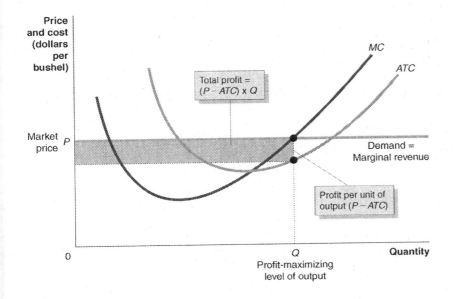

### Figure 11-4

**The Area of Maximum Profit**

A firm maximizes profit at the level of output at which marginal revenue equals marginal cost. The difference between price and average total cost equals profit per unit of output. Total profit equals profit per unit multiplied by the number of units produced. Total profit is represented by the area of the green-shaded rectangle, which has a height equal to $(P - ATC)$ and a width equal to $Q$.

# Solved Problem | 11-3

## Determining Profit-Maximizing Price and Quantity

Suppose that Andy sells basketballs in the perfectly competitive basketball market. His output per day and his costs are as follows:

| OUTPUT PER DAY | TOTAL COST |
|---|---|
| 0 | $10.00 |
| 1 | 15.00 |
| 2 | 17.50 |
| 3 | 22.50 |
| 4 | 30.00 |
| 5 | 40.00 |
| 6 | 52.50 |
| 7 | 67.50 |
| 8 | 85.00 |
| 9 | 105.00 |

a. If the current equilibrium price in the basketball market is $12.50, to maximize profits, how many basketballs will Andy produce, what price will he charge, and how much profit (or loss) will he make? Draw a graph to illustrate your answer. Your graph should be labeled clearly and should include Andy's demand, *ATC*, *AVC*, *MC*, and *MR* curves; the price he is charging; the quantity he is producing; and the area representing his profit (or loss).

b. Suppose the equilibrium price of basketballs falls to $5.00. Now how many basketballs will Andy produce, what price will he charge, and how much profit (or loss) will he make? Draw a graph to illustrate this situation, using the instructions in question (a).

## SOLVING THE PROBLEM:

**Step 1:** **Review the chapter material.** This problem is about using cost curve graphs to analyze perfectly competitive firms, so you may want to review the section "Illustrating Profit or Loss on the Cost Curve Graph," which begins on page 385.

**Step 2:** **Calculate Andy's marginal cost, average total cost, and average variable cost.** To maximize profits, Andy will produce the level of output where marginal revenue is equal to marginal cost. We can calculate marginal cost from the information given in the table. We can also calculate average total cost and average variable cost in order to draw the required graph. Average total cost (*ATC*) equals total cost (*TC*) divided by the level of output (*Q*). Average variable cost (*AVC*) equals variable cost (*VC*) divided by output (*Q*). To calculate variable cost, recall that total cost equals variable cost plus fixed cost. When output equals zero, total cost equals fixed cost. In this case, fixed cost equals $10.00.

| OUTPUT PER DAY (Q) | TOTAL COST (TC) | FIXED COST (FC) | VARIABLE COST (VC) | AVERAGE TOTAL COST (ATC) | AVERAGE VARIABLE COST (AVC) | MARGINAL COST (MC) |
|---|---|---|---|---|---|---|
| 0 | $10.00 | $10.00 | $0.00 | — | — | — |
| 1 | 15.00 | 10.00 | 5.00 | $15.00 | $5.00 | $5.00 |
| 2 | 17.50 | 10.00 | 7.50 | 8.75 | 3.75 | 2.50 |
| 3 | 22.50 | 10.00 | 12.50 | 7.50 | 4.17 | 5.00 |
| 4 | 30.00 | 10.00 | 20.00 | 7.50 | 5.00 | 7.50 |
| 5 | 40.00 | 10.00 | 30.00 | 8.00 | 6.00 | 10.00 |
| 6 | 52.50 | 10.00 | 42.50 | 8.75 | 7.08 | 12.50 |
| 7 | 67.50 | 10.00 | 57.50 | 9.64 | 8.21 | 15.00 |
| 8 | 85.00 | 10.00 | 75.00 | 10.63 | 9.38 | 17.50 |
| 9 | 105.00 | 10.00 | 95.00 | 11.67 | 10.56 | 20.00 |

**Step 3:** **Use the information from the table in step 2 to calculate how many basket-balls Andy will produce, what price he will charge, and how much profit he will earn if the market price of basketballs is $12.50.** Andy's marginal revenue is equal to the market price of $12.50. Marginal revenue equals marginal cost when Andy produces 6 basketballs per day. So, Andy will produce 6 basketballs per day and charge a price of $12.50 per basketball. Andy's profits are equal to his total revenue minus his total costs. His total revenue equals the 6 basketballs he sells multiplied by the $12.50 price, or $75.00. So, his profits equal $75.00 − $52.50 = $22.50.

**Step 4:** **Use the information from the table in step 2 to illustrate your answer to question (a) with a graph.**

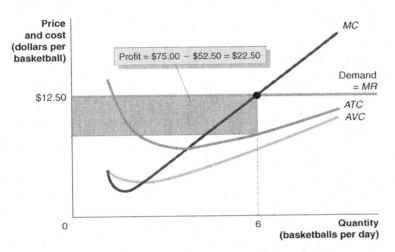

**Step 5:** **Calculate how many basketballs Andy will produce, what price he will charge, and how much profit he will earn when the market price of basketballs is $5.00.** Referring to the table in step 2, we can see that marginal revenue equals marginal cost when Andy produces 3 basketballs per day. He charges the market price of $5.00 per basketball. His total revenue is only $15.00, while his total costs are $22.50, so he will have a loss of $7.50. (Can we be sure that Andy will continue to produce even though he is operating at a loss? We answer this question in the next section.)

**Step 6:** **Illustrate your answer to question (b) with a graph.**

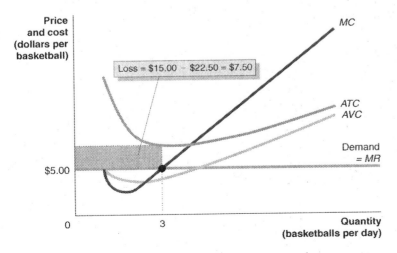

>> End Solved Problem 11-3

## Don't Let This Happen to **YOU!**

### Remember That Firms Maximize Total Profit, Not Profit per Unit

A student examines the following graph and argues, "I believe that a firm will want to produce at $Q_1$, not $Q_2$. At $Q_1$, the distance between price and average total cost is the greatest. Therefore, at $Q_1$, the firm will be maximizing its profits per unit." Briefly explain whether you agree with the student's argument.

The student's argument is incorrect because firms are interested in maximizing their *total* profits and not their profits per unit. We know that profits are not maximized at $Q_1$ because at that level of output, marginal revenue is greater than marginal cost. A firm can always increase its profits by producing any unit that adds more to its revenue than it does to its costs. Only when the firm has expanded production to $Q_2$ will it have produced every unit for which marginal revenue is greater than marginal cost. At that point, it will have maximized profit.

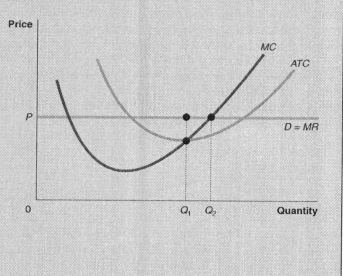

## Illustrating When a Firm Is Breaking Even or Operating at a Loss

We have already seen that to maximize profits, a firm produces the level of output where marginal revenue equals marginal cost. But will the firm actually make a profit at that level of output? It depends on the relationship of price to average total cost. There are three possibilities:

1  $P > ATC$, which means the firm makes a profit.
2  $P = ATC$, which means the firm *breaks even* (its total cost equals its total revenue).
3  $P < ATC$, which means the firm experiences losses.

Figure 11-4 shows the first possibility, where the firm makes a profit. Panels (a) and (b) of Figure 11-5 show the situations where a firm experiences losses or breaks

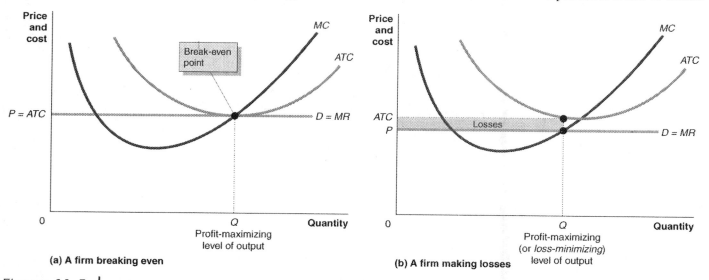

(a) A firm breaking even

(b) A firm making losses

Figure 11-5  |  A Firm Breaking Even and a Firm Experiencing Losses

In panel (a), price equals average total cost, and the firm breaks even because its total revenue will be equal to its total cost. In this situation, the firm makes zero economic profit. In panel (b), price is below average total cost, and the firm experiences a loss.

The loss is represented by the area of the red-shaded rectangle, which has a height equal to $(ATC - P)$ and a width equal to $Q$.

even. In panel (a) of Figure 11-5, at the level of output at which $MR = MC$, price is equal to average total cost. Therefore, total revenue is equal to total cost, and the firm will break even, making zero economic profit. In panel (b), at the level of output at which $MR = MC$, price is less than average total cost. Therefore, total revenue is less than total cost, and the firm has losses. In this case, maximizing profits amounts to *minimizing* losses.

## Making the Connection | Losing Money in the Medical Screening Industry

In a market system, a good or service becomes available to consumers only if an entrepreneur brings the product to market. Thousands of new businesses open every week in the United States. Each new business represents an entrepreneur risking his or her funds trying to earn a profit by offering a good or service to consumers. Of course, there are no guarantees of success, and many new businesses experience losses rather than earn the profits their owners hoped for.

In the early 2000s, technological advance reduced the price of computed tomography (CT) scanning equipment. For years, doctors and hospitals have prescribed CT scans to diagnose patients showing symptoms of heart disease, cancer, and other disorders. The declining price of CT scanning equipment convinced many entrepreneurs that it would be profitable to offer preventive body scans to apparently healthy people. The idea was that the scans would provide early detection of diseases before the customers had begun experiencing symptoms. Unfortunately, the new firms offering this service ran into several difficulties: First, because the CT scan was a voluntary procedure, it was not covered under most medical insurance plans. Second, very few consumers used the service more than once, so there was almost no repeat business. Finally, as with any other medical test, some false positives occurred, where the scan appeared to detect a problem that did not actually exist. Negative publicity from people who had expensive additional—and unnecessary—medical procedures as a result of false-positive CT scans also hurt these new businesses.

As a result of these difficulties, the demand for CT scans was less than most of these entrepreneurs had expected, and the new businesses operated at a loss. For example, the owner of California HeartScan would have broken even if the market price had been $495 per heart scan, but it suffered losses because the actual market price was only $250. The following graphs show the owner's situation.

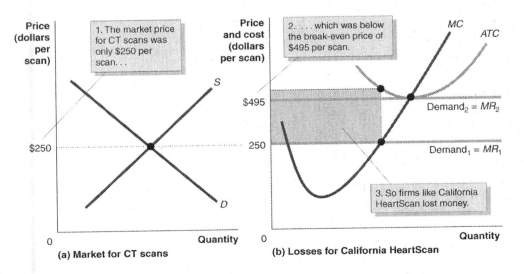

(a) Market for CT scans

(b) Losses for California HeartScan

Why didn't California HeartScan and other medical clinics just raise the price to the level they needed to break even? We have already seen that any firm that tries to raise the price it charges above the market price loses customers to competing firms. By fall 2003, many scanning businesses began to close. Most of the entrepreneurs who had started these businesses lost their investments.

Source: Patricia Callahan, "Scanning for Trouble," *Wall Street Journal*, September 11, 2003, p. B1.

---

**11.4 LEARNING** OBJECTIVE

11.4 | Explain why firms may shut down temporarily.

# Deciding Whether to Produce or to Shut Down in the Short Run

In panel (b) of Figure 11-5, we assumed that the firm would continue to produce, even though it was operating at a loss. In fact, in the short run, a firm suffering losses has two choices:

1  Continue to produce

2  Stop production by shutting down temporarily

In many cases, a firm experiencing losses will consider stopping production temporarily. Even during a temporary shutdown, however, a firm must still pay its fixed costs. For example, if the firm has signed a lease for its building, the landlord will expect to receive a monthly rent payment, even if the firm is not producing anything that month. Therefore, if a firm does not produce, it will suffer a loss equal to its fixed costs. This loss is the maximum the firm will accept. If, by producing, the firm would lose an amount greater than its fixed costs, it will shut down.

A firm will be able to reduce its loss below the amount of its total fixed cost by continuing to produce, provided the total revenue it receives is greater than its variable cost. A firm can use the revenue over and above variable cost to cover part of its fixed cost. In this case, the firm will have a smaller loss by continuing to produce than if it shut down.

**Sunk cost** A cost that has already been paid and that cannot be recovered.

In analyzing the firm's decision to shut down, we are assuming that its fixed costs are *sunk costs*. Remember from Chapter 9 that a **sunk cost** is a cost that has already been paid and cannot be recovered. We assume, as is usually the case, that the firm cannot recover its fixed costs by shutting down. For example, if a farmer has taken out a loan to buy land, the farmer is legally required to make the monthly loan payment whether he grows any wheat that season or not. The farmer has to spend those funds and cannot get them back, so the farmer should treat his sunk costs as irrelevant to his decision making. For any firm, whether total revenue is greater or less than *variable costs* is the key to deciding whether to shut down. As long as a firm's total revenue is greater than its variable costs, it should continue to produce no matter how large or small its fixed costs are.

## Making the Connection | When to Close a Laundry

An article in the *Wall Street Journal* describes what happened to Robert Kjelgaard when he quit his job writing software code at Microsoft and bought a laundry by paying the previous owner $80,000. For this payment, he received 76 washers and dryers and the existing lease on the building. The lease had six years remaining and required a monthly payment of $3,300. Unfortunately, Mr. Kjelgaard had difficulty operating the laundry at a profit. His explicit costs were $4,000 per month more than his revenue.

He tried but failed to sell the laundry. As he told a reporter, "It's hard to sell a business that's losing money." He considered closing the laundry, but as a sole proprietor, he would be responsible for the remainder of the lease. At $3,300 per month for six years, he would be responsible for paying almost $200,000 out of his personal savings. Closing the laundry would still seem to be the better choice because his $3,300 per month in sunk costs were less than the $4,000 per month plus the opportunity cost of his time, which he was losing from operating the laundry.

He finally decided to reorganize his business and hire a professional manager. This change allowed him to return to Microsoft and still reduce his losses to $2,000 per month. Because this amount was less than the $3,300 per month he would lose by shutting down, it made sense for him to continue to operate the laundry. But he was still suffering losses and, according to the article, his wife was "counting the days until the lease runs out."

Source: G. Pascal Zachary, "How a Success at Microsoft Washed Out at a Laundry," *Wall Street Journal*, May 30, 1995.

*Keeping a business open even when suffering losses can sometimes be the best decision for an entrepreneur in the short run.*

One option not available to a firm with losses in a perfectly competitive market is to raise its price. If the firm did raise its price, it would lose all its customers, and its sales would drop to zero. For example, in a recent year, the price of wheat in the United States was $3.16 per bushel. At that price, the typical U.S. wheat farmer lost $9,500. At a price of about $4.25 per bushel, the typical wheat farmer would have broken even. But any wheat farmer who tried to raise his price to $4.25 per bushel would have seen his sales quickly disappear because buyers could purchase all the wheat they wanted at $3.16 per bushel from the thousands of other wheat farmers.

## The Supply Curve of a Firm in the Short Run

Remember that the supply curve for a firm tells us how many units of a product the firm is willing to sell at any given price. Notice that the marginal cost curve for a firm in a perfectly competitive market tells us the same thing. The firm will produce at the level of output where $MR = MC$. Because price equals marginal revenue for a firm in a perfectly competitive market, the firm will produce where $P = MC$. For any given price, we can determine from the marginal cost curve the quantity of output the firm will supply. *Therefore, a perfectly competitive firm's marginal cost curve also is its supply curve.* There is, however, an important qualification to this. We have seen that if a firm is experiencing losses, it will shut down if its total revenue is less than its variable cost:

Total revenue < Variable cost,

or, in symbols:

$$P \times Q < VC.$$

If we divide both sides by $Q$, we have the result that the firm will shut down if:

$$P < AVC.$$

If the price drops below average variable cost, the firm will have a smaller loss if it shuts down and produces no output. *So, the firm's marginal cost curve is its supply curve only for prices at or above average variable cost.* The red line in Figure 11-6 shows the supply curve for the firm in the short run.

Recall that the marginal cost curve intersects the average variable cost where the average variable cost curve is at its minimum point. Therefore, the firm's supply curve is its marginal cost curve above the minimum point of the average variable cost curve. For prices below minimum average variable cost ($P_{MIN}$), the firm will shut down, and its output will fall to zero. The minimum point on the average variable cost curve is called the **shutdown point** and occurs in Figure 11-6 at output level $Q_{SD}$.

**Shutdown point** The minimum point on a firm's average variable cost curve; if the price falls below this point, the firm shuts down production in the short run.

## Figure 11-6

**The Firm's Short-Run Supply Curve**

The firm will produce at the level of output at which $MR = MC$. Because price equals marginal revenue for a firm in a perfectly competitive market, the firm will produce where $P = MC$. For any given price, we can determine the quantity of output the firm will supply from the marginal cost curve. In other words, the marginal cost curve is the firm's supply curve. But remember that the firm will shut down if the price falls below average variable cost. The marginal cost curve crosses the average variable cost at the firm's shutdown point. This point occurs at output level $Q_{SD}$. For prices below $P_{MIN}$, the supply curve is a vertical line along the price axis, which shows that the firm will supply zero output at those prices. The red line in the figure is the firm's short-run supply curve.

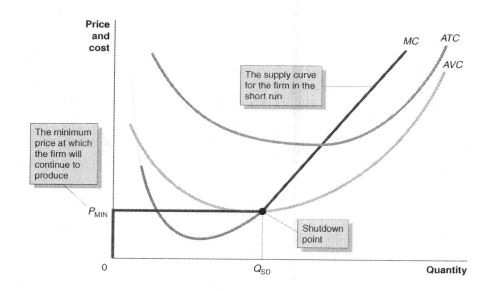

## The Market Supply Curve in a Perfectly Competitive Industry

We saw in Chapter 9 that the market demand curve is determined by adding up the quantity demanded by each consumer in the market at each price. Similarly, the market supply curve is determined by adding up the quantity supplied by each firm in the market at each price. Each firm's marginal cost curve tells us how much that firm will supply at each price. So, the market supply curve can be derived directly from the marginal cost curves of the firms in the market. Panel (a) of Figure 11-7 shows the marginal cost curve for one wheat farmer. At a price of $4, this wheat farmer supplies 8,000 bushels of wheat.

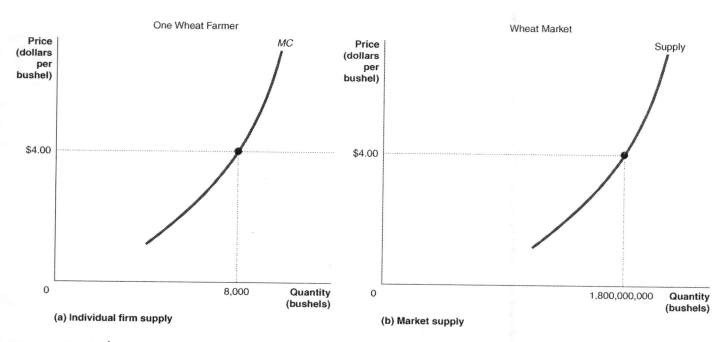

**(a) Individual firm supply**

**(b) Market supply**

## Figure 11-7 | Firm Supply and Market Supply

We can derive the market supply curve by adding up the quantity that each firm in the market is willing to supply at each price. In panel (a), one wheat farmer is willing to supply 8,000 bushels of wheat at a price of $4 per bushel. If every wheat farmer supplies the same amount of wheat at this price and if there are 225,000 wheat farmers,

the total amount of wheat supplied at a price of $4 will equal 8,000 bushels per farmer × 225,000 farmers = 1.8 billion bushels of wheat. This is one point on the market supply curve for wheat shown in panel (b). We can find the other points on the market supply curve by seeing how much wheat each farmer is willing to supply at each price.

If every wheat farmer supplies the same amount of wheat at this price and if there are 225,000 wheat farmers, the total amount of wheat supplied at a price of $4 will be:

8,000 bushels per farmer × 225,000 farmers = 1.8 billion bushels of wheat.

Panel (b) shows a price of $4 and a quantity of 1.8 billion bushels as a point on the market supply curve for wheat. In reality, of course, not all wheat farms are alike. Some wheat farms supply more at the market price than the typical farm; other wheat farms supply less. The key point is that we can derive the market supply curve by adding up the quantity that each firm in the market is willing to supply at each price.

11.5 | Explain how entry and exit ensure that perfectly competitive firms earn zero economic profit in the long run.

# "If Everyone Can Do It, You Can't Make Money at It": The Entry and Exit of Firms in the Long Run

In the long run, unless a firm can cover all its costs, it will shut down and exit the industry. In a market system, firms continually enter and exit industries. In this section, we will see how profits and losses provide signals to firms that lead to entry and exit.

## Economic Profit and the Entry or Exit Decision

To begin, let's look more closely at how economists characterize the profits earned by the owners of a firm. Suppose Anne Moreno decides to start her own business. After considering her interests and preparing a business plan, she decides to start an organic apple farm rather than open a restaurant or gift shop. After 10 years of effort, Anne has saved $100,000 and borrowed another $900,000 from a bank. With these funds, she has bought the land, apple trees, and farm equipment necessary to start her organic apple business. As we saw in Chapter 10, when someone invests her own funds in her firm, the opportunity cost to the firm is the return the funds would have earned in their best alternative use. If Farmer Moreno could have earned a 10 percent return on her $100,000 in savings in their best alternative use—which might have been, for example, to buy a small restaurant—then her apple business incurs a $10,000 opportunity cost. We can also think of this $10,000 as being the minimum amount that Farmer Moreno needs to earn on her $100,000 investment in her farm to remain in the industry in the long run.

Table 11-4 lists Farmer Moreno's costs. In addition to her explicit costs, we assume that she has two implicit costs: the $10,000, which represents the opportunity cost of the

TABLE 11-4

Farmer Moreno's Costs per Year

| EXPLICIT COSTS | |
| --- | --- |
| Water | $10,000 |
| Wages | $15,000 |
| Organic fertilizer | $10,000 |
| Electricity | $5,000 |
| Payment on bank loan | $45,000 |
| **IMPLICIT COSTS** | |
| Foregone salary | $30,000 |
| Opportunity cost of the $100,000 she has invested in her farm | $10,000 |
| Total cost | $125,000 |

funds she invested in her farm, and the $30,000 salary she could have earned managing someone else's farm instead of her own. Her total costs are $125,000. If the market price of organic apples is $15 per box and Farmer Moreno sells 10,000 boxes, her total revenue will be $150,000 and her economic profit will be $25,000 (total revenue of $150,000 minus total costs of $125,000). Recall from Chapter 7 that **economic profit** equals a firm's revenues minus all of its costs, implicit and explicit. So, Farmer Moreno is covering the $10,000 opportunity cost of the funds invested in her firm, and she is also earning an additional $25,000 in economic profit.

**Economic profit** A firm's revenues minus all its costs, implicit and explicit.

***Economic Profit Leads to Entry of New Firms*** Unfortunately, Farmer Moreno is unlikely to earn an economic profit for very long. Suppose other apple farmers are just breaking even by growing apples using conventional methods. In that case, they will have an incentive to convert to organic growing methods so they can begin earning an economic profit. Remember that the more firms there are in an industry, the further to the right the market supply curve is. Panel (a) of Figure 11-8 shows that more farmers entering the market for organically grown apples will cause the market supply curve to shift to the right. Farmers will continue entering the market until the market supply curve has shifted from $S_1$ to $S_2$.

With the supply curve at $S_2$, the market price will have fallen to $10 per box. Panel (b) shows the effect on Farmer Moreno, whom we assume has the same costs as other organic apple farmers. As the market price falls from $15 to $10 per box, Farmer Moreno's demand curve shifts down, from $D_1$ to $D_2$. In the new equilibrium, Farmer Moreno is selling 8,000 boxes at a price of $10 per box. She and the other organic apple growers are no longer earning any economic profit. They are just breaking even, and the return on their investment is just covering the opportunity cost of these funds. New farmers will stop entering the market for organic apples because the rate of return is no better than they can earn elsewhere.

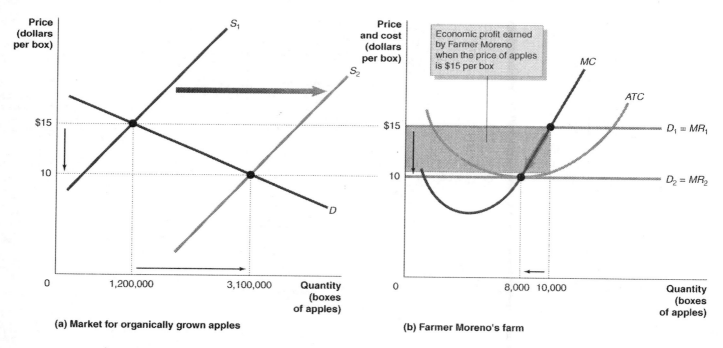

(a) Market for organically grown apples

(b) Farmer Moreno's farm

Figure 11-8 | The Effect of Entry on Economic Profits

We assume that Farmer Moreno's costs are the same as the costs of other organic apple growers. Initially, she and other producers of organically grown apples are able to charge $15 per box and earn an economic profit. Farmer Moreno's economic profit is represented by the area of the green box. Panel (a) shows that as other farmers begin to grow apples using organic methods, the market supply curve shifts to the right, from $S_1$ to $S_2$, and the market price drops to $10 per box. Panel (b) shows that the falling price causes Farmer Moreno's demand curve to shift down from $D_1$ to $D_2$, and she reduces her output from 10,000 boxes to 8,000. At the new market price of $10 per box, organic apple growers are just breaking even: Their total revenue is equal to their total cost, and their economic profit is zero. Notice the difference in scale between the graph in panel (a) and the graph in panel (b).

Will Farmer Moreno continue to grow organic apples even though she is just breaking even? She will because growing organic apples earns her as high a return on her investment as she could earn elsewhere. It may seem strange that new firms will continue to enter a market until all economic profits are eliminated and that established firms remain in a market despite not earning any economic profit. It only seems strange because we are used to thinking in terms of accounting profits, rather than *economic* profits. Remember that accounting rules generally require that only explicit costs be included on a firm's financial statements. The opportunity cost of the funds Farmer Moreno invested in her firm—$10,000—and her foregone salary—$30,000—are economic costs, but neither is an accounting cost. So, although an accountant would see Farmer Moreno as earning a profit of $40,000, an economist would see her as just breaking even. Farmer Moreno must pay attention to her accounting profit when preparing her financial statements and when paying her income tax. But because economic profit takes into account all her costs, it gives a truer indication of the financial health of her farm.

***Economic Losses Lead to Exit of Firms*** Suppose some consumers decide there are no important benefits from eating organically grown apples and they switch back to buying conventionally grown apples. Panel (a) of Figure 11-9 shows that the demand curve for organically grown apples will shift to the left, from $D_1$ to $D_2$, and the market price will fall from $10 per box to $7. Panel (b) shows that as the price falls, a typical organic apple farmer, like Anne Moreno, will move down her marginal cost curve to a lower level of output. At the lower level of output and lower price, she will be suffering an **economic loss** because she will not cover all her costs. As long as price is above average variable cost, she will continue to produce in the short run, even when suffering losses. But in the long run, firms will exit an industry if they are unable to cover all their costs. In this case, some organic apple growers will switch back to growing apples using conventional methods.

    Panel (c) of Figure 11-9 shows that firms exiting the organic apple industry will cause the market supply curve to shift to the left. Firms will continue to exit, and the supply curve will continue to shift to the left until the price has risen back to $10 and the market supply curve is at $S_2$. Panel (d) shows that when the price is back to $10, the remaining firms in the industry will be breaking even.

**Economic loss** The situation in which a firm's total revenue is less than its total cost, including all implicit costs.

# Long-Run Equilibrium in a Perfectly Competitive Market

We have seen that economic profits attract firms to enter an industry. The entry of firms forces down the market price until the typical firm is breaking even. Economic losses cause firms to exit an industry. The exit of firms forces up the equilibrium market price until the typical firm is breaking even. This process of entry and exit results in *long-run competitive equilibrium*. In **long-run competitive equilibrium**, entry and exit have resulted in the typical firm breaking even. The *long-run equilibrium market price* is at a level equal to the minimum point on the typical firm's average total cost curve.

    The long run in the organic apple market is three to four years, which is the amount of time it takes farmers to convert from conventional growing methods to organic growing methods. As discussed at the beginning of this chapter, only during the years from 1997 to 2001 was it possible for organic apple farmers to earn economic profits. By 2002, the entry of new firms had eliminated economic profits in the industry.

    Firms in perfectly competitive markets are in a constant struggle to stay one step ahead of their competitors. They are always looking for new ways to provide a product, such as growing apples organically. It is possible for firms to find ways to earn an economic profit for a while, but to repeat the quote from a Yakima Valley organic apple farmer at the beginning of this chapter, "It's like anything else in agriculture. If people see an economic opportunity, usually it only lasts for a few years." This observation is not restricted to agriculture. In any perfectly competitive market, an opportunity to make economic profits never lasts long. As Sharon Oster, an economist at Yale University, has put it, "If everyone can do it, you can't make money at it."

**Long-run competitive equilibrium** The situation in which the entry and exit of firms has resulted in the typical firm breaking even.

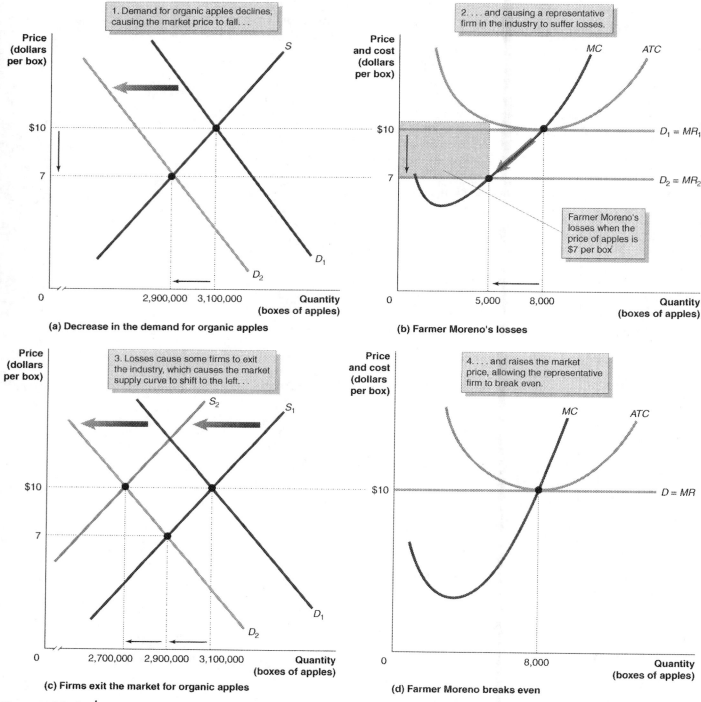

**(a) Decrease in the demand for organic apples**

1. Demand for organic apples declines, causing the market price to fall. . .

**(b) Farmer Moreno's losses**

2. . . . and causing a representative firm in the industry to suffer losses.

Farmer Moreno's losses when the price of apples is $7 per box

**(c) Firms exit the market for organic apples**

3. Losses cause some firms to exit the industry, which causes the market supply curve to shift to the left. . .

**(d) Farmer Moreno breaks even**

4. . . . and raises the market price, allowing the representative firm to break even.

# Figure 11-9 | The Effect of Exit on Economic Losses

When the price of apples is $10 per box, Farmer Moreno and other producers of organically grown apples are breaking even. A total quantity of 3,100,000 boxes is sold in the market. Farmer Moreno sells 8,000 boxes. Panel (a) shows a decline in the demand for organically grown apples from $D_1$ to $D_2$ that reduces the market price to $7 per box. Panel (b) shows that the falling price causes Farmer Moreno's demand curve to shift down from $D_1$ to $D_2$ and her output to fall from 8,000 to 5,000 boxes. At a market price of $7 per box, farmers have economic losses, represented by the area of the red box. As a result, some farmers will exit the market, which shifts the market supply curve to the left. Panel (c) shows that exit continues until the supply curve has shifted from $S_1$ to $S_2$ and the market price has risen from $7 back to $10. Panel (d) shows that with the price back at $10, Farmer Moreno will break even. In the new market equilibrium, total production of organic apples has fallen from 3,100,000 to 2,700,000 boxes.

# The Long-Run Supply Curve in a Perfectly Competitive Market

If the typical organic apple grower breaks even at a price of $10 per box, in the long run, the market price will always return to this level. If an increase in demand causes the market price to rise above $10, farmers will be earning economic profits. This profit will attract additional farmers into the market, and the market supply curve will shift to the right until the price is back to $10. Panel (a) in Figure 11-10 illustrates the long-run effect of an increase in demand. An increase in demand from $D_1$ to $D_2$ causes the market price to temporarily rise from $10 per box to $15. At this price, farmers are making economic profits growing organic apples, but these profits attract entry of new farmers' organic apples. The result is an increase in supply from $S_1$ to $S_2$, which forces the price back down to $10 per box and eliminates the economic profits.

Similarly, if a decrease in demand causes the market price to fall below $10, farmers will experience economic losses. These losses will cause some farmers to exit the market, the supply curve will shift to the left, and the price will return to $10. Panel (b) in Figure 11-10 illustrates the long-run effect of a decrease in demand. A decrease in demand from $D_1$ to $D_2$ causes the market price to fall temporarily from $10 per box to $7. At this price, farmers are suffering economic losses growing organic apples, but these losses cause some farmers to exit the market for organic apples. The result is a decrease in supply from $S_1$ to $S_2$, which forces the price back up to $10 per box and eliminates the losses.

The **long-run supply curve** shows the relationship in the long run between market price and the quantity supplied. In the long run, the price in the organic apple market will be $10 per box, no matter how many boxes of apples are produced. So, as Figure 11-10 shows, the long-run supply curve ($S_{LR}$) for organic apples is a horizontal line at a price of $10. Remember that the reason the price returns to $10 in the long run is that this is the price at which the typical firm in the industry just breaks even. The typical firm breaks even

**Long-run supply curve** A curve that shows the relationship in the long run between market price and the quantity supplied.

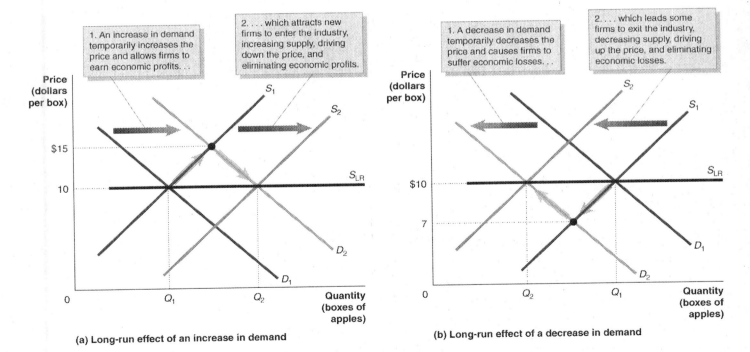

**(a) Long-run effect of an increase in demand**

**(b) Long-run effect of a decrease in demand**

Figure 11-10 | The Long-Run Supply Curve in a Perfectly Competitive Industry

Panel (a) shows that an increase in demand for organic apples will lead to a temporary increase in price from $10 to $15 per box, as the market demand curve shifts to the right, from $D_1$ to $D_2$. The entry of new firms shifts the market supply curve to the right, from $S_1$ to $S_2$, which will cause the price to fall back to its long-run level of $10. Panel (b) shows that a decrease in demand will lead to a temporary decrease in price

from $10 to $7 per box, as the market demand curve shifts to the left, from $D_1$ to $D_2$. The exit of firms shifts the market supply curve to the left, from $S_1$ to $S_2$, which causes the price to rise back to its long-run level of $10. The long-run supply curve ($S_{LR}$) shows the relationship between market price and the quantity supplied in the long run. In this case, the long-run supply curve is a horizontal line.

at this price because it is at the minimum point on the firm's average total cost curve. We can draw the important conclusion that *in the long run, a perfectly competitive market will supply whatever amount of a good consumers demand at a price determined by the minimum point on the typical firm's average total cost curve.*

Because the position of the long-run supply curve is determined by the minimum point on the typical firm's average total cost curve, anything that raises or lowers the costs of the typical firm in the long run will cause the long-run supply curve to shift. For example, if a disease infects apple trees and the costs of treating the disease adds $2 per box to the cost of producing apples, the long-run supply curve will shift up by $2.

## Increasing-Cost and Decreasing-Cost Industries

Any industry in which the typical firm's average costs do not change as the industry expands production will have a horizontal long-run supply curve, like the one in Figure 11-10. Industries, like the apple industry, where this holds true are called *constant-cost industries.* It's possible, however, for the typical firm's average costs to change as an industry expands.

For example, if an input used in producing a good is available in only limited quantities, the cost of the input will rise as the industry expands. If only a limited amount of land is available on which to grow the grapes to make a certain variety of wine, an increase in demand for wine made from these grapes will result in competition for the land and will drive up its price. As a result, more of the wine will be produced in the long run only if the price rises to cover the higher average costs of the typical firm. In this case, the long-run supply curve will slope upward. Industries with upward-sloping long-run supply curves are called *increasing-cost industries.*

Finally, in some cases, the typical firm's costs may fall as the industry expands. Suppose that someone invents a new microwave that uses as an input a specialized memory chip that is currently produced only in small quantities. If demand for the microwave increases, firms that produce microwaves will increase their orders for the memory chip. We saw in Chapter 10 that if there are economies of scale in producing a good, its average cost will decline as output increases. If there are economies of scale in producing this memory chip, the average cost of producing it will fall, and competition will result in its price falling as well. This price decline, in turn, will lower the average cost of producing the new microwave. In the long run, competition will force the price of the microwave to fall to the level of the new lower average cost of the typical firm. In this case, the long-run supply curve will slope downward. Industries with downward-sloping long-run supply curves are called *decreasing-cost industries.*

11.6 | Explain how perfect competition leads to economic efficiency.

## Perfect Competition and Efficiency

Notice how powerful consumers are in a market system. If consumers want more organic apples, the market will supply them. This happens not because a government bureaucrat in Washington, DC, or an official in an apple growers' association gives orders. The additional apples are produced because an increase in demand results in higher prices and a higher rate of return on investments in organic growing techniques. Apple growers, trying to get the highest possible return on their investment, begin to switch from using conventional growing methods to using organic growing methods. If consumers lose their taste for organic apples and demand falls, the process works in reverse.

Making the Connection | **The Decline of Apple Production in New York State**

Although New York State is second only to Washington State in production of apples, its production has been declining during the past 20 years. The decline has been particularly steep in counties close to New York City. In 1985, there were more than 11,000 acres of apple orchards in Ulster County, which is 75 miles north of New York City. Today, fewer than 5,000 acres remain. As it became difficult for apple growers in the county to compete with lower-cost producers elsewhere, the resources these entrepreneurs were using to produce apples—particularly land—became more valuable in other uses. Many farmers sold their land to housing developers. As one apple farmer put it, "Over the last ten years or so, [apple] prices have been stagnant or going down. I didn't see a return on the money, and I didn't want to continue."

In a market system, entrepreneurs will not continue to employ economic resources to produce a good or service unless consumers are willing to pay a price at least high enough for them to break even. Consumers were not willing to pay a high enough price for apples for many New York State apple growers to break even on their investments. As a result, resources left apple production in that state.

Sources: Lisa W. Foderaro, "Where Apples Don't Pay, Developers Will," *New York Times*, June 23, 2001; and USDA, *2002 Census of Agriculture, Volume 1, Chapter 2*, New York County Level Data, Table 31.

*When apple growers in New York State stopped breaking even, many sold their land to housing developers.*

## Productive Efficiency

In the market system, consumers get as many apples as they want, produced at the lowest average cost possible. The forces of competition will drive the market price to the minimum average cost of the typical firm. **Productive efficiency** refers to the situation in which a good or service is produced at the lowest possible cost. As we have seen, perfect competition results in productive efficiency.

The managers of every firm strive to earn an economic profit by reducing costs. But in a perfectly competitive market, other firms quickly copy ways of reducing costs, so that in the long run, only the consumer benefits from cost reductions.

**Productive efficiency** The situation in which a good or service is produced at the lowest possible cost.

# Solved Problem | 11-6

## How Productive Efficiency Benefits Consumers

Writing in the *New York Times* on the technology boom of the late 1990s, Michael Lewis argues "The sad truth, for investors, seems to be that most of the benefits of new technologies are passed right through to consumers free of charge."

a. What do you think Lewis means by the benefits of new technology being "passed right through to consumers free of charge"? Use a graph like Figure 11-8 on page 394 to illustrate your answer.

b. Explain why this result is a "sad truth" for investors.

## SOLVING THE PROBLEM:

**Step 1:** **Review the chapter material.** This problem is about perfect competition and efficiency, so you may want to review the section "Perfect Competition and Efficiency," which begins on page 398.

**Step 2:** **Use the concepts from this chapter to explain what Lewis means.** By "new technologies," Lewis means new products—like cell phones or plasma television sets—or lower-cost ways of producing existing products. In either case, new technologies will allow firms to earn economic profits for a while, but these profits will lead new firms to enter the market in the long run.

**Step 3:** **Use a graph like Figure 11-8 to illustrate why the benefits of new technologies are "passed right through to consumers free of charge."** Figure 11-8 shows the situation in which a firm is making economic profits in the short run but has these profits eliminated by entry in the long run. We can draw a similar graph to analyze what happens in the long run in the market for plasma televisions:

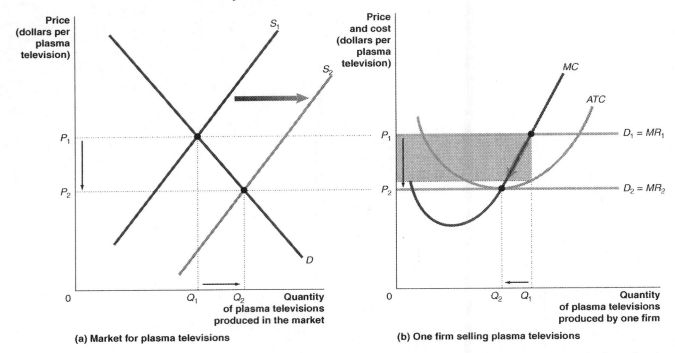

**(a) Market for plasma televisions**

**(b) One firm selling plasma televisions**

When plasma televisions were first introduced, prices were high, and only a few firms were in the market. Panel (a) shows that the initial equilibrium price in the market for plasma televisions is $P_1$. Panel (b) shows that at this price, the typical firm in the industry is earning an economic profit, which is shown by the green-shaded box. The economic profit attracts new firms into the industry. This entry shifts the market supply curve from $S_1$ to $S_2$ in panel (a) and lowers the equilibrium price from $P_1$ to $P_2$. Panel (b) shows that at the new market price, $P_2$, the typical firm is breaking even. Therefore, plasma televisions are being produced at the lowest possible cost, and productive efficiency is achieved. Consumers receive the new technology "free of charge" in the sense that they only have to pay a price equal to the lowest possible cost of production.

**Step 4:** **Answer question (b) by explaining why the result in question (a) is a "sad truth" for investors.** We have seen in answering question (a) that in the long run, firms only break even on their investment in producing high-technology goods. That result implies that investors in these firms are also unlikely to earn an economic profit in the long run.

**EXTRA CREDIT:** Lewis is using a key result from this chapter: In the long run, entry of new firms competes away economic profits. We should notice that, strictly speaking, the high-technology industries Lewis is discussing are not perfectly competitive. Cell phones or plasma televisions, for instance, are not identical, and each cell phone company produces a quantity large enough to affect the market price. However, as we will see in Chapter 12, these deviations from perfect competition do not change the important conclusion that the entry of new firms benefits consumers by forcing prices down to the level of average cost. In fact, the price of plasma televisions dropped by more than 75 percent within five years of their first becoming widely available.

Source: Michael Lewis, "In Defense of the Boom," *New York Times*, October 27, 2002.

## Allocative Efficiency

Not only do perfectly competitive firms produce goods and services at the lowest possible cost, they also produce the goods and services that consumers value most. Firms will produce a good up to the point where the marginal cost of producing another unit is equal to the marginal benefit consumers receive from consuming that unit. In other words, firms will supply all those goods that provide consumers with a marginal benefit at least as great as the marginal cost of producing them. We know this is true because:

1 The price of a good represents the marginal benefit consumers receive from consuming the last unit of the good sold.

2 Perfectly competitive firms produce up to the point where the price of the good equals the marginal cost of producing the last unit.

3 Therefore, firms produce up to the point where the last unit provides a marginal benefit to consumers equal to the marginal cost of producing it.

These statements are another way of saying that entrepreneurs in a market system efficiently *allocate* labor, machinery, and other inputs to produce the goods and services that best satisfy consumer wants. In this sense, perfect competition achieves **allocative efficiency**. As we will explore in the next few chapters, many goods and services sold in the U.S. economy are not produced in perfectly competitive markets. Nevertheless, productive efficiency and allocative efficiency are useful benchmarks against which to compare the actual performance of the economy.

**Allocative efficiency** A state of the economy in which production represents consumer preferences; in particular, every good or service is produced up to the point where the last unit provides a marginal benefit to consumers equal to the marginal cost of producing it.

## Conclusion

The competitive forces of the market impose relentless pressure on firms to produce new and better goods and services at the lowest possible cost. Firms that fail to adequately anticipate changes in consumer tastes or that fail to adopt the latest and most efficient technology do not survive in the long run. In the nineteenth century, the biologist Charles Darwin developed a theory of evolution based on the idea of the "survival of the fittest." Only those plants and animals that are best able to adapt to the demands of their environment are able to survive. Darwin first realized the important role that the struggle for existence plays in the natural world after reading early nineteenth-century economists' descriptions of the role it plays in the economic world. Just as "survival of the fittest" is the rule in nature, so it is in the economic world.

At the start of this chapter, we saw that there are four market structures: perfect competition, monopolistic competition, oligopoly, and monopoly. Now that we have studied perfect competition, in the following chapters we move on to the other three market structures.

# Chapter 9
# Monopoly

Although few firms are monopolies, the economic model of monopoly can still be quite useful. As we saw in Chapter 11, even though perfectly competitive markets are rare, this market model provides a benchmark for how a firm acts in the most competitive situation possible: when it is in an industry with many firms that all supply the same product. Monopoly provides a benchmark for the other extreme, where a firm is the only one in its market and, therefore, faces no competition from other firms supplying its product. The monopoly model is also useful in analyzing situations in which firms agree to *collude*, or not compete, and act together as if they were a monopoly. As we will discuss in this chapter, collusion is illegal in the United States, but it occasionally happens.

Monopolies also pose a dilemma for the government. Should the government allow monopolies to exist? Are there circumstances in which the government should actually promote the existence of monopolies? Should the government regulate the prices monopolies charge? If so, will such price regulation increase economic efficiency? In this chapter, we will explore these public policy issues.

---

**14.1 LEARNING OBJECTIVE**

14.1 | Define monopoly.

# Is Any Firm Ever Really a Monopoly?

**Monopoly** A firm that is the only seller of a good or service that does not have a close substitute.

A **monopoly** is a firm that is the only seller of a good or service that does not have a close substitute. Because substitutes of some kind exist for just about every product, can any firm really be a monopoly? The answer is "yes," provided that the substitutes are not "close" substitutes. But how do we decide whether a substitute is a close substitute? A narrow definition of monopoly that some economists use is that a firm has a monopoly if it can ignore the actions of all other firms. In other words, other firms must not be producing close substitutes if the monopolist can ignore the other firms' prices. For example, candles are a substitute for electric lights, but your local electric company can ignore candle prices because however low the price of candles falls, almost no customers will give up using electric lights and switch to candles. Therefore, your local electric company is clearly a monopoly.

Many economists, however, use a broader definition of monopoly. For example, suppose Joe Santos owns the only pizza parlor in a small town. (We will consider later the question of *why* a market may have only a single firm.) Does Joe have a monopoly? Substitutes for pizzas certainly exist. If the price of pizza is too high, people will switch to hamburgers or fried chicken or some other food instead. People do not have to eat at Joe's or starve. Joe is in competition with the local McDonald's and Kentucky Fried Chicken, among other firms. So, Joe does not meet the narrow definition of a monopoly. But many economists would still argue that it is useful to think of Joe as having a monopoly.

Although hamburgers and fried chicken are substitutes for pizza, competition from firms selling them is not enough to keep Joe from earning economic profits. We saw in Chapter 11 that when firms earn economic profits, we can expect new firms to enter the industry, and in the long run, the economic profits are competed away. Joe's profits will not be competed away as long as he is the *only* seller of pizza. Using the broader definition, Joe has a monopoly because there are no other firms selling a substitute close enough that his economic profits are competed away in the long run.

> *Monopoly –*
> *Only seller of a good/*
> *service that does not*
> *have a close substitute*

## Making *the* Connection | Is Xbox 360 a Close Substitute for PlayStation 3?

In the early 2000s, Microsoft's Xbox and Sony's PlayStation 2 (PS2) were the best-selling video game consoles. When the two companies began work on the next generation of consoles, they had important decisions to make. In developing the Xbox, Microsoft had decided to include a hard disk and a version of the Windows computer operating system. As a result, the cost of producing the Xbox was much higher than the cost to Sony of producing the PlayStation 2. Microsoft was not concerned by the higher production cost because it believed it would be able to charge a higher price for Xbox than Sony charged for PlayStation 2. Unfortunately for Microsoft, consumers considered the Sony PS2 a close substitute for the Xbox. Microsoft was forced to charge the same price for the Xbox that Sony charged for the PS2. So, while Sony was able to make a substantial profit at that price, Microsoft initially lost money on the Xbox because of its higher costs.

In developing the next generation of video game consoles, both companies hoped to produce devices that could serve as multipurpose home-entertainment systems. To achieve this goal, the new systems needed to play DVDs as well as games. Sony developed a new type of DVD called Blu-ray. Blu-ray DVDs can store five times as much data as conventional DVDs and can play back high-definition (HD) video. Sony's decision to give the new PlayStation 3 (PS3) the capability to play Blu-ray DVDs was risky in two ways: First, it raised the cost of producing the consoles. Second, because there is a competing second-generation standard for DVDs, called HD-DVD, the PlayStation 3 would not be capable of playing all available second-generation DVDs, thereby reducing its appeal to some consumers. Microsoft decided to sell its Xbox 360 with only the capability of playing older-format DVDs, while making available an add-on component that would play HD-DVDs.

*To many gamers PlayStation 3 is a close substitute for Xbox.*

Early indications were that Microsoft may have made the better decision. Consumers seemed to consider the PS3 and the Xbox to be close substitutes. In that case, the fact that the PS3's price was $200 higher than the Xbox 360's price was a significant problem for Sony. Ironically, Sony made the same mistake Microsoft made several years before when it launched the Xbox to compete with PS2.

Sources: Stephen H, Wildstrom, "PlayStation 3: It's Got Game," *BusinessWeek*, December 4, 2006; and "Sony: Playing a Long Game," *Economist*, November 16, 2006.

---

14.2 | Explain the four main reasons monopolies arise.

# Where Do Monopolies Come From?

Because monopolies do not face competition, every firm would like to have a monopoly. But to have a monopoly, barriers to entering the market must be so high that no other firms can enter. *Barriers to entry* may be high enough to keep out competing firms for four main reasons:

1 Government blocks the entry of more than one firm into a market.

2 One firm has control of a key resource necessary to produce a good.

3 There are important *network externalities* in supplying the good or service.

4 Economies of scale are so large that one firm has a *natural monopoly*.

## Entry Blocked by Government Action

As we will discuss later in this chapter, governments ordinarily try to promote competition in markets, but sometimes governments take action to block entry into a market. In the United States, government blocks entry in two main ways:

1 By granting a *patent* or *copyright* to an individual or firm, giving it the exclusive right to produce a product.

2 By granting a firm a *public franchise*, making it the exclusive legal provider of a good or service.

**Patent** The exclusive right to a product for a period of 20 years from the date the product is invented.

*Patents and Copyrights* The U.S. government grants patents to firms that develop new products or new ways of making existing products. A **patent** gives a firm the exclusive right to a new product for a period of 20 years from the date the product is invented. Because Microsoft has a patent on the Windows operating system, other firms cannot sell their own versions of Windows. The government grants patents to encourage firms to spend money on the research and development necessary to create new products. If other firms could have freely copied Windows, Microsoft is unlikely to have spent the money necessary to develop it. Sometimes firms are able to maintain a monopoly in the production of a good without patent protection, provided that they can keep secret how the product is made.

Patent protection is of vital importance to pharmaceutical firms as they develop new prescription drugs. Pharmaceutical firms start research and development work on a new prescription drug an average of 12 years before the drug is available for sale. A firm applies for a patent about 10 years before it begins to sell the product. The average 10-year delay between the government granting a patent and the firm actually selling the drug is due to the federal Food and Drug Administration's requirements that the firm demonstrate that the drug is both safe and effective. Therefore, during the period before the drug can be sold, the firm will have substantial costs to develop and test the drug. If the drug does not make it successfully to market, the firm will have a substantial loss.

Once a drug is available for sale, the profits the firm earns from the drug will increase throughout the period of patent protection—which is usually about 10 years—as the drug becomes more widely known to doctors and patients. After the patent has expired, other firms are free to legally produce chemically identical drugs called *generic drugs*. Gradually, competition from generic drugs will eliminate the profits the original firm had been earning. For example, when patent protection expired for Glucophage, a diabetes drug manufactured by Bristol-Myers Squibb, sales of the drug declined by more than $1.5 billion in the first year due to competition from 12 generic versions of the drug produced by other firms. When the patent expired on Prozac, an antidepressant drug manufactured by Eli Lilly, sales dropped by more than 80 percent. Most economic profits from selling a prescription drug are eliminated 20 years after the drug is first offered for sale.

## Making the Connection | The End of the Christmas Plant Monopoly

In December, the poinsettia plant seems to be almost everywhere, decorating stores, restaurants, and houses. Although it may seem strange that anyone can have a monopoly on the production of a plant, for many years the Paul Ecke Ranch in Encinitas, California, had a monopoly on poinsettias.

The poinsettia is a wildflower native to Mexico. It was almost unknown in the United States before Albert Ecke, a German immigrant, began selling it in the early twentieth century at his flower stand in Hollywood, California. Unlike almost every other flowering plant, the poinsettia blossoms in the winter. This timing, along with the plant's striking red and green colors, makes the Poinsettia ideal for Christmas decorating.

Albert Ecke's son, Paul, discovered that by grafting together two varieties of poinsettias, it was possible to have multiple branches grow from one stem. The result was a plant that had more leaves and was much more colorful than conventional poinsettias. Paul Ecke did not attempt to patent his new technique for growing poinsettias. But because the Ecke family kept the technique secret for decades, it was able to maintain a monopoly on the commercial production of the plants. Unfortunately for the Ecke family—but fortunately for consumers—a university researcher discovered the technique and published it in an academic journal.

New firms quickly entered the industry, and the price of poinsettias plummeted. Soon consumers could purchase them for as little as three for $10. At those prices, the Ecke's firm was unable to earn economic profits. Eventually, Paul Ecke III, the owner of the firm, decided to sell off more than half the firm's land to fund new state-of-the-art

*At one time, the Ecke family had a monopoly on growing poinsettias, but many new firms entered the industry.*

greenhouses and research into new varieties of plants that he hoped would earn the firm economic profits once again. One of the firm's new products was a variety of white poinsettias that could be spray-painted in different colors and sold for $10 or more—double the price of plain poinsettias.

Sources: Bart Ziegler, "What Color Is Your Poinsettia?" *Wall Street Journal*, December 14, 2006; Cynthia Crossen, "Holiday's Ubiquitous Houseplant," *Wall Street Journal*, December 19, 2000; and Mike Freeman and David E. Graham, "Ecke Ranch Plans to Sell Most of Its Remaining Land," *San Diego Union-Tribune*, December 11, 2003.

Just as the government grants a new product patent protection, books, films, and software receive **copyright** protection. U.S. law grants the creator of a book, film, or piece of music the exclusive right to use the creation during the creator's lifetime. The creator's heirs retain this exclusive right for 70 years after the creator's death. In effect, copyrights create monopolies for the copyrighted items. Without copyrights, individuals and firms would be less likely to invest in creating new books, films, and software.

> **Copyright** A government-granted exclusive right to produce and sell a creation.

*Public Franchises* In some cases, the government grants a firm a **public franchise** that allows it to be the only legal provider of a good or service. For example, state and local governments often designate one company as the sole provider of electricity, natural gas, or water.

Occasionally, the government may decide to provide certain services directly to consumers through a *public enterprise*. This is much more common in Europe than in the United States. For example, the governments in most European countries own the railroad systems. In the United States, many city governments provide water and sewage service themselves rather than rely on private firms.

> **Public franchise** A designation by the government that a firm is the only legal provider of a good or service.

## Control of a Key Resource

Another way for a firm to become a monopoly is by controlling a key resource. This happens infrequently because most resources, including raw materials such as oil or iron ore, are widely available from a variety of suppliers. There are, however, a few prominent examples of monopolies based on control of a key resource, such as the Aluminum Company of America (Alcoa) and the International Nickel Company of Canada.

For many years until the 1940s, Alcoa either owned or had long-term contracts to buy nearly all of the available bauxite, the mineral needed to produce aluminum. Without access to bauxite, competing firms had to use recycled aluminum, which limited the amount of aluminum they could produce. Similarly, the International Nickel Company of Canada controlled more than 90 percent of available nickel supplies. Competition in the nickel market increased when the Petsamo nickel fields in northern Russia were developed after World War II.

In the United States, a key resource for a professional sports team is a large stadium. The teams that make up the major professional sports leagues—Major League Baseball, the National Football League, and the National Basketball Association—usually have long-term leases with the stadiums in major cities. Control of these stadiums is a major barrier to new professional baseball, football, or basketball leagues forming.

## Making the Connection | Are Diamond Profits Forever? The De Beers Diamond Monopoly

The most famous monopoly based on control of a raw material is the De Beers diamond mining and marketing company of South Africa. Before the 1860s, diamonds were extremely rare. Only a few pounds of diamonds were produced each year, primarily from Brazil and India. Then in 1870,

*De Beers promoted the sentimental value of diamonds as a way to maintain its position in the diamond market.*

enormous deposits of diamonds were discovered along the Orange River in South Africa. It became possible to produce thousands of pounds of diamonds per year, and the owners of the new mines feared that the price of diamonds would plummet. To avoid financial disaster, the mine owners decided in 1888 to merge and form De Beers Consolidated Mines, Ltd.

De Beers became one of the most profitable and longest-lived monopolies in history. The company has carefully controlled the supply of diamonds to keep prices high. As new diamond deposits were discovered in Russia and Zaire, De Beers was able to maintain prices by buying most of the new supplies.

Because diamonds are rarely destroyed, De Beers has always worried about competition from the resale of stones. Heavily promoting diamond engagement and wedding rings with the slogan "A Diamond Is Forever" was a way around this problem. Because engagement and wedding rings have great sentimental value, they are seldom resold, even by the heirs of the original recipients. De Beers advertising has been successful even in some countries, such as Japan, that have had no custom of giving diamond engagement rings. As the populations in De Beers's key markets age, its advertising in recent years has focused on middle-aged men presenting diamond rings to their wives as symbols of financial success and continuing love and on professional women buying "right-hand rings" for themselves.

In the past few years, competition has finally come to the diamond business. By 2000, De Beers directly controlled only about 40 percent of world diamond production. The company became concerned about the amount it was spending to buy diamonds from other sources to keep them off the market. It decided to adopt a strategy of differentiating its diamonds by relying on its name recognition. Each De Beers diamond is now marked with a microscopic brand—a "Forevermark"—to reassure consumers of its high quality. Other firms, such as BHP Billiton, which owns mines in northern Canada, have followed suit by branding their diamonds. Sellers of Canadian diamonds stress that they are "mined under ethical, environmentally friendly conditions," as opposed to "blood diamonds," which are supposedly "mined under armed force in war-torn African countries and exported to finance military campaigns." Whether consumers will pay attention to brands on diamonds remains to be seen, although through 2006, the branding strategy had helped De Beers maintain its 40 percent share of the diamond market.

Sources: Edward Jay Epstein, "Have You Ever Tried to Sell a Diamond?" *Atlantic Monthly*, February 1982; Donna J. Bergenstock, Mary E. Deily, and Larry W. Taylor, "A Cartel's Response to Cheating: An Empirical Investigation of the De Beers Diamond Empire," *Southern Economic Journal*, Vol. 73, No. 1, July 2006, pp. 173–189; Bernard Simon, "Adding Brand Names to Nameless Stones," *New York Times*, June 27, 2002; Blythe Yee, "Ads Remind Women They Have Two Hands," *Wall Street Journal*, August 14, 2003; quote in last paragraph from Joel Baglole, "Political Correctness by the Carat," *Wall Street Journal*, April 17, 2003.

## Network Externalities

**Network externalities** The situation where the usefulness of a product increases with the number of consumers who use it.

There are **network externalities** in the consumption of a product if the usefulness of the product increases with the number of people who use it. If you owned the only cell phone in the world, for example, it would not be very valuable. The more cell phones there are in use, the more valuable they become to consumers.

Some economists argue that network externalities can serve as barriers to entry. For example, in the early 1980s, Microsoft gained an advantage over other software companies by developing MS-DOS, the operating system for the first IBM personal computers. Because IBM sold more computers than any other company, software developers wrote many application programs for MS-DOS. The more people who used MS-DOS–based programs, the greater the usefulness to a consumer of using an MS-DOS–based program. Today, Windows, the program Microsoft developed to succeed MS-DOS, has a 95 percent share in the market for personal computer operating systems (although

Windows has a much lower share in the market for operating systems for servers). If another firm introduced a competing operating system, some economists argue that relatively few people would use it initially, and few applications would run on it, which would limit the operating system's value to other consumers.

eBay was the first Internet site to attract a significant number of people to its online auctions. Once a large number of people began to use eBay to buy and sell collectibles, antiques, and many other products, it became a more valuable place to buy and sell. Yahoo.com, Amazon.com, and other Internet sites eventually started online auctions, but they found it difficult to attract buyers and sellers. On eBay, a buyer expects to find more sellers, and a seller expects to find more potential buyers than on Amazon or other auction sites.

As these examples show, network externalities can set off a *virtuous cycle*: If a firm can attract enough customers initially, it can attract additional customers because its product's value has been increased by more people using it, which attracts even more customers, and so on. With products such as computer operating systems and online auctions, it might be difficult for new firms to enter the market and compete away the profits being earned by the first firm in the market.

Economists engage in considerable debate, however, about the extent to which network externalities are important barriers to entry in the business world. Some economists argue that the dominant positions of Microsoft and eBay reflect the efficiency of those firms in offering products that satisfy consumer preferences more than the effects of network externalities. In this view, the advantages existing firms gain from network externalities would not be enough to protect them from competing firms offering better products. In other words, a firm entering the operating system market with a program better than Windows or a firm offering an Internet auction site better than eBay would be successful despite the effects of network externalities. (We discussed this point in more detail in Chapter 9.)

## Natural Monopoly

We saw in Chapter 10 that economies of scale exist when a firm's long-run average costs fall as it increases the quantity of output it produces. A **natural monopoly** occurs when economies of scale are so large that one firm can supply the entire market at a lower average total cost than two or more firms. In that case, there is really "room" in the market for only one firm.

Figure 14-1 shows the average total cost curve for a firm producing electricity and the total demand for electricity in the firm's market. Notice that the average total cost

**Natural monopoly** A situation in which economies of scale are so large that one firm can supply the entire market at a lower average total cost than can two or more firms.

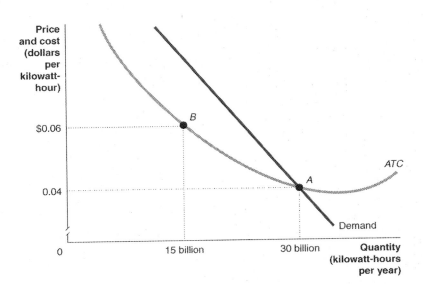

## Figure 14-1

**Average Total Cost Curve for a Natural Monopoly**

With a natural monopoly, the average total cost curve is still falling when it crosses the demand curve (point *A*). If only one firm is producing electric power in the market and it produces where average cost intersects the demand curve, average total cost will equal $0.04 per kilowatt-hour of electricity produced. If the market is divided between two firms, each producing 15 billion kilowatt-hours, the average cost of producing electricity rises to $0.06 per kilowatt-hour (point *B*). In this case, if one firm expands production, it can move down the average total cost curve, lower its price, and drive the other firm out of business.

curve is still falling when it crosses the demand curve at point *A*. If the firm is a monopoly and produces 30 billion kilowatt-hours of electricity per year, its average total cost of production will be $0.04 per kilowatt-hour. Suppose instead that two firms are in the market, each producing half of the market output, or 15 billion kilowatt-hours per year. Assume that each firm has the same average total cost curve. The figure shows that producing 15 billion kilowatt-hours would move each firm back up its average cost curve so that the average cost of producing electricity would rise to $0.06 per kilowatt-hour (point *B*). In this case, if one of the firms expands production, it will move down the average total cost curve. With lower average costs, it will be able to offer electricity at a lower price than the other firm can. Eventually, the other firm will be driven out of business, and the remaining firm will have a monopoly. Because a monopoly would develop automatically—or *naturally*—in this market, it is a natural monopoly.

Natural monopolies are most likely to occur in markets where fixed costs are very large relative to variable costs. For example, a firm that produces electricity must make a substantial investment in machinery and equipment necessary to generate the electricity and in wires and cables necessary to distribute it. Once the initial investment has been made, however, the marginal cost of producing another kilowatt-hour of electricity is relatively small.

---

# Solved Problem | 14-2

## Is the "Proxy Business" a Natural Monopoly?

A corporation is owned by its shareholders, who elect members of the corporation's board of directors and who also vote on particularly important issues of corporate policy. The shareholders of large corporations are spread around the country, and relatively few of them are present at the annual meetings at which elections take place. Before each meeting, corporations must provide shareholders with annual reports and forms that allow them to vote by mail. Voting by mail is referred to as "proxy voting." People who work on Wall Street refer to providing annual reports and ballots to shareholders as the "proxy business." Currently, one company, Broadridge, controls almost all of the proxy business.

According to the *Wall Street Journal,* Don Kittell of the Securities Industry Association has explained Broadridge's virtual monopoly by arguing that, "The economies of scale

and the efficiencies achieved by Broadridge handling all the brokerage business—rather than multiple companies—resulted in savings to [corporations]."

a.  Assuming that Kittell is correct, draw a graph showing the market for handling proxy materials. Be sure that the graph contains the demand for proxy materials and Broadridge's average total cost curve. Explain why cost savings result from having the proxy business handled by a single firm.

b.  According to a spokesperson for Broadridge, the proxy business produces a profit rate of about 7 percent, which is lower than the profit rate the company receives from any of its other businesses. Does this information support or undermine Kittell's analysis? Explain.

## SOLVING THE PROBLEM:

**Step 1:** **Review the chapter material.** This problem is about natural monopoly, so you may want to review the section "Natural Monopoly," which begins on page 479.

**Step 2:** **Answer question (a) by drawing a natural monopoly graph and discussing the potential cost savings in this industry.** Kittell describes a situation of natural monopoly. Otherwise, the entry of another firm into the market would not raise average cost. Draw a natural monopoly graph, like the one in Figure 14-1:

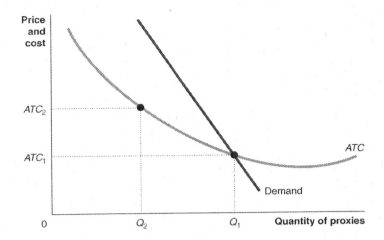

Make sure your average total cost curve is still declining when it crosses the demand curve. If one firm can supply $Q_1$ proxies at an average total cost of $ATC_1$, then dividing the business equally between two firms each supplying $Q_2$ proxies would raise average total cost to $ATC_2$.

**Step 3:** **Answer question (b) by discussing the implications of Broadridge's low profit rate in the proxy business.** If Broadridge earns a low profit rate on its investment in this business even though it has a monopoly, Kittell probably is correct that the proxy business is a natural monopoly.

**EXTRA CREDIT:** Keep in mind that competition is not good for its own sake. It is good because it can lead to lower costs, lower prices, and better products. In certain markets, however, cost conditions are such that competition is likely to lead to higher costs and higher prices. These markets are natural monopolies that are best served by one firm.

Source: Phyllis Plitch, "Competition Remains Issue in Proxy-Mailing Costs," *Wall Street Journal*, January 16, 2002.

>> **End Solved Problem 14-2**

**14.3 LEARNING** OBJECTIVE

14.3 | Explain how a monopoly chooses price and output.

# How Does a Monopoly Choose Price and Output?

Like every other firm, a monopoly maximizes profit by producing where marginal revenue equals marginal cost. A monopoly differs from other firms in that *a monopoly's demand curve is the same as the demand curve for the product.* We emphasized in Chapter 11 that the market demand curve for wheat was very different from the demand curve for the wheat produced by any one farmer. If, however, one farmer had a monopoly on wheat production, the two demand curves would be exactly the same.

## Marginal Revenue Once Again

Recall from Chapter 11 that firms in perfectly competitive markets—such as a farmer in the wheat market—face horizontal demand curves. They are *price takers.* All other firms, including monopolies, are *price makers.* If price makers raise their prices, they will lose some, but not all, of their customers. Therefore, they face a downward-sloping demand curve and a downward-sloping marginal revenue curve as well. Let's review why a firm's marginal revenue curve slopes downward if its demand curve slopes downward.

Remember that when a firm cuts the price of a product, one good thing happens, and one bad thing happens:

- **The good thing.** It sells more units of the product.
- **The bad thing.** It receives less revenue from each unit than it would have received at the higher price.

For example, consider the table in Figure 14-2, which shows the demand curve for Time Warner Cable's basic cable package. For simplicity, we assume that the market has only 10 potential subscribers instead of the millions it actually has. If Time Warner charges a price of $60 per month, it won't have any subscribers. If it charges a price of $57, it sells 1 subscription. At $54, it sells 2, and so on. Time Warner's total revenue is equal to the number of subscriptions sold per month multiplied by the price. The firm's average revenue—or revenue per subscription sold—is equal to its total revenue divided by the quantity of subscriptions sold. Time Warner is particularly interested in marginal revenue because marginal revenue tells the firm how much revenue will increase if it cuts the price to sell one more subscription.

Notice that Time Warner's marginal revenue is less than the price for every subscription sold after the first subscription. To see why, think about what happens if Time Warner cuts the price of its basic cable package from $42 to $39, which increases its subscriptions sold from 6 to 7. Time Warner increases its revenue by the $39 it receives for the seventh subscription. But it also loses revenue of $3 per subscription on the first 6 subscriptions because it could have sold them at the old price of $42. So, its marginal

## Figure 14-2

### Calculating a Monopoly's Revenue

Time Warner Cable faces a downward-sloping demand curve for subscriptions to basic cable. To sell more subscriptions, it must cut the price. When this happens, it gains the revenue from selling more subscriptions but loses revenue from selling at a lower price the subscriptions that it could have sold at a higher price. The firm's marginal revenue is the change in revenue from selling another subscription. We can calculate marginal revenue by subtracting the revenue lost as a result of a price cut from the revenue gained. The table shows that Time Warner's marginal revenue is less than the price for every subscription sold after the first subscription. Therefore, Time Warner's marginal revenue curve will be below its demand curve.

| Subscribers per Month (Q) | Price (P) | Total Revenue (TR = P x Q) | Average Revenue (AR = TR/Q) | Marginal Revenue (MR = ΔTR/ΔQ) |
|---|---|---|---|---|
| 0 | $60 | $0 | — | — |
| 1 | 57 | 57 | $57 | $57 |
| 2 | 54 | 108 | 54 | 51 |
| 3 | 51 | 153 | 51 | 45 |
| 4 | 48 | 192 | 48 | 39 |
| 5 | 45 | 225 | 45 | 33 |
| 6 | 42 | 252 | 42 | 27 |
| 7 | 39 | 273 | 39 | 21 |
| 8 | 36 | 288 | 36 | 15 |
| 9 | 33 | 297 | 33 | 9 |
| 10 | 30 | 300 | 30 | 3 |

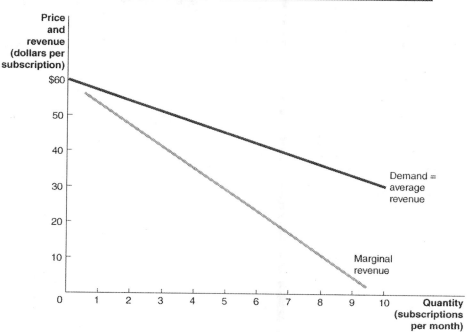

revenue on the seventh subscription is $39 − $18 = $21, which is the value shown in the table. The graph in Figure 14-2 plots Time Warner's demand and marginal revenue curves, based on the information given in the table.

## Profit Maximization for a Monopolist

Figure 14-3 shows how Time Warner combines the information on demand and marginal revenue with information on average and marginal costs to decide how many subscriptions to sell and what price to charge. We assume that the firm's marginal cost and average total cost curves have the usual U shapes we encountered in Chapters 10 and 11. In panel (a), we see how Time Warner can calculate its profit-maximizing quantity and price. As long as the marginal cost of selling one more subscription is less than the marginal revenue, the firm should sell additional subscriptions because it is adding to its profits. As Time Warner sells more cable subscriptions, rising marginal cost will eventually equal marginal revenue, and the firm will be selling the profit-maximizing quantity of subscriptions. This happens with the sixth subscription, which adds $27 to the firm's costs and $27 to its revenues (point A in panel (a) of Figure 14-3). The demand curve tells us that Time Warner can sell 6 subscriptions for a price of $42 per month. We can conclude that Time Warner's profit-maximizing quantity of subscriptions is 6 and its profit-maximizing price is $42.

Panel (b) shows that the average total cost of 6 subscriptions is $30 and that Time Warner can sell 6 subscriptions at a price of $42 per month (point B on the demand curve). Time Warner is making a profit of $12 per subscription—the price of $42 minus the average cost of $30. Its total profit is $72 (6 subscriptions × $12 profit per subscription), which is shown by the area of the green-shaded rectangle in the figure. We could also have calculated Time Warner's total profit as the difference between its total revenue and its total cost. Its total revenue from selling 6 subscriptions is $252. Its total cost equals its average cost multiplied by the number of subscriptions sold, or $30 × 6 = $180. So, its profit is $252 − $180 = $72.

It's important to note that even though Time Warner is earning economic profits, new firms will *not* enter the market. Because Time Warner has a monopoly, it will not face competition from other cable operators. Therefore, if other factors remain unchanged, Time Warner will be able to continue to earn economic profits, even in the long run.

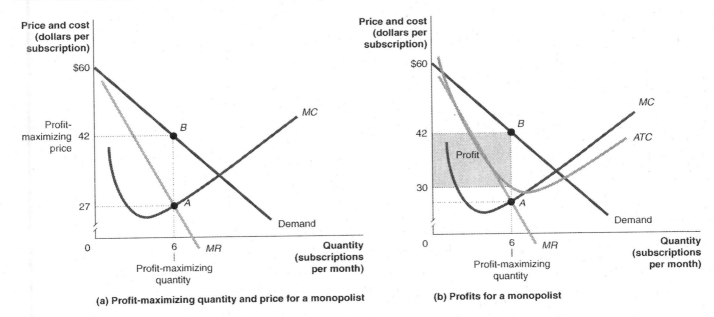

**Figure 14-3** | Profit-Maximizing Price and Output for a Monopoly

Panel (a) shows that to maximize profit, Time Warner should sell subscriptions up to the point that the marginal revenue from selling the last subscription equals its marginal cost (point A). In this case, the marginal revenue from selling the sixth subscription and the marginal cost are both $27. Time Warner maximizes profit by selling 6

subscriptions per month and charging a price of $42 (point B). In panel (b), the green box represents Time Warner's profits. The box has a height equal to $12, which is the price of $42 minus the average total cost of $30, and a base equal to the quantity of 6 cable subscriptions. Time Warner's profit equals $12 × 6 = $72.

# Solved Problem | 14-3

## Finding the Profit-Maximizing Price and Output for a Monopolist

Suppose that Comcast has a cable monopoly in Philadelphia. The following table gives Comcast's demand and costs per month for subscriptions to basic cable (for simplicity, we once again keep the number of subscribers artificially small).

| PRICE | QUANTITY | TOTAL REVENUE | MARGINAL REVENUE $(MR = \Delta TR/\Delta Q)$ | TOTAL COST | MARGINAL COST $(MC = \Delta TC/\Delta Q)$ |
|-------|----------|---------------|------------------|------------|--------------|
| $17 | 3 | | | $56 | |
| 16 | 4 | | | 63 | |
| 15 | 5 | | | 71 | |
| 14 | 6 | | | 80 | |
| 13 | 7 | | | 90 | |
| 12 | 8 | | | 101 | |

**a.** Fill in the missing values in the table.

**b.** If Comcast wants to maximize profits, what price should it charge and how many cable subscriptions per month should it sell? How much profit will Comcast make? Briefly explain.

**c.** Suppose the local government imposes a $2.50 per month tax on cable companies. Now what price should Comcast charge, how many subscriptions should it sell, and what will its profits be?

## SOLVING THE PROBLEM:

**Step 1:** **Review the chapter material.** This problem is about finding the profit-maximizing quantity and price for a monopolist, so you may want to review the section "Profit Maximization for a Monopolist," which begins on page 483.

**Step 2:** **Answer question (a) by filling in the missing values in the table.** Remember that to calculate marginal revenue and marginal cost, you must divide the change in total revenue or total cost by the change in quantity.

| PRICE | QUANTITY | TOTAL REVENUE | MARGINAL REVENUE $(MR = \Delta TR/\Delta Q)$ | TOTAL COST | MARGINAL COST $(MC = \Delta TC/\Delta Q)$ |
|-------|----------|---------------|------------------|------------|--------------|
| $17 | 3 | $51 | — | $56 | — |
| 16 | 4 | 64 | $13 | 63 | $7 |
| 15 | 5 | 75 | 11 | 71 | 8 |
| 14 | 6 | 84 | 9 | 80 | 9 |
| 13 | 7 | 91 | 7 | 90 | 10 |
| 12 | 8 | 96 | 5 | 101 | 11 |

We don't have enough information from the table to fill in the values for marginal revenue or marginal cost in the first row.

**Step 3:** **Answer question (b) by determining the profit-maximizing quantity and price.** We know that Comcast will maximize profits by selling subscriptions up to the point where marginal cost equals marginal revenue. In this case, that means selling 6 subscriptions per month. From the information in the first two columns, we know Comcast can sell 6 subscriptions at a price of $14 each. Comcast's profits are equal to the difference between its total revenue and its total cost: Profit = $84 − $80 = $4 per month.

**Step 4:** **Answer question (c) by analyzing the impact of the tax.** This tax is a fixed cost to Comcast because it is a flat $2.50, no matter how many subscriptions it sells. Because the tax has no impact on Comcast's marginal revenue or marginal cost, the profit-maximizing level of output has not changed. So, Comcast will still sell 6 subscriptions per month at a price of $14, but its profits will fall by the amount of the tax from $4.00 per month to $1.50.

**>> End Solved Problem 14-3**

---

14.4 | Use a graph to illustrate how a monopoly affects economic efficiency.

# Does Monopoly Reduce Economic Efficiency?

We saw in Chapter 11 that a perfectly competitive market is economically efficient. How would economic efficiency be affected if instead of being perfectly competitive, a market were a monopoly? In Chapter 4, we developed the idea of *economic surplus*. Economic surplus provides a way of characterizing the economic efficiency of a perfectly competitive market: *Equilibrium in a perfectly competitive market results in the greatest amount of economic surplus, or total benefit to society, from the production of a good or service.* What happens to economic surplus under monopoly? We can begin the analysis by considering the hypothetical case of what would happen if the market for television sets begins as perfectly competitive and then becomes a monopoly. (In reality, the market for television sets is not perfectly competitive, but assuming that it is simplifies our analysis.)

## Comparing Monopoly and Perfect Competition

Panel (a) in Figure 14-4 illustrates the situation if the market for televisions is perfectly competitive. Price and quantity are determined by the intersection of the demand and supply curves. Remember that none of the individual firms in a perfectly competitive industry has any control over price. Each firm must accept the price determined by the market. Panel (b) shows what happens if the television industry becomes a monopoly. We know that the monopoly will maximize profits by producing where marginal revenue equals marginal cost. To do this, the monopoly reduces the quantity of televisions

---

# Don't Let This Happen to **YOU!**

### Don't Assume That Charging a Higher Price Is Always More Profitable for a Monopolist

In answering question (c) of Solved Problem 14-3, it's tempting to argue that Comcast should increase its price to make up for the tax. After all, Comcast is a monopolist, so why can't it just pass along the tax to its customers? The reason it can't is that Comcast, like any other monopolist, must pay attention to demand. Comcast is not interested in charging high prices for the sake of charging high prices; it is interested in maximizing profits. Charging a price of $1,000 for a basic cable subscription sounds nice, but if no one will buy at that price, Comcast would hardly be maximizing profits.

To look at it another way, before the tax is imposed, Comcast has already determined $14 is the price that will maximize its profits. After the tax is imposed, it must determine whether $14 is still the profit-maximizing price. Because the tax has not affected Comcast's marginal revenue or marginal cost (or had any effect on consumer demand), $14 is still the profit-maximizing price, and Comcast should continue to charge it. The tax cuts into Comcast's profits but doesn't cause it to increase the price of cable subscriptions.

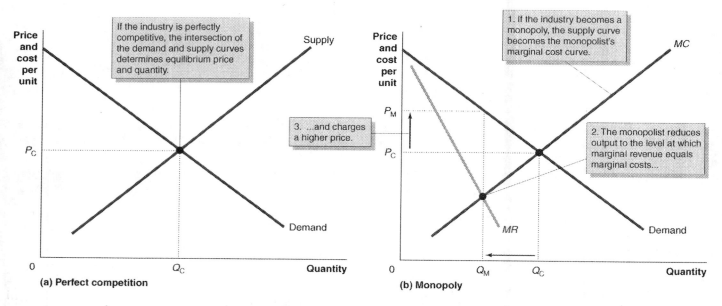

**Figure 14-4** | What Happens If a Perfectly Competitive Industry Becomes a Monopoly?

In panel (a), the market for television sets is perfectly competitive, and price and quantity are determined by the intersection of the demand and supply curves. In panel (b), the perfectly competitive television industry became a monopoly. As a result, the equilibrium quantity falls, and the equilibrium price rises.

1. The industry supply curve becomes the monopolist's marginal cost curve.
2. The monopolist reduces output to where marginal revenue equals marginal cost, $Q_M$.
3. The monopolist raises the price from $P_C$ to $P_M$.

that would have been produced if the industry were perfectly competitive and increases the price. Panel (b) illustrates an important conclusion: *A monopoly will produce less and charge a higher price than would a perfectly competitive industry producing the same good.*

## Measuring the Efficiency Losses from Monopoly

Figure 14-5 uses panel (b) from Figure 14-4 to illustrate how monopoly affects consumers, producers, and the efficiency of the economy. Recall from Chapter 4 that *consumer surplus* measures the net benefit received by consumers from purchasing a good or service. We measure consumer surplus as the area below the demand curve and above the market price. The higher the price, the smaller the consumer surplus. Because a monopoly raises the market price, it reduces consumer surplus. In Figure 14-5, the loss of consumer surplus is equal to rectangle A plus triangle B. Remember that *producer surplus* measures the net benefit to producers from selling a good or service. We measure producer surplus as the area above the supply curve and below the market price. The increase in price due to monopoly increases producer surplus by an amount equal to rectangle A and reduces it by an amount equal to triangle C. Because rectangle A is larger than triangle C, we know that a monopoly increases producer surplus compared with perfect competition.

Economic surplus is equal to the sum of consumer surplus plus producer surplus. By increasing price and reducing the quantity produced, the monopolist has reduced economic surplus by an amount equal to the areas of triangles B and C. This reduction in economic surplus is called *deadweight loss* and represents the loss of economic efficiency due to monopoly.

The best way to understand how a monopoly causes a loss of economic efficiency is to recall that price is equal to marginal cost in a perfectly competitive market. As a result, a consumer in a perfectly competitive market is always able to buy a good if she is willing to pay a price equal to the marginal cost of producing it. As Figure 14-5 shows, the monopolist stops producing at a point where the price is well above marginal cost. Consumers are unable to buy some units of the good for which they would be willing to pay a price greater

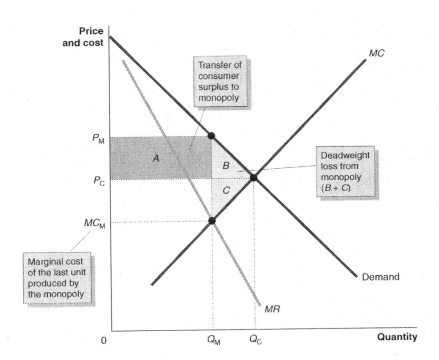

Figure 14-5

**The Inefficiency of Monopoly**

A monopoly charges a higher price, $P_M$, and produces a smaller quantity, $Q_M$, than a perfectly competitive industry, which charges a price of $P_C$ and produces at $Q_C$. The higher price reduces consumer surplus by the area equal to the rectangle $A$ and the triangle $B$. Some of the reduction in consumer surplus is captured by the monopoly as producer surplus, and some becomes deadweight loss, which is the area equal to triangles $B$ and $C$.

than the marginal cost of producing them. Why doesn't the monopolist produce this additional output? Because the monopolist's profits are greater if it restricts output and forces up the price. A monopoly produces the profit-maximizing level of output but fails to produce the efficient level of output from the point of view of society.

We can summarize the effects of monopoly as follows:

1 Monopoly causes a reduction in consumer surplus.

2 Monopoly causes an increase in producer surplus.

3 Monopoly causes a deadweight loss, which represents a reduction in economic efficiency.

## How Large Are the Efficiency Losses Due to Monopoly?

We know that there are relatively few monopolies, so the loss of economic efficiency due to monopoly must be small. Many firms, though, have **market power**, which is the ability of a firm to charge a price greater than marginal cost. The analysis we just completed shows that some loss of economic efficiency will occur whenever a firm has market power and can charge a price greater than marginal cost, even if the firm is not a monopoly. The only firms that do *not* have market power are firms in perfectly competitive markets, who must charge a price equal to marginal cost. Because few markets are perfectly competitive, *some loss of economic efficiency occurs in the market for nearly every good or service.*

Is the total loss of economic efficiency due to market power large or small? It is possible to put a dollar value on the loss of economic efficiency by estimating for every industry the size of the deadweight loss triangle, as in Figure 14-5. The first economist to do this was Arnold Harberger of the University of Chicago. His estimates—largely confirmed by later researchers—indicated that the total loss of economic efficiency in the U.S. economy due to market power is small. According to his estimates, if every industry in the economy were perfectly competitive, so that price were equal to marginal cost in every market, the gain in economic efficiency would equal less than 1 percent of the value of total production in the United States, or about $450 per person.

The loss of economic efficiency is this small primarily because true monopolies are very rare. In most industries, competition keeps price much closer to marginal cost than would be the case in a monopoly. The closer price is to marginal cost, the smaller the size of the deadweight loss.

**Market power** The ability of a firm to charge a price greater than marginal cost.

## Market Power and Technological Change

Some economists have raised the possibility that the economy may actually benefit from firms having market power. This argument is most closely identified with Joseph Schumpeter, an Austrian economist who spent many years as a professor of economics at Harvard. Schumpeter argued that economic progress depended on technological change in the form of new products. For example, the replacement of horse-drawn carriages by automobiles, the replacement of ice boxes by refrigerators, and the replacement of mechanical calculators by electronic computers all represent technological changes that significantly raised living standards. In Schumpeter's view, new products unleash a "gale of creative destruction" that drives older products—and, often, the firms that produced them—out of the market. Schumpeter was unconcerned that firms with market power would charge higher prices than perfectly competitive firms:

> It is not that kind of [price] competition which counts but the competition from the new commodity, the new technology, the new source of supply, the new type of organization . . . competition which commands a decisive cost or quality advantage and which strikes not at the margins of the profits and outputs of the existing firms but at their foundations and their very lives.

Economists who support Schumpeter's view argue that the introduction of new products requires firms to spend funds on research and development. It is possible for firms to raise this money by borrowing from investors or from banks. But investors and banks are usually skeptical of ideas for new products that have not yet passed the test of consumer acceptance in the market. As a result, firms are often forced to rely on their profits to finance the research and development needed for new products. Because firms with market power are more likely to earn economic profits than are perfectly competitive firms, they are also more likely to carry out research and development and introduce new products. In this view, the higher prices firms with market power charge are unimportant compared with the benefits from the new products these firms introduce to the market.

Some economists disagree with Schumpeter's views. These economists point to the number of new products developed by smaller firms, including, for example, Steve Jobs and Steve Wozniak inventing the first Apple computer in Wozniak's garage, and Larry Page and Sergey Brin inventing the Google search engine as graduate students at Stanford. As we will see in the next section, government policymakers continue to struggle with the issue of whether, on balance, large firms with market power are good or bad for the economy.

---

14.5 | Discuss government policies toward monopoly.

# Government Policy toward Monopoly

**Collusion** An agreement among firms to charge the same price or otherwise not to compete.

Because monopolies reduce consumer surplus and economic efficiency, most governments have policies that regulate their behavior. Recall from Chapter 13 that **collusion** refers to an agreement among firms to charge the same price or otherwise not to compete. In the United States, government policies with respect to monopolies and collusion are embodied in the *antitrust laws*. These laws make illegal any attempts to form a monopoly or to collude. Governments also regulate firms that are natural monopolies, often by controlling the prices they charge.

## Antitrust Laws and Antitrust Enforcement

The first important law regulating monopolies in the United States was the Sherman Act, which Congress passed in 1890 to promote competition and prevent the formation of monopolies. Section 1 of the Sherman Act outlaws "every contract, combination in the form of trust or otherwise, or conspiracy in restraint of trade." Section 2 states that "every person who shall monopolize, or attempt to monopolize, or combine or conspire with any other person or persons, to monopolize any part of the trade or commerce . . . shall be deemed guilty of a felony."

The Sherman Act targeted firms in several industries that had combined together during the 1870s and 1880s to form "trusts." In a trust, the firms were operated independently but gave voting control to a board of trustees. The board enforced collusive agreements for the firms to charge the same price and not to compete for each other's customers. The most notorious of the trusts was the Standard Oil Trust, organized by John D. Rockefeller. After the Sherman Act was passed, trusts disappeared, but the term **antitrust laws** has lived on to refer to the laws aimed at eliminating collusion and promoting competition among firms.

The Sherman Act prohibited trusts and collusive agreements, but it left several loopholes. For example, it was not clear whether it would be legal for two or more firms to merge to form a new, larger firm that would have substantial market power. A series of Supreme Court decisions interpreted the Sherman Act narrowly, and the result was a wave of mergers at the turn of the twentieth century. Included in these mergers was the U.S. Steel Corporation, which was formed from dozens of smaller companies. U.S. Steel, organized by J. P. Morgan, was the first billion-dollar corporation, and it controlled two-thirds of steel production in the United States. The Sherman Act also left unclear whether any business practices short of outright collusion were illegal.

To address the loopholes in the Sherman Act, in 1914, Congress passed the Clayton Act and the Federal Trade Commission Act. Under the Clayton Act, a merger was illegal if its effect was "substantially to lessen competition, or to tend to create a monopoly." The Federal Trade Commission Act set up the Federal Trade Commission (FTC), which was given the power to police unfair business practices. The FTC has brought lawsuits against firms employing a variety of business practices, including deceptive advertising. In setting up the FTC, however, Congress divided the authority to police mergers. Currently, both the Antitrust Division of the U.S. Department of Justice and the FTC are responsible for merger policy. Table 14-1 lists the most important U.S. antitrust laws and the purpose of each.

**Antitrust laws** Laws aimed at eliminating collusion and promoting competition among firms.

## Mergers: The Trade-off between Market Power and Efficiency

The federal government regulates business mergers because it knows that if firms gain market power by merging, they may use that market power to raise prices and reduce output. As a result, the government is most concerned with **horizontal mergers**, or mergers between firms in the same industry. Horizontal mergers are more likely to increase market power than **vertical mergers**, which are mergers between firms at different stages of the production of a good. An example of a vertical merger would be a merger between a company making personal computers and a company making computer hard drives.

**Horizontal merger** A merger between firms in the same industry.

**Vertical merger** A merger between firms at different stages of production of a good.

TABLE 14-1

**Important U.S. Antitrust Laws**

| LAW | DATE | PURPOSE |
| --- | --- | --- |
| Sherman Act | 1890 | Prohibited "restraint of trade," including price fixing and collusion. Also outlawed monopolization. |
| Clayton Act | 1914 | Prohibited firms from buying stock in competitors and from having directors serve on the boards of competing firms. |
| Federal Trade Commission Act | 1914 | Established the Federal Trade Commission (FTC) to help administer antitrust laws. |
| Robinson–Patman Act | 1936 | Prohibited charging buyers different prices if the result would reduce competition. |
| Cellar–Kefauver Act | 1950 | Toughened restrictions on mergers by prohibiting any mergers that would reduce competition. |

Regulating horizontal mergers can be complicated by two factors. First, the "market" that firms are in is not always clear. For example, if Hershey Foods wants to merge with Mars, Inc., maker of M&Ms, Snickers, and other candies, what is the relevant market? If the government looks just at the candy market, the newly merged company would have more than 70 percent of the market, a level at which the government would likely oppose the merger. What if the government looks at the broader market for "snacks"? In this market, Hershey and Mars compete with makers of potato chips, pretzels, peanuts, and, perhaps, even producers of fresh fruit. Of course, if the government looked at the very broad market for "food," then both Hershey and Mars have very small market shares, and there would be no reason to oppose their merger. In practice, the government defines the relevant market on the basis of whether there are close substitutes for the products being made by the merging firms. In this case, potato chips and the other snack foods mentioned are not close substitutes for candy. So, the government would consider the candy market to be the relevant market and would oppose the merger on the grounds that the new firm would have too much market power.

The second factor that complicates merger policy is the possibility that the newly merged firm might be more efficient than the merging firms were individually. For example, one firm might have an excellent product but a poor distribution system for getting the product into the hands of consumers. A competing firm might have built a great distribution system but have an inferior product. Allowing these firms to merge might be good for both the firms and consumers. Or, two competing firms might each have an extensive system of warehouses that are only half full, but if the firms merged, they could consolidate their warehouses and significantly reduce their costs.

An example of the government dealing with the issue of greater efficiency versus reduced competition occurred in early 2000, when Time Warner—which owns cable systems with more than 20 million subscribers—and America Online (AOL)—which was the country's largest Internet service provider (ISP), with more than 26 million subscribers—announced plans to merge. The firms argued that the merger would speed the development of high-speed (or "broadband") Internet access and would lead to more rapid growth of services such as interactive television. Some competing firms complained that the new firm created by the merger would have excessive market power. In particular, other ISPs were worried that they would be denied access to the cable systems owned by Time Warner. After more than a year of study, the FTC finally approved the merger, subject to certain conditions. One key condition was that Time Warner was required to allow AOL's competitors to offer their services over Time Warner's high-speed cable lines before AOL would be permitted to offer its services over those lines.

Most of the mergers that come under scrutiny by the Department of Justice and the FTC are between large firms. For simplicity, let's consider a case where all the firms in a perfectly competitive industry want to merge to form a monopoly. As we saw in Figure 14-5, as a result of this merger, prices will rise and output will fall, leading to a decline in consumer surplus and economic efficiency. But what if the larger, newly merged firm actually is more efficient than the smaller firms had been? Figure 14-6 shows a possible result.

If costs are unaffected by the merger, we get the same result as in Figure 14-5: Price rises from $P_C$ to $P_M$, quantity falls from $Q_C$ to $Q_M$, consumer surplus is lower, and a loss of economic efficiency results. If the monopoly has lower costs than the competitive firms, it is possible for price to decline and quantity to increase. In Figure 14-6, to find the new profit-maximizing quantity, note where $MR$ crosses $MC$ after the merger. This new profit-maximizing quantity is $Q_{Merge}$. The demand curve shows that the monopolist can sell this quantity at a price of $P_{Merge}$. Therefore, the price declines after the merger from $P_C$ to $P_{Merge}$ and quantity increases from $Q_C$ to $Q_{Merge}$. We have the following seemingly paradoxical result: *Although the newly merged firm has a great deal of market power, because it is more efficient, consumers are better off and economic efficiency is improved.* Of course, sometimes a merged firm will be more efficient and have lower costs, and other times it won't. Even if a merged firm is more efficient and has lower costs, that may not offset the increased market power of the firm enough to increase consumer surplus and economic efficiency.

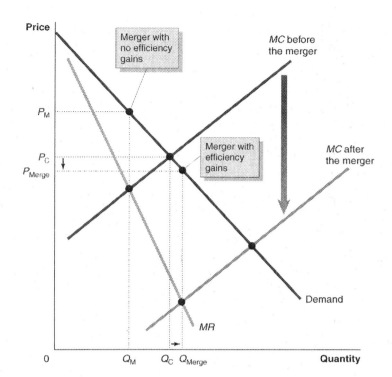

Figure 14-6

**A Merger That Makes Consumers Better Off**

This figure shows the result of all the firms in a perfectly competitive industry merging to form a monopoly. If costs are unaffected by the merger, the result is the same as in Figure 14-5 on page 487: Price rises from $P_C$ to $P_M$, quantity falls from $Q_C$ to $Q_M$, consumer surplus declines, and a loss of economic efficiency results. If, however, the monopoly has lower costs than the perfectly competitive firms, as shown by the marginal cost curve shifting to $MC$ after the merger, it is possible that the price will actually decline from $P_C$ to $P_{Merge}$ and output will increase from $Q_C$ to $Q_{Merge}$ following the merger.

As you might expect, whenever large firms propose a merger, they claim that the newly merged firm will be more efficient and have lower costs. They realize that without these claims, it is unlikely their merger will be approved. It is up to the Department of Justice and the FTC, along with the court system, to evaluate the merits of these claims.

## The Department of Justice and Federal Trade Commission Merger Guidelines

For many years after the passage of the Sherman Antitrust Act in 1890, lawyers from the Department of Justice enforced the antitrust laws. They rarely considered economic arguments, such as the possibility that consumers might be made better off by a merger if economic efficiency were significantly improved. This began to change in 1965, when Donald Turner became the first Ph.D. economist to head the Antitrust Division of the Department of Justice. Under Turner and his successors, economic analysis shaped antitrust policy. In 1973, the Economics Section of the Antitrust Division was established and staffed with economists who evaluate the economic consequences of proposed mergers.

Economists played a major role in the development of merger guidelines by the Department of Justice and the FTC in 1982. The guidelines made it easier for firms considering a merger to understand whether the government was likely to allow the merger or to oppose it. The guidelines have three main parts:

1 Market definition

2 Measure of concentration

3 Merger standards

***Market Definition*** A market consists of all firms making products that consumers view as close substitutes. We can identify close substitutes by looking at the effect of a price increase. If our definition of a market is too narrow, a price increase will cause firms to experience a significant decline in sales—and profits—as consumers switch to buying close substitutes.

Identifying the relevant market involved in a proposed merger begins with a narrow definition of the industry. For the hypothetical merger of Hershey Foods and Mars, Inc., discussed previously in this chapter, we might start with the candy industry. If all firms in the candy industry increased price by 5 percent, would their profits increase or decrease? If profits would increase, the market is defined as being just these firms. If profits would decrease, we would try a broader definition—say, by adding in potato chips and other snacks. Would a price increase of 5 percent by all firms in the broader market raise profits? If profits increase, the relevant market has been identified. If profits decrease, we consider a broader definition. We continue this procedure until a market has been identified.

***Measure of Concentration*** A market is *concentrated* if a relatively small number of firms have a large share of total sales in the market. A merger between firms in a market that is already highly concentrated is very likely to increase market power. A merger between firms in an industry that has a very low concentration is unlikely to increase market power and can be ignored. The guidelines use the *Herfindahl-Hirschman Index (HHI)* of concentration, which squares the market shares of each firm in the industry and adds up the values of the squares. The following are some examples of calculating a Herfindahl-Hirschman Index:

- 1 firm, with 100% market share (a monopoly):

$$HHI = 100^2 = 10,000$$

- 2 firms, each with a 50% market share:

$$HHI = 50^2 + 50^2 = 5,000$$

- 4 firms, with market shares of 30%, 30%, 20%, and 20%:

$$HHI = 30^2 + 30^2 + 20^2 + 20^2 = 2,600$$

- 10 firms, each with market shares of 10%:

$$HHI = 10 \, (10^2) = 1,000$$

***Merger Standards*** The Department of Justice and the FTC use the HHI calculation for a market to evaluate proposed horizontal mergers according to these standards:

- ***Post-merger HHI below 1,000.*** These markets are not concentrated, so mergers in them are not challenged.

- ***Post-merger HHI between 1,000 and 1,800.*** These markets are moderately concentrated. Mergers that raise the HHI by less than 100 probably will not be challenged. Mergers that raise the HHI by more than 100 may be challenged.

- ***Post-merger HHI above 1,800.*** These markets are highly concentrated. Mergers that increase the HHI by less than 50 points will not be challenged. Mergers that increase the HHI by 50 to 100 points may be challenged. Mergers that increase the HHI by more than 100 points will be challenged.

Increases in economic efficiency will be taken into account and can lead to approval of a merger that otherwise would be opposed, but the burden of showing that the efficiencies exist lies with the merging firms:

> The merging firms must substantiate efficiency claims so that the [Department of Justice and the FTC] can verify by reasonable means the likelihood and magnitude of each asserted efficiency. . . . Efficiency claims will not be considered if they are vague or speculative or otherwise cannot be verified by reasonable means.

## Making the Connection

# Should the Government Prevent Banks from Becoming Too Big?

For many years, state and federal regulations kept banks small. Until the 1990s, federal regulations required a bank to operate in only a single state. This restriction on interstate banking meant that there were no nationwide banks. As recently as the 1980s, some states—including Illinois and Texas—did not allow banks to have branches. So, if a bank opened in Chicago, it could not have branches in other cities in Illinois. Today, these regulations have been repealed, and banks are free to have as many branches as they choose and can operate nationwide. Many economists believe that the old regulations on banks reduced economic efficiency. If there are significant economies of scale in banking, then keeping banks artificially small by not allowing them to operate in more than one state will drive up their average cost of providing banking services. As a result, consumers will have to pay higher interest rates on loans and will receive lower interest rates on deposits.

The elimination of government regulations on nationwide banking and on branch banking led to a sharp decline in the number of banks. In the early 1980s, there were 14,500 banks in the United States; today there are fewer than 7,500. Smaller, less efficient banks were acquired by larger banks or went out of business, and some large banks merged with other large banks. There is, however, still one limit on the size of banks. In 1994, when Congress removed restrictions on interstate banking, it wrote into the law a restriction that no bank mergers would be allowed if they resulted in one bank having more than 10 percent of all bank deposits. This provision was included because some smaller, community-based banks were afraid that they would be unable to compete against large, nationwide banks.

**The Top-Five U.S. Banks by Domestic Deposits, Through Sept. 30 of Each Year**

| 2006 | Dometic deposits, in billions | Percentage of all U.S. deposits | 1994 | Dometic deposits, in billions | Percentage of all U.S. deposits |
|---|---|---|---|---|---|
| Bank of America | $584.33 | 9.0% | Bank of America | $125.59 | 4.0% |
| J.P. Morgan Chase | 447.30 | 6.9 | NationsBank | 87.44 | 2.8 |
| Wachovia/Golden West Financial* | 375.61 | 5.8 | Chemical Banking | 66.86 | 2.1 |
| Wells Fargo | 295.14 | 4.6 | Banc One | 64.74 | 2.1 |
| Citigroup | 226.26 | 3.5 | First Union | 52.54 | 1.7 |

Note: Deposit share information is based on FDIC quarterly reports. The Federal Reserve, which approves acquisitions, uses a slightly different definition of deposits.
* Figures are combined to reflect merger which took place Oct. 1, 2006
Source: FDIC call reports

As the chart shows, at the time the government removed restrictions on interstate banking, no bank was near the 10 percent limit. But by the end of 2006, Bank of America had 9 percent of all U.S. deposits and was considering mergers that would have brought its share above 10 percent. Bank of America Chairman and Chief Executive Kenneth D. Lewis began to push for Congress to remove the 10 percent limit. He argued that because other countries did not have limits on the size of banks, foreign banks were able to take advantage of economies of scale beyond what was possible for U.S. banks. In a position paper, Bank of America argued, "In time, the mega-foreign banks will be positioned to acquire the largest U.S. banks." Many community banks, though, remained opposed to lifting the 10 percent limit. Some consumer groups also argued that very large banks would have enough market power to raise interest rates on loans and lower interest rates on deposits because they would have less competition. Members of Congress considering the possibility of changing the law had to face the usual question raised by antitrust policy: Will a potential increase in monopoly power made possible by lifting the 10-percent limit be offset by gains in economic efficiency?

Source: Valerie Bauerlein and Damian Paletta, "Bank of America Quietly Targets Barrier to Growth," *Wall Street Journal*, January 16, 2007, p. A1.

# Regulating Natural Monopolies

If a firm is a natural monopoly, competition from other firms will not play its usual role of forcing price down to the level where the company earns zero economic profit. As a result, local or state *regulatory commissions* usually set the prices for natural monopolies, such as firms selling natural gas or electricity. What price should these commissions set? Recall from Chapter 11 that economic efficiency requires the last unit of a good or service produced to provide an additional benefit to consumers equal to the additional cost of producing it. We can measure the additional benefit consumers receive from the last unit by the price and the additional cost to the monopoly of producing the last unit by marginal cost. Therefore, to achieve economic efficiency, regulators should require that the monopoly charge a price equal to its marginal cost. There is, however, an important drawback to doing so, which is illustrated in Figure 14-7. This figure shows the situation of a typical regulated natural monopoly.

Remember that with a natural monopoly, the average total cost curve is still falling when it crosses the demand curve. If unregulated, the monopoly will charge a price equal to $P_M$ and produce $Q_M$. To achieve economic efficiency, regulators should require the monopoly to charge a price equal to $P_E$. The monopoly will then produce $Q_E$. But here is the drawback: $P_E$ is less than average total cost, so the monopoly will be suffering a loss, shown by the area of the red-shaded rectangle. In the long run, the owners of the monopoly will not continue in business if they are experiencing losses. Realizing this, most regulators will set the regulated price, $P_R$, equal to the level of average total cost at which the demand curve intersects the *ATC* curve. At that price, the owners of the monopoly are able to break even on their investment by producing the quantity $Q_R$.

## Figure 14-7

**Regulating a Natural Monopoly**

A natural monopoly that is not subject to government regulation will charge a price equal to $P_M$ and produce $Q_M$. If government regulators want to achieve economic efficiency, they will set the regulated price equal to $P_E$, and the monopoly will produce $Q_E$. Unfortunately, $P_E$ is below average cost, and the monopoly will suffer a loss, shown by the shaded rectangle. Because the monopoly will not continue to produce in the long run if it suffers a loss, government regulators set a price equal to average cost, which is $P_R$ in the figure.

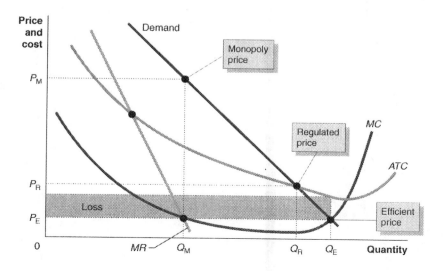

# Conclusion

The more intense the level of competition among firms, the better a market works. In this chapter, we have seen that with monopoly—where competition is entirely absent—price is higher, output is lower, and consumer surplus and economic efficiency decline compared with perfect competition. Fortunately, true monopolies are rare. Even though most firms resemble monopolies in being able to charge a price above marginal cost, most markets have enough competition to keep the efficiency losses from market power quite low.

We've seen that barriers to entry are an important source of market power. Read *An Inside Look at Policy* on the next page for a discussion of how legislation in California is lowering barriers to entry into the cable TV market.

# As Barriers Fall, Will Cable TV Competition Rise?

**WALL STREET JOURNAL, SEPTEMBER 28, 2006**

## Cable Guys

In an era of partisan nastiness and gridlock, the California legislature did something on Aug. 31 that was shockingly harmonious, reasonable and beneficial to consumers. Both parties voted overwhelmingly to allow competition into a sector—cable television—where prices have been elevated and service depressed by the most pernicious monopoly in America.

When Gov. Arnold Schwarzenegger signs the bill, as expected, companies that want a statewide video franchise can go straight to the Public Utility Commission and get approval to operate within 44 days. In the past, in California, as in other states, cable companies had to make separate deals with America's 33,760 municipal units—a process that can take years....

The effect was to create cable monopolies that often infuriated captive customers. According to a 2004 study by the Government Accountability Office, "cable subscribers in about 2% of all markets have the opportunity to choose between two or more wire-based operators." As cable rates rose in the 1980s, the federal government tried to fix the market with more regulation. That attempt, of course, failed. For the five years ending January 2004, the Federal Communications Commission reports that average cable rates increased 7.8% annually, compared with a 2.1% increase in the Consumer Price Index.

Very quietly, things are changing. Seven states, comprising about one-third of the U.S. population, have now passed video franchise laws, which will not only lower monthly subscriber costs but also create new technology jobs—10,000 in California alone, according to one estimate—as Verizon and AT&T, along with cable overbuilders like RCN, jump in with both feet. To bring high-quality video to the home over a technology called Internet protocol, the telcos will make major investments to drive the fiber—which carries the data—much more deeply into their networks. Broadband service will improve; state and local governments will still get their franchise fees. All that will end is a monopoly that drives consumers nuts....

With a national election coming up, you would expect Congress to get on the bandwagon and embrace a version of the state bills, killing the monopoly and taking the credit. Instead, federal legislation is slowed down by measures promoting "net neutrality"—the concept that telecom companies should be barred from asking content providers, like Amazon, to pay extra for higher-speed service the telcos develop—the way that an airline asks more for a first-class seat....

How much will consumers save? A 2004 study by the GAO looked at six markets with cable competition and found that rates were 15% to 41% below similar markets with no competition. Annual savings for U.S. households through competition will total $8 billion, says the Phoenix Center for Advanced Legal and Economic Public Policy.

In Texas, where a statewide franchising law went into effect last year, a study by the American Consumer Institute surveyed consumers and found that 22% switched cable providers and saved an average of $22.30 per month. Subscribers who stayed with incumbent providers saved $26.83 per month because of the downward pressure on prices. Verizon rolled out a service in Keller, Plano and Lewisville, charging $43.95 a month for 180 video and music channels. "Shortly thereafter," writes the Heartland Institute's Steven Titch, Charter, the erstwhile monopoly cable provider, "began offering a bundle of 240 channels and fast Internet service for $50 a month, compared to $68.99 Charter had been charging for the TV package alone." Savings in Texas this year alone will total $599 million, according to the Phoenix Center. Yale Braunstein, an economist at the University of California at Berkeley, estimates that Californians will save between $692 million and $1 billion a year.

Yes, Americans can choose satellite TV, but, for reasons of convenience and service, many find it an inadequate substitute. There's a reason that cable families far outnumber satellite families. "Overall customer satisfaction among satellite subscribers has declined," says Steve Kirkeby, senior director of telecommunication research for J.D. Power and Associates....

*Source: James K. Glassman, "Cable Guys," Wall Street Journal, September 28, 2006. Copyright © 2006 Dow Jones. Reprinted by permission of Dow Jones via Copyright Clearance Center.*

## Key Points in the Article

This article discusses a change in regulatory policy toward cable television in California. The change should make it easier for new cable firms to enter the market. As a result, prices for cable TV should fall, and we should see more firms offering cable TV in California cities. This article indicates that an increase in quantity and a decrease in price occurs as policy makes entry into the cable TV market easier.

## Analyzing the News

**a** In California, the state government's requirement that a cable provider buy a franchise in each jurisdiction was a barrier to entry because of the high cost of franchises. By allowing firms a statewide license, California has made it easier for them to enter the cable TV market in a given jurisdiction, making competition more likely. In fact, the relative lack of competition in many local cable television markets was partly the result of technology—laying more than one set of cables to an individual home would be very expensive—and partly the result of government regulations, which often allowed only one firm to be in the market.

**b** Entry, of course, will reduce the economic profit existing firms earn. The figure illustrates what happens as entry occurs and the market becomes competitive. For simplicity, we assume that the marginal cost of providing cable services is constant, so the marginal cost curve is a horizontal line. Notice that output increases from $Q_M$ to $Q_C$, and price falls from $P_M$ to $P_C$. You can also see that consumer surplus increases from areas $A + E$ to areas $A + E + B + C + D$, and the deadweight loss in the market (area $D$) disappears and becomes consumer surplus. In this figure, what were profits to the monopoly (areas $B + C$) are redistributed to consumers as consumer surplus. Economic profits fall to zero.

**c** One of the benefits of competition is that firms compete not just by cutting prices, but also by improving the services they offer. Here, we see cable systems competing by providing more services and channels to their customers.

## Thinking Critically
## About Policy

1. What is the most a firm would be willing to spend to remain the sole provider of cable television in a market?
2. Even with a statewide franchise, what might prevent new cable TV firms from entering local markets?

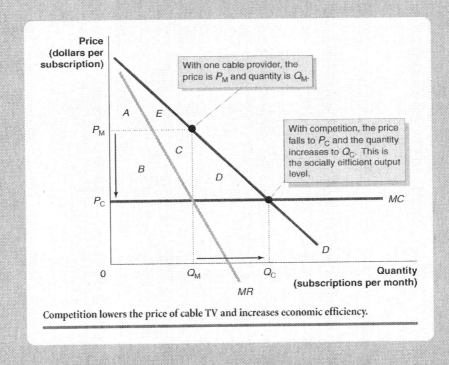

Competition lowers the price of cable TV and increases economic efficiency.

# Chapter 10
# Monopolistic Competitive Industry

**M**any markets in the U.S. economy are similar to the coffeehouse market: They have many buyers and sellers, and the barriers to entry are low, but the goods and services offered for sale are differentiated rather than identical. Examples of these markets include consumer electronics stores, restaurants, movie theaters, supermarkets, and manufacturers of men's and women's clothing. In fact, the majority of the firms you patronize are competing in **monopolistically competitive** markets.

In Chapter 11, we saw how perfect competition benefits consumers and results in economic efficiency. Will these same desirable outcomes also hold for monopolistically competitive markets? This question, which we explore in this chapter, is important because monopolistically competitive markets are so common.

**Monopolistic competition** A market structure in which barriers to entry are low and many firms compete by selling similar, but not identical, products.

**12.1 LEARNING** OBJECTIVE

12.1 | Explain why a monopolistically competitive firm has downward-sloping demand and marginal revenue curves.

# Demand and Marginal Revenue for a Firm in a Monopolistically Competitive Market

If the Starbucks coffeehouse located one mile from your house raises the price for a caffè latte from $3.00 to $3.25, it will lose some, but not all, of its customers. Some customers will switch to buying their coffee at another store, but other customers will be willing to pay the higher price for a variety of reasons: This store may be closer to them, or they may prefer Starbucks caffè lattes to similar coffees at competing stores. Because changing the price affects the quantity of caffè lattes sold, a Starbucks store will face a downward-sloping demand curve rather than the horizontal demand curve that a wheat farmer faces.

## The Demand Curve for a Monopolistically Competitive Firm

Figure 12-1 shows how a change in price affects the quantity of caffè lattes Starbucks sells. The increase in the price from $3.00 to $3.25 decreases the quantity of caffè lattes sold from 3,000 per week to 2,400 per week.

## Figure 12-1

**The Downward-Sloping Demand for Caffè Lattes at a Starbucks**

If a Starbucks increases the price of caffè lattes, it will lose some, but not all, of its customers. In this case, raising the price from $3.00 to $3.25 reduces the quantity of caffè lattes sold from 3,000 to 2,400. Therefore, unlike a perfect competitor, a Starbucks store faces a downward-sloping demand curve.

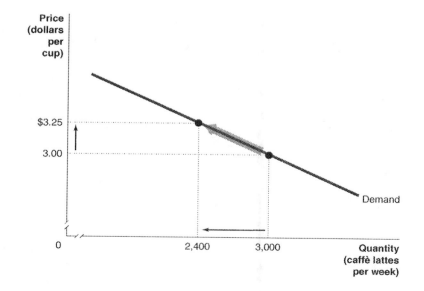

# Marginal Revenue for a Firm with a Downward-Sloping Demand Curve

Recall from Chapter 11 that for a firm in a perfectly competitive market, the demand curve and the marginal revenue curve are the same. A perfectly competitive firm faces a horizontal demand curve and does not have to cut the price to sell a larger quantity. A monopolistically competitive firm, however, must cut the price to sell more, so its marginal revenue curve will slope downward and will be below its demand curve.

The data in Table 12-1 illustrate this point. To keep the numbers simple, let's assume that your local Starbucks coffeehouse is very small and sells at most 10 caffè lattes per week. If Starbucks charges a price of $6.00 or more, all of its potential customers will buy their coffee somewhere else. If it charges $5.50, it will sell 1 caffè latte per week. For each additional $0.50 Starbucks reduces the price, it increases the number of caffè lattes it sells by 1. The third column in the table shows how the firm's *total revenue* changes as it sells more caffè lattes. The fourth column shows the firm's revenue per unit, or its *average revenue*. Average revenue is equal to total revenue divided by quantity. Because total revenue equals price multiplied by quantity, dividing by quantity leaves just price. Therefore, *average revenue is always equal to price*. This result will be true for firms selling in any of the four market structures we discussed in Chapter 11.

The last column shows the firm's marginal revenue, or the amount that total revenue changes as the firm sells 1 more caffè latte. For a perfectly competitive firm, the additional revenue received from selling 1 more unit is just equal to the price. That will not be true for Starbucks because to sell another caffè latte, it has to reduce the price. When the firm cuts the price by $0.50, one good thing and one bad thing happen:

- **The good thing.** It sells one more caffè latte; we can call this the *output effect*.

- **The bad thing.** It receives $0.50 less for each caffè latte that it could have sold at the higher price; we can call this the *price effect*.

Figure 12-2 illustrates what happens when the firm cuts the price from $3.50 to $3.00. Selling the sixth caffè latte adds the $3.00 price to the firm's revenue; this is the output effect. But Starbucks now receives a price of $3.00, rather than $3.50, on the first 5 caffè lattes sold; this is the price effect. As a result of the price effect, the firm's revenue

**TABLE 12-1**

**Demand and Marginal Revenue at a Starbucks**

| CAFFÈ LATTES SOLD PER WEEK (Q) | PRICE (P) | TOTAL REVENUE (TR = P × Q) | AVERAGE REVENUE ($AR = \frac{TR}{Q}$) | MARGINAL REVENUE ($MR = \frac{\Delta TR}{\Delta Q}$) |
|---|---|---|---|---|
| 0 | $6.00 | $0.00 | — | — |
| 1 | 5.50 | 5.50 | $5.50 | $5.50 |
| 2 | 5.00 | 10.00 | 5.00 | 4.50 |
| 3 | 4.50 | 13.50 | 4.50 | 3.50 |
| 4 | 4.00 | 16.00 | 4.00 | 2.50 |
| 5 | 3.50 | 17.50 | 3.50 | 1.50 |
| 6 | 3.00 | 18.00 | 3.00 | 0.50 |
| 7 | 2.50 | 17.50 | 2.50 | –0.50 |
| 8 | 2.00 | 16.00 | 2.00 | –1.50 |
| 9 | 1.50 | 13.50 | 1.50 | –2.50 |
| 10 | 1.00 | 10.00 | 1.00 | –3.50 |

## Figure 12-2

### How a Price Cut Affects a Firm's Revenue

If the local Starbucks reduces the price of a caffè latte from $3.50 to $3.00, the number of caffè lattes it sells per week will increase from 5 to 6. Its marginal revenue from selling the sixth caffè latte will be $0.50, which is equal to the $3.00 additional revenue from selling 1 more caffè latte (the area of the green box) minus the $2.50 loss in revenue from selling the first 5 caffè lattes for $0.50 less each (the area of the red box).

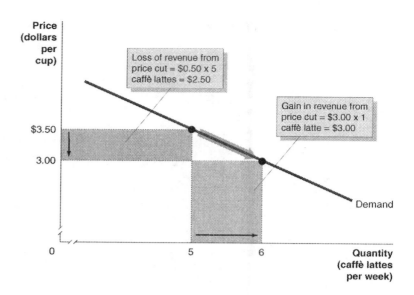

on these 5 caffè lattes is $2.50 less than it would have been if the price had remained at $3.50. So, the firm has gained $3.00 in revenue on the sixth caffè latte and lost $2.50 in revenue on the first 5 caffè lattes, for a net change in revenue of $0.50. Marginal revenue is the change in total revenue from selling one more unit. Therefore, the marginal revenue of the sixth caffè latte is $0.50. Notice that the marginal revenue of the sixth unit is far below its price of $3.00. In fact, for each additional caffè latte Starbucks sells, marginal revenue will be less than price. There is an important general point: *Every firm that has the ability to affect the price of the good or service it sells will have a marginal revenue curve that is below its demand curve.* Only firms in perfectly competitive markets, which can sell as many units as they want at the market price, have marginal revenue curves that are the same as their demand curves.

Figure 12-3 shows the relationship between the demand curve and the marginal revenue curve for the local Starbucks. Notice that after the sixth caffè latte, marginal rev-

## Figure 12-3

### The Demand and Marginal Revenue Curves for a Monopolistically Competitive Firm

Any firm that has the ability to affect the price of the product it sells will have a marginal revenue curve that is below its demand curve. We plot the data from Table 12-1 to create the demand and marginal revenue curves. After the sixth caffè latte, marginal revenue becomes negative because the additional revenue received from selling 1 more caffè latte is smaller than the revenue lost from receiving a lower price on the caffè lattes that could have been sold at the original price.

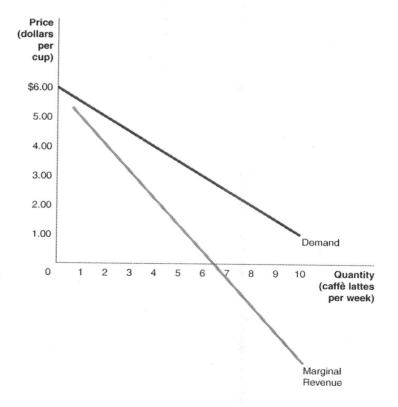

enue becomes negative. Marginal revenue is negative because the additional revenue received from selling 1 more caffè latte is smaller than the revenue lost from receiving a lower price on the caffè lattes that could have been sold at the original price.

12.2 | Explain how a monopolistically competitive firm maximizes profits in the short run.

# How a Monopolistically Competitive Firm Maximizes Profits in the Short Run

All firms use the same approach to maximize profits: They produce where marginal revenue is equal to marginal cost. For the local Starbucks, this means selling the quantity of caffè lattes for which the last caffè latte sold adds the same amount to the firm's revenue as to its costs. To begin our discussion of how monopolistically competitive firms maximize profits, let's consider the situation the local Starbucks faces in the short run. Recall from Chapter 10 that in the short run, at least one factor of production is fixed and there is not enough time for new firms to enter the market. A Starbucks has many costs, including the cost of purchasing the ingredients for its caffè lattes and other coffees, the electricity it uses, and the wages of its employees. Recall that a firm's *marginal cost* is the increase in total cost resulting from producing another unit of output. We have seen that for many firms, marginal cost has a U shape. We will assume that the Starbucks marginal cost has this usual shape.

In the table in Figure 12-4, we bring together the revenue data from Table 12-1 with the cost data for Starbucks. The graphs in Figure 12-4 plot the data from the table. In panel (a), we see how Starbucks can determine its profit-maximizing quantity and price. As long as the marginal cost of selling one more caffè latte is less than the marginal revenue, the firm should sell additional caffè lattes. For example, increasing the quantity of caffè lattes sold from 3 per week to 4 per week increases marginal cost by $1.00 but increases marginal revenue by $2.50. So, the firm's profits are increased by $1.50 as a result of selling the fourth caffè latte.

As Starbucks sells more caffè lattes, rising marginal cost eventually equals marginal revenue, and the firm sells the profit-maximizing quantity of caffè lattes. Marginal cost equals marginal revenue with the fifth caffè latte, which adds $1.50 to the firm's costs and $1.50 to its revenues—point *A* in panel (a) of Figure 12-4. The demand curve tells us the price at which the firm is able to sell 5 caffè lattes per week. In Figure 12-4, if we draw a vertical line from 5 caffè lattes up to the demand curve, we can see that the price at which the firm can sell 5 caffè lattes per week is $3.50 (point *B*). We can conclude that for Starbucks the profit-maximizing quantity is 5 caffè lattes, and its profit-maximizing price is $3.50. If the firm sells more than 5 caffè lattes per week, its profits fall. For example, selling a sixth caffè latte adds $2.00 to its costs and only $0.50 to its revenues. So, its profit would fall from $5.00 to $3.50.

Panel (b) adds the average total cost curve for Starbucks. The panel shows that the average total cost of selling 5 caffè lattes is $2.50. Recall from Chapter 11 that:

$$\text{Profit} = (P - ATC) \times Q.$$

In this case, profit = ($3.50 − $2.50) × 5 = $5.00. The green box in panel (b) shows the amount of profit. The box has a base equal to $Q$ and a height equal to $(P - ATC)$, so its area equals profit.

Notice that, unlike a perfectly competitive firm, which produces where $P = MC$, a monopolistically competitive firm produces where $P > MC$. In this case, Starbucks is charging a price of $3.50, although marginal cost is $1.50. For the perfectly competitive firm, price equals marginal revenue, $P = MR$. Therefore, to fulfill the $MR = MC$ condition for profit maximization, a perfectly competitive firm will produce where $P = MC$. Because $P > MR$ for a monopolistically competitive firm—which results from the marginal revenue curve being below the demand curve—a monopolistically competitive firm will maximize profits where $P > MC$.

| Caffè Lattes Sold per Week (Q) | Price (P) | Total Revenue (TR) | Marginal Revenue (MR) | Total Cost (TC) | Marginal Cost (MC) | Average Total Cost (ATC) | Profit |
|---|---|---|---|---|---|---|---|
| 0 | $6.00 | $0.00 | – | $5.00 | – | – | –$5.00 |
| 1 | 5.50 | 5.50 | $5.50 | 8.00 | $3.00 | $8.00 | –2.50 |
| 2 | 5.00 | 10.00 | 4.50 | 9.50 | 1.50 | 4.75 | 0.50 |
| 3 | 4.50 | 13.50 | 3.50 | 10.00 | 0.50 | 3.33 | 3.50 |
| 4 | 4.00 | 16.00 | 2.50 | 11.00 | 1.00 | 2.75 | 5.00 |
| 5 | 3.50 | 17.50 | 1.50 | 12.50 | 1.50 | 2.50 | 5.00 |
| 6 | 3.00 | 18.00 | 0.50 | 14.50 | 2.00 | 2.42 | 3.50 |
| 7 | 2.50 | 17.50 | –0.50 | 17.00 | 2.50 | 2.43 | 0.50 |
| 8 | 2.00 | 16.00 | –1.50 | 20.00 | 3.00 | 2.50 | –4.00 |
| 9 | 1.50 | 13.50 | –2.50 | 23.50 | 3.50 | 2.61 | –10.00 |
| 10 | 1.00 | 10.00 | –3.50 | 27.50 | 4.00 | 2.75 | –17.50 |

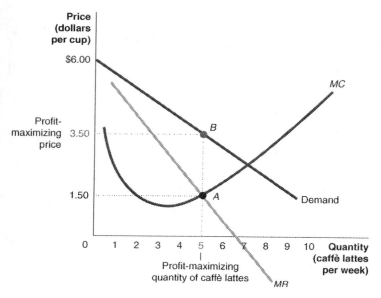

**(a) Profit-maximizing quantity and price for a monopolistic competitor**

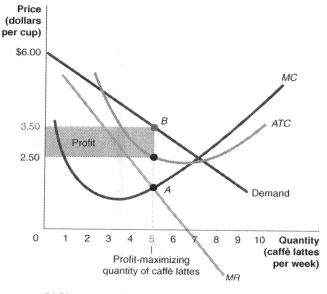

**(b) Short-run profits for a monopolistic competitor**

**Figure 12-4** | Maximizing Profit in a Monopolistically Competitive Market

To maximize profit, a Starbucks coffeehouse wants to sell caffè lattes up to the point where the marginal revenue from selling the last caffè latte is just equal to the marginal cost. As the table shows, this happens with the fifth caffè latte—point A in panel (a)—which adds $1.50 to the firm's costs and $1.50 to its revenues. The firm then uses the demand curve to find the price that will lead consumers to buy this quantity of caffè lattes (point B). In panel (b), the green box represents the firm's profits. The box has a height equal to $1.00, which is the price of $3.50 minus the average total cost of $2.50, and a base equal to the quantity of 5 caffè lattes. So, this Starbucks profit equals $1 × 5 = $5.00.

# Solved Problem | 12-2

## How Not to Maximize Profits at a Publishing Company

In an article in the *New York Times*, Virginia Postrel states that when deciding the "question of whether printing another copy of a given, already published book, is a profitable thing to do," managers at publishing firms begin by calculating the cost of printing one additional copy. But these managers "often fall prey to the mistake of adding up every expense associated with a book, including the overhead like rent and editors' salaries, and then dividing by the number of copies." Will the process described in the previous sentence give an accurate estimate of marginal cost? If you were a manager at a publishing firm, how would you determine whether producing one more copy of a book will increase your profits?

## SOLVING THE PROBLEM:

**Step 1:** **Review the chapter material.** This problem is about how monopolistically competitive firms maximize profits, so you may want to review the section "How a Monopolistically Competitive Firm Maximizes Profits in the Short Run," which begins on page 415.

**Step 2:** **Analyze the costs described in the problem.** We have seen that to maximize profits, firms should produce up to the point where marginal revenue equals marginal cost. Marginal cost is the increase in total cost that results from producing another unit of output. Rent and editors' salaries are part of a publishing company's fixed costs because they do not change as the company increases its output of books. Therefore, managers at publishing companies should not include them in calculating marginal cost.

**Step 3:** **Explain how a manager at a publishing firm should decide whether to publish one more copy of a book.** To determine whether producing one more copy of a book will increase your profits, you need to compare the marginal revenue received from selling the book with the marginal cost of producing it. If the marginal revenue is greater than the marginal cost, producing the book will increase your profits.

Source: Virginia Postrel, "Often, Basic Concepts in Economics Are Taken for Granted," *New York Times*, January 3, 2002.

>> End Solved Problem 12-2

12.3 | Analyze the situation of a monopolistically competitive firm in the long run.

# What Happens to Profits in the Long Run?

Remember that a firm makes an economic profit when its total revenue is greater than all of its costs, including the opportunity cost of the funds invested in the firm by its owners. Because cost curves include the owners' opportunity costs, the Starbucks coffeehouse represented in Figure 12-4 is making an economic profit. This economic profit gives entrepreneurs an incentive to enter this market and establish new firms. If a Starbucks is earning economic profit selling caffè lattes, new coffeehouses are likely to open in the same area.

## How Does the Entry of New Firms Affect the Profits of Existing Firms?

As new coffeehouses open near the local Starbucks, the firm's demand curve will shift to the left. The demand curve will shift because Starbucks will sell fewer caffè lattes at each price when there are additional coffeehouses in the area selling similar drinks. The demand curve will also become more elastic because consumers have additional coffeehouses from which to buy coffee, so Starbucks will lose more sales if it raises its prices. Figure 12-5 shows how the demand curve for the local Starbucks shifts as new firms enter its market.

In panel (a) of Figure 12-5, the short-run demand curve shows the relationship between the price of caffè lattes and the quantity of caffè lattes Starbucks sells per week before the entry of new firms. With this demand curve, Starbucks can charge a price above average total cost—shown as point *A* in panel (a)—and make a profit. But this profit attracts additional coffeehouses to the area and shifts the demand curve for the Starbucks caffè lattes to the left. As long as Starbucks is making an economic profit, there is an incentive for additional coffeehouses to open in the area, and the demand curve will

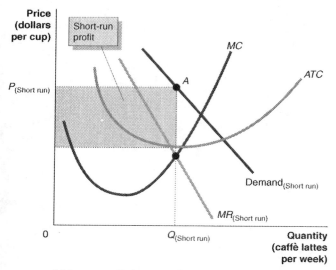

**(a) A monopolistic competitor may earn a short-run profit**

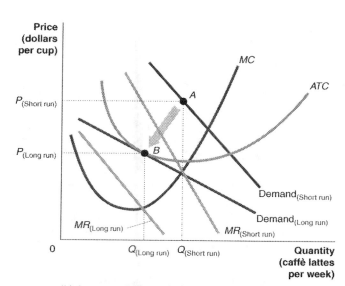

**(b) A monopolistic competitor's profits are eliminated in the long run**

**Figure 12-5** | How Entry of New Firms Eliminates Profits

In the short run—panel (a)—the local Starbucks faces the demand and marginal revenue curves labeled "Short run." With this demand curve, Starbucks can charge a price above average total cost (point A) and make a profit, shown by the green rectangle. But this profit attracts new firms to enter the market, which shifts the demand and marginal revenue curves to the ones labeled "Long run" in panel (b). Because price is now equal to average total cost (point B), Starbucks breaks even and no longer earns an economic profit.

continue shifting to the left. As panel (b) shows, eventually the demand curve will have shifted to the point where it is just touching—or tangent to—the average cost curve.

In the long run, at the point at which the demand curve is tangent to the average cost curve, price is equal to average total cost (point B), the firm is breaking even, and it no longer earns an economic profit. In the long run, the demand curve is also more elastic because the more coffeehouses there are in the area, the more sales Starbucks will lose to other coffeehouses if it raises its price.

Of course, it is possible that a monopolistically competitive firm will suffer economic losses in the short run. As a consequence, the owners of the firm will not be covering the opportunity cost of their investment. We expect that, in the long run, firms will exit an industry if they are suffering economic losses. If firms exit, the demand curve for the output of a remaining firm will shift to the right. This process will continue until the representative firm in the industry is able to charge a price equal to its average cost and break even. Therefore, in the long run, monopolistically competitive firms will experience neither economic profits nor economic losses. Table 12-2 summarizes the short run and the long run for a monopolistically competitive firm.

# Don't Let This Happen to YOU!

## Don't Confuse Zero Economic Profit with Zero Accounting Profit

Remember that economists count the opportunity cost of the owner's investment in a firm as a cost. For example, suppose you invest $200,000 opening a pizza parlor, and the return you could earn on those funds each year in a similar investment—such as opening a sandwich shop—is 10 percent. Therefore, the annual opportunity cost of investing the funds in your own business is 10 percent of $200,000, or $20,000.

This $20,000 is part of your profit in the accounting sense, and you would have to pay taxes on it. But in an economic sense, the $20,000 is a cost. In long-run equilibrium, we would expect that entry of new firms would keep you from earning more than 10 percent on your investment. So, you would end up breaking even and earning zero economic profit, even though you were earning an accounting profit of $20,000.

TABLE 12-2 | **The Short Run and the Long Run for a Monopolistically Competitive Firm**

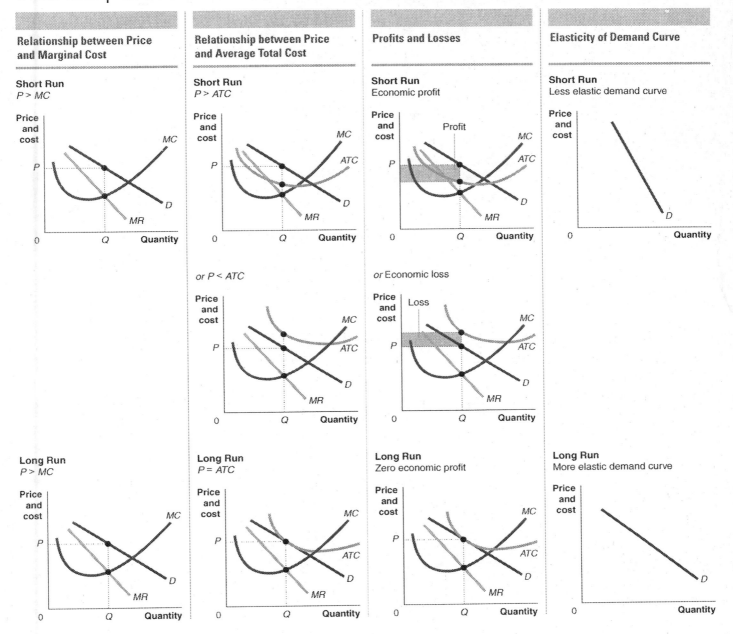

| **Relationship between Price and Marginal Cost** | **Relationship between Price and Average Total Cost** | **Profits and Losses** | **Elasticity of Demand Curve** |
|---|---|---|---|
| **Short Run** P > MC | **Short Run** P > ATC | **Short Run** Economic profit | **Short Run** Less elastic demand curve |
| | *or* P < ATC | *or* Economic loss | |
| **Long Run** P > MC | **Long Run** P = ATC | **Long Run** Zero economic profit | **Long Run** More elastic demand curve |

## Making the Connection | The Rise and Fall of Apple's Macintosh Computer

In 1983, there were more than 15 firms selling personal computers nationally, as well as many smaller firms in local markets selling computers assembled from purchased components. None of these personal computers operated using the current system of clicking on icons with a mouse. Instead, users had to type in commands to call up word processing, spreadsheet, and other software programs. This awkward system required users to memorize many commands or constantly consult computer manuals. In January 1984, Apple Computer introduced the Macintosh, which used a mouse and could be operated by clicking on icons. The average cost of producing Macintoshes was about $500. Apple sold them for prices between $2,500 and $3,000. This price was more than twice that

*Macintosh lost its differentiation, but still has a loyal—if relatively small—following.*

of comparable personal computers sold by IBM and other companies, but the Macintosh was so easy to use that it was able to achieve a 15 percent share of the market. Apple had successfully introduced a personal computer that was strongly differentiated from its competitors. One journalist covering the computer industry has gone so far as to call the Macintosh "the most important consumer product of the last half of the twentieth century."

Microsoft produced the operating system known as MS-DOS (for Microsoft disk operating system), which most non-Apple computers used. The financial success of the Macintosh led Microsoft to develop an operating system that would also use a mouse and icons. In 1992, Microsoft introduced the operating system Windows 3.1, which succeeded in reproducing many of the key features of the Macintosh. By August 1995, when Microsoft introduced Windows 95, non-Apple computers had become as easy to use as Macintosh computers. By that time, most personal computers operated in a way very similar to the Macintosh, and Apple was no longer able to charge prices that were significantly above those that its competitors charged. The Macintosh had lost its differentiation. Although the Macintosh (now known as the iMac) continues to have a loyal following, particularly among graphic designers, today it has only a 6 percent share of the personal computer market.

Source for quote: Steven Levy, *Insanely Great: The Life and Times of Macintosh, the Computer that Changed Everything*, New York: Viking, 1994, p. 7.

# **Solved** Problem | **12-3**

## The Short Run and the Long Run for the Macintosh

Use the information in *Making the Connection* on page 419 to draw a graph that shows changes in the market for Macintosh computers between 1984 and 1995.

### SOLVING THE PROBLEM:

**Step 1:** **Review the chapter material.** This problem is about how the entry of new firms affected the market for the Macintosh, so you may want to review the section "How Does the Entry of New Firms Affect the Profits of Existing Firms?" which begins on page 417.

**Step 2:** **Draw the graph.** The *Making the Connection* about Apple indicates that in 1984, when the Macintosh was first introduced, its differentiation from other computers allowed Apple to make a substantial economic profit. In 1995, the release of Windows 95 meant that non-Macintosh computers were as easy to use as Macintosh computers. Apple's product differentiation was eliminated, as was its ability to earn economic profits. The change over time in Apple's situation is shown in the following graph, which combines panels (a) and (b) from Figure 12-5 in one graph.

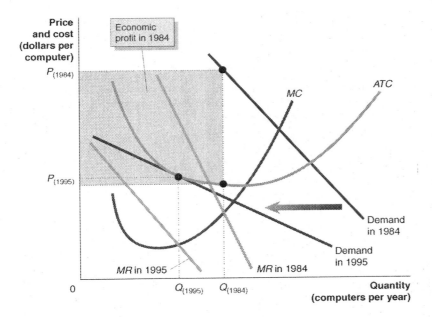

Between 1984 and 1995, Microsoft's development of the Windows operating system eliminated Macintosh's product differentiation. The demand curve for Macintosh shifted to the left and became more elastic throughout the relevant range of prices.

**EXTRA CREDIT:** Note that this analysis is simplified. The Macintosh of 1995 was a different—and better—computer than the Macintosh of 1984. Apple has made changes to the Macintosh, such as the introduction of the colorful iMac computer in 1999, that have sometimes led to increases in sales. The great success of the Apple iPod has also lead some consumers to switch to Apple computers. But the Macintosh has never been able to regain the high demand and premium prices it enjoyed from the mid-1980s to the early 1990s.

>> End Solved Problem 12-3

## Is Zero Economic Profit Inevitable in the Long Run?

The economic analysis of the long run shows the effects of market forces over time. In the case of Starbucks, the effect of market forces is to eliminate the economic profit earned by a monopolistically competitive firm. Owners of monopolistically competitive firms, of course, do not have to passively accept this long-run result. The key to earning economic profits is either to sell a differentiated product or to find a way of producing an existing product at a lower cost. If a monopolistically competitive firm selling a differentiated product is earning profits, these profits will attract the entry of additional firms, and the entry of those firms will eventually eliminate the firm's profits. If a firm introduces new technology that allows it to sell a good or service at a lower cost, competing firms will eventually be able to duplicate that technology and eliminate the firm's profits. *But this result holds only if the firm stands still and fails to find new ways of differentiating its product or fails to find new ways of lowering the cost of producing its product.* Firms continually struggle to find new ways of differentiating their products as they try to stay one step ahead of other firms that are attempting to copy their success. As new coffeehouses enter the area served by the Starbucks coffeehouse, the owners can expect to see their economic profits competed away, unless they can find ways to differentiate their product.

In 2007, Howard Schultz, the chairman of Starbucks, was well aware of this fact. In opening thousands of coffeehouses worldwide, he worried that Starbucks had made the customer experience less distinctive and easier for competitors to copy. Starbucks has used various strategies to differentiate itself from competing coffeehouses. Competitors have found it difficult to duplicate the European espresso bar atmosphere of Starbucks, with its large, comfortable chairs; music playing; and groups of friends dropping in and out during the day. Most importantly, Starbucks has continued to be very responsive to its customers' preferences. As one observer put it, "How many retailers could put up with 'I'll have a grande low-fat triple-shot half-caf white-chocolate mocha, extra hot, easy on the whipped cream. And I'm in a rush'?" But Howard Schultz was worried. In a memo sent to employees, he wrote, "Over the past ten years, in order to achieve the growth, development, and scale necessary to go from less than 1,000 stores to 13,000 stores . . . we have had to make a series of decisions that . . . have led to the watering down of the Starbucks experience." Starbucks has begun serving breakfast sandwiches and installing drive-through windows that make its stores appear similar to other fast-food restaurants. Although at one time Starbucks had been able to maintain greater control over the operations of its coffeehouses, because unlike many of its competitors, all of its coffeehouses were company owned, it now has thousands of *franchises*. A franchise is a business with the legal right to sell a good or service in a particular area. When a firm uses franchises, local businesspeople are able to buy and run the stores in their area. This makes it easier for a firm to finance its expansion but forces the firm to give up some control over its stores.

Starbucks experienced great success during the 1990s and the early 2000s, but history shows that in the long run, competitors will be able to duplicate most of what it does. In the face of that competition, it will be very difficult for Starbucks to continue earning economic profits. As Howard Schultz put it, "Competitors of all kinds, small and large coffee companies, fast food operators, and mom and pops, [have positioned] themselves in a way that creates awareness . . . and loyalty of people who previously have been Starbucks customers." He concluded, "I have said for 20 years that our success is not an entitlement and now it's proving to be a reality."

The owner of a competitive firm is in a position similar to that of Ebenezer Scrooge in Charles Dickens's *A Christmas Carol*. When the Ghost of Christmas Yet to Come shows Scrooge visions of his own death, he asks the ghost, "Are these the shadows of the things that Will be, or are they shadows of things that May be, only?" The shadow of the end of their profits haunts owners of every firm. Firms try to avoid losing profits by reducing costs, by improving their products, or by convincing consumers their products are indeed different from what competitors offer. To stay one step ahead of its competitors, a firm has to offer consumers goods or services that they perceive to have greater *value* than those offered by competing firms. Value can take the form of product differentiation that makes the good or service more suited to consumers' preferences, or it can take the form of a lower price.

## Making the Connection | Staying One Step Ahead of the Competition: Eugène Schueller and L'Oréal

Today, L'Oréal, with headquarters in the Paris suburb of Clichy, is the largest seller of perfumes, cosmetics, and hair care products in the world. In addition to L'Oréal, its brands include Lancôme, Maybelline, Soft Sheen/Carson, Garnier, Redken, Ralph Lauren, and Matrix. Like most other large firms, L'Oréal was started by an entrepreneur with an idea. Eugène Schueller was a French chemist who experimented in the evenings trying to find a safe and reliable hair coloring for women. In 1907, he founded the firm that became L'Oréal and began selling his hair coloring preparations to Paris hair salons. Schueller was able to take advantage of changes in fashion. In the early twentieth century, women began to cut their hair much shorter than had been typical in the nineteenth century, and it had become socially acceptable to spend time and money styling it. The number of hair salons in Europe and the United States increased rapidly. By the 1920s and 1930s, the international popularity of Hollywood films, many starring "platinum blonde bombshells" such as Jean Harlow, made it fashionable for women to color their hair. By the late 1920s, L'Oréal was selling its products throughout Europe, the United States, and Japan.

*Unlike many monopolistically competitive firms, L'Oréal has earned economic profits for a very long time.*

Perfumes, cosmetics, and hair coloring are all products that should be easy for rival firms to duplicate. We would expect, then, that the economic profits L'Oréal earned in its early years would have been competed away in the long run through the entry of new firms. In fact, though, the firm has remained profitable through the decades, following a strategy of developing new products, improving existing products, and expanding into new markets. For example, when French workers first received paid holidays during the 1930s, L'Oréal moved quickly to dominate the new market for suntan lotion. Today, the firm's SoftSheen brand is experiencing rapid sales increases in Africa. When L'Oréal launched a new line of men's skin-care products, including shaving cream, one analyst observed that at L'Oréal, "brands don't stay at home serving the same old clientele. They get spruced up, put in a new set of traveling clothes, and sent abroad to meet new customers." L'Oréal has maintained its ability to innovate by spending more on research and development than do competing firms. The firm has a research staff of more than 1,000.

One reason L'Oréal has been able to follow a focused strategy is that the firm has had only three chairmen in its nearly century of existence: founder Eugène Schueller, François Dalle, and Lindsay Owen-Jones, who became chairman in 1988. Owen-Jones has described the firm's strategy: "Each brand is positioned on a very precise [market] segment, which overlaps as little as possible with the others." The story of L'Oréal shows that it is possible for a firm to stay one step ahead of the competition, but it takes top management committed to an entrepreneurial spirit of continually developing new products.

Source for quotes: Richard Tomlinson, "L'Oréal's Global Makeover," *Fortune*, September 30, 2002.

---

**12.4 LEARNING** OBJECTIVE

12.4 | Compare the efficiency of monopolistic competition and perfect competition.

# Comparing Perfect Competition and Monopolistic Competition

We have seen that monopolistic competition and perfect competition share the characteristic that in long-run equilibrium, firms earn zero economic profits. As Figure 12-6 shows, however, there are two important differences between long-run equilibrium in the two markets:

- Monopolistically competitive firms charge a price greater than marginal cost.

- Monopolistically competitive firms do not produce at minimum average total cost.

## Excess Capacity under Monopolistic Competition

Recall that a firm in a perfectly competitive market faces a perfectly elastic demand curve that is also its marginal revenue curve. Therefore, the firm maximizes profit by producing where price equals marginal cost. As panel (a) of Figure 12-6 shows, in

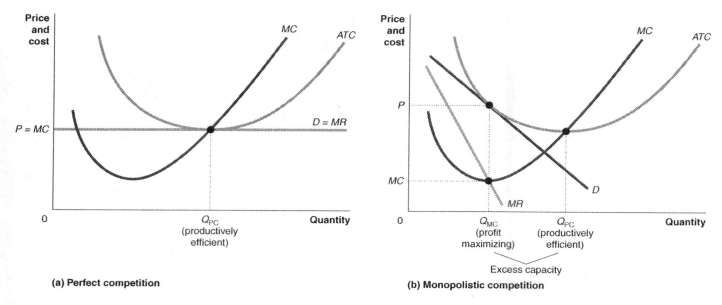

**Figure 12-6** | Comparing Long-Run Equilibrium under Perfect Competition and Monopolistic Competition

In panel (a), the perfectly competitive firm in long-run equilibrium produces at $Q_{PC}$, where price equals marginal cost, and average total cost is at a minimum. The perfectly competitive firm is both allocatively efficient and productively efficient. In panel (b), the monopolistically competitive firm produces at $Q_{MC}$, where price is greater than marginal cost, and average total cost is not at a minimum. As a result, the monopolistically competitive firm is neither allocatively efficient nor productively efficient. The monopolistically competitive firm has excess capacity equal to the difference between its profit-maximizing level of output and the productively efficient level of output.

long-run equilibrium, a perfectly competitive firm produces at the minimum point of its average total cost curve.

Panel (b) of Figure 12-6 shows that the profit-maximizing level of output for a monopolistically competitive firm comes at a level of output where price is greater than marginal cost and the firm is not at the minimum point of its average total cost curve. A monopolistically competitive firm has *excess capacity*: If it increased its output, it could produce at a lower average cost.

## Is Monopolistic Competition Inefficient?

In Chapter 11, we discussed *productive efficiency* and *allocative efficiency*. Productive efficiency refers to the situation where a good is produced at the lowest possible cost. Allocative efficiency refers to the situation where every good or service is produced up to the point where the last unit provides a marginal benefit to consumers equal to the marginal cost of producing it. For productive efficiency to hold, firms must produce at the minimum point of average total cost. For allocative efficiency to hold, firms must charge a price equal to marginal cost. In a perfectly competitive market, both productive efficiency and allocative efficiency are achieved, but in a monopolistically competitive market, neither is achieved. Does it matter? Economists have debated whether monopolistically competitive markets being neither productively nor allocatively efficient results in a significant loss of well-being to society in these markets compared with perfectly competitive markets.

## How Consumers Benefit from Monopolistic Competition

Looking again at Figure 12-6, you can see that the only difference between the monopolistically competitive firm and the perfectly competitive firm is that the demand curve for the monopolistically competitive firm slopes downward, whereas the demand curve for the perfectly competitive firm is a horizontal line. The demand curve for the monopolistically competitive firm slopes downward because the good or service the firm is selling is differentiated from the goods or services being sold by competing firms. The perfectly competitive firm is selling a good or service identical to those being sold by its competitors. A key point to remember is that *firms differentiate their products to appeal to consumers.* When Starbucks coffeehouses begin offering new flavors of coffee, when Blockbuster stores begin carrying more HD-DVDs and fewer regular DVDs, when General Mills introduces Apple-Cinnamon Cheerios, or when PepsiCo introduces caffeine-free Diet Pepsi, they are all attempting to attract and retain consumers through product differentiation. The success of these product differentiation strategies indicates that some consumers find these products preferable to the alternatives. Consumers, therefore, are better off than they would have been had these companies not differentiated their products.

We can conclude that consumers face a trade-off when buying the product of a monopolistically competitive firm: They are paying a price that is greater than marginal cost, and the product is not being produced at minimum average cost, but they benefit from being able to purchase a product that is differentiated and more closely suited to their tastes.

## Making the Connection | Abercrombie & Fitch: Can the Product Be Too Differentiated?

Business managers often refer to differentiating their products as finding a "market niche." The larger the niche you have, the greater the potential profit but the more likely that other firms will be able to compete against you. Too small a niche, however, may reduce competition—but also reduce profits. Some analysts believe that the market niche chosen by the managers of the Abercrombie & Fitch clothing stores is too small. The chief executive, Mike Jeffries, argues that his store's target customer is an "18-to-22 [year old] college guy who has a good body and is aspirational." He admits that this is a narrow niche: "If I exclude people—absolutely. Delighted to do so."

*Did Abercrombie and Fitch narrow its target market too much?*

But is A&F excluding too many people? One analyst argues "they've . . . pushed a lot of people out of the brand." A&F's sales results seemed to indicate that this analyst may be correct. Managers of retail stores closely monitor "same-store sales," which measures how much sales have increased in the same stores from one year to the next. To offset the effects of inflation—or general increases in prices in the economy—same-store sales need to increase at least 2 percent to 3 percent each year. A firm whose strategy of product differentiation succeeds will experience increases in same-store sales of at least 5 percent to 6 percent each year. For several years in the early 2000s, A&F's 350 stores experienced *negative* same-store results. Although sales increased from 2004 through early 2006, negative changes in same-store sales returned in late 2006 and continued through mid 2007. A&F may have gone too far in narrowing its market niche.

Sources: James Covert, "Retail Sales Slide Fuels Concern," *Wall Street Journal*, May 11, 2007; and Shelly Branch, "Maybe Sex Doesn't Sell, A&F Is Discovering," *Wall Street Journal*, December 12, 2003.

---

12.5 | Define marketing and explain how firms use it to differentiate their products.

# How Marketing Differentiates Products

Firms can differentiate their products through marketing. **Marketing** refers to all the activities necessary for a firm to sell a product to a consumer. Marketing includes activities such as determining which product to produce, designing the product, advertising the product, deciding how to distribute the product—for example, in retail stores or

**Marketing** All the activities necessary for a firm to sell a product to a consumer.

through a Web site—and monitoring how changes in consumer tastes are affecting the market for the product. Peter F. Drucker, a leading business strategist, describes marketing as follows: "It is the whole business seen from the point of view of its final result, that is, from the consumer's point of view. . . . True marketing . . . does not ask, 'What do we want to sell?' It asks, 'What does the consumer want to buy?'"

As we have seen, for monopolistically competitive firms to earn economic profits and to defend those profits from competitors, they must differentiate their products. Firms use two marketing tools to differentiate their products: brand management and advertising.

## Brand Management

**Brand management** The actions of a firm intended to maintain the differentiation of a product over time.

Once a firm has succeeded in differentiating its product, it must try to maintain that differentiation over time through **brand management**. As we have seen, whenever a firm successfully introduces a new product or a significantly different version of an old product, it earns economic profits in the short run. But the success of the firm inspires competitors to copy the new or improved product and, in the long run, the firm's economic profits will be competed away. Firms use brand management to postpone the time when they will no longer be able to earn economic profits.

## Advertising

An innovative advertising campaign can make even long-established and familiar products, such as Coke or McDonald's Big Mac hamburgers, seem more desirable than competing products. When a firm advertises a product, it is trying to shift the demand curve for the product to the right and to make it more inelastic. If the firm is successful, it will sell more of the product at every price, and it will be able to increase the price it charges without losing as many customers. Of course, advertising also increases a firm's costs. If the increase in revenue that results from the advertising is greater than the increase in costs, the firm's profits will rise.

Needless to say, advertising campaigns are not always successful. In 1957, the Ford Motor Company introduced a new car, the Edsel, designed to compete with the Buick from General Motors. Ford set up a new division of the company to produce the Edsel in five different models and hired the advertising firm of Foote, Cone & Belding to direct a massive advertising campaign. Among other things, Ford purchased an hour of prime television time on the CBS network to broadcast *The Edsel Show*, hosted by Frank Sinatra, Bing Crosby, and Louis Armstrong, three of the biggest stars of the 1950s. Ford set a sales goal of 200,000 cars during the first year of production. Unfortunately, most of the car-buying public found the styling of the Edsel, with its oversized headlights and elaborate front grill, unappealing. First-year sales were only about 63,000 cars. During the same period, General Motors sold more than 230,000 Buicks. Ford decided to shift its advertising account for the Edsel from Foote, Cone & Belding to Kenyon & Eckhardt. Despite a revised advertising campaign, sales of the Edsel remained very low. Ford sold fewer than 45,000 Edsels during the car's second year of production. In November 1959, after only two years in production, Ford stopped making the Edsel. Even one of the largest advertising campaigns in history had failed to make the Edsel successful.

## Defending a Brand Name

Once a firm has established a successful brand name, it has a strong incentive to defend it. A firm can apply for a *trademark*, which grants legal protection against other firms using its product's name.

One threat to a trademarked name is the possibility that it will become so widely used for a type of product that it will no longer be associated with the product of a specific company. Courts in the United States have ruled that when this happens, a firm is no longer entitled to legal protection of the brand name. For example, "aspirin," "escalator," and "thermos" were originally all brand names of the products of particular firms, but each became so widely used to refer to a type of product that none remains a legally protected brand name. Firms spend substantial amounts of money trying to make sure that this does not happen to them. Coca-Cola, for example, employs workers to travel around the country stopping at restaurants and asking to be served a "Coke" with their meal. If the restaurant serves Pepsi or some other cola, rather than Coke, Coca-Cola's legal department sends the restaurant a letter reminding that "Coke" is a trademarked name and not a generic name for any cola. Similarly, Xerox Corporation spends money on advertising to remind the public that "Xerox" is not a generic term for making photocopies.

Legally enforcing trademarks can be difficult. Estimates are that each year, U.S. firms lose hundreds of billions of dollars in sales worldwide as a result of unauthorized use of their trademarked brand names. U.S. firms often find it difficult to enforce their trademarks in the courts of some foreign countries, although recent international agreements have increased the legal protections for trademarks.

Firms that sell their products through franchises rather than through company-owned stores encounter the problem that if a franchisee does not run his or her business well, the firm's brand may be damaged. Automobile firms send "roadmen" to visit their dealers to make sure the dealerships are clean and well maintained and that the service departments employ competent mechanics and are well equipped with spare parts. Similarly, McDonald's sends employees from corporate headquarters to visit McDonald's franchises to make sure the bathrooms are clean and the French fries are hot.

12.6 | Identify the key factors that determine a firm's success.

# What Makes a Firm Successful?

A firm's owners and managers control some of the factors that make a firm successful and allow it to earn economic profits. The most important of these are the firm's ability to differentiate its product and to produce its product at a lower average cost than competing firms. A firm that successfully does these things creates *value* for its customers. Consumers will buy a product if they believe it meets a need not met by competing products or if its price is below that of competitors.

Some factors that affect a firm's profitability are not directly under the firm's control. Certain factors will affect all the firms in a market. For example, rising prices for jet fuel will reduce the profitability of all airlines. If consumers decide that they would rather watch pay-for-view movies delivered to their homes by cable or satellite than buy DVDs, the profitability of all stores selling DVDs will be reduced.

Sheer chance also plays a role in business, as it does in all other aspects of life. A struggling McDonald's franchise may see profits increase dramatically after the county unexpectedly decides to build a new road nearby. Many businesses in New York City, including restaurants, hotels, and theaters, experienced a marked drop in customers and profits following the September 11, 2001, terrorist attacks. Figure 12-7 illustrates the important point that factors within the firm's control and factors outside the firm's control interact to determine the firm's profitability.

## Figure 12-7

**What Makes a Firm Successful?**

The factors under a firm's control—the ability to differentiate its product and the ability to produce it at lower cost—combine with the factors beyond its control to determine the firm's profitability.

Source: Adapted from Figure 11.3 in David Besanko, David Dranove, Mark Shanley, and Scott Schaefer, *The Economics of Strategy*, 4th ed., New York: Wiley, 2007.

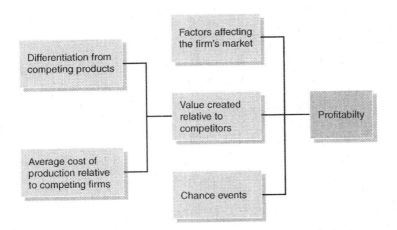

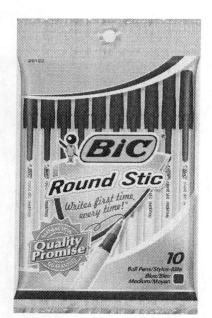

*Although not first to market, Bic ultimately was more successful than the firm that pioneered ballpoint pens.*

# Making the Connection | Is Being the First Firm in the Market a Key to Success?

Some business analysts argue that the first firm to enter a market can have important *first-mover advantages*. By being the first to sell a particular good, a firm may find its name closely associated with the good in the public's mind, as, for instance, Amazon is closely associated with ordering books online or eBay is associated with online auctions. This close association may make it more difficult for new firms to enter the market and compete against the first mover.

Surprisingly, though, recent research has shown that the first firm to enter a market often does *not* have a long-lived advantage over later entrants. Consider, for instance, the market for pens. Until the 1940s, the only pens available were fountain pens that had to be refilled frequently from an ink bottle and used ink that dried slowly and smeared easily. In October 1945, entrepreneur Milton Reynolds introduced the first ballpoint pen, which never needed to be refilled. When it went on sale at Gimbel's department store in New York City, it was an instant success. Although the pen had a price of $12.00—the equivalent of about $135.00 at today's prices—hundreds of thousands were sold, and Milton Reynolds became a millionaire. Unfortunately, it didn't last. Although Reynolds had guaranteed that his pen would write for two years—later raised to five years—in fact, the pen often leaked and frequently stopped writing after only limited use. Sales began to collapse, the flood of pens returned under the company's guarantee wiped out its profits, and within a few years, Reynolds International Pen Company stopped selling pens in the United States. By the late 1960s, firms such as Bic selling inexpensive—but reliable—ballpoint pens dominated the market.

What happened to the Reynolds International Pen Company turns out to be more the rule than the exception. For example, Apple's iPod was not the first digital music player to appear on the U.S. market. Both Seahan's MPMan and Diamond's PMP300 were released in the United States in 1998, three years before the iPod. Similarly, although Hewlett-Packard currently dominates the market for laser printers, with a market share of more than 50 percent, it did not invent the laser printer. Xerox invented the laser printer, and IBM sold the first commercial laser printers. Nor was Procter & Gamble the first firm to sell disposable diapers when it introduced Pampers in 1961. Microsoft's Internet Explorer was not the first Web browser: Before Internet Explorer, there was Netscape; before Netscape, there was Mosaic; and before Mosaic, there were several other Web browsers that for a time looked as if they might dominate the market. In all these cases, the firms that were first to introduce a product ultimately lost out to latecomers who did a better job of providing consumers with products that were more reliable, less expensive, more convenient, or otherwise provided greater value.

Sources: Steven P. Schnaars, *Managing Imitation Strategies: How Later Entrants Seize Markets from Pioneers*, New York: The Free Press, 1994; and Gerard J. Tellis and Peter N. Golder, *Will and Vision: How Latecomers Grow to Dominate Markets*, Los Angeles: Figueroa Press, 2002.

# Conclusion

In this chapter, we have applied many of the ideas about competition we developed in Chapter 11 to the more common market structure of monopolistic competition. We have seen that these ideas apply to monopolistically competitive markets, just as they do to perfectly competitive markets. At the end of Chapter 11, we concluded that "The competitive forces of the market impose relentless pressure on firms to produce new and better goods and services at the lowest possible cost. Firms that fail to adequately anticipate changes in consumer tastes or that fail to adopt the latest and most efficient production technology do not survive in the long run." These conclusions are as true for coffeehouses and firms in other monopolistically competitive markets as they are for wheat farmers or apple growers.

# Chapter 11
# Price Determination

In previous chapters, we saw that entrepreneurs continually seek out economic profit. Pricing strategies are one way firms can attempt to increase their economic profit. One of these strategies is called *price discrimination*. It involves firms setting different prices for the same good or service, as Disney does when setting admission prices at Disney World. In Chapter 14, we analyzed the situation of a monopolist who sets a single price for its product. In this chapter, we will see how a firm can increase its profits by charging a higher price to consumers who value the good more and a lower price to consumers who value the good less.

We will also analyze the widely used strategies of *odd pricing* and *cost-plus pricing*. Finally, we will analyze situations in which firms are able to charge consumers one price for the right to buy a good and a second price for each unit of the good purchased. The ability of Disney to charge for admission to Disney World and also to charge for each ride is an example of this situation, which economists call a *two-part tariff*.

---

**15.1 LEARNING** OBJECTIVE

15.1 | Define the law of one price and explain the role of arbitrage.

# Pricing Strategy, the Law of One Price, and Arbitrage

We saw in the opening to this chapter that sometimes firms can increase their profits by charging different prices for the same good. In fact, many firms rely on economic analysis to practice *price discrimination* by charging higher prices to some customers and lower prices to others. Firms use technology to gather information on the preferences of consumers and their responsiveness to changes in prices. Managers use the information to rapidly adjust the prices of their goods and services. This practice of rapidly adjusting prices, called *yield management*, has been particularly important to airlines and hotels. There are limits, though, to the ability of firms to charge different prices for the same product. The key limit is the possibility in some circumstances that consumers who can buy a good at a low price will resell it to consumers who would otherwise have to buy at a high price.

## Arbitrage

According to the *law of one price*, identical products should sell for the same price everywhere. Let's explore why the law of one price usually holds true. Suppose that a Sony PlayStation Portable (PSP) handheld video game player sells for $249 in stores in Atlanta and for $199 in stores in San Francisco. Anyone who lives in San Francisco could buy PSPs for $199 and resell them for $249 in Atlanta. They could sell them on eBay or ship them to someone they know in Atlanta who could sell them in local flea markets. Buying a product in one market at a low price and reselling it in another market at a high price is referred to as *arbitrage*. The profits received from engaging in arbitrage are referred to as *arbitrage profits*.

As the supply of PSPs in Atlanta increases, the price of PSPs in Atlanta will decline, and as the supply of PSPs in San Francisco decreases, the price of PSPs in San Francisco will rise. Eventually the arbitrage process will eliminate most, but not all, of the price difference. Some price difference will remain because sellers must pay to list PSPs on eBay and to ship them to Atlanta. The costs of carrying out a transaction—by, for example, listing items on eBay and shipping them across the country—are called **transactions costs**. The law of one price holds exactly *only if transactions costs are zero*. As we will soon see, in cases in which it is impossible to resell a product, the law of one price will not hold, and firms will be able to price discriminate. Apart from this important qualification, we expect that arbitrage will result in a product selling for the same price everywhere.

**Transactions costs** The costs in time and other resources that parties incur in the process of agreeing to and carrying out an exchange of goods or services.

# Solved Problem | 15-1

## Is Arbitrage Just a Rip-off?

People are often suspicious of arbitrage. Buying something at a low price and reselling it at a high price exploits the person buying at the high price. Or does it? Is this view correct? If so, do the auctions on eBay serve any useful economic purpose?

## SOLVING THE PROBLEM:

**Step 1:** **Review the chapter material.** This problem is about arbitrage, so you may want to review the section "Arbitrage," which begins on page 508. If necessary, also review the discussion of the benefits from trade in Chapters 2 and 8.

**Step 2:** **Use the discussion of arbitrage and the discussion in earlier chapters of the benefits from trade to answer the questions.** Many of the goods on eBay have been bought at a low price and are being resold at a higher price. In fact, some people supplement their incomes by buying collectibles and other goods at garage sales and reselling them on eBay. Does eBay serve a useful economic purpose? Economists would say that it does. Consider the case of Lou, who buys collectible movie posters and resells them on eBay. Suppose Lou buys a *Spider-Man 3* poster at a garage sale for $30 and resells it on eBay for $60. Both the person who sold to Lou at the garage sale and the person who bought from him on eBay must have been made better off by the deals *or they would not have made them.* Lou has performed the useful service of locating the poster and making it available for sale on eBay. In carrying out this service, Lou has incurred costs, including the opportunity cost of his time spent searching garage sales, the opportunity cost of the funds he has tied up in posters he has purchased but not yet sold, and the cost of the fees eBay charges him. It is easy to sell goods on eBay, so over time, competition among Lou and other movie poster dealers should cause the difference between the prices of posters sold at garage sales and the prices on eBay to shrink until they are equal to the dealers' costs of reselling the posters.

>> **End Solved Problem 15-1**

## Why Don't All Firms Charge the Same Price?

The law of one price may appear to be violated even where transactions costs are zero and a product can be resold. For example, different Internet Web sites may sell what seem to be identical products for different prices. We can resolve this apparent contradiction if we look more closely at what "product" an Internet Web site—or other business—actually offers for sale.

Suppose you want to buy a copy of the book *Harry Potter and the Deathly Hallows*. You use mySimon.com or some other search engine to compare the book's price at various Web sites. You get the results shown in Table 15-1.

Would you automatically buy the book from one of the last two sites listed rather than from Amazon.com or BarnesandNoble.com? We can think about why you might not. Consider what product is being offered for sale. Amazon.com is not just offering *Harry Potter and the Deathly Hallows*; it is offering *Harry Potter and the Deathly Hallows* delivered quickly to your home, well packaged so it's not damaged in the mail, and charged to your credit card using a secure method that keeps your credit card number safe from computer hackers. As we discussed in Chapter 12, firms differentiate the products they sell in many ways. One way is by providing faster and more reliable delivery than competitors.

**TABLE 15-1**

**Which Internet Bookseller Would You Buy From?**

| PRODUCT: *HARRY POTTER AND THE DEATHLY HALLOWS* | |
|---|---|
| COMPANY | PRICE |
| Amazon.com | $18.89 |
| BarnesandNoble.com | 18.89 |
| WaitForeverForYourOrder.com | 17.50 |
| JustStartedinBusinessLastWednesday.com | 16.75 |

Amazon.com and BarnesandNoble.com have built reputations for fast and reliable service. New Internet booksellers who lack that reputation will have to differentiate their products on the basis of price, as the two fictitious firms listed in the table have done. So, the difference in the prices of products offered on Web sites does *not* violate the law of one price. A book Amazon.com offers for sale is not the same product as a book JustStartedinBusinessLastWednesday.com offers for sale.

15.2 | Explain how a firm can increase its profits through price discrimination.

# Price Discrimination: Charging Different Prices for the Same Product

**Price discrimination** Charging different prices to different customers for the same product when the price differences are not due to differences in cost.

We saw at the beginning of this chapter that the Walt Disney Company charges different prices for the same product: admission to Disney World. Charging different prices to different customers for the same good or service when the price differences are not due to differences in cost is called **price discrimination**. But doesn't price discrimination

## Don't Let This Happen to **YOU!**

### Don't Confuse Price Discrimination with Other Types of Discrimination

Don't confuse price discrimination with discrimination based on race or gender. Discriminating on the basis of arbitrary characteristics, like race or gender, is illegal under the civil rights laws. Price discrimination is legal because it involves charging people different prices on the basis of their willingness to pay rather than on the basis of arbitrary characteristics. There is a gray area, however, when companies charge different prices on the basis of race or gender. For example, insurance companies usually charge women lower prices than men for automobile insurance. The courts have ruled that this is not illegal discrimination under the civil rights laws because women, on average, have better driving records than men. Because the costs of insuring men are higher than the costs of insuring women, insurance companies are allowed to charge them higher prices. Notice that this is not actually price discrimination as we have defined it here. Price discrimination involves charging different prices for the same product *where the price differences are not due to differences in cost.*

Insurance companies have been less successful in defending the practice of charging black people higher life insurance prices than white people. The insurance companies had claimed that this practice, which continued into the 1960s, was based on the shorter average life span of black people. Even though most insurance companies stopped the practice in the 1960s for new policies, most companies continued to collect the higher prices on policies that were already in effect. When this became widely known, several state insurance commissions launched investigations. Eventually, most companies reimbursed policyholders for the higher prices and paid substantial fines to the government. MetLife, the largest publicly held life insurance company in the United States, paid $250 million to settle a lawsuit by policyholders and to pay fines imposed by the New York State Insurance Department.

contradict the law of one price? Why doesn't the possibility of arbitrage profits lead people to buy at the low price and resell at the high price?

## The Requirements for Successful Price Discrimination

A successful strategy of price discrimination has three requirements:

1 A firm must possess market power.

2 Some consumers must have a greater willingness to pay for the product than other consumers, and the firm must be able to know what prices customers are willing to pay.

3 The firm must be able to divide up—or *segment*—the market for the product so that consumers who buy the product at a low price are not able to resell it at a high price. In other words, price discrimination will not work if arbitrage is possible.

Note that a firm selling in a perfectly competitive market cannot practice price discrimination because it can only charge the market price. But because most firms do not sell in perfectly competitive markets, they have market power and can set the price of the good they sell. Many firms may also be able to determine that some customers have a greater willingness to pay for the product than others. However, the third requirement—that markets be segmented so that customers buying at a low price will not be able to resell the product—can be difficult to fulfill. For example, some people really love Big Macs and would be willing to pay $10 rather than do without one. Other people would not be willing to pay a penny more than $1 for one. Even if McDonald's could identify differences in the willingness of its customers to pay for Big Macs, it would not be able to charge them different prices. Suppose McDonald's knows that Joe is willing to pay $10, whereas Jill will pay only $1. If McDonald's tries to charge Joe $10, he will just have Jill buy his Big Mac for him.

Only firms that can keep consumers from reselling a product are able to practice price discrimination. Because buyers cannot resell the product, the law of one price does not hold. For example, movie theaters know that many people are willing to pay more to see a movie at night than during the afternoon. As a result, theaters usually charge higher prices for tickets to night showings than for tickets to afternoon showings. They keep these markets separate by making the tickets to afternoon showings a different color or by having the time printed on them, and by having a ticket taker examine the tickets. That makes it difficult for someone to buy a lower-priced ticket in the afternoon and use the ticket to gain admission to an evening showing.

Figure 15-1 illustrates how the owners of movie theaters use price discrimination to increase their profits. The marginal cost to the movie theater owner from another person attending a showing is very small: a little more wear on a theater seat and a few more kernels of popcorn to be swept from the floor. In previous chapters, we assumed that marginal cost has a U shape. In Figure 15-1, we assume for simplicity that marginal cost is a constant $0.50, shown as a horizontal line. Panel (a) shows the demand for afternoon showings. In this segment of its market, the theater should maximize profit by selling the number of tickets for which marginal revenue equals marginal cost, or 450 tickets. We know from the demand curve that the theater can sell 450 tickets at a price of $4.50 per ticket. Panel (b) shows the demand for night showings. Notice that charging $4.50 per ticket would *not* be profit maximizing in this market. At a price of $4.50, the theater sells 850 tickets, which is 225 more tickets than the profit-maximizing number of 625. By charging $4.50 for tickets to afternoon showings and $6.75 for tickets to night showings, the theater has maximized profits.

Figure 15-1 also illustrates another important point about price discrimination: When firms can price discriminate, they will charge customers who are less sensitive to price—those whose demand for the product is *less elastic*—a higher price and charge customers who are more sensitive to price—those whose demand is *more elastic*—a lower price. In this case, the demand for tickets to night showings is less elastic, so the price charged is higher, and the demand for tickets to afternoon showings is more elastic, so the price charged is lower.

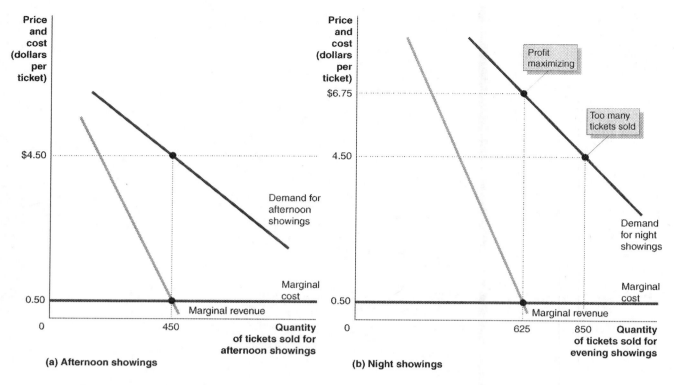

**Figure 15-1** | Price Discrimination by a Movie Theater

Fewer people want to go to the movies in the afternoon than in the evening. In panel (a), the profit-maximizing price for a ticket to an afternoon showing is $4.50. Charging this same price for night showings would not be profit maximizing, as panel (b) shows. At a price of $4.50, 850 tickets would be sold to night showings, which is more than the profit-maximizing number of 625 tickets. To maximize profits, the theater should charge $6.75 for tickets to night showings.

# Solved Problem | 15-2

## How Dell Computer Uses Price Discrimination to Increase Profits

According to an article in the *Wall Street Journal*, "On Dell's Web site recently, the same Optiplex business desktop PC priced at $1,498 for education customers was offered at $1,426 on a page devoted to health-care customers." Why would Dell charge different prices for the same computer, depending on whether the buyer is an education customer or a health-care customer? Draw a graph to illustrate your answer.

### SOLVING THE PROBLEM:

**Step 1:** **Review the chapter material.** This problem is about using price discrimination to increase profits, so you may want to review the section "Price Discrimination: Charging Different Prices for the Same Product," which begins on page 510.

**Step 2:** **Explain why charging different prices to education customers and health care customers will increase Dell's profits.** It makes sense for Dell to charge different prices if education customers have a different price elasticity of demand than do health-care customers. In that case, Dell will charge the market segment with the less elastic demand a higher price and the market segment with the more elastic demand a lower price. Because education customers are being charged the higher price, they must have a less elastic demand than health-care customers.

**Step 3:** **Draw a graph to illustrate your answer.** Your graph should look like the one below, where we have chosen hypothetical quantities to illustrate the ideas. As in the case of movie theaters, you can assume for simplicity that the marginal cost is constant; in the graph we assume that marginal cost is $400.

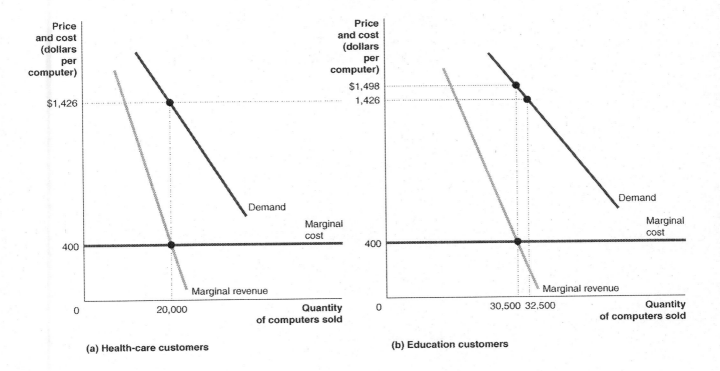

**(a) Health-care customers**          **(b) Education customers**

The graph shows that in the health-care customers segment of the market, marginal revenue equals marginal cost at 20,000 computers sold. Therefore, Dell should charge a price of $1,426 to maximize profits. But if Dell also charged $1,426 in the education customers segment of the market, it would sell 32,500 computers, which is more than the profit-maximizing quantity. By charging $1,498 to education customers, Dell will sell 30,500 computers, the profit-maximizing quantity. We have shown that Dell maximizes its profits by charging education customers a higher price than health care customers. Notice that although the demand curve in panel (a) is more elastic, it is also steeper. This reminds us of the important point from Chapter 5 that elasticity is different from slope.

Source: David Bank and Gary McWilliams, "Picking a Big Fight with Dell, H-P Cuts PC Profits Razor-Thin," *Wall Street Journal*, May 12, 2004.

>> **End Solved Problem 15-2**

# Airlines: The Kings of Price Discrimination

Airline seats are a perishable product. Once a plane has taken off from Chicago for Los Angeles, any seat that has not been sold on that particular flight will never be sold. In addition, the marginal cost of flying one additional passenger is low. This situation gives airlines a strong incentive to manage prices so that as many seats as possible are filled on each flight.

Airlines divide their customers into two main categories: business travelers and leisure travelers. Business travelers often have inflexible schedules, can't commit until the last minute to traveling on a particular day, and, most importantly, are not very sensitive to changes in price. The opposite is true for leisure travelers: They are flexible about when they travel, willing to buy their tickets well in advance, and sensitive to changes in price. Based on what we discussed earlier in this chapter, you can see that airlines will maximize profits by charging business travelers higher ticket prices than leisure travelers, but they need to determine who is a business traveler and who is a leisure traveler. Some airlines do this by requiring people who want to buy a ticket at the leisure price to buy 14 days in advance and to stay at their destination over a Saturday night. Anyone unable to meet these requirements must pay a much higher price. Because business travelers often cannot make their plans 14 days in advance of their flight and don't want to stay over a weekend, they end up paying the higher ticket price. The gap between leisure fares and business fares is often very substantial. For example, in April 2007, the price of a leisure-fare ticket between New York and San Francisco on United Airlines was $308. The price of a business-fare ticket was $1,198.

The airlines go well beyond a single leisure fare and a single business fare in their pricing strategies. Although they ordinarily charge high prices for tickets sold only a few days in advance, they are willing to reduce prices for seats that they expect will not be sold at existing prices. Since the late 1980s, airlines have employed economists and mathematicians to construct computer models of the market for airline tickets. To calculate a suggested price each day for each seat, these models take into account factors that affect the demand for tickets, such as the season of the year, the length of the route, the day of the week, and whether the flight typically attracts primarily business or leisure travelers. This practice of continually adjusting prices to take into account fluctuations in demand is called *yield management*.

Since the late 1990s, Internet sites such as Priceline.com have helped the airlines to implement yield management. On Priceline.com, buyers commit to paying a price of their choosing for a ticket on a particular day and agree that they will fly at any time on that day. This gives airlines the opportunity to fill seats that otherwise would have gone empty, particularly on late night or early morning flights, even though the price may be well below the normal leisure fare. In 2001, several airlines combined to form the Internet site Orbitz, which became another means of filling seats at discount prices. In fact, in the past few years, the chance that you paid the same price for your airline ticket as the person sitting next to you has become quite small. Figure 15-2 shows an actual

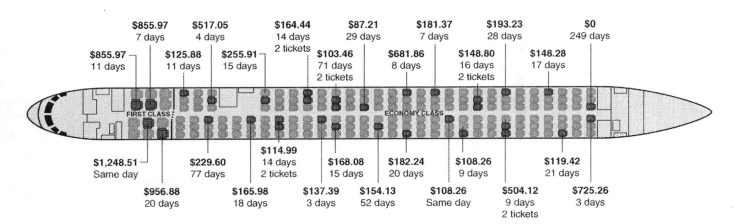

**Figure 15-2 | 33 Customers and 27 Different Prices**

To fill as many seats on a flight as possible, airlines charge many different ticket prices. The 33 passengers on this United Airlines flight from Chicago to Los Angeles paid 27 different prices for their tickets, including one passenger who used frequent flyer miles to obtain a free ticket. The first number in the figure is the price paid for the ticket; the second number is the number of days in advance that the ticket was purchased.
Source: Matthew L. Wald, "So, How Much Did You Pay for Your Ticket?" *New York Times*, April 12, 1998. Used with permission of New York Times Agency.

United Airlines flight from Chicago to Los Angeles. The 33 passengers on the flight paid 27 different prices for their tickets, including one passenger who used frequent flyer miles to obtain a free ticket.

## Making the Connection | How Colleges Use Yield Management

Traditionally, colleges have based financial aid decisions only on the incomes of prospective students. In recent years, however, many colleges have started using yield management techniques, first developed for the airlines, to determine the amount of financial aid they offer different students. Colleges typically use a name like "financial aid engineering" or "student enrollment management" rather than "yield management" to describe what they are doing. There is an important difference between the airlines and colleges: Colleges are interested not just in maximizing the revenue they receive from student tuition but also in increasing the academic quality of the students who enroll.

The "price" of a college education equals the tuition charged minus any financial aid received. When colleges use yield management techniques, they increase financial aid offers to students likely to be more price sensitive, and they reduce financial aid offers to students likely to be less price sensitive. As Stanford economist Caroline Hoxby puts it, "Universities are trying to find the people whose decisions will be changed by these [financial aid] grants." Some of the factors colleges use to judge how sensitive to price students are likely to be include whether they applied for early admission, whether they came for an on-campus interview, their intended major, their home state, and the level of their family's income. Focusing on one of these factors, William F. Elliot, vice president for enrollment management at Carnegie Mellon University, advises, "If finances are a concern, you shouldn't be applying any place [for] early decision" because you are less likely to receive a large financial aid offer.

Many students (and their parents) are critical of colleges that use yield management techniques in allocating financial aid. Some colleges, such as those in the Ivy League, have large enough endowments to meet all of their students' financial aid needs, so they don't practice yield management. Less well-endowed colleges defend the practice on the grounds that it allows them to recruit the best students at a lower cost in financial aid.

*Some colleges use yield management techniques to determine financial aid.*

Sources: Jane J. Kim and Anjali Athavaley, "Colleges Seek to Address Affordability," *Wall Street Journal*, May 3, 2007; and Albert B. Crenshaw, "Price Wars on Campus: Colleges Use Discounts to Draw Best Mix of Top Students, Paying Customers," *Washington Post*, October 15, 2002; and Steve Stecklow, "Expensive Lesson: Colleges Manipulate Financial-Aid Offers, *Wall Street Journal*, April 1, 1996.

## Perfect Price Discrimination

If a firm knew every consumer's willingness to pay—and could keep consumers who bought a product at a low price from reselling it—the firm could charge every consumer a different price. In this case of *perfect price discrimination*—also known as *first-degree price discrimination*—each consumer would have to pay a price equal to the consumer's willingness to pay and, therefore, would receive no consumer surplus. To see why, remember that consumer surplus is the difference between the highest price a consumer is willing to pay for a product and the price the consumer actually pays. But if the price the consumer pays is the maximum the consumer would be willing to pay, there is no consumer surplus.

Figure 15-3 shows the effects of perfect price discrimination. To simplify the discussion, we assume that the firm is a monopoly and that it has constant marginal and average costs. Panel (a) should be familiar from Chapter 14. It shows the case of a monopolist who cannot price discriminate and, therefore, can charge only a single price for its product. The monopolist maximizes profits by producing the level of output where marginal revenue equals marginal cost. Recall that the economically efficient level of output occurs where price is equal to marginal cost, which is the level of output in a perfectly competitive market. Because the monopolist produces where price is greater than marginal cost, it causes a loss of economic efficiency equal to the area of the deadweight loss triangle in the figure.

Panel (b) shows the situation of a monopolist practicing perfect price discrimination. Because the firm can now charge each consumer the maximum the consumer is willing to pay, its marginal revenue from selling one more unit is equal to the price of that unit. Therefore, the monopolist's marginal revenue curve becomes equal to its demand curve, and the firm will continue to produce up to the point where price is equal to marginal cost. It may seem like a paradox, but the ability to perfectly price discriminate causes the monopolist to produce the efficient level of output. By doing so, it converts into profits what in panel (a) had been consumer surplus *and* what had been deadweight loss. In both panel (a) and panel (b), the profit shown is also producer surplus.

Even though the result in panel (b) is more economically efficient than the result in panel (a), consumers clearly are worse off because the amount of consumer surplus has been reduced to zero. We probably will never see a case of perfect price discrimination in the real world because firms typically do not know how much each consumer is willing to pay and therefore cannot charge each consumer a different price. Still, this extreme case helps us to see the two key results of price discrimination:

1 Profits increase.

2 Consumer surplus decreases.

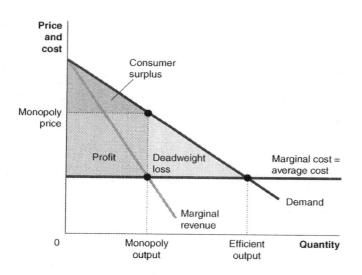

**(a) A monopolist who cannot practice price discrimination**

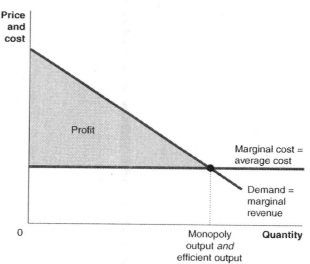

**(b) A monopolist practicing perfect price discrimination**

## Figure 15-3 | Perfect Price Discrimination

Panel (a) shows the case of a monopolist who cannot price discriminate and, therefore, can charge only a single price for its product. The graph, like those in Chapter 14, shows that to maximize profits, the monopolist will produce the level of output where marginal revenue equals marginal cost. The resulting profit is shown by the area of the green rectangle. Given the monopoly price, the amount of consumer surplus in this market is shown by the area of the blue triangle. The economically efficient level of output occurs where price equals marginal cost. Because the monopolist stops production at a level of output where price is above marginal cost, there is a deadweight loss equal to the area of the yellow triangle. In panel (b), the monopolist is able to perfectly price discriminate by charging a different price to each consumer. The result is to convert both the consumer surplus *and* the deadweight loss from panel (a) into profit.

With perfect price discrimination, economic efficiency is improved. Can we also say that this will be the case if price discrimination is less than perfect? Often, less-than-perfect price discrimination will improve economic efficiency. But under certain circumstances, it may actually reduce economic efficiency, so we can't draw a general conclusion.

## Price Discrimination across Time

Firms are sometimes able to engage in price discrimination over time. With this strategy, firms charge a higher price for a product when it is first introduced and a lower price later. Some consumers are *early adopters* who will pay a high price to be among the first to own certain new products. This pattern helps explain why DVD players, digital cameras, and flat-screen plasma televisions all sold for very high prices when they were first introduced. After the demand of the early adopters was satisfied, the companies reduced prices to attract more price-sensitive customers. For example, the price of DVD players dropped by 95 percent within five years of their introduction. Some of the price reductions over time for these products was also due to falling costs as companies took advantage of economies of scale, but some represented price discrimination across time.

Book publishers routinely use price discrimination across time to increase profits. Hardcover editions of novels have much higher prices and are published months before paperback editions. For example, the hardcover edition of Stephen King's novel *Lisey's Story* was published in October 2006 at a price of $28. The paperback edition was published in June 2007 for $9.99. Although this difference in price might seem to reflect the higher costs of hardcover books, in fact, it does not. The marginal cost of printing another copy of the hardcover is about $1.50. The marginal cost of printing another copy of the paperback edition is only slightly less, about $1.25. So, the difference in price between the hardcover and paperback is driven primarily by differences in demand. Stephen King's most devoted fans want to read his next book at the earliest possible moment and are not too sensitive to price. Many casual readers are also interested in King's books but will read something else if the price is too high.

As Figure 15-4 shows, a publisher will maximize profits by segmenting the market—in this case across time—and by charging a higher price to the less elastic market segment and a lower price to the more elastic segment. (This example is similar to our earlier analysis of movie tickets in Figure 15-1 on page 512.) If the publisher had skipped the hardcover and issued only the paperback version at a price of $9.99 when the book was first published in October, its revenue would have dropped by the number of readers who bought the hardcover multiplied by the difference between the price of the hardcover and the price of the paperback, or $500,000 \times (\$28 - 9.99) = \$9,005,000$.

## Can Price Discrimination Be Illegal?

In Chapter 14, we saw that Congress has passed *antitrust laws* to promote competition. Price discrimination may be illegal if its effect is to reduce competition in an industry. In 1936, Congress passed the Robinson–Patman Act, which outlawed price discrimination that reduced competition, but which also contained language that could be interpreted as making illegal *all* price discrimination not based on differences in cost. In the 1960s, the Federal Trade Commission sued the Borden company under this act because Borden was selling the same evaporated milk for two different prices. Cans with the Borden label were sold for a high price, and cans sold to supermarkets to be repackaged as the supermarkets' private brands were sold for a much lower price. The courts ultimately ruled that Borden had not violated the law because the price differences increased, rather than reduced, competition in the market

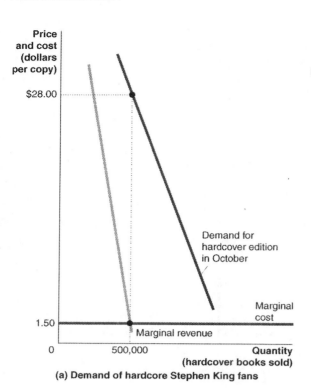

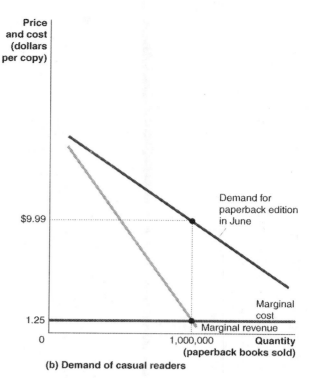

(a) Demand of hardcore Stephen King fans

(b) Demand of casual readers

## Figure 15-4 | Price Discrimination across Time

Publishers issue most novels in hardcover at high prices to satisfy the demand of the novelists' most devoted fans. Later, they publish paperback editions at much lower prices to capture sales from casual readers. In panel (a), with a marginal cost of $1.50 per copy for a hardcover, the profit-maximizing level of output is 500,000 copies, which can be sold at a price of $28. In panel (b), the more elastic demand of casual readers and the slightly lower marginal cost result in a profit-maximizing output of 1,000,000 for the paperback edition, which can be sold at a price of $9.99.

for evaporated milk. In recent years, the courts have interpreted Robinson–Patman narrowly, allowing firms to use the types of price discrimination described in this chapter.

*Why does renting only a few movies get you better service on Netflix?*

**Making** the **Connection**

## Price Discrimination with a Twist at Netflix

Price discrimination usually refers to charging different prices to different consumers for the same good or service. But price discrimination can also involve charging the same price for goods or services of different quality. Netflix, an online DVD rental service, has apparently engaged in this second form of price discrimination. According to a newspaper story, "Netflix customers who pay the same price for the same service are often treated differently, depending on their rental patterns." Netflix subscribers pay a fixed monthly fee to rent a given number of DVDs. For instance, in 2007, Netflix was charging $17.99 per month to rent three DVDs at a time. After a subscriber returns a DVD, Netflix mails that subscriber a new DVD. Subscribers can rent an unlimited number of DVDs per month, although they can have no more than three at any one time. Netflix has become very popular, with more than seven million subscribers by 2007.

But does every Netflix subscriber receive service of the same quality? In particular, does every subscriber have an equal chance of receiving the latest movie released on DVD? Apparently not. Although Netflix does not emphasize it in its advertising, subscribers who rent the fewest movies per month have the best chance of receiving the latest releases and will typically receive their DVDs faster. According to Netflix's Terms of Use (the "fine print" that most subscribers don't read):

> In determining priority for shipping and inventory allocation, we may utilize many different factors. . . . For example, if all other factors are the same, we give priority to those members who receive the fewest DVDs through our service. . . . Also . . . [the service you experience] may be different from the service we provide to other members on the same membership plan.

One Netflix subscriber was quoted in a newspaper article as saying, "Sometimes it would be two or three months before I got [a movie] once it came out on DVD. The longer I was a customer, the worse it got."

Why would Netflix provide better service to subscribers who rent only a few DVDs per month and poorer service to subscribers who rent many DVDs per month? Subscribers who rent many DVDs per month are likely to have less elastic demand— they really like watching movies—than subscribers who rent only a few DVDs per month. As we have seen in this chapter, firms can increase their profits by charging higher prices to consumers with less elastic demand and lower prices to consumers with more elastic demand. But this strategy works only if firms have a way of reliably separating consumers into groups on the basis of how elastic their demand is. When they first subscribe, Netflix has no way of separating their consumers on the basis of how elastic their demand is, so it has to charge the same price to everyone. But after a few months of observing a subscriber's pattern of rentals, Netflix has enough information to determine whether the subscriber's demand is more or less elastic. By reducing the level of service to subscribers with less elastic demand, Netflix is, in effect, raising the price these consumers pay relative to consumers who receive better service. In effect, Netflix is engaging in price discrimination and increasing its profits over what they would be if every subscriber received the same service at the same price.

Sources: Alina Tugend, "Getting Movies from a Store or a Mailbox (or Just a Box)," *New York Times*, August 5, 2006; and "Netflix Critics Slam 'Throttling,'" Associated Press, February 10, 2006.

---

**15.3 LEARNING** OBJECTIVE

15.3 | Explain how some firms increase their profits through the use of odd pricing, cost-plus pricing, and two-part tariffs.

# Other Pricing Strategies

In addition to price discrimination, firms use many different pricing strategies, depending on the nature of their products, the level of competition in their markets, and the characteristics of their customers. In this section, we consider three important strategies: odd pricing, cost-plus pricing, and two-part tariffs.

## Odd Pricing: Why Is the Price $2.99 Instead of $3.00?

Many firms use what is called *odd pricing*—for example, charging $4.95 instead of $5.00, or $199 instead of $200. Surveys show that 80 percent to 90 percent of the products sold in supermarkets have prices ending in "9" or "5" rather than "0." Odd pricing has a long history. In the early nineteenth century, most goods in the United States were sold in general stores and did not have fixed prices. Instead, prices were often determined by haggling, much as prices of new cars are often determined today by haggling on dealers' lots. Later in the nineteenth century, when most products began to sell for a fixed price, odd pricing became popular.

Different explanations have been given for the origin of odd pricing. One explanation is that it began because goods imported from Great Britain had a reputation for high quality. When the prices of British goods in British currency—the pound—were translated into U.S. dollars, the result was an odd price. Because customers connected odd prices with high-quality goods, even sellers of domestic goods charged odd prices. Another explanation is that odd pricing began as an attempt to guard against employee theft. An odd price forced an employee to give the customer change, which reduced the likelihood that the employee would simply pocket the customer's money without recording the sale.

Whatever the origins of odd pricing, why do firms still use it today? The most obvious answer is that an odd price, say $9.99, seems somehow significantly—more than a penny—cheaper than $10.00. But do consumers really have this illusion? To find out, three market researchers conducted a study. We saw in Chapter 3 that demand curves can be estimated statistically. If consumers have the illusion that $9.99 is significantly cheaper than $10.00, they will demand a greater quantity of goods at $9.99—and other odd prices—than the estimated demand curve predicts. The researchers surveyed consumers about their willingness to purchase six different products—ranging from a block of cheese to an electric blender—at a series of prices. Ten of the prices were either odd cent prices—99 cents or 95 cents—or odd dollar prices—$95 or $99. Nine of these 10 odd prices resulted in an odd-price effect, with the quantity demanded being greater than predicted using the estimated demand curve. The study was not conclusive because it relied on surveys rather than on observing actual purchasing behavior and because it used only a small group of products, but it does provide some evidence that using odd prices makes economic sense.

## Why Do Firms Use Cost-Plus Pricing?

Many firms use *cost-plus pricing*, which involves adding a percentage *markup* to average cost. With this pricing strategy, the firm first calculates average cost at a particular level of production, usually equal to the firm's expected sales. It then increases average cost by a percentage amount, say 30 percent, to arrive at the price. For example, if average cost is $100 and the percentage markup is 30 percent, the price will be $130. In a firm selling multiple products, the markup is intended to cover all costs, including those that the firm cannot assign to any particular product. Most firms have costs that are difficult to assign to one particular product. For example, the work performed by the employees in McDonald's accounting and finance departments applies to all of McDonald's products and can't be assigned directly to Big Macs or Happy Meals.

Making | **Cost-Plus Pricing in the**
the | **Publishing Industry**
Connection |

Book publishing companies incur substantial costs for editing, designing, marketing, and warehousing books. These costs are difficult to assign directly to any particular book. Most publishers arrive at a price for a book by applying a markup to their production costs, which are usually divided into plant costs and manufacturing costs. Plant costs include typesetting the manuscript and preparing graphics or artwork for printing. Manufacturing costs include the costs of printing, paper, and binding the book.

Consider the following example for the hypothetical new book by Adam Smith, *How to Succeed at Economics without Really Trying*. We will assume that the book is 250 pages long, the publisher expects to sell 5,000 copies, and plant and manufacturing costs are as given in the following table:

**PLANT COST**

|  | | |
|---|---|---|
| | Typesetting | $3,500 |
| | Other plant costs | 2,000 |

**MANUFACTURING COST**

|  | | |
|---|---|---|
| | Printing | $5,750 |
| | Paper | 6,250 |
| | Binding | 5,000 |

**TOTAL PRODUCTION COST**

|  | | |
|---|---|---|
| | | $22,500 |

With total production cost of $22,500 and production of 5,000 books, the per-unit production cost is $22,500/5,000 = $4.50. Many publishers multiply the unit production cost number by 7 or 8 to arrive at the retail price they will charge customers in bookstores. In this case, multiplying by 7 results in a price of $31.50 for the book. The markup seems quite high, but publishers typically sell books to bookstores at a 40 percent discount. Although a customer in a bookstore will pay $31.50 for the book—or less, of course, if it is purchased from a bookseller that discounts the retail price—the publisher receives only $18.90. The difference between the $18.90 received from the bookstore and the $4.50 production cost equals the cost of editing, marketing, warehousing, and all other costs, including the opportunity cost of the investment in the firm by its owners, plus any economic profit received by the owners.

Source: Beth Luey, *Handbook for Academic Authors*, 4th ed., New York: Cambridge University Press, 2002.

A difficulty that firms face when using cost-plus pricing should be obvious to you. In this chapter, as in the previous four chapters, we have emphasized that firms maximize profit by producing the quantity where marginal revenue equals marginal cost and charging a price that will cause consumers to buy this quantity. The cost-plus approach doesn't appear to maximize profits unless the cost-plus price turns out to be the same as the price that will cause the quantity sold to be where marginal revenue is equal to marginal cost. Economists have two views of cost-plus pricing. One is that cost-plus pricing is simply a mistake that firms should avoid. The other view is that cost-plus pricing is a good way to come close to the profit-maximizing price when either marginal revenue or marginal cost is difficult to calculate.

Small firms often like cost-plus pricing because it is easy to use. Unfortunately, these firms can fall into the trap of mechanically applying a cost-plus pricing rule, which can result in charging prices that do not maximize profits. The most obvious problems with cost-plus pricing are that it ignores demand and focuses on average cost rather than marginal cost. If the firm's marginal cost is significantly different from its average cost at its current level of production, cost-plus pricing is unlikely to maximize profits.

Despite these problems, cost-plus pricing is used by some large firms, such as General Motors, that clearly have the knowledge and resources to devise a better method of pricing if cost-plus pricing fails to maximize profits. Economists conclude that cost-plus pricing may be the best way to determine the optimal price in two situations:

1 When marginal cost and average cost are roughly equal

2 When the firm has difficulty estimating its demand curve

In fact, most large firms that use cost-plus pricing do not just mechanically apply a markup to their estimate of average cost. Instead, they adjust the markup to reflect their best estimate of current demand. At General Motors, for example, a pricing policy committee adjusts prices to reflect its views of the current state of competition in the industry and the current state of the economy. If competition is strong in a weak economy, the pricing committee may decide to set price significantly below the cost-plus price—perhaps by offering buyers a rebate.

In general, firms that take demand into account will charge lower markups on products that are more price elastic and higher markups on products that are less elastic. Supermarkets, where cost-plus pricing is widely used, have markups in the 5 percent to 10 percent range for products with more elastic demand, such as soft drinks and breakfast cereals, and markups in the 50 percent range for products with less elastic demand, such as fresh fruits and vegetables.

## Pricing with Two-Part Tariffs

Some firms can require consumers to pay an initial fee for the right to buy their product and an additional fee for each unit of the product purchased. For example, many golf and tennis clubs require members to buy an annual membership in addition to paying a fee each time they use the tennis court or golf course. Sam's Club requires consumers to pay a membership fee before shopping at its stores. Cellular phone companies charge a monthly fee and then have a per-minute charge after a certain number of minutes have been used. Economists refer to this situation as a **two-part tariff**.

The Walt Disney Company is in a position to use a two-part tariff by charging consumers for admission to Walt Disney World or Disneyland and also charging them to use the rides in the parks. As mentioned at the beginning of this chapter, at one time, the admission price to Disneyland was low, but people had to purchase tickets to go on the rides. Today, you must pay a high price for admission to Disneyland or Disney World, but the rides are free once you're in the park. Figure 15-5 helps us understand which of these pricing strategies is more profitable for Disney. The numbers in the figure are simplified to make the calculations easier.

Once visitors are inside the park, Disney is in the position of a monopolist—no other firm is operating rides in Disney World. So, we can draw panel (a) in Figure 15-5 to represent the market for rides at Disney World. This graph looks like the standard monopoly graph from Chapter 14. (Note that the marginal cost of another rider is quite low. We can assume that it is a constant $2 and equal to the average cost.) It seems obvious—but it will turn out to be wrong!—that Disney should determine the profit-maximizing quantity of ride tickets by setting marginal revenue equal to marginal cost. In this case, that would lead to 20,000 ride tickets sold per day at a price of $26 per ride. Disney's profit from selling *ride tickets* is shown by the area of the light-green rectangle, *B*. It equals the difference between the $26 price and the average cost of $2, multiplied by the 20,000 tickets sold, or ($26 − $2) × 20,000 = $480,000. Disney also has a second source of profit from selling *admission tickets* to the park. Given the $26 price for ride tickets, what price would Disney be able to charge for admission tickets?

Let's assume the following for simplicity: The only reason people want admission to Disney World is to go on the rides, all consumers have the same individual demand curve for rides, and Disney knows what this demand curve is. This last assumption allows Disney to be able to practice perfect price discrimination. More realistic assumptions would make the outcome of the analysis somewhat different but would not affect

**Two-part tariff** A situation in which consumers pay one price (or tariff) for the right to buy as much of a related good as they want at a second price.

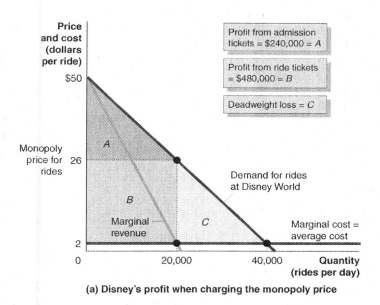

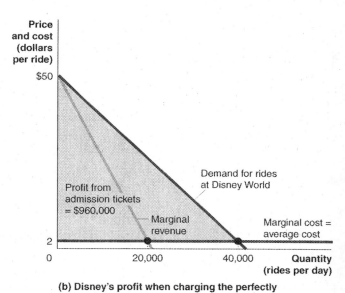

(a) Disney's profit when charging the monopoly price

(b) Disney's profit when charging the perfectly competitive price

**Figure 15-5 | A Two-Part Tariff at Disney World**

In panel (a), Disney charges the monopoly price of $26 per ride ticket and sells 20,000 ride tickets. Its profit from *ride tickets* is shown by the area of the light-green rectangle, *B*, $480,000. If Disney is in the position of knowing every consumer's willingness to pay, it can also charge a price for *admission tickets* that would result in the total amount paid for admission tickets being equal to total consumer surplus from the rides. Total consumer surplus from the rides equals the area of the dark-green trian-

gle, *A*, or $240,000. So, when charging the monopoly price, Disney's total profit equals $480,000 + $240,000, or $720,000. In panel (b), Disney charges the perfectly competitive price of $2, where marginal revenue equals marginal cost, and sells 40,000 ride tickets. At the lower ride ticket price, Disney can charge a higher price for admission tickets, which will increase its total profits from operating the park to the area of the light-green triangle, or $960,000.

the main point of how Disney uses a two-part tariff to increase its profits. With these assumptions, we can use the concept of consumer surplus to calculate the maximum total amount consumers would be willing to pay for admission. Remember that consumer surplus is equal to the area below the demand curve and above the price line, shown by the dark-green triangle, *A*, in panel (a). The area represents the benefit to buyers from consuming the product. In this case, consumers would not be willing to pay more for admission to the park than the consumer surplus they receive from the rides. In panel (a) of Figure 15-5, the total consumer surplus when Disney charges a price of $26 per ride is $240,000. (This number is easy to calculate if you remember that the formula for the area of a triangle is ½ × base × height, or ½ × 20,000 × $24.) Disney can set the price of admission tickets so that the *total* amount spent by buyers would be $240,000. In other words, Disney can set the price of admission to capture the entire consumer surplus from the rides. So, Disney's total profit from Disney World would be the $240,000 it receives from admission tickets plus the $480,000 in profit from the rides, or $720,000 per day.

Is this the most profit Disney can earn from selling admission tickets and ride tickets? The answer is "no." The key to seeing why is to notice that *the lower the price Disney charges for ride tickets, the higher the price it can charge for admission tickets.* Lower-priced ride tickets increase consumer surplus from the rides and, therefore, increase the willingness of buyers to pay a higher price for admission tickets. In panel (b) of Figure 15-5, we assume that Disney acts as it would in a perfectly competitive market and charges a price for ride tickets that is equal to marginal cost, or $2. Charging this price increases consumer surplus—— *and* the maximum total amount that Disney can charge for admission tickets—from $240,000 to $960,000. (Once again, we use the formula for the area of a triangle to calculate the light-green area in panel (b): ½ × 40,000 × 48 × $960,000) Disney's profits from the rides will decline to

TABLE 15-2

Disney's Profits per Day from
Different Pricing Strategies

| | MONOPOLY PRICE FOR RIDES | COMPETITIVE PRICE FOR RIDES |
|---|---|---|
| PROFITS FROM ADMISSION TICKETS | $240,000 | $960,000 |
| PROFITS FROM RIDE TICKETS | 480,000 | 0 |
| TOTAL PROFIT | 720,000 | 960,000 |

zero because it is now charging a price equal to average cost, *but its total profit from Disney World will rise from $720,000 per day to $960,000.* Table 15-2 summarizes this result.

What is the source of Disney's increased profit from charging a price equal to marginal cost? The answer is that Disney has converted what was deadweight loss when the monopoly price was charged—the area of triangle *C* in panel (a)—into consumer surplus. It then turns this consumer surplus into profit by increasing the price of admission tickets.

It is important to note the following about the outcome of a firm using an optimal two-part tariff:

1 Because price equals marginal cost at the level of output supplied, the outcome is economically efficient.

2 All of consumer surplus is transformed into profit.

Notice that, in effect, Disney is practicing perfect price discrimination. As we noted in our discussion of perfect price discrimination on page 515, Disney's use of a two-part tariff has increased the amount of the product—in this case, rides at Disney World—consumers are able to purchase, but has eliminated consumer surplus. Although it may seem paradoxical, consumer surplus was actually higher when consumers were being charged the monopoly price for the rides. The solution to the paradox is that although consumers pay a lower price for the rides when Disney employs a two-part tariff, the overall amount they pay to be at Disney World increases.

Disney actually does follow the profit-maximizing strategy of charging a high price for admission to the park and a very low price—zero—for the rides. It seems that Disney could increase its profits by raising the price for the rides from zero to the marginal cost of the rides. But the marginal cost is so low that it would not be worth the expense of printing ride tickets and hiring additional workers to sell the tickets and collect them at each ride. Finally, note that because the demand curves of Disney's customers are not all the same, and because Disney does not actually know precisely what these demand curves are, Disney is not able to convert all of consumer surplus into profit.

*The rides at Disney World are free—once you have paid to get into the park.*

# Conclusion

Firms in perfectly competitive industries must sell their products at the market price. For firms in other industries—which means, of course, the vast majority of firms—pricing is an important part of the strategy used to maximize profits. We have seen in this chapter, for example, that if firms can successfully segment their customers into different groups on the basis of willingness to pay, they can increase their profits by charging different segments different prices.

Read *An Inside Look* on the next page for a discussion of why colleges do not charge all students the same tuition.

## *WALL STREET JOURNAL*, OCTOBER 11, 2006

# Amid Rising Costs and Criticism, Some Colleges Cut Back Merit Aid

As colleges and universities consider whether to join Harvard and Princeton in abandoning early-admissions programs, some are also trying to roll back another popular recruiting tool: merit aid.

Colleges offer merit aid, which is typically awarded on the basis of grades, class rank and test scores, to students who ordinarily wouldn't qualify for financial help. Because merit aid can be a deciding factor in these students' choice of schools, it has become a major weapon in the bidding wars among colleges for high achievers who can help boost their national rankings. . . .

But the cost of such programs has mounted as their use has expanded and tuition has risen. Meanwhile, criticism has grown that they disproportionately benefit students from wealthier communities with better school systems, siphoning resources away from lower-income students with greater financial need. In some cases, students who qualify for neither need- nor merit-based aid end up paying even more to cover a college's costs. As a result, a small but growing number of schools and university systems are trying to reduce their merit offerings. The University of Florida recently slashed the value of its four-year scholarships for in-state scholars who qualified under the National Merit program by 79% to a total of $5,000. . . .

Allegheny College, in Meadville, Pa., where annual tuition and fees total about $28,300, gave its $15,000-a-year merit scholarships to 15% of this year's freshmen, down from about 33% three years ago. To free up funding for more need-based aid, Rhode Island's Providence College scuttled its smaller merit scholarships and raised the eligibility requirements for its larger ones: A grade-point average of about 3.7 on a 4.0 scale used to be good enough; now it takes around a 3.83. Providence's merit scholarships can run as high as full tuition, which is $26,780 this year. . . .

Efforts to cut back on merit aid also risk setting off a backlash from middle- and upper-income families who don't qualify for need-based aid but are finding the rising cost of a college to be a daunting stretch. "Family income isn't keeping pace with the things driving higher-education costs," says Jim Scannell, a partner at Scannell & Kurz Inc., a Pittsford, N.Y., consulting firm that works with colleges on enrollment issues.

Some high-achieving applicants target schools that have merit-aid programs, hoping to win a tuition break. With tuition and fees at many private schools surpassing $40,000 a year, small private liberal-arts colleges that lack the cachet of the Ivy League but whose tuitions far exceed those of state colleges could have the most to lose from any cutbacks in merit aid. . . .

Many institutions have no intention of cutting back on merit aid. Baylor University, a Baptist college in Waco, Texas, recently increased the value of the merit awards it gives to all incoming freshmen who score at least 1,300 points out of a possible 1,600 on SAT reading and math exams. The awards, which rise in value in tandem with a student's SAT scores, range from $2,000 to $4,000 a year. . . .

For some smaller schools, merit aid is less about boosting rankings than adding revenue by swelling enrollment. In most cases, students are still paying substantial sums for tuition even after receiving a scholarship. "I think in many cases it's misleading to call it merit aid," says Michael McPherson, president of the Spencer Foundation, a Chicago-based educational research group. "It's 'get 'em in the door' aid."

At private Wilkes University, Wilkes Barre, Pa., where tuition and fees are about $23,000 a year, only 81 of this year's 580 incoming freshmen didn't get merit aid. To land a scholarship, which starts at $6,000 a year, students have to have graduated in the top half of their high-school class and to have scored a combined total of at least a 900 on the SAT reading and math exams, not much above average. . . .

Although families with earnings of $100,000 or more might qualify for need-based aid, depending on factors such as how many college-aged children they have, college administrators say many such families usually don't bother to apply for need-based aid because they presume they won't get it. . . .

Source: Robert Tomsho, "Amid Rising Costs and Criticism, Some Colleges Cut Back Merit Aid," Wall Street Journal, October 11, 2006.

## Key Points in the Article

This article highlights a change in the scholarships offered by universities and colleges. In particular, colleges are reducing merit aid and increasing the amount of need-based financial aid. Because many students receive scholarships and other types of aid, they pay a variety of actual tuition prices, which may be very different from the posted tuition price.

## Analyzing the News

**(a)** High-achieving students are typically offered admission by a number of different universities, many of which are good substitutes for each other. As a result, talented high school seniors would have a relatively elastic demand for attending any particular college. Consumers with more elastic demands tend to pay lower prices for goods.

**(b)** Need-based aid can be thought of as a form of price discrimination, separating the market into high-income students (with high demand) and low-income students (with low demand). Panel (a) in the figure below shows two demand curves for college education: one for high-income students and the other for low-income students. Notice that for any quantity, high-income students have a higher willingness to pay for education. So for $Q_1$ of each type of student to be enrolled, the school could charge $P_1$ dollars to high-income students but only $P_2$ dollars to low-income students. Need-based aid makes it possible to charge a lower price to low-income students without changing the tuition price charged to high-income students. You can see in panel (a) that if the school had to charge $P_1$ to both types of students, it would still enroll $Q_1$ high-income students but only $Q_2$ low-income students, so it would not maximize revenue.

**(c)** An additional student adds very little to the cost of running a college or university. As a result, offering merit aid is usually not the difference between a student paying full tuition or reduced tuition; it is the difference between a student enrolling and paying some tuition or not enrolling and paying $0 to the school. Panel (b) in the figure below shows the demand curve for enrollment at a school. Notice that in this example as the price drops from $P_1$ to $P_2$, there is a large increase in quantity, from $Q_1$ to $Q_2$ students. If the demand for education at a particular college is elastic, as it likely is, tuition revenues will increase as the school lowers its price. At the higher price, $P_1$, with $Q_1$ students, revenue is shown as areas $A + B$. If tuition drops, revenue at price $P_2$ with $Q_2$ students will be areas $B + C$. The school will be better off if the increased revenue from additional students is (area $C$) greater than the lost revenue from the lower price now charged to the original $Q_1$ students (area $A$). In this example, area $C$ is greater than area $A$, so the college's revenues increase when it cuts its tuition.

## Thinking Critically

1. If lowering the tuition to some students increases a university's revenue, why don't universities just lower the tuition for everyone?

2. If customers with less elastic demands will pay more for a product when firms can price discriminate, would you expect to see freshmen or seniors pay higher tuition at your college? How might a college charge different classes different levels of tuition?

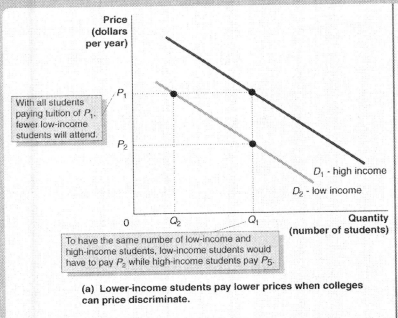

(a) Lower-income students pay lower prices when colleges can price discriminate.

College tuition strategies.

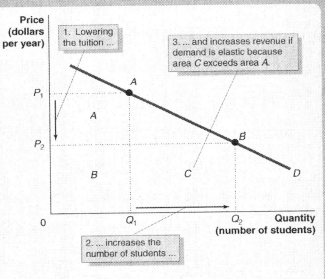

(b) Demand and revenue at different tuition prices.

# Chapter 12
# Oligopoly

**Oligopoly** A market structure in which a small number of interdependent firms compete.

In Chapters 11 and 12, we studied perfectly competitive and monopolistically competitive industries. Our analysis focused on the determination of a firm's profit-maximizing price and quantity. We concluded that firms maximize profit by producing where marginal revenue equals marginal cost. To determine marginal revenue and marginal cost, we used graphs that included the firm's demand, marginal revenue, and marginal cost curves. In this chapter, we will study **oligopoly**, a market structure in which a small number of interdependent firms compete. In analyzing oligopoly, we cannot rely on the same types of graphs we used in analyzing perfect competition and monopolistic competition—for two reasons.

First, we need to use economic models that allow us to analyze the more complex business strategies of large oligopoly firms. Second, even in determining the profit-maximizing price and output of an oligopoly firm, demand curves and cost curves are not as useful as in the cases of perfect competition and monopolistic competition. We are able to draw the demand curves for competitive firms by assuming that the prices these firms charge have no impact on the prices other firms in their industries charge. This assumption is realistic when each firm is small relative to the market. It is not a realistic assumption, however, for firms that are as large relative to their markets as Microsoft, Dell, or Wal-Mart.

When large firms cut their prices, their rivals in the industry often—but not always—respond by also cutting their prices. Because we don't know for sure how other firms will respond to a price change, we don't know the quantity an oligopolist will sell at a particular price. In other words, it is difficult to know what an oligopolist's demand curve will look like. As we have seen, a firm's marginal revenue curve depends on its demand curve. If we don't know what an oligopolist's demand curve looks like, we also don't know what its marginal revenue curve looks like. Not knowing marginal revenue, we can't calculate the profit-maximizing level of output and the profit-maximizing price the way we did for competitive firms.

The approach we use to analyze competition among oligopolists is called *game theory*. Game theory can be used to analyze any situation in which groups or individuals interact. In the context of economic analysis, game theory is the study of the decisions of firms in industries where the profits of each firm depend on its interactions with other firms. It has been applied to strategies for nuclear war, for international trade negotiations, and for political campaigns, among many other examples. In this chapter, we use game theory to analyze the business strategies of large firms.

---

13.1 | Show how barriers to entry explain the existence of oligopolies.

# Oligopoly and Barriers to Entry

*Oligopolies* are industries with only a few firms. This market structure lies between the competitive industries we studied in Chapters 11 and 12, which have many firms, and the monopolies we will study in Chapter 14, which have only a single firm. One measure of the extent of competition in an industry is the *concentration ratio*. Every five years, the U.S. Bureau of the Census publishes four-firm concentration ratios that state the fraction of each industry's sales accounted for by its four largest firms. Most economists believe that a four-firm concentration ratio of greater than 40 percent indicates that an industry is an oligopoly.

The concentration ratio has some flaws as a measure of the extent of competition in an industry. For example, concentration ratios do not include sales in the United States by foreign firms. In addition, concentration ratios are calculated for the national market, even though the competition in some industries, such as restaurants or college bookstores, is mainly local. Finally, competition sometimes exists between firms in different industries. For example, Wal-Mart is included in the discount department stores industry but also competes with firms in the supermarket industry and the retail toy store industry. As we will see in Chapter 14, some economists prefer another measure of competition, known as the *Herfindahl-Hirschman Index*. Despite their shortcomings, concentration ratios can be useful in providing a general idea of the extent of competition in an industry.

Table 13-1 lists examples of oligopolies in manufacturing and retail trade. Notice that the "Discount Department Stores" industry that includes Wal-Mart is highly concentrated. Wal-Mart also operates Sam's Club stores, which are in the highly concentrated "Warehouse Clubs and Supercenters" industry.

## Barriers to Entry

Why do oligopolies exist? Why aren't there many more firms in the discount department store industry, the beer industry, or the automobile industry? Recall that new firms will enter industries where existing firms are earning economic profits. But new firms often have difficulty entering an oligopoly. Anything that keeps new firms from entering an industry in which firms are earning economic profits is called a **barrier to entry**. Three barriers to entry are economies of scale, ownership of a key input, and government-imposed barriers.

*Economies of Scale* The most important barrier to entry is economies of scale. Chapter 10 stated that **economies of scale** exist when a firm's long-run average costs fall as it increases output. The greater the economies of scale, the fewer the number of firms that will be in the industry. Figure 13-1 illustrates this point.

If economies of scale are relatively unimportant in the industry, the typical firm's long-run average cost curve (*LRAC*) will reach a minimum at a level of output ($Q_1$ in Figure 13-1) that is a small fraction of total industry sales. The industry will have room for a large number of firms and will be competitive. If economies of scale are significant, the typical firm will not reach the minimum point on its long-run average cost curve ($Q_2$ in Figure 13-1) until it has produced a large fraction of industry sales. Then the industry will have room for only a few firms and will be an oligopoly.

**Barrier to entry** Anything that keeps new firms from entering an industry in which firms are earning economic profits.

**Economies of scale** The situation when a firm's long-run average costs fall as it increases output.

| RETAIL TRADE | | MANUFACTURING | |
|---|---|---|---|
| **INDUSTRY** | **FOUR-FIRM CONCENTRATION RATIO** | **INDUSTRY** | **FOUR-FIRM CONCENTRATION RATIO** |
| Discount Department Stores | 95% | Cigarettes | 95% |
| Warehouse Clubs and Supercenters | 92% | Beer | 91% |
| Hobby, Toy, and Game Stores | 72% | Aircraft | 81% |
| Athletic Footwear Stores | 71% | Breakfast Cereal | 78% |
| College Bookstores | 70% | Automobiles | 76% |
| Radio, Television, and Other Electronic Stores | 69% | Computers | 76% |
| Pharmacies and Drugstores | 53% | Dog and Cat Food | 64% |

## TABLE 13-1

**Examples of Oligopolies in Retail Trade and Manufacturing**

Source: U.S. Census Bureau, *Concentration Ratios, 2002*, May 2006; and U.S. Census Bureau, *Establishment and Firm Size, 2002*, November 2005.

## Figure 13-1

Economies of Scale Help Determine the Extent of Competition in an Industry

An industry will be competitive if the minimum point on the typical firm's long-run average cost curve ($LRAC_1$) occurs at a level of output that is a small fraction of total industry sales, like $Q_1$. The industry will be an oligopoly if the minimum point comes at a level of output that is a large fraction of industry sales, like $Q_2$.

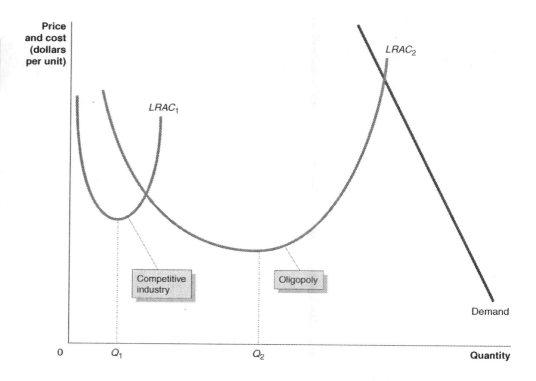

Economies of scale can explain why there is much more competition in the restaurant industry than in the discount department store industry. Because very large restaurants do not have lower average costs than smaller restaurants, the restaurant industry has room for many firms. In contrast, large discount department stores, such as Wal-Mart, have much lower average costs than small discount department stores, for the reasons we discussed in the chapter opener. As a result, just four firms—Wal-Mart, Target, Kmart, and Costco—account for about 95 percent of all sales in this industry.

***Ownership of a Key Input*** If production of a good requires a particular input, then control of that input can be a barrier to entry. For many years, the Aluminum Company of America (Alcoa) controlled most of the world's supply of high-quality bauxite, the mineral needed to produce aluminum. The only way other companies could enter the industry to compete with Alcoa was to recycle aluminum. The De Beers Company of South Africa was able to block competition in the diamond market by controlling the output of most of the world's diamond mines. Until the 1990s, Ocean Spray had very little competition in the market for fresh and frozen cranberries because it controlled almost the entire supply of cranberries. Even today, it controls about 80 percent of the cranberry crop.

***Government-Imposed Barriers*** Firms sometimes try to have the government impose barriers to entry. Many large firms employ *lobbyists* to convince state legislators and members of Congress to pass laws favorable to the economic interests of the firms. There are tens of thousands of lobbyists in Washington, DC, alone. Top lobbyists command annual salaries of $300,000 or more, which indicates the value firms place on their activities. Examples of government-imposed barriers to entry are patents, licensing requirements, and barriers to international trade. A **patent** gives a firm the exclusive right to a new product for a period of 20 years from the date the product is invented. Governments use patents to encourage firms to carry out research and development of new and better products and better ways of producing existing products. Output and living standards increase faster when firms devote resources to research and development, but a firm that spends money to develop a new product may not earn much profit if other firms can copy the product. For example, the pharmaceutical company Merck spends more than $3 billion per year to develop new prescription drugs. If rival compa-

**Patent** The exclusive right to a product for a period of 20 years from the date the product is invented.

nies could freely produce these new drugs as soon as Merck developed them, most of the firm's investment would be wasted. Because Merck can patent a new drug, the firm can charge higher prices during the years the patent is in force and make an economic profit on its successful innovation.

The government also restricts competition through *occupational licensing*. The United States currently has about 500 occupational licensing laws. For example, doctors and dentists in every state need licenses to practice. The justification for the laws is to protect the public from incompetent practitioners, but by restricting the number of people who can enter the licensed professions, the laws also raise prices. Studies have shown that states that make it harder to earn a dentist's license have prices for dental services that are about 15 percent higher than in other states. Similarly, states that require a license for out-of-state firms to sell contact lenses have higher prices for contact lenses. When state licenses are required for occupations like hair braiding, which was done several years ago in California, restricting competition is the main result.

Government also imposes barriers to entering some industries by imposing tariffs and quotas on foreign competition. As we saw in Chapter 8, a *tariff* is a tax on imports, and a *quota* limits the quantity of a good that can be imported into a country. A quota on foreign sugar imports severely limits competition in the U.S. sugar market. As a result, U.S. sugar companies can charge prices that are more than twice as high as those charged by companies outside the United States.

In summary, to earn economic profits, all firms would like to charge a price well above average cost, but earning economic profits attracts new firms to enter the industry. Eventually, the increased competition forces price down to average cost, and firms just break even. In an oligopoly, barriers to entry prevent—or at least slow down—entry, which allows firms to earn economic profits over a longer period.

---

13.2 | Use game theory to analyze the strategies of oligopolistic firms.

# Using Game Theory to Analyze Oligopoly

As we noted at the beginning of the chapter, economists analyze oligopolies using *game theory*, which was developed during the 1940s by the mathematician John von Neumann and the economist Oskar Morgenstern. **Game theory** is the study of how people make decisions in situations in which attaining their goals depends on their interactions with others. In oligopolies, the interactions among firms are crucial in determining profitability because the firms are large relative to the market.

In all games—whether poker, chess, or Monopoly—the interactions among the players are crucial in determining the outcome. In addition, games share three key characteristics:

1 *Rules* that determine what actions are allowable

2 *Strategies* that players employ to attain their objectives in the game

3 *Payoffs* that are the results of the interaction among the players' strategies

In business situations, the rules of the "game" include not just laws that a firm must obey but also other matters beyond a firm's control—at least in the short run—such as its production function. A **business strategy** is a set of actions that a firm takes to achieve a goal, such as maximizing profits. The *payoffs* are the profits earned as a result of a firm's strategies interacting with the strategies of the other firms. The best way to understand the game theory approach is to look at an example.

**Game theory** The study of how people make decisions in situations in which attaining their goals depends on their interactions with others; in economics, the study of the decisions of firms in industries where the profits of each firm depend on its interactions with other firms.

**Business strategy** Actions taken by a firm to achieve a goal, such as maximizing profits.

## A Duopoly Game: Price Competition between Two Firms

In this simple example, we use game theory to analyze price competition in a *duopoly*—an oligopoly with two firms. Suppose that an isolated town in Alaska has only two stores: Wal-Mart and Target. Both stores sell the new Sony PlayStation 3. For simplicity, let's

## Figure 13-2

### A Duopoly Game

Wal-Mart's profits are in blue, and Target's profits are in red. Wal-Mart and Target would each make profits of $10,000 per month on sales of PlayStation 3 if they both charged $600. However, each store manager has an incentive to undercut the other by charging a lower price. If both charge $400, they would each make a profit of only $7,500 per month.

**Payoff matrix** A table that shows the payoffs that each firm earns from every combination of strategies by the firms.

assume that no other stores stock PlayStation 3 and that consumers in the town can't buy it on the Internet or through mail-order catalogs. The manager of each store decides whether to charge $400 or $600 for the PlayStation. Which price will be more profitable depends on the price the other store charges. The decision regarding what price to charge is an example of a business strategy. In Figure 13-2, we organize the possible outcomes that result from the actions of the two firms into a *payoff matrix*. A **payoff matrix** is a table that shows the payoffs that each firm earns from every combination of strategies by the firms.

Wal-Mart's profits are shown in blue, and Target's profits are shown in red. If Wal-Mart and Target both charge $600 for the PlayStation, each store will make a profit of $10,000 per month from sales of the game console. If Wal-Mart charges the lower price of $400, while Target charges $600, Wal-Mart will gain many of Target's customers. Wal-Mart's profits will be $15,000, and Target's will be only $5,000. Similarly, if Wal-Mart charges $600, while Target is charging $400, Wal-Mart's profits will be only $5,000, while Target's profits will be $15,000. If both stores charge $400, each will earn profits of $7,500 per month.

Clearly, the stores will be better off if they both charge $600 for the PlayStation. But will they both charge this price? One possibility is that the manager of the Wal-Mart and the manager of the Target will get together and *collude* by agreeing to charge the higher price. **Collusion** is an agreement among firms to charge the same price or otherwise not to compete. Unfortunately, for Wal-Mart and Target—but fortunately for their customers—collusion is against the law in the United States. The government can fine companies that collude and send the managers involved to jail.

**Collusion** An agreement among firms to charge the same price or otherwise not to compete.

The manager of the Wal-Mart store legally can't discuss his pricing decision with the manager of the Target store, so he has to predict what the other manager will do. Suppose the Wal-Mart manager is convinced that the Target manager will charge $600 for the PlayStation. In this case, the Wal-Mart manager will definitely charge $400 because that will increase his profit from $10,000 to $15,000. But suppose instead the Wal-Mart manager is convinced that the Target manager will charge $400. Then the Wal-Mart manager also definitely will charge $400 because that will increase his profit from $5,000 to $7,500. In fact, whichever price the Target manager decides to charge, the Wal-Mart manager is better off charging $400. So, we know that the Wal-Mart manager will choose a price of $400 for the PlayStation.

Now consider the situation of the Target manager. The Target manager is in the identical position to the Wal-Mart manager, so we can expect her to make the same decision to charge $400 for the PlayStation. In this situation, each manager has a *dominant strategy*. A **dominant strategy** is the best strategy for a firm, no matter what strategies other firms use. The result is an equilibrium where both managers charge $400 for the PlayStation. This situation is an equilibrium because each manager is maximizing profits, *given the price chosen by the other manager*. In other words, neither firm can increase its profits by changing its price, given the price chosen by the other firm. An equilibrium where each firm chooses the best strategy, given the strategies chosen by other firms, is called a **Nash equilibrium**, named after Nobel laureate John Nash of Princeton University, a pioneer in the development of game theory.

**Dominant strategy** A strategy that is the best for a firm, no matter what strategies other firms use.

**Nash equilibrium** A situation in which each firm chooses the best strategy, given the strategies chosen by other firms.

## Making the Connection | A Beautiful Mind: Game Theory Goes to the Movies

John Nash is the most celebrated game theorist in the world, partly because of his achievements and partly because of his dramatic life. In 1948, at the age of 20, Nash received bachelor's and master's degrees in mathematics from the Carnegie Institute of Technology (now known as Carnegie Mellon University). Two years later, he received a Ph.D. from Princeton for his 27-page dissertation on game theory. It was in this dissertation that he first discussed the concept that became known as the *Nash equilibrium*. Nash appeared to be on his way to a brilliant academic career until he developed schizophrenia in the 1950s. He spent decades in and out of mental hospitals. During these years, he roamed the Princeton campus, covering blackboards in unused classrooms with indecipherable writings. He became known as the "Phantom of Fine Hall." In the 1970s, Nash gradually began to recover. In 1994, he shared the Nobel Prize in Economics with John Harsanyi of the University of California, Berkeley, and Reinhard Selten of Rheinische Friedrich–Wilhelms Universität, Germany, for his work on game theory.

In 1998, Sylvia Nasar of the *New York Times* wrote a biography of Nash, titled *A Beautiful Mind*. Three years later, the book was adapted into an award-winning film starring Russell Crowe. Unfortunately, the (fictitious) scene in the film that shows Nash discovering the idea of Nash equilibrium misstates the concept. In the scene, Nash is in a bar with several friends when four women with brown hair and one with blonde hair walk in. Nash and all of his friends prefer the blonde to the brunettes. One of Nash's friends points out that if they all compete for the blonde, they are unlikely to get her. In competing for the blonde, they will also insult the brunettes, with the result that none of them will end up with a date. Nash then gets a sudden insight. He suggests that they ignore the blonde and each approach one of the brunettes. That is the only way, he argues, that each of them will end up with a date.

Nash immediately claims that this is also an economic insight. He points out that Adam Smith had argued that the best result comes from everyone in the group doing what's best for himself. Nash argues, however, "The best result comes from everyone in the group doing what's best for himself *and* the group." But this is not an accurate description of the Nash equilibrium. As we have seen, in a Nash equilibrium, each player uses a strategy that will make him as well off as possible, *given the strategies of the other players*. The bar situation would not be a Nash equilibrium. Once the other men have chosen a brunette, each man will have an incentive to switch from the brunette he initially chose to the blonde.

*In the film* A Beautiful Mind, *Russell Crowe played John Nash, winner of the Nobel Prize in Economics.*

## Don't Let This Happen to YOU!

### Don't Misunderstand Why Each Manager Ends Up Charging a Price of $400

It is tempting to think that the Wal-Mart manager and the Target manager would each charge $400 rather than $600 for the PlayStation because each is afraid that the other manager will charge $400. In fact, fear of being undercut by the other firm's charging a lower price is not the key to understanding each manager's pricing strategy. Notice that charging $400 is the most profitable strategy for each man-

ager, no matter which price the other manager decides to charge. For example, even if the Wal-Mart manager somehow knew for sure that the Target manager intended to charge $600, he would still charge $400 because his profits would be $15,000 instead of $10,000. The Target manager is in the same situation. That is why charging $400 is a dominant strategy for both managers.

## Firm Behavior and the Prisoners' Dilemma

Notice that the equilibrium in Figure 13-2 is not very satisfactory for either firm. The firms earn $7,500 profit each month by charging $400, but they could have earned $10,000 profit if they had both charged $600. By "cooperating" and charging the higher price, they would have achieved a *cooperative equilibrium*. In a **cooperative equilibrium**, players cooperate to increase their mutual payoff. We have seen, though, that the outcome of this game is likely to be a **noncooperative equilibrium**, in which each firm pursues its own self-interest.

A situation like this, in which pursuing dominant strategies results in noncooperation that leaves everyone worse off, is called a **prisoners' dilemma**. The game gets its name from the problem faced by two suspects the police arrest for a crime. If the police lack other evidence, they may separate the suspects and offer each a reduced prison sentence in exchange for confessing to the crime and testifying against the other criminal. Because each suspect has a dominant strategy to confess to the crime, they will both confess and serve a jail term, even though they would have gone free if they had both remained silent.

**Cooperative equilibrium** An equilibrium in a game in which players cooperate to increase their mutual payoff.

**Noncooperative equilibrium** An equilibrium in a game in which players do not cooperate but pursue their own self-interest.

**Prisoners' dilemma** A game in which pursuing dominant strategies results in noncooperation that leaves everyone worse off.

---

# Solved Problem | 13-2

## Is Advertising a Prisoners' Dilemma for Coca-Cola and Pepsi?

Coca-Cola and Pepsi both advertise aggressively, but would they be better off if they didn't? Their commercials are not designed to convey new information about the products. Instead, they are designed to capture each other's customers. Construct a payoff matrix using the following hypothetical information:

- If neither firm advertises, Coca-Cola and Pepsi both earn profits of $750 million per year.

- If both firms advertise, Coca-Cola and Pepsi both earn profits of $500 million per year.

- If Coca-Cola advertises and Pepsi doesn't, Coca-Cola earns profits of $900 million and Pepsi earns profits of $400 million.

- If Pepsi advertises and Coca-Cola doesn't, Pepsi earns profits of $900 million and Coca-Cola earns profits of $400 million.

a. If Coca-Cola wants to maximize profit, will it advertise? Briefly explain.

b. If Pepsi wants to maximize profit, will it advertise? Briefly explain.

c. Is there a Nash equilibrium to this advertising game? If so, what is it?

### SOLVING THE PROBLEM:

**Step 1:** **Review the chapter material.** This problem uses payoff matrixes to analyze a business situation, so you may want to review the section "A Duopoly Game: Price Competition between Two Firms," which begins on page 445.

**Step 2:** **Construct the payoff matrix.**

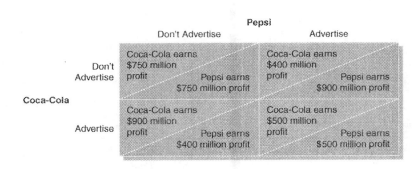

Step 3: **Answer question (a) by showing that Coca-Cola has a dominant strategy of advertising.** If Pepsi doesn't advertise, then Coca-Cola will make $900 million if it advertises but only $750 million if it doesn't. If Pepsi advertises, then Coca-Cola will make $500 million if it advertises but only $400 million if it doesn't. Therefore, advertising is a dominant strategy for Coca-Cola.

Step 4: **Answer question (b) by showing that Pepsi has a dominant strategy of advertising.** Pepsi is in the same position as Coca-Cola, so it also has a dominant strategy of advertising.

Step 5: **Answer question (c) by showing that there is a Nash equilibrium for this game.** Both firms advertising is a Nash equilibrium. Given that Pepsi is advertising, Coca-Cola's best strategy is to advertise. Given that Coca-Cola is advertising, Pepsi's best strategy is to advertise. Therefore, advertising is the optimal decision for both firms, *given the decision by the other firm.*

**EXTRA CREDIT:** This is another example of the prisoners' dilemma game. Coca-Cola and Pepsi would be more profitable if they both refrained from advertising, thereby saving the enormous expense of television and radio commercials and newspaper and magazine ads. Each firm's dominant strategy is to advertise, however, so they end up in an equilibrium where both advertise, and their profits are reduced.

>> **End Solved Problem 13-2**

## Making the Connection | Is There a Dominant Strategy for Bidding on eBay?

An auction is a game in which bidders compete to buy a product. The payoff in winning an auction is equal to the difference between the subjective value you place on the product being auctioned and the amount of the winning bid. On the online auction site eBay, more than 200 million items valued at more than $10 billion are auctioned each year.

eBay is run as a *second-price auction*, where the winning bidder pays the price of the second-highest bidder. If the high bidder on a DVD of *Spider-Man 3* bids $15, and the second bidder bids $10, the high bidder wins the auction and pays $10. It may seem that your best strategy when bidding on eBay is to place a bid well below the subjective value you place on the item in the hope of winning it at a low price. In fact, bidders on eBay have a dominant strategy of entering a bid equal to the maximum value they place on the item. For instance, suppose you are looking for a present for your parents' anniversary. They are Rolling Stones fans, and someone is auctioning a pair of Stones concert tickets. If the maximum value you place on the tickets is $200, that should be your bid. To see why, consider the results of strategies of bidding more or less than $200.

There are two possible outcomes of the auction: Either someone else bids more than you do, or you are the high bidder. First, suppose you bid $200 but someone else bids more than you do. If you had bid less than

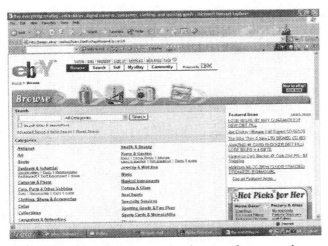

*On eBay, bidding the maximum value you place on an item is a dominant strategy.*

$200, you would still have lost. If you had bid more than $200, you might have been the high bidder, but because your bid would be for more than the value you place on the tickets, you would have a negative payoff. Second, suppose you bid $200 and you are the high bidder. If you had bid less than $200, you would have run the risk of losing the tickets to someone whose bid you would have beaten by bidding $200. You would be worse off than if you had bid $200 and won. If you had bid more than $200, you would not have affected the price you ended up paying—which, remember, is equal to the amount bid by the second-highest bidder. Therefore, a strategy of bidding $200—the maximum value you place on the tickets—dominates bidding more or less than $200.

Even though making your first bid your highest bid is a dominant strategy on eBay, many bidders don't use it. After an auction is over, a link leads to a Web page showing all the bids. In many auctions, the same bidder bids several times, showing that the bidder had not understood his or her dominant strategy.

## Can Firms Escape the Prisoners' Dilemma?

Although the prisoners' dilemma game seems to show that cooperative behavior always breaks down, we know it doesn't. People often cooperate to achieve their goals, and firms find ways to cooperate by not competing on price. The reason the basic prisoners' dilemma story is not always applicable is that it assumes the game will be played only once. Most business situations, however, are repeated over and over. Each month, the Target and Wal-Mart managers will decide again what price they will charge for PlayStation 3. In the language of game theory, the managers are playing a *repeated game*. In a repeated game, the losses from not cooperating are greater than in a game played once, and players can also employ *retaliation strategies* against those who don't cooperate. As a result, we are more likely to see cooperative behavior.

Figure 13-2 on page 446 shows that Wal-Mart and Target are earning $2,500 less per month by both charging $400 instead of $600 for the PlayStation 3. Every month that passes with both stores charging $400 increases the total amount lost: Two years of charging $400 will cause each store to lose $60,000 in profit. This lost profit increases the incentive for the store managers to cooperate by *implicitly* colluding. Remember that *explicit* collusion—such as the managers meeting and agreeing to charge $600—is illegal. But if the managers can find a way to signal each other that they will charge $600, they may be within the law.

Suppose, for example, that Wal-Mart and Target both advertise that they will match the lowest price offered by any competitor—in our simple example, they are each other's only competitor. These advertisements are signals to each other that they intend to charge $600 for the PlayStation. The signal is clear because each store knows that if it charges $400, the other store will automatically retaliate by also lowering its price to $400. The offer to match prices is a good *enforcement mechanism* because it guarantees that if either store fails to cooperate and charges the lower price, the competing store will automatically punish that store by also charging the lower price. As Figure 13-3 shows, the stores have changed the payoff matrix they face.

With the original payoff matrix (a), there is no matching offer, and each store makes more profit if it charges $400 when the other charges $600. The matching offer changes the payoff matrix to (b). Now the stores can charge $600 and receive a profit of $10,000 per month, or they can charge $400 and receive a profit of $7,500 per month. The equilibrium shifts from the prisoners' dilemma result of both stores charging the low price and receiving low profits to a result where both stores charge the high price and receive high profits. An offer to match competitors' prices might seem to benefit consumers, but game theory shows that it actually may hurt consumers by helping to keep prices high.

## Figure 13-3

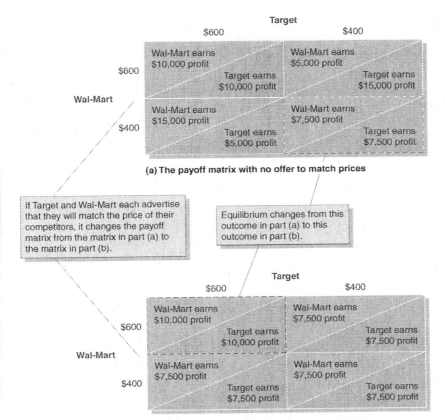

**Target**

(a) The payoff matrix with no offer to match prices

If Target and Wal-Mart each advertise that they will match the price of their competitors, it changes the payoff matrix from the matrix in part (a) to the matrix in part (b).

Equilibrium changes from this outcome in part (a) to this outcome in part (b).

**Target**

(b) The payoff matrix with an offer to match prices

### Changing the Payoff Matrix in a Repeated Game

Wal-Mart and Target can change the payoff matrix by advertising that they will match their competitor's price. This retaliation strategy provides a signal that one store charging a lower price will be met automatically by the other store charging a lower price. In payoff matrix (a), there is no matching offer, and each store benefits if it charges $400 when the other charges $600. In payoff matrix (b), with the matching offer, the companies have only two choices: They can charge $600 and receive a profit of $10,000 per month, or they can charge $400 and receive a profit of $7,500 per month. The equilibrium shifts from the prisoners' dilemma result of both stores charging the low price and receiving low profits to both stores charging the high price and receiving high profits.

One form of implicit collusion occurs as a result of *price leadership*. With **price leadership**, one firm takes the lead in announcing a price change, which is then matched by the other firms in the industry. For example, through the 1970s, General Motors would announce a price change at the beginning of a model year and Ford and Chrysler would match GM's price change. In some cases, such as the airline industry, firms have attempted to act as price leaders, but failed when other firms in the industry declined to cooperate.

**Price leadership** A form of implicit collusion where one firm in an oligopoly announces a price change, which is matched by the other firms in the industry.

## Making the Connection | American Airlines and Northwest Airlines Fail to Cooperate on a Price Increase

Coordinating prices is easier in some industries than in others. Fixed costs in the airline industry are very large, and marginal costs are very small. The marginal cost of flying one more passenger from New York to Chicago is no more than a few dollars: the cost of another snack served and a small amount of additional jet fuel. As a result, airlines often engage in last-minute price cutting to fill the remaining empty seats on a flight. Even a low-price ticket will increase marginal revenue more than marginal cost. As with other oligopolies, if all airlines cut prices, industry profits will decline. Airlines therefore continually adjust their prices while at the same time monitoring their rivals' prices and retaliating against them either for cutting prices or failing to go along with price increases.

*The airlines have trouble raising the price this business traveler pays for a ticket.*

Consider the following fairly typical events from the spring of 2002. American Airlines decided to raise some of its ticket prices in a roundabout way. Business travelers are usually willing to pay higher prices for airline tickets than are leisure travelers. Business travelers also often must make their flight plans only a few days before they leave. Airlines take advantage of this fact by requiring 10- to 14-day advance reservations to get a fully discounted ticket. A smaller discount is available with a 3-day advance reservation. This smaller discount is aimed at business travelers. American decided to increase to 7 days the advance purchase requirement for the business travel discount. Because many business travelers cannot make their reservations that far in advance, they would have to buy full-fare tickets.

Continental Airlines matched American's change, but the other airlines refused to go along. They hoped that by not matching American's price increase, they would gain some of its customers. American then retaliated by offering very low $99 one-way tickets in 10 markets where Northwest Airlines, United Airlines, Delta Air Lines, and US Airways offered nonstop service. American did not offer the $99 fares in the markets where Continental offered nonstop service. An airline industry consultant observed that "American is trying to slap the hands of people who wouldn't go along with its increase."

Northwest immediately responded by offering $99 fares in 20 markets where American offers nonstop service. American retaliated by offering the low fare in 10 additional markets served by Northwest. Northwest then further retaliated by offering the low fare in a total of 160 markets served by American. After several days of very low fares and lost profits, American and Northwest restored their normal fares, and American went back to a 3-day advance reservation requirement for discounted business-travel tickets.

Did American's aggressive retaliation make it easier for airlines to agree on ticket price increases in the future? Apparently not. A few weeks later, Continental raised its prices for round-trip discounted tickets by $20. Every airline but Northwest matched the price increase. Rather than lose customers to Northwest, Continental and the other airlines rolled back the price increase.

Sources: Scott McCartney, "Airfare Wars Show Why Deals Arrive and Depart," *Wall Street Journal*, March 19, 2002; and Scott McCartney, "Airlines Drop $20 Fare Increase after Northwest Fails to Join In," *Wall Street Journal*, April 16, 2002.

## Cartels: The Case of OPEC

In the United States, firms cannot legally meet to agree on what prices to charge and how much to produce. But suppose they could. Would this be enough to guarantee that their collusion would be successful? The example of the Organization of Petroleum Exporting Countries (OPEC) indicates that the answer to this question is "no." OPEC has 11 members, including Saudi Arabia, Kuwait, and other Arab countries, as well as Iran, Venezuela, Nigeria, and Indonesia. Together, these countries own 75 percent of the world's proven oil reserves, although they pump a smaller share of the total oil sold each year. OPEC operates as a **cartel**, which is a group of firms that collude to restrict output to increase prices and profits. The members of OPEC meet periodically and agree on quotas, quantities of oil that each country agrees to produce. The quotas are intended to reduce oil production well below the competitive level, to force up the price of oil, and to increase the profits of member countries.

**Cartel** A group of firms that collude by agreeing to restrict output to increase prices and profits.

Figure 13-4 shows world oil prices from 1972 to 2006. The blue line shows the price of a barrel of oil in each year. Prices in general have risen since 1972, which has reduced the amount of goods and services that consumers can purchase with a dollar. The red line corrects for general price increases by measuring oil prices in terms of the dollar's purchasing power in 2006. Although political unrest in the Middle East and other factors also affect the price of oil, the figure shows that OPEC had considerable success in raising the price of oil during the mid-1970s and early 1980s. Oil prices, which had been below $3 per barrel in 1972, rose to more than $35 per barrel in 1981, which was almost

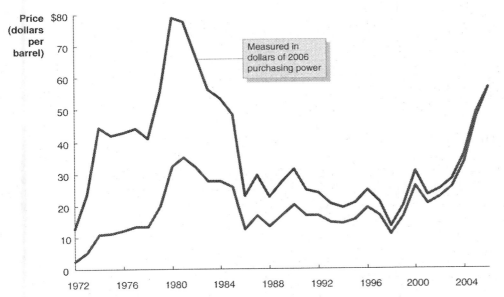

## Figure 13-4

### World Oil Prices, 1972–2006

The blue line shows the price of a barrel of oil in each year. The red line measures the price of a barrel of oil in terms of the purchasing power of the dollar in 2006. By reducing oil production, the Organization of Petroleum Exporting Countries (OPEC) was able to raise the world price of oil in the mid-1970s and early 1980s. Sustaining high prices has been difficult over the long run, however, because members often exceed their output quotas.

Source: U.S. Energy Information Agency, *Monthly Energy Review*, March 2007, Table 9.1.

$78 measured in dollars of 2006 purchasing power. The figure also shows that OPEC has had difficulty sustaining the high prices of 1981 in later years, although beginning in 2004, oil prices rose, in part due to increasing demand from China and India.

Game theory helps us understand why oil prices have fluctuated. If every member of OPEC cooperates and produces the low output level dictated by its quota, prices will be high, and the cartel will earn large profits. Once the price has been driven up, however, each member has an incentive to stop cooperating and to earn even higher profits by increasing output beyond its quota. But if no country sticks to its quota, total oil output will increase, and profits will decline. In other words, OPEC is caught in a prisoners' dilemma.

If the members of OPEC always exceeded their production quotas, the cartel would have no effect on world oil prices. In fact, the members of OPEC periodically meet and assign new quotas that, at least for a while, enable them to restrict output enough to raise prices. OPEC's occasional success at behaving as a cartel can be explained by two factors. First, the members of OPEC are participating in a repeated game. As we have seen, this increases the likelihood of a cooperative outcome. Second, Saudi Arabia has far larger oil reserves than any other member of OPEC. Therefore, it has the most to gain from high oil prices and a greater incentive to cooperate. To see this, consider the payoff matrix shown in Figure 13-5. To keep things simple, let's assume that OPEC has only two members:

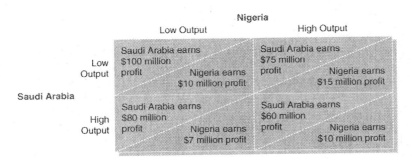

## Figure 13-5 | The OPEC Cartel with Unequal Members

Because Saudi Arabia can produce so much more oil than Nigeria, its output decisions have a much larger effect on the price of oil. In the figure, "low output" corresponds to cooperating with the OPEC-assigned output quota, and "high output" corresponds to producing at maximum capacity. Saudi Arabia has a dominant strategy to cooperate and produce a low output. Nigeria, however, has a dominant strategy not to cooperate and produce a high output. Therefore, the equilibrium of this game will occur with Saudi Arabia producing a low output and Nigeria producing a high output.

Saudi Arabia and Nigeria. In Figure 13-5, "low output" corresponds to cooperating with the OPEC-assigned output quota, and "high output" corresponds to producing at maximum capacity. The payoff matrix shows the profits received per day by each country.

We can see that Saudi Arabia has a strong incentive to cooperate and maintain its low output quota. By keeping output low, Saudi Arabia can by itself significantly raise the world price of oil, increasing its own profits as well as those of other members of OPEC. Therefore, Saudi Arabia has a dominant strategy of cooperating with the quota and producing a low output. Nigeria, however, cannot by itself have much effect on the price of oil. Therefore, Nigeria has a dominant strategy of not cooperating and producing a high output. The equilibrium of this game will occur with Saudi Arabia producing a low output and Nigeria producing a high output. In fact, OPEC often operates in just this way. Saudi Arabia will cooperate with the quota, while the other 10 members produce at capacity. Because this is a repeated game, however, Saudi Arabia will occasionally produce more oil than its quota to intentionally drive down the price and retaliate against the other members for not cooperating.

---

**13.3 LEARNING OBJECTIVE**

13.3 | Use sequential games to analyze business strategies.

# Sequential Games and Business Strategy

We have been analyzing games in which both players move simultaneously. In many business situations, however, one firm will act first, and then other firms will respond. These situations can be analyzed using *sequential games*. We will use sequential games to analyze two business strategies: deterring entry and bargaining between firms. To keep things simple, we consider situations that involve only two firms.

## Deterring Entry

We saw earlier that barriers to entry are a key to firms continuing to earn economic profits. Can firms create barriers to deter new firms from entering an industry? Some recent research in game theory has focused on this question. To take a simple example, suppose a town in South Dakota currently has no discount department stores. Executives at Wal-Mart decide to enter the market and are considering what size store to build. To break even by covering the opportunity cost of the funds involved, the store must provide a minimum rate of return of 15 percent on the firm's investment. If Wal-Mart builds a small store in the town, it will earn economic profits by receiving a return of 30 percent. If Wal-Mart builds a large store, its costs will be somewhat higher, and it will receive a return of only 22 percent.

It seems clear that Wal-Mart should build the small store, but the executives are worried that Target may also build a store in this market. If Wal-Mart builds a small store and Target enters the market, both firms will earn an 18 percent return on their investment in this market. If Wal-Mart builds a large store and Target enters, the stores will have to cut prices, and the firms will each earn only 10 percent return on their investments, which is below the 15 percent return necessary for either firm to break even.

We can analyze a sequential game by using a *decision tree*, like the one shown in Figure 13-6. The boxes in the figure represent *decision nodes*, which are points when the firms must make the decisions contained in the boxes. At the left, Wal-Mart makes the initial decision of what size store to build, and then Target responds by either entering the market or not. The decisions made are shown beside the arrows. The *terminal nodes* at the right side of the figure show the resulting rates of return.

Let's start with Wal-Mart's initial decision. If Wal-Mart builds a large store, then the arrow directs us to the upper red decision node for Target. If Target decides to enter, it will earn only a 10 percent rate of return on its investment, which represents an economic loss because it is below the opportunity cost of the funds involved. If Target doesn't enter, Wal-Mart will earn 22 percent, and Target will not earn anything in this

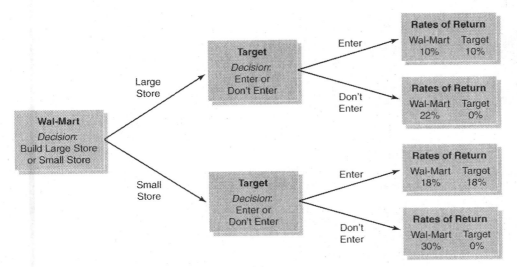

## Figure 13-6

**The Decision Tree for an Entry Game**

Wal-Mart earns its highest return if it builds a small store and Target doesn't enter the market. If Wal-Mart builds a small store, Target will enter because it will earn economic profit by receiving an 18 percent return on its investment. Therefore, the best decision for Wal-Mart is to build a large store to deter Target's entry. Once Wal-Mart has built a large store, Target knows that if it enters this market, it will earn only 10 percent on its investment, which represents an economic loss, so it won't enter the market.

market. Wal-Mart executives can conclude that if they build a large store, Target will not enter, and Wal-Mart will earn 22 percent on its investment.

If Wal-Mart decides to build a small store, then the arrow directs us to the lower red decision node for Target. If Target decides to enter, it will earn an 18 percent rate of return. If it doesn't enter, Wal-Mart will earn 30 percent, and Target will not earn anything in this market. Wal-Mart executives can conclude that if they build a small store, Target will enter, and Wal-Mart will earn 18 percent on its investment.

This analysis should lead Wal-Mart executives to conclude that they can build a small store and earn 18 percent—because Target will enter—or they can build a large store and earn 22 percent by deterring Target's entry.

# Solved Problem | 13-3

## Is Deterring Entry Always a Good Idea?

Whether deterring entry makes sense depends on how costly it is to the firm doing the deterring. Use the following decision tree to decide whether Wal-Mart should deter Target from entering this market. Assume that each firm must earn a 15 percent return on its investment to break even.

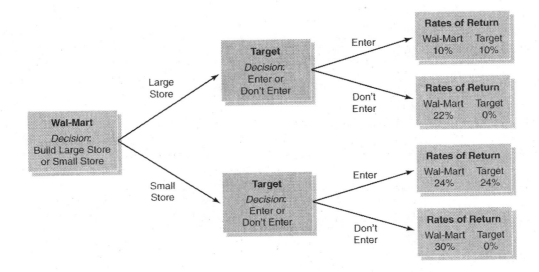

## SOLVING THE PROBLEM:

**Step 1:** **Review the chapter material.** This problem is about sequential games, so you may want to review the section "Deterring Entry," which begins on page 454.

**Step 2:** **Determine how Target will respond to Wal-Mart's decision.** If Wal-Mart builds a large store, Target will not enter this market because the return on its investment represents an economic loss. If Wal-Mart builds a small store, Target will enter because it will earn a return that represents an economic profit.

**Step 3:** **Given how Target will react, determine which strategy maximizes profits for Wal-Mart.** If Wal-Mart builds the large store, it will have deterred Target's entry, and the rate of return on its investment will be 22 percent. If it builds the small store, Target will enter, but Wal-Mart will actually earn a higher return of 24 percent.

**Step 4:** **State your conclusion.** Like any other business strategy, deterrence is worth pursuing only if its costs are not too high. In this case, the high cost of building a large store lowers Wal-Mart's economic profits below what it earns by building a small store, even given that Target will enter the market.

>> **End Solved Problem 13-3**

## Bargaining

The success of many firms depends on how well they bargain with other firms. For example, firms often must bargain with their suppliers over the prices they pay for inputs. Suppose that TruImage is a small firm that has developed software that improves how pictures from a digital camera are displayed on computer screens. TruImage currently sells its software only on its Web site and earns profits of $2 million per year. Dell Computer informs TruImage that it is considering installing the software on every new computer Dell sells. Dell expects to sell more computers at a higher price if it can install TruImage's software on its computers. The two firms begin bargaining over what price Dell will pay TruImage for its software.

The decision tree in Figure 13-7 illustrates this bargaining game. At the left, Dell makes the initial decision on what price to offer TruImage for its software, and then TruImage responds by either accepting or rejecting the contract offer. First, suppose that Dell offers TruImage a contract price of $30 per copy for its software. If TruImage accepts this contract, its profits will be $5 million per year, and Dell will earn $10 million in additional profits. If TruImage rejects the contract, its profits will be the $2 million per year it earns selling its software on its Web site, and Dell will earn zero additional profits.

Now, suppose Dell offers TruImage a contract price of $20 per copy. If TruImage accepts this contract, its profits will be $3 million per year, and Dell will earn $15 million in additional profits. If TruImage rejects this contract, its profits will be the $2 million it earns selling its software on its Web site, and Dell will earn zero additional profits. Clearly, for Dell, a contract of $20 per copy is more profitable, while for TruImage, a contract of $30 per copy is more profitable.

Suppose TruImage attempts to obtain a favorable outcome from the bargaining by telling Dell that it will reject a $20-per-copy contract. If Dell believes this threat, then it will offer TruImage a $30-per-copy contract because Dell is better off with the $10 million profit that will result from TruImage's accepting the contract than with the zero profits Dell will earn if TruImage rejects the $20-per-copy contract. This result is a Nash equilibrium because neither firm can increase its profits by changing its choice—*provided that Dell believes TruImage's threat.* But is TruImage's threat credible? Once Dell has offered TruImage the $20 contract, TruImage's choices are to accept the contract and earn $3 million or reject the contract and earn only $2 million. Because rejecting the

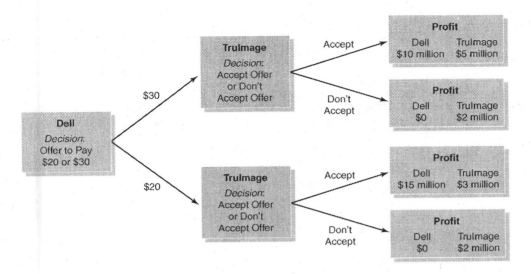

**Figure 13-7** | The Decision Tree for a Bargaining Game

Dell earns the highest profit if it offers a contract price of $20 per copy and TruImage accepts the contract. TruImage earns the highest profit if Dell offers it a contract of $30 per copy and it accepts the contract. TruImage may attempt to bargain by threatening to reject a $20-per-copy contract. But Dell knows this threat is not credible because once Dell has offered a $20-per-copy contract, TruImage's profits are higher if it accepts the contract than if it rejects it.

contract reduces TruImage's profits, TruImage's threat to reject the contract is not credible, and Dell should ignore it.

As a result, we would expect Dell to use the strategy of offering TruImage a $20-per-copy contract and TruImage to use the strategy of accepting the contract. Dell will earn additional profits of $15 million per year, and TruImage will earn profits of $3 million per year. This outcome is called a *subgame-perfect equilibrium*. A subgame-perfect equilibrium is a Nash equilibrium in which no player can make himself better off by changing his decision at any decision node. In our simple bargaining game, each player has only one decision to make. As we have seen, Dell's profits are highest if it offers the $20-per-copy contract, and TruImage's profits are highest if it accepts the contract. Typically, in sequential games of this type, there is only one subgame-perfect equilibrium.

Managers use decision trees like those in Figures 13-6 and 13-7 in business planning because they provide a systematic way of thinking through the implications of a strategy and of predicting the reactions of rivals. We can see the benefits of decision trees in the simple examples we considered here. In the first example, Wal-Mart managers can conclude that building a large store is more profitable than building a smaller store. In the second example, Dell managers can conclude that TruImage's threat to reject a $20-per-copy contract is not credible.

---

**13.4 LEARNING** OBJECTIVE

13.4 | Use the five competitive forces model to analyze competition in an industry.

# The Five Competitive Forces Model

We have seen that the number of competitors in an industry affects a firm's ability to charge a price above average cost and earn an economic profit. The number of firms is not the only determinant of the level of competition in an industry, however. Michael Porter of Harvard Business School has drawn on the research of a number of economists to develop a model that shows how five competitive forces determine the overall level of competition in an industry. Figure 13-8 illustrates Porter's model.

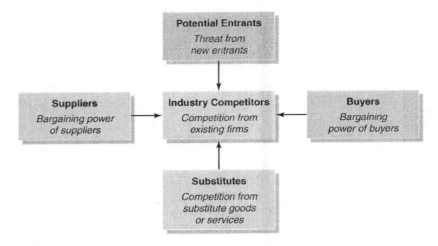

Figure 13-8 | The Five Competitive Forces Model

Michael Porter's model identifies five forces that determine the level of competition in an industry: (1) competition from existing firms, (2) the threat from new entrants, (3) competition from substitute goods or services, (4) the bargaining power of buyers, and (5) the bargaining power of suppliers.
Source: Reprinted with the permission of The Free Press, a Division of Simon & Schuster Adult Publishing Group, from Michael E. Porter, *Competitive Strategy: Techniques for Analyzing Industries and Competitors.* Copyright © 1980, 1998 by The Free Press. All rights reserved.

We now look at each of the five competitive forces: (1) competition from existing firms, (2) the threat from potential entrants, (3) competition from substitute goods or services, (4) the bargaining power of buyers, and (5) the bargaining power of suppliers.

## Competition from Existing Firms

We have already seen that competition among firms in an industry can lower prices and profits. To take another example: The Educational Testing Service (ETS) produces the Scholastic Aptitude Test (SAT) and the Graduate Record Exam (GRE). The GRE is taken by students applying to graduate school. In 2007, the Educational Testing Service charged a price of $43 to take the SAT, but $140 to take the GRE. Part of the explanation for these large price differences is that ETS faces competition in the market for tests given to high school seniors applying to college, where the SAT competes with the ACT Assessment, produced by ACT, Inc. But there is no competition for the GRE test. As we saw earlier in this chapter, when there are only a few firms in a market, it is easier for them to implicitly collude and to charge a price close to the monopoly price. In this case, however, competition from a single firm was enough to cause ETS to keep the price of the SAT near the competition level.

Competition in the form of advertising, better customer service, or longer warranties can also reduce profits by raising costs. For example, online booksellers Amazon.com, BarnesandNoble.com, and Buy.com have competed by offering low-cost—or free—shipping, by increasing their customer service staffs, and by building more warehouses to provide faster deliveries. These activities have raised the booksellers' costs and reduced their profits.

## The Threat from Potential Entrants

Firms face competition from companies that currently are not in the market but might enter. We have already seen how actions taken to deter entry can reduce profits. In our hypothetical example in the previous section, Wal-Mart built a larger store and earned less profit to deter Target's entry. Business managers often take actions aimed at deterring entry. Some of these actions include advertising to create product loyalty, introducing new products—such as slightly different cereals or toothpastes—to fill market niches, and setting lower prices to keep profits at a level that would make entry less attractive.

## Competition from Substitute Goods or Services

Firms are always vulnerable to competitors introducing a new product that fills a consumer need better than their current product does. Consider the encyclopedia business. For decades, many parents bought expensive and bulky encyclopedias for their children attending high school or college. By the 1990s, computer software companies were offering electronic encyclopedias that sold for a small fraction of the price of the printed encyclopedias. Encyclopedia Britannica and the other encyclopedia publishers responded by cutting prices and launching advertising campaigns aimed at showing the superiority of printed encyclopedias. Still, profits continued to decline, and by the end of the 1990s, most printed encyclopedias had disappeared.

## The Bargaining Power of Buyers

If buyers have enough bargaining power, they can insist on lower prices, higher-quality products, or additional services. Automobile companies, for example, have significant bargaining power in the tire market, which tends to lower tire prices and limit the profitability of tire manufacturers. Some retailers have significant buying power over their suppliers. For instance, Wal-Mart has required many of its suppliers to alter their distribution systems to accommodate Wal-Mart's need to control the stocks of goods in its stores.

## The Bargaining Power of Suppliers

If many firms can supply an input and the input is not specialized, the suppliers are unlikely to have the bargaining power to limit a firm's profits. For instance, suppliers of paper napkins to McDonald's restaurants have very little bargaining power. With only a single or a few suppliers of an input, the purchasing firm may face a high price. During the 1930s and 1940s, for example, the Technicolor Company was the only producer of the cameras and film that studios needed to produce color movies. Technicolor charged the studios high prices to use its cameras, and it had the power to insist that only its technicians could operate the cameras. The only alternative for the movie studios was to make black-and-white movies.

As with other competitive forces, the bargaining power of suppliers can change over time. For instance, when IBM chose Microsoft to supply the operating system for its personal computers, Microsoft was a small company with very limited bargaining power. As Microsoft's Windows operating system became standard in more than 90 percent of personal computers, this large market share increased Microsoft's bargaining power.

Making the Connection | **Is Southwest's Business Strategy More Important Than the Structure of the Airline Industry?**

For years, economists and business strategists believed that market structure was the most important factor in explaining the ability of some firms to continue earning economic profits. For example, most economists argued

*Southwest's business strategy allowed it to remain profitable when many other airlines faced heavy losses.*

that during the first few decades after World War II, steel companies in the United States earned economic profits because barriers to entry were high, there were few firms in the industry, and competition among firms was low. In contrast, restaurants were seen as less profitable because barriers to entry were low and the industry was intensely competitive. One problem with this approach to analyzing the profitability of firms is that it does not explain how firms in the same industry can have very different levels of profit.

Today, economists and business strategists put greater emphasis on the characteristics of individual firms and the strategies their managements use to continue to earn economic profits. This approach helps explain why Nucor continues to be a profitable steel company while Bethlehem Steel, at one time the second-largest steel producer in the United States, was forced into bankruptcy. It also explains why Dell, which began as a small company run by Michael Dell from his dorm room at the University of Texas, went on to become extremely profitable and an industry leader, while other computer companies have disappeared.

Many economists argue that the best strategy for a company is to identify a segment of the market and then shape the company to fit that segment. This strategy makes it more difficult for rivals to compete in that part of the market. For example, Southwest Airlines concentrates on customers who fly relatively short distances and who want a low-price, no-frills airline flight. Every aspect of the company is focused on this goal. Southwest's planes have no first-class or business sections—only coach seats are available. By flying primarily between midsize cities, Southwest can avoid the delays at the crowded airports near big cities and can keep its planes at the airport gate for only 15 minutes—much less time than other airlines. This lowers its costs by allowing it to keep its planes in the air longer and to offer more flights with fewer planes. Southwest also lowers costs by not serving meals, flying only Boeing 737s to standardize maintenance, not assigning passengers to particular seats, and not checking luggage through to connecting flights.

It is very difficult for the other full-service airlines, such as Delta, American, and United, to compete with Southwest. Because they fly out of larger, more congested airports, those airlines have no hope of turning around their planes at the gate as quickly as Southwest does. Because many of their passengers are flying longer distances—often using connecting flights—they have to serve meals and check luggage through. Many of the other airlines' customers want upgraded seats and service, so those airlines must offer first-class and business-class seats. Even when Delta, American, and United have tried to offer stripped-down service on certain routes in direct competition with Southwest, they have not been successful. Southwest's complete focus on providing low-cost, low-price service has proven very difficult for the other airlines to copy. While other airlines suffered heavy losses in 2003–2004 as fuel prices rose and demand declined as a result of the war in Iraq and the spread of the disease SARS (severe acute respiratory syndrome), Southwest continued to earn profits. In 2006, it remained the leading airline in on-time arrivals and fewest customer complaints.

Southwest's corporate strategy, rather than the structure of the airline industry, explains why Southwest earns economic profits.

Source: Scott McCartney, "A Report Card on the Nation's Airlines," *Wall Street Journal*, February 6, 2007, p. D1.

# Conclusion

Firms are locked in a never-ending struggle to earn economic profits. As noted in the two preceding chapters, competition erodes economic profits. Even in the oligopolies discussed in this chapter, firms have difficulty earning economic profits in the long run. We have seen that firms attempt to avoid the effects of competition in various ways. For example, they can stake out a secure niche in the market, they can engage in implicit collusion with competing firms, or they can attempt to have the government impose barriers to entry. Read *An Inside Look* on the next page for a discussion of the business strategy Target uses to compete with Wal-Mart in the market for generic prescription drugs.

# Can Target Compete with Wal-Mart in the Market for Generic Drugs?

**USA TODAY, SEPTEMBER 23, 2006**

## Target Says It Will Match Wal-Mart's $4 Generic Drug Price

(a) Chain store Target said late Thursday that it will match rival Wal-Mart's $4 price on 150 generic drug prescriptions in the Tampa Bay area. Target's brief press release didn't say whether it would keep pace with Wal-Mart's plan to take the lower prices nationwide, but it did say it has a "long-standing practice to be price competitive with Wal-Mart."

Wal-Mart, the nation's third-largest seller of prescription drugs, said earlier Thursday that it will offer the $4 price on about 150 generic drugs to the insured and uninsured alike, starting immediately in the Tampa area, and will take the program statewide by January.

"We intend to take it nationwide next year," says Bill Simon, Wal-Mart's executive vice president of the Professional Services Division. For uninsured consumers, the $4 price for some generics is below what they would pay at most pharmacy counters and is less than typical $10 to $15 co-payments on generics offered by many insurance plans.

Wal-Mart's move could save modest amounts for some consumers. It may also draw more customers to its stores or prompt a price war with other pharmacies. Savings could be less than $1 per prescription to more than $20, depending on the drug and pharmacy where customers shop, according to information from Wal-Mart and prices of other retailers posted at MyFloridarx.com, a state-run website.

That could draw more customers to Wal-Mart, already the largest seller of groceries and toys, possibly forcing other chain drugstores to cut their prices, says Ed Kaplan of the Segal Co., a benefits consulting firm. "Customers who take five or seven medications a month and can save $10 on each might switch," says Kaplan.

The move caused share prices for generic drug and pharmacy companies to drop Thursday.

Wal-Mart says the $4 for 30-day supply price would save customers $7.98 a month for blood-pressure drug Lisinopril, $3.85 for diabetes drug metformin and 80 cents for blood-pressure drug atenolol.

(b) Simon says the $4 generics are not expected to be a "loss leader," meaning Wal-Mart doesn't expect to lose money on the drugs in hopes of attracting more customers to buy other products. That's because the drugs offered are longtime generics that have multiple manufacturers and they are already inexpensive on the wholesale market. Large companies such as Wal-Mart can often buy in bulk for less than the $4 cost.

Wal-Mart's press release said 291 drugs will be covered, a total that includes different dosage strengths of the same drugs. When the differing dosage strengths are taken out, the list includes fewer than 150 products, including treatments for high blood pressure, infection and diabetes, along with some vitamins and painkiller ibuprofen. That's a fraction of the estimated 2,100 generic products available.

"This is a much narrower list than they're giving the impression it is," says drug-industry expert Stephen Schondelmeyer at the University of Minnesota. Simon says the drugs chosen for the list represent 20% of the prescriptions Wal-Mart currently fills and cover a wide range of medical needs. More products may be added, he says.

(c) The move comes as Wal-Mart works to counter critics who say the firm doesn't make health insurance affordable for many of its workers. "Providing low-cost drugs is a good thing. But not providing affordable health care to workers is not a good thing. Why can't Wal-Mart address the serious health care crisis in its own stores?" says Chris Kofinis, with WakeUpWalmart.com.

Some praised Wal-Mart's move. "That's a great price for a 30-day supply of drugs and will be a tremendous boon for seniors," says Devon Herrick, economist at the National Center for Policy Analysis.

*Source: Julie Appley, "Target Says It Will Match Wal-Mart's $4 Generic Drug Price," USA Today, September 23, 2006. Reprinted by permission of USA Today.*

## Key Points in the Article

This article illustrates Target's plan to match Wal-Mart's low price on generic prescription drugs. As we have seen in this chapter, when a market is an oligopoly, there are only a few firms. So, each firm must take into account the actions of its competitors. When a competitor changes the price it charges, the other firms in the industry must decide how to react. In this case, Target determined that its profits would be higher by matching Wal-Mart's price.

## Analyzing the News

(a) In an oligopoly market, a firm's profits depend not only on the price it chooses, but on the price its rivals choose. In this case, Target had to choose how to respond to Wal-Mart's pricing decision. From Target's action, we can assume that it believes its profits will be higher with a low price, given that Wal-Mart is charging a low price. The figure is helpful in analyzing whether Wal-Mart can profitably sell generic

drugs at a price of $4. In both panel (a) and panel (b), the rate of return by Wal-Mart is higher when it offers generics at $4 regardless of what Target does. So, Wal-Mart has a dominant strategy of charging $4.

Target faces the choice of whether to match this price. In panel (a), if Target matches the price it earns an 8 percent return, while if it does not match the price it will earn a return of 0 percent. Target prefers the 8 percent return and will choose to match Wal-Mart's $4 generic drug price.

But suppose that Target determines that given its competitive position relative to Wal-Mart the situation is actually that shown in panel (b). Wal-Mart still has a dominant strategy of charging $4 for generic prescription, but now Target faces the choice of a 3 percent return if it matches Wal-Mart's price, or a 5 percent return if it does not match Wal-Mart's price. In this case, Target would be better off not matching the $4 generic price.

(b) Larger stores sometimes cut the price of a product even if this means they will take a loss on sales of the product, if the store manager believes the low price will attract new customers. If low prescription prices attract more customers to Wal-Mart stores, we would expect that Wal-Mart would earn additional profits from the other goods those customers purchased while in Wal-Mart.

(c) As mentioned in the chapter opener, Wal-Mart is facing increased criticism over its corporate policies. Just as Wal-Mart has to decide how to respond to the market behavior of its rivals, such as pricing, it must also decide how to respond to the behavior of its critics.

## Thinking Critically

1. Suppose that you manage a small pharmacy in a local town. How will you decide whether to match the lower generic drug prices of Wal-Mart and Target?

2. Suppose that Congress passes legislation that places a price floor on generic drugs. Who would likely gain from such a law? Who would likely lose? Use a graph to show changes in producer surplus and consumer surplus.

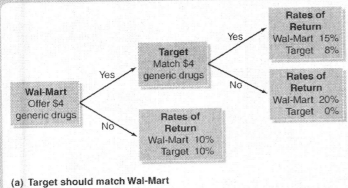

**(a) Target should match Wal-Mart**

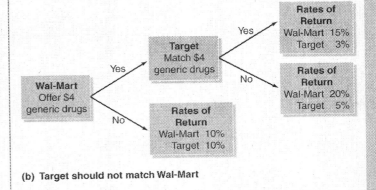

**(b) Target should not match Wal-Mart**

Wal-Mart analyzes whether to offer generic drugs at a price of $4.

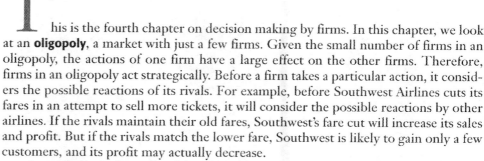

- **oligopoly**
  A market served by a few firms.

- **game theory**
  The study of decision making in strategic situations.

- **concentration ratio**
  The percentage of the market output produced by the largest firms.

This is the fourth chapter on decision making by firms. In this chapter, we look at an **oligopoly**, a market with just a few firms. Given the small number of firms in an oligopoly, the actions of one firm have a large effect on the other firms. Therefore, firms in an oligopoly act strategically. Before a firm takes a particular action, it considers the possible reactions of its rivals. For example, before Southwest Airlines cuts its fares in an attempt to sell more tickets, it will consider the possible reactions by other airlines. If the rivals maintain their old fares, Southwest's fare cut will increase its sales and profit. But if the rivals match the lower fare, Southwest is likely to gain only a few customers, and its profit may actually decrease.

**Game theory** is the study of decision making in strategic situations. The theory can be applied to the game of chess as well as the decisions of oligopolists. A chess player develops a strategy to win the game, anticipating his opponent's reaction to each of his moves. Similarly, an oligopolist develops a strategy to maximize profit, anticipating the reactions of rival firms. We'll use game theory to discuss three business strategies: conspiring to fix prices, preventing another firm from entering the market, and advertising.

# 12.1 | WHAT IS AN OLIGOPOLY?

In an oligopoly, a few firms have market power—the power to control prices. Economists use **concentration ratios** to measure the degree of concentration in a market, computed as the percentage of the market output produced by the largest firms. For example, a four-firm concentration ratio is the percentage of total output in a market produced by the four largest firms. In Table 12.1, the four-firm concentration ratio for cigarettes is 95 percent, indicating that the largest four firms produce 95 percent of the cigarettes in the United States.

An alternative measure of market concentration is the *Herfindahl-Hirschman Index (HHI)*. It is calculated by squaring the market share of each firm in the market and then summing the resulting numbers. For example, consider a market with two firms, one with a 60-percent market share and a second with a 40-percent share. The HHI for the market is 5,200:

$$HHI = 60^2 + 40^2 = 3,600 + 1,600 = 5,200$$

In contrast, for a market with 10 firms, each with a 10-percent market share, the HHI is 1,000:

$$HHI = 10^2 \times 10 = 100 \times 10 = 1,000$$

According to the guidelines established by the U.S. Department of Justice in 1992, a market is "unconcentrated" if the HHI is below 1,000 and "highly concentrated" if it is above 1,800. For example, a market with five firms, each with a 20-percent market share, has a HHI of 2,000 and would be considered highly concentrated:

$$HHI = 20^2 \times 5 = 400 \times 5 = 2,000$$

An oligopoly—a market with just a few firms—occurs for three reasons:

1 *Government barriers to entry.* As we saw in Chapters 6 and 10, the government may limit the number of firms in a market by issuing patents or controlling the number of business licenses.

2 *Economies of scale in production.* As we saw in Chapter 10, a natural monopoly occurs when there are relatively large economies of scale in production, so a single firm produces for the entire market. In some cases, scale economies are not large enough to generate a natural monopoly, but are large enough to generate a natural oligopoly, with a few firms serving the entire market.

3 *Advertising campaigns.* In some markets, a firm cannot enter a market without a substantial investment in an advertising campaign. For example, the breakfast-cereal oligopoly results from the huge advertising campaigns required to get a foothold in the market. As in the case of economies of scale in production, just a few firms will enter the market.

| Table 12.1 | CONCENTRATION RATIOS IN SELECTED MANUFACTURING INDUSTRIES | |
|---|---|---|
| **Industry** | **Four-Firm Concentration Ratio (%)** | **Eight-Firm Concentration Ratio (%)** |
| Primary copper smelting | 99 | Not available |
| House slippers | 97 | 99 |
| Guided missiles and space vehicles | 96 | 99 |
| Cigarettes | 95 | 99 |
| Soybean processing | 95 | 99 |
| Household laundry equipment | 93 | Not available |
| Breweries | 91 | 94 |
| Electric lamp bulbs | 89 | 90 |
| Military vehicles | 88 | 93 |
| Primary battery manufacturing | 87 | 99 |
| Beet sugar processing | 85 | 98 |
| Household refrigerators and freezers | 85 | 95 |
| Small arms (weapons) | 84 | 90 |
| Breakfast cereals | 82 | 93 |
| Motor vehicles and car bodies | 81 | 91 |
| Flavoring syrup | Not available | 89 |

*SOURCE:* U.S. Bureau of the Census, 2002 Economic Census, Manufacturing, *Concentration Ratios: 2002* (Washington, D.C.: U.S. Government Printing Office, 2006).

# 12.2 | CARTEL PRICING AND THE DUOPOLISTS' DILEMMA

One of the virtues of a market economy is that firms compete with one another for customers, and this leads to lower prices and larger quantities. But in some markets, firms cooperate instead of competing with one another. Eighteenth-century economist Adam Smith recognized the possibility that firms would conspire to raise prices: "People of the same trade seldom meet together, even for merriment and diversion, but the conversation ends in a conspiracy against the public, or in some contrivance to raise prices."[1] We'll see that raising prices is not simply a matter of firms getting together and agreeing on higher prices. An agreement to raise prices is likely to break down unless the firms find some way to punish a firm that violates the agreement.

We'll use a market with two firms—a **duopoly**—to explain the key features of an oligopoly. The basic insights from a duopoly apply to oligopolies with more than two firms. Consider a duopoly in the market for air travel between two hypothetical cities. The two airlines can use prices to compete for customers, or they can cooperate and conspire to raise prices. To simplify matters—and to keep the numbers manageable—let's assume that the average cost of providing air travel is constant at $100 per passenger. As shown in Figure 12.1, the average cost is constant, which means that marginal cost equals average cost.

A **cartel** is a group of firms that act in unison, coordinating their price and quantity decisions. In our airline example, the two airlines could form a cartel and choose the monopoly price. In Figure 12.1, the firm-specific demand curve for a monopolist is the market-demand curve, and the marginal-revenue curve intersects the marginal-cost curve at a quantity of 60 passengers per day (point *a*). If the two airlines act as one, they will pick the monopoly price of $400 and split the monopoly output, so each will have 30 passengers per day. The average cost per passenger is $100, so each airline earns a daily profit of $9,000:

profit = (price − average cost) × quantity per firm = ($400 − $100) × 30 = $9,000

* **duopoly**
A market with two firms.

* **cartel**
A group of firms that act in unison, coordinating their price and quantity decisions.

► **FIGURE 12.1**

**A Cartel Picks the Monopoly Quantity and Price**

The monopoly outcome is shown by point *a*, where marginal revenue equals marginal cost. The monopoly quantity is 60 passengers and the price is $400. If the firms form a cartel, the price is $400 and each firm has 30 passengers (half the monopoly quantity). The profit per passenger is $300 (equal to the $400 price minus the $100 average cost), so the profit per firm is $9,000.

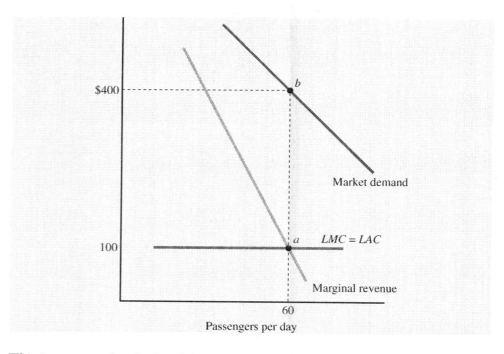

• **price-fixing**
An arrangement in which firms conspire to fix prices.

This is an example of **price-fixing**, an arrangement in which firms conspire to fix prices. As we'll see later in the chapter, cartels and price-fixing are illegal under U.S. antitrust laws.

What would happen if the two firms competed rather than conspiring to fix the price? If they do, each firm will have its own demand curve. As we saw in the previous chapter, the firm-specific demand curve for the typical firm lies to the left of the market demand curve because consumers can choose from two firms. At a particular price, consumers will be divided between the two firms, so each firm will serve only part of the market. In Figure 12.2, the demand curve for the typical duopolist is below the market demand curve. For example, at a price of $300, point *d* shows that the market quantity is 80 passengers, while point *b* shows that each firm has 40 passengers.

► **FIGURE 12.2**

**Competing Duopolists Pick a Lower Price**

**(A)** The typical firm maximizes profit at point *a*, where marginal revenue equals marginal cost. The firm has 40 passengers.
**(B)** At the market level, the duopoly outcome is shown by point *d*, with a price of $300 and 80 passengers. The cartel outcome, shown by point *c*, has a higher price and a smaller total quantity.

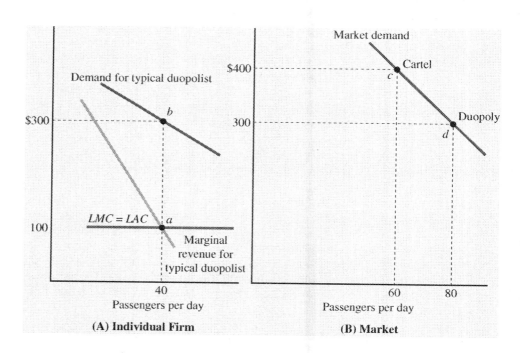

**(A) Individual Firm**     **(B) Market**

Panel A in Figure 12.2 shows the quantity and price choice of an individual firm. Given the firm-specific demand curve and marginal-revenue curve, the marginal principle is satisfied at point *a*, where marginal revenue equals marginal cost. The firm has 40 passengers at a price of $300 (point *b*). The two firms are identical, so each has 40 passengers at a price of $300. Given an average cost of $100, each firm earns a profit of $8,000:

profit = (price – average cost) × quantity per firm = ($300 – $100) × 40 = $8,000

## Price-Fixing and the Game Tree

Clearly, each firm will earn more profit under a price-fixing cartel, but will a cartel succeed, or will firms cheat on a cartel agreement? We can answer this question with the help of a **game tree**, a graphical representation of the consequences of different actions in a strategic setting. Each firm must choose a price for airline tickets, either the high price (the $400 cartel price) or the low price (the duopoly price of $300). Each firm can use the game tree to pick a price, knowing that the other firm is picking a price too.

Figure 12.3 shows the game tree for the price-fixing game. Let's call the managers of the airlines Jack and Jill. The game tree has three components:

- The squares are decision nodes. Each square has a player (Jack or Jill) and a list of the player's possible actions. For example, the game starts at square *A*, where Jill has two options: high price or low price.

- The arrows show the possible paths of the game from left to right. Jill chooses her price first, so we move from square *A* to one of Jack's decision nodes, either square *B* or square *C*. If Jill chooses the high price, we move from square *A* to square *B*. Once we reach one of Jack's decision nodes, he chooses a price—high or low—and then we move to one of the rectangles. For example, if Jack chooses the high price too, we move from square *B* to rectangle 1.

- The rectangles show the profits for the two firms. When we reach a rectangle, the game is over, and the players receive the profits shown in the rectangle. There is a profit rectangle for each of the four possible outcomes of the price-fixing game.

We've already computed the profits for two payoff rectangles. Rectangle 1 shows what happens when each firm chooses the high price. This is the cartel or price-fixing outcome, with each firm earning $9,000. Rectangle 4 shows what happens when each

> **game tree**
> A graphical representation of the consequences of different actions in a strategic setting.

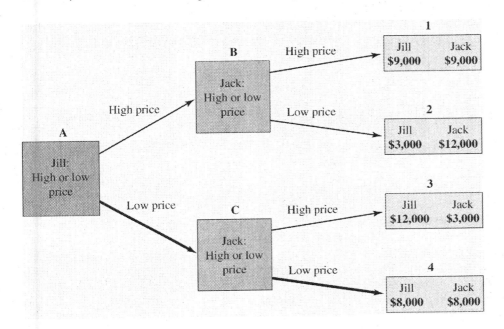

◄ **FIGURE 12.3**
**Game Tree for the Price-Fixing Game**
The equilibrium path of the game is square *A* to square *C* to rectangle *4*: Each firm picks the low price and earns a profit of $8,000. The duopolists' dilemma is that each firm would make more profit if both picked the high price, but both firms pick the low price.

**Table 12.2 | DUOPOLISTS' PROFITS WHEN THEY CHOOSE DIFFERENT PRICES**

|  | Jill: High Price | Jack: Low Price |
|---|---|---|
| Price | $400 | $300 |
| Average cost | $100 | $100 |
| Profit per passenger | $300 | $200 |
| Number of passengers | 10 | 60 |
| Profit | $3,000 | $12,000 |

firm chooses the low price. This is the duopoly outcome, when firms compete and each firm earns a profit of $8,000.

What would happen if the two firms chose different prices? If Jill chooses the high price and Jack chooses the low price, Jack will capture a large share of the market and gain at Jill's expense. In the first column of Table 12.2, Jill charges the high price and has only 10 passengers at a price of $400, so her profit is $3,000:

$$\text{profit} = (\text{price} - \text{average cost}) \times \text{quantity per firm} = (\$400 - \$100) \times 10 = \$3,000$$

In the second column, Jack charges the low price and has 60 passengers at a price of $300 so his profit is $12,000:

$$\text{profit} = (\text{price} - \text{average cost}) \times \text{quantity per firm} = (\$300 - \$100) \times 60 = \$12,000$$

This is shown by rectangle 2 in Figure 12.3: The path of the game is square $A$ to square $B$ to rectangle 2. The other underpricing outcome is shown by rectangle 3. In this case, Jill chooses the low price and Jack chooses the high price, so Jill gains at Jack's expense. The roles are reversed, and so are the numbers in the profit rectangle.

### Equilibrium of the Price-Fixing Game

We can predict the equilibrium of the price-fixing game by a process of elimination. We'll eliminate the rectangles that would require one or both firms to act irrationally, leaving us with the rectangle showing the equilibrium of the game:

- If Jill chooses the high price, we'll move along the upper branches of the tree and eventually reach rectangle 1 or 2, depending on what Jack does. Although Jill would like Jack to choose the high price, too, this would be irrational for Jack. He can earn $12,000 profit by choosing the low price, compared to $9,000 with the high price. Therefore, we can eliminate rectangle 1.

- If Jill chooses the low price, we'll move along the lower branches of the tree and eventually reach rectangle 3 or 4, depending on Jack's choice. Jack won't choose the high price because he can earn $8,000 with the low price, compared to $3,000 with the high price. Therefore, we can eliminate rectangle 3.

We've eliminated the two profit rectangles that involve a high price for Jack—rectangles 1 and 3. That means that the low price is a **dominant strategy** for Jack: Regardless of what Jill does, Jack's best choice is the low price.

Two profit rectangles are left—2 and 4—and Jill's action will determine which rectangle is the equilibrium. Jill knows that Jack will choose the low price regardless of what she does. She could choose the high price and allow Jack to capture most of the market, leaving her with a profit of only $3,000 in rectangle 2. A better choice is to pick the low price and get a profit of $8,000 in rectangle 4. In other words, it would be irrational for Jill to allow herself to be underpriced, so the outcome of the game is shown by profit rectangle 4: Each player chooses the low price. The thick arrows show the equilibrium path of the game, from square $A$ to square $C$ to rectangle 4.

• **dominant strategy**
An action that is the best choice for a player, no matter what the other player does.

Both firms will be unhappy with this equilibrium because each could earn a higher profit with rectangle 1. To get there, however, each firm must choose the high price. The **duopolists' dilemma** is that although both firms would be better off if they both chose the high price, each firm chooses the low price. The dilemma occurs because there is a big payoff from underpricing the other firm and a big penalty from being underpriced, so both firms pick the low price. As we'll see later in the chapter, to avoid the dilemma the firms must find some way to prevent underpricing.

• **duopolists' dilemma**
A situation in which both firms in a market would be better off if both chose the high price, but each chooses the low price.

## Nash Equilibrium

We have used a game tree to find the equilibrium in a price-fixing game. It is an equilibrium in the sense that each player (firm) is doing the best he or she can, given the actions of another player. The label for such an equilibrium is **Nash equilibrium**. This concept is named after John Nash, the recipient of the 1994 Nobel Prize in economics, who developed his equilibrium concept as a 21-year-old graduate student at Princeton University. His life story, which includes a 25-year bout with schizophrenia and a dramatic recovery, is chronicled in the book *A Beautiful Mind*, later made into a movie starring Russell Crowe as John Nash.[2]

• **Nash equilibrium**
An outcome of a game in which each player is doing the best he or she can, given the action of the other players.

In the price-fixing game, the Nash equilibrium is for both firms to pick the low price. Each firm is doing the best it can, given the action of the other firm:

- If Jill picks the low price, Jack's best action is to pick the low price.
- If Jack picks the low price, Jill's best action is to pick the low price.

What about the other potential outcomes? Consider first the possibility that both firms pick the high price. This is not a Nash equilibrium because neither firm is doing the best it can, given the action of the other firm:

- If Jill picks the high price, Jack's best action is to pick the low price.
- If Jack picks the high price, Jill's best action is to pick the low price.

Consider next the possibility that Jill picks the low price and Jack picks the high price. This is not a Nash equilibrium because Jack is not doing the best he can, given Jill's choice:

- If Jill picks the low price, Jack's best action is to pick the low price.

The concept of the Nash equilibrium has been applied to a wide variety of decisions. Later in the chapter, we will use it to predict the outcome of games involving entry deterrence and advertising. In addition to strategic decisions for firms, it has been used to analyze the nuclear arms race, terrorism, evolutionary biology, art auctions, environmental policy, and urban development.

# 12.3 | OVERCOMING THE DUOPOLISTS' DILEMMA

The duopolists' dilemma occurs because the two firms are unable to coordinate their pricing decisions and act as one. Each firm has an incentive to underprice the other firm because the low-price firm will capture a larger share of the market and earn a larger profit. The dilemma can be avoided in two ways: low-price guarantees, and repetition of the pricing game, with retaliation for underpricing.

## Low-Price Guarantees

The duopolists' dilemma occurs because the payoff from underpricing the other firm is too lucrative to miss. To eliminate the possibility for underpricing, one firm can guarantee that it will match a lower price of a competitor. Suppose Jill places the following advertisement in the local newspaper:

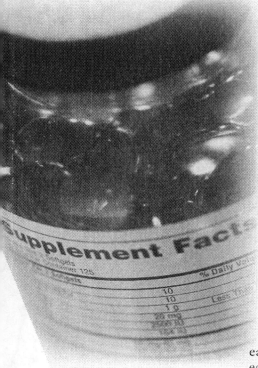

# APPLICATION

## VITAMIN INC. GETS BUSTED

**APPLYING THE CONCEPTS #1:** How do firms conspire to fix prices?

In April 2000, four former executives of drug companies pled guilty to conspiring to fix the prices of bulk vitamins worldwide. It was the largest price-fixing case in U.S. history. The leading companies involved in the illegal cartel were Hoffman-La Roche (with 60 percent of the U.S. vitamin market), BASF AG (28 percent), and Rhone-Poulenc (7 percent). They were joined by other vitamin producers from Japan, Switzerland, and Canada. The announcement brought the number of Swiss and German executives imprisoned for the case to six, with fines for the individual executives and their companies totaling $1 billion.

For almost a decade, these executives conspired to stifle competition around the globe by fixing prices on vitamins A, B2, B5, C, E, and beta carotene. The executives called their group "Vitamin Inc." and met regularly in hotel rooms to carve up the market. Market shares for each region were specified down to a half percentage point, and prices for each vitamin were agreed upon down to the penny. For vitamin "premixes" (used for livestock feed and human food such as breakfast cereals), the executives rigged the bidding process for contracts, specifying a price and designating a "winner" for each contract. To help prevent cheating, they had "budget meetings" to check each other's data on sales and market shares. The cartel managed to boost the prices of vitamins, with markups averaging about 20 percent, or even more at the high-end of the vitamin price range. For example, the price of vitamin A nearly doubled, from about $12 per pound to $20.

Hoffman-LaRoche ultimately paid a fine of $500 million, about half of its annual revenue from its vitamin business in the United States. BASF AG paid a fine of $225 million. Rhone-Poulenc broke ranks early in the investigation, and by cooperating with U.S. Justice Department investigators the firm avoided any fines. A group of Japanese companies paid a total of $137 million. **Related to Exercises 2.8 and 2.9.**

SOURCE: David Barboza, "Tearing Down the Facade of 'Vitamin Inc.'" *New York Times*, October 10, 1999, Section 3, p. 1; Department of Justice, "Four Foreign Executives of Leading European Vitamin Firms Agree to Plead Guilty to Participating in International Vitamin Cartel," Press Release, April 6, 2000.

---

If you buy an airline ticket from me and then discover that Jack offers the same trip at a lower price, I will pay you the price difference. If I charge you $400 and Jack's price is only $300, I will pay you $100.

• **low-price guarantee**
A promise to match a lower price of a competitor.

Jill's **low-price guarantee** is a credible promise because she announces it in the newspaper. Suppose Jack makes a similar commitment to match a lower price from Jill.

Figure 12.4 shows the effect of low-price guarantees on the game tree. Jill now has two decision nodes. As before, she starts the game in square *A*. If Jill picks the high price and then Jack picks the high price, we end up at rectangle 1, as before. But if Jill picks the high price and Jack picks the low price, we get to square *D*. Jill will issue a refund of $100 to each of her consumers. In effect, she has retroactively chosen the

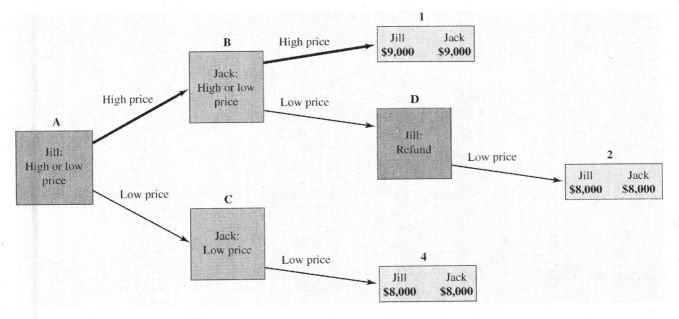

**▲ FIGURE 12.4**

**Low-Price Guarantees Increase Prices**

When both firms have a low-price guarantee, it is impossible for one firm to underprice the other. The only possible outcomes are a pair of high prices (rectangle 1) or a pair of low prices (rectangles 2 or 4). The equilibrium path of the game is square A to square B to rectangle 1. Each firm picks the high price and earns a profit of $9,000.

low price, and payoff rectangle 2 is the duopoly outcome, with both firms picking the low price. For the lower half of the game tree, recall that Jack has committed to match a lower price by Jill, so the old payoff rectangle 3 disappears, leaving us with rectangle 4, where both firms choose the low price and get the duopoly profit.

The thick arrows show the path of the game with low-price guarantees. Consider Jack's decision first:

- If Jill picks the high price, Jack chooses between payoff rectangles 1 and 2, a pair of high prices or a pair of low prices. His profit is higher at $9,000 with a pair of high prices (rectangle 1), so if Jill picks the high price, he will, too.
- If Jill picks the low price, Jack is committed to the low price, too.

Consider Jill's decision. She knows that Jack will match her price—either high or low—meaning that she chooses between profit rectangles 1 and 4. Profit is higher with rectangle 1, so she will pick the high price.

The low-price guarantee eliminates the possibility of underpricing, so it eliminates the duopolists' dilemma and promotes cartel pricing. The firms don't have to create a formal cartel to get the benefits from cartel pricing. The motto of a low-price guarantee is "Low for one means low for all," so both firms charge the high price. Once the possibility of underpricing has been eliminated, the duopoly will be replaced by an informal cartel, with each firm picking the price that would be picked by a monopolist.

## Repeated Pricing Games with Retaliation for Underpricing

Up to this point, we've assumed that the price-fixing game is played only once. Each firm chooses a price and keeps that price for the lifetime of the firm. What happens when two firms play the game repeatedly, picking prices over an extended period of time? We'll see that repetition makes price-fixing more likely because firms can punish a firm that cheats on a price-fixing agreement, whether it's formal or informal.

# APPLICATION

## LOW-PRICE GUARANTEES AND EMPTY PROMISES

### APPLYING THE CONCEPTS #2: Does a low-price guarantee lead to higher or lower prices?

If you shop around for a new car stereo, you'll notice that most sellers have a low-price guarantee. If you buy a stereo from firm A and later discover that firm B sells the same stereo at a lower price, firm A will pay you the difference in price. The guarantee typically excludes discontinued and closeout products, and the other store must be an authorized dealer of the product you bought. Will the low-price guarantee lead to lower prices? As we've seen, a low-price guarantee eliminates the possibility that one firm will underprice the other and, thus leads to high prices.

To most people, the notion that a low-price guarantee leads to higher prices is surprising. After all, if firm A promises to give refunds if its price exceeds firm B's price, we might expect firm A to keep its price low to avoid handing out a lot of refunds. In fact, firm A doesn't have to worry about giving refunds because firm B will also choose the high price. In other words, the promise to issue refunds is an *empty* promise. Although consumers might think that a low-price guarantee will protect them from high prices, it means that consumers are more likely to pay the high price. **Related to Exercises 3.5 and 3.6.**

Firms use several strategies to maintain a price-fixing agreement. Continuing our airline example, suppose Jack and Jill pick their prices at the beginning of each month. Jill chooses the cartel price for the first month and will continue to choose the cartel price as long as Jack does too. Jill could use one of the following strategies to punish Jack if he underprices her:

1 *A duopoly pricing strategy.* Jill chooses the lower duopoly price for the remaining lifetime of her firm. Once Jill is underpriced, she abandons the idea of cartel pricing and accepts the duopoly outcome, which is less profitable than the cartel outcome but more profitable than being underpriced by the other firm.

2 *A grim-trigger strategy.* When Jack underprices Jill, she responds by dropping her price to a level at which each firm will make zero economic profit. This is called the **grim-trigger strategy**, because grim consequences are triggered by Jack's underpricing.

3 *A tit-for-tat strategy.* Starting in the second month, Jill chooses whatever price Jack chose the preceding month. This is the **tit-for-tat** strategy—one firm chooses whatever price the other firm chose in the preceding period. As long as Jack chooses the cartel price, the cartel arrangement will persist. But if Jack underprices Jill, the cartel will break down.

Figure 12.5 shows how a tit-for-tat system works. Jack underprices Jill in the second month, so Jill chooses the low price for the third month, resulting in the duopoly outcome. To restore the cartel outcome, Jack must eventually choose the high price,

- **grim-trigger strategy**
  A strategy where a firm responds to underpricing by choosing a price so low that each firm makes zero economic profit.

- **tit-for-tat**
  A strategy where one firm chooses whatever price the other firm chose in the preceding period.

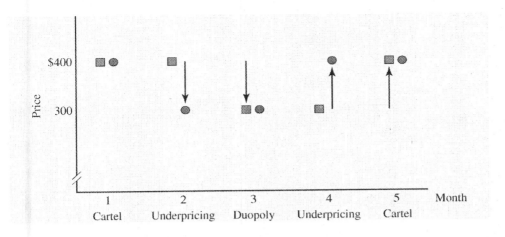

allowing Jill to underprice him for one month. This happens in the fourth month, and the cartel is restored in the fifth month. Although Jack can gain at Jill's expense in the second month, if he wants to restore cartel pricing, he must allow her to gain at his expense during some other month. Under a tit-for-tat strategy, a duopolist does exactly what his or her rival did the last round. This encourages firms to cooperate rather than compete. Several studies have shown that a tit-for-tat strategy is the most effective strategy to promote cooperation.[3]

These three pricing schemes promote cartel pricing by penalizing the firm that underprices the other firm. To decide whether to underprice Jill, Jack must weigh the short-term benefit against the long-term cost:

- The short-term benefit is the increase in profit in the current period. If Jack underprices Jill, he can increase his profit from the cartel profit of $9,000 to the $12,000 earned by a firm that underprices the other firm. Therefore, the short-term benefit of underpricing is $3,000.

- The long-term cost is the loss of profit in later periods. Jill will respond to Jack's underpricing by cutting her price, and this decreases Jack's profit. For example, if Jill retaliates with the duopoly price, Jack's future profit will be $8,000 per day instead of the $9,000 he could have earned by going along with the cartel price. The cost of underpricing is the daily loss of $1,000 in profit.

If the two firms expect to share the market for a long time, the long-term cost of underpricing will exceed the short-term benefit, so underpricing is less likely. The threat of punishment makes it easier to resist the temptation to cheat on the cartel.

## Price-Fixing and the Law

Under the Sherman Antitrust Act of 1890 and subsequent legislation, explicit price-fixing is illegal. It is illegal for firms to discuss pricing strategies or methods of punishing a firm that underprices other firms. In one of the early price-fixing cases (*Addyston Pipe*, 1899), six manufacturers of cast-iron pipe met to fix prices. Several months after the Supreme Court ruled that their cartel pricing was illegal, the firms merged into a single firm, so instead of acting like a monopolist, they became a monopolist. Here are some other examples of price-fixing:

1 *Electric generators (1961)*. Executives from General Electric and Westinghouse were convicted of fixing prices for electrical generators, resulting in fines of over $2 million and imprisonment or probation for 30 corporate executives.

2 *Infant formula (1993)*. The three major U.S. producers of infant formula—Abbott Labs, Mead Johnson, and American Home Products—which together served 95 percent of the market, paid a total of $200 million to wholesalers and retailers to settle lawsuits claiming that they had conspired to fix prices.

**3** *Carton-board pricing in Europe (1994).* The European Union Commission fined 19 manufacturers of carton board a total of 132 million euros ($165 million) for operating a cartel that fixed prices at secret meetings in luxury Zurich hotels.

**4** *Food additives (1996).* An employee of Archer Daniels Midland (ADM), a huge food company, provided audio and videotapes of ADM executives conspiring to fix prices. ADM pleaded guilty to the charges of price-fixing and was fined $100 million.

**5** *Music distribution (2000).* In exchange for advertising subsidies, music retailers agreed to adhere to the minimum advertised prices (MAP) specified by distributors. Any retailer that advertised a CD for less than the MAP would lose all of its "cooperative advertising" funds from the distributor. In May 2000, the Federal Trade Commission reached an agreement with music distributors to end the MAP scheme. The FTC estimated that the MAP scheme imposed an annual cost of $160 million on U.S. music consumers.[4]

# 12.4 | ALTERNATIVE MODELS OF OLIGOPOLY PRICING

We've explored a model of cartel pricing, an arrangement under which firms conspire to fix prices at the monopoly level. In this part of the chapter, we consider two alternative models of oligopoly pricing: A model of price leadership and the model of the kinked demand curve.

## Price Leadership

- **price leadership**
  A system under which one firm in an oligopoly takes the lead in setting prices.

Because explicit price-fixing is illegal, firms sometimes rely on implicit pricing agreements to fix prices at the monopoly level. Under the model of **price leadership**, one of the oligopolists plays the role of price leader. The leading firm picks a price, and other firms match the price. Such an agreement allows firms to cooperate without actually discussing their pricing strategies.

The problem with an implicit pricing agreement is that it relies on indirect signals that are often garbled and misinterpreted. Suppose that two firms have cooperated for several years, both sticking to the cartel price. When one firm suddenly drops its price, the other firm could interpret the price cut in one of two ways:

- *A change in market conditions.* Perhaps the first firm observed a change in demand or production cost and decides that both firms would benefit from a lower price.
- *Underpricing.* Perhaps the first firm is trying to increase its market share and profit at the expense of the second firm.

The first interpretation would probably cause the second firm to match the lower price of the first firm, and price-fixing would continue at the lower price. In contrast, the second interpretation could trigger a price war, undermining the price-fixing agreement.

## The Kinked Demand Curve Model

- **kinked demand curve model**
  A model in which firms in an oligopoly match price cuts by other firms, but do not match price hikes.

The **kinked demand curve model** of oligopoly gets its name from its assumptions about how firms in an oligopoly respond when one firm changes its price. The model assumes that when one firm cuts its price, the other firms will match the price cut. But if one firm raises its price, other firms don't match the price hike.

The firm-specific demand curve in Figure 12.6 incorporates the assumptions of the kinked demand curve model. The demand curve shows the demand facing Kirk, one of three firms in the oligopoly. Suppose each of the three firms starts out with a price of $6, and Kirk sells 30 units of output (point *k*). What happens if Kirk changes his price?

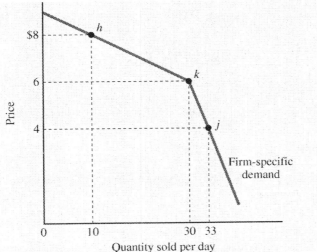

- If Kirk decreases his price, the other firms will decrease their prices too. Kirk will have the same price as the other firms, so his quantity will increase by a relatively small amount—from 30 to 33 units.

- If Kirk increases his price, the other firms will not change their prices. Kirk will have a higher price than the other firms, so his quantity will decrease by a relatively large amount—from 30 to 10 units.

In this model, the demand curve of the typical firm has a kink at the prevailing price. It is relatively flat for higher prices because other firms won't match a higher price. It is relatively steep for lower prices because other firms *will* match a lower price. Once a price has been established, it will tend to persist. The benefit of cutting the price is relatively small because the other firms will match a lower price. Moving in the other direction, the penalty for an increase in price is relatively large because the other firms won't match a higher price.

The model of kinked demand is a model of pessimism. Each firm assumes the worst about how its fellow oligopolists will respond to a change in price: The other firms will not go along with a higher price, but will match a lower price. Although this model may have some intuitive appeal, there is no evidence that firms act this way. Starting in 1947, various studies of oligopolies have failed to find compelling evidence to support the kinked demand model of oligopoly.[5]

# 12.5 | SIMULTANEOUS DECISION MAKING AND THE PAYOFF MATRIX

So far we have considered a game with sequential decisions. Jill chooses her price first, and then Jack observes her choice and then makes his own. An alternative scenario is that the two firms make their decisions simultaneously, so each firm picks its price without knowing the other firm's price. The analysis of a simultaneous game requires a different tool. A **payoff matrix** shows, for each possible outcome of a game, the consequences—or payoffs—for each player.

◆ **payoff matrix**
A matrix or table that shows, for each possible outcome of a game, the consequences for each player.

## Simultaneous Price-Fixing Game

Figure 12.7 shows the payoff matrix for the price-fixing game. Each cell in the matrix shows the payoffs from a potential outcome of the game. In the northwest corner of the matrix, if both firms pick the high price, each firm earns a profit of $9,000. In the southeast corner, if both firms pick the low price, each firm earns a profit of $8,000. If

► **FIGURE 12.7**
Payoff Matrix for the Price-Fixing Game
Jill's profit is in red, and Jack's profit is in blue. If both firms pick the high price, each firm earns a profit of $9,000. Both firms will pick the low price, and each firm will earn a profit of only $8,000.

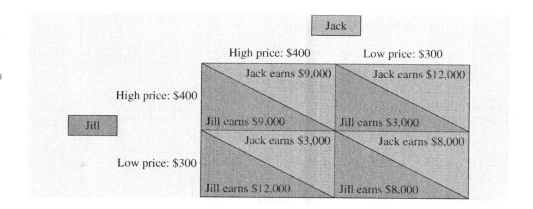

one firm picks the low price and the other picks the high price, the low-price firm earns $12,000 and the high-price firm earns only $3,000. For example, in the northeast corner, if Jill picks the high price and Jack picks the low price, Jill earns a profit of $3,000 and Jack earns a profit of $12,000.

We can use the payoff matrix to predict the equilibrium of the price-fixing game. In a simultaneous-decision game, Jack doesn't know whether Jill will pick the low price or the high price. There are two possibilities:

- If Jill picks the high price, we will be in the upper half of the matrix, and Jack's best response is the low price. In the northeast corner of the matrix, he can earn $12,000 by picking the low price. This is better than the $9,000 he can earn by picking the high price in the northwest corner.

- If Jill picks the low price, we will be in the lower half of the matrix, and Jack's best response is the low price. In the southeast corner of the matrix, he can earn $8,000 by picking the low price. This is better than the $3,000 he can earn by picking the high price in the southwest corner.

In other words, the low price is the dominant strategy for Jack. Jill knows this, so she realizes that the equilibrium will be in the eastern half of the matrix. Her best response is the low price. In the southeast corner of the matrix, she can earn $8,000 by picking the low price. This is better than the $3,000 she can earn in the northeast corner by picking the high price. Therefore, the equilibrium is the same as with the game-tree approach: Both firms pick the low price.

### The Prisoners' Dilemma

We can gain some insight into the duopolists' dilemma by examining the classic prisoners' dilemma. Consider two people, Bonnie and Clyde, who have been accused of committing a crime. The police give each person an opportunity to confess to the crime. The traditional version of the story involves a simultaneous decision-making game: The two are put in separate rooms, and each makes a choice without knowing the other's choice.

The police confront Bonnie and Clyde with the payoff matrix in Figure 12.8. If both confess, each gets five years in prison, as shown in the southeast corner of the matrix. If neither confesses, the police can convict both of them on a lesser charge, and each gets two years, as shown in the northwest corner of the matrix. If only one confesses, he or she will implicate the other prisoner. The confessor is rewarded with a one-year prison sentence, while the other prisoner gets 10 years. If Bonnie confesses and Clyde does not, we are in the southwest corner of the matrix. If the roles are reversed, we are in the northeast corner.

We can use the payoff matrix to predict the equilibrium of the prisoner game. In a simultaneous-decision game, Clyde doesn't know whether Bonnie will confess or not:

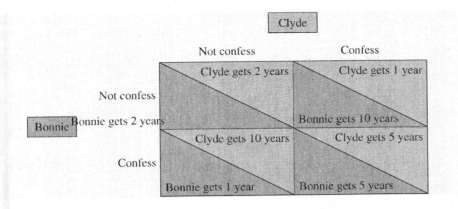

◀ FIGURE 12.8
Payoff Matrix for the Prisoners' Dilemma
The prisoners' dilemma is that each prisoner would be better off if neither confessed, but both people confess. The Nash equilibrium is shown in the southeast corner of the matrix. Each person gets five years of prison time.

- If Bonnie does not confess, we are in the upper half of the matrix, and Clyde's best response is to confess. In the northeast corner of the matrix, he gets one year in prison if he confesses. This is better than the two years he would get in the northwest corner by not confessing.
- If Bonnie confesses, we are in the lower half of the matrix, and Clyde's best response is to confess. In the southeast corner of the matrix, he gets five years in prison. This is better than the 10 years he would get in the southwest corner by not confessing.

In other words, confessing is the dominant strategy for Clyde. Bonnie knows this, so she realizes that the equilibrium will be in the eastern half of the matrix. Her best response is to confess. In the southeast corner of the matrix, she gets five years in prison. This is better than the 10 years she would get in the northeast by not confessing.

In the Nash equilibrium, both prisoners confess and each gets five years in prison. This is a Nash equilibrium because each prisoner is doing the best he or she can, given the actions of the other prisoner. Although both criminals would be better off if they both kept quiet, they implicate each other because the police reward them for doing so. There is an incentive for squealing, just as there is an incentive for one duopolist to underprice the other.

# 12.6 | THE INSECURE MONOPOLIST AND ENTRY DETERRENCE

We've seen what happens when two duopolists try to act as one, fixing the price at the monopoly level. Consider next how a monopolist might try to prevent a second firm from entering its market. We will use some of the numbers from our airline example, although we will look at a different city with a different cast of characters.

Suppose that Mona initially has a secure monopoly in the market for air travel between two cities. When there is no threat of entry, Mona uses the marginal principle (marginal revenue equals marginal cost) to pick a quantity and a price. In Figure 12.9, we start at point $c$ on the market demand curve, with a quantity of 60 passengers per day and a price of $400 per passenger. Her profit is $18,000:

$$\text{profit} = (\text{price} - \text{average cost}) \times \text{quantity per firm} = (\$400 - \$100) \times 60 = \$18,000$$

If Mona discovers that a second airline is thinking about entering the market, what will she do? Now that her monopoly is insecure, she has two options: She can be passive and allow the second airline to enter the market, or she can try to prevent the other firm from entering the market.

### The Passive Approach

The passive approach will lead to the duopoly outcome we saw earlier in the chapter. In Figure 12.9, if the second firm enters the market, we move downward along the market demand curve from point $c$ to point $d$. In a duopoly, each firm charges a price

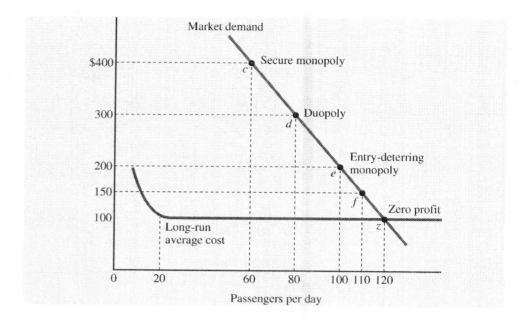

of $300 and serves 40 passengers, half the total quantity demanded at a price of $300. For each duopolist, the daily profit is $8,000:

$$\text{profit} = (\text{price} - \text{average cost}) \times \text{quantity per firm} = (\$300 - \$100) \times 40 = \$8,000$$

## Entry Deterrence and Limit Pricing

The second option is to take actions to prevent the second firm from entering the market. To decide whether to deter the entry of the other firm, Mona must answer two questions:

- What must she do to deter entry?
- Given what she must do to deter entry, is deterrence more profitable than being passive and sharing the market with the second firm?

To prevent the second firm from entering the market, Mona must commit herself to serving a large number of passengers. If she commits to a large passenger load, there won't be enough passengers left for a potential entrant to make a profit. Suppose there are economies of scale in providing air travel, and the minimum entry quantity is 20 passengers per day: That is, it would be impractical for a firm to serve fewer than 20 passengers. In Figure 12.9, the long-run average cost curve is negatively sloped for relatively low levels of output, and the average cost for the minimum entry quantity of 20 passengers is just over $100, say $101.

Mona must compute the quantity of output that is just large enough to prevent the second firm from entering the market. In Figure 12.9, point z shows the point of zero economic profit in the market: If the two firms serve a total of 120 passengers per day and split the market equally, with 60 passengers each, the price ($100) equals average cost, so each firm would earn zero economic profit. The quantity required to prevent the entry of the second firm is computed as follows:

$$\text{deterring quantity} = \text{zero profit quantity} - \text{minimum entry quantity}$$
$$100 = 120 - 20$$

If Mona commits to serve 100 passengers and a second firm were to enter with the minimum quantity of 20 passengers, the price would drop to $100. Mona, with an average cost of $100 to serve 100 passengers, would break even. The second firm, with an average cost just above $100, would lose money. Specifically, if the average cost of 20 passengers is $101, the second firm would lose $1 per passenger, or $20 in total.

It's important to note that Mona cannot simply announce that she will serve 100 passengers. She must take actions that ensure that her most profitable output is in fact 100 passengers. In other words, she must commit to 100 passengers. She could commit to the larger passenger load by purchasing a large fleet of airplanes and signing labor contracts that require her to hire a large workforce.

Which is more profitable, entry deterrence or the passive duopoly outcome? The deterrence strategy, shown by point $e$ in Figure 12.9, generates a price of $200 and a profit of $10,000:

profit = (price − average cost) × quantity per firm = ($200 − $100) × 100 = $10,000

This is larger than the $8,000 profit under the passive approach, so deterrence is the best strategy.

Figure 12.10 uses a game tree to represent the entry-deterrence game. Mona makes the first move, and she considers the consequences of her two options:

- If Mona is passive and commits to serve only 40 passengers, we reach the upper branch of the game tree. The best response for Doug, the manager of the second firm, is to enter to earn a profit of $8,000, as shown by rectangle 1.

- If Mona commits to serve 100 passengers, we reach the lower branch of the game tree. If Doug enters with the minimum entry quantity of 20 passengers, his average cost will be $101, which exceeds the market price of $100. Therefore, the best response is to stay out of the market and avoid losing money.

Mona can choose between rectangles 1 and 4. Mona's profit is higher in rectangle 4, so that's the equilibrium. The equilibrium path of the game is square $A$ to square $C$ to rectangle 4.

Mona's entry-deterrence strategy generates a market price of $200, which is less than the $400 price charged by a secure monopolist and less than the $300 price with two competing firms. Mona can keep the second firm out of the market, but only by producing a large quantity and charging a relatively low price. This is known as **limit pricing**: To prevent a firm from entering the market, the firm reduces its price.

* **limit pricing**
The strategy of reducing the price to deter entry.

◄ **FIGURE 12.10**
**Game Tree for the Entry-Deterrence Game**
The path of the game is square $A$ to square $C$ to rectangle 4. Mona commits to the entry-deterring quantity of 100, so Doug stays out of the market. Mona' profit of $10,000 is less than the monopoly profit but more than the duopoly profit of $8,000.

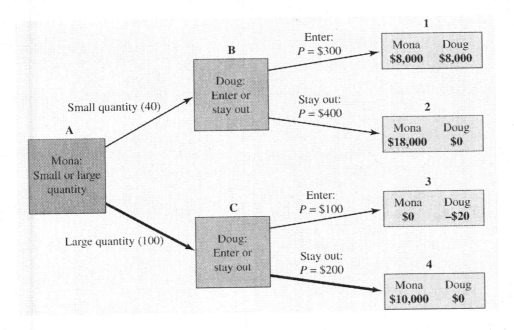

# 3

# APPLICATION

## LEGAL AND ILLEGAL ENTRY DETERRENCE

**APPLYING THE CONCEPTS #3:** What means—legal and illegal—do firms use to prevent other firms from entering a market?

When firms use limit pricing to prevent other firms from entering the market, entry deterrence is legal. For example, between 1893 and 1940, the Aluminum Company of America (Alcoa) had a monopoly on aluminum production in the United States. During this period, Alcoa kept other firms out of the market by producing a large quantity and keeping its price relatively low. Although a higher price would have generated more profit in the short run, the entry of other firms would have eventually reduced Alcoa's profit.

In recent years, the European Commission has uncovered many examples of entry deterrence that are illegal under the rules of the European Union. Van den Bergh Foods, a subsidiary of Unilever, held a dominant position in the market for ice cream in Ireland in 1998. The company provided "free" freezer cabinets to retailers, under the condition that the cabinets were to be used exclusively for the storage of Unilever's products. Irish retailers were reluctant to replace Unilever cabinets, so 40 percent of retailers sold only Unilever ice-cream products. The Commission concluded that this practice constituted an abuse of Unilever's dominant position. In 2003, the European Court of First Instance ordered Unilever to share the freezer cabinets with its competitors, including the Mars Company, which had argued that it was unable to sell its ice cream in many retail outlets in Ireland. ***Related to Exercise 6.8.***

SOURCES: Leonard W. Weiss, *Economics and American Industry* (New York: Wiley, 1963), pp. 189–204; European Commission, *Report on Competition Policy 1998*, pp. 35–39.

### Examples: Microsoft Windows and Campus Bookstores

For an example of limit pricing, consider the pricing of the Windows operating system by Microsoft. The Windows operating system runs about 90 percent of the world's personal computers, so it is natural to think that Microsoft has a monopoly in the market for operating systems. According to economist Richard Schmalensee, Microsoft's profit-maximizing monopoly price is between $900 and $2,000. That's the amount Microsoft would charge if it acted like a secure monopolist.[6] The fact that Microsoft charges only $99 for Windows suggests that Microsoft is an insecure monopolist, and that it picks a lower price to discourage entry and preserve its monopoly. If Microsoft charged $2,000 for its operating system, there would be a greater incentive for other firms to develop competing operating systems.

We can apply the notion of entry deterrence to your favorite monopoly: your campus bookstore. On most college campuses, the campus bookstore has a monopoly on the sale of textbooks. Other organizations are prohibited, usually by the state government or the college, from selling textbooks on campus. The recent growth of Internet commerce has given students another option: Order textbooks over the Web and have them shipped by mail, UPS, FedEx, or Airborne Express. Several Web booksellers charge less than the campus bookstore, and the growth of Web book sales threatens the campus bookstore monopoly. If your campus bookstore suddenly feels insecure about its monopoly position, it could cut its prices to prevent Web booksellers from capturing too many of its customers. If it does this, you will pay lower prices even if you don't patronize the Web seller.

## Entry Deterrence and Contestable Markets

We've seen that an insecure monopolist may cut its price to prevent a second firm from entering the market. The same logic applies to a market that has a few firms and could potentially have many firms. The mere existence of a monopoly or oligopoly does not necessarily generate high prices and large profits. To protect its market share, an oligopolist may act like a firm in a market with many firms, leading to relatively low prices.

The threat of entry faced by an insecure monopolist underlies the theory of market contestability. A **contestable market** is a market with low entry and exit costs. The few firms in a contestable market will be threatened constantly by the entry of new firms, so prices and profits will be relatively low. In the extreme case of perfect contestability, firms can enter and exit a market at zero cost. In this case, the price will be the same as the price that would occur in a competitive market. Although few markets are perfectly contestable, many markets are contestable to a certain degree, and the threat of entry tends to decrease prices and profits.

• **contestable market**
A market with low entry and exit costs.

## When Is the Passive Approach Better?

Although our example shows that entry deterrence is the best strategy for Mona, it won't be the best strategy for all insecure monopolists. The key variable is the minimum entry quantity. Suppose that the scale economies in air travel were relatively small, so a second firm could enter the market with as few as 10 passengers. In this case, if Mona commits to serving only 100 passengers, that won't be enough to deter entry: A firm entering with 10 passengers will still make a profit. If the minimum entry quantity is 10 passengers, the entry-deterring quantity rises to 110 passengers:

$$\text{deterring quantity} = \text{zero profit quantity} - \text{minimum entry quantity}$$
$$110 = 120 - 10$$

Mona can commit to serving 110 passengers and thus prevent the second firm from entering the market, but is this the most profitable strategy? As shown by point $f$ in Figure 12.9, the limit price associated with an entry-deterring quantity is $150. Mona's profit from entry deterrence would be $5,500:

$$\text{profit} = (\text{price} - \text{average cost}) \times \text{quantity per firm} = (\$150 - \$100) \times 110 = \$5,500$$

This is less than the $8,000 profit she could earn by being passive and letting the second firm enter the market. In this case, the minimum entry quantity is relatively small, so the entry-deterring quantity is large and the limit price is low. As a result, sharing a duopoly is more profitable than increasing output and cutting the price to keep the other firm out.

# 12.7 | THE ADVERTISERS' DILEMMA

We have explored two sorts of strategic behavior of firms in an oligopoly—price-fixing and entry deterrence. A third type of strategy concerns advertising. As we'll see, firms in an oligopoly may suffer from an advertisers' dilemma: Although both firms would be better off if neither spent money on advertising, each firm advertises.

# 4

# APPLICATION

## REYNOLDS INTERNATIONAL TAKES THE MONEY AND LEAVES THE MARKET

**APPLYING THE CONCEPTS #4:** When is it sensible for a monopolist not to take measures to prevent other firms from entering the market?

In 1945, Reynolds International Pen Corporation introduced a revolutionary product: the ballpoint pen. The new type of pen could be produced with a very simple production technology. For three years, Reynolds earned enormous profits on this innovative product. In 1948, Reynolds stopped producing pens, dropping out of the market entirely. What happened?

The key to solving this puzzle is the fact that Reynolds earned enormous profits for a short time. The simple technology of the ballpoint pen could be copied easily by other producers, so the price required to deter entry—the limit price—was low. The limit price was so low that it was better for Reynolds to charge a high price and squeeze out as much profit as possible from a short-lived monopoly. Reynolds sold its pens for $12.50, about 16 times the average production cost of $0.80. By 1948, a total of 100 firms had entered the ballpoint market, and the price had fallen to the average cost of production, so each firm made zero economic profit. *Related to Exercises 6.9, 6.10, and 6.11.*

SOURCE: Thomas Whiteside, "Where Are They Now?" *New Yorker*, February 17, 1951, pp. 39–58.

Consider the producers of two brands of aspirin. Each firm must decide whether to spend $7 million on an advertising campaign for its product. In Table 12.3, the first two columns show what happens if neither firm advertises. Each firm earns $8 million in net revenue (revenue minus production cost) and spends no money on advertising, so each firm earns $8 million in profit. The third and fourth columns show what happens if each firm spends $7 million on advertising. The net revenue for each firm increases by only $5 million, so the profit of each firm drops by $2 million, to $6 million.

What happens if one firm advertises and the other does not? As shown in the last two columns in Table 12.3, a firm can increases its profit by advertising. If Adeline spends $7 million on advertising and Vern spends nothing, Adeline's net revenue increases to $17 million and her profit increases to $10 million. Adeline's advertisements cause some of Vern's consumers to switch to Adeline, and Vern's profit drops to $5 million.

We can use the data in Table 12.3 to construct a game tree for the advertising game. In Figure 12.11, Adeline makes her decision first, followed by Vern:

- If neither firm advertises, we go from square $A$ to square $C$ to rectangle 4, and each firm gets a profit $8 million.

- If both firms advertise, we go from square $A$ to square $B$ to rectangle 1, and each firm earns a profit of $6 million.

- If Adeline advertises and Vern does not, we go from square $A$ to square $B$ to rectangle 2. Adeline earns $10 million, while Vern earns $5 million. If the roles are reversed, we end up in rectangle 3, with Vern the advertiser earning $10 million and Adeline earning only $5 million.

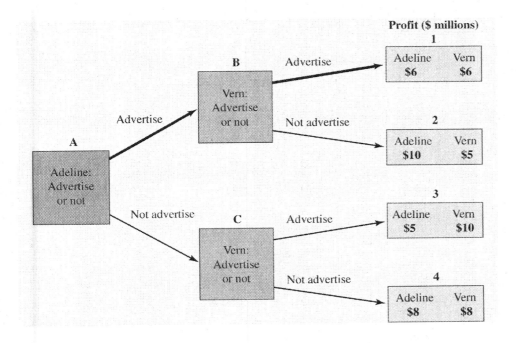

**Profit ($ millions)**

◄ **FIGURE 12.11**
**Game Tree for the Advertisers'
Dilemma**
Adeline moves first, choosing to advertise
or not. Vern's best response is to advertise
no matter what Adeline does. Knowing
this, Adeline realizes that the only possible
outcomes are shown by rectangles 1 and
3. From Adeline's perspective, rectangle 1
($6 million) is better than rectangle 3 ($5
million), so her best response is to advertise. Both Adeline and Vern advertise, and
each earns a profit of $6 million.

**Table 12.3 | ADVERTISING AND PROFIT**

|  | Neither Advertises | | Both Advertise | | Adeline Advertises | |
|---|---|---|---|---|---|---|
|  | Adeline | Vern | Adeline | Vern | Adeline | Vern |
| Net revenue from sales ($ million) | $8 | $8 | $13 | $13 | $17 | $5 |
| Cost of advertising ($ million) | 0 | 0 | 7 | 7 | 7 | 0 |
| Profit ($ million) | 8 | 8 | 6 | 6 | 10 | 5 |

To determine the outcome of this advertising game, let's start with Vern's possible
actions:

- If Adeline advertises, we move along the upper branches of the game tree from
  square *A* to square *B*. Vern will earn $6 million if he advertises (rectangle 1), but
  only $5 million if he does not advertise (rectangle 2). Therefore, Vern's best
  response is to match Adeline's campaign.

- If Adeline does not advertise, we move along the lower branches from square *A*
  to square *C*. Vern will earn $10 million if he advertises, but only $8 million if he
  does not. Therefore, if Adeline does not advertise, Vern's best response is to
  advertise.

Advertising is Vern's dominant strategy because it is the best response no matter what
Adeline does.

Consider next the options faced by Adeline. She will figure out that advertising is
a dominant strategy for Vern, so she realizes that that the only possible outcomes are
shown by rectangles 1 and 3. To get to rectangle 1, she advertises and gets a profit of
with $6 million. This is better than not advertising and going to rectangle 3, with a
profit of $5 million. So her best response is to advertise. The thick arrows show the
equilibrium path of the game, from square *A* to square *B* to rectangle 1. In equilibrium, both firms advertise and each earns a profit of $6.

What is the advertisers' dilemma? Both Adeline and Vern would be better off if
neither advertised. Each would get a profit of $8 million if neither advertised, com-
pared to $6 million when they both advertise. But each firm has an incentive to use

advertising to increase its sales at the expense of the other. Stuck in the dilemma, each firm earns $2 million less than it would if neither advertised.

Why does the advertisers' dilemma occur? In general, it happens when advertising causes a relatively small increase in the total sales of the industry, but allows a firm that advertises to gain at the expense of firms that don't. In our example, a pair of advertising campaigns costing a total of $14 million increases the net revenue of the entire industry by only $10 million. The increase in revenue is less than the cost of advertising, so advertising decreases total profit. Nonetheless, each firm has an incentive to advertise to take sales away from the other firm. If the increase in industry-wide net revenue were larger, advertising could benefit both firms.

## SUMMARY

In this chapter, we've seen that when a few firms share a market they have an incentive to act strategically. Firms in an oligopoly try to use cartel pricing—price-fixing—to avoid competition and keep prices high. A monopolist may commit to a large quantity and a low price in order to prevent a second firm from entering the market. Oligopolists may use advertising to increase their sales at the expense of competitors. Here are the main points of the chapter:

1 Each firm in an oligopoly has an incentive to underprice the other firms, so price-fixing will be unsuccessful unless firms have some way of enforcing a price-fixing agreement.

2 One way to maintain price-fixing is a low-price guarantee: One firm chooses the high price and promises to match any lower price of its competitor.

3 Price-fixing is more likely to occur if firms choose prices repeatedly and can punish a firm that chooses a price below the cartel price.

4 To prevent a second firm from entering the market, an insecure monopolist may commit itself to producing a relatively large quantity and accepting a relatively low price.

5 The advertisers' dilemma is that both firms would be better off if neither firm advertised.

# Chapter 13
# Factor Markets

**Factors of production** Labor, capital, natural resources, and other inputs used to produce goods and services.

Firms use **factors of production**—such as labor, capital, and natural resources—to produce goods and services. For example, the Chicago Cubs use labor (baseball players), capital (Wrigley Field), and natural resources (the land on which Wrigley Field sits) to produce baseball games. In this chapter, we will explore how firms choose the profit-maximizing quantity of labor and other factors of production. The interaction between firm demand for labor and household supply of labor determines the equilibrium wage rate.

Because there are many different types of labor, there are many different labor markets. The equilibrium wage in the market for baseball players is much higher than the equilibrium wage in the market for college professors. We will explore why this is true. We will also explore how factors such as discrimination, unions, and compensation for dangerous or unpleasant jobs help explain differences among wages. We will then look at *personnel economics*, which is concerned with how firms can use economic analysis to design their employee compensation plans. Finally, we will analyze the markets for other factors of production.

16.1 | Explain how firms choose the profit-maximizing quantity of labor to employ.

# The Demand for Labor

**Derived demand** The demand for a factor of production that is derived from the demand for the good the factor produces.

Up until now we have concentrated on consumer demand for final goods and services. The demand for labor is different from the demand for final goods and services because it is a *derived demand*. A **derived demand** is the demand for a factor of production that is based on the demand for the good the factor produces. You demand an Apple iPod because of the utility you receive from listening to music. Apple's demand for the labor to make iPods is derived from the underlying consumer demand for iPods. As a result, we can say that Apple's demand for labor depends primarily on two factors:

1. The additional iPods Apple will be able to produce if it hires one more worker

2. The additional revenue Apple receives from selling the additional iPods

## The Marginal Revenue Product of Labor

Consider the following example. To keep the main point clear, let's assume that in the short run, Apple can increase production of iPods only by increasing the quantity of labor it employs. The table in Figure 16-1 shows the relationship between the quantity of workers Apple hires, the quantity of iPods it produces, the additional revenue from selling the additional iPods, and the additional profit from hiring each additional worker.

For simplicity, we are keeping the scale of Apple's factory very small. We will also assume that Apple is a perfect competitor both in the market for selling digital music players and in the market for hiring labor. This means that Apple is a *price taker* in both markets. Although this is not realistic, the basic analysis would not change if we assumed that Apple can affect the price of digital music players and the wage paid to workers. Given these assumptions, suppose that Apple can sell as many iPods as it wants at a price of $200 and can hire as many workers as it wants at a wage of $600 per week. Remember from Chapter 10 that the additional output a firm produces as a result of hiring one more worker is called the **marginal product of labor**. In the table, we calculate the marginal product of labor as the change in total output as each additional worker is hired. As we saw in Chapter 10, because of *the law of diminishing returns*, the marginal product of labor declines as a firm hires more workers.

**Marginal product of labor** The additional output a firm produces as a result of hiring one more worker.

When deciding how many workers to hire, a firm is not interested in how much *output* will increase as it hires another worker but in how much *revenue* will increase as it hires another worker. In other words, what matters is how much the firm's revenue will rise when it sells the additional output it can produce by hiring one more worker.

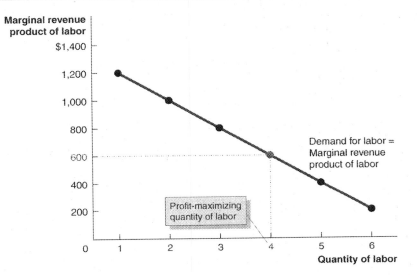

| Number of Workers | Output of iPods per Week | Marginal Product of Labor (iPods per week) | Product Price | Marginal Revenue Product of Labor (dollars per week) | Wage (dollars per week) | Additional Profit from Hiring One More Worker (dollars per week) |
|---|---|---|---|---|---|---|
| L | Q | MP | P | MRP = P × MP | W | MRP − W |
| 0 | 0 | — | $200 | — | $600 | — |
| 1 | 6 | 6 | 200 | $1,200 | 600 | $600 |
| 2 | 11 | 5 | 200 | 1,000 | 600 | 400 |
| 3 | 15 | 4 | 200 | 800 | 600 | 200 |
| 4 | 18 | 3 | 200 | 600 | 600 | 0 |
| 5 | 20 | 2 | 200 | 400 | 600 | −200 |
| 6 | 21 | 1 | 200 | 200 | 600 | −400 |

## Figure 16-1

**The Marginal Revenue Product of Labor and the Demand for Labor**

The marginal revenue product of labor equals the marginal product of labor multiplied by the price of the good. The marginal revenue product curve slopes downward because diminishing returns cause the marginal product of labor to decline as more workers are hired. A firm maximizes profits by hiring workers up to the point where the wage equals the marginal revenue product of labor. The marginal revenue product of labor curve is the firm's demand curve for labor because it tells the firm the profit-maximizing quantity of workers to hire at each wage. For example, using the demand curve shown in this figure, if the wage is $600, the firm will hire 4 workers.

We can calculate this amount by multiplying the additional output produced by the product price. This amount is called the **marginal revenue product of labor** (*MRP*). For example, consider what happens if Apple increases the number of workers hired from 2 to 3. The table in Figure 16-1 shows that hiring the third worker allows Apple to increase its weekly output of iPods from 11 to 15, so the marginal product of labor is 4 iPods. The price of the iPods is $200, so the marginal revenue product of the third worker is 4 × $200, or $800. In other words, Apple adds $800 to its revenue as a result of hiring the third worker. In the graph, we plot the values of the marginal revenue product of labor at each quantity of labor.

To decide how many workers to hire, Apple must compare the additional revenue it earns from hiring another worker to the increase in its costs from paying that worker. The difference between the additional revenue and the additional cost is the additional profit (or loss) from hiring one more worker. This additional profit is shown in the last column of the table in Figure 16-1 and is calculated by subtracting the wage from the marginal revenue product of labor. As long as the marginal revenue product of labor is greater than the wage, Apple's profits are increasing, and it should continue to hire more workers. When the marginal revenue product of labor is less than the wage, Apple's profits are falling, and it should hire fewer workers. When the marginal revenue product of labor is equal to the wage, Apple has maximized its profits by hiring the optimal number of workers. The values in the table show that Apple should hire 4 workers. If the company hires a fifth worker, the marginal revenue product of $400 will be less than the wage of $600, and its profits will fall by $200. Table 16-1 summarizes the relationship between the marginal revenue product of labor and the wage.

**Marginal revenue product of labor** (*MRP*) The change in a firm's revenue as a result of hiring one more worker.

## TABLE 16-1

**The Relationship between the Marginal Revenue Product of Labor and the Wage**

| WHEN . . . | THEN THE FIRM . . . |
|---|---|
| $MRP > W$, | should hire more workers to increase profits. |
| $MRP < W$, | should hire fewer workers to increase profits. |
| $MRP = W$, | is hiring the optimal number of workers and is maximizing profits. |

We can see from Figure 16-1 that if Apple has to pay a wage of $600 per week, it should hire 4 workers. If the wage were to rise to $1,000, then applying the rule that profits are maximized where the marginal revenue product of labor equals the wage, Apple should hire only 2 workers. Similarly, if the wage is only $400 per week, Apple should hire 5 workers. In fact, the marginal revenue product curve tells a firm how many workers it should hire at any wage rate. In other words, *the marginal revenue product of labor curve is the demand curve for labor.*

# Solved Problem | 16-1

## Hiring Decisions by a Firm That Is a Price Maker

We have assumed that Apple can sell as many iPods as it wants without having to cut the price. Recall from Chapter 11 that this is the case for firms in perfectly competitive markets. These firms are *price takers.* Suppose instead that a firm has market power and is a *price maker,* so that to increase sales, it must reduce the price.

Suppose Apple faces the situation shown in the following table. Fill in the blanks and then determine the profit-maximizing number of workers for Apple to hire. Briefly explain why hiring this number of workers is profit maximizing.

| (1) QUANTITY OF LABOR | (2) OUTPUT OF iPODS PER WEEK | (3) MARGINAL PRODUCT OF LABOR | (4) PRODUCT PRICE | (5) TOTAL REVENUE | (6) MARGINAL REVENUE PRODUCT OF LABOR | (7) WAGE | (8) ADDITIONAL PROFIT FROM HIRING ONE ADDITIONAL WORKER |
|---|---|---|---|---|---|---|---|
| 0 | 0 | — | $200 | | — | $500 | — |
| 1 | 6 | 6 | 180 | | | 500 | |
| 2 | 11 | 5 | 160 | | | 500 | |
| 3 | 15 | 4 | 140 | | | 500 | |
| 4 | 18 | 3 | 120 | | | 500 | |
| 5 | 20 | 2 | 100 | | | 500 | |
| 6 | 21 | 1 | 80 | | | 500 | |

## SOLVING THE PROBLEM:

**Step 1:** **Review the chapter material.** This problem is about determining the profit-maximizing quantity of labor for a firm to hire, so you may want to review the section "The Demand for Labor," which begins on page 536.

**Step 2:** **Fill in the blanks in the table.** As Apple hires more workers, it sells more iPods and earns more revenue. You can calculate how revenue increases by multiplying the number of iPods produced—shown in column 2—by the price—shown in column 4. Then you can calculate the marginal revenue product of labor as the change in revenue as each additional worker is hired. (Notice that in this case marginal revenue product is *not* calculated by multiplying the marginal product by the product price. Because Apple is a price maker, its marginal revenue from selling additional iPods is less than the price of iPods.) Finally, you can calculate the additional profit from hiring one more worker by subtracting the wage—shown in column 7—from each worker's marginal revenue product.

| (1) QUANTITY OF LABOR | (2) OUTPUT OF iPODS PER WEEK | (3) MARGINAL PRODUCT OF LABOR | (4) PRODUCT PRICE | (5) TOTAL REVENUE | (6) MARGINAL REVENUE PRODUCT OF LABOR | (7) WAGE | (8) ADDITIONAL PROFIT FROM HIRING ONE ADDITIONAL WORKER |
|---|---|---|---|---|---|---|---|
| 0 | 0 | — | $200 | $0 | — | $500 | — |
| 1 | 6 | 6 | 180 | 1,080 | $1,080 | 500 | $580 |
| 2 | 11 | 5 | 160 | 1,760 | 680 | 500 | 180 |
| 3 | 15 | 4 | 140 | 2,100 | 340 | 500 | –160 |
| 4 | 18 | 3 | 120 | 2,160 | 60 | 500 | –440 |
| 5 | 20 | 2 | 100 | 2,000 | –160 | 500 | –660 |
| 6 | 21 | 1 | 80 | 1,680 | –320 | 500 | –820 |

**Step 3:** **Use the information in the table to determine the profit-maximizing quantity of workers to hire.** To determine the profit-maximizing quantity of workers to hire, you need to compare the marginal revenue product of labor with the wage. Column 8 does this by subtracting the wage from the marginal revenue product. As long as the values in column 8 are positive, the firm should continue to hire workers. The marginal revenue product of the second worker is $680, and the wage is $500, so column 8 shows that hiring the second worker will add $180 to Apple's profits. The marginal revenue product of the third worker is $340, and the wage is $500, so hiring the third worker would reduce Apple's profits by $160. Therefore, Apple will maximize profits by hiring 2 workers.

>> End Solved Problem 16-1

# The Market Demand Curve for Labor

We can determine the market demand curve for labor in the same way we determine a market demand curve for a good. We saw in Chapter 9 that the market demand curve for a good is determined by adding up the quantity of the good demanded by each consumer at each price. Similarly, the market demand curve for labor is determined by adding up the quantity of labor demanded by each firm at each wage, holding constant all other variables that might affect the willingness of firms to hire workers.

# Factors That Shift the Market Demand Curve for Labor

In constructing the demand curve for labor, we held constant all variables that would affect the willingness of firms to demand labor—except for the wage. An increase or a decrease in the wage causes *an increase or a decrease in the quantity of labor demanded,* which we show by a movement along the demand curve. If any variable other than the wage changes, the result is *an increase or a decrease in the demand for labor,* which we show by a shift of the demand curve. The five most important variables that cause the labor demand curve to shift are the following:

- *Increases in human capital.* **Human capital** represents the accumulated training and skills that workers possess. For example, a worker with a college education generally has more skills and is more productive than a worker who has only a high school diploma. If workers become more educated and are therefore able to produce

**Human capital** The accumulated training and skills that workers possess.

more output per day, the demand for their services will increase, shifting the labor demand curve to the right.

- *Changes in technology.* As new and better machinery and equipment are developed, workers become more productive. This effect causes the labor demand curve to shift to the right over time.

- *Changes in the price of the product.* The marginal revenue product of labor depends on the price a firm receives for its output. A higher price increases the marginal revenue product and shifts the labor demand curve to the right. A lower price shifts the labor demand curve to the left.

- *Changes in the quantity of other inputs.* Workers are able to produce more if they have more machinery and other inputs available to them. The marginal product of labor in the United States is higher than the marginal product of labor in other countries in large part because U.S. firms provide workers with more machinery and equipment. Over time, workers in the United States have had increasing amounts of other inputs available to them, and that has increased their productivity and caused the demand for labor to shift to the right.

- *Changes in the number of firms in the market.* If new firms enter the market, the demand for labor will shift to the right. If firms exit the market, the demand for labor will shift to the left. This effect is similar to that which increasing or decreasing the number of consumers in a market has on the demand for a good.

---

**16.2 LEARNING** OBJECTIVE

16.2 | Explain how people choose the quantity of labor to supply.

# The Supply of Labor

Having discussed the demand for labor, we can now consider the supply of labor. Of the many trade-offs each of us faces in life, one of the most important is how to divide up the 24 hours in the day between labor and leisure. Every hour spent watching television, walking on the beach, or in other forms of leisure is one less hour spent working. Because in devoting an hour to leisure, we give up an hour's earnings from working, the *opportunity cost* of leisure is the wage. The higher the wage we could earn working, the higher the opportunity cost of leisure. Therefore, as the wage increases, we tend to take less leisure and work more. This relationship explains why the labor supply curve for most people is upward sloping, as Figure 16-2 shows.

## Figure 16-2

**The Labor Supply Curve**

As the wage increases, the opportunity cost of leisure increases, causing individuals to supply a greater quantity of labor. Therefore, the labor supply curve is upward sloping.

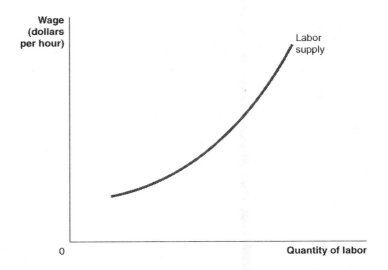

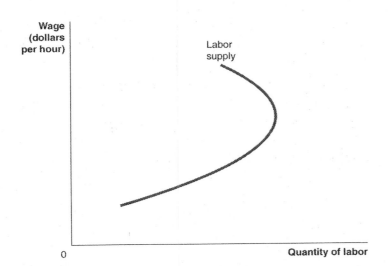

**Wage (dollars per hour)**

Labor supply

0    Quantity of labor

Figure 16-3

**A Backward-Bending Labor Supply Curve**

As the wage rises, a greater quantity of labor is usually supplied. As the wage climbs above a certain level, the individual is able to afford more leisure even though the opportunity cost of leisure is high. The result may be a smaller quantity of labor supplied.

Although we normally expect the labor supply curve for an individual to be upward sloping, it is possible that at very high wage levels, the supply curve of an individual might be *backward bending*, so that higher wages actually result in a *smaller* quantity of labor supplied, as shown in Figure 16-3. To understand why, recall the definitions of the *substitution effect* and the *income effect*, which we introduced in Chapter 3 and discussed more fully in Chapter 9. The substitution effect of a price change refers to the fact that an increase in price makes a good more expensive *relative* to other goods. In the case of a wage change, the substitution effect refers to the fact that an increase in the wage raises the opportunity cost of leisure and causes a worker to devote *more* time to working and less time to leisure.

The income effect of a price change refers to the change in the quantity demanded of a good that results from changes in consumer purchasing power as a result of a price change. An increase in the wage will clearly increase a consumer's purchasing power for any given number of hours worked. For a normal good, the income effect leads to a larger quantity demanded. Because leisure is a normal good, the income effect of a wage increase will cause a worker to devote *less* time to working and more time to leisure. So, the substitution effect of a wage increase causes a worker to supply a larger quantity of labor, but the income effect causes a worker to supply a smaller quantity of labor. Whether a worker supplies more or less labor following a wage increase depends on whether the substitution effect is larger than the income effect. Figure 16-3 shows the typical case of the substitution effect being larger than the income effect at low levels of wages—so the worker supplies a larger quantity of labor as the wage rises—and the income effect being larger than the substitution effect at high levels of wages—so the worker supplies a smaller quantity of labor as the wage rises. For example, suppose an attorney has become quite successful and can charge clients very high fees. Or suppose a rock band has become very popular and receives a large payment for every concert it performs. In these cases, there is a high opportunity cost for the lawyer to turn down another client to take a longer vacation or for the band to turn down another concert. But because their incomes are already very high, they may decide to give up additional income for more leisure. For the lawyer or the rock band, the income effect is larger than the substitution effect, and a higher wage causes them to supply *less* labor.

## The Market Supply Curve of Labor

We can determine the market supply curve of labor in the same way we determine a market supply curve of a good. We saw in Chapter 11 that the market supply curve of a good is determined by adding up the quantity of the good supplied by each firm at each price. Similarly, the market supply curve of labor is determined by adding up the quantity of labor supplied by each worker at each wage, holding constant all other variables that might affect the willingness of workers to supply labor.

## Factors That Shift the Market Supply Curve of Labor

In constructing the market supply curve of labor, we hold constant all other variables that would affect the willingness of workers to supply labor, except the wage. If any of these other variables change, the market supply curve will shift. The following are the three most important variables that cause the market supply curve of labor to shift:

- *Increases in population.* As the population grows because of natural increase and immigration, the supply curve of labor shifts to the right. The effects of immigration on labor supply are largest in the markets for unskilled workers. In some large cities in the United States, for example, the majority of taxi drivers and workers in hotels and restaurants are immigrants. Some supporters of reducing immigration argue that wages in these jobs have been depressed by the increased supply of labor from immigrants.

- *Changing demographics.* *Demographics* refers to the composition of the population. The more people who are between the ages of 16 and 65, the greater the quantity of labor supplied. During the 1970s and 1980s, the U.S. labor force grew particularly rapidly as members of the baby boom generation—born between 1946 and 1964—first began working. In contrast, a low birth rate in Japan has resulted in an aging population. The number of working-age people in Japan actually began to decline during the 1990s, causing the labor supply curve to shift to the left.

  A related demographic issue is the changing role of women in the labor force. In 1900, only 21 percent of women in the United States were in the labor force. By 1950, this had risen to 30 percent, and today, it is 60 percent. This increase in the *labor force participation* of women has significantly increased the supply of labor in the United States.

- *Changing alternatives.* The labor supply in any particular labor market depends, in part, on the opportunities available in other labor markets. For example, the telecommunications industry bust in 2001 reduced the opportunities for optical engineers. Many workers left this market—causing the labor supply curve to shift to the left—and entered other markets, causing the labor supply curves to shift to the right in those markets. People who have lost jobs or who have low incomes are eligible for unemployment insurance and other payments from the government. The more generous these payments are, the less pressure unemployed workers have to quickly find another job. In many European countries, it is much easier than in the United States for unemployed workers to receive a greater replacement of their wage income from government payments. In one case that received widespread publicity, an unemployed German banker received payments of $2,400 per month from the German government to help pay for his apartment in Miami Beach in a gated community with a swimming pool and sauna. The banker's psychiatrist reportedly argued that the banker needed to remain in sunny Florida because the overcast weather in his hometown in Germany might worsen his depression. Although cases like this are extreme, many economists believe generous unemployment benefits help explain the higher unemployment rates experienced in Europe. For example, in the 10 years from 1997 to 2006, the average of the unemployment rates in the United Kingdom, France, Germany, Italy, and Spain was 9 percent, while in the United States, the unemployment rate averaged just under 5 percent. There have been proposals in some European countries to reduce the size of these government payments in the hope of increasing the labor supply.

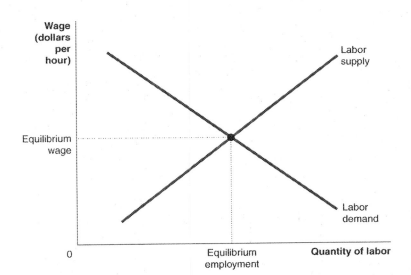

## Figure 16-4

**Equilibrium in the Labor Market**

As in other markets, equilibrium in the labor market occurs where the demand curve for labor and the supply curve of labor intersect.

16.3 | Explain how equilibrium wages are determined in labor markets.

# Equilibrium in the Labor Market

In Figure 16-4, we bring labor demand and labor supply together to determine equilibrium in the labor market. We can use demand and supply to analyze changes in the equilibrium wage and the level of employment for the entire labor market, or we can use it to analyze markets for different types of labor, such as baseball players or college professors.

## The Effect on Equilibrium Wages of a Shift in Labor Demand

In many labor markets, increases over time in labor productivity will cause the demand for labor to increase. As Figure 16-5 shows, if labor supply is unchanged, an increase in labor demand will increase both the equilibrium wage and the number of workers employed.

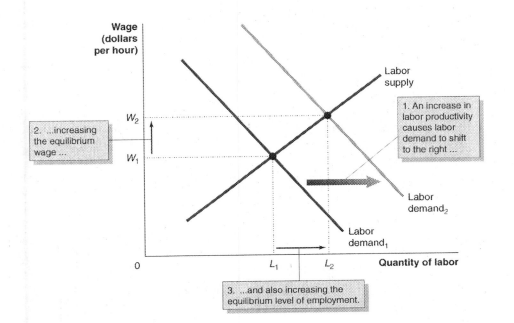

## Figure 16-5

**The Effect of an Increase in Labor Demand**

Increases in labor demand will cause the equilibrium wage and the equilibrium level of employment to rise.
1. If the productivity of workers rises, the marginal revenue product increases, causing the labor demand curve to shift to the right.
2. The equilibrium wage rises from $W_1$ to $W_2$.
3. The equilibrium level of employment rises from $L_1$ to $L_2$.

Making
the
Connection

# Will Your Future Income Depend on Which Courses You Take in College?

Most people realize the value of a college education. As the following chart shows, in 2007, full-time workers ages 25 and over with a college degree earned more per week than other workers; for example, they earned 2.5 times as much as high school dropouts.

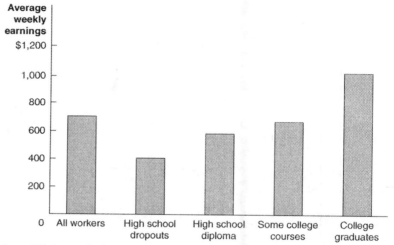

*Source:* U.S. Bureau of Labor Statistics, "Usual Weekly Earnings of Wage and Salary Workers," April 18, 2007.

Why do college graduates earn more than others? The obvious answer would seem to be that a college education provides skills that increase productivity. Some economists, though, advocate an alternative explanation, known as the *signaling hypothesis*, first proposed by Nobel laureate A. Michael Spence of Stanford University. This hypothesis is based on the idea that job applicants will always have more information than will potential employers about how productive the applicants are likely to be. Although employers attempt through job interviews and background checks to distinguish "good workers" from "bad workers," they are always looking for more information.

According to the signaling hypothesis, employers see a college education as a signal that workers possess certain desirable characteristics: self-discipline, the ability to meet deadlines, and the ability to make a sustained effort. Even if these characteristics are not related to the specifics of a particular job, employers value them because they usually lead to success in any activity. People generally believe that college graduates possess these characteristics, so employers often require a college degree for their best-paying jobs. In this view, the signal that a college education sends about a person's inherent characteristics—which the person presumably already possessed *before* entering college—is much more important than any skills the person may have learned in college. Or, as a college math professor of one of the authors put it (only half-jokingly), "The purpose of college is to show employers that you can succeed at something that's boring and hard."

Recently, though, several economic studies have provided evidence that the higher incomes of college graduates are due to their greater productivity rather than the signal that a college degree sends to employers. Orley Ashenfelter and Cecilia Rouse of Princeton University studied the relationship between schooling and income among 700 pairs of identical twins. Identical twins have identical genes, so differences in their inherent abilities should be relatively small. Therefore, if they have different numbers of years in school, differences in their earnings should be mainly due to the effect of schooling on their productivity. Ashenfelter and Rouse found that identical twins had returns of about 9 percent per additional year of schooling, enough to account for most of the gap in income between high school graduates and college graduates.

Daniel Hamermesh and Stephen G. Donald of the University of Texas have studied the determinants of the earnings of college graduates 5 to 25 years after graduation. They collected extensive information on each person in their study, including the person's SAT scores, rank in high school class, grades in every college course taken, and college major. Hamermesh and Donald discovered that, holding constant all other factors, business and engineering majors earned more than graduates with other majors. They also discovered a large impact on future earnings of taking science and math courses: "A student who takes 15 credits of upper-division science and math courses and obtains a B average in them will earn about 10 percent more than an otherwise identical student in the same major . . . who takes no upper-division classes in these areas." This result held even after adjusting for a student's SAT score. The study by Hamermesh and Donald contradicts the signaling hypothesis because if the signaling hypothesis is correct, the choice of courses taken in college should be of minor importance compared with the signal workers send to employers just by having completed college.

Sources: Orley Ashenfelter and Cecilia Rouse, "Income, Schooling, and Ability: Evidence from a New Sample of Identical Twins," *Quarterly Journal of Economics*, Vol. 113, No. 1 (February 1998), pp. 253–284; Daniel S. Hamermesh and Stephen G. Donald, "The Effect of College Curriculum on Earnings: Accounting for Non-Ignorable Non-Response Bias," National Bureau of Economic Research working paper 10809, September 2004.

## The Effect on Equilibrium Wages of a Shift in Labor Supply

What is the effect on the equilibrium wage of an increase in labor supply due to population growth? As Figure 16-6 shows, if labor demand is unchanged, an increase in labor supply will decrease the equilibrium wage but increase the number of workers employed.

Whether the wage rises in a market depends on whether demand increases faster than supply. For example, after the success of Walt Disney's animated film *The Lion King* in 1994, most movie studios increased production of animated films, increasing the

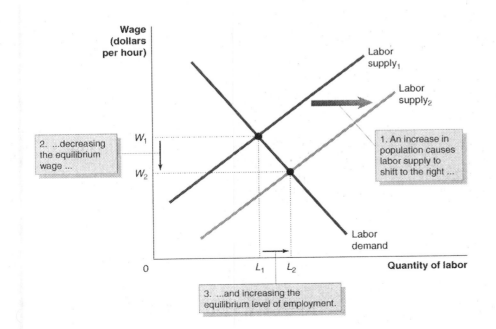

**Figure 16-6**

**The Effect of an Increase in Labor Supply**

Increases in labor supply will cause the equilibrium wage to fall but the equilibrium level of employment to rise.
1. As population increases, the labor supply curve shifts to the right.
2. The equilibrium wage falls from $W_1$ to $W_2$.
3. The equilibrium level of employment increases from $L_1$ to $L_2$.

demand for animators much faster than the supply of animators was increasing. The annual salary for a top animator rose from about $125,000 in 1994 to $550,000 in 1999. These high salaries led more people with artistic ability to choose to get training as film animators, causing the supply of animators to increase after 1999. Several of the animated films released between 1999 and 2001 failed to earn profits, which caused some companies to stop making these films, thereby decreasing the demand for animators. The decrease in demand for animators and the increase in supply caused the salaries of top animators to fall from $550,000 in 1999 to $225,000 in 2002.

*The flower industry is one of many industries in the United States that rely on immigrant workers.*

## Making the Connection | Immigration and Wages, Then and Now

Between 1900 and the outbreak of World War I in 1914, about 13.4 million immigrants arrived in the United States. Relative to the U.S. population—which was about 76 million in 1900—this was the largest wave of immigration in the history of the world. Many commentators at the time predicted that this great increase in the U.S. labor supply would cause a sharp fall in wages. Figure 16-6 shows that this is a reasonable prediction of the effect of an increase in labor supply on the equilibrium wage, *but only if the demand for labor remains unchanged.* In fact, the demand for labor increased rapidly during these years as technological progress, such as electrification and the development of mass-production techniques, increased the productivity of labor.

As a result, the demand for labor shifted to the right faster than the supply of labor, and wages rose. The following figure shows the situation in manufacturing. Both demand and supply increased, but because the shift in demand was greater than the shift in supply, average hourly earnings rose from less than $0.18 in 1900 to $0.22 in 1914, or by almost 25 percent. (The data for both years use 1914 prices to correct for the effects of inflation.) During the same years, employment in manufacturing rose from about 5.5 million workers to almost 9 million.

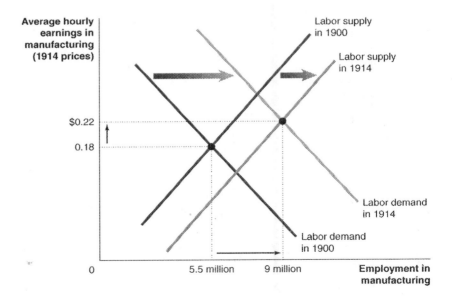

In 2007, the economics of immigration was once again in the forefront during the debate over a proposal by President George W. Bush to revise the immigration laws. President Bush proposed allowing the approximately 12 million illegal immigrants in the United States to enter a process that would allow them to become legal permanent residents. He also proposed strengthening security at the country's borders to reduce future illegal immigration. The figure below shows estimates by the Pew Hispanic Center indicating that illegal immigrants had become a substantial part of the labor supply in a number of industries.

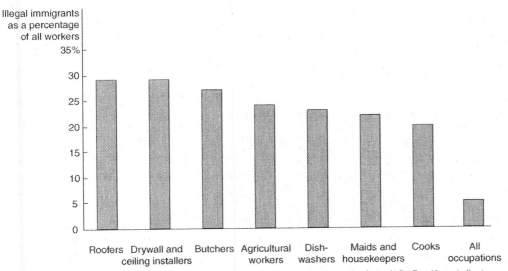

Source: Jeffrey S. Passel, "The Size and Characteristics of the Unauthorized Migrant Population in the U.S.," Pew Hispanic Center Research Report, March 7, 2006, Table 1, p. 12.

Economists have debated the impact of illegal immigrants on the wages of unskilled workers. As the figure indicates, illegal immigrants have substantially increased the supply of labor in some occupations. Some economists argue that illegal immigration may have significantly contributed to the distribution of income becoming more unequal in recent years. Illegal immigration increases income inequality if the supply of illegal workers reduces the wages of low-income workers relative to high-income workers. Claudia Goldin and Lawrence Katz, economists at Harvard University, have recently estimated that immigration—both legal and illegal—can explain only about 10 percent of the increase in the gap between the wages of college-educated workers and the wages of high school-educated workers during the years between 1980 and 2005. George Borjas, of Harvard, Jeffrey Grogger, of the University of Chicago, and Gordon Hanson, of the University of California, San Diego, find a significant impact of immigration on the employment opportunities of African Americans. They find that if as a result of immigration there is a 10 percent increase in the supply of labor with a particular skill, the wages of African Americans with that skill fall by 4 percent, the employment rate of African Americans falls by 3.5 percentage points, and the fraction of African Americans in jail increases by 1 percentage point.

The economic impact of immigration is certain to remain a hotly debated issue for the foreseeable future.

Source: U.S. Department of Commerce, *Historical Statistics of the United States*, Washington, DC: USGPO, 1976; Jeffrey S. Passel, "The Size and Characteristics of the Unauthorized Migrant Population in the U.S.," Pew Hispanic Center Research Report, March 7, 2006; Claudia Goldin and Lawrence F. Katz, "The Race Between Education and Technology," NBER Working Paper, No. 12984, March 2007; and George J. Borjas, Jeffrey Grogger, and Gordon H. Hanson, "Immigration and African-American Employment Opportunties," NBER Working Paper No. 12518, May 2007.

16.4 | Use demand and supply analysis to explain how compensating differentials, discrimination, and labor unions cause wages to differ.

# Explaining Differences in Wages

A key conclusion of our discussion of the labor market is that the equilibrium wage equals the marginal revenue product of labor. The more productive workers are and the higher the price workers' output can be sold for, the higher the wages workers will receive. At the beginning of the chapter, we raised the question of why major league baseball players are paid so much more than college professors. We are now ready to use demand and supply analysis to answer this question. Figure 16-7 shows the demand and supply curves for major league baseball players and the demand and supply curves for college professors.

Consider first the marginal revenue product of baseball players, which is the additional revenue a team owner will receive from hiring one more player. Baseball players are hired to produce baseball games that are then sold to fans who pay admission to baseball stadiums and to radio and television stations that broadcast the games. Because a major league baseball team can sell each baseball game for a large amount, the marginal revenue product of baseball players is high. The supply of people with the ability to play major league baseball is also very limited. As a result, the average annual salary of the 750 major league baseball players is about $2,700,000.

The marginal revenue product of college professors is much lower than for baseball players. College professors are hired to produce college educations that are then sold to students and their parents. Although one year's college tuition is quite high at many colleges, hiring one more professor allows a college to admit at most a few more students. So, the marginal revenue product of a college professor is much lower than the marginal revenue product of a baseball player. There are also many more people who possess the skills to be a college professor than possess the skills to be a major league baseball player. As a result, the country's 663,000 college professors are paid an average salary of about $73,000.

This still leaves unanswered the question raised at the beginning of this chapter: Why are the Chicago Cubs willing to pay Alfonso Soriano more than the Washington Nationals were? Soriano's marginal product——which we can think of as the extra games a

## Figure 16-7

### Baseball Players Are Paid More Than College Professors

The marginal revenue product of baseball players is very high, and the supply of people with the ability to play major league baseball is low. The result is that the 750 major league baseball players receive an average wage of $2,700,000. The marginal revenue product of college professors is much lower, and the supply of people with the ability to be college professors is much higher. The result is that the 663,000 college professors in the United States receive an average wage of $73,000, far below that of baseball players.

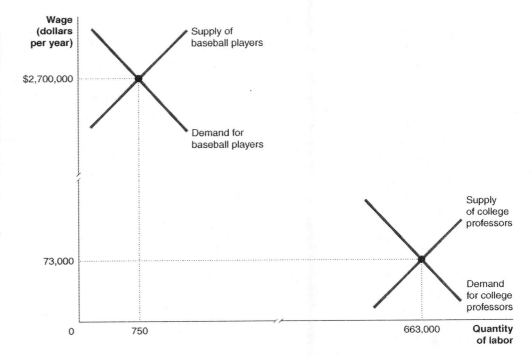

# Don't Let This Happen to **YOU!**

## Remember That Prices and Wages Are Determined at the Margin

You have probably heard some variation of the following remark: "We could live without baseball, but we can't live without the garbage being hauled away. In a more rational world, garbage collectors would be paid more than baseball players." This remark seems logical: The total value to society of having the garbage hauled away certainly is greater than the total value of baseball games. But wages—like prices—do not depend on total value but on *marginal* value. The *additional* baseball games the Chicago Cubs expect to win by signing Alfonso Soriano will result in millions of dollars in increased revenue. The supply of people with the ability to play major league baseball is very limited. The supply of people with the ability to be trash haulers is much greater. If a trash-hauling firm hires another worker, the *additional* trash-hauling services it can

now offer will bring in a relatively small amount of revenue. The *total* value of baseball games and the *total* value of trash hauling are not relevant in determining the relative salaries of baseball players and garbage collectors.

This point is related to the diamond and water paradox first noted by Adam Smith. On the one hand, water is very valuable—we literally couldn't live without it—but its price is very low. On the other hand, apart from a few industrial uses, diamonds are used only for jewelry, yet their prices are quite high. We resolve the paradox by noting that the price of water is low because the supply is very large and the additional benefit consumers receive from the last gallon purchased is low. The price of diamonds is high because the supply is very small, and the additional benefit consumers receive from the last diamond purchased is high.

team will win by employing him—should be about the same in Chicago as it was in Washington, DC. But his *marginal revenue product* will be higher in Chicago. Because the population of the Chicago metropolitan area is about twice as large as the population of the Washington metropolitan area, winning more games will result in a greater increase in attendance at Chicago Cubs games than it would at Washington Nationals games. It will also result in a greater increase in viewers for Cubs games on television. Therefore, the Cubs are able to sell the extra wins that Soriano produces for much more than the Washington Nationals can. This difference explains why the Cubs were willing to pay Soriano $18 million per year when he had made "only" $10 million with the Nationals.

## Making the Connection | Technology and the Earnings of "Superstars"

The gap between Alfonso Soriano's salary and the salary of the lowest-paid baseball players is much greater than the gap between the salaries paid during the 1950s and 1960s to top players such as Mickey Mantle and Willie Mays and the salaries of the lowest-paid players. Similarly, the gap between the $20 million Julia Roberts is paid to star in a movie and the salary paid to an actor in a minor role is much greater than the gap between the salaries paid during the 1930s and 1940s to stars such as Clark Gable and Cary Grant and the salaries paid to bit players. In fact, in most areas of sports and entertainment, the highest-paid performers—the "superstars"—now have much higher incomes relative to other members of their professions than was true a few decades ago.

The increase in the relative incomes of superstars is mainly due to technological advances. The spread of cable television has increased the number of potential viewers of Cubs games, but many of those viewers will watch only if the Cubs are winning. This increases the value to the Cubs of winning games and, therefore, increases Soriano's marginal revenue product and the salary he can earn.

With DVDs, Internet streaming video, and pay-per-view cable, the value to movie studios of producing a hit movie has risen greatly. Not surprisingly, movie studios have also increased their willingness to pay large salaries to stars like Julia Roberts or Brad Pitt because they think these superstars will significantly raise the chances of a film being successful.

*Why does Julia Roberts earn more today relative to the typical actor than stars did in the 1940s?*

This process has been going on for a long time. For instance, before the invention of the motion picture, anyone who wanted to see a play had to attend the theater and see a live performance. Limits on the number of people who could see the best actors and actresses perform created an opportunity for many more people to succeed in the acting profession, and the gap between the salaries earned by the best actors and the salaries earned by average actors was relatively small. Today, when a hit movie starring Julia Roberts appears on DVD, millions of people will buy or rent it, and they will not be forced to spend money to see a lesser actress, as their great-great-grandparents might have been.

Differences in marginal revenue products are the most important factor in explaining differences in wages, but they are not the whole story. To provide a more complete explanation for differences in wages, we must take into account three important aspects of labor markets: compensating differentials, discrimination, and labor unions. We begin with compensating differentials.

## Compensating Differentials

Suppose Paul runs a video rental store and acquires a reputation for being a bad boss who yells at his workers and is generally unpleasant. Two blocks away, Brendan also runs a video rental store, but Brendan is always very polite to his workers. We would expect in these circumstances that Paul will have to pay a higher wage than Brendan to attract and retain workers. Higher wages that compensate workers for unpleasant aspects of a job are called **compensating differentials**.

**Compensating differentials** Higher wages that compensate workers for unpleasant aspects of a job.

If working in a dynamite factory requires the same degree of training and education as working in a semiconductor factory but is much more dangerous, a larger number of workers will want to work making semiconductors than will want to work making dynamite. As a consequence, the wages of dynamite workers will be higher than the wages of semiconductor workers. We can think of the difference in wages as being the price of risk. As each worker decides on his or her willingness to assume risk and decides how much higher the wage must be to compensate for assuming more risk, wages will adjust so that dynamite factories will end up paying wages that are just high enough to compensate workers who choose to work there for the extra risk they assume. Only when workers in dynamite factories have been fully compensated with higher wages for the additional risk they assume will dynamite companies be able to attract enough workers.

One surprising implication of compensating differentials is that *laws protecting the health and safety of workers may not make workers better off.* To see this, suppose that dynamite factories pay wages of $25 per hour, and semiconductor factories pay wages of $20 per hour, with the $5 difference in wages being a compensating differential for the greater risk of working in a dynamite factory. Suppose that the government passes a law regulating the manufacture of dynamite in order to improve safety in dynamite factories. As a result of this law, dynamite factories are no longer any more dangerous than semiconductor factories. Once this happens, the wages in dynamite factories will decline to $20 per hour, the same as in semiconductor factories. Are workers in dynamite factories any better or worse off? Before the law was passed, their wages were $25 per hour, but $5 per hour was a compensating differential for the extra risk they were exposed to. Now their wages are only $20 per hour, but the extra risk has been eliminated. The conclusion seems to be that dynamite workers are no better off as a result of the safety legislation.

This conclusion is only true, though, if the compensating differential actually does compensate workers fully for the additional risk. George Akerlof of the University of California, Berkeley, and William Dickens of the Brookings Institution have argued that the psychological principle known as *cognitive dissonance* might cause workers to underestimate the true risk of their jobs. According to this principle, people prefer to think of themselves as intelligent and rational and tend to reject evidence that seems to contradict this image. Because working in a very hazardous job may seem irrational, workers in such jobs may refuse to believe that the jobs really are hazardous. Akerlof and Dickens present evidence that workers in chemical plants producing benzene and workers in nuclear power plants underestimate the hazards of their jobs. If this is true, the wages of these workers will not be high enough to compensate them fully for the risk they have assumed. So, in this situation, safety legislation may make workers better off.

## Discrimination

Table 16-2 shows that in the United States, white males on average earn more than other groups. One possible explanation for this is **economic discrimination**, which involves paying a person a lower wage or excluding a person from an occupation on the basis of an irrelevant characteristic such as race or gender.

**Economic discrimination** Paying a person a lower wage or excluding a person from an occupation on the basis of an irrelevant characteristic such as race or gender.

If employers discriminate by hiring only white males for high-paying jobs or by paying white males higher wages than other groups working the same jobs, white males would have higher earnings, as Table 16-2 shows. However, excluding groups from certain jobs or paying one group more than another has been illegal in the United States since the passage of the Equal Pay Act of 1963 and the Civil Rights Act of 1964. Nevertheless, it is possible that employers are ignoring the law and practicing economic discrimination.

Most economists believe that only a small amount of the gap between the wages of white males and the wages of other groups is due to discrimination. Instead, most of the gap is explained by three main factors:

1 Differences in education

2 Differences in experience

3 Differing preferences for jobs

*Differences in Education* Some of the difference between the incomes of whites and the incomes of blacks can be explained by differences in education. Historically, African Americans have had less schooling than whites. Although the gap has closed significantly over the years, 90 percent of adult non-Hispanic white males in 2005 had graduated from high school, but only 80 percent of adult African American males had. Whereas 33 percent of white males had graduated from college, only 17 percent of African American males had. These statistics understate the true gap in education between blacks and whites because many blacks receive a substandard education in inner-city schools. Not surprisingly, studies have shown that differing levels of education can account for a significant part of the gap between the earnings of white and black males.

| GROUP | ANNUAL EARNINGS |
|---|---|
| White males | $46,746 |
| White females | 34,464 |
| Black males | 33,248 |
| Black females | 29,749 |
| Hispanic males | 26,769 |
| Hispanic females | 24,402 |

## TABLE 16-2

**Why Do White Males Earn More Than Other Groups?**

*Note:* The values are median annual earnings for persons who worked full time, year round in 2005. Persons of Hispanic origin can be of any race.

Source: U.S. Bureau of the Census, Table PINC-10, Current Population Survey, *Annual Social and Economic Supplement,* March 2006.

***Differences in Experience*** Women are much more likely than men to leave their jobs for a period of time after having a child. Women with several children will sometimes have several interruptions in their careers. Some women leave the workforce for several years until their children are of school age. As a result, on average, women with children have less workforce experience than do men of the same age. Because workers with greater experience are, on average, more productive, the difference in levels of experience helps to explain some of the difference in earnings between men and women. One indication of this is that, on average, married women earn about 39 percent less than married men, but women who have never been married—and whose careers are less likely to have been interrupted—earn only about 10 percent less than men who have never been married.

***Differing Preferences for Jobs*** Significant differences exist between the types of jobs held by women and men. As Table 16-3 shows, women are overrepresented in some jobs where average weekly earnings are less than $500 per week, and men are overrepresented in some jobs where weekly earnings are greater than $700 per week.

Although the patterns shown in Table 16-3 could be explained by women being excluded from some occupations, it is likely that they reflect differences in job preferences between men and women. For example, because many women interrupt their careers—at least briefly—when their children are born, they are more likely to take jobs where work experience is less important. Women may also be more likely to take jobs, such as teaching, that allow them to be home in the afternoons when their children return from school.

**TABLE 16-3**

"Men's Jobs" Often Pay More Than "Women's Jobs"

| "WOMEN'S JOBS" | | | "MEN'S JOBS" | | |
|---|---|---|---|---|---|
| OCCUPATION | WEEKLY EARNINGS | PERCENTAGE OF WORKERS WHO ARE WOMEN | OCCUPATION | WEEKLY EARNINGS | PERCENTAGE OF WORKERS WHO ARE WOMEN |
| Preschool and kindergarten teachers | $521 | 96% | Electricians | $713 | 2% |
| Dental assistants | 474 | 95 | Fire fighters | 944 | 4 |
| Childcare workers | 332 | 93 | Aircraft mechanics | 919 | 6 |
| Receptionists | 466 | 92 | Aircraft pilots | 1,366 | 6 |
| Hairdressers | 416 | 91 | Engineering managers | 1,788 | 10 |
| Teacher assistants | 398 | 91 | Aerospace engineers | 1,366 | 11 |
| Nursing aides | 388 | 89 | Civil engineers | 1,138 | 13 |
| Maids and housekeeping cleaners | 335 | 87 | Computer software engineers | 1,401 | 21 |
| Cashiers | 336 | 75 | Chief executives | 1,834 | 24 |

*Note:* Earnings are for men and women in the occupation and are "median usual weekly earnings of full-time wage and salary workers."

Source: U.S. Department of Labor, Bureau of Labor Statistics, *Highlights of Women's Earnings in 2005*, Report 995, Table 2, September 2006.

# Solved Problem | 16-4

## Is "Comparable Worth" Legislation the Answer to Closing the Gap between Men's and Women's Pay?

As we have seen, either because of discrimination or differing preferences, certain jobs are filled primarily by men, and other jobs are filled primarily by women. On average, the "men's jobs" have higher wages than the "women's jobs." Some observers have argued that many "men's jobs" are more highly paid than "women's jobs," despite the jobs being comparable in terms of the education and skills required and the working conditions involved. These observers have argued that the earnings gap between men and women could be closed at least partially if the government required employers to pay the same wages for jobs that have *comparable worth*. Many economists are skeptical of

these proposals because they believe allowing markets to determine wages results in a more efficient outcome.

Suppose that electricians are currently being paid a market equilibrium wage of $700 per week, and dental technicians are being paid a market equilibrium wage of $400 per week. Comparable-worth legislation is passed, and a study finds that an electrician and a dental technician have comparable jobs, so employers will now be required to pay workers in both jobs $550 per week. Analyze the effects of this requirement on the market for electricians and on the market for dental technicians. Be sure to use demand and supply graphs.

## SOLVING THE PROBLEM:

**Step 1:** **Review the chapter material.** This problem is about economic discrimination, so you may want to review the section "Discrimination," which begins on page 551.

**Step 2:** **Draw the graphs.** We saw in Chapter 4 that when the government sets the price in a market, the result is a surplus or a shortage, depending on whether the government-mandated price is above or below the competitive market equilibrium. A wage of $550 per week is below the market wage for electricians and above the market wage for dental technicians. Therefore, we expect the requirement to result in a shortage of electricians and a surplus of dental technicians.

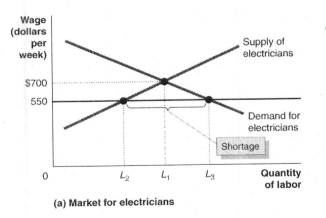

**(a) Market for electricians**

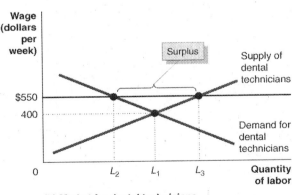

**(b) Market for dental technicians**

In panel (a), without comparable-worth legislation, the equilibrium wage for electricians is $700, and the equilibrium quantity of electricians hired is $L_1$. Setting the wage for electricians below equilibrium at $550 reduces the quantity of labor supplied in this occupation from $L_1$ to $L_2$ but increases the quantity of labor demanded by employers from $L_1$ to $L_3$. The result is a shortage of electricians equal to $L_3 - L_2$, as shown by the bracket in the graph.

In panel (b), without comparable-worth legislation, the equilibrium wage for dental technicians is $400, and the equilibrium quantity of dental technicians hired is $L_1$. Setting the wage for dental technicians above equilibrium at $550 increases the quantity of labor supplied in this occupation from $L_1$ to $L_3$ but reduces the quantity of labor demanded by employers from $L_1$ to $L_2$. The result is a surplus of dental technicians equal to $L_3 - L_2$, as shown by the bracket in the graph.

**EXTRA CREDIT:** Most economists are skeptical of government attempts to set wages and prices, as comparable-worth legislation would require. Supporters of comparable-worth legislation, by contrast, see differences between men's and women's wages as being mainly due to discrimination and are looking to government legislation as a solution.

>> **End Solved Problem 16-4**

***The Difficulty of Measuring Discrimination*** When two people are paid different wages, discrimination may be the explanation. But differences in productivity or preferences may also be an explanation. Labor economists have attempted to measure what part of differences in wages between blacks and whites and between men and women is due to discrimination and what part is due to other factors. Unfortunately, it is difficult to measure precisely differences in productivity or in worker preferences. As a result, we can't know exactly the extent of economic discrimination in the United States today. Most economists do believe, however, that most of the differences in wages between different groups are due to factors other than discrimination.

***Does It Pay to Discriminate?*** Many economists argue that economic discrimination is no longer a major factor in labor markets in the United States. One reason is that *employers who discriminate pay an economic penalty.* To see why this is true, let's consider a simplified example. Suppose that men and women are equally qualified to be airline pilots and that, initially, airlines do not discriminate. In Figure 16-8, we divide the airlines

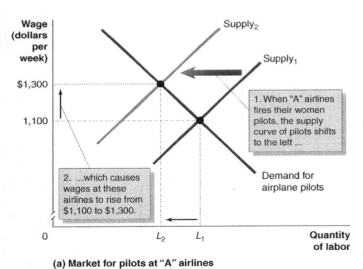

(a) Market for pilots at "A" airlines

(b) Market for pilots at "B" airlines

## Figure 16-8 | Discrimination and Wages

In this hypothetical example, we assume that initially neither "A" airlines nor "B" airlines discriminate. As a result, men and women pilots receive the same wage of $1,100 per week at both groups of airlines. We then assume that "A" airlines discriminates by firing all their women pilots. Panel (a) shows that this reduces the supply of pilots to "A" airlines and raises the wage paid by these airlines from $1,100 to $1,300. Panel (b) shows that this increases the supply of pilots to "B" airlines and lowers the wage paid by these airlines from $1,100 to $900. All the women pilots will end up being employed at the nondiscriminating airlines and will be paid a lower wage than the men who are employed by the discriminating airlines.

into two groups: "A" airlines and "B" airlines. If neither group of airlines discriminates, we would expect them to pay an equal wage of $1,100 per week to both men and women pilots. Now suppose that "A" airlines decide to discriminate and to fire all their women pilots. This action will reduce the supply of pilots to these airlines and, as shown in panel (a), that will force up the wage from $1,100 to $1,300. At the same time, as women fired from the jobs with "A" airlines apply for jobs with "B" airlines, the supply of pilots to "B" airlines will increase, and the equilibrium wage will fall from $1,100 to $900. All the women pilots will end up being employed at the nondiscriminating airlines and be paid a lower wage than the men who are employed by the discriminating airlines.

But this situation cannot persist for two reasons. First, male pilots employed by "B" airlines will also receive the lower wage. This lower wage gives them an incentive to quit their jobs at "B" airlines and apply at "A" airlines, which will shift the labor supply curve for "B" airlines to the left and the labor supply curve for "A" airlines to the right. Second, "A" airlines are paying $1,300 per week to hire pilots who are no more productive than the pilots being paid $900 per week by "B" airlines. As a result, "B" airlines will have lower costs and will be able to charge lower prices. Eventually, "A" airlines will lose their customers to "B" airlines and be driven out of business. The market will have imposed an economic penalty on the discriminating airlines. So, discrimination will not persist, and the wages of men and women pilots will become equal.

Can we conclude from this analysis that competition in markets will eliminate all economic discrimination? Unfortunately, this optimistic conclusion is not completely accurate. We know that until the Civil Rights Act of 1964 was passed, many firms in the United States refused to hire blacks. Even though this practice had persisted for decades, nondiscriminating competitors did not drive these firms out of business. Why not? There were three important factors:

1 **Worker discrimination.** In many cases, white workers refused to work alongside black workers. As a result, some industries—such as the important cotton textile industry in the South—were all white. Because of discrimination by white workers, a businessperson who wanted to use low-cost black labor might need to hire an all-black workforce. Some businesspeople tried this, but because blacks had been excluded from these industries, they often lacked the skills and experience to form an effective workforce.

2 **Customer discrimination.** Some white consumers were unwilling to buy from companies in certain industries if they employed black workers. This was not a significant barrier in manufacturing industries, where customers would not know the race of the workers producing the good. It was, however, a problem for firms in industries in which workers came into direct contact with the public.

3 **Negative feedback loops.** Our analysis in Figure 16-8 assumed that men and women pilots were equally qualified. However, if discrimination makes it difficult for a member of a group to find employment in a particular occupation, his or her incentive to be trained to enter that occupation is reduced. Consider the legal profession as an example. In 1952, future Supreme Court Justice Sandra Day O'Connor graduated third in her class at Stanford University Law School and was an editor of the *Stanford Law Review*, but for some time she was unable to find a job as a lawyer because in those years, many law firms would not hire women. Facing such bleak job prospects, it's not surprising that relatively few women entered law school. As a result, a law firm that did not discriminate would have been unable to act like the nondiscriminating airlines in our example by hiring women lawyers at a lower salary and using this cost advantage to drive discriminating law firms out of business. In this situation, an unfortunate feedback loop was in place: Few women prepared to become lawyers because many law firms discriminated against women, and nondiscriminating law firms were unable to drive discriminating law firms out of business because there were too few women lawyers available.

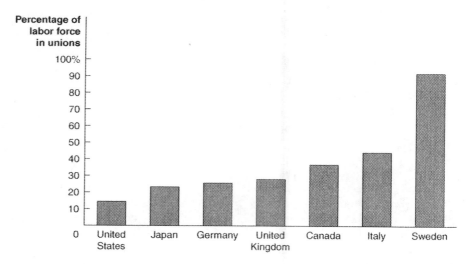

Figure 16-9 | The United States Is Less Unionized Than Most Industrial Countries

In 2006, the percentage of the labor force belonging to unions was lower in the United States than in most other industrial countries.
Source: International Labour Organization.

Most economists agree that the market imposes an economic penalty on firms that discriminate, but because of the factors just discussed, it may take the market a very long time to eliminate discrimination entirely. The passage of the Civil Rights Act of 1964, which outlawed hiring discrimination on the basis of race and sex, greatly sped up the process of reducing economic discrimination in the United States.

## Labor Unions

**Labor union** An organization of employees that has the legal right to bargain with employers about wages and working conditions.

Workers' wages can differ depending on whether the workers are members of labor unions. **Labor unions** are organizations of employees that have the legal right to bargain with employers about wages and working conditions. If a union is unable to reach an agreement with a company, it has the legal right to call a *strike*, which means its members refuse to work until a satisfactory agreement has been reached. As Figure 16-9 shows, a smaller fraction of the U.S. labor force is unionized than in most other industrial countries.

As Table 16-4 shows, in the United States, workers in unions receive higher wages than workers who are not in unions. Do union members earn more than nonunion members because they are in unions? The answer might seem to be "yes," but many union workers are in industries, such as automobile manufacturing, in which their marginal revenue products are high, so their wages would be high even if they were not unionized. Economists who have attempted to estimate statistically the impact of unionization on wages have concluded that being in a union increases a worker's wages about 10 percent, holding constant other factors, such as the industry the worker is in. A

TABLE 16-4

**Union Workers Earn More Than Nonunion Workers**

| | AVERAGE WEEKLY EARNINGS |
|---|---|
| **UNION WORKERS** | $833 |
| **NONUNION WORKERS** | 642 |

*Note:* "Union workers" includes union members as well as workers who are represented by unions but who are not members of them.

Source: U.S. Bureau of Labor Statistics, *Union Members Summary*, January 25, 2007.

related question is whether unions raise the total amount of wages received by all workers, whether unionized or not. Because the share of national income received by workers has remained roughly constant over many years, most economists do not believe that unions have raised the total amount of wages received by workers.

---

16.5 | Discuss the role personnel economics can play in helping firms deal with human resources issues.

# Personnel Economics

Traditionally, labor economists have focused on issues such as the effects of labor unions on wages or the determinants of changes in average wages over time. They have spent less time analyzing *human resources issues*, which address how firms hire, train, and promote workers and set their wages and benefits. In recent years, some labor economists, including Edward Lazear of Stanford University and William Neilson of Texas A&M University, have begun exploring the application of economic analysis to human resources issues. This new focus has become known as **personnel economics**.

Personnel economics analyzes the link between differences among jobs and differences in the way workers are paid. Jobs have different skill requirements, require more or less interaction with other workers, have to be performed in more or less unpleasant environments, and so on. Firms need to design compensation policies that take into account these differences. Personnel economics also analyzes policies related to other human resources issues, such as promotions, training, and pensions. In this brief overview, we look only at compensation policies.

**Personnel economics** The application of economic analysis to human resources issues.

## Should Workers' Pay Depend on How Much They Work or on How Much They Produce?

One issue personnel economics addresses is when workers should receive *straight-time pay*—a certain wage per hour or salary per week or month—and when they should receive *commission* or *piece-rate pay*—a wage based on how much output they produce.

Suppose, for example, that Anne owns a car dealership and is trying to decide whether to pay her salespeople a salary of $800 per week or a commission of $200 on each car they sell. Figure 16-10 compares the compensation a salesperson would receive under the two systems, according to the number of cars the salesperson sells.

With a straight salary, the salesperson receives $800 per week, no matter how many cars she sells. This outcome is shown by the horizontal line in Figure 16-10. If she receives a commission of $200 per car, her compensation will increase with every car she sells. This outcome is shown by the upward-sloping line. A salesperson who sells fewer than 4 cars per week would earn more by receiving a straight salary of $800 per week. A salesperson who sells more than 4 cars per week would be better off receiving the $200-per-car commission. We can identify two advantages Anne would receive from paying her salespeople commissions rather than salaries: She would attract and retain the most productive employees, and she would provide an incentive to her employees to sell more cars.

Suppose that other car dealerships were all paying salaries of $800 per week. If Anne pays her employees on commission, any of her employees who are unable to sell at least 4 cars per week can improve their pay by going to work for one of her competitors. By the same token, any salespeople at Anne's competitors who can sell more than 4 cars per week can raise their pay by quitting and coming to work for Anne. Over time, Anne will find her least productive employees leaving, while she is able to hire new employees who are more productive.

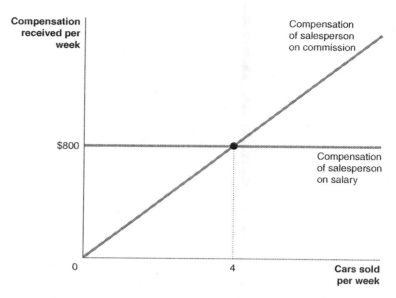

**Figure 16-10** | Paying Car Salespeople by Salary or by Commission

This figure compares the compensation a car salesperson receives if she is on a straight salary of $800 per week or if she receives a commission of $200 for each car she sells. With a straight salary, she receives $800 per week, no matter how many cars she sells. This outcome is shown by the horizontal line in the figure. If she receives a commission of $200 per car, her compensation will increase with every car she sells. This outcome is shown by the upward-sloping line. If she sells fewer than 4 cars per week, she would be better off with the $800 salary. If she sells more than 4 cars per week, she would be better off with the $200-per-car commission.

Paying a commission also increases the incentive Anne's salespeople have to sell more cars. If Anne paid a salary, her employees would receive the same amount no matter how few cars they sold. An employee on salary might decide on a particularly hot or cold day that it was less trouble to stay inside the building than to go out on the car lot to greet potential customers. An employee on commission would know that the additional effort expended on selling more cars would be rewarded with additional compensation.

*A piece-rate system at Safelite AutoGlass led to increased worker wages and firm profits.*

Making | **Raising Pay, Productivity, and Profits**
the |
Connection | **at Safelite AutoGlass**

Safelite Group, headquartered in Columbus, Ohio, is the parent company of Safelite AutoGlass, the nation's largest installer of auto glass, with 600 repair shops. In the mid-1990s, Safelite shifted from paying its glass installers hourly wages to paying them on the basis of how many windows they installed. Safelite already had in place a computer system that allowed it to track easily how many windows each worker installed per day. To make sure quality did not suffer, Safelite added a rule that if a workmanship-related defect occurred with the installed windshield, the worker would have to install a new windshield and would not be paid for the additional work.

Edward Lazear analyzed data provided by the firm and discovered that under the new piece-rate system, the number of windows installed per worker jumped 44 percent. Lazear estimates that half of this increase was due to increased productivity from workers who continued with the company and half was due to new hires being more productive than the workers they replaced who had left the company. Worker pay rose on average by about 9.9 percent. Ninety-two percent of workers experienced a pay increase, and one-quarter received an increase of at least 28 percent. Safelite's profits also increased as the cost to the company per window installed fell from $44.43 under the hourly wage system to $35.24 under the piece-rate system.

Sociologists sometimes question whether worker productivity can be increased through the use of monetary incentives. The experience of Safelite AutoGlass provides a clear example of workers reacting favorably to the opportunity to increase output in exchange for higher compensation.

Source: Edward P. Lazear, "Performance Pay and Productivity," *American Economic Review*, Vol. 90, No. 5, December 2000, pp. 1346–1361.

## Other Considerations in Setting Compensation Systems

The discussion so far indicates that companies will find it more profitable to use a commission or piece-rate system of compensation rather than a salary system. In fact, many firms continue to pay their workers salaries, which means they are paying their workers on the basis of how long they work rather than on the basis of how much they produce. Firms may choose a salary system for several good reasons:

- *Difficulty in measuring output.* Often it is difficult to attribute output to any particular worker. For example, projects carried out by an engineering firm may involve teams of workers whose individual contributions are difficult to distinguish. On assembly lines, such as those used in the automobile industry, the amount produced by each worker is determined by the speed of the line, which is set by managers rather than by workers. Managers at many firms perform such a wide variety of tasks that measuring their output would be costly, if it could be done at all.

- *Concerns about quality.* If workers are paid on the basis of the number of units produced, they may become less concerned about quality. An office assistant who is paid on the basis of the quantity of letters typed may become careless about how many typos the letters contain. In some cases, there are ways around this problem; for example, the assistant may be required to correct the mistakes on his or her own time without pay.

- *Worker dislike of risk.* Piece-rate or commission systems of compensation increase the risk to workers because sometimes output declines for reasons not connected to the worker's effort. For example, if there is a very snowy winter, few customers may show up at Anne's auto dealership. Through no fault of their own, her salespeople may have great difficulty selling any cars. If they are paid a salary, their income will not be affected, but if they are on commission, their incomes may drop to low levels. The flip side of this is that by paying salaries, Anne assumes a greater risk. During a snowy winter, her payroll expenses will remain high even though her sales are low. With a commission system of compensation, her payroll expenses will decline along with her sales. But owners of firms are typically better able to bear risk than are workers. As a result, some firms may find that workers who would earn more under a commission system will prefer to receive a salary to reduce their risk. In these situations, paying a lower salary may reduce the firm's payroll expenses compared with what they would have been under a commission or piece-rate system.

Personnel economics is a relatively new field, but it holds great potential for helping firms deal more efficiently with human relations issues.

16.6 | Show how equilibrium prices are determined in the markets for capital and natural resources.

# The Markets for Capital and Natural Resources

The approach we have used to analyze the market for labor can also be used to analyze the markets for other factors of production. We have seen that the demand for labor is determined by the marginal revenue product of labor because the value to a firm from hiring another worker equals the increase in the firm's revenue from selling the additional output it can produce by hiring the worker. The demand for capital and natural resources is determined in a similar way.

## The Market for Capital

Physical capital includes machines, equipment, and buildings. Firms sometimes buy capital, but we will focus on situations in which firms rent capital. A chocolate manufacturer renting a warehouse and an airline leasing a plane are examples of firms renting capital. Like the demand for labor, the demand for capital is a derived demand. When a firm is considering increasing its capital by, for example, employing another machine, the value it receives equals the increase in the firm's revenue from selling the additional output it can produce by employing the machine. The *marginal revenue product of capital* is the change in the firm's revenue as a result of employing one more unit of capital, such as a machine. We have seen that the marginal revenue product of labor curve is the demand curve for labor. Similarly, the marginal revenue product of capital curve is also the demand curve for capital.

Firms producing capital goods face increasing marginal costs, so the supply curve of capital goods is upward sloping, as are the supply curves for other goods and services. Figure 16-11 shows equilibrium in the market for capital. In equilibrium,

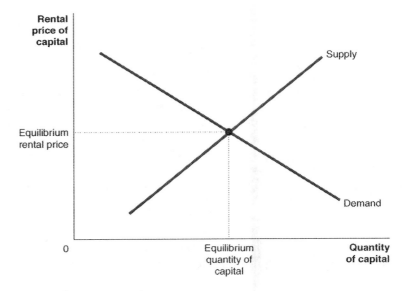

**Figure 16-11** | Equilibrium in the Market for Capital

The rental price of capital is determined by equilibrium in the market for capital. In equilibrium, the rental price of capital is equal to the marginal revenue product of capital.

suppliers of capital receive a rental price equal to the marginal revenue product of capital, just as suppliers of labor receive a wage equal to the marginal revenue product of labor.

## The Market for Natural Resources

The market for natural resources can be analyzed in the same way as the markets for labor and capital. When a firm is considering employing more natural resources, the value it receives equals the increase in the firm's revenue from selling the additional output it can produce by buying the natural resources. So, the demand for natural resources is also a derived demand. The *marginal revenue product of natural resources* is the change in the firm's revenue as a result of employing one more unit of natural resources, such as a barrel of oil. The marginal revenue product of natural resources curve is also the demand curve for natural resources.

Although the total quantity of most natural resources is ultimately fixed—as the humorist Will Rogers once remarked, "Buy land; They ain't making any more of it"—in many cases, the quantity supplied still responds to the price. For example, although the total quantity of oil deposits in the world is fixed, an increase in the price of oil will result in an increase in the quantity of oil supplied during a particular period. The result, as shown in panel (a) of Figure 16-12, is an upward-sloping supply curve. In some cases, however, the quantity of a natural resource that will be supplied is fixed and will not change as the price changes. The land available at a busy intersection is fixed, for example. In panel (b) of Figure 16-12, we illustrate this situation with a supply curve that is a vertical line, or perfectly inelastic. The price received by a factor of production that is in fixed supply is called an **economic rent** (or **pure rent**) because, in this case, the price of the factor is determined only by demand. For example, if a new highway diverts much of the traffic from a previously busy intersection, the

**Economic rent** (or **pure rent**) The price of a factor of production that is in fixed supply.

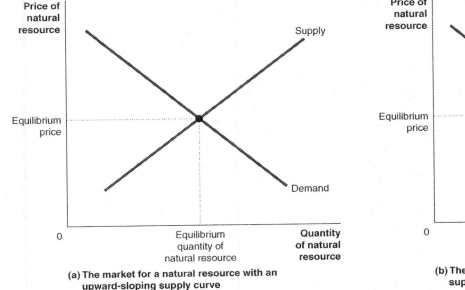

(a) The market for a natural resource with an upward-sloping supply curve

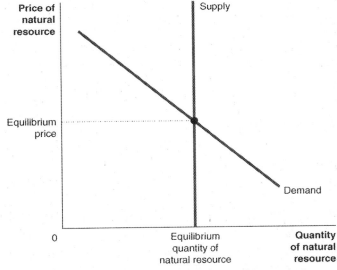

(b) The market for a natural resource with a vertical supply curve

Figure 16-12 | Equilibrium in the Market for Natural Resources

In panel (a), the supply curve of a natural resource is upward sloping. The price of the natural resource is determined by the interaction of demand and supply. In panel (b), the supply curve of the natural resource is a vertical line, indicating that the quantity supplied does not respond to changes in price. In this case, the price of the natural resource is determined only by demand. The price of a factor of production with a vertical supply curve is called an *economic rent* or a *pure rent*.

demand for the land will decline and the price of the land will fall, but the quantity of the land will not change.

## Monopsony

**Monopsony** The sole buyer of a factor of production.

In Chapter 14, we analyzed the case of *monopoly*, where a firm is the sole *seller* of a good or service. What happens if a firm is the sole *buyer* of a factor of production? This case, which is known as **monopsony**, is comparatively rare. An example is a firm in an isolated town—perhaps a lumber mill in a small town in Washington or Oregon—that is the sole employer of labor in that location. In the nineteenth and early twentieth centuries, some coal mining firms were the sole employers in certain small towns in West Virginia and some pineapple planta- tions were the sole employ- ers on certain small islands in Hawaii. In these cases, not only would the firm own the mill, mine, or plantation, but it would also own the stores and other businesses in the town. Workers would have the choice of working for the sole employer in the town or moving to another town.

*With only one lumber mill in town, the wages of these loggers won't be as high.*

We know that a firm with a monopoly in an out- put market takes advantage of its market power to reduce the quantity supplied to force up the market price and increase its profits. A firm that has a monopsony in a factor market would employ a similar strategy: It would restrict the quantity of the factor demanded to force down the price of the factor and increase profits. A firm with a monopsony in a labor market will hire fewer workers and pay lower wages than would be the case in a competitive market. Because fewer workers are hired than would be true in a competitive market, monopsony results in a deadweight loss. Monopoly and monopsony have similar effects on the economy: In both cases a firm's market power results in a lower equilibrium quantity, a deadweight loss, and a reduction in economic efficiency compared with a competitive market.

In some cases, monopsony in labor markets is offset by worker membership in a labor union. A notable example of this is professional sports. For instance, Major League Baseball (MLB) effectively has a monopsony on employing professional base- ball players. (Although independent baseball leagues exist, none of the best players play for these teams, and the teams pay salaries that are a small fraction of those paid by MLB teams.) The monopsony power of the owners of MLB teams is offset by the power of the Major League Baseball Players Association, the union that represents baseball players. Bargaining between the representatives of MLB and the players union has resulted in baseball players being paid something close to what they would be receiving in a competitive market.

## The Marginal Productivity Theory of Income Distribution

We have seen that in equilibrium, each factor of production receives a price equal to its marginal revenue product. We can use this fact to explain the distribution of income. Marginal revenue product represents the value of a factor's marginal contribution to producing goods and services. Therefore, individuals will receive income equal to the marginal contributions to production from the factors of production they own, including their labor. The more factors of production an individual owns and the more productive those factors are, the higher the individual's income will be. This approach to explaining the distribution of income is called the **marginal productivity theory of income distribution**. The marginal productivity theory of income distribution was developed by John Bates Clark, who taught at Columbia University in the late nineteenth and early twentieth centuries.

> **Marginal productivity theory of income distribution** The theory that the distribution of income is determined by the marginal productivity of the factors of production that individuals own.

## Conclusion

In this chapter, we used the demand and supply model from Chapter 3 to explain why wages differ among workers. The demand for workers depends on their productivity and on the price that firms receive for the output the workers produce. The supply of workers to an occupation depends on the wages and working conditions offered by employers and on the skills required. The demand and supply for labor can also help us analyze such issues as economic discrimination and the impact of labor unions.

# Glossary

**Absolute advantage** The ability of an individual, a firm, or a country to produce more of a good or service than competitors, using the same amount of resources.

**Accounting profit** A firm's net income measured by revenue minus operating expenses and taxes paid.

**Adverse selection** The situation in which one party to a transaction takes advantage of knowing more than the other party to the transaction.

**Aggregate demand and aggregate supply model** A model that explains short-run fluctuations in real GDP and the price level.

**Aggregate demand curve** A curve that shows the relationship between the price level and the quantity of real GDP demanded by households, firms, and the government.

**Aggregate expenditure (AE)** The total amount of spending in the economy: the sum of consumption, planned investment, government purchases, and net exports.

**Aggregate expenditure model** A macroeconomic model that focuses on the relationship between total spending and real GDP, assuming that the price level is constant.

**Allocative efficiency** A state of the economy in which production represents consumer preferences; in particular, every good or service is produced up to the point where the last unit provides a marginal benefit to consumers equal to the marginal cost of producing it.

**Antitrust laws** Laws aimed at eliminating collusion and promoting competition among firms.

**Arrow impossibility theorem** A mathematical theorem that holds that no system of voting can be devised that will consistently represent the underlying preferences of voters.

**Asset** Anything of value owned by a person or a firm.

**Asymmetric information** A situation in which one party to an economic transaction has less information than the other party.

**Autarky** A situation in which a country does not trade with other countries.

**Automatic stabilizers** Government spending and taxes that automatically increase or decrease along with the business cycle.

**Autonomous expenditure** An expenditure that does not depend on the level of GDP.

**Average fixed cost** Fixed cost divided by the quantity of output produced.

**Average product of labor** The total output produced by a firm divided by the quantity of workers.

**Average revenue (AR)** Total revenue divided by the quantity of the product sold.

**Average tax rate** Total tax paid divided by total income.

**Average total cost** Total cost divided by the quantity of output produced.

**Average variable cost** Variable cost divided by the quantity of output produced.

## B

**Balance of payments** The record of a country's trade with other countries in goods, services, and assets.

**Balance of trade** The difference between the value of the goods a country exports and the value of the goods a country imports.

**Balance sheet** A financial statement that sums up a firm's financial position on a particular day, usually the end of a quarter or year.

**Bank panic** A situation in which many banks experience runs at the same time.

**Bank run** A situation in which many depositors simultaneously decide to withdraw money from a bank.

**Barrier to entry** Anything that keeps new firms from entering an industry in which firms are earning economic profits.

**Behavioral economics** The study of situations in which people make choices that do not appear to be economically rational.

**Black market** A market in which buying and selling take place at prices that violate government price regulations.

**Bond** A financial security that represents a promise to repay a fixed amount of funds.

**Brand management** The actions of a firm intended to maintain the differentiation of a product over time.

**Bretton Woods System** An exchange rate system that lasted from 1944 to 1971, under which countries pledged to buy and sell their currencies at a fixed rate against the dollar.

**Budget constraint** The limited amount of income available to consumers to spend on goods and services.

**Budget deficit** The situation in which the government's expenditures are greater than its tax revenue.

**Budget surplus** The situation in which the government's expenditures are less than its tax revenue.

**Business cycle** Alternating periods of economic expansion and economic recession.

**Business strategy** Actions taken by a firm to achieve a goal, such as maximizing profits.

## C

**Capital account** The part of the balance of payments that records relatively minor transactions, such as migrants' transfers, and sales and purchases of nonproduced, nonfinancial assets.

**Capital controls** Limits on the flow of foreign exchange and financial investment across countries.

**Capital** Manufactured goods that are used to produce other goods and services.

**Cartel** A group of firms that collude by agreeing to restrict output to increase prices and profits.

**Cash flow** The difference between the cash revenues received by a firm and the cash spending by the firm.

**Catch-up** The prediction that the level of GDP per capita (or income per capita) in poor countries will grow faster than in rich countries.

**Centrally planned economy** An economy in which the government decides how economic resources will be allocated.

**Ceteris paribus ("all else equal")** The requirement that when analyzing the relationship between two variables—such as price and quantity demanded—other variables must be held constant.

**Circular-flow diagram** A model that illustrates how participants in markets are linked.

**Closed economy** An economy that has no interactions in trade or finance with other countries.

**Coase theorem** The argument of economist Ronald Coase that if transactions costs are low, private bargaining will result in an efficient solution to the problem of externalities.

**Collusion** An agreement among firms to charge the same price or otherwise not to compete.

**Command and control approach** An approach that involves the government imposing quantitative limits on the amount of pollution firms are allowed to emit or requiring firms to install specific pollution control devices.

**Commodity money** A good used as money that also has value independent of its use as money.

**Common resource** A good that is rival but not excludable.

**Comparative advantage** The ability of an individual, a firm, or a country to produce a good or service at a lower opportunity cost than competitors.

**Compensating differentials** Higher wages that compensate workers for unpleasant aspects of a job.

**Competitive market equilibrium** A market equilibrium with many buyers and many sellers.

**Complements** Goods and services that are used together.

**Constant returns to scale** The situation when a firm's long-run average costs remain unchanged as it increases output.

**Consumer price index (CPI)** An average of the prices of the goods and services purchased by the typical urban family of four.

**Consumer surplus** The difference between the highest price a consumer is willing to pay and the price the consumer actually pays.

**Consumption function** The relationship between consumption spending and disposable income.

**Consumption** Spending by households on goods and services, not including spending on new houses.

**Contractionary monetary policy** The Federal Reserve's adjusting the money supply to increase interest rates to reduce inflation.

**Cooperative equilibrium** An equilibrium in a game in which players cooperate to increase their mutual payoff.

**Copyright** A government-granted exclusive right to produce and sell a creation.

**Corporate governance** The way in which a corporation is structured and the effect a corporation's structure has on the firm's behavior.

**Corporation** A legal form of business that provides the owners with limited liability.

**Coupon payment** An interest payment on a bond.

**Cross-price elasticity of demand** The percentage change in quantity demanded of one good divided by the percentage change in the price of another good.

**Crowding out** A decline in private expenditures as a result of an increase in government purchases.

**Currency appreciation** An increase in the market value of one currency relative to another currency.

**Currency depreciation** A decrease in the market value of one currency relative to another currency.

**Current account** The part of the balance of payments that records a country's net exports, net investment income, and net transfers.

**Cyclical unemployment** Unemployment caused by a business cycle recession.

**Cyclically adjusted budget deficit or surplus** The deficit or surplus in the federal government's budget if the economy were at potential GDP.

## D

**Deadweight loss** The reduction in economic surplus resulting from a market not being in competitive equilibrium.

**Deflation** A decline in the price level.

**Demand curve** A curve that shows the relationship between the price of a product and the quantity of the product demanded.

**Demand schedule** A table showing the relationship between the price of a product and the quantity of the product demanded.

**Demographics** The characteristics of a population with respect to age, race, and gender.

**Derived demand** The demand for a factor of production that is derived from the demand for the good the factor produces.

**Devaluation** A reduction in a fixed exchange rate.

**Direct finance** A flow of funds from savers to firms through financial markets, such as the New York Stock Exchange.

**Discount loans** Loans the Federal Reserve makes to banks.

**Discount rate** The interest rate the Federal Reserve charges on discount loans.

**Discouraged workers** People who are available for work but have not looked for a job during the previous four weeks because they believe no jobs are available for them.

**Diseconomies of scale** The situation when a firm's long-run average costs rise as the firm increases output.

**Disinflation** A significant reduction in the inflation rate.

**Dividends** Payments by a corporation to its shareholders.

**Dominant strategy** A strategy that is the best for a firm, no matter what strategies other firms use.

**Dumping** Selling a product for a price below its cost of production.

## E

**Economic discrimination** Paying a person a lower wage or excluding a person from an occupation on the basis of an irrelevant characteristic such as race or gender.

**Economic efficiency** A market outcome in which the marginal benefit to consumers of the last unit produced is equal to its marginal cost of production and in which the sum of consumer surplus and producer surplus is at a maximum.

**Economic growth** The ability of an economy to produce increasing quantities of goods and services.

**Economic growth model** A model that explains growth rate changes in real GDP per capita in the long run.

**Economic loss** The situation in which a firm's total revenue is less

than its total cost, including all implicit costs.

**Economic model** A simplified version of reality used to analyze real-world economic situations.

**Economic profit** A firm's revenues minus all its costs, implicit and explicit.

**Economic rent (or pure rent)** The price of a factor of production that is in fixed supply.

**Economic surplus** The sum of consumer surplus and producer surplus.

**Economic variable** Something measurable that can have different values, such as the wages of software programmers.

**Economics** The study of the choices people make to attain their goals, given their scarce resources.

**Economies of scale** The situation when a firm's long-run average costs fall as it increases output.

**Efficiency wage** A higher-than-market wage that a firm pays to increase worker productivity.

**Elastic demand** Demand is elastic when the percentage change in quantity demanded is *greater* than the percentage change in price, so the price elasticity is *greater* than 1 in absolute value.

**Elasticity** A measure of how much one economic variable responds to changes in another economic variable.

**Endowment effect** The tendency of people to be unwilling to sell a good they already own even if they are offered a price that is greater than the price they would be willing to pay to buy the good if they didn't already own it.

**Entrepreneur** Someone who operates a business, bringing together the factors of production——labor, capital, and natural resources—to produce goods and services.

**Equity** The fair distribution of economic benefits.

**Euro** The common currency of many European countries.

**Excess burden** The efficiency loss to the economy that results from a tax causing a reduction in the quantity of a good produced; also known as the deadweight loss.

**Excess reserves**  Reserves that banks hold over and above the legal requirement.

**Exchange rate system**  An agreement among countries on how exchange rates should be determined.

**Excludability**  The situation in which anyone who does not pay for a good cannot consume it.

**Expansion path**  A curve that shows a firm's cost-minimizing combination of inputs for every level of output.

**Expansion**  The period of a business cycle during which total production and total employment are increasing.

**Expansionary monetary policy**  The Federal Reserve's increasing the money supply and decreasing interest rates to increase real GDP.

**Explicit cost**  A cost that involves spending money.

**Exports**  Goods and services produced domestically but sold to other countries.

**External economies**  Reductions in a firm's costs that result from an increase in the size of an industry.

**Externality**  A benefit or cost that affects someone who is not directly involved in the production or consumption of a good or service.

## F

**Factor markets**  Markets for the factors of production, such as labor, capital, natural resources, and entrepreneurial ability.

**Factors of production**  Labor, capital, natural resources, and other inputs used to produce goods and services.

**Federal funds rate**  The interest rate banks charge each other for overnight loans.

**Federal Open Market Committee (FOMC)**  The Federal Reserve committee responsible for open market

operations and managing the money supply in the United States.

**Federal Reserve System**  The central bank of the United States.

**Fiat money**  Money, such as paper currency, that is authorized by a central bank or governmental body and that does not have to be exchanged by the central bank for gold or some other commodity money.

**Final good or service**  A good or service purchased by a final user.

**Financial account**  The part of the balance of payments that records purchases of assets a country has made abroad and foreign purchases of assets in the country.

**Financial intermediaries**  Firms, such as banks, mutual funds, pension funds, and insurance companies, that borrow funds from savers and lend them to borrowers.

**Financial markets**  Markets where financial securities, such as stocks and bonds, are bought and sold.

**Financial system**  The system of financial markets and financial intermediaries through which firms acquire funds from households.

**Fiscal policy**  Changes in federal taxes and purchases that are intended to achieve macroeconomic policy objectives, such as high employment, price stability, and high rates of economic growth.

**Fixed costs**  Costs that remain constant as output changes.

**Fixed exchange rate system**  A system under which countries agree to keep the exchange rates among their currencies fixed.

**Floating currency**  The outcome of a country allowing its currency's exchange rate to be determined by demand and supply.

**Foreign direct investment (FDI)**  The purchase or building by a corporation of a facility in a foreign country.

**Foreign portfolio investment**  The purchase by an individual or

a firm of stocks or bonds issued in another country.

**Fractional reserve banking system**  A banking system in which banks keep less than 100 percent of deposits as reserves.

**Free market**  A market with few government restrictions on how a good or service can be produced or sold or on how a factor of production can be employed.

**Free riding**  Benefiting from a good without paying for it.

**Free trade**  Trade between countries that is without government restrictions.

**Frictional unemployment**  Short-term unemployment that arises from the process of matching workers with jobs.

## G

**Game theory**  The study of how people make decisions in situations in which attaining their goals depends on their interactions with others; in economics, the study of the decisions of firms in industries where the profits of each firm depend on its interactions with other firms.

**GDP deflator**  A measure of the price level, calculated by dividing nominal GDP by real GDP and multiplying by 100.

**Globalization**  The process of countries becoming more open to foreign trade and investment.

**Government purchases**  Spending by federal, state, and local governments on goods and services.

**Gross domestic product (GDP)**  The market value of all final goods and services produced in a country during a period of time, typically one year.

## H

**Horizontal merger**  A merger between firms in the same industry.

**Human capital**  The accumulated knowledge and skills that workers acquire from education and training or from their life experiences.

## I

**Implicit cost**  A nonmonetary opportunity cost.

**Imports**  Goods and services bought domestically but produced in other countries.

**Income effect**  The change in the quantity demanded of a good that results from the effect of a change in price on consumer purchasing power, holding all other factors constant.

**Income elasticity of demand**  A measure of the responsiveness of quantity demanded to changes in income, measured by the percentage change in quantity demanded divided by the percentage change in income.

**Income statement**  A financial statement that sums up a firm's revenues, costs, and profit over a period of time.

**Indifference curve**  A curve that shows the combinations of consumption bundles that give the consumer the same utility.

**Indirect finance**  A flow of funds from savers to borrowers through financial intermediaries such as banks. Intermediaries raise funds from savers to lend to firms (and other borrowers).

**Industrial Revolution**  The application of mechanical power to the production of goods, beginning in England around 1750.

**Inelastic demand**  Demand is inelastic when the percentage change in quantity demanded is *less* than the percentage change in price, so the price elasticity is *less* than 1 in absolute value.

**Inferior good**  A good for which the demand increases as income falls and decreases as income rises.

**Inflation targeting**  Conducting monetary policy so as to commit the central bank to achieving a publicly announced level of inflation.

**Interest rate**  The cost of borrowing funds, usually expressed as a percentage of the amount borrowed.

**Intermediate good or service**  A good or service that is an input into another good or service, such as a tire on a truck.

**International Monetary Fund (IMF)**  An international organization that provides foreign currency loans to central banks and oversees the operation of the international monetary system.

**Inventories**  Goods that have been produced but not yet sold.

**Investment**  Spending by firms on new factories, office buildings, machinery, and additions to inventories, and spending by households on new houses.

**Isocost line**  All the combinations of two inputs, such as capital and labor, that have the same total cost.

**Isoquant**  A curve that shows all the combinations of two inputs, such as capital and labor, that will produce the same level of output.

## K

**Keynesian revolution**  The name given to the widespread acceptance during the 1930s and 1940s of John Maynard Keynes's macroeconomic model.

## L

**Labor force**  The sum of employed and unemployed workers in the economy.

**Labor force participation rate**  The percentage of the working-age population in the labor force.

**Labor productivity**  The quantity of goods and services that can be produced by one worker or by one hour of work.

**Labor union**  An organization of employees that has the legal right to bargain with employers about wages and working conditions.

**Law of demand**  The rule that, holding everything else constant, when the price of a product falls, the quantity demanded of the product will increase, and when the price of a product rises, the quantity demanded of the product will decrease.

**Law of diminishing marginal utility**  The principle that consumers experience diminishing additional satisfaction as they consume more of a good or service during a given period of time.

**Law of diminishing returns**  The principle that, at some point, adding more of a variable input, such as labor, to the same amount of a fixed input, such as capital, will cause the marginal product of the variable input to decline.

**Law of supply**  The rule that, holding everything else constant, increases in price cause increases in the quantity supplied, and decreases in price cause decreases in the quantity supplied.

**Liability**  Anything owed by a person or a firm.

**Limited liability**  The legal provision that shields owners of a corporation from losing more than they have invested in the firm.

**Long run**  The period of time in which a firm can vary all its inputs, adopt new technology, and increase or decrease the size of its physical plant.

**Long-run aggregate supply curve**  A curve that shows the relationship in the long run between the price level and the quantity of real GDP supplied.

**Long-run average cost curve**  A curve showing the lowest cost at which a firm is able to produce a given quantity of output in the long run, when no inputs are fixed.

**Long-run competitive equilibrium**  The situation in which the entry and exit of firms has resulted in the typical firm breaking even.

**Long-run economic growth**  The process by which rising productivity increases the average standard of living.

**Long-run supply curve**  A curve that shows the relationship in the long run between market price and the quantity supplied.

**Lorenz curve**  A curve that shows the distribution of income by arraying incomes from lowest to highest on the horizontal axis and indicating the cumulative fraction of income earned by each fraction of households on the vertical axis.

## M

**M1**  The narrowest definition of the money supply: The sum of currency in circulation, checking account deposits in banks, and holdings of traveler's checks.

**M2**  A broader definition of the money supply: M1 plus savings account balances, small-denomination time deposits, balances in money market deposit accounts in banks, and noninstitutional money market fund shares.

**Macroeconomics**  The study of the economy as a whole, including topics such as inflation, unemployment, and economic growth.

**Managed float exchange rate system**  The current exchange rate system, under which the value of most currencies is determined by demand and supply, with occasional government intervention.

**Marginal analysis**  Analysis that involves comparing marginal benefits and marginal costs.

**Marginal benefit**  The additional benefit to a consumer from consuming one more unit of a good or service.

**Marginal cost**  The change in a firm's total cost from producing one more unit of a good or service.

**Marginal product of labor**  The additional output a firm produces as a result of hiring one more worker.

**Marginal productivity theory of income distribution**  The theory that the distribution of income is determined by the marginal productivity of the factors of production that individuals own.

**Marginal propensity to consume (MPC)**  The slope of the consumption function: The amount by which consumption spending changes when disposable income changes.

**Marginal propensity to save (MPS)**  The change in saving divided by the change in disposable income.

**Marginal rate of substitution (MRS)**  The slope of an indifference curve, which represents the rate at which a consumer would be willing to trade off one good for another.

**Marginal rate of technical substitution (MRTS)**  The slope of an isoquant, or the rate at which a firm is able to substitute one input for another while keeping the level of output constant.

**Marginal revenue (MR)**  Change in total revenue from selling one more unit of a product.

**Marginal revenue product of labor (MRP)**  The change in a firm's revenue as a result of hiring one more worker.

**Marginal tax rate**  The fraction of each additional dollar of income that must be paid in taxes.

**Marginal utility (MU)**  The change in total utility a person receives from consuming one additional unit of a good or service.

**Market**  A group of buyers and sellers of a good or service and the institution or arrangement by which they come together to trade.

**Market demand**  The demand by all the consumers of a given good or service.

**Market economy**  An economy in which the decisions of households and firms interacting in markets allocate economic resources.

**Market equilibrium**  A situation in which quantity demanded equals quantity supplied.

**Market failure**  A situation in which the market fails to produce the efficient level of output.

**Market for loanable funds**  The interaction of borrowers and lenders that determines the market interest rate and the quantity of loanable funds exchanged.

**Market power**  The ability of a firm to charge a price greater than marginal cost.

**Marketing**  All the activities necessary for a firm to sell a product to a consumer.

**Median voter theorem** The proposition that the outcome of a majority vote is likely to represent the preferences of the voter who is in the political middle.

**Menu costs** The costs to firms of changing prices.

**Microeconomics** The study of how households and firms make choices, how they interact in markets, and how the government attempts to influence their choices.

**Minimum efficient scale** The level of output at which all economies of scale are exhausted.

**Mixed economy** An economy in which most economic decisions result from the interaction of buyers and sellers in markets but in which the government plays a significant role in the allocation of resources.

**Monetarism** The macroeconomic theories of Milton Friedman and his followers; particularly the idea that the quantity of money should be increased at a constant rate.

**Monetary growth rule** A plan for increasing the quantity of money at a fixed rate that does not respond to changes in economic conditions.

**Monetary policy** The actions the Federal Reserve takes to manage the money supply and interest rates to pursue macroeconomic policy objectives.

**Money** Assets that people are generally willing to accept in exchange for goods and services or for payment of debts.

**Monopolistic competition** A market structure in which barriers to entry are low and many firms compete by selling similar, but not identical, products.

**Monopoly** A firm that is the only seller of a good or service that does not have a close substitute.

**Monopsony** The sole buyer of a factor of production.

**Moral hazard** The actions people take after they have entered into a transaction that make the other party to the transaction worse off.

**Multinational enterprise** A firm that conducts operations in more than one country.

**Multiplier effect** The series of induced increases in consumption spending that results from an initial increase in autonomous expenditure.

**Multiplier** The increase in equilibrium real GDP divided by the increase in autonomous expenditure.

## N

**Nash equilibrium** A situation in which each firm chooses the best strategy, given the strategies chosen by other firms.

**Natural monopoly** A situation in which economies of scale are so large that one firm can supply the entire market at a lower average total cost than can two or more firms.

**Natural rate of unemployment** The normal rate of unemployment, consisting of frictional unemployment plus structural unemployment.

**Net exports** Exports minus imports.

**Net foreign investment** The difference between capital outflows from a country and capital inflows, also equal to net foreign direct investment plus net foreign portfolio investment.

**Network externalities** The situation where the usefulness of a product increases with the number of consumers who use it.

**New classical macroeconomics** The macroeconomic theories of Robert Lucas and others, particularly the idea that workers and firms have rational expectations.

**New growth theory** A model of long-run economic growth which emphasizes that technological change is influenced by economic incentives and so is determined by the working of the market system.

**Nominal exchange rate** The value of one country's currency in terms of another country's currency.

**Nominal GDP** The value of final goods and services evaluated at current-year prices.

**Nominal interest rate** The stated interest rate on a loan.

**Nonaccelerating inflation rate of unemployment (NAIRU)** The unemployment rate at which the inflation rate has no tendency to increase or decrease.

**Noncooperative equilibrium** An equilibrium in a game in which players do not cooperate but pursue their own self-interest.

**Normal good** A good for which the demand increases as income rises and decreases as income falls.

**Normative analysis** Analysis concerned with what ought to be.

## O

**Oligopoly** A market structure in which a small number of interdependent firms compete.

**Open economy** An economy that has interactions in trade or finance with other countries.

**Open market operations** The buying and selling of Treasury securities by the Federal Reserve in order to control the money supply.

**Opportunity cost** The highest-valued alternative that must be given up to engage in an activity.

## P

**Partnership** A firm owned jointly by two or more persons and not organized as a corporation.

**Patent** The exclusive right to a product for a period of 20 years from the date the product is invented.

**Payoff matrix** A table that shows the payoffs that each firm earns from every combination of strategies by the firms.

**Pegging** The decision by a country to keep the exchange rate fixed between its currency and another currency.

**Perfectly competitive market** A market that meets the conditions of (1) many buyers and sellers, (2) all firms selling identical products, and (3) no barriers to new firms entering the market.

**Perfectly elastic demand** The case where the quantity demanded is infinitely responsive to price, and the price elasticity of demand equals infinity.

**Perfectly inelastic demand** The case where the quantity demanded is completely unresponsive to price, and the price elasticity of demand equals zero.

**Personnel economics** The application of economic analysis to human resources issues.

**Per-worker production function** The relationship between real GDP per hour worked and capital per hour worked, holding the level of technology constant.

**Phillips curve** A curve showing the short-run relationship between the unemployment rate and the inflation rate.

**Pigovian taxes and subsidies** Government taxes and subsidies intended to bring about an efficient level of output in the presence of externalities.

**Positive analysis** Analysis concerned with what is.

**Potential GDP** The level of GDP attained when all firms are producing at capacity.

**Poverty line** A level of annual income equal to three times the amount of money necessary to purchase the minimal quantity of food required for adequate nutrition.

**Poverty rate** The percentage of the population that is poor according to the federal government's definition.

**Present value** The value in today's dollars of funds to be paid or received in the future.

**Price ceiling** A legally determined maximum price that sellers may charge.

**Price discrimination** Charging different prices to different customers for the same product when the price differences are not due to differences in cost.

**Price elasticity of demand**  The responsiveness of the quantity demanded to a change in price, measured by dividing the percentage change in the quantity demanded of a product by the percentage change in the product's price.

**Price elasticity of supply**  The responsiveness of the quantity supplied to a change in price, measured by dividing the percentage change in the quantity supplied of a product by the percentage change in the product's price.

**Price floor**  A legally determined minimum price that sellers may receive.

**Price leadership**  A form of implicit collusion where one firm in an oligopoly announces a price change, which is matched by the other firms in the industry.

**Price level**  A measure of the average prices of goods and services in the economy.

**Price taker**  A buyer or seller that is unable to affect the market price.

**Principal–agent problem**  A problem caused by an agent pursuing his own interests rather than the interests of the principal who hired him.

**Prisoners' dilemma**  A game in which pursuing dominant strategies results in noncooperation that leaves everyone worse off.

**Private benefit**  The benefit received by the consumer of a good or service.

**Private cost**  The cost borne by the producer of a good or service.

**Private good**  A good that is both rival and excludable.

**Producer price index (PPI)**  An average of the prices received by producers of goods and services at all stages of the production process.

**Producer surplus**  The difference between the lowest price a firm would be willing to accept and the price it actually receives.

**Product markets**  Markets for goods—such as computers—

and services—such as medical treatment.

**Production function**  The relationship between the inputs employed by a firm and the maximum output it can produce with those inputs.

**Production possibilities frontier (PPF)**  A curve showing the maximum attainable combinations of two products that may be produced with available resources and current technology.

**Productive efficiency**  The situation in which a good or service is produced at the lowest possible cost.

**Profit**  Total revenue minus total cost.

**Progressive tax**  A tax for which people with lower incomes pay a lower percentage of their income in tax than do people with higher incomes.

**Protectionism**  The use of trade barriers to shield domestic firms from foreign competition.

**Public choice model**  A model that applies economic analysis to government decision making.

**Public franchise**  A designation by the government that a firm is the only legal provider of a good or service.

**Public good**  A good that is both nonrivalrous and nonexcludable.

**Purchasing power parity**  The theory that in the long run, exchange rates move to equalize the purchasing powers of different currencies.

## Q

**Quantity demanded**  The amount of a good or service that a consumer is willing and able to purchase at a given price.

**Quantity supplied**  The amount of a good or service that a firm is willing and able to supply at a given price.

**Quantity theory of money**  A theory of the connection between money and prices that assumes that the velocity of money is constant.

**Quota**  A numeric limit imposed by a government on the quantity of a good that can be imported into the country.

## R

**Rational expectations**  Expectations formed by using all available information about an economic variable.

**Real business cycle model**  A macroeconomic model that focuses on real, rather than monetary, causes of the business cycle.

**Real exchange rate**  The price of domestic goods in terms of foreign goods.

**Real GDP**  The value of final goods and services evaluated at base-year prices.

**Real interest rate**  The nominal interest rate minus the inflation rate.

**Recession**  The period of a business cycle during which total production and total employment are decreasing.

**Regressive tax**  A tax for which people with lower incomes pay a higher percentage of their income in tax than do people with higher incomes.

**Rent seeking**  The attempts by individuals and firms to use government action to make themselves better off at the expense of others.

**Required reserve ratio**  The minimum fraction of deposits banks are required by law to keep as reserves.

**Required reserves**  Reserves that a bank is legally required to hold, based on its checking account deposits.

**Reserves**  Deposits that a bank keeps as cash in its vault or on deposit with the Federal Reserve.

**Revaluation**  An increase in a fixed exchange rate.

**Rivalry**  The situation that occurs when one person's consuming a unit of a good means no one else can consume it.

**Rule of law**  The ability of a government to enforce the laws of the country, particularly with

respect to protecting private property and enforcing contracts.

## S

**Saving and investment equation**  An equation that shows that national saving is equal to domestic investment plus net foreign investment.

**Scarcity**  The situation in which unlimited wants exceed the limited resources available to fulfill those wants.

**Separation of ownership from control**  A situation in a corporation in which the top management, rather than the shareholders, control day-to-day operations.

**Short run**  The period of time during which at least one of a firm's inputs is fixed.

**Shortage**  A situation in which the quantity demanded is greater than the quantity supplied.

**Short-run aggregate supply curve**  A curve that shows the relationship in the short run between the price level and the quantity of real GDP supplied by firms.

**Shutdown point**  The minimum point on a firm's average variable cost curve; if the price falls below this point, the firm shuts down production in the short run.

**Simple deposit multiplier**  The ratio of the amount of deposits created by banks to the amount of new reserves.

**Social benefit**  The total benefit from consuming a good or service, including both the private benefit and any external benefit.

**Social cost**  The total cost of producing a good or service, including both the private cost and any external cost.

**Sole proprietorship**  A firm owned by a single individual and not organized as a corporation.

**Speculators**  Currency traders who buy and sell foreign exchange in an attempt to profit from changes in exchange rates.

**Stagflation**  A combination of inflation and recession, usually resulting from a supply shock.

**Stock**   A financial security that represents partial ownership of a firm.

**Stockholders' equity**   The difference between the value of a corporation's assets and the value of its liabilities; also known as net worth.

**Structural relationship**   A relationship that depends on the basic behavior of consumers and firms and remains unchanged over long periods.

**Structural unemployment**   Unemployment arising from a persistent mismatch between the skills and characteristics of workers and the requirements of jobs.

**Substitutes**   Goods and services that can be used for the same purpose.

**Substitution effect**   The change in the quantity demanded of a good that results from a change in price making the good more or less expensive relative to other goods, holding constant the effect of the price change on consumer purchasing power.

**Sunk cost**   A cost that has already been paid and cannot be recovered.

**Supply curve**   A curve that shows the relationship between the price of a product and the quantity of the product supplied.

**Supply schedule**   A table that shows the relationship between the price of a product and the quantity of the product supplied.

**Supply shock**   An unexpected event that causes the short-run aggregate supply curve to shift.

**Surplus**   A situation in which the quantity supplied is greater than the quantity demanded.

# T

**Tariff**   A tax imposed by a government on imports.

**Tax incidence**   The actual division of the burden of a tax between buyers and sellers in a market.

**Tax wedge**   The difference between the pretax and posttax return to an economic activity.

**Taylor rule**   A rule developed by John Taylor that links the Fed's target for the federal funds rate to economic variables.

**Technological change**   A change in the quantity of output a firm can produce using a given quantity of inputs.

**Technology**   The processes a firm uses to turn inputs into outputs of goods and services.

**Terms of trade**   The ratio at which a country can trade its exports for imports from other countries.

**Total cost**   The cost of all the inputs a firm uses in production.

**Total revenue**   The total amount of funds received by a seller of a good or service, calculated by multiplying price per unit by the number of units sold.

**Trade**   The act of buying or selling.

**Trade-off**   The idea that because of scarcity, producing more of one good or service means producing less of another good or service.

**Tragedy of the commons**   The tendency for a common resource to be overused.

**Transactions costs**   The costs in time and other resources that parties incur in the process of agreeing to and carrying out an exchange of goods or services.

**Transfer payments**   Payments by the government to individuals for which the government does not receive a new good or service in return.

**Two-part tariff**   A situation in which consumers pay one price (or tariff) for the right to buy as much of a related good as they want at a second price.

# U

**Underground economy**   Buying and selling of goods and services that is concealed from the government to avoid taxes or regulations or because the goods and services are illegal.

**Unemployment rate**   The percentage of the labor force that is unemployed.

**Unit-elastic demand**   Demand is unit-elastic when the percentage change in quantity demanded is *equal to* the percentage change in price, so the price elasticity is equal to 1 in absolute value.

**Utility**   The enjoyment or satisfaction people receive from consuming goods and services.

# V

**Value added**   The market value a firm adds to a product.

**Variable costs**   Costs that change as output changes.

**Velocity of money**   The average number of times each dollar in the money supply is used to purchase goods and services included in GDP.

**Vertical merger**   A merger between firms at different stages of production of a good.

**Voluntary exchange**   The situation that occurs in markets when both the buyer and seller of a product are made better off by the transaction.

**Voluntary export restraint (VER)**   An agreement negotiated between two countries that places a numeric limit on the quantity of a good that can be imported by one country from the other country.

**Voting paradox**   The failure of majority voting to always result in consistent choices.

# W

**Winner's curse**   The idea that the winner in certain auctions may have overestimated the value of the good, thus ending up worse off than the losers.

**World Trade Organization (WTO)**   An international organization that oversees international trade agreements.

# Subject Index

# Credits

## Photo

**Chapter 1**, *pages 2, 3, 19*, © Phototex/Sipa Press/0501050124; *page 13*, Brian Lee, CORBIS–NY.

**Chapter 2**, *pages 36, 37, 59*, © Car Culture/CORBIS, All Rights Reserved; *page 41*, Getty Images, Inc.; *page 51 top*, Jupiter Images Picturequest–Royalty Free; *right*, Dan Lim, Masterfile Corporation; *bottom*, Photolibrary.com; *left*, David Young Wolff, Getty Images Inc.–Stone Allstock; *page 53*, © Apple Computer/Court Mast/Handout/Reuters/Corbis; *page 55*, Imagination Photo Design.

**Chapter 3**, *pages 66, 67, 91*, © Glow Images/Alamy; *page 72*, Getty Images, Inc; *page 75*, Getty Images, Inc.

**Chapter 4**, *pages 98, 99, 123*, © Ambient Images Inc./Alamy; *page 113*, Neil Guegan, Corbis Zefa Collection; *page 119*, Bill Aron, PhotoEdit, Inc.

**Chapter 5**, *pages 136, 137, 165*, Mariusz Szachowski, Shutterstock; *page 146*, AP Wide World Photos; *page*, Paul A. Souders, Corbis/Bettmann.

**Chapter 6**, *pages 172, 173, 199*, Getty Images, Inc.; *page 181*, Michelle D. Bridwell PhotoEdit Inc.; *page 186*, Getty Images, Inc.

**Chapter 7**, *pages 208, 209, 227*, AP Wide World Photos; *page 211*, Ed Pritchard, Getty Images Inc.–Stone Allstock; *page 219*, David McIntyre, Black Star.

**Chapter 8**, *pages 242, 243*, David R. Frazier, Photolibrary, Inc., Alamy Images; *page 246*, © Chung Sung-Jun/Getty Images; *page 254*, Ron Sherman, Photographer; *page 263*, Pallava Bagla, Corbis/Sygma; *page 265*, AP Wide World Photos; *page 280*, Michael Newman, PhotoEdit Inc.

**Chapter 9**, *pages 284, 285, 311*, © Frank Micelotta/Getty Images; *page 298*, Chris Carlson, AP Wide World Photos; *page 302*, Getty Images, Inc.; *page 305*, Janet Bailey, Masterfile Stock Image Library; *page 307*, Larry Kolvoord, The Image Works.

**Chapter 10**, *pages 332, 333, 355*, Yoshikazu Tsuno/AFP/Getty Images; *page 334*, Getty Images, Inc.; *page 336*, Getty Images–Stockbyte; *page 340*, © Indranil Mukherjee/AFP/Getty Images; *page 350*, Keystone, Getty Images Inc.–Hulton Archive Photos; *page 372*, © Chris McGrath/Getty Images.

**Chapter 11**, *pages 376, 377, 403*, © Bob Daemmrich/The Image Works; *page 391*, Raymond Forbes, SuperStock, Inc.; *page 399*, Richard Heinzen, SuperStock, Inc.

**Chapter 12**, *pages 410, 411, 431*, Bernard Boutrit, Woodfin Camp & Associates; *page 420*, © Up The Resolution (uptheres)/Alamy; *page 423*, © Adam Berry/Bloomberg News/Landov; *page 425*, James A. Finley, AP Wide World Photos; *page 428*, Courtesy of BIC Corporation.

**Chapter 13**, *pages 440, 441, 463*, Ralf-Finn Hestoft, Corbis/Bettmann; *page 447*, Dreamworks/Universal/Eli Reed, Picture Desk, Inc./Kobal Collection; *page 449*, These materials have been reproduced with the permission of eBay Inc. Copyright © 2006 EBAY INC. All Rights Reserved; *page 451*, Ken Reid, Getty Images, Inc.–Taxi; *page 460*, David Frazier, The Image Works.

**Chapter 14**, *pages 472, 473, 497*, Getty Images, Inc.; *page 475*, REUTERS/Toshiyuki Aizawa/Landov; *page 476*, Sean Cayton, The Image Works; *page 478*, Niall McDiarmid, Alamy Images.

**Chapter 15**, *pages 506, 507*, John M. Greim/CreativeEye/MIRA.com. Disney characters © Disney Enterprises, Inc. Used by permission from Disney Enterprises, Inc.; *page 515*, Bruce Newman, AP Wide World Photos; *page 518*, David Young-Wolff, PhotoEdit Inc.; *page 524*, Gerd Ludwig, The Image Works.

**Chapter 16**, *pages 534, 535*, Getty Images, Inc.; *page 546*, Getty Images, Inc.; *page 549*, The Kobal Collection/Columbia Pictures; *page 558*, Safelite Group; *page 562*, Willard Culver/National Geographic Image Collection.

**Chapter 17**, *pages 574, 575, 591*, © Bubbles Photolibrary/Alamy; *page 582*, Getty Images, Inc.; *page 586*, **www.indexopen.com**; *page 587*, Bruce Laurance/Image Bank/Getty Images; *page 588*, © 2005 Kristen Brochmann/Fundamental Photographs.

**Chapter 18**, *pages 598, 599*, Anthony P. Bolante, Corbis/Bettmann; *page 611*, Spencer Grant, PhotoEdit Inc.; *page 614*, Paul Sakuma, AP Wide World Photos.

## Text

**Chapter 1**, *page 5*, "In Estonia, Paying Women to Have Babies Is Paying Off" by Marcus Walker from *Wall Street Journal*, October 20, 2006, p. A1. Copyright © 2006 Dow Jones. Reprinted by permission of Dow Jones via Copyright Clearance Center; *page 18*, "Nightmare Scenarios" from *The Economist*, October 7, 2006. Copyright © 2006 The Economist. Reprinted by permission of *The Economist* via Copyright Clearance Center.

**Chapter 2**, *page 58*, Jim Duplessis, "BMW Expects Turnaround," *Knight Ridder Tribune Business News*, January 25, 2007, p. 1. Reprinted by permission of The Permissions Group.

**Chapter 3**, *page 90*, "Apple Coup: How Steve Jobs Played Hardball in iPhone Birth" by Armol Sharma, Nick Wingfield, and Li Yuan from *Wall Street Journal*, February 17, 2007, p. A1. Copyright © 2007 Dow Jones. Reprinted by permission of Dow Jones via Copyright Clearance Center.

**Chapter 4**, *page 122*, Diane Wedner, "The Landlords: Two Sides of a Coin," *Los Angeles Times*, Jan. 14, 2007, p. K1. Copyright © 2007 Los Angeles Times. Reprinted by permission.

**Chapter 5**, *page 164*, Kevin Morrison, "Next Carbon Trading Phase Promises to Clean Up Anomalies," *Financial Times*, Feb. 7, 2007, p. 38. Reprinted by permission.

**Chapter 6**, *page 181*, Jerry A. Hausman, "The Price Elasticity of Demand for Breakfast Cereal," in *The Economics of New Goods*, TF Bresnahan & RJ Gordon, eds. Used with permission of The University of Chicago Press; *page 198*, "Borders Slashes Buyer Rewards, Cuts Discounts," by Jeffrey Trachtenberg from *Wall Street Journal*, March 28, 2007, p. D1. Copyright © 2007 Dow Jones. Reprinted by permission of Dow Jones via Copyright Clearance Center.

**Chapter 7**, *page 217*, "Stock Prices from Abercrombie and Fitch" from *The Wall Street Journal*, March 6, 2007. Copyright © 2007 Dow Jones. Reprinted by permission of Dow Jones via Copyright Clearance Center; *page 226*, Michael Liedtke, "Google CEO, Co-Founders Get $1 Salary," Associated Press, April 4, 2007, 4:52PM ET version. Available at: **http://hosted.ap.org/ dynamic/stories/G/GOOGLE_ APRIL_FOOLS?SITE=TXKER&S ECTION=HOME&TEMPLATE= DEFAULT&CTIME=2007-04-02- 09-57-41.** Reprinted by permission of Associated Press via Reprint Management Services.

**Chapter 8**, *page 265*, Gordon H. Hanson, "What Has Happened to Wages in Mexico Since NAFTA? Implications for Hemispheric Free Trade" in Toni Estevadeordal, Dani Rodrick, Alan Taylor Andres Velasco, eds., *FTAA and Beyond: Prospects for Integration in the Americas*, Cambridge: Harvard University Press, 2004; *page 278*, The Top 25 Multinational Corporations 2006 from "Fortune Global 500"

*Fortune*, July 24, 2006. © 2007 Time Inc. All rights reserved. Reprinted by permission.

**Chapter 9**, *page 284*, Can Jay-Z Get You to Drink Cherry Coke? from Kenneth Hein, "Cherry Coke Gets Fresh Jay-Z Remix," *Brandweek*, January 29, 2007, p. 4; *page 310*, "Mariah Signs Scent Deal with Arden" by Julie Naughton from *WWD*, April 7, 2006, Vol. 191, No. 74, p. 11. Copyright © 2006 Conde Nast Publications. All rights reserved. Reprinted by permission.

**Chapter 10**, *page 354*, "Flat-Panel TVs, Long Touted, Finally are Becoming the Norm" by Evan Ranstad from *Wall Street Journal Online*, April 15, 2006. Copyright © 2006 Dow Jones. Reprinted by permission of Dow Jones via Copyright Clearance Center.

**Chapter 11**, *page 402*, Pallavi Gogoi, "Wal-Mart's Organic

Offensive," *BusinessWeek*, March 29, 2006 (from *BusinessWeek Online*).

**Chapter 12**, *page 430*, "Brewing Battle: Dunkin' Donuts Tries to Go Upscale, But Not Too Far," by Janet Adamy from *Wall Street Journal*, April 8, 2006. p. A1. Copyright © 2006 Dow Jones. Reprinted by permission of Dow Jones via Copyright Clearance Center.

**Chapter 13**, *page 462*, "Savings, Shakeup Seen in $4 Drug Plan; Wal-Mart May 'Take It Nationwide Next Year' " by Julie Appleby from *USA TODAY*, September 22, 2006, p. 1A. Reprinted by permission of *USA TODAY*.

**Chapter 14**, *page 496*, James K. Glassman, "Cable Guys," *Wall Street Journal Online*, September 28, 2006. Copyright © 2006 Dow Jones. Reprinted by permission

of Dow Jones via Copyright Clearance Center.

**Chapter 16**, *page 564*, "Racing Teams Recruit Athletes and Train Them Hard; The $60,000 Tire Carrier" by Neal E. Boudette, Staff Reporter of *Wall Street Journal*, June 16, 2005, p. A1. Copyright © 2005 Dow Jones. Reprinted by permission of Dow Jones via Copyright Clearance Center.

**Chapter 17**, *page 590*, "Your Money: Bad Credit Can Inflate Car Insurance Premiums" by Sandra Block from *USA TODAY*, June 11, 2007. Reprinted by permission *USA TODAY*.

**Chapter 18**, *page 624*, "The Grand Bargainer" by Steven Pearlstein from *Washington Post*, Wednesday, February 7, 2007, p. D1. Copyright © 2007 Dow Jones. Reprinted with permission of Dow Jones via Copyright Clearance Center.